HUMANIST POETICS

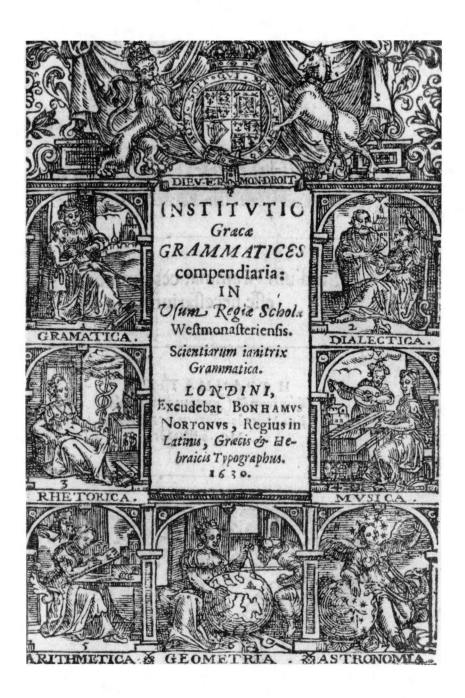

DIEV·ET·MON·DROIT

INSTITVTIO
Græcæ
GRAMMATICES
compendiaria:
IN
Vsum Regiæ Scholæ
Weſtmonaſterienſis.

Scientiarum ianitrix
Grammatica.

LONDINI,
Excudebat BONHAMVS
NORTONVS, Regius in
Latinis, Græcis & He-
braicis Typographus.
1630.

GRAMATICA.

DIALECTICA.

RHETORICA.

MVSICA.

ARITHMETICA. GEOMETRIA. ASTRONOMIA.

Humanist Poetics

THOUGHT, RHETORIC, AND FICTION

IN SIXTEENTH-CENTURY

ENGLAND

ARTHUR F. KINNEY

THE UNIVERSITY OF MASSACHUSETTS PRESS

AMHERST

1986

Copyright © 1986 by The University of Massachusetts Press
All rights reserved
Printed in the United States of America
Set in Caslon on a APS-5, by Compositors, Inc.
Printed by Cushing-Malloy, Inc. and bound by John Dekker & Sons

Library of Congress Cataloging–in–Publication Data

Kinney, Arthur F., 1933–
Humanist poetics.
Bibliography: p.
Includes index.
1. English fiction—Early modern, 1500–1700—
History and criticism. 2. Humanism in literature.
3. Humanists—England. 4. Rhetoric—1500–1800.
5. England—Intellectual life—16th century. I. Title.
PR833.K5 1986   823'.3'09384   85–20828
ISBN 0–87023–485–4

This publication has been supported by the
National Endowment for the Humanities, a federal agency
which supports the study of such fields as
history, philosophy, literature, and languages.

Frontispiece: Mason M.5. Used with permission of the
Curators of the Bodleian Library

For my colleagues in the English Department,
University of Massachusetts, Amherst

Titled Elizabethans: A Directory of State and Church Officers in
England, Scotland, and Wales, 1558–1603

Elizabethan Backgrounds:
Historical Documents in the Age of Elizabeth I

Markets of Bawdrie: The Dramatic Criticism of Stephen Gosson

Rogues, Vagabonds, and Sturdy Beggars

H. R.'s *Mythomystes*

Rhetoric and Poetic in Thomas More's *Utopia*

Nicholas Hilliard's *The Art of Limning*
(with Linda Bradley Salamon)

Sir Philip Sidney: 1576 and the Making of a Legend
(with Dominic Baker-Smith and Jan Van Dorsten)

Essential Articles for the Study of Sir Philip Sidney
(editor)

Someone said "The dead writers are remote from us
because we know so much more than they did."
Precisely, and they are that which we know.

T. S. ELIOT

In rhetoric, more than in anything else, the continuity
of the old European tradition was embodied. Older
than the Church, older than Roman Law, older than all Latin
literature, it descends from the age of the
Greek Sophists. Like the Church and the law it survives the
fall of the empire, rides the *renascentia* and the
Reformation like waves, and penetrates far into the eighteenth
century; through all these ages not the tyrant, but the
darling of humanity, *soavissima,* as Dante says, "the sweetest
of all the other sciences." Nearly all our older poetry
was written and read by men to whom the distinction
between poetry and rhetoric, in its modern form,
would have been meaningless.

C. S. LEWIS

CONTENTS

WE HAVE NEARLY LOST at present any broad and deep knowledge of our classical past; and the loss is incalculable. For one thing, it decisively separates us from the spirit and substance of much of the Renaissance, especially the literary achievement of the Tudors. For in the joy of discovering their cultural ancestors they reshaped their civilization. This study is about a part of that reshaping, and it tries to understand their work, as they did, by locating and appreciating the antique bases for it.

Such bases pay particular tribute to the attitudes and values of humanism, because it was the humanists who fostered such study and so gave rise to the sudden magnificent rush of creativity that marks the Elizabethan age. Beginning with Erasmus and More in the reign of Henry VIII, the poetics of the Tudors was a decidedly *humanist* poetics. It hewed closely to the lessons of Tudor humanist grammar schools and univeristy curricula, which taught the value of human dignity, encouraging self-respect through philosophic discussions of man's educability—even perfectibility—in its constant concern with nurture, and the challenging rewards of inquiry and argumentation pursued by means of imaginative and persuasive rhetoric drawn from Plato and Isocrates, Cicero and Quintilian.

Yet, from the start, humanist poetics was not merely bookish, although it maintained an abiding admiration for the Greek and Roman texts that stubbornly remained at the roots of its thought and accomplishment. Humanist poetics was also a communal effort serving the state and its people. This, too, the Renaissance learned from its inherited past. What became increasingly clear, however, as the sixteenth century proceeded through expansion, war, religious persecution and reformation, and expansion once again, was that the human values preached from a classical past when aligned with Christianity could not always account for subsequent observation and experience. Discrepancies multiplied, and the writers of humanist poetics, wishing to secure the values of their humanist training, turned increasingly to the branches of imaginative poetry to explore the usefulness and, increasingly, the limitations, of the past.

Nowhere in their many efforts of creative will is this struggle clearer than in humanist fiction. Although we have grossly misjudged and underestimated that part of the Tudor literary achievement, the brilliant and searching minds of Lyly and Sidney, Nashe and Lodge forge individual poetic means to register their own humanist faith—or their profound discontent. By concentrating on the writers of humanist fiction, I hope to demonstrate some of the significant ways in which a humanist poetics, once formed, inspired several generations of writers and readers and directed them to some of the most revealing and important works of the English Renaissance.

This study is for me conclusive proof that research and teaching are inseparable; the tough questions raised by successive terms of graduate and undergraduate students led to this project. Such inquiries were central but not swift or easy of answer: What precisely was the humanist movement in England, and why did it have such lasting effect? If the humanist movement were so strong, did it survive the Reformation and, if so, in what ways? What finally brought about its collapse? Other tough questions involved particular writers and what they chose to do. Although we could rather easily establish the brilliant wordplay of Lyly, the engaging wit of Sidney, and the serious scorn of Nashe, why did these writers—whose hands touched many genres—put their more important and more sustained efforts in fiction, a genre we now place considerably lower than poetry and drama on our scale of Renaissance literary forms? The answer, of course, is that for the Elizabethans (and for their Henrician and Continental counterparts) fiction was a genre of high calling. This study attempts to explain why.

The argument that follows took eight long years to investigate and to write; many times, the project seemed endless. I can remember when it began. It was when Dr. James Thorpe tapped me on the shoulder as a Huntington Library Fellow and asked me to present a seminar on my findings, and I realized I had to pull together some scattered hypotheses and begin to make sense of them; fittingly enough, the research and writing of the book ended at the Huntington Library, too, on a second fellowship for which I am grateful. Between these two periods, I have been supported by two Independent Research Fellowships from the National Endowment for the Humanities, by a Folger Library Senior Fellowship, by a Hays-Fulbright Research Fellowship to Oxford University, by grants-in-aid from the American Philosophical Society, and by various paid and unpaid leaves from the University of Massachusetts at Amherst. I am grateful for all of these opportunities to further my investigations.

A study that has taken so much of my attention for so long a time has also involved the attention—whether they wished it or not—of many of my colleagues and students, and I have tried to make particular cases of indebtedness clear in my quotations and notes. But I have been informed by so many on so many occasions that I can no longer recall them all, or recall when a particular idea first came to mind; I can only say that much of the encouragment and many of the examples came from giving earlier drafts of these chapters as lectures. Over the years, Humanist Poetics has been the subject of a course of eight public lectures delivered during Trinity term 1977 at Oxford University and of individual lectures at the Modern Language Association (English 4), the Southeastern Renaissance Conference, the Newberry Library International Conference on Rhetoric, and the Southern California Renaissance Conference, as well as two Huntington Library seminars and formal presentations at the following institutions: Amherst College; Arizona State University; University of Arizona at Tucson; Brandeis University; Brown University; Bryn Mawr College; California State College at Long Beach; University of California at Berkeley, at Davis, at Irvine, at Los Angeles, and at Santa Barbara; Duke University; Emory University; University of Florida at Gainesville; Georgia State University; Georgia Technological University; University of Georgia at Athens; University of London; University of Maryland at College Park; University of Massachusetts at Amherst; Mt. Holyoke College; University of Newcastle on Tyne; University of New Mexico; North Carolina State University; University of North Carolina at Chapel Hill and at Greensboro; University of Nottingham; University of Ottawa; Rice University; Smith College; University of South Carolina; University of Texas at Austin and at El Paso; University of Toronto; Tulane University; and Vanderbilt University. I am indebted to the administrations and to the faculty and students at all these institutions. The editors and staff of *English Literary Renaissance* have excused me from responsibilities for three prolonged absences when I was fortunate enough to use the Bodleian, British Museum, Huntington, Folger, and Houghton libraries; the Olin Library at Cornell University; the Lambeth Palace Library; and various public records offices (especially those of Norwich and Westminster). Previous versions have also appeared in print in radically different form, and I am indebted to the editors of *ELH, SEL,* and *Renaissance Papers,* to the UCLA Center for Medieval and Renaissance Studies, and to the University of California Press (as publishers of *Renaissance Eloquence,* ed. J. J. Murphy) for permission to use and reuse various phrases and passages here.

Warren D. Anderson, John Demaray, Walter R. Davis, and R. J. Schoeck read this manuscript at earlier stages, and made many useful suggestions. Charles Fister and Edward Curran aided with proofreading. I am also grateful for the wisdom and support of Richard Martin, to Barbara Palmer for her superb editing of a long and difficult manuscript, Pam Wilkinson for her patience and care throughout the publishing process, and Barbara Werden for her elegant design. Claire Hopley has supplied the Index.

A NOTE ON THE TEXTS

A CONTEXTUAL AND developmental study such as the present one needs to strike some sort of balance between the texts used by the writers under discussion and texts accessible to present-day readers. I have, therefore, cited both sixteenth-century editions of works (from which quotations are taken) and their equivalents in standard modern editions. The attempt to re-create the matrix out of which Elizabethan writers of fiction worked also means that the Latin, French, and Italian texts are cited when that is what they knew or used. The same premise accounts for varied spellings.

With few exceptions, Loeb translations of classical texts have been used; specific translators and editions are given in the notes.

HUMANIST POETICS

In principio erat Verbum: The Fashioning of
a Humanist Poetics

The Mind of Man is this worlds true dimension;
and *Knowledge* is the measure of the minde:
And as the minde, in her vast comprehension,
Contains more worlds than all the world can finde:
  So Knowledge doth it selfe farre more extend,
  Than all the minds of Men can comprehend.
    FULKE GREVILLE

"IMMORTAL GOD! WHAT A
WORLD I SEE DAWNING: WHY
CAN I NOT GROW YOUNG AGAIN?"
("SED TAMEN IN PRAESENTIA PENE
LIBEAT ALIQUANTISPER REIUVENE-
SCERE"): SO ERASMUS WRITES TO HIS
friend Wolfgang Capito on 26 February 1517.[1] His dramatic self-
consciousness displays the essential spirit of Renaissance humanists—vital,
immediate, durable; it is the direct consequence of their rediscovery of
Greek texts, especially Plato. The revolutionary influence of these pagan
writings released men from their concentrated study of the Church
Fathers, of spiritual contemplation and the afterlife, taking them, with
fresh excitement, to a new sense of personal liberty and accomplishment
that was the chief historical legacy of Greek culture as the Renaissance
redrew it, what Frederick B. Artz has labeled "the greatest originating
force which history has known."[2] This fundamental impulse of Florentine
and northern humanists, a glorification of man broadly promulgated in
Tudor England, has countless classical roots, of course—the myth of
Prometheus and the second chorus of Sophocles' *Antigone* are perhaps two
of the best known—while Varro gives full credit to Socrates in an
important passage of Cicero's *Academica.*

Socrates . . . primus a rebus occultis et ab ipsa natura involutis, in quibus
omnes ante eum philosophi occupati fuerunt, avocavisse philosophiam et ad
vitam communem adduxisse, ut de virtutibus et vitiis omninoque de bonis

rebus et malis quaereret, caelestia autem vel procul esse a nostra cognitione censeret vel, si maxime cognita essent, nihil tamen ad bene vivendum.

(Socrates was the first person who summoned philosophy away from mysteries veiled in concealment by nature herself, upon which all philosophers before him had been engaged, and led it to the subject of ordinary life, in order to investigate the virtues and vices, and good and evil generally, and to realize that heavenly matters are either remote from our knowledge or else, however fully known, have nothing to do with the good life.)[3]

Plato's emphasis on man and his concern with potentiality is also the basis of much humanist thought. Yet, with such earlier precedents, Paul Oskar Kristeller has recently written, "we cannot escape the impression that after the beginnings of Renaissance humanism, the emphasis on man and his dignity becomes more persistent, more exclusive, and ultimately more systematic than it ever had been during the preceding centuries and even during classical antiquity."[4]

Thus the heightened value of man and of human achievement initially owes its force—even among the Tudors—to Florentine philosophy. The idea of the dignity of man developed by Plotinus and later Greek philosophers, along with their notions of natural law and the solidarity of mankind, is the basis of the influential work of Marsilio Ficino. In his massive *Theologica Platonica* (1482), Ficino insists on man's inherent capacities because of the universality of the human mind and sees in this man's fundamental affinity with God. The soul tends to know all of truth and to attain all goodness, according to Ficino; it tries to become all things, including God. Although the soul is unable to attain the Godhead, its glory is its diversity; if God alone actually *remains* all things, he tells us, man's soul tends to *become* all things (14.2–5). The earliest important Tudor humanists, William Grocyn and John Colet, studied the works of Ficino; Colet corresponded with him;[5] and Thomas More translated the life of Ficino's protégé Pico della Mirandola from the original biography by Pico's nephew. And it is Pico who extends still further Ficino's ideas into a memorable fable that must have lingered in the minds of many of the first generation of English humanists. It is presented in the first part of Pico's *Oration* of 1486, the undelivered speech he had prepared in order to defend his 900 theses on man and the universe. Kristeller sums it this way:

When the creation of the whole universe had been completed, the Creator decided to add a being capable of meditating on the reasons of the world, loving its beauty, and admiring its greatness. Thus He undertook the creation of man. All gifts had by then been distributed among the other creatures. . . . Hence, the Creator decided that the being for which nothing had been left as its peculiar property might in turn have a share of all the gifts that had first been assigned singly to the various other beings. Man, therefore, has no clearly determined essence or nature. He is neither celestial nor earthly, neither mortal nor immortal. On the contrary, he may become all of this through his own will. The Creator gave him the germs of every sort of life. Depending on whatever potentiality he develops, he may become a plant, an animal, a celestial being, an angel, or he may even be unified with God Himself. Man therefore possesses all possibilities within himself. It is his task to overcome the lower forms of life and to elevate himself toward God.[6]

This incredible vision—it is nothing less than Jacob's ladder of ascending and descending angels in which man has displaced the inhabitants of Heaven—is likewise a root cause of the humanists' exuberance and optimism.

Pico's ideas concerning the nature of man were considerably furthered and modified by the Aristotelian Pomponazzi in the next generation. Pomponazzi's *Tractatus de immortalitate animae,* his treatise on the soul's immortality (1516), begins with the Neoplatonic observation that man's medial placement between mortal and immortal creatures renders his nature fundamentally ambiguous; he is neither purely eternal nor purely temporal because he participates in both natures by having the power to assume either one. But where the Platonists had taught that the goal of human life is ascension toward contemplation, Pomponazzi argues that this goal is attainable only in a future life; it follows, then, that man should concentrate in his mortal life on earthly virtues. His focus should center on virtuous daily behavior. In this way, the dignity of man is maintained and man's earthly life is invested with greater intrinsic value. Man should not depend on any hopes or fears for the future, according to Pomponazzi, but should concentrate on an ethical life where virtue is its own reward, vice its own punishment (14).[7]

This matrix of assorted ideas—consolidated and extended by synergistic ideas in Plato, Aristotle, and Cicero—is the beginning of Tudor humanist thought. It explains much of its extraordinary faith and energy. For, discovering the texts of the antique civilizations, Roman as well as Greek, and inheriting through Colet and others the concordant ideas of the Florentine Neoplatonists, the Tudor humanists came to an increasing certainty that they could fashion and refashion themselves, and so fashion and refashion society. Being educable, man might also be perfectible. This is the single, overriding idea which in England found reinforcement and fulfillment at the hands of teachers and writers, mostly if not solely in their development, use, and defense of rhetoric.

About such amazing possibilities Tudor humanists were increasingly clear. "I will first examin the naturall abilities, which ar to be perfited, & how natur hirself doth forward the perfectiō," Richard Mulcaster proclaims openly at the start of *The First Part of the Elementarie,* his philosophic treatise on education; "thē I will shew, how those principles, which art hath deuised for the furtherance of natur, do answer vnto those abilities of natur both for sufficiencie in number, and fitnesse to perfection" (sig. D3).[8] The programmatic Mulcaster is representative; he reveals, as Ficino, Pico, and Pomponazzi do on the Continent and as More, Sidney, and Nashe will in humanist fiction, a distinctive combination of involvement, arrogance, and determination. All of them share the conviction that proper education can bring about an ideal state for which Periclean Athens and—more importantly for the Tudors—Augustan Rome stood as guaranteeing precedents. For these humanists, *nihil humani alienum* (nothing concerning man is outside the active range of their interests). All of it, moreover, could be promulgated by teaching proper rhetoric, which would not only guarantee its continuation but also achieve some of its highest and most imaginative explorations. Such fundamental beliefs and practices, in fact, are what joined together for the Tudors such fictional characters as More-persona, Euphues, Menaphon, Pyrocles, Jack Wilton, and Rosalynde.

MAN'S TOTAL FREEDOM for self-fashioning, then, created a vital need for humanist teaching; educ-ation, being led out of the best thought of the ancients, demanded symbiotic in-struction as the necessary coordinate. An urgent, widespread need to learn lessons from the past promulgated by humanist philosophy led to an explosion of grammar schools. Foundations began with Colet's establishment of St. Paul's School, London, in 1512, with the help of the Mercers' Company; by the end of the century there were 109 endowed and 49 unendowed schools in England, Wales, and Scotland: "There are not many corporat townes now vnder the queenes dominion, that hath not one Grammar schoole at the least," William Harrison writes in his *Description of the Iland of Britaine* in 1587 (sig. O3). This new golden age of Tudor education is also the richest era of great schools (St. Paul's, Ipswich, Shrewsbury, Westminster, Merchant Taylors', Rugby, Harrow) and of great schoolmasters (Lily, Coote, Mulcaster, Brinsley, Kempe, Holland, Udall, Camden, Knowlles, Hyrd, Cagan, even Wolsey for a time), each school averaging 42 boys or one for every 375 of the population. Such a widespread dissemination of humanist thought and belief had a massive effect on learning and activity in Tudor England, and such a total revolution caused the Tudor priest to be replaced, as the center of society in polysemic ways, by the schoolmaster: we remember that even Holofernes has his moment of authority in Navarre.

And from the beginning Tudor educators, like their counterparts on the Continent, saw the wisdom of the ancients as most easily accessible by way of the rhetorical forms they taught and employed. What may at first be startling, but is nevertheless essential to understand, is that philosophy was displaced by rhetoric among humanists and humanist educators. Thus the humanist movement quickly focused on both teaching the past and training judgment by reemphasizing the medieval trivium of grammar, rhetoric, and logic. Reason, as man's distinguishing characteristic, was to be realized primarily through speech. *Oratio* is next to *ratio,* as Sidney puts it in the *Defence of Poesie.*[9] God, after all, created the universe by speech (Gen. 1:3); in the beginning was always the Word. We can see this wherever we look. Thomas Wilson's account of humanist eloquence realizing God's grace in the preface to his 1553 *Arte of Rhetorique,* for instance, taken over directly from Cicero's remarks in *De Oratore* (1.8.33), becomes a significant commonplace for Tudor humanist educators. "Where as Menne lyued Brutyshlye in open feldes, hauing neither house to shroude them in, nor attyre to clothe their backes, nor yet anye regarde to seeke theire best auayle," he teaches,

> these appoynted of God called theim together by vtteraunce of speache, and perswaded with them what was good, what was badde, and what was gainefull for mankynde. And although at firste, the rude coulde hardelie learne, & either for straungenes of the thing, would not gladlye receyue the offer, or els for lacke of knoweledge could not perceyue the goodnes: yet being somewhat drawē and delighted with the pleasaūtnes of reason, & the swetenes of vtteraūce: after a certaine space, thei became through nurture and good aduisement, of wilde, sober: of cruel, gentle: of foles, wise: and of beastes, men. Suche force hath the tongue, and such is the power of eloquence and reason, that most men are forced euen to yelde in that, whiche most standeth againste their will. [Sig. A(3)v]

Such faith in eloquence would have been unacceptable and even incomprehensible to the Tudor humanists, however, if they did not also mean by this, as Quintilian remarks chorically, that the orator is a good man (*vir bonus dicendi peritus*). "Verily," Thomas Elyot hedges in *Of The Knowledeg That maketh a wise man* (1533),

> there may no mā be an excellent poet nor oratour / vnlasse he haue parte of all other doctrine specially of noble philosophie. And to say the trouth / no man can apprehēde the very delectation that is in the lessons of noble poets / vnlasse he haue radde very moche / and in diuers autours of diuers lernynges. . . specially of that parte of philosophie named morall: whiche instructeth men in vertue and politike gouernaunce. [Sig. G4v]

Conversely, Roger Ascham warns in *The Scholemaster* 2 (1570),

Ye know not, what hurt ye do to learning, that care not for wordes, but for matter, and so make a deuorse betwixt the tong and the hart. For marke all aiges: looke vpon the whole course of both the Greeke and Latin tonge, and ye shall surelie finde, that, whan apte and good wordes began to be neglected, and properties of those two tonges to be confounded, then also began, ill deedes to spring: strange maners to oppresse good orders, newe and fond opinions to striue with olde and trewe doctrine, first in Philosophie: and after in Religion: right iudgement of all thinges to be peruerted, and so vertue with learning is cõtemned, and studie left of: of ill thoughtes cummeth peruerse iudgement: of ill deedes springeth lewde taulke. [Sig. O2v]

This conjunction of idea, language, and attitudes further helps to clarify the curriculum of an exemplary humanist school such as St. Paul's, which combined a radically new course of study based on ancient Latin and Greek texts and an emphasis on rhetoric with a more traditional religious ceremony at its edges: the picture of Christ in the classroom, the morning prayers for the boys of proven intellectual capacity, the "godly lessons" attached by their schoolmaster William Lily to the end of their accidence.

Reinforced by recent discoveries of key Roman texts (Cicero's *Pro Archia* at Liège and the *Epistolae ad Atticum* at Verona, as well as his *Epistolae ad familiares* discovered by Salutati, and Quintilian's *Institutio Oratoria* found by Poggio Bracciolini), Tudor humanists formulated a plan of lessons centered on the trivium of the *ars disserendi,* or the arts of speaking correctly, speaking well, and arguing well. Together such verbal studies would lead men toward individual perfection while also training them to be ideal citizens through reasoning by Aristotelian *pisteis* (modes of persuasion). We may find it difficult now to imagine the typical schoolboy spending eight to ten hours a day for six days a week in all but about seven weeks a year studying verbal art—Latin grammar through single and double translations, compositions, memorized recitations, declamations, and disputations. But he was restricted to language study, even using Latin while at play and in recess. So thorough was his training and so frequent and repetitive the drills that, at the end of three years, the Tudor student knew well his *syntaxis, figura,* and *prosodia:* a child of eleven or twelve could construe simple, compound, and complex Latin sentences, recognize a large number of figures of speech and so constantly rearrange his own writing, and scan Latin verse in a variety of meters.

A. D. Leach locates one of the fullest accounts of a Tudor plan for such study in the statutes of the cathedral school at Durham (1593):

As soon as any boy had "any perceyving" in Latin he was to "make one epistle weekly and everie weeke of his own mind both in matter and words ... according to the principles of Erasmus or Ludovicus Vives in their booke De scribendis, which shall be showed ... upon Saterday." Next he was to learn to make "a theame according to the precepts of Apthonius." Thirdly, ... "he shall have redd unto him the bookes of Cicero ad Heremium, wherein the schoolemaister shall teach the schollers to frame and make an oration according to the precepts of Rhetorick ... thus: the schoolemaister shall propound a theame or argument which shall have two parties, and two schollers shall be appointed, the one shall take the first part, the other the second ... and upon Saterday ... shall shew their orations. ... Fourthlie, for the practise and exercise of versifying ... the schoolemaister shall read to them the versifying rules sett downe in the latter end of our common grammer."[10]

This is what constituted for the humanists a New Learning, and we understand Tudor poetics when we fix these subjects and forms in our own minds, for much of what we call "English Renaissance literature" relies on them. First, *epistles:* Erasmus's *Modus conscribendi epistolas,* he explains in the *De Ratione Studii* for St. Paul's School, precedes all else and teaches boys to propound both themes and arguments in the vernacular (525D); it also leads to perceiving and composing what we would call fictions. According to the statutes for the Rivington grammar school, to cite one instance, themes were varied by

devising and writing sundry epistles, to sundry persons, of sundry matters, as of chiding, exhorting, comforting, counselling, praying, lamenting; some to friends, some to foes, some to strangers; of weighty matters, or merry, as shooting, hunting, etc.; of adversity, of prosperity, of war and peace, divine and profane, of all sciences and occupations, some long and some short.[11]

A number of English texts provided precise and rather simple models, such as William Fulwood's *Enimie of Idlenesse* (1568), a translation of *Le stile et manière de composer, dicter, et escrire toute sorte d'épistre* (Lyons, 1566). Second, *themes:* Aphthonius's *Progymnasmata* (1520), translated into Latin by Reinhard Lorich in 1542 and into English by Richard Rainolde in 1563, came to be the basic grammar school text for models of short themes. Rainolde's book contains nineteen classical themes for imitation, from Aesop's fables of the ant and the grasshopper and the shepherd and the wolves to historical speeches by Richard III and Julius Caesar, a confutation of the battle of Troy, the description of Xerxes, and "A narracion Poeticall vpon a Rose" (sig. D4). Such exercises get progressively more difficult, while reinforcing by practice the art of *ethopoeia,* or impersonations (sig. N1), for themes or theses (we might say "stories") on things uncertain or fictitious (sig. O1). Third, *orations:* From Aristotle, Cicero, and Quintilian, Tudor grammar schools taught all three kinds of formal declamations—symbouleutic or deliberative, dicanic or judicial (forensic), epideictic or demonstrative. These too had considerable influence in formulating a basis for humanist fiction. When Thomas Wilson, for instance, writes of the demonstrative oration, in his *Rhetorique,* that "There are diuerse thynges, whiche are praised, and dispraised, as menne, Countreis, Citees, Places, Beastes, Hilles, Riuers, Houses, Castles, dedes doen by worthy menne, and pollicies inuented by greate warriers, but moste commonly men are praised, for diuerse respectes, before any of the other thynges are taken in hande" (sig. b2v), he seems to be outlining Thomas More's *Utopia.* The deliberative oration "wherby we do perswade, or disswade, entreate, or rebuke, exhorte, or dehorte, commende, or cōforte any man" (sig. D4) reminds us of Lyly's *Euphues.* And the judicial oration, "an earnest debatyng in open assemblie of some weightie matter before a iudge" (sig. M3), is the formulary Philip Sidney selects for the grand conclusion of the *Arcadia.* These divisions, accompanied by descriptions and practices, ultimately have their origin in Aristotle's *Rhetoric* (1.3), but among the most popular Tudor models was the *Tusculan Disputations* of Cicero, adopted by statute at Rivington in 1566, St. Bees in 1583 and Blackburn in 1597, among others.

Debates grew out of orations dealing with laws real or imagined, the *legislatio,* one of the most popular being Cicero's defense of Milo. Leonard Coxe presents this chestnut in his *Art or crafte of Rhetoryke* (1532):

> In olde tyme there was greate enuy betwene two noble men of Rome / of whō the one was called Milo / & the other Clodius / which malice grew so fer[c]e that Clodius layd wayte for Milo on a season when he sholde ryde out of the Citie / and in his iourney set vpon hym / and there as it chaunced: Clodius was slayne / where vpon this Clodius frendes accused Milo to the Cenate of murder. Tully whiche in tho days was a great Aduocate in Rome sholde plede Miloes cause. Now it was open that Milo had slayne Clodius / but whether he had slayn hym laufully or nat was the doubte. So than the Theme of Tullies oraciō or plee for Milo was this / that he had slayne Clodius laufully / and therfore he ought nat to be punisshed / for the confirmacion wherof (as dothe appere in Tullies oracion) he dyd brynge out of places of Rhetoryque argumentes to pue his sayd Theme or purpose. And likewyse must we do whan we haue any mater to speke or comun of. [Sigs. A4–A5]

Boys found a number of models, culminating in John Stockwood's *Dispvtationcvlarvm Grammaticalivm libellus* (1598), that showed them how to argue for or against an action or person following the customary parts of the declamation; the *exordium,* or opening anecdote; the *propositio,* or statement of the case; the *partitio,* or issues involved; the *confirmatio,* or proof; the *refutatio,* or arguments that deny the opposition; the *conclusio,* or summing up; and the *peroratio,* or closing remarks. The aim in such Tudor exercises resembles that of the Romans where, writes Donald Lemen Clark, the purpose "was not in general to make truth prevail, but to make one side of a debatable question seem as plausible as possible and then turn around and make the other side of the question seem just as plausible."[12] This sense of language—its resourcefulness, flexibility, and fictionality—is More's chief strategy for fiction, as we shall see; later it becomes the chief joke for Gascoigne, a necessary condition for Lyly, a clear and present danger for Nashe, and an inescapable burden for Lodge.

Many of these lessons overlap, of course. And common and natural to all these writers of Tudor humanist fiction because common to teaching all the *ars disserendi* was the method of *imitatio*—the art of writing by following specific models, even playing on allusions to them. The authority most notably cited is Quintilian: "In art no small portion of our task lies in imitation," he instructs, "since, although invention came first and is all-important, it is expedient to imitate whatever has been invented with success" ("quin artis pars magna contineatur imitatione. Nam ut invenire primum fuit estque praecipuum, sic ea, quae bene inventa sunt, utile sequi") (10.2.1).[13]

Surprisingly, what may seem to us at first harmfully confining or dismayingly reductive was for the Tudors a liberating means to creativity. It was a habit of thought and composition beyond question, as the correspondence between Sidney and his tutor Hubert Languet in late 1573 and early 1574 regarding the imitation of Pietro Bizarro illustrates. Such a means of education had classical roots, too—in Pliny (*Epistolae* 7.9), for example, as well as in Plato (*The Sophist* 236) and Cicero (*De Inventione* 2.2.4; *De Oratore* 1.34.156–57).

Yet, no matter what the source of imitatio, support of it is enthusiastic and the practice everywhere. The schoolmaster John Brinsley, in *Lvdvs Literarivs; or, The Grammar Schoole* (1612), advocates this practice in training art, behavior, and thought. "Both experience and reason do shew it to be the surest," he tells us, "to let them haue first the moste excellent patterns, & neuer to rest vntil they haue the very patterns in their heads, and as it were euer before their eies; for then they wil be able to go forwards of themselues with delight & cōmendations" (sig. Ee1). Tudor humanist schoolmasters teaching their students thus imitated parents setting patterns of behavior for their children, a method advocated by Plutarch (*Moralia* 3F); this same need for a model was employed by monarchs instructing their subjects and poets their readers. Sir Henry Sidney advises his son Robert in 1578 to imitate his older brother Philip, and Philip captures this idea as the premise for Euarchus's speeches in *Arcadia* 5. Lyly makes imitatio part of his plot and his characterization in *Euphues* as Greene does in *Pandosto* and Lodge does in *Robert second Duke of Normandy*. The more we study even Nashe's tumbling and erratic prose, the more we find behind it too this single, stabilizing concept. He sets out the idea of imitatio in his very first work, his *Anatomie of Absvrditie* (1589):

> Since then the onely ende of knowledge, ought to be to learne to liue well, let vs propound this vse and end vnto our selues, least after so many yeres paines, we misse of the marke whereat our parents in our education aymed. Turning ouer Histories, and reading the liues of excellent Orators and famous Philosophers, let vs with *Themistocles,* set before our eyes one of the excellentest to imitate, in whose example insisting, our industry may be doubled, to the adequation of his praise.[14]

And in his late, best work, *The Unfortunate Traueller* (1594), the fiction revolves around the protagonist Jack Wilton's growing inability to find any exemplary behavior in a world that is morally bankrupt.

TUDOR HUMANISTS, teachers, and fiction writers most frequently practiced their chief conceptual principle of imitatio by thinking, debating, and writing by means of *topoi,* common places, sources of received ideas and expressions. So the "ten first and chiefe heads of reasoning," Brinsley instructs us out of Aristotle and, following him, Wilson's *Arte of Rhetorique,* are "Causes, Effects, Subjects, Adiuncts, Disagreeable things, Comparisons, Notations, Distributions, Definitions, Testimonies"; "Let them practice when they would inuent matter, but to runne through those places curiously in their mindes" (sig. Aa4). *Places* become conceptual ways of "locating" or "discovering" varying definitions or statements that could be used for evidence, illustration, or decoration. Writers and speakers should make collections of such expressions as others collect tools for farming, Plutarch directs (*Moralia* 8B), while Juan Luis Vives urges students to keep at hand a notebook to jot down festive, elegant, or thoughtful things read or heard (*Exercitatio Linguae Latinae* 172). The Tudor schoolboy also had several ready-made collections at hand: Cato's *Disticha de moribus* (translated in 1477 as the *Dictes and Sayings of the Philosophers*); Erasmus's *Adagia* (1539 et seq.) and *Apophthegmata* (translated in 1542); Richard Tavener's *Garden of Wysdom* and his *Secōd Booke of the Garden of Wysedome* (both 1559); William Baldwin's extremely popular *Treatise of Morall Phylosophie* (1547), which went through many editions; Thomas Blage's *Schole of wise Conceyts* (1569); and W[illiam] Phist[on]'s *Welspring of wittie Conceites* (1584).

Understanding now this building process as a way of thinking, "inventing," and creating, we can understand why *copia* is so important a part of humanist poetics. Cicero's *Orator* shows ways of varying and embellishing a single subject at some length (40.136–39). Quintilian accords (12.4.1). For him, embellishment—which has its own pronounced suasiveness and beauty—may be executed in both words and ideas (8.4.1–3). And what is true for words and ideas must also be true of images. As Quintilian is quick to point out, rhetorical stockpiling carries undeniable force and an extraordinary vividness.

Sine dubio enim, qui dicit expugnatam esse civitatem, complectitur omnia quaecunque talis fortuna recipit, sed in adfectus minus penetrat brevis hic velut nuntius. At si aperias haec, quae verbo uno inclusa erant, apparebunt effusae per domos ac templa flammae et ruentium tectorum fragor et ex diversis clamoribus unus quidam sonus, aliorum fuga incerta, alii extremo complexu suorum cohaerentes et infantium feminarumque ploratus et male usque in illum diem servati fato senes; tum illa profanorum sacrorumque direptio, efferentium praedas repetentiumque discursus et acti ante suum quisque praedonem catenati et conata retinere infantem suum mater et, sicubi maius lucrum est, pugna inter victores. Licet enim haec omnia, ut dixi, complectatur eversio, minus est tamen totum dicere quam omnia. Consequemur autem, ut manifesta sint, si fuerint verisimilia; et licebit etiam falso adfingere quidquid fieri solet.

For the mere statement that the town was stormed, while no doubt it embraces all that such a calamity involves, has all the curtness of a dispatch, and fails to penetrate to the emotions of the hearer. But if we expand all that the one word "stormed" includes, we shall see the flames pouring from house and temple, and hear the crash of falling roofs and one confused clamour blent of many cries: we shall behold some in doubt whither to fly, others clinging to their nearest and dearest in one last embrace, while the wailing of women and children and the laments of old men that the cruelty of fate should have spared them to see that day will strike upon our ears. Then will come the pillage of treasure sacred and profane, the hurrying to and fro of the plunderers as they carry off their booty or return to seek for more, the prisoners driven each before his own inhuman captor, the mother struggling to keep her child, and the victors fighting over the richest of the spoil. For though, as I have already said, the sack of a city includes all these things, it is less effective to tell the whole news at once than to recount it detail by detail. And we shall secure the vividness we seek, if only our descriptions give the impression of truth, nay, we may even add fictitious incidents of the type which commonly occur. [8.3.67–70]

In *De Duplici Copia Verborum ac Rerum,* Erasmus transfers such technique to a major and influential humanist textbook; and there he varies a single sentence, such as "Your letter has delighted me very much," by providing synonymous words and phrases for each original word in turn

(1.33) while copying verbatim the illustration of the captured town from
Quintilian (1569 ed., sigs. D8v–F8). Erasmus's *De Copia* had great impact.
Written at Colet's request for use at St. Paul's School, it was first published
by Badius in Paris in 1512 and then, as a school handbook, went through
180 editions in the sixteenth century, 144 of them before 1572. To aid the
student still further in seeking ways to amplify and vary, the Tudor
humanists produced a number of texts of tropes, figures, and schemes of
rhetoric, such as that appended by Angel Day to *The English Secretorie*
(1586). The distant sources for such figural rhetorics remained Cicero and
Quintilian, the intermediate source Erasmus, and the direct source
Johannes Susenbrotus, whose *Epitome troporum ac schematum* (Zurich,
1540) led in England to Richard Sherry's *Treatise of Schemes & Tropes*
(1550) and *Treatise of the Figures of Grammer and Rhetorike* (1555) and
Henry Peacham's *Garden of Eloquence* (1577; 1593).

SURELY WHAT STRIKES us now is how potentially rich the new
emphasis on eloquence in the Tudor grammar school might prove to be; we
are struck, too, by how essentially *literary* humanist education was, even in
its basic classroom drills.[15] In learning the proper structure for themes and
orations, for instance, grammar school boys were given set patterns not only
from antique speeches and treatises but from narratives in fables or
anecdotes and models of conversations in Erasmus's *Colloquia* (1519).[16]
Such lessons were occasionally augmented by learning and staging school
plays.[17] This persistent humanist emphasis on the ars disserendi continued
in the courses of study Tudor humanists devised at the various colleges of
Oxford and Cambridge. An extant handlist of books at Magdalen College,
Oxford, includes a number of books in rhetoric and poetry.[18] At Cambridge,
the university twice declared its intention to reserve the first year of college
for rhetoric exclusively.[19] Furthermore, the declamation and disputation
remained the chief form of instruction and examination.[20] "A man's friends
attended his disputations and doubtless tried to encourage him as much as
decorum allowed," Craig R. Thompson writes.

> Each disputant gave arguments, cross-examined the other speaker or
> speakers, and attempted to refute them, always attacking or defending by
> means of syllogisms and indeed by any other weapons of logic which he
> could lay hands on. . . . whatever the questions at issue, skill in argument
> was what mattered most. Rhetorical resourcefulness, cogency, the tactics
> of logic and eloquence combined: these carried the day.[21]

Although Henry VIII founded the richest colleges at both universities—
King's and Christ Church— and in 1540 at Cambridge and 1546 at Oxford
founded the Regius professorships in rhetoric, it was Elizabeth I who,

among the Tudors' royal patrons, seems most representative in her enjoyment of university disputations. During her visit to Oxford in 1566, she sat on Tuesday through four hours of philosophical debate in Latin on the powers that governed the world of nature, the influence of the moon upon the tides, and the comparative value of elective and hereditary princes; on Wednesday she heard disputations on the effect of war on civil rights and the effect of a depreciated coinage upon contracts; on Thursday she returned once more to listen to arguments on whether the medical art might prolong life and whether subjects might take arms against an unjust prince. Other topics that have come down to us are both serious and fanciful, once more showing the range of possibilities invited by the humanists' rhetorical culture: in 1589 at Oxford candidates for the degree disputed whether Heaven had made Englishmen stronger than Spaniards; in 1609 they debated a man's rights in the taming of a shrew. The queen's pleasure, moreover, was shared at all levels. Richard Madox, a fellow of All Souls, Oxford, records in his diary that life at school there in 1582 was saturated in words and wordplay.

> 8. (*Mon.*) we went a clubbyng owt of al howses in the town, some, abowt 400, with drome, bagpipe and other melody. At nyght we cam home with . . . torches and at Unyversytie College Latware of St. Johns welcomed us in verse with a fy*ne* oration in the name of kyng Aulredē, crownd us with 2 fayr garlonds and offered the third but I answering his oration gave hȳm the third and crowned hym poet lawreat. So marched we up to Carfox where Sir Abbots of Bayly Colledg had an oration in prose com*mending* us for taking the savage who did ther an*swer* and yelded his hollyn club being with his . . . al in yvy. So went we to Trynyty *Colledg* and at the gate Sir Wurford receved me with an oration and my brother had an other of Sir Poticary. Then at the entry M. Marvin had one by Sir ———. We supt at the presidents lodging and after had the Supposes handeled in the ha̧ul indifferently.[22]

"Mineruium Oxoniense numerosum est diatribis: in quibus p̱fitentur & disputant omnium scientiarum / et liberalium artium principes et candidati"; "The schole strete in Oxforde is full of scholys: to rede / and dispute in euery facultye / or scyence to p̱ocede in," reads one of William Horman's *Vulgaria* (1519), a grammar school text for construing Latin (sig. Q4v). In such a heady atmosphere of ingenious wordplay, Erasmus's *Encomium Moriae* and Lyly's *Euphues* were both enormously popular.

BUT WE COMPREHEND humanist interest in the ars disserendi more fully if we recognize that for the humanist teachers and students speeches were not simply performances (although they seem always to have been that, too) but, by means of varying copia, rearranged topoi, and opposing arguments and narratives or fables, explorations after truth and restatements of truth—so far as truth could be discerned and conveyed. Erasmus's fiction is a clear example of this, in its delineation of the virtues and vices of the estates of man: the concerns More will take into Utopia and Sidney into Arcadia. Thus it follows that the Grand Tour, which the humanists also inaugurated, was conceived as a geographical exploration succeeding a rhetorical one. I learn, writes Ascham in *The Scholemaster,* "not onelie by reading of bookes in my studie, but also by experience of life, abrode in the world" (sig. C4v); "Endeuour to adde vnto Arte Experience," Nashe directs us in his *Anatomie of Absvrditie,* "experience is more profitable voide of arte, then arte which hath not experience" (sig. E2v; 1:46). The Grand Tour follows naturally, too, the basic humanist interest in theory coupled with practice. Such is the conscious division governing the two parts of Thomas Elyot's *Toxophilus* and Ascham's *Scholemaster* or, reversed, More's *Utopia;* and such leads to Sidney's insistence in the *Defence of Poesie* on both *gnosis* and *praxis* (knowledge and action). In *A Method for Trauell* (1598) Robert Dallington concurs. "The end of his *Trauell,*" he argues for the humanist student, "is his ripening in knowledge; and the end of his knowledge is the seruice of his countrie, which of right challengeth, the better part of vs" (sig. b1).

Dallington's book is largely concerned with France, but it was more likely the journeys of the first humanists to Italy from England—Humphrey, duke of Gloucester; John Tiptoft; William Selling—that planted the idea. By the time the Tudor humanists began traveling abroad in larger numbers, the practice had taken on a decidedly Tudor coloration of pragmatism and utility; the purpose of such a trip, they counsel, is to learn about foreign governments and economies so as to aid England, as Philip Sidney does before urging his brother Robert to do the same. "Wee must marke how in euery kinde of gouernment, the Empire is ether continued, or increased, or lost," Jerome Turler advises fellow humanists in *The Traveiler* (1575), "and with what new lawes, officers, and Maiestrates, they vse to furnishe themselues when they perceaue their state to bee in perill" (sig. E5v). Dallington also recommends "a Giornale, wherein from day to day, he shall set downe, the diuers Prouinces he passeth, with their commodities, the townes, with their manner of buildings, the names, & benefit of the riuers, the distance of places, the condition of the soile, manners of the people, and what else his eye meeteth by the way remarqueable" (sig. c1v). There was ritual involved, of course, as there was in the grammar school with themes and the college halls with disputations; the young wandering scholar often signed his name to various matriculation books, took lessons from a fencing master, or through letters of introduction made his way into European courts. And such a "varietie of companie" as he might meet, says Robert Johnson in his *Essaies* of 1601, "bettereth behauiour, subtelizeth artes, awaketh and exerciseth wit, ripeneth iudgement, confirmeth wisedome, and enricheth the mind with many worthy and profitable obseruations" (sig. E2v).[23] Such wider fields of learning extended the possible sources from which humanists might come to understand and improve themselves and so understand and improve their own society.

Perhaps this is best seen in the fiction of Rabelais, where crucial ties between proper education and wise and eloquent citizenship in Books 1 and 2 give way, in the later books, to the need to find instruction in foreign and increasingly fabulous territories of the human mind and spirit. The Divine Oracle of the Holy Bottle—to drink in learning by a kind of holy communion of the sacred and the secular—is both a concrete and a resolutely abstract response. But it clearly serves in turn as a model imitated by Euphues and Eubulus, Menaphon, and Pyrocles and Musidorus in the subsequent fiction of Lyly, Greene, and Sidney. It also sharply delineates the failing vision of the last important Tudor fiction writers— Nashe and Lodge—when Jack Wilton and Duke Robert find in their travels that it has become more man's nature to be cruel than to be kind, and that a rhetoric that attempts to persuade men otherwise is wishful, deceptive, and even dangerous.

ELOQUENCE COULD THEREFORE be a two-edged sword. Just as Erasmus's Folly could talk wisdom or foolishness—and who would distinguish?—so might More's Hythlodaye. Just as Rabelais's word of prophecy might also be the direction for perpetual inebriation—and who would decide?—so Lyly's Eubulus might lead Euphues down the right, or the wrong, path. It is true (as we shall soon discover) that as the sixteenth century progressed, doubts about the basic premises of humanism became more widespread, and the wordplay characterizing Erasmus, More, and Gascoigne took on a kind of fabulous quality with Lyly, Greene, and Sidney that Nashe and Lodge would find had no resources in the actual world around them. But such potential failings and delusions of eloquence were known by humanist writers of fiction from the start. It was not a new discovery that would characterize Nashe and Lodge. Far from it. They were always, as they knew, in an inherently problematic tradition fostered by humanism. The tradition foundered because it had rested its lessons on the educability of men who seemed, after a century of lessons, to be unteachable. But the dangers of a permanent and exclusive faith in eloquence had been the birthright of humanism alongside the glorious possibilities of rhetoric, which could instill virtue and free the imagination.

Cicero, for instance, clearly understands such potential dangers when he distinguishes in his rhetorical treatises between the philosophic ends of eloquence as man's civilizing art and the rhetorical means or *techne* (Latin *ars*). In his early work, *De Inventione,* Cicero notes that the words of the orator may be quite distinct from the author's intention (1.13.17); in *De Oratore* 2 he instructs the speaker on how to attain his peculiar end: how to capitalize on strong points without slurring the weaker ones, how to choose the most effective kinds of proof, and how to appeal to feelings as well as to reason (2.71.289–75.306). Both works thus enlarge on the Aristotelian ideas of *ethos* (by which the speaker develops a persona) and *pathos* (by which the speaker puts the audience into a particular frame of mind.)[24] Cicero wrote for statesmen; his disciple Quintilian wrote especially for lawyers. But here, too, in an earlier age of eristics, victory is the end that is actually sought. A clear example of this is Quintilian's use of a commonplace example to explain *definition:* if the lawyer must defend a thief whose crime occurred in a temple and the fact of the theft is widely known, according to Quintilian, he may win his case by changing the charge of the prosecution from theft to sacrilege (4.2.8). Quintilian further argues in *Institutio* 4 for persuasive statements employing lies if necessary to win the case; *narratio* in argument can become for him indistinguishable from *narratio* meaning "myth" or "fiction." The *Institutio* instructed Tudor humanists. It also instructs us on how to read them. Their practice repeatedly shows us how, in following Quintilian, they could also see through him. For, although Quintilian means to teach acuity, he also reveals a sense of language as manipulable: words, rather than pointing to particular shared meanings, can be shaped to personal ends. Language can be made relative,[25] the act of formulating it *creative*.

Such a practice goes back at least to Homer's Odysseus, especially as the Tudors recast him as their model for the crafty orator and spinner of tales, but it seems not to have become especially profitable until the fifth century B.C. with Gorgias of Leontini. Implicit in his instruction to the Athenians was the premise that one could control his audience by controlling speech, an idea that led the contemporary sophist Protagoras to remark that it was possible to argue for or against any proposition and to go so far as to claim that he could make the worse appear better. In the hands of Protagoras, rhetoric was allied to dialectic and both reduced to eristics. Socrates, who had his own vested interest in the utility and power of language, was outraged: "Sophist and orator," he tells Callicles near the end of the dialogue *Gorgias* (520A), "are the same thing, or very much of a piece." For him this attack was abiding. In the *Protagoras* Socrates locates the weakness of the sophists in their exclusion of matter for manner (312D). He presses the attack further yet in the *Phaedrus:* a man should train himself "not to undergo for the sake of speaking and acting before men, but that he may be able to [please] the gods" (273E–274A). The sophists were unable to answer these various charges. But, as we might expect, Aristotle replied to Plato and in doing so adumbrated Cicero and Quintilian and their defense of rhetoric: such personal use of language, Aristotle maintains, is necessary for a man's self-defense, and also for the affairs of state (1355*b*).

The sixteenth century championed the Aristotelian perspective in its grammar schools where a renewed emphasis on rhetoric was nearly total; from grammar, rhetoric took over the study of syntax, etymology, and allusion for its own ends; and from dialectic it appropriated the artificial constructs of debate—syllogism, maxim, and analogy—converting them to techniques of persuasion. Among the Tudors, "rhetoric produced individuals predisposed to approach any subject by taking a side, because they were not formally trained to do anything else: any side, perhaps, but some side certainly," Walter J. Ong comments. "The life of the mind was exciting because it was framed in conflict."[26] This attitude was forwarded by the Tudors' use, in grammar school and university classrooms, of classical *controversiae,* fixed paradoxes presented by ambiguous or contradictory (but often actual) Roman laws that gave formal models for disputations. Such controversiae—really the exemplars of Tudor fiction— are presented in detail by Seneca the Elder, Seneca Rhetor, along with epigrams and amusing anecdotes; they appear too in Livy. According to the pseudo-Cicero, they are often couched in the inherent multiplicity of meanings that a copious rhetoric shares with fiction when it turns narrative situations or language into ambiguity (and, we should add, metaphor).

Ex ambiguo controversia nascitur cum scriptum duas aut plures sententias significat, hoc modo: Paterfamilias cum filium heredem faceret, testamento vasa argentea uxori legavit: "Heres meus uxori meae xxx pondo vasorum argenteorum dato, quae volet." Post mortem eius vasa pretiosa et caelata magnifice petit mulier. Filius se quae ipse vellet in xxx pondo ei debere dicit. Constitutio est legitima ex ambiguo.

A controversy is created by Ambiguity when a text presents two or more meanings, as follows: The father of a family, when making his son his heir, in his will bequeathed silver vessels to his wife: "Let my heir give my wife thirty pounds' weight of silver vessels, 'such as shall be selected.' " After his death the widow asks for some precious vessels of magnificent relief-work.

The son contends that he owes her thirty pounds' weight of vessels "such as shall be selected" *by him.* Here is a Legal Issue established from Ambiguity. [*Ad Herennium* 1.12.20]

Leonard Coxe, in his *Art or crafte of Rhetoryke,* cites another instance in the case of a man who leaves to each of his two maiden daughters 100 sheep to be delivered to them on the days of marriage "suche as they wyll": here, he asks, does "they" refer to daughters or to the executors who have kept the sheep (sigs. F4–F4v)?

Two or more truths might be construed from a single remark or a single situation, then, and the task of the antique or Tudor rhetor was to judge one of them paramount and to persuade his audience to adopt an identical position: not only words but also conclusions—or operative truths—might be relative. The fullest collection of such exercises that Tudor educators inherited from their Roman sources has unfortunately survived only in fragments. But, reviewing these models from Seneca Rhetor now, we are struck by how frequently, especially in forensic rhetoric, truth must be established in the course of argumentation; we also note how far from their own experiences—as remote as fictions themselves—are the exemplars Tudor schoolboys came to know so well and work so often.

> A girl who has been raped may choose either marriage to her ravisher without a dowry or his death. On a single night a man rapes two girls. One demands his death, the other marriage. Speeches for and against the man. [*Controversiae* 1.3]
>
> A man disinherits his son; the disinherited son goes to a prostitute and acknowledges a son by her. He falls ill and sends for his father; when the father arrives, he entrusts his son to the old man and dies. After his death the father adopts the boy. He is accused of insanity by his other son. [2.4]
>
> While a certain city is at war, a hero loses his weapons in battle and removes the arms from the tomb of a dead hero. He fights heroically, then puts the weapons back. He gets his reward, and is accused of violating the tomb. [4.4]
>
> A man is caught in bed with the wife of a tyrant and snatches the sword from the tyrant's hand and kills him. He asks for the reward. There is an objection. [4.7]

Tudor students were taught that such rhetorical problems rotate around three axes of concern: *an sit* (did it happen?), *quid sit* (how do we define what happened?), and *quale sit* (how do we interpret an act?). Such questions, we see at once, rhetoric shares with poetics. The problem of actualizing, defining, and interpreting Folly or Utopia (Nowhere)—and later such places as Arcadia and Arden—derive directly from such playful and yet such vital concerns. Indeed, another popular controversia supplied by Cicero in *De Inventione* led to an inventive, playful competition between two exemplars of Elizabeth fiction, Erasmus and More. It concerns tyrannicide.

> Lex: Qui tyrannum occiderit, Olympionicarum praemia capito et quam volet sibi rem a magistratu deposcito et magistratus ei concedito. Et altera lex: Tyranno occiso quinque eius proximos cognatione magistratus necato. Alexandrum, qui apud Pheraeos in Thessalia tyrannidem occuparat, uxor sua, cui Thebe nomen fuit, noctu, cum simul cubaret, occidit. Haec filium suum, quem ex tyranno habebat, sibi in praemi loco deposcit. Sunt qui ex lege occidi puerum dicant oportere. Res in iudicio est.

> Law: A tyrannicide shall receive the reward commonly given to victors at the Olympic games and he shall ask the magistrate for whatever he wishes, and the magistrate shall give it to him. Another law: When a tyrant has been slain the magistrate shall execute his five nearest blood-relations. Alexander, who had set himself up as tyrant at Pherae in Thessaly, was killed by his wife, named Thebe, at night, when he was in bed with her. She demands as a reward her son whom she had by the tyrant. Some say that the boy ought to be executed according to law. The case is brought before a court. [2.49.144]

Cicero's accompanying advice relies solely on adeptness at law. Where the same topics of invention may favor either side, he tells the readers of *De Inventione,* the lawyer must consider what is expedient, honorable, or necessary; which law was passed most recently, because it is considered the most important; which law requires an action and which permits an action, the former having more force and authority; which law carries a greater or lesser penalty; and so on (2.49.144–46). A combination of the most helpful issues to a particular cause may shape the argument. In one telling moment, Cicero even reports to us that he takes clients into their cells and argues both sides of their cases with them—holding a small controversia of his own—in order to determine the strongest—not the truest, most just, or most moral, but the strongest—possible argument (*De Oratore* 2.24.102).

In promoting the study of rhetoric, then, the Tudors saw language as a logomachy, or contention, and promoted the study of antilogy, the ability to argue either side of a question with comparable ease and equivalent skill. Indeed, as early as grammar school there was considerable practice—after 1581 with Le Sylvain's *Epitomes de cent histories tragicques,* Englished by Lazarus Piot as *The Orator: Handling a Hundred Several Discourses, in forme of Declamations.* Here the themes include the controversiae concerning the wife who slew her tyrant husband and the ravisher of two women, as well as the man who repudiated his agreement to allow the foster father of his exposed children to keep one of them, the brave veteran without hands accused of murder, and the maternal grandfather who kidnapped his grandson. Such possibilities invite the student to frame narratives and characters in conflict: the authentic roots of western fiction, they set the imagination leaping. And such lessons were repeated in the frequent disputations at the university. Father William T. Costello notes—he writes particularly of early seventeenth-century Cambridge, but the same was true of both Tudor Oxford and Cambridge—"the opponent follows a carefully plotted line of syllogisms designed to trap the answerer into a position where he may be logically forced, step by step, into admitting the exact opposite of his thesis."[27] This was even more frequently pursued at the Inns of Court where, Margaret Hastings assures us, even in the fifteenth century mornings were spent in attendance at Westminster or other courts, afternoons were spent in disputation, and evenings in more formally conducted arguments or mootings.[28] In all these situations—and at all levels of humanist schooling—any evidence that was sufficiently potent and pointed was employed, and Cicero's careful and once useful distinctions among *fabula, historia,* and *argumentum* in the *De Inventione* (1.19.27) were eroded past recall.[29] "So long as a theme did indeed force the student to think through an intricate lawyer's puzzle, the teachers seemed not to care even if the theme involved the acceptance of impossibilities, perversions of history, and nonexistent laws," Donald Lemen Clark has written of these Roman originals.[30] The same holds true for the Tudors, in practice—we think of Hythlodaye's defense of *Utopia* or Euphues' defense of nature—as it does in theory. In this context of Tudor thought and training, Thomas Wilson's early statement in his *Arte of Rhetorique* about the end of humanist rhetoric is especially revealing. "The findyng out of apte matter," he proposes, "called otherwise Inuencion, is a searchyng out of thynges true, *or thynges likely,* the whiche maie reasonably sette furth a matter, and make it *appere* probable" (sig. A3v; my italics). Nor can there be a better definition of Arcadia or, according to Nashe, the world of *The Unfortunate Traueller,* than this.

THE LINE BETWEEN a developing rhetoric and a developing poetic for fiction thus becomes perilously thin. "Thynges likely" take many forms, but the most popular figures used by Tudor humanists as rhetorical techne are *prosopographia* and *prosopopoeia.* The former is an impersonation of a historical individual. Once again, it was first taught in the humanist grammar schools; once more, the models are given us by Seneca the Elder, this time in his *Suasoriae.* Here, in the first of seven, Alexander debates whether to sail the ocean (as the Loeb edition titles it), and the speaker must *imagine himself* one of the sailors, Alexander wishing to go, or his mother wishing to prevent him. In other exercises, the student is to take the part of Sparta at Thermopylae pressing his companions to stand and fight the Persians *or else* urging them to retreat; in a third, the speaker as Agamemnon tells Calchas why he refuses to sacrifice his daughter Iphigenia.[31] It is important to note that students were required, again and again, to play opposing roles, to simulate varying personalities, to *create characters*. Even more popular than prosopographia—and more distant from truth, most like poetry—is the impersonation known as prosopopoeia, or what George Puttenham calls in *The Arte of English Poesie* (1589) the feigning of a person who is fictional (sig. Dd2v), "when," as Angel Day has it in his *Declaration of all such Tropes, Figures, or Schemes* (1592), "to things without life we frame an action, speech, or person, fitting a man" (1595 ed., sig. Mm4). Abraham Fraunce's enthusiasm for this figure in particular in *The Arcadian Rhetorike* (1588) is shared with most Tudor rhetoricians. "*Prosopopoia* is a fayning of any person, when in our speech we represent the person of anie, and make it speake as though he were there present," he writes; "an excellent figure, much vsed of Poets, wherein wee must diligentlie take heede" (sig. G2). Impersonation is repeatedly the device that gives to *suasoria* and *controversia,* to declamation and disputation, their vividness, energy, and emotional conviction. Gascoigne, Nashe, and Lodge follow More and Lyly in making fictional characters persuasive, admonitory, and even exemplary, and Sidney singles out David's Psalms in the *Defence* because "his notable *Prosopopeias* . . . maketh you as it were see God comming in his maiestie" (sig. B4; 77).

Aristotle's *Rhetoric 2,* with its discussion of ethos and pathos, is another creative use of language to manipulate responses (and thoughts). Nor is Cicero unaware—or unsupportive—of still other possibilities. As early as the youthful *De Inventione,* he stresses the probable nature of argumentation and notes that, in assumptive issues unable to be proven, the rhetorician will rely on extraneous circumstances, shifting charges, or confession and avoidance (2.24.71 ff.). In the *Brutus* he acknowledges " 'the privilege . . . conceded to rhetoricians to distort history in order to give more point to their narrative' " ("inquit, arbitratu, quoniam quidem concessum est rhetoribus ementiri in historiis, ut aliquid dicere possint argutius" (10.42).[32] Even the inner dynamics of Cicero's *De Oratore* must have been strikingly instructive to the Tudors: although Crassus is presented as Cicero's ideal teacher, all the theory he establishes in this dialogue is undercut by the remarks and practices of Antonius, much as the activities of Thomas More's *Utopia* will be undermined in Hythlodaye's naiveté. Once we are alerted, we see how persistently Cicero transforms dialogue into inherent disputation—in which the judgment of the wider boundaries of rhetoric and the use and abuse of rhetoric are ours alone to make (cf. 2.27.115; 2.42.178; 2.17.72). As if recognizing that the Greek word for persuasion, *psychagogia,* would likewise be translated as "enchantment of the soul"—"a word," Eugene M. Waith reminds us, "which was used first of the conjuring of the souls of the dead and then applied metaphorically to the magic of words by which the mind may be directed"[33]—Quintilian in his *Institutio* devotes a surprising series of references to just those *techne* that would seem to us (and to Tudor humanists) to undermine his understanding, simply put, of the *rhetor* as *vir bonum.* This is true for each part of the traditional declamation: for the *exordium* (4.1.43), the *propositio* (4.3.19), the *confirmatio* (5.8.7), the *refutatio* (5.8.2) where even documents can be refuted on occasion (5.5.1), and the *peroratio* (6.1.1). In addition, there is room for appeals to the emotions (4.2.111). Wesley Trimpi has already made note of this. "The early writers of forensic manuals taught students how to pick out the weakest terms of their opponents in order to discredit them," he says, "and made no effort to educate them in any other way."[34] Coxe puts it rather differently, and more pungently: he finds that the rhetorician depends on "high and excellent quicke wyt" (sig. E2v), like Euphues—or Jack Wilton.

AT ITS BEST, then, at its most imaginative and playful, such agility and wit led to *paranomasia,* a kind of wordplay in which the rhetorician never betrays himself because he never insists on a single meaning for words or situations that are capable of more than one construction. As Sidney remarks of Plato in the *Defence,* he never lies as a poet precisely because he never affirms. Erasmus has fun, for example, with the word *bellum* in his serious adage on war:

> Necque non viderunt haec Grammatici, quorum alii bellum, dictum volunt, quod nihil habeat neque bonum, neque bellum: nec alia ratione bellum esse bellum, quam Furiae sunt Eumenides. Alii malunt à bellua deductum, quod belluarum sit, non hominum, in mutuum exitium congredi. At mihi sane plus quam ferinum, plus quam belluinum esse videtur, armis confligere. [*Adagia,* 953F]

> The grammarians perceyued right welle these thynges, of the whiche, some wyl, that warre haue his name by contrary meanyng of the worde *Bellum,* that is to seye fayre, bycause it hathe nothynge good nor feyre. Nor *bellum,* that is to sey warre, is none other wyse called *Bellum,* that is to seye fayre: then the furies are called *Eumenides,* that is to seye meke: by cause they are

woode and contrarye to all mekenes. And somme grammaryans thynke rather, that *Bellum* warre, shoulde be deryuied out of this worde *Belua,* that is for to say, a brute beaste: for soo moche as hit belongeth to brute beastie, and not vnto menne to runne to ge ther, eche to distroye other. But it semeth to me to passe farre all wylde and all brute beastlynes, to fyght to gether with weapons. [1533 trans., sigs. A7v–A8].

Such cleverness is meant to reveal indirectly both wise judgment and forceful eloquence, matter joined with manner. It suggests at once the interest in creativity and the desire to break loose from strictly formulaic presentation. Conversely, wit can openly parody traditional forms, as Proteus and Speed do in *Two Gentlemen of Verona:*

> *Speed.* The shepherd seeks the sheep, and not the sheep the shepherd; but I seek my master, and my master seeks not me: therefore, I am no sheep.
> *Proteus.* The sheep for fodder follow the shepherd, the shepherd for food follow not the sheep; thou for wages followest thy master, thy master for wages follows not thee: therefore thou art a sheep. [1.1.86–92]

Agility with language was approved by grammar school and university; and it was also forwarded by the Church, which meant to teach theologians how to attack heresies and win against tricky heretical arguments by bettering those who attacked the Church at their own game. It is this—as well as the joys of education—that Brinsley has in mind when he calls his book, subtitled *The Grammar Schoole, Lvdvs Literarivs.* This development of humanist rhetoric has its consequences for humanist fiction, too: in the wonderful spoof of the *Encomium Moriae* where Folly audaciously asks us to listen to her despite the fact that she wears the ass's ears of Midas, or when Rabelais addresses us—and significantly—as most noble boozers, or when Thomas More can insist we pay attention to, take time reading about, and even dispute Nowhere and Nothing.

Richard A. Lanham catches this spirit and also the situation: "Rhetorical man is trained not to discover reality but to manipulate it."[35] So does Ben Jonson. "It is an Art," he comments in *Discoveries,* "to have so much judgment, as to apparell a Lye well, to give it a good dressing; that though the nakednesse would shew deform'd and odious, the suiting of it might draw their Readers" (sig. M4v). The ends of words and wordplay did in fact "discover" realities at times by creating them, not merely by accumulating suitable or persuasive topoi but by imagining personae through sharply imaging prosopopoeia. But humanist educators did not always approve such fanciful writing. The result could be, as Thomas Elyot defines clearly in his *Dictionary* of 1538, the corruption of *sophia* ("wysedome") by the *sophos* ("a wyse man") into *sophisma* ("a craftye and deceytefull sentence, an Oracyon or inuention, whiche seemeth to be trewe, whan it is false") by a *sophista* ("a dissembler of wysedome, a deceyuer vnder an eloquente or crafty speakynge" (sig. Aal). His definitions echo Aristotle's observation in the appendix to his *Topica,* referring to Gorgias and Protagoras, that "the sophistic art consists in apparent and not real wisdom, and the sophist is one who makes money from apparent and not real wisdom" (*De Sophisticis Elenchis* 1.20–23)[36] and his own sophistical practice in his *Rhetoric* (1.9). Such a situation gave natural rise to Greek skepticism, most notably in the work of Sextus Empiricus. "Rhetoric declares this to be its main task," he writes,

> how, for instance, we are to make small things great and great things small, or how just things may be made to appear unjust, and the unjust just. And in general, as rhetoric consists of opposite statements, one cannot say that the refined speaker is an orator, but the unrefined no longer an orator. For the orator, of whatever sort he may be, must certainly practise himself in contradictory speeches, and injustice is inherent in contradictions; therefore every orator, being an advocate of injustice, is unjust.[37]

In his *Outlines of Pyrrhonism,* Sextus goes even farther by parodying disjunctive propositions the better to expose the possible abuse of dialectic and rhetoric.

> Some argue also as follows: If Socrates was born, Socrates became either when Socrates existed not or when Socrates already existed; but if he shall be said to have become when he already existed, he will have become twice; and if when he did not exist, Socrates was both existent and non-existent at the same time—existent through having become, non-existent by hypothesis. And if Socrates died, he died either when he lived or when he died. Now he did not die when he lived, since he would have been at once both alive and dead; nor yet when he died, since he would have been dead twice. Therefore Socrates did not die. And by applying this argument in turn to each of the things said to become or perish it is possible to abolish becoming and perishing.[38]

Little wonder that in light of all this Plato, in the *Gorgias* (463A–C), accuses sophists and rhetoricians alike of practicing neither art nor poetry but a kind of trade such as cookery, face painting, fawning, or bewitching— that is, being tricky, deceitful, immoral, or superficial—and exclaims to Callicles, at the end of the dialogue (520A), "Sophist and orator, my estimable friend, are the same thing, or very much of a piece."[39] For Plato, the rhetorician undertaking the art of persuasion was willing to accept any helpful arguments, even fallacious ones, from the sophist, whereas the symbiotic sophist, in his turn, would learn from the rhetorician seductive figures of speech. This goes some distance in explaining why Plato, when he apparently praises the inspired poet in the *Ion* for suppressing the intellect, actually compares him to one possessed, one without true reason (533C–534), and, further, why he feels he must banish any poet as one who imitated mere imitations rather than truths (*Republic,* 568B–C, 607B). And it is a decisive statement in helping us to place Euphues' sophistry as Lyly meant to depict it. Or, in another instance more similar than we might at first think, it helps us to place Jack Wilton's seductive teacher Surrey, whose fond poetry and love of the tournament never touch real life but, like a Roman pleasure garden, seduce and threaten Jack's very existence.

THE PROBLEM, then, whether admitting or denying wordplay, was to forge a usable poetic, to preserve the possibilities of the imagination in full awareness of these dangers in it. Cicero signals the need at the start of *De Inventione:* "Saepe et multum hoc mecum cogitavi, bonine an mali plus attulerit hominibus et civitatibus copia dicendi ac summum eloquentiae studium"; "I have often seriously debated with myself whether men and communities have received more good or evil from oratory and a consuming devotion to eloquence" (1.1). Isocrates had been even more clear-sighted and condemnatory. "Indeed, who can fail to abhor, yes to contemn, those teachers [of eristics]," he writes, "who devote themselves to disputation, since they pretend to search for truth, but straightway at the beginning of their professions attempt to deceive us with lies," adding they "have no interest whatever in the truth."[40] Such absolute distrust causes George Puttenham, in the single 1589 edition of his *Arte of English Poesie,* to urge that the judges of the Areopagus acted wisely in forbidding "all manner of figuratiue speaches to be vsed before them in their consistorie of Iustice, as meere illusions to the minde, and wresters of vpright iudgement," because "to allow such manner of forraine, & coloured talke to make the iudges affectioned, were all one as if the carpenter before he began to square his timber would make his squire crooked" (sigs. S2v–S3).

In retrospect, we can see how naturally the wit of an Erasmus or a More, the extravagant burlesque or jest of a Gascoigne, who shared an abiding trust in humanist nature and humanist language, could quickly lead to such denunciations. But it also seems to threaten the very grounds of fiction. It squelches poetry by denying creativity and by voiding the use of metaphor and image. It invites *dis*trust, an elemental and threatening skepticism. Plato seems to have been the first to foresee this, to sense the endangering possibilities. In rescuing a rhetoric for a usable poetic while confronting such dangers openly, he established grounds for a fiction that might reliably teach. He gave philosophic and rhetorical validity and purpose, that is, for More to create Utopia, Castiglione his Urbino, or Sidney Arcadia. Put another way, Plato paved the way for Lyly to imagine a Euphues, Greene a Perimides, and Nashe a Jack Wilton who could figuratively, metaphorically, discern through language both the danger and the vision of humanist belief and rhetoric.

And Plato manages to reserve grounds for establishing a usable poetic at precisely the point we have also reached—he discusses *good art* as the *avoidance of sophistry*. This statement of Plato's comes where we might hope to find it, in the middle or late dialogue *The Sophist,* which by its title doubtless attracted the attention of humanist thinkers like Elyot and Wilson as well as humanist writers of fiction. Here an Elean Stranger informs Theaetetus (in the presence of Theodorus and Socrates) of two fundamental kinds of art, icastic and fantastic. Both kinds of art are what the Stranger calls *productive* rather than *acquisitive* (219A–C), for they are not acquired from things already existing but bring into being something new. Thus both permit fiction. But these two kinds of art, according to Plato, are different in process and so identifiably distinct in their final products. Icastic or "likeness-making art" occurs "whenever anyone produces the imitation by following the proportions of the original in length, breadth, and depth, and giving, besides, the appropriate colours to each part" (235D)—when the artist records simply, without an intervenient imagination. Fantastic art, on the other hand, either creates that which does not exist or gives a disproportionate, faulty representation of the object being imitated—it "produces appearance," Plato says, "but not likeness" (236C). Icastic art copies the original precisely. Fantastic art is exemplified by

> those who produce some large work of sculpture or painting. For if they reproduced the true proportions of beautiful forms, the upper parts, you know, would seem smaller and the lower parts larger than they ought, because we see the former from a distance, the latter from near at hand. . . . So the artists abandon the truth and give their figures not the actual proportions but those which seem to be beautiful . . . but which would not even be likely to resemble that which it claims to be like, if a person were able to see such large works adequately. [235E–236B][41]

Representation, re-presentation, is the end of both forms of art, but the means are radically opposed. Icastic art conveys by reproducing an object; fantastic art re-creates the appearance only, not the substance; it succeeds because it allows for a subjective, or displaced, perspective. It *persuades* the viewer to accept the fantastic art form as icastic, to accept what *seems* to be for what is *known* to be. Plato's terms, already a nascent poetics because his examples are drawn from paintings and sculpture, are meant to divide truth from sophistry in his own sophistic age.

This passing example in Plato's abiding attack on the abuse of speech and Logos as a threat to philosophy became a central concern for humanist theorists in the Renaissance, eager as they were to locate in the classical heritage supplied by the New Learning a basis for inviolable (and justifiable) defenses of poetry. So we find such cinquecento critics as Patrizi, Castelvetro, and Mazzoni significantly agreeing with their authority Plato while making a chief issue of icastic as opposed to fantastic art. Patrizi, in *La deca disputata,* also prefers the figure of icastic art (which he calls *effigy*) as truthful and reliable in its contrast with the *image* of fantastic art, because effigies for him particularize ideas. In the *Poetica,* Castelvetro tests all inventions by their icastic properties, dismissing fantastic art because it is not verisimilar. One of the few exceptions to the general preference for icastic art is made in the *Della difesa della Commedia di Dante* 3, where Mazzoni finds icastic art too close to history and elects something more akin to fantastic art, which he describes as "marvelous-credible." Debate in humanist Italy on icastic and fantastic art came finally to rest on the widespread distinction made between Tasso's *Gerusalemme liberata* with its imitatio of biblical truth—Tasso's own 1585 *Apologia in difesa della sua Gerusalemme agli Accademici della Crusca* says he was influenced by Plato's definitions in *The Sophist* when he began his epic—and the opposing alternative, Ariosto's *Orlando Furioso,* which imitates nothing at all and is generally considered to be the epitome of fantastic art.[42] Tudor humanists as apologists for poetry in a second high age of rhetoric continue to argue for icastic art because of its lifelike properties, its truth, and its reliability. In his dedication to *The Revenge of Bussy D'Ambois* (1613), George Chapman argues that the poet creates not truth, but "things like truth" (sig. A3v), while Ben Jonson, in *Discoveries,* agrees that a "fainer" is one who "writes things like the Truth" (sig. R1). A fantastic poetics, on the other hand, results in unreal, freakish images. "This imagination," Juan Huarte Navarro writes in his *Examen de Ingeniis,* Englished by R. C. in 1594, "hath force not onely to compound a figure possible with another, but doth ioyne also (after the order of nature) those which are vnpossible, and of them growes to shape mountains of gold, and calues that flie" (sig. K2v). Such a commonplace attitude lies behind the complaint of John Davies of Hereford in *Mirum in modum* (1602) that "*Fantacie* / . . . doth so forme, reforme, [that] it deformes" (sig. B3) and behind Spenser's figure of Phantastes in *The Faerie Queene* (1590) with his chamber filled with "leasings, tales, and lies" (2.9.51; sig. X2).

Like their Italian counterparts, the Tudor humanists also developed the Platonic dichotomy in their own ways. For Puttenham, proportion and disproportion become infused with humanist reason; he distinguishes in *The Arte of English Poesie* between ordered and disordered art, or what he calls the "eufantastic" and the "fantastic." "Wherefore such persons as be illuminated with the brightest irradiations of knowledge and of the veritie and due proportion of things," he writes,

> they are called by the learned men not *phaentastici* but *euphantasiote* and of this sorte of phantasie are all good Poets, notable Captaines stratagema-tique, all cunning artificers and enginers, all Legislators Polititiens & Counsellours of estate, in whose exercises the inuentiue part is most employed and is to the sound & true iudgement of man most needful. [Sig. D4]

As for Sidney, his Puritan leanings caused yet another metamorphosis inspired by an openly pragmatic, explicitly Christian humanism while using nearly the same illustration we first find in Plato.

> For I will not denie, but that mans wit may make *Poesie*, which should be [*eikastike*] which some learned haue defined figuring foorth good things to be [*phantastike*] which doth contrariwise infect the fancie with vnwoorthie obiects, as the Painter should giue to the eye either some excellent perspectiue, or some fine Picture fit for building or fortification, or containing in it some notable example, as *Abraham* sacrificing his sonne *Isaak, Iudith* killing *Holofernes, Dauid* fighting with *Golias,* may leaue those, and please an ill pleased eye with wanton shewes of better hiddē matters. [Sig. G2; 104]

Sidney links the infected will with fantastic art and the erected wit with icastic art because it is icastic art, truly representing God's creation through the poet's analogous creative act, which moves men to virtue. For Sidney, poets counterfeit by establishing appealing alternative, but not deceptive, worlds: poetry is truth, the poet never lieth. More astonishing yet, *orator fit, poeta nascitur:* Erasmus's adage is turned back upon itself and so aborted. The poet, now using all the rhetorical devices instructed by humanist educators, can turn them to the perfection of the self and the welfare of society by using them to define and persuade men to truth through fiction. Humanist thought had struggled and so won the way for humanist literature, for the Tudor flowering of fiction under Elizabeth I.

VARIOUS FASHIONINGS of humanist fiction, from More's copia on an ideal commonwealth to Lyly's disputations on *euphues* or "good endow-ment," and from Sidney's foreconceit of Arcadia to Greene's wondrous fictions eliciting an instructive purpose for the marvelous, are diverse creative acts all proceeding directly from humanist lessons in classical rhetoric. The ancients anticipated such poetic possibilities in rhetoric. "Est enim finitimus oratori poeta, numeris astrictior paulo, verborum autem licentia liberior, multis vero ornandi generibus socius, ac paene par," Cicero argues in *De Oratore* 1; "The truth is that the poet is a very near kinsman of the orator, rather more heavily fettered as regards rhythm, but with ampler freedom in his choice of words, while in the use of many sorts of ornament he is his ally and almost his counterpart" (1.16.70). In the Renaissance, Erasmus for one is joyous over such a blurring of boundaries, as he comments in a letter to Andrew Ammonius on 21 December 1513: "me vehementer delectat poema rhetoricum et rhetor poeticus, vt et in oratione soluta carmen agnoscas et in carmine rhetoricam phrasin"; "What especially delights me is a rhetorical poem and a poetical oration, in which you can see the poetry in the prose and the rhetorical expression in the poetry."[43]

But if there was a certain joy for poets with the infusion of the vigor and vividness of rhetorical force and creativity in their work, in a second high age of rhetoric the potentiality for confusion between the eloquent use of antique techne for teaching wisdom and the misuse of similar (or even identical) techne to pursue the ends of sophistry grew acute. Trained readers from grammar schools, universities, and Inns of Court, alerted to the possibilities of multiple signification, interpreted or reinterpreted narrative and speech: this was, Richard A. Lanham reminds us, "a world of contingent purpose, of perpetual cognitive dissonance, plural orchestration."[44] Clearly, what the humanist writers needed—and what humanist poetics demanded—was still another classical authority from the New Learning that would help them in promulgating the ideas of Plato and the later Cicero while still employing the strategies of Aristotle, the earlier Cicero, and Quintilian. They found just such a resource in the philosopher (not the rhetorician) Seneca, whose ideas were particularly congenial to the fundamental tenets of humanist educators.

> Virtus non contingit animo nisi instituto et edocto et ad summum adsidua exercitatione perducto. Ad hoc quidem, sed sine hoc nascimur et in optimis quoque, antequam erudias, virtutis materia, non virtus est.

> Virtue is not vouchsafed to a soul unless that soul has been trained and taught, and by unremitting practice brought to perfection. For the attainment of this boon, but not in the possession of it, were we born; and even in the best of men, before you refine them by instruction, there is but the stuff of virtue, not virtue itself.[45]

Seneca's own awareness of sophistic rhetoric, moreover, caused him to develop for himself a poetics that moves considerably beyond that of Plato and Aristotle. It is a key passage in his Letter 65 on the nature of matter and art, and it is so crucial that it bears quoting at some length.

Omnis ars naturae imitatio est. Itaque quod de universo dicebam, ad haec transfer, quae ab homine facienda sunt. Statua et materiam habuit, quae pateretur artificem, et artificem, qui materiae daret faciem. Ergo in statua materia aes fuit, causa opifex. Eadem condicio rerum omnium est; ex eo constant, quod fit, et ex eo, quod facit. Stoicis placet unam causam esse, id, quod facit. Aristoteles putat causam tribus modis dici: "Prima," inquit, "causa est ipsa materia, sine qua nihil potest effici; secunda opifex. Tertia est forma, quae unicuique operi inponitur tamquam statuae"; nam hanc Aristoteles idos vocat. "Quarta quoque," inquit, "hic accedit, propositum totius operis." Quid sit hoc, aperiam. Aes prima statuae causa est. Numquam enim facta esset, nisi fuisset id, ex quo funderetur ducereturve. Secunda causa artifex est. Non potuisset enim aes illud in habitum statuae figurari, nisi accessissent peritae manus. Tertia causa est forma. Neque enim statua ista doryphoros aut diadumenos vocaretur, nisi haec illi esset inpressa facies. Quarta causa est faciendi propositum. Nam nisi hoc fuisset, facta non esset. Quid est propositum? Quod invitavit artificem, quod ille secutus fecit; vel pecunia est haec, si venditurus fabricavit, vel gloria, si laboravit in nomen, vel religio, si donum templo paravit. Ergo et haec causa est, propter quam fit; an non putas inter causas facti operis esse numerandum, quo remoto factum non esset?

His quintam Plato adicit exemplar, quam ipse idean vocat; hoc est enim, ad quod respiciens artifex id, quod destinabat, effecit. Nihil autem ad rem pertinet, utrum foris habeat exemplar, ad quod referat oculos, an intus, quod ibi ipse concepit et posuit. Haec exemplaria rerum omnium deus intra se habet numerosque universorum, quae agenda sunt, et modos mente complexus est; plenus his figuris est, quas Plato ideas appellat, immortales, immutabiles, infatigabiles. Itaque homines quidem pereunt, ipsa autem humanitas, ad quam homo effingitur, permanet, et hominibus laborantibus, intereuntibus illa nihil patitur. Quinque ergo causae sunt, ut Plato dicit: id ex quo, id a quo, id in quo, id ad quod, id propter quod. Novissime id quod ex his est. Tamquam in statua, quia de hac loqui coepimus, id ex quo aes est, id a quo artifex est, id in quo forma est, quae raptatur illi, id ad quod exemplar est, quod imitatur is, qui facit, id propter quod facientis propositum est, id quod ex istis est, ipsa statua est. Haec omnia mundus quoque, ut ait Plato, habet. Facientem: hic deus est. Ex quo fit: haec materia est. Formam: haec est habitus et ordo mundi, quem videmus. Exemplar, scilicet, ad quod deus hanc magnitudinem operis pulcherrmi fecit. Propositum, propter quod fecit. Quaeris, quod sit propositum deo? Bonitas. Ita certe Plato ait: "Quae deo faciendi mundum fuit causa? Bonus est; bono nulla cuiusquam boni invidia est. Fecit itaque quam optimum potuit." Fer ergo, iudex, sententiam et pronuntia, quis tibi videatur verissimum dicere, non quis verissimum dicat. Id enim tam supra nos est quam ipsa veritas.

All art is but imitation of nature; therefore, let me apply these statements of general principles to the things which have to be made by man. A statue, for example, has afforded matter which was to undergo treatment at the hands of the artist, and has had an artist who was to give form to the matter. Hence, in the case of the statue, the material was bronze, the cause was the workman. And so it goes with all things,—they consist of that which is made, and of the maker. The Stoics believe in one cause only,—the maker; but Aristotle thinks that the word "cause" can be used in three ways: "The first cause," he says, "is the actual matter, without which nothing can be created. The second is the workman. The third is the form, which is impressed upon every work,—a statue, for example." This last is what Aristotle calls the *idos*. "There is, too," says he, "a fourth,—the purpose of the work as a whole." Now I shall show you what this last means. Bronze is the "first cause" of the statue, for it could never have been made unless there had been something from which it could be cast and moulded. The "second cause" is the artist; for without the skilled hands of a workman that bronze could not have been shaped to the outlines of the statue. The "third cause" is the form, inasmuch as our statue could never be called The Lance-Bearer or The Boy Binding his Hair, had not this special shape been stamped upon it. The "fourth cause" is the purpose of the work. For if this purpose had not existed, the statue would not have been made. Now what is this purpose? It is that which attracted the artist, which he followed when he made the statue. It may have been money, if he has made it for sale; or renown, if he has worked for reputation; or religion, if he has wrought it as a gift for a temple. Therefore this also is a cause contributing towards the making of the statue: or do you think we should avoid including, among the causes of a thing which has been made, that element without which the thing in question would not have been made?

To these four Plato adds a fifth cause,—the pattern which he himself calls the "idea"; for it is this that the artist gazed upon when he created the work which he had decided to carry out. Now it makes no difference whether he has his pattern outside himself, that he may direct his glance to it, or within himself, conceived and placed there by himself. God has within himself these patterns of all things, and his mind comprehends the harmonies and the measures of the whole totality of things which are to be carried out; he is filled with these shapes which Plato calls the "ideas,"— imperishable, unchangeable, not subject to decay. And therefore, though men die, humanity itself, or the idea of man, according to which man is moulded, lasts on, and though men toil and perish, it suffers no change. Accordingly, there are five causes, as Plato says: the material, the agent, the

make-up, the model, and the end in view. Last comes the result of all these. Just as in the case of the statue,—to go back to the figure with which we began,—the material is the bronze, the agent is the artist, the make-up is the form which is to be adapted to the material, the model is the pattern imitated by the agent, the end in view is the purpose in the maker's mind, and, finally, the result of all these is the statue itself. The universe also, in Plato's opinion, possesses all these elements. The agent is God; the source, matter; the form, the shape and the arrangement of the visible world. The pattern is doubtless the model according to which God has made this great and most beautiful creation. The purpose is his object in so doing. Do you ask what God's purpose is? It is goodness. Plato, at any rate, says: "What was God's reason for creating the world? God is good, and no good person is grudging of anything that is good. Therefore, God made it the best world possible." Hand down your opinion, then, O judge; state who seems to you to say what is truest, and not who says what is absolutely true. For to do that is as far beyond our ken as truth itself. [3–11][46]

The need so decidedly pronounced here is the need to pass beyond the four causes of the Aristotelian *Organon* which, as limned in the *Prior Analytics,* was susceptible to the fallacious arguments detailed in the *Rhetoric* and potential grounds for sophistry and eristics. It is a need felt by the humanists for a model. It is not just the method of imitatio as a means of instruction but, rather, an ideal model that grounds humanist language in humanist values and ideas, serving as a stable guide. It is a model that is the starting point for their poetry. The *fifth* cause, this Platonic or Senecan original, as we might term it, is that basis of humanist poetics that takes rhetoric and poetics past the dangers (if *not* the techne; there is no need for that) of sophistry. It is this use of a correct model and correct technique that according to Plato achieves both the good and the pleasurable (*Republic,* 607C–E).

This is not at all surprising, of course, given the centrality of the exemplar to the humanist process of cultivation. But, as Wesley Trimpi has recently commented, by placing the fifth cause between the formal and final causes Seneca opens up the possibilities of creation while preventing the possibilities of incoherence or chaos.[47] On the one hand, this allows fiction writers to appeal implicitly to Alexandrian romance as well as to Longinus's sense of wonder (or something akin to it), as Greene does, every bit as much as it allows More, in creating *Utopia,* to identify what humanists can accept in Hythlodaye's vision by playing it off against Plato's *Republic* and Plutarch's *Lycurgus,* or Nashe, in writing *The Unfortunate Traueller,* to insinuate Juvenal's first Satire and the Book of Revelation as equally central to his meaning. At the same time that this fifth cause allows a humanist poetics that frees fiction without letting it become unmoored entirely, it also allows a surface levity that can complement or counter the serious *significatio;* as the exemplar of the Silenus allows us to chart the meaning, as well as the jokes, of the *Encomium Moriae,* Erasmus's best-known fiction, and the humor of the symbolic disguises shaping the declamations and disputations of Pyrocles and Musidorus in the *Arcadia* points out that novel's intention to teach through its serious underpinning in the political philosophy of Aristotle and Cicero. It is only fitting that in this teaching fiction of humanist poetics, Thomas Lodge, still struggling to validate and extend Christian humanist values in later years, returns to translating Seneca himself—and sees this as a logical outgrowth of his earlier humanist novels, *Rosalynde* and *A Margarite of America.* For Lodge, an exemplary model for fictional characters and Stoic and Christian models for actual lives are finally indistinguishable.

At the deepest conceptual roots, then, humanist poetics is both philosophically and rhetorically grounded; it marries both chief interests of the humanist educators. Ethical and stylistic models are alike appealed to—and they may be identical, or spoken of in identical terms, as Hanna H. Gray has written.[48] Humanist poetics is, moreover, a poetics that directs thoughts, always, toward abstractions; it leads away from the circumstances and confinements of a mundane world toward more universal conceptualizations which from the start appealed to the humanist temperament and turn of mind and emphasized the usefulness (and compatibility; indeed, the necessity) of the Platonic concept of Form while making it seductive and persuasive through rhetorical patternings. F. M. Cornford in a neglected but brilliant essay of 1932 states this important characteristic succinctly from the viewpoint of the antique philosophers.

> In mathematical proof, the mind "travels" down through an argument limited by the premises assumed, "as if the mind could not mount above its hypotheses." ... Dialectic includes an opposite movement of thought, upwards, "treating its hypotheses not as principles but literally as *hypo-theses,* positions laid down, like steps which discourse can mount upon and take off from, in order that, advancing all the way to that which rests on no hypothesis—to the principle of the whole—it may apprehend that.[49]

It is a short and natural step to move from the *thesis* of the *declamatio* or *suasoria* to a linked sequence of such *theses* in *disputatio;* it is not difficult either to imagine Thomas More, observing the wordplay of Erasmus in his copious development of *folly,* replying with his own variations on *nowhere, Nusquam,* or on *utopia* and *eutopia*—or to imagine Lyly teased into fictional theses and hypotheses on *nature* and *nurture,* or Nashe on *travel* and *travail.* What such writers sense, however, is that for the sequence to work it cannot be random, and for aesthetic pleasure to be awakened it must have rhetorical form. Given such prerequisites, fiction can evolve into—even transcend—the highest of universal ideas and values: into wisdom for Lyly; into justice for Sidney; into wonder for Greene. Such spiraling intellectual organicism is, finally, as far removed from Aristotle's *Poetics* as the *Utopia* and *Arcadia* are from the *Oedipus Tyrannus*. Humanist poetics is a poetics of discovery as well as of recovery, at once inductive and deductive.

SUCH A POETICS signals a kind of intellectual and imaginative liberty that was given sudden and glorious warrant by the advent of humanism. Erasmus's analogy of his period with the dawn of civilization captures the Tudor humanists' enthusiasm, their joy—and their naiveté. The powerful forces of humanism and their various educational programs were at first sufficient to block from men's minds the periodic threats posed by nationalism, poverty, plague, and illiteracy and the various ambitions and tactics of popes and kings. Such dazzling forces of a world splendidly reborn on the road to perfection even override the last years of Henry VIII and move into the reign of Edward VI, halted only by the shaky religious and political actions that threaten a continuous sense of Tudor well-being, and then temporarily. For after the bloodshed and bitterness, the quarrels and treachery that mark the brief reign of the Counter-Reformation in England, an untarnished humanism surfaces again, with new means toward glory in the new courtly behavior and values first fictionally limned of Urbino by Castiglione but, it would seem, perpetually realizable during the peaceful years under Elizabeth I. If the initial wordplay and paradox of More and Gascoigne are subsequently muted—in Greene, say—there is renewed attention to elegance and eloquence. It is, in fact, only when the peculiar glories of humanist philosophy renewed by Christian humanism and captured by humanist fiction move widely away from the workaday world of the reader that we find fiction writers fumbling for new models, new and sufficient Senecan and Platonic originals.

The history of Tudor humanist fiction thus develops out of and parallels the history of Tudor humanism. At first charged with the beliefs of Erasmus and the expansive, inquiring joy of More, humanist fiction comes into question (if deftly and temporarily) with Gascoigne, who finds the early humanist confidence in man's nature and nurture innocent of contrary experience and self-serving in the employment of sophistry. The human capacity for self-improvement implied by Folly and by Hythlodaye is optimistic, even when Erasmus and More consider such human shortcomings as pride and ignorance. All things, they imply, can be mended.

The possibilities for amelioration and advancement remain eternal and infinite. But such fiction does not contemplate so powerful a movement as the Protestant Reformation with its brutal wars and its ugly pronouncements on man's natural depravity, and it is left for Gascoigne's *Adventures of Master F. J.* in 1573, when a buried humanism is resurfacing, to bring into question what More and Erasmus had trusted by exploring the possibility of self-deception by wit as a deliberate, continual disguise of more primitive and selfish desires. In the early decades of Elizabeth, humanist fiction enters a second phase in which an eloquent style as a testament to man's innate capacities attempts to chart humanist ideas of perfectibility in the larger realm of the human imagination. The emphasis now is not so much on words—on the play of wit—as on man's actions in social, marital, and political relationships. Humanist improvement is sought through the security of humanist fiction as becoming that Senecan or Platonic model which before it only drew from for a patterning. Lyly's detailed examinations of worldly experience against the pale lessons from books epitomized first by Eubulus and later by Euphues, Greene's use of wonder to awaken a sense of desirable discipline and improvement, and Sidney's attempt to achieve total harmony among philosophy, polity, and poetry embrace an evolution from clever sophistry to hard-won spirituality, informed by both pagan and Christian texts. But this second cycle repeats the first; in asking readers to judge the validity and utility of their fictions as a way to promote and prolong humanist values and thoughts of perfectibility, Lyly, Greene, and Sidney all call attention to the fact that fiction cannot substitute for life, that its success still rests on the contingencies of actuality. It is to the credit of Nashe and Lodge, coming in such twilight days of humanism when the perfectibility of man no longer seems viable and the perfection of language no longer seems possible, that they attempt, for one last time, to concentrate (as Nashe does) on the possibility of reformation or (as Lodge does) on the need for redemption. That these two writers learn through bitter experience in writing fiction that man's art gives way to God's providence shows their work at the borderline of the imagination, where the edges between fiction and treatise become (it would seem permanently) blurred.

The authentic rise of the novel in England, then, is a major consequence of humanist thought and humanist rhetoric. But that, seen in retrospect, was both its blessing and its curse. Initially, fiction could share the exuberance and freedom enjoyed by humanist thoughts of disciplining, cultivating, and fashioning men to perfection. It exercised wit and wisdom through a copiousness that at times seems almost endless. This is possible because the trust humanists held in men generally, and educated men especially, allowed writers of fiction to see their work, even at its most creative, as instructive, as significant, and as thoughtful contributions to burgeoning culture. Fiction writers could explore, experiment, and test ways that stretched literature in numerous directions and gave to image and metaphor both immediacy and importance. But with the severe testing of time—through war, religious strife, plague, and poverty—the idea (or ideal) of human perfectibility receded to the last reaches of man's vision, and a fiction that rested on such claims had to find, through other Senecan or Platonic models, new reasons to exist. In the end, it gave way to the satire of pamphlet and drama, and the early novels of English literature, for a time, lost their influence. But when the English novel again takes root in a major way in the eighteenth century, with a new and different, a proletarian, audience, it is instructive that Swift draws for a Senecan model on More, as Richardson does on Sidney, and Fielding on Nashe. Despite the severity of the challenges the writers of humanist fiction had to face, sooner or later, they discovered for all time the sources of fiction that have prevailed to the present day, as well as anticipating, in today's nonfiction novels, the very limits of the form.

I

THE POETICS OF WORDPLAY

He who enters in this school
Learns a new and wondrous rule:—
"Who hath never been a fool,
Wisdom's scholar cannot be."
JACOPONE DA TODI

ONE

Introduction

 "OUTSIDE ITALY," A. J. KRAILSHEIMER WRITES, "ERASMUS IS UNQUESTIONABLY THE POINT OF DEPARTURE FROM WHICH ALMOST EVERYTHING ELSE STEMS."[1] HE IS ALSO THE IMMEDIATE CONTINENTAL source of a Tudor humanist poetics for fiction. His *Encomium Moriae,* which Johan Huizinga once called "the perfect work of art,"[2] is an exacting paradigm, a kind of Senecan original, for the Tudor fiction of Thomas More and George Gascoigne. As a classical speech of praise defending indefensible folly, it demonstrates the power of humanist oratory and the skill and ingenuity available to the humanist rhetorician. At the same time it displays in the passionate and irrefragable commitment beneath the ludic surface its serious aim to defend learning and reason. All of these features bear some examination here because they will help us to understand, as the early Tudor humanists did, what More attempts in the *Utopia* and Gascoigne intends in *The Adventures of Master F. J.* Moreover, the techniques Erasmus is the first to discover are precisely those that More will use to expose Hythlodaye and Gascoigne will employ to examine, through various levels of fictive wordplay, the pretense of the gentle life grounded in Petrarchanism.

Nor was Erasmus's work ignored by generations of English humanists to follow: Sidney in his *Defence of Poesie* remarks that in the *Encomium Moriae* Erasmus "had an other foundation then the superficiall part would promise" and so honored its wit,[3] and nearly a century later the young Milton still finds the *Encomium* in everyone's hands at Cambridge, "Et cuique jam in manibus est ingeniosissimum illud Moriae encomium non infimi Scriptoris opus."[4] We might speculate that the carnival atmosphere of the crowd that applauds Folly on her entrance at the beginning of Erasmus's fiction and the infectious vitality and joy of Folly in her subsequent self-praise could have led the amused humanists of the sixteenth century to think of the *Encomium Moriae* itself as the supreme act of folly, as the theologians and monks exemplified by Martin Dorp did, but they were never misled by Folly in this way. Erasmus "neuer shewed more arte,

nor witte, in any the grauest boke he wrote, than in this his praise of Folie,"
Thomas Chaloner remarks in his preface to the first English translation
(1549), although he was well aware that the reader "maie chaunce to see
his own image more liuely described [there] than in any peincted table"
(sigs. A3v, A2v). As one of the early English humanists, Chaloner was less
concerned with the open satire on scholasticism and the Church than with
the cleverness of Erasmus's idea and the deftness of his execution. "Folie
in al poincts is not (as I take it) so straunge vnto vs, but that hir name maie
well be abidden, as long as will we or nill we, she will be sure to beare a
stroke in most of our dooyngs" (sig. A2). By extrapolating again and again
so as to make clear in his translation Erasmus's humor and meaning in the
original Latin, Chaloner sees—as Sidney and Milton do—that the
Encomium Moriae is an Aphthonian fable, defined by Richard Rainolde in
his *Foundacion of Rhetorike* (1563) as "a forged tale, cōtaining in it by the
colour of a lie, a matter of truthe" (sig. A2v).

Their ready appreciation stems from a humanist education all of them
share: "Better unborn than untaught" was one of the more popular
Erasmian adages. The sources of the *Encomium Moriae* can be traced to
Erasmus's early schooling with the Brethren of the Common Life at
Deventer where the young boy found himself "swept onwards towards the
New Learning by a hidden and overpowering instinct: *occulta naturae vi
rapiebar ad bonas literas.*"[5] The Brethren, who "exerted their crowning
activities in the seclusion of the schoolroom and the silence of the writing
cell,"[6] instilled in Erasmus the love of ancient texts, pagan and patristic,
texts to which More, Lyly, and Sidney would turn in their fiction. The
Brethren led Erasmus, too, to classical satires such as those recorded in
later editions of the *Encomium Moriae* as additional remarks, the *parerga:*
Seneca's *In Mortem Claudii Caesaris,* which applies elevated classical
allusions to the paltry facts of the present, and Synesius's *De Laudibus
Calvicii,* which uses formal oratory for trivial subjects,[7] the sort of witty
tradition that would later inspire writers like Gascoigne, Lyly, and Nashe.
Likewise imbued with the Brethren's *Devotio Moderna,* which emphasized
individual religious experience and cultivated an ethical rather than a
sacramental piety, and which he later transformed into his own *Philosophia
Christi,* Erasmus seems particularly important when we read the later
humanist fiction of Lodge and of Greene.

The *Encomium Moriae*—published with two titles, not one: *Morias
engkomion; Stultitiae laus*—pulls together all of Erasmus's interests in one
great act of humanist fiction that is at once profoundly philosophic and,
with its surface levity, an apparent *jeu d'esprit.* Allegedly drafted in seven
days in London in 1509 when Erasmus was forty-three, revised and

augmented for publication in Paris in 1511 when he was forty-five, it makes obvious use of humanist purpose, thought, and rhetoric as well as a standard technique of classical forensic declamation—irony. *Stultitia loquitur:* Folly speaks, we learn at the beginning, rather than Wisdom, but, like any earnest student of humanism, she hopes through humanist eloquence to become *sophas,* to become wise.

> Lubitum est enim paulisper apud vos Sophistam agere, non quidem hujus generis quod hodie nugas quasdam anxias inculcat pueris, ac plusquam muliebrem rixandi pertinaciam tradit, sed veteres illos imitabor, qui quo infamem Sophorum appellationem vitarent, *Sophistae* vocari maluerint. Horum studium erat, Deorum ac fortium virorum laudes encomiis celebrare. Encomium igitur audietis, non Herculis, neque Solonis, sed meum ipsius, hoc est, Stultitiae.

> I purpose a season to become a *Sophiste,* mistake me not I praie you, as if I saied Sophistrer, suche as now a daies driue into childers heads, certaine tangled trifuls, with more than womens stubbournesse and skoldyng in their disputacions. But I meane the other, who to the ende they myght shonne that presumptuous name of *Sophi* or wysemen, did rather take vpon them to be called *Sophistes:* Whose study and profession it was, to aduaunce, and set foorth in theyr writyngs the praises bothe of the Godds, and of men also, suche as were famous and worthies here in earth. Ye shall heare therfore the praise set foorth, not of *Hercules,* nor yet of *Solon,* but rather of myne owne selfe, That is to saie of Folie.[8]

This emblem passage contains within it all the strands of Folly's prosopopoeia. She will speak in the respected tradition of the best of the ancients, although they disclaimed the name of wisdom for that of *rhetor,* which Folly's syntax makes antonymous.[9] Alternatively, she will be straightforward with us—"Mihi porro semper gratissimum fuit dicere" (*LB* 4:408A); "it hath euer best lyked me to speake streight what so euer laie on my tongues ende" (sig. A2v)—unlike those orators whose public character was merely a role for the end of persuasion and despite being a woman, which figured for her day fickleness, ignorance, and temptation.[10]

As consequence, Folly's intentions and behavior are divorced from the start. She claims it needless to follow "vulgarium istorum Rhetorum consuetudinem, me ipsam finitione explicem porro ut dividam, multo minus"; ("these common Sophisters and Rhetoriciens maner, [to] go about to shew by diffinicion what I am, and muche lesse vse any diuision" (*LB* 4:408A; sig. A2v), yet that is exactly what she does. She presents a classical declamation in the five parts that Cicero and Quintilian teach. The partitioning of her argument is clear, as is her parsing of issues; she thus lectures *about* her audience while lecturing *to* them. Folly's speech is throughout both wise and foolish; it is learned in its allusions but absurd in its quotations, wrenched as they are from context;[11] and in both ways her speech is a deliberate parody of the sort that Erasmus—whom Ascham calls "the honor of learning of all oure time" in *The Scholemaster* (sig. G3)—had earlier hired himself out to compose for Philip of Burgundy.[12] Although Folly denies speaking in any traditional oratorical form, that is precisely her method, as Hoyt Hudson and Walter Kaiser have long since shown us.[13]

The title mirrors this factual dissembling. The genitive *Moriae* is syntactically ambiguous, either subjective or objective: it may mean that Folly is doing the praising, or it may mean that Folly is being praised. *Encomium Moriae,* written at Thomas More's house at the Old Barge, Bucklersbury, can likewise be doubly translated as *The Praise of Folly* or *In Praise of More.* Raising all these possibilities for his "*small Declamation*" (sig. A2v) in a prefatory letter to "*disputant*" More (sig. A4), Erasmus refuses to choose between them. "*I conceiv'd this exercise of wit, would not be least approv'd by you,*" he continues, allowing "wit" (*ingenii*) to mean "wisdom" or "foolery"—the same deliberate ambiguity More will use in *Utopia*—and adds,

> *Deinde suspicabar hunc ingenii nostri lusum tibi praecipue probatum iri, propterea quod soleas hujus generis jocis, hoc est, ni fallor, nec usquequaque insulsis, impendio delectari, & omnino in communi mortalium vita Democritum quemdam agere. Quamquam tu quidem, ut pro singulari quadam ingenii tui perspicacitate, longe lateque a vulgo dissentire soles, ita pro incredibili morum sua vitate facilitatque cum omnibus omnium horarum hominem agere, & potes & gaudes.*
>
> *inasmuch as you are wont to be delighted with such kind of mirth, that is to say, neither unlearned, if I am not mistaken, nor altogether insipid, and in the whole course of your life have play'd the part of a* Democritus. *And though, such is the excellence of your Iudgement, that 'twas ever contrary to that of the peoples, yet such is your incredible affability, and sweetness of temper that you both can, and delight to carry your self to all men, a man of all hours.* [LB 4:401-2; sig. A2v]

The portrait that emerges here is one of More as intellectual recluse—and *because* of his "*excellence of . . . Iudgement*"—yet one who mingles with those common people from whom his wisdom estranges him. Thus, in a letter written for us rather than for Thomas More (for it tells More nothing he does not already know), More himself becomes the foolishly wise Folly, as the implicit equation of the punning title says.[14]

But "The reader hauing any consideraunce," Chaloner also notes in his preface, "shall soone espie, how in euery mattier, yea almost euery clause, is hidden besides the myrth, some deeper sence and purpose" (sig. A3v). This admonition proves instructive. Folly begins her self-praise with a brief biography. Her parents, she tells us unequivocally, are the god Plutus, god of riches, and a nymph named Youth; she was conceived out of wedlock, when her father was inebriated (*LB* 4:410A; sig. A4), on the Fortunate Isles (*LB* 4:410B; sig. A4v).[15] This is obvious joking, but it is also a little puzzling when we consider that repeatedly Folly sees materialism as evil (as we do), a foolishness she herself cannot abide. What she implies, then, is not that she is Riches or Youth but that she is the singular product of both; and it is the riches *of* youth, which she redefines as instinctual pleasure and beauty, that she calls again and again the basis of a wisdom *misjudged* to be folly. As further self-definition, she identifies her chief companions as Madness and Oblivion, again outrageous on the face of it (*LB* 4:410A–B, 412D; sigs. A4v–B2).[16] But, by the close of her oration, we will realize that this is seriously meant, for only in states of madness and oblivion, both seen synonymously as meaning self-delusion from the wickedness and pain of the world, does wisdom reside.

Repeatedly, the worse appears the better part: *hoc est hominem esse;* at the heart of Folly's argument is the issue of semantics, or the very root of sophistical rhetoric. So, for Folly (often speaking wisely and drawing on classical myth and contemporary proverb as authority), a father's foolish love for his squint-eyed son solders family unity (*LB* 4:420A; sig. C4v); foolish youths can likewise be seen as carefree men rather than experienced hypocrites; drunkenness can be a necessary sedative; blindness makes marriage possible; cities and empires are preserved by flattery; and self-love can lead to contentment and that in turn to generosity: for how can we love our neighbors as ourselves if, first, we do not love—that is, respect—ourselves?[17] And how, then, do we maintain art?

> [Nisi adsit dextra haec Philautia].... Tolle hoc vitae condimentum & protinus frigebit cum sua actione Orator, nulli placebit cum suis numeris Musicus, explodetur cum sua gesticulatione Histrio, ridebitur una suis cum Musis Poëta, sordebit cum arte Pictor.... Ut ne dicam interim, nullum egregium facinus adiri, nisi meo impulsu, nullas egregias artes, nisi me auctore fuisse repertas.

> Take awaie this saulce of *Selflikyng* [Philautia], which is euin the verie relesse [release] of mans life and doynges, and by and by ye shal see the *Oratour* cold in his mattier, the *Musicien* mislyked withall his discant, the *Plaier* hissed out of the place, the *Poete* and his muses taught to skorne, the *Peincter* and his art naught set by. [*LB* 4:421E–F, 422C; sig. D2v]

In sum, "I recke not much, to passe ouer vntouched, how no maner arte, or noble deede was euer attempted, nor any arte or science inuented, other, than of whiche I might fully beholden first author" (sig. D3).

This brief catalogue of putative folly redefined as wisdom is an accurate microcosmos of the larger anthology that is Folly's *confirmatio*—and most of her oration: what Erasmus calls elsewhere an *argumentum fictum*.[18] She herself provides an initial index to it with her citation of the Socratic Silenus.

> Principio constat res omnes humanas, velut Acibiadis Silenos, binas habere facies nimium inter sese dissimiles. Adeo ut quod prima, ut ajunt, fronte mors est, si interius inspicias, vita sit: contra quod vita, mors: quod formosum, deforme: quod opulentum, id pauperrimum: quod infame, gloriosum: quod doctum, indoctum: quod robustum, imbecille: quod generosum, ignobile; quod laetum, triste: quod prosperum, adversum: quod amicum, inimicum: quod salutare, noxium: breviter, omnia repente versa reperies, si Silenum aperueris.

> For fyrst it is not vnknowen, how all humaine thyngs lyke the *Silenes or duble images of Alcibiades,* haue two faces muche vnlyke and dissemblable, that what outwardly seemed death, yet lokyng within ye shulde fynde it lyfe: and on the other side what semed life, to be death: what fayre, to be foule: what riche, beggerly: what cunnyng, rude: what stronge, feable: what noble, vile: what gladsome, sadde: what happie, vnlucky: what friendly, vnfriendly: what healthsome, noysome. Briefely the Silene ones beyng vndone and disclosed, ye shall fynde all thyngs tourned into a new semblance. [*LB* 4:428A–B; sig. E3][19]

As an emblem of myriad potentiality, the Silenus drawn from Socrates himself schemes man as *sub specie moriae*. Thus Folly realizes the possibilities of her own persona in the mirroring symbol drawn from the Senecan original, the series of disputations in Plato's *Symposium*. In rhetorical terms, she has transformed the apparent declamation into a disputation between what is said and its very opposite.[20] Understanding this, we can only marvel at Folly's attempt—or Erasmus's, for they are one—to master rhetorical sophistry and convert it through an analogical and metaphoric exemplar into a usable poetics.

Recognizing Folly's customary dichotomizing thus allows us to locate our own responses more consciously. Sometimes we agree with Folly, and she seems to side with us; at other times she is outrageous, and she attacks us: "qui se sapientiae studio dediderunt"; "this kynde of men, that are bookisshe" are thereby "peuisshe" (sig. D4v; *LB* 4:423). Folly's only real maneuverability is from one extreme to the other, from witnessing to ideal life as we would have her if she were wisdom (on the one hand) and reporting actual life as folly (on the other). Thus her apparent joke, to find folly in wisdom or wisdom in folly as Erasmus claims in his letter to More, is in fact her single point.[21] The only complication is that, in love with rhetoric yet a bit fearful of its redounding on her, she would assume *both* the role of defendant and that of respondent so as to assure herself the victory in the argument.

The remainder of her oration realizes the continuing value of the Silenic disputation as poetic form. And, having recovered her own Senecan original, she becomes more leisurely in developing her twinned themes— for, in love with the disputation, she seems limited to doublets—in the notions of wisdom in madness and life in oblivion. Her observations, nonbookish, are drawn from witnessing life: in this too she cannot help addressing a basic concern of humanism.

> Principio si rerum usu constat prudentia, in utrum magis competet ejus cognominis honos, in sapientem, qui partim ob pudorem, partim ob animi timiditatem nihil aggreditur, an in stultum, quem neque pudor quo vacat, neque periculum, quod non perpendit, ab ulla ne deterret? Sapiens ad libros Veterum consugit, atque hinc meras vocum argutias ediscit. Stultus adeundis cominusque periclitandis rebus, veram, ni fallor, prudentiam colligit. Id quod vidisse videtur Homerus, etiam si caecus, cum ait ῥὲχθὲν δέ τε νήπιος ἔγνω. Sunt enim duo praecipua ad cognitionem rerum parandam obstacula, pudor qui fumum offundit animo, & metus, qui, ostenso periculo, dehortatur ab adeundis facinoribus. At his magnifice liberat Stultitia. Pauci mortales intelligunt ad quam multas alias quoque commoditates conducat, numquam pudescere, & nihil non audere.

> And fyrst of all, if *Prudence* consisteth in longe practise and experience of thyngs, vnto whether of these maie the honour of that name better square? Either to this wyseman, who partly for shame, and partly for dastardnesse of herte, attempteth nothyng, or els that foole, whom neither shame, beyng shameles, nor perill, beyng reckeles, maie feare from prouyng any thyng. A wyseman reports hym selfe to his bokes, and there learneth naught but mere triflyng distinctions of woords. A foole in ioepardyng, and goyng presently where thyngs are to be knowne, gathereth (vnles I am deceiued) the perfect true prudence. Whiche *Homer* seemeth, notwithstandyng his blindnesse to haue seen, whan he said thus, *A foole knoweth the thyng, that is ones dooen.* For there be two stronge lettes againste such knowlage of thyngs to be gathered, that is to saie, shame and dreade: shame, that casts a mist before mens myndes: and dreade, that shewyng the perilles, discounsaileth men from ventryng any enterprises. But I Folie maie, and am wonte to wype those lettes cleane awaie. Yea, few men consider, how many ways els it auaileth to bloushe at nothyng, and dare dooe euery thyng. [*LB* 48, 417C–418A; sigs. E2v–E3]

Men hang on to life; "lothe they are to die yet" (sig. F2). "So that how lesse cause they haue, why they shoulde lyue, yet so muche leefer is life vnto theim, not that they fele any combraunce of the same" (sig. F2); ("ut ne tum quidem libeat vltam relinquere cum exacto Paracarum stamine, ipsa jam dudum eos relinquit vita, quoque minus sit causae, cur in vita manere debeant, hoc magis juvet vivere, tantum abest, ut ullo vitae taedio tangantur"; *LB* 4:431C). Folly's gift is her lesson teaching us the value of experiential learning, yet this is also inescapably the occasion for human folly as well.

> Fucis assidue vultum oblinere, nusquam a speculo discedere, infirmae pubis silvam vellere, vietas ac putres ostentare mammas, tremuloque gannitu languentem sollicitare cupidinem, potitare, misceri puellarum choris, litterulas amatorias scribere.
>
> [Old women, for example] still daube theyr lither chekes with peintyng, neuer goe from the glasse, shew out; theyr flaggie and pendant duggs, prouoke theyr stale nature with hote restoritiues, sitte vp at bankettes, daunce galierds, write loueletters, &c. [sig. F2v; *LB* 4:432B–433A]

Man's insight can be a delusion; his hope, his despair; his pride, his ridiculousness.

As a consequence, Folly logically devotes the second half of her oration to a series of mordacious illustrations at the urging of "these eluishe *Sophistrers*" (sig. F3), illustrations of foolish humanists who put living before learning, in which we would agree with her.

> Est, inquiunt, homini peculiariter addita disciplinarum cognitio, quarum adminiculis id quod natura diminutum est, ingenio penset.
>
> *The knowlage* (saie they) *of disciplines is peculierly geuin to man, throughe helpe wherof, what he lacketh by nature, he maie supplie with his witte and learnyng.* [*LB* 4:433C; sig. F3]

They and not Folly are now the agents of excess: "nihil ultra sortem sapere velle"; "nothing can be more foolisshe than wisedome out of place" (*LB* 4:429C; sig. E4). She scoffs at the neoteric applications of grammar, logic, and rhetoric, of law and science (cf. *LB* 4:457A ff.; sigs. K3v ff.).[22] The golden world, she claims, had no need for them; only the iron age has turned to science and superstition.

> Atque in hoc ipso genere, quo quisque indoctior, audacior, incogitantior-que, hoc pluris fit etiam apud torquatos istos Principes.
>
> Yea and commenly the rasher, the vncunnynger, and lesse circumspect the vndertaker of any of those vsuall sciences is, the more yet is he regarded & allowed euen amonges great men also. [*LB* 4:434B–D; sig. F4]

Such men are broken, spurred, girded, hampered, whipped, laden, bound, and imprisoned with their own foolish desires [*LB* 4:435D–436A; sigs. F4v–G1]. The passage adumbrates a longer diatribe that, encomium made invective, defense turned prosecution, assaults nearly all the secular seven liberal arts (*LB* 4:457A ff.; sigs. K3v ff.) and sacred practices and rituals—all leveled to indulgences in both senses of that word—of the Holy Roman Church (*LB* 4:481B ff.; sigs. o3v ff.).[23] In abruptly dismissing "*Stoickes Syllogismes*" (*Stoicis enthymematis*), for "some familiar exemple" (*LB* 4:436C; sig. G1v), she prefers Grillus to Ulysses, "for all his deepe witte" (*LB* 4:436B; sig. G1), because wit leads only to suffering and chance. In her penchant for pushing to extremes so as to clarify true wisdom and true folly, Folly invites from us a moderation divorced from either alternative of her spiraling sophistry—we would not eliminate the education derived from experience, yet not all experience would be equally educational—and so aligns the *effects* of her oration with a usable poetics.

The other continuing metaphor that Folly uses to complement and extend indefinitely that of the Silenus is the *topos* that Ernst Curtius has found in her declamation turned disputation, first employed by Lucian, that "all the world is a stage" (*totus mundus agit histrionem*).[24] It is the second leitmotif of her work. It appears first just after her discussion of the Silenus.

> Si quis histrionibus in scena fabulam agentibus personas detrahere conetur, ac spectatoribus veras nativasque facies ostendere, nonne is fabulam omnem perverterit, dignusque habentur, quem omnes e theatro velut lymphatum saxis ejiciant? . . . Porro mortalium vita omnis quid aliud est, quam fabula quaepiam, in qua alii aliis obtecti personis procedunt, aguntique suas quisque partes, donec choragus educat e proscenio? . . . Haud equidem inficias inverim, modo fateantur illi vicissim hoc esse, vitae fabulam agere.

> If one at a solemne stage plaie, woulde take vpon hym to plucke of the plaiers garmentes, whiles they were saiyng theyr partes, and so disciphre vnto the lokers on, the true and natiue faces of eche of the plaiers, shoulde he not (trow ye) marre all the mattier? . . . all this life of mortall men, what is it els, but a certaine kynde of stage plaie? whereas men come foorthe disguised one in one arraie, an other in an other, eche plaiyng his parte, till at last the maker of the plaie, or bokebearer causeth theim to auoyde the skaffolde . . . . to dissemble, or erre so, is the right plaiyng of the pageants of this life. [*LB* 4:428B–C, 428C, 429D; sigs. E3–E3v, E3v, E4]

This accumulation of references suggests the ever-present immanence of folly by suggesting the impermanence of human action. Later Folly returns to this metaphor.

Neque perperam sensit Argivus ille, qui hactenus insaniebat, ut totos dies solus desideret in theatro, ridens, plaudens, gaudens, quod crederet illic miras agi tragoedias, cum nihil omnino ageretur, cum in caeteris vitae officiis probe sese gereret, *jucundus amicis, comis in uxorem, posset qui ignoscere servis, Et signo laesa non insaniere lagena.*

Lykewyse *Argiuus,* he whom *Horace* writeth of, iudged not muche amysse. Who this farsoorth raued, that whole daies togethers he woulde sitte alone in the *Theatre* (a place where the commen plaies were plaied) laughyng, and clappyng his handes, and reioysyng muche to hym selfe, because hym seemed verily that some excellent *Tragedies* were in plaiyng there, whereas in deede he sawe nothyng at all. Whan yet for all that as to other respects, he behaued hym selfe wysely enough, beyng welbeloued of his friends, gentill to his wyfe, and easie to his seruants, without fallyng in any rage with theim, whan he founde a backe faulset set in his wyne vessell. Now whan his kinsfolkes procurement, geuyng hym medecines therfore, had healed his disease, and restored hym to his former wittes, marke ye, how he fell out with theim, in blamyng their thanklesse and double diligence. *Ye haue slaine, and not saued me, ò my friendes (quod he) in wrestyng my pleasure from me in this sort, and by force bereuyng me suche a most delectable errour of my mynde. [LB* 4:440A–B; sig. G4v]

This Grecian's act of looking at an empty stage was not mad but the sane choice of a distinguishing perspective.[25] Yet to realize this is to take not the view of the man in the theater applauding the empty stage because it remains empty, or the view of his family that he is altogether mad, but a third view that can reconcile the other two. We see his distraction as a poetic alternative to mundane reality. We judge the man as both sane *and* mad. Again, when pressed by Folly to dismiss her superb description of a stag hunt as coarse butchery (*LB* 4:441B–C; sigs. H1v–H2),[26] we find it contains three alternative commonplaces: the joy of sport, the beauty of the hunt, and the cruelty of slaying. Likewise, when we are confronted by Folly's gross reduction of national traits for England, Scotland, France, Italy, Turkey, Spain, and Germany (*LB* 4:448–449A; sig. I2), we see at once the basis for them—and the need to moderate her excessive and reductive claims. *Encomium Moriae* consistently asks us, then, to endorse not the double perspective of inside–outside (as with the Silenus) or defendant–respondent (as with Folly's disputation) but the third view of a judge. Not to do this would render us functionless before Folly's serial satires, which, finally drawing Erasmus (both the real-life martyr and the actual author) into the fictive frame of reference, blurs all boundaries on which we may rely for meaning in fiction.

His rursum adfines sunt ii, qui sibi stultam quidem, sed tamen jucundam persuasionem induerunt, futurum, ut si ligneum, aut pictum aliquem

Polyphemum Christophorum adspexerint, eo die non sint perituri, aut qui sculptam Barbaram praescriptis verbis salutarit, sit incolumis praelio rediturus, aut si quis Erasmum certis diebus, certis cereolis, certisque preculis convenerit, brevi sit dives evasurus.

Than againe next neyghbours to [those who tell old wives' tales], are suche as haue a foolisshe, but yet a pleasant perswasion to theim selues, that what daie thei see a woodden or a peincted image of the geant saincte *Christopher,* no mischaunce shall betide theim. Or of thei grete the grauen image of saincte *Barbara,* with some praier prescribed for that vse, they can not but retourne hurtelesse from the warres. Or if vpon the sondaies they woorship saincte *Erasmus,* with certaine tapers and *Paternosters,* thei shall in short space become riche men. [*LB* 4:443A–D; sig. H3]

Here we must condemn the practice but not its needs or motive; we can contemn the medals but not the saints they demean. The same requirement is levied when Folly condemns herself, and Erasmus this work for More. "This is the best sporte of all," she mocks, "to see theim present eche others with *epistles, with verses, and with mattiers of prose,* sent from fooles, to fooles: and from asses, to asses" ("Illud autem lepidissimum, cum mutuis epistolis, carminibus, encomiis sese vicissim laudant, stulti stultos, indoctos indocti") (sigs. L2v–L3; *LB* 4:460C).[27] The encomium—both encomia— have point as well as sport, but we must redefine the attack to see why; to say simply that this is both true and untrue (that is, paradoxical) is insufficient. Confronted, therefore, with such a tumbling perspective, such apparently crumbling logic, and yet such apparently surefooted rhetoric— for Erasmus is never anacoluthic—we are forced to independent judgment. Our own reason—the need for a logic, the preservation of a rhetoric—is clearly at stake. So we develop a third view, a view that like the many roles we play in a single life depends on the judge, the occasion, and the context. Such continuing participatory judgment and revision are, in fact, required of us as readers: we *must,* as Erasmus was so in the habit of doing throughout his lifetime, *translate* the text.[28]

But what we work out so carefully the humanists, accustomed to imitatio and to the means of rhetoric and dialectic, must have seen almost intuitively. The triangular presentation, for instance, by which we are asked to take every statement as a possible hypothesis, the *hypo-thesis* that will become a distinguishing characteristic of *all* humanist fiction, was nowhere better known among the humanists than in the dialogues of Plato, whose own trust in human reason and judgment is an important foundation of humanist philosophy. The clue of the Silenus takes on a more pronounced significance when we see the dim allusions to the *Symposium* in the *Encomium Moriae.* Like Plato's dialogue on love, Erasmus's *Encomium* begins with a search for a suitable topic for panegyric, continues with several voices making their own additions to a various and accretive encomium, moves from earthly vicissitudes of human love to the more satisfying wholeness of the intellectual love of God, and ends with praise for the highest forms of folly as love. Read against the *Symposium,* the *Encomium* renews the form of classical dialectic; just as significantly, it follows the curve of Plato's presentation. Erasmus's final witty comment is that no man yet has achieved what Folly achieves in experiencing mystical ecstasy as the highest form of pleasure, an experience she shares through the *Symposium* with the historical Socrates.

The *Symposium,* we know, was not only fundamental to the thought of the early Italian and English humanists; it was also a particular favorite of Ficino, Pico, and Colet (who came to represent Plato to Erasmus).[29] But in turning to Plato at a critical juncture in her argument, at the definition of love as the common distinctive frenzy of poets, prophets, and lovers (*LB* 4:439B; sig. G4), Folly alludes not only to Plato's *Symposium* but also to his *Phaedrus.*[30] And it is this later dialogue, which focuses as Folly does on the twin concerns of rhetoric and love, or the necessary coordinates of form and substance, that most closely resembles—and so helps to explain—the *Encomium Moriae.* The titular character Phaedrus, like the titular Folly, has an extraordinary attraction to rhetoric (242A),[31] and his encounter with Socrates after hearing a speech by Lysias, which he takes with him so as to memorize it exactly, leads to a dialogue that is, thematically, identical to the *Encomium Moriae.* In aligning poor judgment with poor rhetoric—a classical belief that becomes a basis of the New Learning of the humanists—Socrates warns Phaedrus "of those whose opinions are at variance with facts and who are deceived" (262B; 521–23/75–76). Like Folly, the youthful Phaedrus cannot tell the bad from the good because he relies on appearances. Rather, as Socrates has told his friend and student earlier, "in reality the greatest of blessings come to us through madness, when it is sent as a gift of the gods" (244A; 465/46). The *Phaedrus* deals with the definition of love, as the *Encomium* deals centrally with the nature and power of love both to cement human society and to lead to mystical unity with God. Congruent with the *Encomium,* the *Phaedrus* pursues this line of thought in a tripartite dialectic whose resemblances to Folly's oration show on her part an imitation of the classics that astonishes us with its frequency. Plato's dialogue, like Erasmus's, opens with an unusual concern paid to describing the scene, in this instance a plane tree on the banks of the Ilissus River outside Athens, as uncustomary a place for Socrates (as he acknowledges) as Folly claims the pulpit is in which we find her at the outset. The first stage of Plato's dialogue, comparable to Folly's amusing and ironic catalogue of commonplace fools and foolish behavior, is Lysias's foolish and nearly incoherent speech, an encomium on love that Phaedrus has tucked under his toga but not yet memorized, as the good rhetorician should. When he reads it to Socrates and to us, we find that this encomium is, like Folly's, inextricably wise and foolish because it too is scattered in its presentation and jumbled in its thought (231D; 427/27). In the second section of the *Phaedrus,* in which Socrates provides an alternative panegyric by way of parodic correction, his attack on foolish lovers is sufficiently stern to provide a startling contrast in tone (240C–241C; 453–57/40–41); the same sharp break in Folly's genial presentation also introduces the second part of her encomium (*LB* 4:432A–433A; sig. F2). The remainder of the middle section of the *Phaedrus* is given over to the marvelous myth of the soul as a charioteer with two horses, one representing spirit and one appetite, emphasizing the dichotomy so striking by this time in Folly's encomium; the pain and cruelty of appetite discussed first by Plato in terms of the various social classes of man (248) find their counterpart in Folly's shrill attack on man's estates. Socrates' myth concludes, in the third section of the *Phaedrus,* with a realization of the intellectual and mystical love of God, which subdues the part of the soul containing the seeds of vice, setting forth only virtue. Out of gratitude Socrates ends his speech with a prayer (256–57). Folly, in her turn, concludes in mystical ecstasy and with an invitation to partake of Holy Communion, a merging of love with the divine. In thus duplicating in broad outline one of the central Socratic panegyrics for the humanists in writing his own encomium on love, Erasmus reiterates the close relationship between *bonae litterae* and *sacrae litterae* that is at the heart of his humanist thinking.[32]

Yet, despite the triadic arrangement of Plato's dialogue, the *Phaedrus* ends not on the note of a higher love but on lessons Socrates provides for Phaedrus in practical rhetoric. The instruction at first seems distracting and irrelevant to understanding the *Encomium Moriae.* But, actually, the opening speech by the sophist Lysias, like Socrates' opening speech in a style clearly meant to imitate the sophist Isocrates, is corrected by the final speech on higher love. Such a progression suggests that false rhetoric relies on appearances, true rhetoric on Platonic Forms. Bad rhetoric is itself betrayed by "likeness to truth" (273D), and it is this—which has led Lysias, Phaedrus, and Folly (at the first) astray—that Socrates is at some pains to prevent when he teaches his young pupil about definition (265A–B), places (270C–D), and propriety (275) so that he in turn may teach others. For

> serious discourse . . . is far nobler, when one employs the dialectic method
> and plants and sows in a fitting soul intelligent words which are able to
> help themselves and him who planted them, which are not fruitless, but

yield seed from which there spring up in other minds other words capable
of continuing the process for ever, and which make their possessor happy,
to the farthest possible limit of human happiness. [276E–277A; 569–71/99]

We recall that Folly tells us at the outset that she will play the sophist with
us while presuming to be one of the *sophie,* or wise men (*LB* 4, 406C–D;
sig. A1v); in the course of the *Encomium,* she too is transformed into the
wise woman she hopes to become because of her discovery of Christian
love. Not only does the *Encomium Moriae* save Folly; it also means, by
insinuating Plato's dialogues as Senecan originals, as we have seen, to
redeem rhetoric.[33]

Likewise, the *Encomium Moriae* provides and redeems a poetics for
humanist fiction with the "forged tale" Rainolde teaches in 1563 that
actually instructs us in "matter[s] of truthe." Whether Rainolde was
thinking of Erasmus or the close imitation of Erasmus by Thomas More in
the *Utopia* and whether Gascoigne had this grammar school definition in
mind when writing *The Adventures of Master F. J.,* we have no sure way
of knowing. But the evidence of the first two important Tudor works of
humanist fiction suggests strongly that something like the ideas and
techniques established by Erasmus were formative for English fiction.
More's *Utopia,* for instance, also begins with joking prefatory matter to
introduce what appears at first to be a lighthearted debate about the
possibilities of Nowhere, yet this work too grows increasingly serious and
even grim when it comes to portray the crime and poverty in England
during the reign of Henry VIII. Hythlodaye's charges regarding the
inadequacy of Tudor law are as telling as Folly's attacks on the monks of
an earlier period, although Hythlodaye, whose name transcribes him into
a version of Folly, wishes to prove his point by repeatedly citing a country
only he has visited. In the *Utopia* as in the *Encomium Moriae,* then, the
mingling of the foolish and the serious proceeds in Book 2 to extend the
debate between Hythlodaye and More-character in Book 1. What looks at
first to be a formal classical oration by Hythlodaye in Book 2 is actually,
from the very outset, a disputation in which Hythlodaye's increasingly
deluded advocacy must awaken in us as readers, as it does in an auditor like
the More-persona, reasonable and substantial doubts. Following the lesson
of the *Encomium Moriae,* More causes the patterns of humanist rhetoric
so to intersect that he signals to his humanist audience their fundamental
understanding that all orations are potentially single sides of a *controversia.*
Like Folly, Hythlodaye seems to report when actually he is persuading, and
in the act of persuasion he invites from his Tudor audience traditional
speculation and questioning. The contest of words that *Utopia* embodies is
also a contest of wills, between those who, like More-persona, would

improve actual conditions and those who, like Hythlodaye, would over-throw the present government entirely, but such a dichotomy between what is and what is not, in an absolutist way, is fatal at either end. At the moderating center of the *Utopia* we as readers find precisely the poetic and dynamic we find in the *Encomium Moriae.*

The techniques implementing such a poetics are likewise similar in the two works. Both rely on a divided perspective, neither of which alone would be sufficient as a blueprint for action. Yet neither can be entirely dismissed. Just as we cannot blink away the forms of folly that Folly exposes, so we can ignore only at our own peril the sort of inequity and hardship that Hythlodaye castigates. However much we choose to dis-believe Folly or Hythlodaye, we cannot accept the alternative at the other end of the spectrum from where they stand. Like the Silenus, Utopia—once we examine the inside—looks very unlike our first impression. But, if we must develop a third viewpoint in an act of triangulation, that is not the viewpoint of the narrator, for another Erasmian strategy is to place the narrator squarely within the narrative and make him or her, Hythlodaye or Folly, a subject of the argument the narrative is meant to provide. The reader is left, then, to judge by contextual standards within the work as well as by exterior traditions and texts of humanist learning which seem clear models against which the fiction of an Erasmus or a More seems to be playing—the Senecan originals. The end of such a dynamics of fiction is not merely to entertain or challenge the reader but to instruct him. It is another event that can discipline and cultivate—teach—the mind. In growing out of humanism, humanist fiction guarantees its continuing activity of education.

More's *Utopia* is frequently misgauged because the context in which it was written—and an understanding of the audience for whom it was intended—is ignored. But when the *Encomium Moriae* is placed directly alongside the *Utopia,* certain puzzling elements in More's fiction become clear, both in how they work and in what they mean to do and say. George Gascoigne's *Adventures of Master F. J.* seems considerably more distant in time and structure, yet Chaloner's translation of Erasmus was much in circulation, and his summary, when reapplied by Gascoigne to the courtly behavior he may well have witnessed, shows how timely Erasmus's fiction could be. "Folie in al poincts is not (as I take it) so straunge vnto vs, but that hir name maie well be abidden, as long as will we or nill we, she will be sure to beare a stroke in most of our dooyngs," Chaloner had written (sig. A2). Gascoigne's basic series of epistles—parodying a humanist form other than the oration—also come to work as an emerging disputation between the participants who write them, such as F. J., and the narrator who records them, G. T. G. T.'s reserved judgment of the heated pro-

nouncements by F. J. reminds us of More's measured reactions to Hythlodaye's exclusive and heightened praise of all Utopian practices. But we
soon discover that G. T. is also a part of the narrative, much as he might
wish not to be, and that his participation is a variant form of folly. Once
more the authority on which we must come to rely can only be our
own.

Gascoigne practices other techne of rhetoric in writing fiction that we
find in Erasmus and More. There is much wordplay in *The Adventures of
Master F. J.,* and once again the framing devices of the prefatory matter
so multiply the perspectives brought to bear on G. T.'s account that his
narration becomes one of many possible arguments to be structured from
the "facts," much as Tudor students would structure different roles from
the contradictory Roman laws set out by Seneca Rhetor. Still, all this is
possible because both More and Gascoigne, like Erasmus, have a residual
trust in their readers to doubt and debate what is presented as, after all, a
hypothesis, a hypo-thesis. It is fiction and not fact, argument and not report.
Like Erasmus, too, More and Gascoigne can engage in wordplay because
they can rely on readers who understand that although words are a
necessary means to knowledge they are also always multiple in their
referents and at best approximate meanings in their capacity to convey
thought. The very certain values that humanists initially place on oratory,
on rhetoric, and on virtue—the orator as a *vir bonum,* despite what the
characters in a debate might become—allow for More and Gascoigne a
kind of infectious high spirits that marks the first major period of Tudor
humanist fiction, as we shall see now in turning to two major texts.

TWO

Encomium Sapientiae: Thomas More and *Utopia*

 *RESPONDE STULTO SECUN-DUM STULTITIAM EJUS:* "AN-SWER A FOOL ACCORDING TO HIS FOLLY" (PROV. 26:5). THOMAS MORE'S FICTIONAL *UTOPIA* OF 1516— THE EARLY MASTERPIECE OF TUDOR humanist poetics—began as a deliberate reply to the fictional *Encomium Moriae* of Erasmus. In a letter to Ulrich von Hutten, Erasmus claims that More composed his response in much the same way, beginning with a wise and witty declamation, a monologic praise of wisdom, which would also fulfill, at least on its surface, the demands of a petulant Martin Dorp.[1] This oration, which became Book 2 of *Utopia,* was written prior to the completion of Book 1 and was at first intended as the entire work. Consequently, *Utopia* 2 is in form analogous to the *Moriae,* a self-contained and self-referential speech in praise of the ideal commonwealth,[2] and Raphael Hythlodaye, who delivers it to us, is in his combination of the reasonable and the unreasonable, the desirable and the mad, a reification of Folly herself.[3] Hythlodaye is

> uergentis ad senium aetatis, uultu adusto, promissa barba, penula neglec-tim ab humero dependente, qui mihi ex uultu atque habitu nauclerus esse uidebatur.

> a certeyne straunger a man well stryken in age wyth a blake sonne burned face, a longe bearde and a cloke caste homely aboute hys shoulders, whom by hys fauour & apparrel forthwythe I iudged to be a maryner.[4]

He is also "both hermit/prophet and sea captain/voyager."[5] That is to say, he is also a humanist student who benefits both from the works of Plato and Cicero and from his Grand Tour, although he admires without reservation all he has seen and learned of Utopia, a country where "Moriones in delitijs habentur"; "They sette great store by fooles" (192; sig. N8; 102). But Hythlodaye's stubborn orthopraxy, we find, is the ironic result of his misguided, self-righteous orthodoxy. Like Erasmus, Thomas More conceived of his early exercise in *joculatio* as a "trifle," *meas nugas;* but, revealingly, two years later he was publishing it with his epigrams as his *Lucubrationes,* his "serious writing." Both *Encomium Moriae* and *Utopia,* transforming humanist thought and rhetoric into a usable poetics, then, are sober examinations of human nature and behavior, especially speech.

Yet from the start this Tudor masterpiece is rhetorically the more complex. Although Thomas More selects some of the same targets as Erasmus—education and sport, logic and law, court life and Church, even philosophy and religion—his spokesman Hythlodaye not only praises, he *commends. Utopia* 2 is thus more than an encomium; it is a demonstrative oration in full dress, which Thomas Wilson defines in *The Arte of Rhetorique* as "a meane wherby we do praise, or dispraise thynges, as vertue, vice, tounes, citees, castles, woddes, waters, hilles, and moūntaines"; confirm them by proofs showing their honesty, profit, and execution; and then "teache men the truth of it." Only then "it were wel done & Oratourlike." Because a successful work of demonstrative rhetoric requires not merely praise but also truth, "the Logician shewes hymselfe" in the six places of logic that together account for Hythlodaye's presentation of Utopia to Peter Giles, John Clement, the More-persona, and us: definition, causes, parts, effects, things adjoining, and contraries. "I do not se otherwise," Wilson concludes, but that "these [places] of Logique must first be mynded ere thother can well be had" (sigs. C4v–D1). Although we may be surprised at how closely *Utopia* 2 conforms to Wilson's prescription, we should also note with what clarity this distinguishes it from the *Encomium Moriae.* Folly asks only that we commend her to our delight; Hythlodaye, as Thomas More's prolocutor, insists that everywhere we find him *reasonable,* sound in his ideas and in the sequence of his thoughts.

To complicate matters still further, we soon learn that Hythlodaye means to give us, by borrowing from its form, a *deliberative* oration as well. Once again Wilson's definition, although long, is strikingly apposite.

> An Oration deliberatiue is a meane, wherby we do perswade, or disswade, entreate, or rebuke, exhorte, or dehorte, commende, or cōforte any man. In this kynd of Oration we do not purpose wholly to praise any body, nor yet to determine any matter in cōtrouersie, but the whole compasse of this cause is, either to aduise our neighbour to that thyng, whiche we thynke most nedeful for hym or els to cal him backe frō that folie, which hindereth muche his estimacion. As for exāple, if I would counseil my frende to trauaile beyond the Seas for knowlege of the tongues, & experience in forein countries: I might resorte to this kinde of Oration, & finde matter to cōfirme my cause plentifully. And the reasons which are commonly vsed to enlarge suche matters, are these that folowe.

The thynge is honest.	Saufe.	Lawful and meete.
Profitable.	Easie.	Praise worthie.
Pleasaunt.	Harde.	Necessarie.

...Where I spake of profite, this is to be learned, that vnder the same is comprehended the gettyng of gaine, and the eschewyng of harme. Againe, concernyng profite (which also beareth the name of goodnesse) it partely perteineth to the bodie, as beautie, strength, and healthe, partely to the mynde, as the encrease of witte, the gettyng of experience, and heaping together of muche learnyng: and partely to fortune (as Philosophers take it) wherby bothe wealth, honor, and frendes are gotten. Thus he that diuideth profite, can not want matter. . . . In declaryng it is pleasaunt, I might heape together the varietie of pleasures, whiche comme by trauaile, firste the swetnesse of the tongue, the holsomnesse of the ayer in other countries, the goodly wittes of the ientlemen, the straunge and auncient buildynges, the wonderful monumentes, the great learned Clerckes in al faculties, with diuerse other like, and almost infinite pleasures. [Sigs. D4–D4v]

So too with Hythlodaye: such later humanist directives seem in retrospect to determine the order and content of his description of Utopia, which is forensic and hortatory; he means us not only to *believe in* Utopia but to *desire to imitate it*. We, rather than More's text, are made the final products of humanist imitatio.

Hythlodaye's Utopia is therefore eudaemonic, a country characterized by peace, stability, and democracy, and one that practices parliamentary government, a cooperative economy, and religious toleration. Utopia is also a state that advocates work and relaxation, family and social unity, special fare for the sick and elderly, and individual cultivation of learning and morality. This sempiternal land, finally, has learned how to eliminate crime, poverty, war, and capital punishment and has therefore released its citizenry from grief, from illness, and from despair. Such matters have real force for Hythlodaye: his praise is heightened by the seriousness of his issues and the desirability of his ends. He notes that "Ita tota insula uelut una familia est"; "the hole Ilande is as it were one famelie, or housholde" (148; sig. K4v; 76), supplying its people with abundant food, adequate housing, clean streets, and spacious and well-equipped hospitals. Such reason as provides this support and directs an efficient administration is grounded in studying the wisdom of the ancients; for instance, because the land is governed by those who are classically trained, many Utopians take up instrumental or vocal music, drawing on the Greeks' understanding that "ita rei sensum quendam melodiae forma repraesentat, ut animos auditorum mirum in modum afficiat, penetret, incendat"; "the fassion of the melodye doethe so represente the meaning of the thing, that it doth wonderfullye moue, stire, pearce, and enflame the hearers myndes" (236; sigs. R5v–R6; 129; cf. Plato, *Republic,* 402C). Their religion is as admirable as their deeds and thoughts. In prayers at their annual services of consecration,

In his deum & creationis, & gubernationis, & caeterorum praeterea bonorum omnium, quilibet recognoscit auctorem, tot ob recepta beneficia gratias agit.

Man recogniseth and knowlegeth God to be hys maker, hys gouernoure, and the principal cause of all other goodnes, thankyng him for so many benefits receaued at hys hande. [236; sig. R6; 129–30]

Like Folly, who concludes her own encomium by concentrating on holiness, Hythlodaye ends *his* encomium by miraculously fusing an Ovidian golden age with a Platonic visionary republic and the prayers of Christ's apostles.[6] Such an ideal existence is made credible, at least at the first, by the wealth of Hythlodaye's detail and by the authority of his own experience: "there ys no man this daye lyuynge," Giles tells More-persona, "that can tell you of so manye strange and vnknowne peoples and countreis as this man can" ("Nam nemo uiuit hodie mortalium omnium, qui tantam tibi hominum, terrarumque incognitarum narrare possit historiam") (48; sig. B3; 15).[7] In addition, Hythlodaye's account is a deliberate reminder of those actual lands discovered by Amerigo Vespucci. In the description of Utopian natives, their society, their beliefs, and their values, Hythlodaye imitates the descriptions of Vespucci's *Quatuor Navigationes* appended to Martin Waldseemüller's *Cosmographiae Introductio* (1507) and offers an explanation for what happened to twenty-four of Vespucci's men who were involuntarily left behind at Cape Frio with arms and a six-month supply of provisions.[8] In all these particular matters, Hythlodaye reminds us that he, like Folly, is not altogether foolish. Moreover, the issues he raises are vital, even urgent ones, as Robert M. Adams has recently noted.

The first part propounds a set of riddles which every sincere man who enters public life is bound to ask himself. . . . He must think, What good can I do as an honorable man in a society of power-hungry individuals? What evil will I have to condone as the price of the good I accomplish? And how can I tell when the harm I am doing, by acting as window-dressing for evil, outweighs my potential for good? The second part of *Utopia* offers a set of no less disturbing questions. For example, Can a community be organized for the benefit of all, and not to satisfy the greed, lust, and appetite for domination of a few? How much repression is a good society justified in exercising in order to retain its goodness? And finally, When we give some persons power in our society (as we must), and appoint others to watch them (as we'd better), who is going to watch the watchers? Can we really stand a society in which everybody watches everybody?[9]

The ideas here are as important as Folly's are in the *Encomium Moriae,* or as Tommaso Campanella's in his later imitatio of *Utopia,* the *dialogo poetico* called *La Città del Sole* (*The City of the Sun.*)[10]

Yet form alone does not guarantee function—or authenticity. For the tone of Raphael Hythlodaye's account is disturbing; it is too shrill, too insistent. Moreover, he seems to have withdrawn any doubts; he refuses to entertain More-persona's questions; he doth protest too much. His is a speech of "passionate rhetoric," Richard S. Sylvester reminds us; "Once started, his flow of words cannot be checked."[11] He is also, writes W. S. Campbell, "impatient, presumptuous, inexperienced and unbalanced in judgment."[12] Like the Utopians whom he comes to resemble, and who also learn from the Greeks and Romans but who stoutly refuse to share that learning or their own, Hythlodaye refuses to modify his approbation of Utopia or translate it into useful counsel for the European societies of his own time. Like the humanists Giles, Clement, and More-persona, he is a student of a primarily literary education—"when I was determyned to enter into my .iiii. voyage I caste into the shippe in the steade of marchandyse a pretye fardell of bookes" ("librorum sarcinam mediocrem loco mercium") (180; sig. N1; 95), Hythlodaye remarks with some pride—yet he misreads Lucian, along with the Utopians, as only "facetijs ac lepore"; "merye conceytes and iestes" (182; sig. N1; 95), and he fails to be tested or enlightened by his experience to see the hypocrisy of courtiers in Utopia or his own very real success in advising Cardinal Morton in England. Beyond his lopsided presentation—his assurance here echoing that of Folly—there are troubling aspects to his report. The very first sentences of *Utopia* 2, for instance, are an emblem of the whole, and they too figure an impossible strangeness. Hythlodaye begins:

> VTOPIENSIVM INSVLA in media sui parte (nam hac latissima est) millia passuum ducenta porrigitur, magnumque per insulae spatium non multo angustior, fines uersus paulatim utrinque tenuatur. hi uelut circunducti eircino quingentorum ambitu millium, insulam totam in lunae speciem renascentis effigiant.

> The Ilande of Vtopia, conteyneth in breadthe in the myddell part of it (for there it is brodest) CC. miles. Whiche bredthe continueth through the moste parte of the lande. Sauyng that by lytle and lytle it commeth in, and waxeth narrower towardes both the endes. Whiche fetchynge about a circuite or compasse of .vc. myles, do fassion the hole Ilande lyke to the newe mone. [110; sigs. G5–G5v; 55]

The image he gives us is placid, a small island surrounding protected waters. It is a land characterized by pleasure and virtue, by "formam, uires, agilitatem"; "bewtye, strengthe, nemblenes" (176; sig. M6; 93). But the island also images Luna, which for More's day shone with borrowed, not original light and signified inconstancy and minor misfortune. Beyond that, Hythlodaye's account is in factual error: if there is indeed a crescent shape and an inner bay, then the greatest breadth of land must be substantially less than the diameter of the circumference, or approximately 160 miles (500 pi), or there would be no inner bay. Thomas More, in the fictional presence of his close friend Cuthbert Tunstall (46; sig. B1; 13), vice-chancellor, master of the rolls, and later author of a popular book on arithmetic, *De arte supputandi libri quattuor* (1522), would surely know that.[13] So either the shape of the island has been misjudged by Hythlodaye or the dimensions are wrong; he cannot have it both ways. Nor can he possibly allow fifty-four cities of 645 square miles each on an island of only 31,000 square miles.[14]

Now these are jokes that might slip past a quick or careless reader, but not the wit of an Erasmus or any of the other humanists to whom More and Erasmus so proudly rushed manuscript copies of the completed *Utopia*.[15] In what H. G. Wells in 1935 called "one of the most profoundly inconsistent of books,"[16] other flaws, more obvious ones, fly at us thick and fast, for "Like Socrates," notes J. Churton Collins, More "moved in an atmosphere of irony."[17] So we are amused that Hythlodaye would tell the lawyer Thomas More, son of the distinguished lawyer John More, about an ideal land where lawyers are not permitted.[18] We notice that, in their democratic form of government, those annually elected officers, unlike the lifelong sinecures, are the only representatives unable to vote, and the king of the putative monarchy seems to have disappeared altogether; only the secret voting of the syphogrants allows some men to abjure manual labor for scholarly pursuits. We read further that this land, which boasts of cooperation—of communism, in fact, a form of government shared by Greek philosophy, canon law and the cenobitic way of life young Thomas More experienced in the Charterhouse—promotes a competition in gardens,

> uicorum quoque inuicem de suo cuiusque horti cultu certamen accendit.
>
> stryffe and contentyon that is betwene streete and strete concerynynge the trymmynge husbanding and furnyshyng. [120; sig. H3v; 61]

In Utopia they also rotate the houses of all citizens every ten years lest they take a personal interest in them and erect statues of notable men in the marketplace. Hythlodaye's rational scheme shows the irrational process of communism which, appealing to man's baser instincts, promises him what he has *not* earned.

Such inconsistencies are for us soon epidemic, ineluctable. The Utopians, we are told, believe in a beneficent nature (and love mankind); yet, led by the eponymous King Utopus, their first historic acts are to cut themselves from the mainland, to raise a garrison in the midst of their bay, and to allow hidden rocks there to destroy strangers: their history begins in divisiveness, military defensiveness, and planned treachery. This treachery is reinforced by deceit; although they erect landmarks on shore for themselves, "His in diuersa translatis loca, hostium quamlibet numerosam classem facile in perniciem traherent"; "By turning translatynge & remouinge this markes into other places they maye destroye their enemies nauies be thei neuer so many" (110; sig. G6; 56). Although Utopians promote a nearly monastic community, they nevertheless adopt the hierarchy of Church polity. Utopians pool labor forces and products, yet in fact engineer a surplus of goods for which they must create artificial markets through colonization. They emphasize personal freedom yet draft young men into farm service, all city men into harvesting crops each year, and all men and women into learning some craft under supervision, and they remain partially dependent on slavery. They scorn luxury, yet their children wear jewelry—learn, that is, and indulge a taste for adornment. They eat flesh but despise butchery. They argue for pleasure of a high order, but Hythlodaye's word for it, *voluptas*, means sensual gratification.[19] They desire peace, yet they have no hesitation in annexing territory not their own; they claim selflessness yet remain imperialistic.[20] Such irrationality becomes in time deliberately comic. Chickens born from incubators follow human beings as their parents, and slaves are chained in gold, the softest of metals, saving iron, actually needful in war, to fashion chamberpots.[21] Surely C. S. Lewis has a point when he argues "that as long as we take the *Utopia* for a [serious] philosophical treatise it will 'give' wherever we lean our weight";[22] it works, adds Dominic Baker-Smith, by "a violation of expectation."[23]

But as with the *Encomium Moriae,* where Folly invites us to a game only to involve us, to turn up our own portraits on her face cards, so in *Utopia* 2 the picture darkens. Hythlodaye's recalcitrant view is not what we had expected, is finally casuistic and dystopian. For he teaches us that Utopians make war not only to combat invasion of their own lands but also to remain ever ready to infiltrate peoples "they coūt their chieffe aduersaries" (204; sig. o8v; 109) and by proclamations offer rewards for such enemies, dead, alive, or voluntarily surrendering. By a ruthless logic, "The Utopians are provided with the *casus belli* against any land they choose," Father Edward J. Surtz tells us (*CW* 4: 499).

> Itaque fit celeriter, ut & caeteros mortales suspectos habeant, & sibi inuicem ipsi, neque fidentes satis, neque fidi sint, maximoque in metu & non minore periculo uersentur. Nam saepenumero constat euenisse, uti bona pars eorum & princeps in primis ipse ab his proderentur, in quibus maximam spem reposuerint.

> Therfore it quickely commeth to passe that they haue al other men in

suspicion, and be vnfaithfull and mistrusting among themselfes as one to another, liuing in great feare and in lese ieopardye. For it is well knowen that dyuers times the most part of them, and specially the prince him selfe hath bene betraied of thē in whome they put their most hoope and trust [204; sig. o8v; 109–10]

They even hire mercenaries they do not mind seeing killed,

> rati de genere humano maximam merituros gratiam se, si tota illa colluuie populi tam tetri, ac nepharij orbem terrarum purgare possent.

> For they beleue that they should doo a very good deade for all mankind, if they could ridde out of ye worlde all that fowle stinkinge denne of that most wicked and cursed people. [208; sig. P3v; 112]

Public policy of the Utopians undermines Hythlodaye's claims and exposes his ignorance.

Such intimidation and violence abroad take scarcely subtler forms in domestic policy: "Non poenis tantum, deterrent a flagitijs, sed propositis quoque honoribus ad uirtutes inuitant"; "They do not only feare theire people frō doinge euell by punyshmentes, but also allure them to vertue with rewardes of honoure" (192; sig. O1; 102–3). But some of their means for maintaining their regimented society are means we cannot condone. We are told that the Utopians, with "geometric rationalism,"[24] must maintain a standard family size, are reared in the same way regardless of skills, wear prescribed clothing (to distinguish only sex and marital state), change equivalent houses on schedule, and are restricted in their travel. This is congruent with the restriction against killing animals on the farms or in the shambles (lest men come to enjoy it), or with the regulation that each betrothed Utopian couple see each other naked before sealing the marriage contract. Plainly enough, the Utopians *do not trust each other*. The spring that is made into a city reservoir for the principal metropolis of Amaurote, we are told further, is fenced in lest someone poison the water! Nowhere do the Utopians show a humanist faith in humanity; rather, their state adumbrates a totalitarian regimen in which men and farms, like cities, become faceless. "He that knoweth one of them," Hythlodaye admits of Utopians in the aggregate, "knoweth them all" ("VRbium qui unam norit, omnes nouerit") (116; sig. Hlv; 59).[25] Their culture—a product of unalloyed, unadorned reason—resembles Swift's imitative land of Houyhnhmns; "a continual irony," writes Robbin S. Johnson, "tugs at the edges" and "ultimately consumes the human being it would reform."[26] The Tudor translator Robynson may well have seen this, too, for he changes his title for Book 2 from "of the Godly gouernment" (1551 ed., sig. G5) to "of the politike gouernement" (1556 ed., sig. G5v).

Carefully studied, then, Utopia turns bleak because the declamation turns disputation *within* Hythlodaye's definition of reason. As for Folly's foolery, any praise we offer to Hythlodaye sooner or later turns back on us. Like the *Encomium Moriae,* too, the poetics of *Utopia* derives from an implicit argument, a *mock encomium,* because it places the fictional against the actual. For in defining Utopia Hythlodaye does not merely describe a self-isolated autarchy as an improvement on England; he also describes a country that at times *is* England. The map of one nearly superimposes the other exactly: both are islands with a major river flowing by a major town, the fifty-three English shires and London correlating to the fifty-four cities of Utopia. Erasmus writes that More represented chiefly Britain, of which he has acquired a profound analysis and knowledge,[27] and a colligation persistently obtains: in Utopia as in England, agriculture is the basic means of economy, the family is the primary social unit, and the kingdom is a monarchy with a governing parliament of two houses. In both lands there is a strong, hierarchical sense of place that promises security as it tends to limit personal freedom and liberty. Utopia, like Folly's propositions, is thus an endless fun house of mirrors: wherever we turn, there our desires and dreams are reflected, but in twisted and distorted configurations. Where we thought we were being persuaded by Hythlodaye, we are in fact opposed to him[28]—and once again fictional dialogue opens not into colloquy but into a controversia.[29]

Consult *Utopia* anywhere, and this is so. In open imitation of the *Encomium Moriae,* More awards his book not one title but two: *A fruteful and pleasaunt worke of the beste state of a publyque weale, and of the newe yle called Vtopia* (*De Optimo Reipvblicae Statu Deqve noua insula Vtopia*). The titles are antonymous. "The first half calls attention to those numerous discussions of ideal governments which, from Plato on, had occupied the minds of many philosophical writers," Sylvester notes, and "The second half of the title points directly to Book 2, which is not a dialogue at all but a fervently eulogistic monologue in which the new island is described."[30] As Hythlodaye's "praise of wisdom" fails to satisfy More-persona at the close of Book 2, and thus fails to answer the quest of Book 1, so *Utopia* fails to respond adequately to *De Optimo Reipvblicae Statu.* Yet, if that is clear enough, the full title still bewilders. *Topia* means "place," but Greek *u* means "no" (hence, Noplace; More wittily alludes to this when he remarks in the first letter to Giles that in this book "I thinke nothing could fall out of my minde" [40; sig. +8v; 18]). But Greek *eu* means "good" (hence, Utopia images the *good place*).[31] Budé adds another suggestion in a letter to Lupset: Udepotia or Never-Land.[32] As a further complication yet, the family name of the man who shares his vision of the ideal land is Hythlodaye, Latin for "expert in nonsense." But his given name is Raphael, Greek for "messenger from God"—Milton's use of him in *Paradise Lost* is based on this—and Hebrew for "God has healed"; he is the angel St. Thomas Aquinas uses for the highest of purposes (*Summa Theologica* 3.2).[33] Raphael's sole appearance in the Bible is in the apocryphal book of Tobit; there, rather like Hythlodaye, he takes on human form (as Azarias) to become Tobias's traveling companion and guide, and to lead him into a providential land (Rages)—that hides the devil in it![34] In an analogy to the nomenclature used in the *Encomium Moriae,* then, we are rhetorically invited to believe in a good place that may be noplace and never, a chimerical country that may image England, from an account told by a divine messenger who cannot be trusted. In More as in Erasmus circumstances and details so puzzle and accounts are transformed to such ambivalences and ambiguities that the work no longer declares but generates, no longer *tells us* but *depends on us* for its tellings, its meanings. For the antimonies of name and idea continually put before us an equivocation between Hythlodaye's yearning and the More-persona's nonpossession, between desire and inaccessibility, between what even the well-educated man can want and believe and what he can have and know. The two stand alike yet opposed, the prosopographia of More-persona alongside the prosopopoeia of Hythlodaye, the real made to seem fictional and the fictional real by way of the alchemy of humanist rhetoric. Ambrosius Holbein sees this, too, engraving an illustration for the 1518 edition in which Hythlodaye leans toward More-persona and More-persona leans in perfect static balance toward Hythlodaye while John Clement and Peter Giles, also in perfect and static balance, look on. Only we readers are left to assess and interpret such frozen equipoise.[35]

This inherent division of meanings must have come easily to More, trained in law, for he was seen as "a man of so incomparable witte, of so profounde knowledge, of so absolute learning, & of so fine eloquence," as Robynson describes him to William Cecil (sig. +3v), that his matter always "conteineth frutefull & profitable" ideas (sig. +4) conveyed with More's abiding *festivitas*. It is a wit that unlike his later, obscene parodies (in the *Responsio ad Lutherum* especially) comes from the genial training of the humanist classrooms. More was educated at St. Anthony's grammar School in London (the school John Stow praises as the inevitable champion in the annual contests at disputation at Smithfield) and tutored at the home of the archbishop of Canterbury, John Cardinal Morton. Later he attended Canterbury College (now Christ Church), Oxford, before proceeding to the study of law at New Inn and Lincoln's Inn. He learned his lessons well, for he seems always to have been successful at law and oratory. He was a reader at Furnivall's Inn for three years (1501–4) and was later named Autumn Reader at Lincoln's Inn (1510) and Lent Reader there (1514), the highest honor the school could bestow: all he lacked was a serjeanty to lead him to knighthood and to the bench. Throughout this period More remained close to other leading London humanists—to Colet, his *vitae magister;* to Grocyn, with whom he studied Greek; to Thomas Linacre (of the Royal College of Physicians), with whom he studied Aristotle's *Meteorologica;* and to William Lily, with whom he translated part of the witty, epigrammatic Greek Anthology. "I never see him without his sending me away better informed and more attached to him than ever," Niccolò Sagundino writes to Marcus Musurus in Venice in 1517; "his wonderful elegance as a writer, his noble periods, his choice of words and well-rounded sentences are universally admired, but not more so than his keen mind and his polished Latin, set off by fairness, humour, wit and courtesy."[36] Concurrently, he took up residency with the Carthusians: his son-in-law William Roper tells us in his biography of More that he "gaue himselfe to devotion *and* prayer in the Charter house of London, religiously lyvinge there, without vowe, about iiij^{er} yeares."[37] He also, we learn from Roper, lectured on Augustine's *City of God* before a learned audience at Grocyn's parish church (St. Lawrence Jewry), much as Pico planned public lectures, and his earliest surviving letter describes his attendance at Grocyn's lectures in St. Paul's Cathedral on Dionysius the Aereopagite, the Syrian Neoplatonist of the sixth century. Indeed, More seems at this period to have been drawn to Pico as a kind of exemplar: he translated a life of Pico (by his nephew Francis) and quotes Pico's *Oration* at a critical juncture in the *Utopia*. Like his predecessor Pico, More too combined serious scholarship, religious devotion, and public service. It is in this last capacity that most Londoners knew him best: in 1510 he was nominated as undersheriff of London; in 1514 he was nominated to membership in the Mercers' Company and appointed commissioner of the sewers, where he learned about city planning; in 1515 he was invited to be orator for the City of London at the reception of the new Venetian ambassador and, later that year, to represent the Mercers' Company on an embassy to Brussels, to which he refers at the start of *Utopia* 1. It is in this role that he chooses to introduce his self-projected character in *Utopia,* lending an air of veracity to the book.

What consistently characterizes Thomas More in all his many roles is an abiding perspective on theoretical and practical affairs in which wit and wisdom remain inseparable. He was, writes his modern biographer R. W. Chambers, one "of the greatest masters of irony who ever lived";[38] his near contemporary Beatus Rheananus characterizes him as "every inch pure jest."[39] "Rebus etiam grauissimis facetias ita intermiscuit, vultus tamen totius corporis externa grauitate nihil prorsus immutata," Thomas Stapleton confirms in the *Vita Thomae Mori* of his apologist's *Tres Thomae* (1588); "He often introduced humour even into most serious business, without the slightest change in his features or the gravity of his demeanour."[40] Before such an intriguing and puzzling personality the Tudor chronicler Edward Halle in *The Vnion of the two noble and illustre famelies of Lancastre & Yorke* seems almost to falter: "I cannot tell whether I should call him a foolishe wyseman, or a wise foolishman," he sums, "for vndoubtedly he beside his learnyng had a great witte, but it was so myngled with tauntyng and mocking, that it seemed to them that best knew him, that he thought nothyng to be wel spoken except he had ministred some mocke in the communicacion . . . ; with a mocke he ended his life" (1548 ed., sig. 3P4v).

But this engaging and disarming wit does not escape explanation altogether. It has classical roots; More's perspective agrees with that of the *Epistulae Morales ad Lucilium* of Seneca—one of the two Roman writers whom, according to Peter Giles, Hythlodaye has studied and so, it is implied, one of the sources of the *Utopia*. In Seneca's Letter 48, for instance, he has just the sort of fun with syllogisms that Socrates does when demolishing an opponent such as Lysias in the *Phaedrus* and that More has in his letter to Giles prefacing *Utopia:*

> "Mus syllaba est. Mus autem caseum rodit; syllaba ergo caseum rodit." Puta nunc me istuc non posse solvere. Quod mihi ex ista inscientia periculum inminet? Quod incommodum? Sine dubio verendum est, ne quando in muscipulo syllabas capiam aut ne quando, si neglegentior fuero, caseum liber comedat. Nisi forte illa acutior est collectio: "Mus syllaba est. Syllaba autem caseum non rodit; mus ergo caseum non rodit." O pueriles ineptias! In hoc supercilia subduximus? In hoc barbam demisimus? Hoc est, quod tristes docemus et pallidi?

> " 'Mouse' is a syllable. Now a mouse eats cheese; therefore, a syllable eats cheese." Suppose now that I cannot solve this problem; see what peril hangs over my head as a result of such ignorance! What a scrape I shall be in! Without doubt I must beware, or some day I shall be catching syllables in a mousetrap, or, if I grow careless, a book may devour my cheese! Unless, perhaps, the following syllogism is shrewder still: " 'Mouse' is a syllable. Now a syllable does not eat cheese. Therefore a mouse does not eat cheese." What childish nonsense! Do we knit our brows over this sort of problem? Do we let our beards grow long for this reason? Is this the matter which we teach with sour and pale faces? [6–7][41]

This is the same witty philosopher who in his younger days wrote for Nero a witty panegyric on Claudius, the recitation of which, Tacitus records, reduced the audience to helpless laughter (*Annales* 13.3), a classical encomium that is a precedent for Folly and for Hythlodaye. It is also the pseudo-Seneca of the *Apocolocyntosis,* an imaginary tale of Claudius who is refused admission to Heaven when he arrives at its portals, a tale that may have suggested to Erasmus the *Julius Exclusus* and to More Hythlodaye's exclusion of everyone (including, apparently, himself) from his precious Utopia. Here, then, as in the later letters, Seneca plays with the inherent fictional possibilities of rhetoric.

But Seneca doubtless attracted humanists such as More because of a rhetoric that seems to us, as Robin Campbell notes, "highly wrought and polished. The exploitation of such figures as antithesis, alliteration, homeoteleuta and all manner of other plays upon words, paradox and oxymoron, apposition and asyndeton, the use of cases and prepositions in uncommon connotations, all contribute to the twin aims of brevity and sparkle."[42] Seneca was never as much admired as Cicero (or Aristotle) by the Tudor humanists, but the style of his letters was nevertheless an alternative model for Latin lessons at the humanist grammar schools, and it is difficult to believe that for the more astute youngsters such as More it would not be apparent how supple and manipulative—and, finally, how insubstantial—language can become when one sees the range of its possible applications alongside a truth that requires unequivocal communication. Often, language was up for imaginative play (as with Folly's varying of her own name) or even up for hire (as the dialogue on counsel in *Utopia* 1 confirms), but for the humanists, truth—especially philosophic truth—is never up for play or hire. It is just this dilemma that humanist poetics confronts in both the *Ecomium Moriae* and the *Utopia* even as it seems to indulge in illustrating the problem; and it is just this concern, which Seneca faced so dramatically as counselor to Nero, that makes the invocation to him in the opening pages of the *Utopia* so appropriate.

Whatever grammar school boys thought of Seneca's letters, we know they enjoyed staging plays they thought his, such as the *Thyestes* and *Octavia.*[43] The *Octavia* earns special reference in the *Utopia* as a part of More's continuing concern with life as a play and man's behavior as the playing of actors because, beneath this, he sees the need for a more permanently reliable counsel. "Sed est alia philosophia ciuilior," More-persona tells Hythlodaye,

> quae suam nouit scenam, eique sese accommodans, in ea fabula quae in manibus est, suas partes concinne & cum decoro tutatur. Hac utendum est tibi. Alioquin dum agitur quaepiam Plauti comoedia, nugantibus inter se uernulis, si tu in proscenium prodeas habitu philosophico, & recenseas ex

Octauia locum in quo Seneca disputat cum Nerone, nonne praestiterit egisse mutam personam, quam aliena recitando talem fecisse tragico-moediam? Corruperis enim, peruerterisque praesentem fabulam, dum diuersa permisces, etiam si ea quae tu affers meliora fuerint. Quaecunque fabula in manu est, eam age quam potes optime. neque ideo totam perturbes, quod tibi in mentem uenit alterius, quae sit lepidior.

But ther is an other philosophye more cyuyle, whyche knoweth as ye wolde saye her owne stage, and thereafter orderynge and behauynge herselfe in the playe that she hathe in hande, playethe her parte accordynglye wyth comlynes, vtterynge nothynge owte of dewe ordre and fassyon. And thys ys the phylosophye that yowe muste vse. Orels whyles a commodye of Plautus is playinge, and the vyle bondemen shoffynge and tryffelynge amonge themselfes, yf yowe shoulde sodenlye come vpon the stage in a philosophers apparrell, and reherse owte of Octauia the place wherin Seneca dysputeth with Nero: had it not bene better for yowe to haue played the domme persone, then by rehersynge that, which serued nother for the tyme nor place to haue made such a tragycall comedye or gallym alfreye? For by bryngynge in other stuffe that nothynge apperteyneth to the presente matter, yowe must nedys marre and peruert the play that ys in hande, thoughe the stuffe that yowe brynge be much better. What parte soeuer yowe haue taken vpon yowe playe that aswell as yowe canne and make the beste of yt: And doo not therefore dysturbe and brynge owte of ordre the hole matter, bycause that an other whyche is meryere and bettere cummethe to yowre remembraunce. [98; sigs. F5–F6; 58]

The *exemplum* is more than an attractive tribute to Erasmus with its echo of his Horatian allusion to the man who spent his time in the theater, for More means to take us back as well to the Senecan play as especially apt to his purpose. The central scene of *Octavia,* the fulcrum between the opening and closing scenes, is the significant disputation between Nero and Seneca on the proper behavior of the ruler—Seneca's own dialogue of counsel. Like Hythlodaye, Seneca too has wished to retire from the pain and danger of life at court as well as its apparent futility:

> melius latebam procul ab invidiae malis
> remotus inter Corsici rupes maris,
> ubi liber animus et sui iuris mihi
> semper vacabat studia recolenti mea.

Better was I hid, far out of the reach of envy's sting, midst the crags of Corsica, facing on the sea, where my spirit, free and its own lord, had ever time to contemplate my favourite themes. [381–84]

He feels this loss with special keenness because his own advice is so contrary to Nero's temperament and policy. Still he perseveres:

Pulcrum eminere est inter illustres viros,
consulere patriae, parcere afflictis, fera
caede abstinere tempus atque irae dare,
orbi quietem, saeculo pacem suo.
haec summa virtus, petitur hac caelum via.
sic ille patriae primus Augustus parens
complexus astra est colitur et templis deus.

'Tis glorious to tower aloft amongst great men, to have care for father-land, to spare the downtrodden, to abstain from cruel bloodshed, to be slow to wrath, give quiet to the world, peace to one's time. This is virtue's crown, by this way is heaven sought. So did that first Augustus, his country's father, gain the stars, and is worshipped in the temples as a god. [472–78]

The method he advocates resembles More's technique with Henry VIII, principled wit, and so illustrates the sort of compromising language that More-persona urges on Hythlodaye.

SENECA: Nihil in propinquos temere constitui decet.
NERO: Iustum esse facile est cui vacat pectus metu.
SENECA: Magnum timoris remedium clementia est.
NERO: Extinguere hostem maxima est virtus ducis.
SENECA: Servare cives maior est patriae patri.
NERO: Praecipere mitem convenit pueris senem.
SENECA: Regenda magis est fervida adolescentia.
NERO: Aetate in hac sat esse consilii reor.
SENECA: Vt facta superi comprobent semper tua.
NERO: Stulte verebor, ipse cum faciam, deos.
SENECA: Hoc plus verere quod licet tantum tibi.

SENECA: 'Tis not becoming to proceed rashly 'gainst one's friends.
NERO: 'Tis easy to be just when the heart is free from fear.
SENECA: A sovereign cure for fear is clemency.
NERO: To destroy foes is a leader's greatest virtue.
SENECA: For the father of his country to save citizens, is greater still.
NERO: A mild old man should give schooling to boys.
SENECA: More needful 'tis that fiery youth be ruled.
NERO: I deem that at this age we are wise enough.
SENECA: May thy deeds be ever pleasing to the gods.
NERO: Foolish I'd be to fear the gods, when I myself make them.
SENECA: Fear thou the more, that so great power is thine. [440–50]

Seneca's pleas for rational behavior, the protection of Roman citizens, and love rather than fear as the basis of the relationship between the ruler and the ruled[44] suggest that More's means of breaking the fictional deadlock in *Utopia* is through positing its exact classical counterpart, in which the source of our sympathy is never in doubt. That Nero fails to heed Seneca leads to Octavia's tragic exile and death: the parallel furnishes a darker undercurrent to the witty disputation on the surface of Utopia 1. Most significant of all, however, is More's reference to the one Senecan play in which the author is himself a character (like More-persona), and the situation (like More's own diplomatic journey to the Low Countries, the occasion for More-persona's meeting with Hythlodaye)[45] is likewise factual and autobiographical. The allusion not only gives More-persona classical authority for his advice on the need for diplomatic counsel and the tragic consequences if such counsel is not given; it may also point to Hythlodaye's accuracy in remarking that such counsel would be unwelcome and so ignored. More's use of Seneca thus furthers the equivocation basic to humanist poetics, but at a much more serious level.

What this use of the *Octavia* clearly suggests is that wordplay in the *Utopia* is at root, as in the *Encomium Moriae,* conceptual rather than merely verbal. More's chief exemplar in the *Utopia* is not Seneca, however, but Plato; More seems to have found Plato early in his studies and never to have left the master. We have Stapleton's testimony regarding More's enduring interest in Plato—"Inter philosophos Platonem & Platonicos maximè legit, & libentius euoluit, tanquam ad Rempub regendam & ciuilem conuersationē magis idoneos." "Amongst the philosophers he read especially Plato and his followers, delighting in their study because he considered their teaching most useful in the government of the State and the preservation of civic order"—while Erasmus notes that the young More composed a dialogue in which he defended Plato's communism.[46] The numerous textual references to Plato in *Utopia* are pointers for our reading of More's text; Plato "contributed more to *Utopia*," Craig R. Thompson writes representatively, "than any other author ancient or modern."[47] Perhaps the most important Platonic legacy in *Utopia* is the form of the dialogue itself, for it gives to More's fiction a range of possibilities in subtlety and variety of argument and understanding not available to Erasmus in his *Ecomium Moriae* and advances enormously the technical possibilities for humanist fiction. It not only allows more nuance of idea and feeling but expands the room for surprise and paradox, irony and satire. Within this general form of dialogue, the shadow of one book—Plato's splendid *Republic*—is behind much of the *Utopia*. It is the fifth cause of the *Utopia,* the Senecan original, the model against which, by comparison or contrast, much of the meaning of More's fiction is conveyed with a certainty not otherwise available in a work so shifting and witty as this discussion of Nowhere.

"Vna ego terrarum omnium absque philosophia/Ciuitatem philosophicam expressi mortalibus," says the poem at the outset of the 1518

Utopia and subsequent editions; "Alone of all lands, without the aid of abstract philosophy, I have represented for mortals the philosophical city" (*CW* 4: 19). Hythlodaye confirms this allusion to the *Republic;* he means to admire and reveal "quae fingit Plato in sua Republica aut ea quae faciunt Vtopienses in sua"; "those thynges that Plato fayneth in hys weale publique: or that the utopians do in theires" (86; sig. F6v; 48). Hythlodaye's premise, like that of Plato's *Republic* (473C–D), is that philosophers should be kings (86; sig. F5; 48). To this end, says Socrates—perhaps suggesting to More Hythlodaye's role—the true visionaries are the true navigators (*Republic,* 488D). Thus the land that Hythlodaye describes has much in common with Plato's ideal community: the republican form of government, for one thing, insures a strong central authority working through a rigid social and class system for the peace and well-being of the entire population. In Plato's Republic as in Hythlodaye's Utopia, there is an emphasis on the exercise of reason to balance and direct impulses. The end of both rational states is a stratified community of faceless citizens. The premium Plato places on education—with its regulated readings, its aesthetics of morality, and its use of literature as self-fulfilling propaganda—is surely meant to correspond to the society Hythlodaye reports to More, where readings at mealtime as well as channeled leisure activities all serve individuals by serving the state through them. The state is self-perpetuating in both instances, while economically it rests on the abolition of private ownership, the sharing of all property, and the labor of the whole citizenry toward common ends. Classes, rather than families, are the organizing units of Plato's Republic, but there are a number of more specific correspondences, such as military training and preparedness, slavery, and the decreasing distinction between men and women, all traced frequently by previous critics.[48]

What is often forgotten, however, is that the *Republic* is not simply Socrates' *declamatio* in praise of the ideal state but a disputation in which Socrates, especially in Books 8 and 9, advances the possibility of the moral degeneration and corruption of man. In defining imperfect societies—the timarchy, which creates a split community that encourages the use of force and relies on an evil lack of intelligence; the democracy, which harbors anarchy and eternal class struggle; and the tyranny, which frees man's criminal instincts—he realizes the full possibilities of the Foundation Myth, which makes humanity at various stages of perfection or imperfection analogous to the metals of the earth. This double edge of Socrates' understanding of man and his institutions is more dramatic and explicit than Hythlodaye's fatuous report on Utopia, but it is precisely the obviousness of this pattern that allows More to work largely through insinuation. In this, he follows the Erasmian structural principle of the Socratic Silenus, which demands our active interpretation each step of the way. This triangular presentation, introduced in the fiction of the *Encomium Moriae*—two opposing arguments to be reconciled by the active collaboration of the reader, much as a judge at a disputation reviews and chooses—is continued in the *Utopia* by the introduction of two characters expressing the two opposing viewpoints, Hythlodaye and More-persona, as in the earlier pattern of the *Republic* Socrates employs Glaucon and Adeimantus as stalking horses. But the triangular *process* in Erasmus is confirmed and forwarded by the triadic *structure,* in which the notion of the holy fool reconciles innocent and serious folly. This structured principle operates in the *Republic* as well; the apparent excrescence of *Republic* 10, which discusses a theory of art as an imitation twice removed from reality, as the image of a bed is removed from both the object of a bed and the ideal Form of Bedness (597 ff.), and Socrates' related understanding of the divine soul of the world, which both guarantees and sanctions immortality, are alike meant to validate the Form of the Republic despite its absence in human history. Comprehension of the Form secures the possibility of the object. This validation, which Socrates arrives at by analogy (the underlying method of Hythlodaye's definition of Utopia, in terms of an implied analogy to the Europe of Antwerp), gives both purpose and end to human endeavor, or first and fourth cause to the discussion of an ideal city-state. Erasmus has something similar in mind when Folly's holy fool suggests at the end of *Encomium Moriae* an immortal Form in the pattern of Christ, which all rational and spiritual beings more or less imitate. More's patterned arrangement in *Utopia* appears to be similar, especially to the *Republic,* but incomplete: the truncated disputation between Hythlodaye and More-persona leaves resolution beyond the text, where Socrates and Folly leave only the correct interpretation of the resolution for the reader to determine. This decisive change is a telling one, and an important step in the development of a humanist poetics. The inconclusiveness of the *Utopia* extends the use of irony significantly.

The allusion to the lost island of Atlantis in the unknown whereabouts of Utopia further suggests that in studying the *Republic* More also studied the trilogy of which it formed a part, including the *Timaeus* (the Platonic work most easily absorbed by the early and medieval Christian Church) and the unfinished *Critias.*[49] There the Senecan poetic is forcefully enunciated by Socrates when he defines the act of creation in the Platonic terms of being and becoming.

> Now first of all we must, in my judgement, make the following distinction. What is that which is Existent always and has no Becoming?

And what is that which is Becoming always and never is Existent? Now the one of these is apprehensible by thought with the aid of reasoning, since it is ever uniformly existent; whereas the other is an object of opinion with the aid of unreasoning sensation, since it becomes and perishes and is never really existent. Again, everything which becomes must of necessity become owing to some Cause; for without a cause it is impossible for anything to attain becoming. But when the artificer of any object, in forming its shape and quality, keeps his gaze fixed on that which is uniform, using a model of this kind, that object, executed in this way, must of necessity be beautiful; but whenever he gazes at that which has come into existence and uses a created model, the object thus executed is not beautiful. [*Timaeus,* 27D–28B][50]

This is perhaps Socrates' most encapsulated statement of his own poetic; and it comes in one of his most extraordinary and fascinating works. The *Timaeus* begins by reviewing the *Republic* but moves beyond and behind the proposal of an ideal city-state to summarize, in one brief, thickly textured declamation by Timaeus, all that the ancient Greek world of his day knew of cosmology, geography, anatomy, and chemistry. The Platonic poetic about creating a philosophic work of art is made deliberately analogous to its greater shadow of Form in the Creation of the World. This central analogy is also More's: he too implies a perfect world by addressing the imperfect reality of England and Europe. But we do not knowingly and willingly address imperfection; and More takes from the *Timaeus* not simply the idea of Seneca's fourth cause but the dramatic technique of distancing "real" persons (Socrates, More-persona) by several layers of fiction. This pattern comes not in Timaeus's scientific account of reality but in Critias's introduction to his report of Atlantis.

Listen, then, Socrates, to a tale which, though passing strange, is yet wholly true, as Solon, the wisest, of the Seven, once upon a time declared. Now Solon—as indeed he often says himself in his poems—was a relative and very dear friend of our great-grandfather Dropides; and Dropides told our grandfather Critias—as the old man himself, in turn, related to us—that the exploits of this city in olden days, the record of which had perished through time and the destruction of its inhabitants, were great and marvellous, the greatest of all being one which it would be proper for us now to relate. [20D–21A]

Report within report, box within box, a method readily adapted by many of the later Tudor writers of humanist fiction (especially Gascoigne) allows the possibility of fact to be retained, much as Hythlodaye's final court of appeal does ("I have been there and so I know"). Here More conceives of the Utopians telling Hythlodaye, so that he may tell More-persona, who will (as More) write a version of the account for Peter

Giles. The joke of it—for there is still the inescapable wit and conceptual wordplay with More—is that he will double the fun: the story of *Utopia* is set on a mission to Bruges that moves on to Antwerp and then, inexplicably, into Peter Giles's garden there. Such intricacies, however, rather than diminishing the power or significance of the story, most surely serve to preserve its importance. More also alludes to the *Critias,* by which Plato returns to the ideal state and the communistic society and, in the description of the island of Atlantis surrounded by ditches and fortifications, lends something to the geography of Utopia. But Plato did not finish the *Timaeus* trilogy: as his theory of an ideal if fabulous Athenian past drew closer to the present, he turned his attention to his final work, the more realistic *Laws.* This too, like the *Utopia,* is incomplete.[51]

Plato's descriptions of imperfect societies (like More's) refer to actual governments—the discussion of timarchy refers to Lycurgus's Sparta, for example, an allusion Busleiden for one saw in the *Utopia*[52]—but it is difficult to tell now whether this reference, or the communism shared by Sparta and Plato's ideal Republic, or the reference to Solon (with whom Plutarch compares and contrasts Lycurgus, the other classical lawmaker) in the *Timeaus* recalled to More's mind Plutarch's life of Lycurgus. In following the Senecan poetic of creating fiction by imitating an implied exemplar, however, and in taking the form of a dialogic fiction from Plato's trilogy of dialogues, what More needed badly was content. It is this that Plutarch's life of Lycurgus supplies. A swift survey of only a few of More's borrowings will show how frequently—and how comprehensively—he means Plutarch's life to be discerned as a model behind *Utopia.* Among Lycurgus's innovations are

> his institution of a senate, or Council of Elders, . . . by making the power of the senate a sort of ballast for the ship of state and putting her on a steady keel, it achieved the safest and the most orderly arrangement, since the twenty-eight senators always took the side of the kings when it was a question of curbing democracy, and, on the other hand, always strengthened the people to withstand the encroachments of tyranny. [5.6–7]

> He persuaded his fellow-citizens to make one parcel of all their territory and divide it up anew, and to live with one another on a basis of entire uniformity and equality. [8.2]

> Next, he undertook to divide up their movable property also, in order that every vestige of unevenness and inequality might be removed; and when he saw that they could not bear to have it taken from them directly, he took another course, and overcame their avarice by political devices. In the first place, he withdrew all gold and silver money from currency, and ordained the use of iron money only. [9.1–2]

With a view to attack luxury still more and remove the thirst for wealth, he introduced his third and most exquisite political device, namely, the institution of common messes, so that they might eat with one another in companies, of common and specified foods, and not take their meals at home, reclining on costly couches at costly tables, delivering themselves into the hands of servants and cooks to be fattened in the dark, like voracious animals. [10.1]

For one of the noble and blessed privileges which Lycurgus provided for his fellow-citizens, was abundance of leisure. [24.2]

He did not permit them to live abroad at their pleasure and wander in strange lands, assuming foreign habits and imitating the lives of peoples who were without training and lived under different forms of government. [27.3]

[Lycurgus] trained his fellow-citizens to have neither the wish nor the ability to live for themselves; but like bees they were to make themselves always integral parts of the whole community, clustering together about their leader. [25.3][53]

Senators are elected for life terms (26.3), Lycurgus drives away visitors (27.3–4), lawsuits vanish (24.4), and burials are made simple and free of superstition (27.1–2): Plutarch means this state to be exemplary, and in this half of the disputation comparing Lycurgus the Greek and Numa the Roman it is Lycurgus who is meant to elicit our respect. But there is another side to the argument. The boys are separated from the girls in Sparta and subjected to stern discipline by older men; they practice sodomy to relieve themselves (17.1); they turn effeminate (22.1)—practices that would not disturb Plutarch would signal a corrupted world to the humanists. Lycurgus's society earns a legendary distinction for simplicity; it is a life based on hard physicality with little advantage, no luxury, no splendor, and little joy. We find here the basis for various portions of More's satire of Hythlodaye and of Utopia. But we must also realize, as Plato does, that the Spartans are a minority dependent on their Helot slaves, who constitute a majority of the population. The Spartan government is, ultimately, untenable—even if Utopia could approximate it by using mercenaries as the Spartans use the Helots. Socrates realizes this, too, when he ridicules Sparta and its system of government in *Republic* 8. The *Utopia* is thus hugely dependent on the *Republic*—and on our knowledge of the *Republic* and of the *Lycurgus*—to show us how the classicist Hythlodaye has spun his visionary dream, and also to show how he has neglected to see how fundamentally unrealistic it is.

More also turns to Cicero, both to supply detail for Hythlodaye's ideal land and further to point the irony of Hythlodaye's partial comprehension of it; and, significantly, it is not the Cicero of the rhetorics and the political orations but the mature Cicero of moral philosophy on whom More draws. His major Ciceronian source for *Utopia* is Book 1 of the *De Finibus,* the summary discussion of Epicureanism that becomes the basis of the Utopian philosophy. Here we find Cicero's full explication of a system of belief in pleasure as the chief good (1.9.29 ff.), a pleasure that, naturally perceived, sought, and achieved, leads to natural fulfillment and therefore to wisdom, temperance, and reason (1.14.46–47).

> O praeclaram beate vivendi et apertam et simplicem et directam viam! Cum enim certe nihil homini possit melius esse quam vacare omni dolore et molestia perfruique maximis et animi et corporis voluptatibus, videtisne quam nihil praetermittatur quod vitam adiuvet, quo facilius id quod propositum est summum bonum consequamur? Clamat Epicurus, is quem vos nimis voluptatibus esse deditum dicitis, non posse iucunde vivi nisi sapienter, honeste iusteque vivatur nec sapienter, honeste, iuste nisi iucunde.

> Here is indeed a royal road to happiness—open, simple, and direct! For clearly man can have no greater good than complete freedom from pain and sorrow coupled with the enjoyment of the highest bodily and mental pleasures. Notice then how the theory embraces every possible enhancement of life, every aid to the attainment of that Chief Good which is our object. Epicurus, the man whom you denounce as a voluptuary, cries aloud that no one can live pleasantly without living wisely, honourably and justly, and no one wisely, honourably and justly without living pleasantly. (1.18.57).[54]

Cicero's *De Finibus* is also a disputation, however, for Book 2 is the wise Cicero's refutation of Epicureanism on several grounds—that, for instance, pleasure leads not only to happiness but to pride and utility (2.8.23–25) as it does in *Utopia* and, negatively, that it leaves out of account virtue and moral worth. This in turn relates *De Finibus* to the *Republic,* where virtue is the end Socrates seeks, and thence back to the *Utopia,* where virtue and moral worth are the fundamental humanist concerns finally *missing* from Hythlodaye's account. Boxes within boxes, classical sources and allusions nestled within one another, the world of humanist learning serves to point the way to proper understanding of *Utopia* then and now as well as to a constructive and pioneering development of a humanist poetics of fiction.

What is alone missing in these sources is tone; and that is Lucianic. It is this kind of wit that for More distinguishes philosophy from what we might call literature, as he himself confesses in the letter to Thomas Ruthall that prefaces his portion of the translations of Lucian he performed with Erasmus:

Si qvisqvam fuit unquam, uir doctissime, qui Horatianum praeceptum impleuerit, uoluptatemque cum utilitate coniunxerit, hoc ego certe Lucianum in primis puto praestitisse. Qui & superciliosis abstinens Philosophorum praeceptis, & solutioribus Poetarum lusibus, honestissimis simul & facetissimis salibus, uitia ubique notat atque insectatur mortalium.

If, most learned Sir, there was ever anyone who fulfilled the Horatian maxim and combined delight with instruction, I think Lucian certainly ranked among the foremost in this respect. Refraining from the arrogant pronouncements of the philosophers as well as from the wanton wiles of the poets, he everywhere reprimands and censures, with very honest and at the same time very entertaining wit, our human frailties.[55]

Perhaps in writing the *Utopia* More was cognizant that Lucian was one of the important Greek writers of the antique world who refused to take Plato seriously but who nevertheless satirized fraud and hypocrisy and set out, through infinite jest of his own, to urge reform. Like the classical Plato and like the sixteenth-century humanists, he means through writing to educate. In the Lucianic wit, which is so similar to More's own, we find further characteristics of More's fictional technique: the same comic fantasy and the same use of a fictional character as "his mouthpiece for the moment, [who] will put forward a false sentiment or an outrageous proposition—which, however, is an accepted element of the life or thought of his day—and, by allowing it to be carried through to its logical conclusion in the course of the dialogue, will expose its pretentiousness or its falsity," as T. S. Dorsch has it.[56] The longest piece More translated from Lucian is the *Philopseudes,* an attack on liars—really an examination of human credulity (*read* Hythlodaye)—who, overcome by a sense of the oracular or of divine possession (38), need the powerful antidote of truth and sound reason (40). Equally applicable to the *Utopia* is the central passage of the *Menippus* where Menippus tells us from the perspective of visiting the underworld that "it seemed to me that human life is like a long pageant, and that all its trappings are supplied and distributed by Fortune, who arrays the participants in various costumes of many colours." Again, it is not simply the metaphor that all the world is a stage that is important but what happens midway in Menippus's conceptualization of the metaphor.

> Often, in the very middle of the pageant, she [Fortune] exchanges the costumes of several players; instead of allowing them to finish the pageant in the parts that had been assigned to them, she re-apparels them, forcing Croesus to assume the dress of a slave and a captive, and shifting Maeandrius, who formerly paraded among the servants, into the imperial habit of Polycrates. For a brief space she lets them use their costumes, but

when the time of the pageant is over, each gives back the properties and lays off the costume along with his body, becoming what he was before his birth, no different from his neighbour. Some, however, are so ungrateful that when Fortune appears to them and asks her trappings back, they are vexed and indignant, as if they were being robbed of their own property, instead of giving back what they had borrowed for a little time. [16][57]

Folly uses the ideal of life as a pageant, but More again goes Erasmus one better: in *realizing* the metaphor in the characterization of Hythlodaye, he presents one who assumes the role of oracle, who parades his knowledge in reporting on Utopia, and who will brook no opposition; he too is angered when More-persona suggests, however deftly, that there may be another side to his argument at the close of *Utopia* 2.

More's own naturally witty inclination toward jest and irony—toward various means of satire generally—is what is missing in Plato, Plutarch, Cicero, and even Seneca: they share the dry seriousness of Hythlodaye. But it is precisely this *festivitas,* More knew, that would achieve the dictates of Horatian art, win the interest and pleasure of his fellow humanists, and earn their approval. It would also make his work a fitting complement to (and so a compliment of) Erasmus's *Encomium,* which had been dedicated to him, a house gift written in his house. It is Lucianic irony in its widest and most varied sense, then, that finally distinguishes the humanist thought and inventive strategy of *Utopia:* in this way, More insists that, acknowledging the patterns in the sources and ideas behind the *Utopia,* we come to question them too.

But, as More also knew, irony can often turn back on itself, fooling even the wise. In a sense, "the humor and sense of irony [only] tempered the rigour of his mind," to paraphrase John Hayes.[58] Thus, to be certain of distancing his readers and requiring their active interpretation and judgment—and not simply to supply contextual circumstantiality for Hythlodaye's account—More felt it necessary to compose Book 1: Hythlodaye's smug but inane babbling at the conclusion of *Utopia* 2 alongside the antipathetic doubts expressed by More-persona, sufficient for a bifocal disputation, was apparently not enough.[59] Yet again, in gaining access by *Utopia* 1, we must look out for overtones and undertones because More's aesthetic does not provide a third viewpoint openly. Thus we find, for example, that Hythlodaye praises John Cardinal Morton, yet it was Morton, for all More's tribute, who was popularly held responsible among More's fellow Tudors for heavy taxation under Henry VII, historically analogous to Wolsey and fictionally a subtle countercurrent to Hythlodaye's naive perception of England. Here as in *Utopia* 2 Hythlodaye attempts to persuade by the eloquence of his manner rather than his knowledge or his logic. His formal arrangements employ a number of devices common to a humanist rhetoric made into a humanist poetics—parallelism, chiasmus, balanced antithesis, and synonymy; enallage, antonomasia, periphrasis, onomatopoeia, and paragoge; synecdoche and hyperbole; simile and metaphor:[60] so impressive is he verbally that More-persona invites young John Clement to join the others in the garden to hear Hythlodaye. And Hythlodaye's new speech in *Utopia* 1 tracks domestic, international, and fiscal policy in Europe, leading him to a simplified solution to European ills in the establishment of a communistic economy, a solution whose very simplicity lends it undeniable potency. This answer shows also the static quality of his mind, for it agrees exactly with his later description:

> Contra hic, ubi omnia omnium sunt nemo dubitat (curetur modo, ut plena sint horrea publica) nihil quicquam priuati cuiquam defuturum. Neque enim maligna rerum destributio est, neque inops, neque mendicus ibi quisquam. & quum nemo quicquam habeat, omnes tamen diuites sunt.

> There where all thynges be commen to euerye man, it is not to be dowted that anye man shal lacke anye thynge necessarye for hys pryuate vses: so that the commen store houses and barnes be sufficientlye stored. For there nothynge is distrybuted after a nyggyshe sorte, nother there is any poore man or begger. And though no man haue any thynge, yet euerye man is ryche. [238; sigs. R7–R7v; 131]

Hythlodaye remains stuck in one groove, the consistency of his thought and vision stubbornly unopen to and unaware of other circumstances or possibilities.

Still More continues here to insinuate an inherent *controversia* rather than a simple *suasoria*, even when More-persona declines to argue with Hythlodaye. For, as Hythlodaye's case becomes more rhetorically forceful, the lands on which he bases his argument grow more and more distant, more and more *fictional;* they recede from Morton's actual household in the near past to an imagined incident at the French court, thence to the imaginary Polylerites who dwell near an authentic Persia to the wholly imaginary Utopia.[61] As he grows more assertive and more argumentative, Hythlodaye indiscriminately mixes fact with fiction. He cites theft, which was indeed widespread under Henry VIII, alongside the evil of enclosures, which, except perhaps in the Midlands, seems to have been thought generally beneficial—and in any event less frequent than it had been a century or so earlier.[62] Furthermore, Hythlodaye's account of Europe verges on the nonsensical. He argues that, because both thieves and murderers are sentenced to capital punishment, killing is encouraged:

"Itaque dum fures nimis atrociter studemus perterrefacere, in bonorum incitamus perniciem"; "Therfore whyles we goo about wyth suche crueltye to make theues afered, we prouoke thē to kyll good men" (74; sig. D5; 31). Superficially, the reaction may be logical enough, but the spurious and witty reasoning cannot withstand scrutiny. Hythlodaye ignores the purpose of the law, its first cause: in a country overpopulated with the poor, it is a nice question whether murder is worse; in a country in short supply, theft is tantamount to a capital offense. More revealingly, he does not discriminate between stealing and killing. Stealing needs sterner control because, driven by debt, we are more apt to steal than to slay; English law knows us if Hythlodaye does not. Most revealing of all, thieves in Utopia—where they are seen as insurrectionists—are also punished by death. Hythlodaye's vision of Utopia has not so much awakened him to the possibilities of human society as it has blinded him to the potentialities of human nature and the inherent evils of Utopia.[63]

More is insistent that we understand Hythlodaye's lack of wit and wisdom here by causing him to offer More-persona two kinds of alternatives. One involves inhumane tortures as practiced by the Romans:

> administrandae reipublicae peritissimis? Nempe hi magnorum facinorum conuictos in lapidicinas, atque folienda metalla damnabant, perpetuis adseruandos vinculis.

> Men in thadmynystratyon of a weale publyque moste experte polytque and cunnyng [send convicted thieves] condempned into ston quarris, and in myenes to dygge mettalle, there to be kepte in cheynes all the dayes of theyr life. [74; sig. D5; 32]

The other alternative is irrational (and, in Europe as portrayed, impossible). In Persia, Hythlodaye claims, men make restitution of stolen goods and then, if they have committed a felony, also are condemned to forced labor (76; sig. D6; 31). They may also be physically mutilated, Hythlodaye blandly reports (76; sig. D7; 33). Thus, caught between humane treatment of petty criminals and the need for realistic political law, we side neither with Hythlodaye nor with English practice but chart a third, more moderate course. Our tendency to support the moderation of a sixteenth-century humanist is therefore reinforced.[64]

Beneath and beyond Hythlodaye's remarks, we must also interpret his actions. We must ask why he is in Antwerp, then headquarters of international commerce and banking, the center of the world's capitalism; we are tempted to ask why he ever left Utopia,[65] since he says he wishes to share his knowledge of Utopia yet steadfastly declines to counsel rulers with that knowledge. His discussion with More-persona is, additionally, surreal. Amidst sickness and starvation, poverty and disease, they hold a teatime conversation in a garden, a conversation somewhat wandering in style and loose in syntactic construction which, given the darker tones surrounding their talk and the immensity of the issues at hand, cannot help but remind us of other gardens in literature: of Eden, where the language of persuasion initiated the Fall of Man; of Vergil's gardens, unreal because enclosed, shut off from the problems, dangers, and struggles of life; and of medieval gardens, where man's vision of the City of God proved to be only a dream.[66] The torpor of this setting sharpens when the otiose Hythlodaye attacks drones who live on the labors of others, for here too is a startling if naive act of self-condemnation. A master of rhetoric, Hythlodaye stubbornly refuses to enter into a disputation with others—either at the home of Cardinal Morton in Book 1 or with More-persona at the close of Book 2. Rather, the pride he condemns he also reveals in his sense of discovery at the start of *Utopia* 1 and in his intractable superiority at the close of *Utopia* 2. Yet, in fact, by the book's end his apocalyptic oration leads him into an uncontrolled denunciation at the opposite extreme from Folly's ecstatic vision—and so weakens him intellectually, physically, and verbally that More-persona must help him out of his garden and indoors. As a consequence, we are so alienated from Hythlodaye finally—although we admit to reason much of the value he argues for it—that when he charges Europe with allowing sheep to eat men, surely our response is that in Utopia men are not human but, rather, resemble sheep.[67]

It is to keep us alert to such a subtext and to moderating responses to it that More introduces early in *Utopia* 1 the symbol of the magnetic compass. The mariners of Utopia, he recalls from Hythlodaye, are

> maris ac caeli non imperiti. Sed miram se narrabat inisse gratiam, tradito magnetis usu, cuius antea penitus erant ignari. ideoque timide pelago consueuisse sese, neque alias temere, quam aestate credere. Nunc uero eius fiducia lapidis contemnunt hyemem, securi magis, quam tuti, ut periculum sit, ne quae res magno eis bono futura putabatur, eadem per imprudentiam magnorum causa malorum fiat.

> also verye experte and connynge both in the sea and in the wether. But he sayde that he founde great fauour and fryndeshyppe amonge them for teachynge them the feate and vse of the lode stone. Whych to them before that tyme was vnknowne. And therefore they were wonte to be verye tymerous and fearefull vpon the sea. Nor to venter vpon it, but onlye in the somer time. But nowe they haue such a confidence in that stone, that they feare not stormy wynter, in so doynge ferther frome care then ieopardye. In so muche that it is greatlye to be doubtyd, leste that thynge thoroughe theyre owne folyshe hardynes shall tourne them to euyll and harme,

whyche at the fyrste was supposyde shoulde be to them good and commodyous. [52; sigs. B5v–B6; 17–18]

We must remember that the man with the magnetic needle is also *our* pilot in *Utopia* 2.

And if we study this emblem passage carefully enough, we see that it does not offer us two mutually exclusive alternatives as irony and paradox frequently do, both interdependent. Implied instead are multiple alternatives: we can use the compass along with great caution in winters, trust it in winter but not when the weather is stormy, or lay it aside forever. What we are offered is a *range* of possibilities in which the missing fact is our individual self and our own judgment—the triangularity of defendant, respondent, and judge. So too the greater range More gives us between the pedestrian view of Europe and the ecstatic vision of Utopia. For Hythlodaye is made to look both visionary ("tamen aequatis rebus omnia abundant omnibus"; "all thynges beynge ther common, euerye man hath abundaunce of euery thynge" [102; sig. G1; 50]) and shortsighted ("Nam quo pacto suppetat copia rerum, unoquoque ab labore subducente se?"; "For how can there by abundañce of gooddes, or of any thing where euery mā withdraweth his hāde frō labour?" [106; sig. G2v; 52]) while, in his most open tribute to the *Encomium Moriae,* More-persona (*Morus,* folly) repeats the advice that the sane man must not spoil the design of the play (98; sigs. F5v–F6; 47). It is significant that More and Hythlodaye first meet outside Notre Dame in Antwerp, a potentially powerful cathedral then being rebuilt but still unfinished.

Erasmus's letter to More preceding the *Encomium Moriae* (which, we recall, helped us understand Erasmus's irony) has its parallel in the letter to Peter Giles—a man of "prudente symplycyte" (*simplicitas inest prudentior*) (48; sig. B2v; 14)—with which More prefaces the *Utopia,* and it confirms our reading.[68] "The introductory letter," Harry Berger, Jr., comments,

> not only anticipates the body of the work, it also contains the past experience in miniature form. It reveals the continuing pressure of actual affairs on More, the insufficiency of time, the discordant claims of pleasure and business, desire and obligation. It portrays a world in which ideal conditions are something man may rather wish for than hope after.[69]

Yet, if More seems at times to reduplicate Hythlodaye's own despair and pessimism in the self-portrayal here, there is more to it than this: the mere act of writing the letter, and the *Utopia,* suggests an abiding faith in man on the part of More, which Hythlodaye like the Utopians is incapable of sharing; we shall see this extrapolated in *Utopia* 1 when More-persona argues that the humanist should counsel the prince and Hythlodaye replies that such action would be futile (54; sig. C1; 20).[70] All their characters are encapsulated in this interchange: More-persona is flexible, open, optimistic, practical; Hythlodaye is inflexible, authoritarian, cynical, selfish. The double choice that Hythlodaye offers More-persona is meant to imply others—one may counsel in some instances and keep silent in others, or counsel in various ways at different times and from changing motives. The humanists who knew their Seneca and the *Octavia* would see the point quickly enough.

That we are left to resolve the differences between Hythlodaye and More-persona by ourselves is also signaled in the difference of opinion over the river Anyder in More's prefatory letter to Giles. The More-persona recalls that the bridge spanning the river is 500 paces long. But, in a book where More refuses to allow any serious statement to be absolute, the More-persona swiftly adds that his memory may be faulty, the more so since his pupil-servant John Clement remembers with certainty that the river is not more than 300 paces wide (40; sigs. +8v–A1; 8). Surely this is meant to be a false dilemma: the answer is that the bridge extends 200 paces over the land. A solution so simple and so near to hand must be a ploy to let us know at the outset that here as elsewhere we will be invited to supply the missing third view, the unstated conclusion to stated premises, resolutions to dilemmas more apparent than real.[71]

This dynamics of response holds true finally for the very first dichotomy More presents to us. It comes in his apology to Giles for the lateness of his narrative and the roughness of its style in those parts outlined in humanist textbooks—in *inventio, dispositio,* and *elocutio.*

> quippe quum scires mihi demptum in hoc opere inueniendi laborem, neque de dispositione quicquam fuisse cogitandum, cui tantum erant ea recitanda, quae tecum una pariter audiui narrantem Raphaelem. quare nec erat quod in eloquendo laboraretur, quando nec illius sermo potuit exquisitus esse, quum esset primum subitarius, atque extemporalis, deinde hominis, ut scis, non perinde Latine docti quam Graece, & mea oratio quanto accederet propius ad illius neglectam simplicitatem, tanto futura sit propior ueritati, cui hac in re soli curam & debeo & habeo.

> For you knewe welenough, that I was already disbourdened of all that labour & study belōging to the inuention in this work, and that I had no nede at all to trouble my braynes about the dispositiō, or cōueyaunce of the matter: & therfore had herin nothing els to do, but only to rehearse those thinges, which you and I togethers hard maister Raphaell tel and declare. Wherefore there was no cause whie I shold study to set forth that matter with eloquēce: for asmuch as his talke cold not be fine & eloquent, being

firste not studied for, but sodein and vnpremeditate, and then, as you know, of a mā better sene in the greke language, then in the latine tong. And my writing, the nigher it shold approche to his homely playne, and simple speche, somuch the higher shold it go to the trueth: whiche is the only marke, wherunto I do and ought to direct all my travail and study herin. [38; sigs. +6v–+7; 6][72]

The problem of language, then, is one of careless yet eloquent truth versus controlled but self-generated opinion, a comment on the florid rhetoricians of More's day surely but specifically, here, on the formal self-conscious *learned* presentation of Hythlodaye in *both* orations, *Utopia* 1 and *Utopia* 2. More is proposing that Hythlodaye's account of Utopia—naked, undisciplined eloquence, hence sophistry—could not be further from the truth. It is not absolutely clear whether More means Hythlodaye's account is untrue because it is a fiction or untrue because it is invalid or incivil or psychologically unrealistic. But it does not matter, for again the distinction is false; there is no quantitative difference between More's style and that of Hythlodaye within the fiction of the book—either they are both eloquent and lying, or they are both unpolished and truthful. Still, this is so only if we insist on paradox, for the four terms make other combinations available to us. "A mind like More's was full of light like a house made of windows," G. K. Chesteron once advised, "but the windows looked out on all sides and in all directions. We might say that, as the jewel has many facets, so the man had many faces; only none of them were masks."[73]

In sum, *Utopia* is "a dialogue of the mind with itself";[74] and, where the dialogue becomes monologue, nearly 200 marginal notations restore the fundamental force of the disputation.[75] Even within the narrative, Hythlodaye's questionable presentation (as well as his inconsistent ideas) supplies its own argumentation. Thus he finds the Utopian ritual for betrothal foolish and ridiculous—and proceeds in his very next comments to explain and justify it; he is astonished by Utopian epicureanism yet defends it, *as the Utopians do,* by Utopian religious principles. Ironically, he juxtaposes his descriptions of Utopian marriage and Utopian slavery; he argues that communism eliminates pride and social injustice, and yet the communistic Utopians display both within their patriarchal repressionism. He does not see that his perfect heterocosm[76] also knows suicide and euthanasia. Utopia is realized as a community only by arguing paradoxically that man is most free and fully realized when he loses self-awareness and liberty in a community that is itself in the process of becoming. "What an infinitely wise—infinitely foolish—book [*Utopia*] is!" John Ruskin wrote F. S. Ellis in July 1870. "Right in all it asks—insane, in venturing to ask it all at once—so making its own wisdom folly for evermore; and becoming perhaps the most really mischievous book ever written."[77]

As Thomas Wilson can supply significant rhetorical paradigms for *Utopia,* as we saw at the beginning of our discussion, so another Tudor rhetorician, Richard Rainolde, may supply the criteria for judgment, for the Tudors and for us. "Nature hath indued euery man, with a certain eloquence, and also subtilitee to reason and discusse, of any question or proposicion propounded," Rainolde writes in 1563, looking to his Aristotle; "These gifts of nature, singuler doe flowe and abounde in vs, accordyng to the greate and ample indumente and plentuousnes of witte and wisedome, lodged in vs" (*Foundacion of Rhetorike,* sig. A1). We are back in a land of folly, and of Folly—and of man's further inclination to vision, to fantasy and dream. More's jest was so good and so earnest that, four months later, he reported to Erasmus,

> Itaque nescis nunc quantum gestio, quantum creui, quanto memet altiorem gero: its mihi assidue versatur ob oculos perpetuum destinari mihi principatum ab Vtopianis meis, quin iam nunc mihi videor incedere coronatus insigni illo diademate frumentaceo, conspicuus paludamento Franciscano, praeferens venerabile sceptrum e manipulo frugis, stipatus insigni Amauratorum comitatu atque ita celebri pompa legatis atque principibus aliarum gentium occurrere, miseris plane pre nobis, stulte videlicet superbientibus, quod veniant ornati pueriliter et mundo muliebri onusti, vinctique auro illi despuibili, purpura et gemmis atque allis bullatis nugis deridiculi. Quanquam nolim aut te aut Tunstallum nostrum ex aliorum ingeniis aestimare me, quorum fortuna mores mutat. Equidem esti superis visum est nostram humilitatem ad hoc fastigii et sublimitatis euehere, cui nullum regum posse conferri censeo, veteris tamen illius consuetudinis mihi olim priuato fuit vobiscum, nunquam me sentietis immemorem. Quod si non grauemini tantillum viae facere vt Vtopiam venitatis ad me, profecto efficiam vt mortales omnes quos clementiae nostrae regit imperium, id honoris exhibeant vobis quem debent eis quos intelligunt ipsorum principi esse charissimos.
>
> Prosecuturus eram longius hoc dulcissimum somnium, sed Aurora consurgens, veh misero, discussit somnium et principatu me excussit, atque in pistrinum meum me, hoc est in forum, reuocat. Hoc tamen me consolor, quod vera regna video non multo prolixiora.
>
> Vale, charissime Erasme.

You have no idea how thrilled I am; I feel so expanded, and I hold my head high. For in my daydreams I have been marked out by my Utopians to be their king forever; I can see myself now marching along, crowned with a diadem of wheat, very striking in my Franciscan frock, carrying a handful of wheat as my sacred scepter, thronged by a distinguished retinue of Amaurotians, and, with this huge entourage, giving audience to foreign ambassadors and sovereigns; wretched creatures they are, in comparison with us, as they stupidly pride themselves on appearing in childish garb and feminine finery, laced with that despicable gold, and ludicrous in their purple and jewels and other empty baubles. Yet, I would not want either you or our friend, Tunstal, to judge me by other men, whose character shifts with fortune. Even if heaven has decreed to waft me from my lowly estate to this soaring pinnacle which, I think, defies comparison with that of kings, still you will never find me forgetful of that old friendship I had with you when I was but a private citizen. And if you do not mind making the short trip to visit me in Utopia, I shall definitely see to it that all mortals governed by my kindly rule will show you the honor due to those who, they know, are very dear to the heart of their king.

I was going to continue with this fascinating vision, but the rising Dawn has shattered my dream—poor me!—and shaken me off my throne and summons me back to the drudgery of the courts. But at least this thought gives me consolation: real kingdoms do not last much longer.

Farewell, dearest Erasmus.[78]

"The best state of a commen wealthe" (40; sig. B1; [13]), to which More invites us on the title page of *Utopia,* then, is a state of self-examination; Hythlodaye's journey of body and spirit contains not only mad prophecies but exploratory visions. More's little book, *hunc libellum,* is also a *laus hominis* in which wise men become fools while those we thought foolish can still teach us how to escape the seduction of dreams on our own way to wisdom.

THREE

Aliquid Salis: Narrative Wordplay and Gascoigne's *Adventures of Master F. J.*

 GEORGE GASCOIGNE, THE MOST IMPORTANT WRITER OF HUMANIST FICTION AMONG THE SECOND GENERATION OF TUDOR HUMANISTS, WAS BORN IN 1539 AND DIED BEFORE REACHING THE AGE OF forty. Still, in such a remarkably short lifetime he became, as Merritt Lawlis has it, "one of the two or three most versatile writers of the entire century."[1] His most experimental and influential work remains *The Adventures of Master F. J.,* originally published (in *A Hundreth Sundry Flowres* [1573]) shortly after Elizabeth I ascended to the throne, and the first important humanist fiction written in England subsequent to More's *Utopia.* This fiction (similar to Gascoigne's later prodigal-son play, *The Glasse of Gouernement* of 1575) is a deliberate examination of the fundamental premises of Roger Ascham's *Scholemaster,* posthumously published only three years previously. Yet Ascham's remarks sound strange alongside the humanist wit of *Utopia,* because they divide poetry from rhetoric as no other humanist work does. "For this I know," Ascham argues in one of the most important Elizabethan treatises of humanist doctrine,

> not onelie by reading of bookes in my studie, but also by experience of life, abrode in the world, that those, which be commonlie the wisest, the best learned, and best men also, when they be olde, were neuer commonlie the quickest of witte, when they were yonge. The causes why, amongst other, which be many, that moue me thus to thinke, be these fewe, which I will recken. Quicke wittes commonlie, be apte to take, vnapte to keepe: soone hote and desirous of this and that: as colde and sone wery of the same againe: more quicke to enter spedelie, than hable to pearse farre: euen like ouer sharpe tooles, whose edges be verie soone turned. Soch wittes delite them selues in easie and pleasant studies, and neuer passe farreforward in hie and hard sciences. And therfore the quickest wittes commonlie may proue the best Poetes, but not the wisest Orators. [Sig. C4v]

Of this new division Ascham is adamant.

> Moreouer commonlie, men, very quicke of witte, be also, verie light of
> conditions: and thereby, very readie of disposition, to be caried ouer
> quicklie, by any light cumpanie, to any riot of vnthriftines when they be
> yonge: and therfore seldome, either honest of life, or riche in liuing, when
> they be olde. . . . Quicke wittes also be, in most part of all their doinges,
> ouerquicke, hastie, rashe, headie, and brainsicke. . . . They be like trees,
> that shewe forth, faire blossoms & broad leaues in spring time, but bring out
> small and not long lasting fruite in haruest time: and that onelie soch, as
> fall, and rotte, before they be ripe, and so, neuer, or seldome, cum to any
> good at all. For this ye shall finde most true by experience, that amongest
> a number of quicke wittes in youthe, fewe be found, in the end, either verie
> fortunate for them selues, or verie profitable to serue the common wealth.
> [Sig. D1]

But it is not only a critique of humanist wordplay Ascham attacks; it is also
a crucial point of humanist education that Ascham raises: whether the
humanist curriculum in rhetoric has the power and means to nurture weak,
wayward, or corrupted natures—quick wits—which have no staying
power and may therefore remain beyond the capacity of humanist schools
to instruct and redeem. Gascoigne's putative poet-protagonist F. J. is just
such a quick wit whose inflated "adventures" anatomize his inherent and
learned capabilities—his "epic" experiences actually diminish him in
size—just as the putative narrator, G. T., is an older, wiser orator whose
ability to judge is also under scrutiny. More basic still, F. J. pushes the
problem of a usable humanism still farther in one of his early poems.

> *What may be sayd, where truth cannot preuayle?*
> *What plea may serue, where will it selfe is Iudge?*
> *What reason rules, where right and reason fayle?*[2]

Blunt inquiries, laughable in the context of F. J.'s adolescent passions but
far more serious in the intellectual context in which the work was written,
these questions register an urgent, because explicit, confrontation with
eristics. Enriched and inventive with its constant wordplay on Petrarchan
language and its exploratory conceptual play on framing narrative devices,
Gascoigne's contribution to a creative humanist poetics is also the climax
of a humanist fiction of wordplay that began with Erasmus's *Encomium
Moriae*. Finally, it is a glorious extravaganza of humanist poetics in its own
right, made so because, unlike any earlier humanist fiction, it examines the
validity of humanist ideas and rhetoric in a society characterized by
gentlemanly pretense and courtly sophistry. Even Erasmus's copia had not
had to be sustained in so slippery and unreliable a context: with Gascoigne

we confront wordplay neither as a technique of satiric exuberance nor as a *jeu d'esprit* but as an inescapable condition of the times in which the fiction writer pursued his art.

The Adventures of Master F. J.—"an artistic triumph";[3] "a brilliantly conceived and ingeniously executed work of imaginative fiction, incomparably the most entertaining comic narrative of the Elizabethan age"[4]—is a twice-told tale, simultaneously unfolding in the heated, poetic present of F. J. and coolly related from a more prosaic, retrospective past by G. T. Although the two tales are different in form and perspective, each of them focuses from the start on life created by and through language. Each tale is self-reflexive and self-adulatory, like the encomia of Folly and Hythlodaye. Indeed, *The Adventures of Master F. J.* glows throughout with Erasmian wit. E. K. says of Gascoigne while glossing Spenser's *Shepheardes Calender* (1579) that "gifts of wit and naturall promptnesse appeare in hym abundantly";[5] and nothing in *The Adventures,* Gascoigne remarks, is "so barreyne, but that (in my iudgmēt) had in it *Aliquid Salis,*" some wit (sig. A3). In using the two tales of F. J. and G. T. as the basis for a kind of Erasmian doubleness, Gascoigne addresses the theme of education, making the humanist need for self-government, the *de regimine principum,* an inverted *speculum principis* that mirrors a world turned upside-down, a madcap praising of Tudor folly.

Not all of this—perhaps none of this—may at first seem especially pertinent. On the face of it, *The Adventures of Master F. J.* is a loose sonnet sequence in both poetry and prose links that unfolds a rather predictable if lively Petrarchan narrative; it tells of F. J.'s adulterous love for Elinor, the discovery of it, and her abandonment of him. Yet, if we heed the opening words of G. T., the work also announces its concern with that humanist dilemma we have seen inherent in Erasmus and More and central to their fictions: the trust or distrust of language and of man's innate capacity to learn and so improve himself. In Gascoigne, humanist thought and rhetoric, oratory and poetry, are *indivisible.* G. T. therefore speaks of the doctrine of imitatio as the emulation of wisdom—and also as the efficacy of poetry, to teach and to demonstrate what one is taught.

> The most frosty bearded *Philosopher,* maye take iust occasion of honest recreation, not altogether without holsome lessons, tending to the reformation of manners. For who doubteth but that Poets in their most feyned fables and imaginations, haue metaphorically set forth vnto vs the right rewardes of vertues, and the due punnishments for vices? [Sig. A2; 50]

It is this splendid audaciousness that so summons us at the start of Gascoigne's fiction: not only is man's capacity for learning by precept as much as by experience at stake—as it always is with the humanists—but so is the very nature of narrative, the "feyned fable." In a self-conscious fiction that will examine self-conscious fictions, we are to see if the story can hold true amidst disclaiming sophistry.[6]

Gascoigne openly tests language throughout *The Adventures* in poems that often sound like Petrarch's more rhetorical set pieces, in declamations on (and protestations of) love, in the implied dialectic of self-examining soliloquies, and even in the inset parables of disdain, suspicion, and infidelity, all of which adhere to another of Ascham's fundamental principles in *The Scholemaster,* that manner and matter should never be separate (sig. O2). The last of the three inset tales, the one on infidelity, for instance, is told by Fraunces one evening. When the husband of her story within a story finds his wife unfaithful, he leaves slips for her each time they enjoy themselves to remind her of her wantonness until eventually she repents and agrees to end her adultery with a young courtier. Fraunces's story is simple, but it is not innocent, for she has requested to tell it as a game when F. J., as governor for the evening, must judge it. Except for the slips (which may or may not be true), what Fraunces proposes is not a fable at all but fact: she tells F. J. about himself in the character of the young lover and warns him, encoding her message within her fiction, of the outcome of his present affair with the married Lady Elinor. Her tale is deliberately analogous; she rehearses, she tells F. J., "a straunge historie, not fayned, neither borowed out of any olde aucthoritie, but a thing done in deede of late daies, and not farre distant from this place where wee nowe remayne" (sig. K3v; 96). She has thus turned a riddle into a disputation in which the truth lies as well with the respondent, who can verify and validate the fable she has proposed. Furthermore, in her rhetorical hypotyposis Fraunces publicly reveals her own friendly disposition toward F. J. in contrast to Elinor's insincerity. Fiction thus coincident and collusive with fact, as in allegory and parable, would seem to authenticate both.

But the utility of such counterfeiting for Gascoigne, when employed within the artful (and artificial) society of courtly love, is in no way certain. When Fraunces asks F. J. who of the three principals of her fable is most wronged, he answers the riddle correctly—"I think the husbands perplexitie greatest, bicause his losses abounded aboue the rest, & his iniuries were vncomparable" (sig. L3; 100)—but he fails to see that in doing so he condemns his own present actions. Just as the parable is both fiction and fact (or correlative to fact), so it is only partly successful, then, and the efficacy of any fiction—and of rhetoric generally—remains in doubt. Even the three parables presented to F. J. to judge on successive nights and in the ascending order of a lover's mistaken disdain, a husband's unwarranted suspicion, and a wife's actual infidelity, encode in greater and greater degree for him the same personal message, which he continually fails to perceive. Simpler than the Protean representations of Folly and the sophistry of Hythlodaye, these stories that resemble or exaggerate fact—set before us in a larger story that is probably fiction[7]—are, besides being comic, Gascoigne's plainest commentary on the consequences for poetics in a highly rhetorical world.

Rather like Erasmus and More, then, Gascoigne structures his work as a nest of continually larger boxes. Beyond the confines of so straightforward an exemplum as Fraunces's tale of courtly love condemned and reconciled is the larger story of F. J.'s affair with Elinor. F. J. appears by his letters and verses to be bright, self-centered, even arrogant. Yet he possesses few of the courtly graces, shows little skill at hunting and writing, and so is anxious to improve himself. His ambitions are propelled by his energies. The conventions of his early compacted letters and poems disclose a natural affinity for the petty deceits and deployments of courtly love; but, even so, his very first poem is puzzling.

> *Fayre Bersabe the bright once bathing in a Well,*
> *With deawe bedimmed King Dauids eyes that ruled Israell,*
> *And Salomon him selfe, the source of sapience,*
> *Against the force of such assaultes could make but small defěce:*
> *To it the stoutest yeeld, and strongest feele like woo [woe]*
> *Bold Hercules and Sompson both, did proue it to be so.*
> *What wonder seemeth then? when starres stand thicke in skies,*
> *If such a blasing starre haue power to dim my dazled eyes?*
> Lenuoie.
> To you these fewe suffise, your wittes be quicke and good,
> You can coniect by chaunce of hew, what humors feede my blood.
> F. J.

[Sig. A4; 52]

Inner discordances here force our interpretation as readers. The poem may be the early work of a poetaster straining for classical and scriptural *figurae,* an imitative humanist act and a poor one at that. If so, F. J. may be confusing the chaste Corinna, whom Ovid viewed bathing naked in a pool, with the prostitute Bathsheba who was not normally a subject for pagan love poetry. Or perhaps F. J. means to be salacious and seductive by connecting Bathsheba with the following line on *"assaultes."* Either F. J. seems not to know what to say, and so betrays his naiveté; or he does mean what he implies, and the innocence that is here imaged is actually only feigned. Elinor's response is also open to our own best judgment: her teasing reply is suitable to the decorum of courtly love but may in fact protest an honest bafflement. Each (or both) shares the calculated innocence portrayed in Gascoigne's *Dan Bartholomew of Bathe* (also 1573) or the genuine naiveté of Ergasto in Gascoigne's translation of the *I Suppositi* of Ariosto. His prologue to this play, in fact, shows a similar intention to the idea behind *The Adventures of Master F. J.*

> I Suppose you are assembled here, supposing to reape the fruite of my traualyes: and to be playne, I meane presently to presente you with a Comedie called Supposes, the verye name wherof may peraduenture driue into euery of your heades a sundry Suppose, to suppose the meaning of our supposes. Some percase will suppose we meane to occupie your eares with sophisticall handling of subtill Suppositions. Some other will suppose we go about to discipher vnto you some queint conceipte, which hitherto haue bene onely supposed as it were in shadowes: and some I see smyling as though they supposed we would trouble you with the vaine suppose of some wanton Suppose [Sig. B2v; John W. Cunliffe, ed. (Cambridge, 1907), 1:188]

Clearly this wordplay attracts Gascoigne because it allows him to parody both rhetoric and logic at a kind of verbal jointure where the whole is encased in a dramatic *bildung* that examines (and parodies) humanist principles of education. In this, Gascoigne's practice is at one with his theory in "Certayne notes of Instruction *concerning the making of verse or ryme in English*" (1575), which advocates the delight of unusual invention.

Whether or not F. J. means to hint (and thereby test) the possibility of his own victory or defeat in his opening poem to Elinor, his next detailed correspondence with her reverses the situation; he suggests Elinor's surrender by imaging her as Narcissus.

> *The cause of myne affection, I suppose you behold dayly. For (self loue auoyded) euery wight may iudge of themselues as much as reason pers-wadeth: the which if it be in your good nature suppressed with bashfulnes, then mighty loue graunt, you may once behold my wan cheekes washed in woe, that therein my salt teares may be a myrrour to represent your owne shadow, and that like vnto Narcissus you may bee constrayned to kisse the cold waues, wherein your coūterfait is so liuely portrayed.* [Sig. B1; 54]

This is perhaps a pretty conceit, more successful than the allusion to Bathsheba (although still a bit peculiar), by which F. J. calls attention to the fact of his own suffering as if to validate his words; perhaps it is a challenge to Elinor by attributing to her a genuine (or feigned) position of strength. Interpretive possibilities are multiple.

Our whole understanding of F. J., that is, rests on our appreciation of his attempts at artifice in this artificial society: he is callow, clever, or too clever by half. G. T.'s narrative passages do not help us determine which, however, while F. J.'s own writing retains its intrinsic ambiguity. His subsequent attempts to reach Elinor through the command of his rhetoric, and the poem that does bring about their first close encounter, are no better. He poses three pretty riddles summed in the first of them:

> *What reason first persuades the foolish Fly*
> *(As soone as shee a candle can discerne)*
> *To play with flame, till shee bee burnt thereby?*
> [Sig. B2; 55]

But his own metaphoric aptness is erased by the nearly unmediated note of pain on which the poem concludes:

> *And as the Byrd once caught (but woorks her woe)*
> *That stryues to leaue the lymed winges behind:*
> *Euen so the more I straue to parte thee fro,*
> *The greater grief did growe within my minde:*
> *Remediles then must I yeeld to thee,*
> *And craue no more, thy seruaunt but to bee.*
> [Sig. B2v; 56]

By transferring his attention from conventionally wan cheeks to a weakened and tormented mind, F. J. may mean to disclose the very real anxieties of love. Subsequent passages of *The Adventures* supplied to us by F. J. sustain these various postures. At times, he suffers the symptoms of the spurned and despairing courtly lover: he grows sick; his fondest hopes betray him. At other times, he becomes lustful, his passions rising uncontrollably at *"beauties tickle trade"* (sig. C4; 62). "F. J. is taken in by his own imagination," Frank B. Fieler tells us,[8] and, ravished with insatiable desire, his poems become pornographic. "A Friday's Breakfast," one instance of several, celebrates a day associated with fasting by making it an occasion for physical rather than spiritual devotion in F. J.'s corrupted religion of love.

> *And lo, my Lady of hir wonted grace,*
> *First lent hir lippes to me (as for a kisse:)*
> *And after that hir body to embrace,*
> *Wherein dame nature wrought nothing amisse.*
> *What followed next, gesse you that knowe the trade,*
> *For in this sort, my Frydayes feast I made.*
> [Sig. F1v; 74]

"Truth is compted but a toy," comments Gascoigne drily elsewhere, "when such fond fancies reign" (sig. O2; 116).

F. J. pushes such language to its bizarre limits, as M. R. Rohr Philmus puts it,[9] and by that means recovers a trustworthy lexicon. He learns to employ poetry honestly, cathartically. The first stanza of his last work, incorporating Elinor's final angry dismissal of him, is the text for a new autobiographical poetry that is also simple, proverbial wisdom.

> *And if I did what then?*
> *Are you agreeu'd therfore?*
> *The Sea hath fishe for euery man,*
> *And what would you haue more?*
>
> *Thus did my Mistresse once,*
> *Amaze my mind with doubt:*
> *And popt a question for the nonce,*
> *To beate my braynes about.*
>
> *Wherto I thus replied,*
> *Each fisherman can wishe,*
> *That all the Sea at euery tyde,*
> *Were his alone to fishe.*
>
> *And so did I (in vaine,)*
> *But since it may not be:*
> *Let such fishe there as find the gaine,*
> *And leaue the losse for me.*
> [Sigs. M2–M2v; 105]

Together, F. J.'s poems "trace the ideal story of F. I.'s growth as a poet";[10] they also graph his coming of age as he uses poetry increasingly to disclose rather than conceal truth. The crudities of his middle poems destroy his early artificiality and so align his art with his nature. As a consequence, F. J.'s portions of *The Adventures* (in the poems) finally make words conjunct with experience and supply us with a language superior even to that of Fraunces's parables or "feyned fables."

We can see this design in *The Adventures of Master F. J.* because we have always been invited to observe and judge F. J. with a critical eye through G. T.'s detached prose narration: *quot homines, tot sententiae* (so many men, so many minds).[11] As "the reader's garrulous and intimate companion,"[12] G. T. is from the outset our chief informant, inquiring into F. J.'s story, accumulating facts, and relaying information. He is the *histor*.[13] His knowledge, moreover, is firsthand. "*F. J.* tolde me himself," he claims; "My friend *F. J.* hath told me"; "as I haue heard him say." Interested but apparently uninvolved, sympathetic but seemingly never surprised or indulgent, G. T.'s version of F. J.'s story sketches a medieval courtly romance with a cast of men and women of gentle birth gathered at a castle or manor house in northern England who spend their time shooting, feasting, dancing, conversing, and making love. Into their midst comes a young man, G. T. informs us, who, taking instructions from courtly convention, presses suit on the married daughter-in-law of the lord who is his host by way of secret messages and nighttime assignations. Their adulterous affair, beginning one summer and ending by autumn, is doomed from the start, for Dame Elinor is already the mistress of her secretary, an ugly dwarf whose sudden departure gives F. J. a temporary advantage in his presumed courtship. With infinitely greater skill than the Reporter who narrates Gascoigne's *Dan Bartholomew of Bathe,* G. T. shows us in *The Adventures of Master F. J.* a young man whose earnestness offsets his innocence. This more admirable portrait of F. J. is strengthened by the support the boy gains from Fraunces. Her devotion to him—in word and deed—is consistent, beyond question. But her concern for F. J. and her teasing of him do not mar her own abilities: she is as clever as any one of the characters at repartee, and her sense of the comic is the most highly developed in G. T.'s story—her understanding of irony exceeds that of the more sober G. T. himself. Together G. T. and Fraunces supply Gascoigne and us with a humanist fiction of prodigality as well as a spirited divertissement on the wanton woman, the infatuated lover, and the understanding, self-sacrificing friend, the whole concluding in F. J.'s putative motto *Si fortunatus infoelix,* (If I am fortunate, then I am unhappy).

Gascoigne's fiction is thus cross-grained. "Prosatext und Gedichte sind Teile eines Ganzen, in dem sie gleichberechtigt nebeneinander stehen, ja, sich gegenseitig ergänzen," Alfred Anderau reminds us; "The prose and poems are parts of one whole, in which they are situated equally together, truly mutually supplementary."[14] They continuously function dialectically, in the way More-persona and Hythlodaye do. Similarly, too, to More, Gascoigne points for the learned in his audience to a number of contemporary and ancient texts that were common property to humanist training and humanist poetics. For Gascoigne was as familiar with humanist training and perspectives as any humanist of his time. A student at Trinity College, Cambridge, and later at Gray's Inn, as well as an Elizabethan courtier, a member of Parliament for Bedford, and a soldier in the Low Countries, Gascoigne adopted the motto *Tam Marti, Quam Mercvrio* (Both Mars and Mercury), war and words, to suggest his belief in the humanist training in both experience and books. Indeed, he seems to have been adept at many languages—Latin, French, Italian, and Dutch[15]—

and his education in the New Learning prompted him to take its thought and rhetoric, through imitation, into several forms for Renaissance England. He translated the Greek tragedy *Jocasta* (from the Italian) into the English vernacular and put it on the English stage; he translated the Italian comedy *I Suppositi* into prose and also saw it produced (at Gray's Inn); he composed and published the first sonnet sequence, the first literary masque, and the first treatise on English poetry (in which he defends the vernacular as a literary language by examining prosodic, orthographic, and linguistic changes in the sixteenth century); and his personal reportage of the 1576 siege of Antwerp, the gathering point of the Dutch humanists, makes him the first English war correspondent. "Who euer my priuate opinion condemneth as faultie, Maister *Gascoigne* is not to bee abridged of his deserued esteeme," Thomas Nashe will sum in his preface to Robert Greene's *Menaphon* (1579), for he "first beate the path to that perfection which our best Poets haue aspired to since his departure" (sig. B1v).

And like his predecessors in humanist fiction, Gascoigne also followed Seneca's fourth cause by imitating several models in writing *The Adventures of Master F. J.* rather than just one. Of all his sources, the most obvious is the *Rerum vulgarium fragmenta* of the first of the humanists, Petrarch. In these *rime sparse* (scattered rhymes), the poet whom Thomas Goddard Bergin calls "the prince of the humanists, the intimate of princes,"[16] transforms Andreas Capellanus's code of courtly love behavior into an autobiographical sequence of poems. The ideas, sentiments, and even images of Petrarch's canzone are copied over in less inspired verse by F. J., such as Petrarch's Rime 134:

> Pace non trove et non ò da far guerra,
> e temo et spero, et ardo et son un ghiaccio,
> et volo sopra 'l cielo et giaccio in terra,
> et nulla stringo et tutto 'l mondo abbraccio.
> Tal m'à in pregion che non m'apre né serra,
> né per suo mi riten né scioglie il laccio,
> et non m'ancide Amore et non mi sferra,
> né mi vuol vivo né mi trae d'impaccio.
> Veggio senza occhi, et non ò lingua et grido,
> et bramo di perir et cheggio aita,
> et ò in odio me stesso et amo altrui.
> Pascomi di dolor, piangendo rido,
> egualmente mi spiace morte et vita.
> In questo stato son, Donna, per vui.

Peace I do not find, and I have no wish to make war; and I fear and hope, and burn and am of ice; and I fly above the heavens and lie on the ground; and I grasp nothing and embrace all the world.

One has me in prison who neither opens nor locks, neither keeps me for his own nor unties the bonds; and Love does not kill and does not unchain me, he neither wishes me alive nor frees me from the tangle.

I see without eyes, and I have no tongue and yet cry out; and I wish to perish and I ask for help; and I hate myself and love another.

I feed on pain, weeping I laugh; equally displeasing to me are death and life. In this state am I, Lady, on account of you.[17]

Well known to the Tudors through the transliterations of both Wyatt and Surrey, this particular Petrarchan lyric is imitated by F. J. in his first letter to Elinor, "*I haue found fire in frost*" (sig. A3v; 52), and his subsequent poem, "*Loue, hope, and death, do stirre in me such strife*" (sig. C1v; 59–60). Of this latter poem, G. T. comments, in fact, "I haue heard *F. I.* saye, that he borrowed th'inuention of an *Italian:* but were it a translation or inuention (if I be Iudge) it is both prety and pithy" (sig. C1v; 60). His observation is accurate but shortsighted; he might have found elsewhere in F. J.'s poems and letters echoes of such other Petrarchan canzone as 119 ("Una donna più bella assai che'l sole") or 132 ("S'amor non 'e, che dunque è quel ch'io sento?"), which concludes "tremo a mezza state, ardendo il verno"; "I shiver in midsummer, burn in winter." Here are all the conflicting passions, the unreleased anxieties, and the recurrent suffering that characterize F. J. The narrative that emerges from the chronological and dramatic ordering of Petrarch's sonnets and songs, moreover, the fashioning of which began in his youth but continued to the day of his death, follows a literary pattern in its turn, that of Dante's *Vita Nuova*. In forcing this particular analogy by repeatedly citing such efforts as the song "*Dame Cinthia hir selfe that shines so bright*" (sigs. E2v–E3v; 70–72) or the blazon "*The stately Dames of Rome, their Pearles did wear*" (sigs. F3–F3v; 77), G. T. attempts to elevate F. J. in his eyes and in our own.

It is in the foolishness of this analogy too that Gascoigne locates much of his wit and wordplay. And it is here that G. T.'s shortcomings are made evident, not only in what he includes but also in what he omits—as Hythlodaye's partial understanding of the *Republic* and the *Lycurgus* is a significant means of More's fictional strategy. For Petrarch's conscious self-posturing and rhetorical set pieces are placed alongside his lyrics of struggling self-definition and anguished self-confrontation, what Bergin calls Petrarch's "profound and moving concern for the welfare of his soul."[18] Petrarch's poems unite two poetic traditions, Provençal lyrics (which made frequent use of the *tenson,* or dispute, often a debate between two singers) and Tuscan songs (such as the *rimes* of Guinizelli or Cavalcanti), which are essentially metaphysical, transcendent, and spiritual. In Petrarch, not only the will but the mind and spirit are captivated by love: "Unde fit ut tolerabilior sit defectus eloquentiae aut scientiae, quam virtutis, quod illae scilicet sint paucorum, haec est omnium," he writes to a friend; "the lack of eloquence or knowledge is more tolerable than that of virtue, for those qualities belong to a few, but this to everybody."[19] It is this very interest in the state of the soul and the woman as the embodiment of virtue that is missing in F. J.'s poetry—and in G. T.'s references and statements of appreciation. The omission is the joke.

Gascoigne's use of a relatively contemporary humanist work rather than an antique text as a primary model is something new to humanist poetics; but, as the *Utopia* suggests classical texts as well as contemporary ones, so *The Adventures of Master F. J.* also suggests the Greek text on love most revered by the humanists and one we have briefly met before in connection with Erasmus, Plato's *Symposium*. This comparison too is instructive in locating Gascoigne's comments on his characters and on the society they emulate. In the *Symposium*, for instance, Socrates' disciple Phaedrus concludes, like F. J., that Love is "the most venerable and valuable of the gods, and that he has sovereign power to provide all virtue and happiness for men whether living or departed,"[20] causing Pausanias, unlike G. T., to reply that such a simplistic panegyric is an *encomium moriae*.

> I do not consider, Phaedrus, our plan of speaking a good one, if the rule is simply that we are to make eulogies of Love. If Love were only one, it would be right; but, you see, he is not one, and this being the case, it would be more correct to have it previously announced what sort we ought to praise. Now this defect I will endeavour to amend, and will first decide on a Love who deserves our praise, and then will praise him in terms worthy of his godhead. We are all aware that there is no Aphrodite or Love-passion without a Love. True, if that goddess were one, then Love would be one: but since there are two of her, there must needs be two Loves also. Does anyone doubt that she is double? Surely there is the elder, of no mother born, but daughter of Heaven, whence we name her Heavenly; while the younger was the child of Zeus and Dione, and her we call Popular. It follows then that of the two Loves also the one ought to be called Popular, as fellow-worker with the one of those goddesses, and the other Heavenly. All gods, of course, ought to be praised: but none the less I must try to describe the faculties of each of these two. For of every action it may be observed that as acted by itself it is neither noble nor base. For instance, in our conduct at this moment, whether we drink or sing or converse, none of these things is noble in itself; each only turns out to be such in the doing, as the manner of doing it may be. For when the doing of it is noble and right, the thing itself becomes noble; when wrong, it becomes base. So also it is with loving, and Love is not in every case noble or worthy of

celebration, but only when he impels us to love in a noble manner.
[180C–181A]

The pattern defined here is what lies behind *The Adventures of Master F. J.* Using the language reserved for the Heavenly Aphrodite, however, F. J.'s understanding is limited to Love in her more popular form. Gascoigne makes this clear by drawing Elinor and F. J. in the terms first laid down by Pausanias, who distinguishes the two forms of Love, continuing,

> Now the Love that belongs to the Popular Aphrodite is in very truth popular and does his work at haphazard: this is the Love we see in the meaner sort of men; . . . where they love, they are set on the body more than the soul; and . . . they choose the most witless people they can find, since they look merely to the accomplishment and care not if the manner be noble or no. Hence they find themselves doing everything at haphazard, good or its opposite, without distinction. [181B]

F. J.'s overtures and Elinor's responses, Fraunce's warnings and G. T.'s interpolations constitute a second symposium that is both statement and counterstatement of its Platonic and Petrarchan antecedents, but Gascoigne's witty point is that, unlike the traditions they apparently mean to emulate, they see only the Popular and not the Heavenly goddess of Love and practice troubadour earthiness without any saving Tuscan grace.

That G. T. is just as vulnerable as the rest to misunderstanding the situation he describes is a focal point of Gascoigne's humanist poetics of wit. This is not clear at first, however, because in a number of ways G. T. satirizes the lovers' antihumanist misuse of rhetoric: he ridicules the lovers' compliments, their jejune use of rhetorical questions, their impasses in conversation, and their remarks and actions when they are at cross-purposes. What is true of his broader characterizations is also true of his reports of more specific incidents. It is the secretary, not Elinor, who understands F. J.'s initial advances and so responds to them; it is Elinor, not Pergo, who makes the affair public; and it is Fraunces, not Elinor, who steals F. J.'s sword as a kind of phallic symbol to fondle. By such multiple comic means, G. T. points to the deviations and perversions inherent in a society of courtly love constructed as a kind of fiction, in a false rhetoric. But G. T. is not only a witness and commentator; he is also a participant and promulgator. He takes shameless delight in F. J.'s instantaneous love poems stuffed into Elinor's bosom or left in her chamber—and, like F. J., he seems not to perceive F. J.'s oversight in using the name Helen (or what it might reveal). In telling us that "the *Secretary* hauing bin of long time absēt, & therby his quile & pēnes not worn so neer as they were wont to be, did now prick such faire large notes, that his Mistres liked better to sing faburden vnder him, thā to descant any longer vppon *F. I.* playne song" (sig. I4v; 93), G. T. resorts to farcical situations in obscene overtones. Such remarks of open, pure sexuality remind us of a coarser Folly; here they corrode and finally destroy the pretended gentleness, grace, honor, and refined morality of G. T. and of his characters. Detached from his own work, G. T. resembles, as Lynette F. McGrath notes, the Lucianic narrator,[21] the growing outrageousness of his observations distancing us irremediably from his ostensibly sympathetic judgment. The evenness of G. T.'s tone through his tumbling medley of commentary and incident reminds us most of Erasmus's implacable Folly, while the angle of his vision—always slightly awry—fragments his presentation so that the closer analogue might actually be to an Erasmian colloquy.

But G. T. does not intend to be only a critic of Petrarchan manners and mores; he means to criticize Petrarchan poetry as well. He is a literary critic as much as he is a social commentator. He says, for example, of *"Loue, hope, and death, do stirre in me such strife,"* that "it is both prety and pithy" (sig. C1v; 59–60), while *"In prime of lustie yeares"* (sigs. C4–C4v; 62–63) calls forth a certain reservation:

> These verses are more in number than do stand with contentation of some iudgements, and yit the occasion throughly considered, I can commend them with the rest, for it is (as may be well termed) *continua oratio,* declaring a full discourse of his first loue: wherin (ouer and besides that the Epythetes are aptly applied, & the verse of it self pleasant enough) I note that by it he ment in cloudes to discipher vnto Mistres *Fraunces* such matter as she wold snatch at, and yit could take no good hold of the same.
> [Sig. D1; 64]

Like Gascoigne in "Certayne notes of Instruction," G. T. is concerned first with invention, what Gascoigne defines as "some good and fine deuise, shewing the quicke capacitie of a writer" (ed. Cunliffe, sig. T2; 1:465), in reference to Ascham's division of quick and slow wits; then with the propriety of diction; and finally with tradition, imitation, and originality. So, seeming to take his own literary comments seriously "by apologizing for the poem," as Ronald C. Johnson puts it, "he directly criticizes the critical tastes of those influential persons who decide on a poem's merit."[22]

All this is, as the humanists would quickly see, a flatulent, even deleterious misconception of such model rimes as 134 that place love in a frozen equipoise of warring moods and responses that is psychologically penetrating if conceptually frustrating and intellectually unenlightening. Beside the turgid attempts of F. J., neither pretty nor pithy, we can place a representative Petrarchan rime like 122:

> Dicesette anni à già rivolto il cielo
> poi che 'mprima arsi, et giamai non mi spensi;
> quando aven ch' al mio stato ripensi,
> sento nel mezzo de le fiamme un gelo.
> Vero è 'l proverbio ch' altri cangia il pelo
> anzi che 'l vezzo, et per lentar i sensi
> gli umani affetti non son meno intensi;
> ciò ne fa l'ombra ria del grave velo.
> Oi me, lasso! e quando fia quel giorno
> che mirando il fuggir de gli anni miei
> esca del foco et di sì lunghe pene?
> Vedrò mai il dì che pur quant' io vorrei
> quell'aria dolce del bel viso adorno
> piaccia a quest'occhi, e quanto si convene?

The heavens have already revolved seventeen years since I first caught fire, and still my fire is not extinguished; when I reflect on my state, I feel in the midst of the flames a chill.

True is the proverb, one's hair will change before one's habits, and human passions are no less intense because of the slackening of sense; the bitter shadow of the heavy veil does that to us.

Ah me, alas! and when will that day be when gazing at the flight of my years I may come out of the fire and out of so long a sorrow?

Will I ever see the day when the sweet air of that lovely face will please these eyes only as much as I wish and as much as is fitting?

The constant alternations in Petrarch of the concrete image (fire) and the abstract *significatio* (my state) make the inner state of man and the outer landscape interchangeable and inseparable, further circumscribing and enclosing the wretched thinking, feeling poet. Furthermore, "The Petrarchan speaker's rhetorical strategy of alternating and suspending contrarieties within his own *ethos*," William J. Kennedy writes,

in fact generates structural transformations in each poem. His expression of joy and lament, hope and despair, certitude and doubt characteristically balance thesis against antithesis, statement against counterstatement, and reversal against counter-reversal, allowing a dialectical unity to evolve out of multiplicity through patterns of shading and contrast, challenge and fulfillment, assertion and negation. The result of such a rhetorical patterning is a careful structural proportioning of the poetic utterance into antithetically balanced words, phrases, lines, couplets, tercets, and quatrains, all combining to form antithetically balanced sestets and octaves.[23]

The constant shifting of the poet through a wide range of roles—lover, servant, soldier—and through many moods—as a man victimized, victorious, frustrated, isolated—is one of the artistic glories of the *rime sparse,* while Petrarch's continual extensions to patriotic and national concern (rime 128) and to divine love (rimes 122, 123) extend the poet's emotional and philosophic domains. "The figure of oxymoron inherent in these relationships," Kennedy adds, "establishes itself as the normative elocutionary strategy of Petrarchan poetry" (p. 21). Grief within Petrarch's persona becomes a universal sorrow and, finally, a *contemptus mundi,* which in F. J.'s hands either is ignored or degenerates into mere self-pity. Whereas Petrarch constantly widens the implications of his poems, F. J. stubbornly narrows them onto the single self. Clearly, in his adulation of F. J., G. T. displays his own ignorance and writes his own encomium moriae.

This too Gascoigne charts by reaching past Petrarch to suggest an analogy with their common source in the *Symposium* of Plato. There the remarks of Pausanias are balanced with and finally superseded by the mystical philosophy of Diotima, who according to Socrates first explained to him the mysteries of love by showing how the love of physical things and persons eventually gives way to a love of transcendent values, like love of the good. It is the origin of Florentine Neoplatonism, as we have seen, and of the thought of Pico and Ficino that initially inspired humanism in England; and it did so in part by reawakening interest in Plato's *Symposium*—particularly in Ficino's commentary on it—and in Petrarch's *rime sparse,* revitalizing them, and making them appear prophetic. G. T. ignores Diotima, as F. J. does. He aligns himself instead with the erotic Pausanias whose passions—in the words of the dialogue if not in his deeds at this particular drinking party—are not heterosexual but homosexual. It is in Pausanias's elaborate lesson about love that the nature of F. J. and the interests of G. T. are best seen.

> Thus far, then, we have ground for supposing that here in our city both loving some one and showing affection to one's lover are held in highest honour. But it happens that fathers put tutors in charge of their boys when they are beloved, to prevent them from conversing with their lovers: the tutor has strict injunctions on the matter, and when they observe a boy to be guilty of such a thing his playmates and fellows reproach him, while his reproachers are not in their turn withheld or upbraided by their elders as speaking amiss. . . .
> Now our law has a sure and excellent test for the trial of these persons, showing which are to be favoured and which to be shunned. In the one

case, accordingly, it encourages pursuit, but flight in the other, applying ordeals and tests in each case, whereby we are able to rank the lover and the beloved on this side or on that. And so it is for this reason that our convention regards a quick capitulation as a disgrace: for there ought, first, to be a certain interval—the generally approved touchstone—of time; and, second, it is disgraceful if the surrender is due to gold or public preferment, or is a mere cowering away from the endurance of ill-treatment, or shows the youth not properly contemptuous of such benefits as he may receive in pelf or political success. For in these there appears nothing steadfast or abiding, unless it be the impossibility of their producing a noble friendship. One way remains in our custom whereby a favourite may rightly gratify his lover: it is our rule that, just as in the case of the lovers it was counted no flattery or scandal for them to be willingly and utterly enslaved to their favourites, so there is left one sort of voluntary thraldom which is not scandalous; I mean, in the cause of virtue. [183C–184C]

This corruption of education by a love that promises virtue but is first based in physical satisfaction is the most sophistic speech in the *Symposium,* and its antihumanism transforms Gascoigne's fiction into delicious humanist parody. So does the sly connection made between Pausanias and G. T. and his young lover and F. J. There are, then, at least three ways in which Plato's *Symposium* is made apposite to *The Adventures of Master F. J.:* it defines love as both good and bad, an ongoing dialectic that must continually be reperceived; it shows by G. T.'s failure to refer to Diotima or to her understanding of love a partial understanding of man's passion, with a dangerous ignorance closely akin to F. J.'s own; and it proposes the possibility of a frustrated relationship, unspoken but poorly concealed, between the narrator and his protagonist as between Pausanias and Phaedrus. There may be others. Humanist fiction has once more left interpretation of a final sort open to the reader, who in the process of examining the text and weighing the evidence is himself educated.

Yet, for all the possibility of Greek antecedents for Gascoigne's fiction—in addition to Plato, the Tudor humanists knew Lucian's series of dialogues of courtesans and Plutarch's apposite love stories (*Moralia,* 771E–775E) and essay on virtue (*Moralia,* 440D–452D)—Gascoigne's subject and spirit are even more Roman in orientation: his first use of Roman poets and satirists is his second important contribution to an evolving humanist poetics for fiction. There are references and patterns in *The Adventures of Master F. J.* that relate it to two stories from Ovid's *Metamorphoses.* The particular story of Narcissus (3.352–510) is meant to point to the essential narcissism of all Gascoigne's characters, converting an image into a major motif and thematic understatement. The overall analogy of F. J., Elinor, and the lord (or G. T.) draws on the story of Mars,

Venus, and Vulcan (4.169–89) where Leuconoe's narration relates the discovery of Venus's adultery to the sun, making adultery a universal phenomenon among the servants of love. It is Ovid's superb ability to combine a detached witty irony and an engaged sympathetic understanding of his characters in both the stories that Gascoigne emulates. The *satiric* portrayal of Echo, for instance, anticipates and underscores the satiric positioning of Fraunces.

> ergo ubi Narcissum per devia rura vagantem
> vidit et incaluit, sequitur vestigia furtim,
> quoque magis sequitur, flamma propiore calescit,
> non aliter quam cum summis circumlita taedis
> admotas rapiunt vivacia sulphura flammas.
> o quotiens voluit blandis accedere dictis
> et mollis adhibere preces! natura repugnat
> nec sinit, incipiat, sed, quod sinit, illa parata est
> exspectare sonos, ad quos sua verba remittat.

Now when she saw Narcissus wandering through the fields, she was inflamed with love and followed him by stealth; and the more she followed, the more she burned by a nearer flame; as when quick-burning sulphur, smeared round the tops of torches, catches fire from another fire brought near. Oh, how often does she long to approach him with alluring words and make soft prayers to him! But her nature forbids this, nor does it permit her to begin; but as it allows, she is ready to await the sounds to which she may give back her own words.[24]

The comic dialogue that follows prepares us intellectually but not tonally for the subsequent *sympathetic* portrayal of Narcissus when he is victimized by Nemesis.

> iste ego sum: sensi, nec me mea fallit imago;
> uror amore mei: flammas moveoque feroque.
> quid faciam? roger anne rogem? quid deinde rogabo?
> quod cupio mecum est: inopem me copia fecit.
> o utinam a nostro secedere corpore possem!
> votum in amante novum, vellem, quod amamus, abesset.
> iamque dolor vires adimit, nec tempora vitae
> longa meae superant, primoque exstinguor in aevo.
> nec mihi mors gravis est posituro morte dolores,
> hic, qui diligitur, vellem diuturnior esset;
> nunc duo concordes anima moriemur in una."

Oh, I am he! I have felt it, I know now my own image. I burn with love of my own self; I both kindle the flames and suffer them. What shall I do? Shall I be wooed or woo? Why woo at all? What I desire, I have; the very abundance of my riches beggars me. Oh, that I might be parted from my own body! and, strange prayer for a lover, I would that what I love were absent from me! And now grief is sapping my strength; but a brief space of life remains to me and I am cut off in my life's prime. Death is nothing to me, for in death I shall leave my troubles; I would he that is loved might live longer; but as it is, we two shall die together in one breath. [3.463–73]

As in any developed fiction, one shade of meaning and attitude implies other shades that are not present; and in *The Adventures of Master F. J.* our own desire to laugh at F. J. while feeling a sympathy for his all-too-human passions enrich Gascoigne's narrative as they enrich Ovid's. Such shades can be multiple, too, and nearly simultaneous, as in the "discovery scene" in the story of Mars and Venus that displays ingenuity, joy, craft, danger, embarrassment, and justice. Leuconoe tells us that

> hunc quoque, siderea qui temperat omnia luce,
> cepit amor Solem: Solis referemus amores.
> primus adulterium Veneris cum Marte putatur
> hic vidisse deus; videt hic deus omnia primus.
> indoluit facto Iunonigenaeque marito
> furta tori furtique locum monstravit, at illi
> et mens et quod opus fabrilis dextra tenebat
> excidit: extemplo graciles ex aere catenas
> retiaque et laqueos, quae lumina fallere possent,
> elimat. non illud opus tenuissima vincant
> stamina, non summo quae pendet aranea tigno;
> utque levis tactus momentaque parva sequantur,
> efficit et lecto circumdata collocat arte.
> ut venere torum coniunx et adulter in unum,
> arte viri vinclisque nova ratione paratis
> in mediis ambo deprensi amplexibus haerent.
> Lemnius extemplo valvas patefecit eburnas
> inmisitque deos; illi iacuere ligati
> turpiter, atque aliquis de dis non tristibus optat
> sic fieri turpis; superi risere, diuque
> haec fuit in toto notissima fabula caelo.

Even the Sun, who with his central light guides all the stars, has felt the power of love. The Sun's loves we will relate. This god was first, 'tis said, to see the shame of Mars and Venus; this god sees all things first. Shocked at the sight, he revealed her sin to the goddess' husband, Vulcan, Juno's son, and where it was committed. Then Vulcan's mind reeled and the work upon which he was engaged fell from his hands. Straightway he fashioned a net of fine links of bronze, so thin that they would escape detection of the

eye. Not the finest threads of wool would surpass that work; no, not the
web which the spider lets down from the ceiling beam. He made the web
in such a way that it would yield to the slightest touch, the least movement,
and then he spread it deftly over the couch. Now when the goddess and her
paramour had come thither, by the husband's art and by the net so
cunningly prepared they were both caught and held fast in each other's
arms. Straightway Vulcan, the Lemnia, opened wide the ivory doors and
invited in the other gods. There lay the two in chains, disgracefully. The
gods were merry, and someone prayed that he might be so disgraced. The
gods laughed, and for a long time this story was the talk of heaven.
[169–89]

The court of love where F. J. is asked to govern and his bedroom where
he is tended by Pergo, Fraunces, and Elinor are such scenes where we are
the discoverers, looking in on characters whose postures with one another
shift and fluctuate—and *metamorphose*—as these narrative scenes entrap
them before us on the page.

Nor is the connection to Ovid the only connection to popular grammar
school textbooks that Gascoigne makes in *The Adventures of Master F. J.*
Tudor schoolboys learned to construe good Latin from other Roman
writers too: from the courtesans and impetuous youth of Plautus, in which
the seduction of the young and the duping of the old were recurrent themes
(as in *Mostellaria*), and from the works of Terence, which likewise
emphasize intrigue (as in *Phormio*) and seduction (*Andria; Eunuchus*).
Some records indicate the boys also learned the parts in these plays and
staged them to further their Latin lessons. Such Roman models for *F. J.*
suggest the satiric intentions in Gascoigne's portraits—and what is true for
F. J. is also true for G. T. For his simpleminded presentation of adolescent
love in a society of feigned virtues and superficial manners renders him just
as naive—and his attempt to convey his own moral and intellectual
superiority to his putative hero just as self-serving. Scorning such widespread behavior, Juvenal notes (in another satire popular among Tudor
grammar school masters) that "there are but few who can distinguish true
blessings from their opposites, putting aside the mists of error," and adds,
ruefully, "Many a man has met death from the rushing flood of his own
eloquence" ("Pauci dinoscere possunt / vera bona atque illis multum
diversa, remota / erroris nebula. . . . / torrens dicendi copia multis / et sua
mortifera est facundia.")[25]

Thus, to see G. T. as he wishes to be seen, as narrator, satirist, and
literary critic—to see him, in short, as our teacher and guide, as we might
have viewed Hythlodaye were we not careful—is to see him at our peril.
For although G. T. conveys to us "a set of poems placed deliberately in a

prose context that aims to show them up as pure rhetoric" or sophistry, as Richard A. Lanham warns,[26] we are also told that the selection and arrangement of those poems that create F. J.'s autobiography are not F. J.'s doing at all but, rather, the calculated guesswork of G. T. He is, in fact, very open about this. "The workes of your friend and myne Master *F. I.* and diuers others," G. T. writes in his prefatory letter to H. W., "the which when I had with long trauayle confusedly gathered together, I thought it then *Opere precium,* to reduce them into some good order. The which I haue done according to my barreyne skill in this written Booke" (sig. A2v; 50–51). And this must be the premise or hypo-thesis, for he repeats this account of his book's genesis to us a page later.

> When I had with no small entreatie obteyned of Master *F. I.* and sundry other toward young gentlemen, the sundry copies of these sundry matters, then aswell for that the number of them was great, . . . I did with more labour gather them into some order, and so placed them in this register. Wherein as neare as I could gesse, I haue set in the first places those which Master *F. I.* did compyle. [Sig. A3; 51]

But if we detach the Petrarchan poems from the first half of G. T.'s (rather than F. J.'s) "story," we shall find that they are all interchangeable. No increasing depth of emotion or ability at poetry is evident, as G. T. so urgently maintains in his running narrative and critical commentary: it is pure rhetoric as smoke screen.

What *does* give shape to *The Adventures of Master F. J.* is the prototypical narrative which, incorporating a compendium of poems, is itself a compendium of conventions from medieval courtly romance. It explains why, with no apparent warning or preparation, the prose takes over the poetry in *F. J.,* subordinates it, and finally supersedes it: G. T.'s real adeptness in literary mode is in prose romance. He gives us the basic situation of love intrigue borrowed from the *novelles* of Boccaccio, Bandello, and Cinthio; there are the love letters such as we find in Belleforest, Painter, and Fenton; there is the election of kings and the telling of stories as in Boccaccio's *Filocolo;* and the combination of narrative and poetry by then easily available in Montemayor's *Diana,* Bembo's *Asolani,* and pastoral romances generally.[27] Even the use of allegory is related to *questioni d'amore* and the stories told by Castiglione's courtiers. Moreover, as G. T.'s narrative gathers force, it consumes more and more of his attention, often displacing or eliminating F. J.'s contributions for long stretches of time,[28] while G. T.'s language is, in the course of the story, taken over from Elinor's and F. J.'s letters and poems. This borrowing surprises and instructs us: Gascoigne's fiction, announced as another thoughtful examination of the place of reason in a work openly in the tradition of humanist poetics, has G. T. (not F. J.) substitute medieval and Renaissance romance for ancient philosophy. G. T.'s worst error of all—instantly available to students of humanism—is that *his* humanist fiction is the product of a contemporary decadent Italy instead of the wiser precepts of an exemplary antique Greece and Rome.

Once we are aware of this, the satire is revealed, and the multilayered, multinarrated work is at last made coherent. G. T. is drawn more and more to F. J.'s putative attutudes than to his own. He too is attracted to Elinor; he too despises the secretary; he dismisses swiftly, as F. J. does, the potentially wholesome effects that Fraunces might instill. When he pretends to literary judgments, G. T. praises F. J.'s formulaic and demonstrably bad poems while failing to comment on the honest and bearably good ones; he even calls F. J. a "valiant Prince" (sig. B1v; 54) when he is at best woefully adolescent. We can measure the seriousness of G. T.'s self-delusion when he finally loses mastery of his story altogether, even as he attempts to shape more and more of it. For *The Adventures of Master F. J.* is finally not, as G. T. means it to be, an archetypal story of Petrarchan romance or even a fruitful warning. It departs too radically from even that pattern. Rather, in G. T.'s transfiguration of events, Elinor is successfully seduced and raped; the innocent lover is the rapist. Breaking tradition, G. T.'s lady is openly promiscuous, and F. J., ignorant of any rival, for some time knows no jealousy. Although the characters of courtly love should be relatively static, as G. T. thinks they are, in his comedy of errors they become Protean—the lord would be F. J.; F. J. would be the secretary; and the devoted Fraunces imitates Elinor in trimming up F. J.'s bed. It is therefore a celebration of metamorphoses that G. T. discloses. G. T.'s narrative, moreover, should conclude on a note of elevated Platonic love—even if the lover is in despair—rather than lapse into scurrility. But G. T. has always had a penchant for the pornographic, from the sexual overtones of Elinor's nosebleed and F. J.'s erect sword to the wordplay on the secretary's penis, from the initial act of love on the cold, bare floor to the act of rape that follows F. J.'s accusations regarding Elinor's faithlessness. At odds even with the frank poem by F. J. that he chooses to place at the end of his story, G. T. concludes his "thriftlesse Historie" (sig. M2v; 105) with sudden and unwarranted sentiment, allowing pretended fact to be truly fiction. Thus, instead of improving F. J.'s language, G. T. is seduced by it; and his reliance on F. J.'s revelations for his own authority is increasingly ironic. G. T.'s judgments and attitudes are so clearly attuned to those of F. J. and so obviously discrepant with the superior value he places on them that *The Adventures of Master F. J.*

becomes, as we read it, no more than layers of rhetoric. G. T.'s persistent inclination to see himself reflected in F. J. (as Folly sees herself all around her and Hythlodaye finds himself mirrored in Utopians), along with the intimacy of his knowledge, suggests that G. T. may even be F. J. at a later stage in life. In any event, he *relives* F. J.'s experiences in his account of them.

As if to assure himself further that we will not fully sanction G. T.'s narrative, Gascoigne first presents us not with G. T.'s prefatory letter, which promises "iust occasion of honest recreation" in a fable that will "metaphorically set forth vnto vs the right rewardes of vertues, and the due punishments for vices" (sig. A2; 50), but with another, contradictory letter by one H. W.[29] He acknowledges that G. T. gave him a cópy of *The Adventures* and

> charged me, that I should vse them onely for mine owne particuler commoditie, and eftsones safely deliuer the originall copie to him againe, wherein I must confesse my selfe but halfe a marchant, for the copie vnto him I haue safely redeliuered. But the worke (for I thought it worthy to be published) I haue entreated my friend *A. B.* to emprint: as one that thought better to please a number by common commoditie then to feede the humor of any priuate parson by nedelesse singularitie. . . . I my selfe haue reaped this commoditie, to sit and smile at the fond deuises of such as haue enchayned them selues in the golden fetters of fantasie, and hauing bewrayed them selues to the whole world, do yet coniecture that they walke vnseene in a net. [Sigs. A1–A1v; 49]

For H. W., *The Adventures of Master F. J.* is unlikely to teach anyone moral wisdom—"the wiser sort," he notes, "wold turne ouer the leafe as a thing altogether fruitlesse" (sig. A1; 49)—but he sees it as fine entertainment, containing what he paradoxically terms "the golden fetters of fantasie" (sig. A1; 49), recalling the story of Mars, Venus, and Vulcan. His confusion of purpose suggests that none of what he says may be trustworthy. Again it is rhetoric as a smoke screen: H. W.'s real purpose, as he unwittingly discloses in his repetition of a single word, is the work's potential worth as a "commoditie"—he would make money on F. J.'s luckless affair.

H. W.'s letter is preceded by still another, this one from the printer A. B. himself. As the first letter we find upon opening Gascoigne's volume, it has the greatest initial claim on our credibility. Thus A. B.'s introductory comments tend to measure the authenticity of both subsequent letters and the narrative that follows them.[30] But we are attuned, reading backward, to anticipate a doubleness—even a duplicity—in whatever is presented here. The printer confirms such expectations. He tells us that, although

H. W. ordered *The Adventures of Master F. J.* to be published because it is a "pleasant Pamphlet" and G. T. claims that he "woulde by no meanes haue it published," nevertheless "these two gentlemen were of one assent compact to haue it imprinted" (prel. sig. A2; 47). A. B. has, then, merely consented to them both. But A. B. turns out to be a man for all seasons himself. He acknowledges "two or three wanton places passed ouer in the discourse of an amorous enterprise" (prel. sig. A2; 47) but knows "the discrete reader may take a happie example by the most lasciuious histories" (prel. sig. A2v; 47). Beyond G. T., H. W., and A. B. is Gascoigne himself, and he appears to resemble them in his own slipperiness. "I haue also sundrie tymes chaunged mine owne worde or deuise," he admits in a prefatory letter to the second, 1575, edition, "And no meruaile: For he that wandereth much in those wildernesses, shall seldome continue long in one minde." As further explanation, he adds, "And by that it proceedeth, that I haue so often chaunged my Posie or worde. For when I did compile any thing at the request of other men, if I had subscribed the same with mine owne vsuall mot or deuise, it might haue bewrayed the same to haue beene of my doing" (sig. ¶¶¶2; 1:17). Even this is part truth, part falsehood: he scrupulously removed any signs of his authorship in the 1573 edition, but he was ready enough in *The Whole Woorkes* (1575) to bring G. T. and F. J. into the same story, rename F. J. and Elinor as Ferdinando Jeronimi and Leonara de Valasco, assign as his source the make-believe Italian writer "Bartello" (sig. S1; 1:383),[31] and admit his responsibility for the recension. He also apologizes in a prefatory letter "*To the reuerende Deuines*" for the bawdiness, which had been attacked in the first edition. "My reuerende and welbeloued," he begins,

> whatsoeuer my youth hath seemed vnto the grauer sort, I woulde bee verie loth nowe in my middle age to deserue reproch: more loth to touch the credite of any other, and most loth to haue mine own name become vnto you odious. For if I shoulde nowe at this age seeme as carelesse of reproch, as I was in greene youth readie to goe astray, my faults might quicklie growe double, & my estimation shoulde bee woorthie to remaine but single. I haue learned that although there maie bee found in a Gentleman whereby to be reprehended or rebuked, yet ought hee not to be worthie of reproofe or condemnation. [Sigs. ¶2–1:3]

But, in fact, only two brief years have elapsed; and although Gascoigne does eliminate the scenes of rape, the stag hunt of F. J. and the lord with its obscene joking, and the poem that follows with its wordplay on "seed" and "horns," the sexual imagery remains in the poetry and the suggestive scenes remain in the prose text in large measure undisturbed (cf. sig. Y1; 1:433-34).[32] The "three-tiered framing device" of the first edition, as Penelope Scambly Schott terms it,[33] is thus replaced by a different set of *paragena* which, following the letters of Lupset, Giles, and Busleiden to later editions of the *Utopia,* goes More one better by making changes that are apparent but not real. Perhaps taking further direction from the ambiguous prologues of Erasmus and More, Gascoigne affixes a new motto to this second edition, *"Euer or neuer"* (sig. Z5v; 1:453), as a substitution for his original conclusion in 1573 that, in the guise of G. T., he was "one that had rather leaue [his work] vnperfect than make it to plaine" (sig. M2v; 105). Gascoigne's vowed repentance is therefore made to seem suspect or, as Charles W. Smith argues,[34] it becomes an act of contempt since, in another letter in the new series of *paragena* addressed "to al young Gentlemen," (¶¶1; 1:9) Gascoigne refers to his critics as both "curious carpers, ignorant readers" and "graue Philosophers" (sig. ¶¶1v; 1:10). Such shifting and elusive borderlines between fact and fiction renew the concerns and strategies of earlier works by Gascoigne, such as *Dan Bartholomew of Bathe,* where the protagonist Dan and the narrator, called simply the Reporter, turn out to be the same person; or the later *Noble Arte of Venerie* (1576), where Gascoigne signs some verses praising his own unsigned translation of a French treatise on hunting.[35] These tricks provoked Gabriel Harvey's disgust. "Sum vanity: & more leuity," he writes in the margin of Gascoigne's work, "his special faulte."[36]

In time Gascoigne came to agree. Although he was uncannily adept at a humanist poetics of wordplay and wit, this style finally constitutes a decidedly secondary strain in his work. Even at the beginning of his career, when he was transforming *I Suppositi* for a student performance at the Inns of Court, Gascoigne was also translating a Reformationist *Jocasta* with Francis Kinwelmershe, a drama that in their hands becomes a stark, unrelieved sermon on the destructiveness of wrathful pride, misused power, public vengeance, and civil war. Apparently Gascoigne was an Edwardian rather than an Elizabethan in outlook, for his other works collate with this more serious beginning. *The Steele Glas* (1575), a poem "conceived ... as a piece of oratory,"[37] is similarly grim; in tracing "blinde desire" (1587 ed., sig. D2v; *Works,* 2:153) and naked will through all the estates of man and all the liberal arts and sciences of a humanist education, Gascoigne locates an intransigent sense of sin that characterizes the Reformation and comes to dominate his later work. In *The Glasse of Gouernement* (1575), for instance, the "godly" schoolmaster Gnomaticus is chosen for his rectitude; and his lessons from the outset represent the view of Dutch Protestantism.

Let vs in the holy name of God begin, and he for his mercy geue me grace to vtter, and you to digest such holesome lessons as may be for the saluation of your soules, the comfort of your lyfe, and the profitte of your Countrey. . . .

Your first chapter and lesson shall then be, that in all your actions you haue an especiall eye and regard to almighty God, and in that consideration I commend vnto your memory, first God himselfe, and secondarily his ministers. As touching your duties vnto God him self, although they be infinite, yet shall we sufficiently conteine them in three especiall poynts to be perfourmed: that is to say, *Feare, Loue, & Trust.* [Sigs. B2–B2v; 2:17–19]

The sentiment here is not merely Reformist; it is Calvinist, and *anti*humanist.

This seems to us now and must have seemed to humanists then a considerable narrowing of Quintilian's premise that rhetoric is the art of speaking well but the art of speaking well by good men. Yet this sentiment also finds support in Thomas Wilson, whose *Arte of Rhetorique* (1553) is composed with a keen awareness of Aristotelian psychology by which the imagination controls the will and the will in turn usurps reason. Such a paradigm schemes not only the doomed brothers Phylautus and Phylosarchus in *The Glasse of Gouernement,* in which the glass may also be a *speculum malorum,* but F. J. and his rapid subservience to the traditions and hypocrisies of courtly love. "Affections therefore (called Passions)," Wilson tells us, "are none other thyng, but a stirryng, or forcyng of the mynde, either to desier, or elles to detest, and lothe any thyng, more vehemently then by nature we are commonly wonte to doe" (sig. S3v). The act of perceiving, according to the lessons taught by English humanists, involves the act of evaluating; fact and value are inseparable. When the *forma,* or image of the thing, is misconceived because of the affections or because of misperception, judgment is skewed and language is perverted. So the poor choice G. T. makes in selecting the corrupted values of courtly love, which cheapen and falsify Platonic thought and the long, later development of Neoplatonic philosophy, suggests his own perverted judgment and his consequent inability to teach worthwhile behavior by instructive and implicitly exemplary fictions. Elinor's apparent resemblance to the perfect *image* of the beloved in courtly love theory misdirects F. J., and his difficulty is compounded by his reliance on a debased Petrarchan lexicon. By con-forming, F. J. is de-formed, and his poetry—his rhetoric generally—is corrupted. For Gascoigne as for Wilson, F. J.'s perceptions and his poetry are duplicative; and each functions to reveal the other. Gascoigne thus confirms the Aristotelian psychology as Wilson sets it forth in his textbook on rhetoric.

In the second part of his *Arte of Rhetorique,* especially in the section on the techniques of narration in a deliberative oration, Wilson describes those strategies employed by G. T. to arrange F. J.'s poetry and his own critical and sentimental observations into his ideal (and falsely exemplary) fable of courtly love. As the best-known classical rhetorician among the Tudors, Wilson was often the authority, and his *Arte* was common coin at Cambridge as well as at the Inns of Court. His idea of invention—"The findyng out of apte matter" (sig. a3v)—agrees with Gascoigne's, and his definition of *pragmatographia,* or vivid description of an event, and *periphrasis,* or circumlocution (for G. T., by way of his own opinionated interruptions), forms the basis of Gascoigne's *dispositio.* Citing the desirability of such opposing actions as Gascoigne develops through F. J.'s rising passion juxtaposed to Elinor's decreasing interest in him, Wilson notes that "It is an excellent kynd of Amplifiyng when thynges encreased, and thynges diminished are both set together, that the one may the rather beautifie the other" (sig. S3).

Such connections between humanist rhetoric and Gascoigne's fiction remind us that the 1573 text is a final major illustration of the humanist poetics of wordplay that flourished in England in the first seven decades of the sixteenth century; but such connections will not accommodate the stark Reformationist view that enters much of Gascoigne's work two brief years later—they have little relevance to the 1575 text of *The Adventures of Master F. J.* although, given the darkening tone of his other work, that later letter to the divines in 1575 looks less like a hoax and far more like the uneasy apology of a man who feels compelled to couch any version of his earlier fiction of courtly love in a language more acceptable to the growing Protestant movement, even if he no longer wishes to spend much of his time revising the body of his work. Seen in this more sober light, Gascoigne's most brilliant work appears to have found one last model in a Reformist Tudor fiction allied to Gascoigne's subsequent prose essays: William Baldwin's *Beware the Cat.* This satiric narrative is extraordinarily successful and deserves to be much better known;[38] it appears to have been written shortly after the evening it describes (28 December 1552) in the waning days of Edward VI and Protector Somerset, hidden during the Marian years, and brought out for publication at least by 1570. The occasion for the narrative is an imminent production of one of Aesop's fables by the King's Players to celebrate the Christmas season; it raises the "controuersie . . . whether Birds and beasts had reasn" because for Baldwin "it was not Comicall to make either speechlesse things to speake: or brutish things to commen resonably" (sig. A4; 27). Baldwin tells his story until he is replaced by Gregory Streamer, who in turn gives way to a servant who recounts a story he heard of talking cats. Others participate by telling still other stories, some relating to incidents forty years previously in Ireland. The large number of narrative frames within frames makes the tripartite *paragena* preceding *The Adventures of Master F. J.* look simple indeed; and F. J. has an antecedent in Streamer who, attempting to understand cats by taking a magic potion he reads of in a treatise reportedly by Albertus Magnus, gets the concoction wrong, takes it at the wrong time, and follows a recipe that is meant to help him understand not cats but birds. Nevertheless, Streamer miraculously hears a long defense by the cat Mousleyer of her chastity. Although by this point Baldwin's narrative has satirized medicine, astrology, and superstition rather than courtly love, the object of attack now narrows. Mousleyer recalls a blind woman who has her sight restored by a priest who hears her confession and celebrates Mass. She is "A ioly perswading knaue" (sigs. D5–D5v; 50), a wanton who runs a house of prostitution but who says her Rosary and prays to the Virgin each evening (sig. D7v; 52); he is a terrified priest who is humiliated when he comes to say Mass against the devil (sigs. E6v–E7; 58). "Woven into the fabric of the narrative," Stephen Gresham sums, "are the commonplace strands of anti-Catholic satire: allusions to the cruelty and gluttony of the pope; attacks on transubstantiation; similarities drawn between witchcraft and unwritten verities; and vignettes of superstitious priests."[39] The complicated game of narrative wordplay and wit takes us through one story into the next to discover finally that to believe Streamer means to believe in all the legendary traditions claimed by the Roman Church—and just those traditions opposed by the Protestants under Edward VI. Take away these beliefs, and the whole structure Streamer conveys—both the Catholic beliefs and the narrative—collapses. Similarly, *The Adventures of Master F. J.* relies on our willingness to accept, at least as a hypothesis for social action, the rituals of courtly love. Discrediting the narrator or the belief in each instance discredits the other and eliminates here the possibility of fiction.

Beware the Cat is heavy with moral doctrine. So are the works that Gascoigne crowded into his final four years. *The Spoyle of Antwerpe* (1576) is an eye-witness account, the "plaine truthe" (sig. A3), which looks forward, quite specifically, to the fiction of Thomas Nashe. It concerns an attack by Catholic Spain in which Gascoigne claims 4,000 Spaniards and support troops entered the city, filling it with smoke, death, and destruction (sigs. A5v ff.; 2.590 ff.); "I list not to recken the infinite nombers of poore Almains, who lay burned in their armour: som thentrailes skorched out, & all the rest of the body free, some their head and shoulders burnt of: so that you might looke down into the bulk & brest and there take an Anatomy of the secrets of nature" (sig. C1). His reportage is a sequel to *The fruites of Warre* (1573?), an extended threnody on the Erasmian adage *Dulce bellum inexpertis,* but without any of the grace of Erasmian wit. *The Grief of Joye* (also 1576) is a collection of elegies that speak of the discommodities and sorrows of lusty youth, the vanities of beauty, the faults of force and strength, and the pride of vain delights. *The Droomme of Doomes day* (again 1576) is partitioned into three sections: the view of worldly vanities; the shame of sin; and the needle's eye, "wherein wee are taught the right rules of a true Christian life, and the straight passage vnto euerlasting felicitie" (sig. ** 1v; *Works,* 2:210). By 1577 he was dead.

The Adventures of Master F. J. is, then, the last fine work—and the last stage—in the developing humanist fiction of wordplay and wit. Religious conflict under Edward VI, savage bloodshed under Mary I, widespread religious warfare on the Continent, and good English humanists exiled for their beliefs in Geneva and elsewhere all circumscribed and darkened the vision of Erasmus, More, and the early Gascoigne in a world bright with wonder and ripe with idealistic possibilities to be realized through the cultivation of a classical past. Midcentury (at least until Baldwin and Gascoigne) sees a lacuna in a serious pursuit of humanist poetics and humanist fiction; when it returns, it gains a new direction, that of eloquence, and its impetus—once again from Italy—is very different indeed. It comes not from the historic Florence of Ficino and Pico or the courtly world of Petrarch but from the imagined Urbino of Castiglione.

II

THE POETICS OF ELOQUENCE

Poets were also from the beginning the best
perswaders and their eloquence the first
Rhetoricke of the world.

GEORGE PUTTENHAM

FOUR

Introduction

AN EXTRAORDINARY ITALIAN
WORK OF HUMANIST FICTION
OF THE SIXTEENTH CENTURY, *IL
LIBRO DEL CORTEGIANO* OF BAL-
DASSARRE CASTIGLIONE, HERALDS A
SECOND AND FAR MORE INFLUENTIAL
period of humanist poetics and a new era of humanist eloquence. It is, in
its way, as profoundly influential as any of the works of Erasmus or More.
But it is far different. "In the subtly controlled art of Castiglione's
Courtier," Wayne A. Rebhorn has recently written,

> as in the art of its significantly greater coevals—Raphael's Stanza della
> Segnatura and Michelangelo's Sistine Chapel ceiling—the humanism of
> the fifteenth century comes to glorious fruition and strikes a momentary
> balance with the love of beauty, elegance, and refinement that would soon
> become the hallmark of later Mannerist courts. For just two short decades
> at the beginning of the sixteenth century, these masterpieces of High
> Renaissance culture magically harmonize moral ideals with elegant
> manners, optimistic ideals of political and social action with aesthetic
> self-cultivation, and virile, directed energy with grace and refinement.[1]

Seen in retrospect, Castiglione's reifying consonance of the physical,
intellectual, and spiritual attributes of man begun with the revived ancient
Greek and Roman texts urged by the humanists is vital, spectacular, and
visionary. In its revolutionary and widespread influence no text in Western
cultural history can match it. Humanist templates of behavior instruct
thought and speech, gesture and act, political purpose and social response
in ways that are consentaneously educative, moral, eloquent, *felicific*.
Human possibilities prophesied by the New Learning are epitomized in the
contagious conceptualizations provided by Castiglione's *Cortegiano*: it
supplies all Europe with an idealistic self-portrait in an apparent pursuit of
life in which substance and style are inseparable, coterminous, even
synonymous, promising a *speculum principis* for shaping the noble qualities
and ennobling reason inherent in all men and women. What sets the style
of Castiglione's Urbino in 1528 sets the style for Elizabeth's London by

1576, a style resulting from the highest of principles, as Thomas Hoby makes clear to Lord Henry Hastings in the epistle preceding his English translation.[2] "To men growen in yeres," Hoby writes, *Il Cortegiano* is "a pathway to the behoulding and musing of the minde, and to whatsoeuer elles is meete for that age: To yonge Gentlemen, an encouraging to garnishe their minde with morall vertues, and their bodye with comely exercises, and both the one and the other with honest qualities to attaine vnto their noble ende" (sig. A3v). For Hoby such values, all stemming from "the behoulding and musing of the minde," are insistent, admonitory, obsessive. "You may see him confirme with reason the Courtly facions, comely exercises, and noble vertues," he reiterates, "that vnawares haue from time to time crept in to you and already with practise and learning taken custome in you" (sig. A3v).

The primary humanist yearning for the moral perfectibility of man always lurks just beneath the polished surfaces of *Il Cortegiano*. All the postured rhetoric of the debates and dialogues in Castiglione's Urbino about the many-sided man, the *uomo universale,* in fact, and all the definitions of courtier and prince rest on an unending pursuit of debating and *proving* man is educable, moral, and potentially perfectible. And such a task is not only monumental but also urgent, because the subjects, Castiglione tells us, are dead or dying. Indeed, Castiglione reveals his own troubling doubts about the inherent nature of his friends, all suffering mortality, even with remarkably diversified and pointed references to humanist teachings. In designing (or redesigning) life at the ducal palace of Urbino by persistently invoking the moral and rhetorical values of Cicero's villa near Tusculum—a significant Senecan model for the Urbino of *Il Cortegiano*—Castiglione prevails on antique texts for his every direction to the present. "Hardly a page of *The Courtier* turns without a bold plagiarism," George Bull notes after translating *Il Cortegiano*,[3] as if Castiglione meant his single literary achievement to be a contemporary encyclopedia of classical learning. Even in his own day his close friend Raphael signaled Castiglione's reliance—or his dependence—by creating a fresco for the Vatican in which Castiglione (as Zoroaster) stands between Aristotle, carrying a copy of the *Ethics* written for his son Nicomachus, and Plato holding a copy of his *Timaeus*.[4] It is as if, by resurrecting the past in the refinements of his own idealized civilization, Castiglione like Raphael would force time to have a stop. The twin motives that inspire and govern *Il Cortegiano* (and in turn govern us) are, then, the inductive establishment of the pure humanist community and the securing of its permanence. Such impulses resemble those of Hythlodaye. The fatal difficulty is that, in so shaping Urbino, Castiglione insists on realizing perfectibility in an imperfect society whose flaws are caught in a discernible time and place. Yet, confronted by the problems of mortality, Castiglione has, by a courageous act of the imagination, made his men and women *im*mortal, impervious to time, by rendering them into the verbal art of a book, *Il Libro*, of the courtier.

Because of such fundamental problems, which Castiglione faced with vision and learning, *Il Libro del Cortegiano* was hugely significant in its time; however foreign it might seem, written as it was in a highly cultivated Continental society, the Tudors under Elizabeth nevertheless mined it, at times exclusively, for its thought and its style. We can explain this effect in part by seeing how it supplied a model for behavior and standards for action by the newly established Elizabethan court, one in need of direction. But there were deeper ties between Castiglione's Italy and, say, Lyly's England, ties of understanding reinforced by a shared humanist culture. The common antique texts from which both societies drew their fundamental ideas and beliefs, as well as their rhetorical pursuit of those ideas and beliefs, help to show us why Lyly found in Castiglione an important Senecan model for style, Greene found there a useful tone, and Sidney, the greatest borrower of them all, found resources not only for verbal strategies but for the alliance of philosophy and politics with morality and manners.

We can trace the underlying junctures of *Il Cortegiano* and a Tudor humanist fiction of eloquence more precisely by looking briefly at those Senecan models which, used and developed by Castiglione, were just those texts taught in Tudor schoolrooms. In arranging his four colloquia on the proper life of a courtier, for instance, Catiglione drew on such classical historians as Livy and Sallust, who served him with both characters and conversations, elevating men and events to exemplary emblems. Yet the best known of Castiglione's Senecan originals is not a history at all but a rhetoric that was also central to Tudor education. This is Cicero's *De Oratore*, a dialogue between Cicero's two teachers, the theorist Crassus and the practitioner Antonius, which like Castiglione's work is an attempt to preserve the memory of those now dead (2.2.8). There is testimony that this source was also widely recognized by the Tudors themselves (as Hoby says in his letter to Lord Hastings). Nor need we seek far to understand why. The premise of *De Oratore* is clearly Castiglione's starting point in *Il Cortegiano* 1.12:

Quare ego tibi oratorem sic iam instituam, si potuero, ut, quid efficere possit, ante perspiciam. Sit enim mihi tinctus litteris; audierit aliquid, legerit, ista ipsa praecepta acceperit: tentabo quid deceat, quid voce, quid viribus, quid spiritu, quid lingua efficere possit. Si intellegam posse ad summos pervenire, non solum hortabor, ut elaboret, sed etiam, si vir quoque bonus mihi videbitur esse, obsecrabo: tantum ego in excellenti oratore, et eodem viro bono, pono esse ornamenti universae civitati.

"And so I shall now begin making an orator for you, if I can, by first discovering the extent of his capacity. I would have him be a man of some learning, who has done some listening and some reading, and received those very teachings we have mentioned; I will make trial of what suits him, and of his powers of intonation, physique, energy and fluency. If I find him capable of reaching the highest class, I will not merely encourage him to work out his purpose but will positively implore him so to do, provided that I also think his character sound—so much glory to the whole community do I see in an outstanding orator who is also a man of worth."[5]

Cicero's ideal orator, the model for Castiglione's ideal courtier as well as for the protagonists of Lyly, Greene, and Sidney, is a man of natural gifts (*De Oratore* 1.28.128) and a liberal education (1.34.158–59), "a man of finish, accomplishment, and taste" ("hominem significant, quod eruditum, quod urbanum," 2.58.236), who is taught by cultivation (2.31.88–89) and imitatio.

Ergo hoc sit primum in praeceptis meis, ut demonstremus, quem imitetur atque ita ut, quae maxime excellant in eo, quem imitabitur, ea diligentissime persequatur. Tum accedat exercitatio, qua illum, quem delegerit, imitando effingat, atque ita exprimat.

"Let this then be my first counsel, that we show the student whom to copy, and to copy in such a way as to strive with all possible care to attain the most excellent qualities of his model. Next let practice be added, whereby in copying he may reproduce the pattern of his choice." [2.22.90]

By precept and practice, Cicero's ideal orator as an ideal student will be a master of language, will be educated in physical and intellectual skills, and will use his talents and training to serve the political and social life of the state. Other debts are more specific in *Il Cortegiano*—Castiglione's discussion of wit and several of his jokes are taken directly from Cicero's long digression in 2.54.219–71.290, for instance—but the attractive feature to Castiglione was doubtless his view of *De Oratore* as a superb defense of eloquence, " 'flexanima atque omnium regina rerum' ", " 'the soulbending sovereign of all things' " (2.44.187), which serves as "oratoris vis illa divina virtusque cernitur . . . ornate, copiose varieque dicere"; "the orator's godlike power and excellence . . . a style elegant, copious and diversified" (2.27.120). In addition, the heightened fluency of Ciceronian language in *De Oratore*, especially in the declamation by Crassus in *De Oratore 3*, is perhaps the work's greatest legacy to Castiglione in his own shaping of a poetics of eloquence; it permeates every sentence of *Il Cortegiano,* as Rebhorn has recently noted (*Courtly Performances,* p. 92). Nowhere in Castiglione do we find the misuse of rhetoric, the tricks of verbal manipulation that Cicero outlines (2.24.101–42.178) and that we find in Erasmus, More, and Gascoigne; in *Il Cortegiano,* oratory remains a high and serious art. Castiglione's view of Cicero, by selective imitation, is that promoted by Strebaeus Remensis in his commentary on *De Oratore* (Basel, 1541):

> Rhetorica Ciceronis ad Quintum fratrem, citra omnem controversiam superant omnia quae de arte dicendi & a Graecis, & a Latinis memoriae sunt prodita. . . . Nusquam tam magnifice honore vestitur orator, nusquam ita graviter & ornate demonstratur oratoria facultas. . . . Sic iudico, omnes omnium rhetorum scriptas observationes in unum coactas, cum hoc uno opere neque gravitate, neque varietate, neque elegantia neque alia laude comparari posse.

> Disputes aside, Cicero's rhetoric to his brother Quintus surpasses everything recorded on the subject of eloquence by both Greeks and Latins. . . . Nowhere is the orator clad in such splendid dignity, nowhere is oratory described so gravely and ornately. . . . I maintain that the writings of all the other teachers of oratory united together cannot stand comparison with this one work either in terms of gravity, or variety, or elegance, or any other merit.[6]

In *De Oratore* this polished style is openly assigned to Crassus (1,2) and illustrated in his long speech, which climaxes the work (3). The startling poignancy that also characterizes *De Oratore* stems from the opening passage about the death of Crassus (and hence of true eloquence, 3.1.1), followed by mourning for the fates of others (3.3) and a general *cri de coeur* for mortality:

> O fallacem hominum spem fragilemque fortunam, et inanes nostras contentiones, quae medio in spatio saepe franguntur et corruunt et ante in ipso cursu obruuntur quam portum conspicere potuerunt!

> Ah, how treacherous are men's hopes, how insecure their fortunes! How hollow are our endeavours, which often break down and come to grief in the middle of the race, or are shipwrecked in full sail before they have been able to sight the harbour! [3.2.7]

The deaths of the great Roman poets and orators who taught Cicero eloquence stand just behind Castiglione's moving memorial to Urbino.

In many ways, however, an even closer model for *Il Cortegiano,* and so a model too for a poetics of eloquence in Tudor humanist fiction, was a second Ciceronian treatise on rhetoric written a decade later, the *Orator.*

Addressed to Cicero's friend Brutus, this also begins with an attempt to fashion the ideal orator, but now Cicero is filled with misgiving in doing so.

> Si id quod vis effecero eumque oratorem quem quaeris expressero, tandem studia multorum, qui desperatione debilitati experiri id nolent quod se assequi posse diffidant. Sed par est est omnis omnia experiri, qui res magnas et magno opere expetendas concupiverunt. Quodsi quem aut natura sua aut illa praestantis ingenii vis forte deficiet aut minus instructus erit magnarum artium disciplinis, teneat tamen eum cursum quem poterit. Prima enim sequentem honestum est in secundis tertiisque consistere.

> I am afraid that if I do what you wish and portray that ideal orator, I may discourage the studies of many who in the weakness of despair will refuse to try what they have no hope of being able to attain. But it is fair that men should leave nothing untried if they have aspired to great and ambitious undertakings. In case anyone happens to lack physical endowment or outstanding intellectual ability, or is insufficiently trained in cultural studies, let him at least maintain the best course he can. For it is no disgrace for one who is striving for the first place to stop at second or third.[7]

The perfect orator, like the perfect courtier as perfect fictional hero, has never existed. It is, as Castiglione's courtier is, a verbal construct, a figure of the mind.

> Ego in summo oratore fingendo talem informabo qualis fortasse nemo fuit. Non enim quaero quis fuerit, sed quid sit illud quo nihil esse possit praestantius, quod in perpetuitate dicendi non saepe atque haud scio an nunquam in aliqua autem parte eluceat aliquando, idem apud alios densius, apud alios fortasse rarius. Sed ego sic statuo, nihil esse in ullo genere tam pulchrum, quo non pulchrius id sit unde illud ut ex ore aliquo quasi imago exprimatur. Quod neque oculis neque auribus neque ullo sensu percipi potest, cogitatione tamen et mente complectimur.

> In delineating the perfect orator I shall be portraying such a one as perhaps has never existed. Indeed I am not inquiring who was the perfect orator, but what is that unsurpassable ideal which seldom if ever appears throughout a whole speech but does shine forth at some times and in some places, more frequently in some speakers, more rarely perhaps in others. But I am firmly of the opinion that nothing of any kind is so beautiful as not to be excelled in beauty by that of which it is a copy, as a mask is a copy of a face. This ideal cannot be perceived by the eye or ear, nor by any of the senses, but we can nevertheless grasp it by the mind and the imagination. [2.7–8]

The analogy for Cicero, as for the courtiers at Urbino, is thus with art, a definition anticipating the poetics of Raphael, Castiglione, or Lyly (as we shall soon see).

Itaque et Phidiae simulacris, quibus nihil in illo genere perfectius videmus, et eis picturis quas nominavi cogitare tamen possumus pulchriora. Nec vero ille artifex cum faceret Iovis formam aut Minervae, contemplabatur aliquem e quo similitudinem duceret, sed ipsius in mente insidebat species pulchritudinis eximia quaedam, quam intuens in eaque defixus ad illius similitudinem artem et manum dirigebat. Ut igitur in formis et figuris est aliquid perfectum et excellens, cuius ad cogitatam speciem imitando referuntur ea quae sub oculos ipsa non cadunt, sic perfectae eloquentiae speciem animo videmus, effigem auribus quaerimus. Has rerum formas appellat ἰδέαι ille non intellegendi solum sed etiam dicendi gravissimus auctor et magister Plato, easque gigni negat et ait semper esse ac ratione et intellegentia contineri; cetera nasci, occidere, fluere, labi, nec diutius esse uno et eodem statu. Quicquid est igitur de quo ratione et via disputetur, id est ad ultimam sui generis formam speciemque redigendum.

For example, in the case of the statues of Phidias, the most perfect of their kind that we have ever seen, and in the case of the paintings I have mentioned, we can, in spite of their beauty, imagine something more beautiful. Surely that great sculptor, while making the image of Jupiter or Minerva, did not look at any person whom he was using as a model, but in his own mind there dwelt a surpassing vision of beauty; at this he gazed and all intent on this he guided his artist's hand to produce the likeness of the god. Accordingly, as there is something perfect and surpassing in the case of sculpture and painting—an intellectual ideal by reference to which the artist represents those objects which do not themselves appear to the eye, so with our minds we conceive the ideal of perfect eloquence, but with our ears we catch only the copy. These patterns of things are called ἰδέαι or ideas by Plato, that eminent master and teacher both of style and thought; these, he says, do not "become"; they exist for ever and depend on intellect and reason; other things come into being and cease to be, they are in flux and do not remain long in the same state. Whatever, then, is to be discussed rationally and methodically, must be reduced to the ultimate form and type of its class. [2.8–3.10]

The perfect sculpture, for Cicero, is not an accurate imitation of reality but the extension of the idea of perfect beauty by the sculptor—who is alone responsible for its conception as much as for its execution—and its perfection is confirmed by the way in which it stimulates further acts of imagination in those who behold it. The artist, then, is indivisible from his art just as an ideal orator is indivisible from perfect eloquence (*perfectae eloquentiae*); and the *Orator* is given over to "our task of delineating that ideal orator and moulding him in that eloquence which Antonius had discovered in no one" ("Referamus igitur nos ad eum quem volumus incohandum et ea quidem eloquentia informandum quam in nullo cognovit Antonius,"9.33). Cicero means to establish "the form and likeness of

surpassing eloquence" ("excellentis eloquentiae speciem et formam adum-
brabimus," 14.43), just as the courtiers at Urbino, and later in Lyly and
Sidney, following Lodovico, fashion the courtier through a *sprezzatura* that
embodies, guarantees, and furthers his qualifications to be an ideal courtier,
(*un perfetto cortegiano*). For Cicero too the key is *performance*.

> Sed iam illius perfecti oratoris et summae eloquentiae species exprimenda
> est. Quem hoc uno excellere, id est oratione, cetera in eo latere indicat
> nomen ipsum. Non enim inventor aut compositor aut actor qui haec
> complexus est omnia, sed et Graece ab eloquendo ῥήτωρ et Latine eloquens
> dictus est. Ceterarum enim rerum quae sunt in oratore partem aliquam sibi
> quisque vindicat, dicendi autem, id est eloquendi, maxima vis soli huic
> conceditur.

> We must now turn to the task of portraying the perfect orator and the
> highest eloquence. The very word "eloquent" shows that he excels because
> of this one quality, that is, in the use of language, and that the other
> qualities are overshadowed by this. For the all-inclusive word is not
> "discoverer," or "arranger," or "actor," but in Greek he is called ῥήτωρ
> from the word "to speak," and in Latin he is said to be "eloquent." For
> everyone claims for himself some part of the other qualities that go to make
> up an orator, but the supreme power in speaking, that is eloquence, is
> granted to him alone. [19.61]

Yet the style Cicero proposes in this dedicated declamation to Brutus is
decidedly not the grandiloquent style, which proclaimed splendid power of
thought and majesty of diction, or the plain style, refined, concise, and
stripped of ornament, but something between them.

> Est autem quidam interiectus inter hos medius et quasi temperatus nec
> acumine posteriorum nec fulmine utens superiorum, vicinus amborum, in
> neutro excellens, utriusque particeps vel utriusque, si verum quaerimus,
> potius expers, isque uno tenore, ut aiunt, in dicendo fluit nihil afferens
> praeter facultatem et aequalitatem aut addit aliquos ut in corona toros
> omnemque orationem ornamentis modicis verborum sententiarumque
> distinguit.

> Between these two there is a mean and I may say tempered style, which
> uses neither the intellectual appeal of the latter class nor the fiery force of
> the former; akin to both, excelling in neither, sharing in both, or, to tell the
> truth, sharing in neither, this style keeps the proverbial "even tenor of its
> way," bringing nothing except ease and uniformity, or at most adding a few
> posies as in a garland, and diversifying the whole speech with simple
> ornaments of thought and diction. [6.21]

The "well-knit rhythm of prose" realizes the Aristotelian mean. "Meae
quidem et perfecto completoque verborum ambitu gaudent et curta senti-

unt nec amant redundantia," Cicero insists; "My ear, at any rate, rejoices in a full and rounded period; it feels a deficiency, and does not like an excess" (50.168). Such a moderate style is verbally analogous to the courtier who must constantly juggle disguise and reality in performing a verisimilitudinous sprezzatura; and it is just such a balancing act that is for Cicero the function of a successful orator. Indeed, the orator fashions his speech to the occasion just as Castiglione's courtier must.

> Semper oratorum eloquentiae moderatrix fuit auditorum prudentia. Omnes enim qui probari volunt voluntatem eorum qui audiunt intuentur ad eamque et ad eorum arbitrium et nutum totos se fingunt et accommodant.

> The eloquence of orators has always been controlled by the good sense of the audience, since all who desire to win approval have regard to the goodwill of their auditors, and shape and adapt themselves completely according to this and to their opinion and approval. [8.24]

This is not only the cardinal but the universal rule in oratory as in life (21.71), and he describes in more detail than Castiglione's courtiers how one performs appropriately for particular audiences (36.124–25). To this end, and for this end only, Cicero catalogues figures of rhetoric for Brutus, both the figures of style (39.135) and the figures of thought (39.136–40.139), as well as various strategies of disposition (44.149–67.226)—the basis for a subsequent poetics of eloquence to be practiced especially by Lyly, Greene, and Sidney. If Castiglione has *De Oratore* in mind during such particular passages as those on mortality and wit, it is likelier he took his understanding of fashioning an idea, of a poetics of eloquence and sprezzatura, from this later work of Cicero's most mature period. He may also have found ready resource in Quintilian's derivative portrait of the ideal orator in *Institutio Oratoria* 12, as one who is brilliant, sublime and opulent of speech, and lord and master of all the resources of eloquence whose affluence surrounds him ("Nitidus ille et sublimis et locuples circumfluentibus undique eloquentiae copiis imperat").[8]

Yet, if Castiglione's humanist fiction originated in Cicero—as so much work by the humanists does—its expansion and refinements come in holograph additions taken from Aristotle; Castiglione's poetics is equally rooted in the *Politics* (especially Book 8) and the *Nicomachean Ethics* (particularly Book 2).[9] In the *Ethics,* for instance, education is seen as an ongoing process for Aristotle, as it is for Castiglione, a matter of *praktikè,* or human endeavor—less stable than the natural phenomena of *theoretikè,* or scientific observation, and thus more needful of constant study, practice, and discipline. The student is for Aristotle, in short, *fashioned;* and it is in this sense of fashioning that Castiglione proposes *di formar un perfetto cortegiano.* Although Castiglione's Ottaviano takes his psychology (4.16) from the *Ethics* and his discussion of governments (4.21) from the *Politics,* as Castiglione himself takes examples of joking from *De Oratore,* it is the sense of Aristotelian epistemology that constitutes another Senecan pattern operating behind *Il Cortegiano.* In forming his perfect courtier of the mind, Castiglione shapes all four of his books of the courtier, in their final revision, by the progressive sense of learning—of education—in the *Ethics* (something Sidney will do, too, in a more concentrated way in *Arcadia* 5). Castiglione builds the courtier through lessons in *technē,* or skill (Aristotle, 6.4); *phronēsis,* or prudence, practical wisdom (6.5); *nous,* or intelligence, rational wisdom (6.6); and *sophia,* or wisdom (6.7). As Erasmus and More relied on organizing patterns for the *Encomium Moriae* and the *Utopia,* so too Castiglione shapes Book 1 by describing the skills of the ideal courtier, Book 2 by showing how these skills are put to practical use, Book 3 by illustrating the wisdom of women through their intuitive responses when their courage or intelligence is tested, and Book 4 through both the rational wisdom of Ottaviano and the mystical and enraptured wisdom of Bembo.

The powerful vision of Bembo, transcending the events of the past and present and even language itself, is Castiglione's final and most moving, most memorable, portrait of an orator. In the thin, high mountain air of the ducal palace, set far above the busy city of Urbino and placed some rooms from the impotent Duke Guidobaldo Montrefeltro's thirty or forty copyists still busy day and night transcribing authentic Greek and Latin manuscripts, Bembo hints ecstatically of the ineffable. He passes beyond even the courtiers' more earthbound art of sprezzatura, where art and nature, style and subject, are somehow reconciled. Even if the details of Bembo's vision elude us, the power and the glory of it do not: here not only time but language has its stop. Here all is one, at eternal rest. Here *Il Cortegiano* passes before us, refined, refining us in turn. It is what it is about. In thus sustaining his central paradox of perfecting what is known to be imperfectible, Castiglione oscillates for a time, before joining them, between the twin concerns of Cicero: an ideal state realized by the ideal orator. By eventually bringing the two together through his own imaginary work of humanist eloquence, Castiglione, in his closing pages, realizes the Greek term *paradoxon* (Latin *para doxa*), which both Cicero and Quintilian translate appropriately elsewhere with words derived from the Latin verb *admiror* (to wonder or marvel at). It is an observation Puttenham makes too in his *Arte of English Poesie* (1589) when he considers paradox as a figure of speech by calling it, instructively, "the Wondrer" (sig. Cc1). It is in this deeper, richer, and more significant sense of a unifying and inspiring poetics of eloquence that Castiglione profoundly affects humanist fiction in Tudor England, and not merely in the elevation of style for its own sake.

To narrow and underscore Castiglione's achievement, then, we can do no better than to repeat Hoby's own acute summary. Castiglione, he says, writes of "the behoulding and musing of the minde." And it is the power of the mind to explore, realize, construct, and imagine that prompts the best of the Tudor humanist fictions by John Lyly, Robert Greene, and Sir Philip Sidney. Their work varies enormously, as their temperaments do, but all of it clearly derives from Castiglione and, behind him, from the philosophy and rhetoric of Aristotle and Cicero. Lyly, for instance, has a keen sense that style and substance must echo one another, work together, and appear, finally, inseparable. In this sense his eloquence resembles that of Castiglione's Ottaviano in Book 4 of *Il Cortegiano*. But Lyly seems also to be keenly aware of Castiglione's warning that oratory can make man seem godlike. The seductive power of language can finally seduce the seducer. Given this fundamental equivocation, Lyly's own inventive and playful mind works out the implications wittily, in the techne derived from Cicero and Castiglione, which at first deliberately lacks the prudence it must learn. Nor is such a lesson an easy one: Castiglione's courtiers, like Cicero's interlocutors, have urged imitation as the means to a prudent language, but who is a man to imitate, and who is to make that choice? Lyly's *Euphues* and *Euphues and his England* are both attempts by a humanist writer of fiction to explore the unexplored inconsistencies and paradoxes found at the heart of humanist philosophy and practice while still employing its own kind of eloquence.

Greene's concern with the legacy of Castiglione is somewhat different. He too is a humanist writer who respects and elevates the use of eloquence as a sign of wisdom and self-discipline; but he is concerned, as Castiglione seems to be at the end of *Il Cortegiano,* with the marvel of it. Greene like Bembo sees eloquence as a result of inspiration, and such visions as inspire can lead to *admiratio,* to the ineffable. Indeed, Greene is much taken with the ineffable and the inexplicable. He may have in mind Cicero's passage on the death of Crassus recalled by Castiglione—

O fallacem hominum spem fragilemque fortunam, et inanes nostras contentiones, quae medio in spatio saepe franguntur et corruunt et aute in ipso cursu obruuntur quam portum conspicere potuerunt!

Ah, how treacherous are men's hopes, how insecure their fortunes! How hollow are our endeavours, which often break down and come to grief in the middle of the race, or are shipwrecked in full sail before they have been able to sight the harbour! [*De Oratore,* 3.2.7]

—or simply the erratic passages on fortune and fate to which he repeatedly points. But the fragility of mortality *in spite of* man's education and eloquence leads Greene not only to a keen sense of guilt and despair but also—and this is the cause of his abiding attraction—to the equally human states of admiration and wonder.

Yet, of all three of the great Tudor writers of eloquence, it is Sir Philip Sidney who comes closest to Castiglione. In the beholding and musing of his mind, Sidney creates an Arcadia that seems a later, English version of Urbino. Sidney too is concerned in some detail with the proper education of the humanist courtier, the training in the skills of techne, the strengths of the body, the discipline of prudence, and the cultivation of wisdom. Such lessons for Sidney, even more than for Castiglione, are learned in the arena of life's hard adventures and rugged challenges, but equally too in life's debates, whether such debates involve the flirtations of courtship, the quelling of an angry and rebellious mob, or the trial of guilt and innocence where real lives hang in the balance. For Sidney pays greatest respect to two of Castiglione's primary authorities, Aristotle and Cicero; and like them, he too sees their philosophy *and* their rhetoric, *ratio* and *oratio,* as indivisible. But Sidney develops at considerable length what Castiglione only hints at—that man's life is unfulfilled if it lacks continual social and political engagement. Techne and prudence cannot achieve wisdom without continuing service to persons and to state—that is, to civilization. In exploring such an idea, Sidney places Cicero in a more reliable context even than Castiglione, for Sidney will draw on the philosophy as well as the rhetoric of Cicero, just as he will draw on both Aristotelian philosophy and rhetoric. In this way, Sidney redefines the substance and the style that Castiglione has already made inseparable. In this way, too, Sidney works his own witty way to his own interpretation of wonder.

Such brief summaries of the three most important Elizabethan writers of the fiction of humanist eloquence are of course an act of considerable injustice. Each of them draws on far more than *Il Libro del Cortegiano.* Each of them weaves a dense, complicated, independent, and original poetics of fiction drawing, as they all do, on humanist thought and humanist rhetoric. It is time now, then, to examine each of them in turn in something like the detail each deserves.

FIVE

"Singuler eloquence and braue composition":

John Lyly, *Euphues,* and Its Sequel

 THE INITIAL HEIR APPARENT TO CASTIGLIONE IS JOHN LYLY. BOTH MEN SHARE AN INTEREST IN VERBAL BEHAVIOR AS AN INDEX TO THE DISPOSITION OF THE MIND AND SOUL, IN HUMAN SUSCEPTIBILITY TO dissimulation through the manipulation of language, and a steady focus on manner as indicative of meaning.[1] So fundamental and so pervasive are their similarities, in fact, that Lyly may have found in the early stages of composing *Euphues* (1578) a validation for his own distinguishing style if not an initial suggestion for it in *Il Libro del Cortegiano.*

> I modi del parlare & le figure, che hanno gratia, i ragionamenti gravi & seueri, quasi sempre anchor stanno ben nelle facetie, & giochi. Vedete che le parole contraposte, danno ornamento assai, quando una clausula contraria s'oppone all'altra. Il medesimo modo spesso è facetissimo.

> The termes of speache and fygures that haue ane grace, and graue talke, are likewise (in a maner) alwaies comely in *Iestes* and merry pleasantnesse. See howe woordes placed contrarywyse giue a great ornament, whan one contrarye clause is sett agaynst another. The same maner is often times verye merrye and pleasant.[2]

Or both may share as an ultimate source Cicero's *De Oratore 2*: "Materiam aliam esse ioci, aliam severitatis; gravium autem et iocorum unam esse rationem. Ornant igitur in primis orationem verba relata contrarie, quod idem genus saepe est etiam facetum"; "Though the [subject matter] of jesting and austerity lie wide apart, yet the methods of seriousness and jesting are identical. So the opposition of verbal contradictories is one of the chief embellishments of diction, and this same device is often witty as well" (65.262–63). A self-conscious style of balance characterizes them both; in commenting on Lyly's "refined taste, his feeling for elegance and grace, his delicate lyrical gift, his wit, his moderate learning," Morris W. Croll could be as easily referring to Castiglione.[3]

The point is a salient one, because we tend to forget how forcefully such a style impressed the Renaissance, how it initially stirred men's imaginations as much as any English prose style has before or since.[4] Later parodies attest to its familiarity. And *Euphues* itself was an unparalleled success for its time, with five editions in three years, while *Euphues and his England* went through four editions in a single year; both fictions enjoyed twenty-six separate and three joint editions by 1630.[5] The compacted craft of Lyly's prose and his dense imagery and allusion, defending and using the humanists' antique heritage, elicited much spontaneous and enthusiastic support. So William Webbe gives Lyly special recognition in his *Discourse of English Poetrie* (1586):

> Among whom I thinke there is none that will gainsay, but Master *Iohn Lilly* hath deserued moste high commendations, as he which hath stept one steppe further therein then any either before or since he first began the wyttie discourse of his *Euphues*. Whose workes, surely in respecte of his singuler eloquence and braue composition of apt words and sentences, let the learned examine and make tryall thereof thorough all the partes of Rethorike, in fitte phrases, in pithy sentences, in gallant tropes, in flowing speeche, in plaine sence, and surely in my iudgment, I thinke he wyll yeelde him that verdict, which *Quintilian* giueth of bothe the best Orators *Demosthenes* and *Tully,* that from the one, nothing may be taken away, to the other, nothing may be added. [Sig. E1v]

Lyly's fiction still excites and amuses us, too, because of its "power to display wit while anatomizing wit."[6]

Nevertheless, style alone could not account for the peculiar distinctions awarded to Lyly's fiction or explain its stunning power of endurance. To appreciate that, we must also acknowledge that, like Castiglione, Lyly writes a fiction of serious aim. The two most vexing concerns of Renaissance English humanism—the capacities of man and the efficacies of a humanist education—are directly addressed in Lyly's chief works of humanist poetics, *Euphues* and *Euphues and his England* (1580). "If nature canne no waye resist the furye of affection," asks one of the characters in *Euphues,* "howe shall it be stayed by wisdome?" The question is an urgent one for Lucilla, whose name pointedly means "little light," for her life is especially vertiginous and it is learning that has created her difficulty as she tries to reason her way to an appropriate and felicitous behavior. Lucilla's noetic response defines the object of her love, Euphues, with language taken from her storehouse of humanist rhetoric as a means of resolving her dilemma.

> I knowe so noble a minde could take no originall but from a noble man, for as no Bird can looke against the Sunne but those that bee bredde of the

Eagle, neither any Hawke soare so high as the broode of the Hobby, so no wight can haue suche excellent qualyties except he descende of a noble race, neither he of so highe capacitie, vnlesse hee issue of a high progeny.

But to love Euphues is to break her pledge to Philautus, and this reminds her, with equal force, of historical examples of nobility—Myrrha, Byblis, Phaedra—who were victimized by passions similar to hers, which they could not control. Her education in the past as exemplary for the present is so broad that it sanctions *all* possibilities: her humanist learning results in a stalemate, fixed by balancing sets of allusions that cause her very thinking and language to freeze in stasis. Her father, Ferardo, seizing this opportunity, interrupts her in defense of Philautus, to whom she is also confessing.

> *Lucilla,* as I am not presently to graunt my good wil, so meane I not to reprehend thy choyce, yet wisedome willeth me to pawse, vntill I haue called what may happen to my remembraunce, and warneth thee to be circumspect, least thy rash conceipt bring a sharpe repentaūce. [sigs. I2v–I3; 1:231).[7]

This correspondingly wide-ranging answer with its own accumulation of possibilities—I do not like this; I will not rebuke (censure) your choice in men; I will delay responding until all this blows over; I will wait until I can determine the cause of your defection; do whatever you wish, if you must, but be discreet about it—only bewilders Lucilla and compounds her problem as well as Philautus's. The father as schoolmaster, the family authority most respected by humanist tradition, likewise knows and says too much. His learning reveals his *in*sufficiency, just as the rush of his rhetoric tries to conceal it. What Lucilla senses Euphues had earlier told *his* proposed schoolmaster, Eubulus ("good counsel"), openly. "If nature be of strength or force," Euphues reasons, "what auaileth discipline or nurture? If of none, what helpeth nature?" (sig. S2; 1:192). The inquiry pentrates humanism to its very core. But it is of a piece with the rest of the work: Lyly's *Euphues: The Anatomy of Wit* opens with a humanist counselor who is ineffective and a prodigal student who is the protagonist, the two from the start turning the world of the book into their world as schoolroom. Thus Lyly's fiction works precisely the way Castiglione's does but in the opposite direction—it implies the universal need for sprezzatura through individual cases rather than by discussing sprezzatura in theory and then citing a series of illustrations. *Euphues* witnesses to the process of life as the progress of learning, playing on the scholastic use of anatomization or analysis as the chief means to wisdom while, through disputations on wit and wisdom, nature and nurture, concupiscence and conscience, it analyzes and parodies more recent means to know and to understand. Thus it is not merely the extravagance but the entirety of Lyly's audacious examination of humanism that now so fixes us: humanist ideas as well as humanist rhetoric are seen from multiple view and become the *total* matter and manner of his fiction.

"*Euphues* is a truly intellectual work in that it considers also the limitations of intellectuality," Merritt Lawlis contends; "What appears to interest [Lyly] is not ideas so much as the process of reasoning, not the ideas themselves but the manipulation of them."[8] The opening debate between Euphues and Eubulus is a case in point. Eubulus presents the traditional argument of the humanist who distrusts untutored human nature; his doctrine and language are standard, and his speech to Euphues is heavily proverbial. It is the major premise of all the syllogisms underlying *Euphues*.

> As thy byrth doth shewe the expresse and liuely Image of gentle bloud, so thy bringing vp seemeth to mee to bee a great blotte to the lynage of so noble a brute, so that I am enforced to thinke that either thou diddest want one to giue thee good instructions, or that thy parentes made thee a wanton with too much cockering, eyther they were too foolish in vsing no discipline, or thou too froward in reiecting their doctrine: either they willing to haue thee idle, or thou wilful to be il employed. [Sig. B3; 1:187]

Such speeches at first seem contrived, static, ceremonial, but Lyly invariably makes the most obvious rhetorical set piece first narrative (in its context) and then dramatic (in its forwarding action); here such bifurcated thinking gives way to multiple if inherent discontinuities: "Did they not remember that which no man ought to forgette, that the tender youth of a childe is like the tempering of new Waxe, apt to receiue any forme?" (sig. B3; 1:187).

Still, the abstractions of Eubulus are so general and so clichéd as to insult Euphues, known for his "sharpe capacity of minde" (sig. B1; 1:184), and to appear meretricious to us. Moreover, Eubulus is a citizen of Naples and, as we learn from the symbolic geography of the book, Naples is "a place of more pleasure then profit, & yet of more profit then pietie" (sig. B2; 1:185), the city of self-delusion where Jerome Turler, in *The Traveiler* (1575) could find talk "full of bragginge and boastinge, insomutche that they despise the counsell of othermen, and prefer their owne wittes before al others" (sigs. N4v–N5).[9] Forgetting, then, even his own doubts about Euphues' nature, Eubulus appoints himself instructor to the boy whom his parents could not teach. His classical lessons slide deliberately into biblical commandments.

Descend into thine owne conscience, and consider with thy selfe, the great
difference betweene staring and starke blynde, witte and wisedome, loue
and lust: be merry, but with modestie: be sober, but not too sullen: be
valyaunt, but not too venterous. Let thy attyre bee comely, but not costly:
thy dyet wholesome, but not excessiue: vse pastime as the word importeth
to passe the time in honest recreation. Mistrust no man without cause,
neither be thou credulus without proofe: be not lyght to follow euery mans
opinion, nor obstinate to stande in thine owne conceipt. Serue GOD, loue
God, feare God, and god will so blesse thee, as eyther heart canne wish or
thy friends desire. [Sig. B4v; 1:189–90][10]

The stability of Eubulus's prophylactic position balances the regnant
hypocrisy of the place in which he resides—in this he matches Hythlodaye
in Antwerp—just as his argument for restraint counteracts the atmosphere
of freedom that he feels will threaten him, the particularization of his
illustrations (the Trojans, Lacedaemonians, Persians, and Parthians) in
counterpoise with the more general precepts, which have permitted some
critics to compare him with Polonius.[11]

But "so many men so many mindes" (sig. B4v; 1:190): in a work formed
by repeatedly contrasted equivalencies, by pairs of words, clauses, attitudes,
and events that stamp it with the impress of the disputation, the other half
of Eubulus's advice is to be sought in Euphues' reply (the book's minor
premise). Euphues' quick wit—making him for Ascham in *The Scholemaster* (1570), we recall, one of "the best Poetes, but not the wisest Orators"
(sig. C4v), rather like F. J.—seizes on the discrepancy between Eubulus's
propositio and his *confirmatio*. Eubulus has consented to Euphues' good
nature by ignoring it in his arguments for good nurture. So Euphues, aware
of the possibilities of language, rephrases Eubulus's premise: "If nature
beare no sway," he replies, "why vse you this adulation? If nature worke
the effect, what booteth any education?" (sig. C2; 1:192). The response is
both logical and rhetorical and employs a basic humanist rhetorical
technique, the disjunctive proposition that was also associated in humanist
minds with the skeptic Sextus Empiricus: (a) If my nature insures my
goodness, then I do not need your training; and (b) If I need your training,
then you have just proven yourself too unwise to give me lessons, for you
said I was well endowed without it. The dilemma Euphues employs as
respondent is unanswerable; pointedly, he displaces the Aristotelian use of
classical precedent known to Erasmus and More with the flashier Ramist
logic that, in his own day, had come to stress schemes and tropes divorced
from logic, style severed from substance. Not that Euphues is without
subtlety: his opposing proposition is one advocated by later humanists—
hence the Grand Tour for experiential education[12]—but, by dividing the

essential position of the traditional humanist, he can beat Eubulus at his own game.[13] Yet it is Lyly's authorial wit that produces the final ironic comment—Euphues, who knows the Greek meaning of his name ("clever," "well-endowed"), apparently does not use his Greek to translate that of Eubulus. In love with his own skill at manipulating words, Euphues reaches the dead end of pure sophistry. "It is ye disposition of the thought," he claims, "that altereth ye nature of the thing" (sig. C2v; 1:193).

If Eubulus shows a deficiency in the use of persuasive rhetorical structures, Euphues shows excess—so much so that Lyly is forced to add his own authoritative voice to the debate so as to reassert the narrative shape (sig. C4; 1:195) and restore the Aristotelian balance (such as we would find in Castiglione). Eubulus and Euphues miss the resolution of the moderating middle ground, much as they choose the "pleasure" or "pietie" of Naples without recognizing the saving middle term of profit inscribed by Lyly. But without such a corrective resolution "wit may be seen as wit praising wit," as Richard Haber remarks, "as self-praise in *The Praise of Folly*."[14] Self-revelation is thereby confounded with self-congratulation, self-righteousness with self-infatuation, before Philautus enters the fiction. Only the narrative voice remains to address the gentlemen readers.

> Too much studie doth intoxicate their braines, for (say thay) although yron the more it is vsed the brighter it is, yet siluer with much wearing doth wast to nothing: though the Cammocke the more it is bowed the better it serueth, yet the bow the more it is bent & occupied, the weaker it waxeth: though the Camomill the more it is troden and pressed downe, the more it spreadeth, yet the Violet the oftner it is handeled and touched, the sooner it withereth and decayeth. [Sigs. C4–C4v; 1:195–96]

The formal speech of adjudication is raised here to the pitch of a dramatic chorus.

This first debate in *Euphues* is an accurate paradigm of the entire work. Behind such contrary and apparently irreconcilable positions voiced by Eubulus and Euphues lie the dual environments of Euphues' education: Athens, which figures the values of classical Greece, Oxford University, and humanist teaching; and Naples, which images contemporary Renaissance Rome, London, and corrupting centers of experience.[15] From the first, Lyly asks us if both locations are potentially complementary or mutually destructive—or if one is sufficient alone. It is the same issue More-persona poses to Hythlodaye and Castiglione poses to us.

Lyly excuses nothing from his examination. The actions of life are captured in explicit and implicit disputations laden with classical and biblical references, literary allusions, and popular maxims. Without the liminary advice of Eubulus, however, the incipient Euphues is soon adrift in the inconstant and unpredictable world of Naples, the book's landscape reduplicating the confused mind of its hero. The Aristotelian moderation that Lyly has suggested authorially is countered by Aristotelian epistemology, which holds that the imagination controls the will and impedes wisdom, and by Euphues' own self-description out of Plutarch whereby he likens his unformed mind to wax, open to all experiences indiscriminately. Wisdom is thus put squarely in opposition to will. The two cancel each other out—or at least weaken each other temporarily—and Euphues descends more and more frequently to eristics, his logic irrational, his analogies frequently false, his allusions contradictory, and some evidence pretending to be accurate unnatural natural history even made up by Euphues in self-defense. Through his cleverness Euphues learns that both the classical oration and the Ramist logic of dichotomies assume truths they do not provide. Repeatedly Euphues tries to clarify his position as well as his argument by defining polarities, only to learn that, rather than illuminate the inner consistency of an organic world as he might have supposed from his training in Greece, they in fact display affinities at some points, destructive antipathies at other points, and ambiguities at still other points. Soon Euphues is forced to admit to himself the inherent fluidity of rhetoric, that words are not in themselves things; as the book progresses, he likewise learns that the very process of human reason, logic, is subject to mistaking all conclusions as self-evident truths. *Euphues: The Anatomy of Wit* thus analyzes the evolution of the fallen—that is, the irrational, undignified—intellect.

Euphues, like us, needs to place his faith in some capacity, if not some process of human thought, however. Rejecting Eubulus, whose precepts are too distant from the desires and activities of his daily life, Euphues finds a new instructor in Philautus. From the beginning, he sees their friendship as a new means for education.

> Wayinge with my selfe the form of friendshippe by the effects, I studyed euer since my first comming to *Naples* to enter league with such a one as might direct my steps being a stranger, and resemble my manners being a scholler, the which two qualities as I find in you able to satisfie my desire, so I hope I shal finde a hearte in you willinge to accomplish my request. [Sig. D2; 1:198]

But "No lofty philosophic speculation is safe from contamination in Lyly's fictive universe," Joseph W. Houppert reminds us (*John Lyly,* p. 60); seeking a companion for purely selfish reasons, Euphues falls in love with himself once again: "I view in him the liuely Image of *Euphues*" (sig. D1v;

1:197). In an elaborate rhetoric—what Thomas Elyot calls "an artifyciall fourme of spekyng" in *The Boke Named the Gouernour* (1531; sig. G1)—Philautus shows himself equally blinded.

> And seeing we reseble (as you say) each other in qualities, it cannot be yt the one should differ from the other in curtesie, seing the sincere affection of the minde cannot be expressed by the mouth, & that no art can vnfolde the entire loue of ye heart, I am earnestly to beseech you not to measure the firmenesse of my faith, by ye fewnes of my wordes, but rather thinke that the ouerflowing waues of good wil, leaue no passage for many words. [Sigs. D2–D2v; 1:198–99]

Eubulus has seen learning as a struggle (sig. B4v; 1:189–90), but in choosing the satisfaction of an agreeable friend both Euphues and Philautus mistake feeling for learning. In making their encomia essentially autobiographical, they (like Folly) deceive themselves.

How blind to reason self-love has made Euphues is apparent when Philautus takes him to supper to meet Lucilla and Livia. As earlier with Philautus, here Euphues is again invited to speak on either learning or love; and, no longer confusing the two, he chooses love alone. In participating in such *dubii,* debates on love after the manner of Castiglione, Euphues reveals his corrupted motives through the baseness of his proposition and the directness of his speech. He chooses to debate "whether the qualities of the minde, or the composition of the man, cause women most to lyke, or whether beautie or wit moue men most to loue" (sig. D4; 1:201).[16] The very language of debate now betrays the self-deceived Euphues.

> The foule Toade hath a faire stone in his head, the fine golde is found in the filthy earth: the sweet kernell lyeth in the hard shell. . . . Heere I could enter into discourse of such fine dames as being in loue with their owne lookes, make such course accompt of their passionate louers: for commonly if they be adorned with beautie, they be straight laced, and made so high in the insteppe, that they disdaine them most that most desire them. . . . Two things do they cause their seruants to vow vnto them, secrecie, & souereintie: the one to conceale their entising sleights, by the other to assure themselues of their only seruice. . . . Let not Gentlewomen therefore make to much of their painted sheath, let them not be so curious in their owne conceit, or so currish to their loyal louers. When the black Crowes foote shall appeare in their eye, or the blacke Oxe treade on their foote, when their beautie shall be lyke the blasted Rose, their wealth wasted, their bodies worne, their faces wrinkled, their fingers crooked, who wil like of them in their age, who loued none in their youth? If you will be cherished when you be olde, be courteous while you be young. [Sigs. D4–E1; 1:202–3]

Whereas in a play like Lyly's *Endimion* the stichomythic dialogue destroys the possibility of reflection and necessitates honest revelation,[17] in *Euphues* formal declamations encourage both artifice and unrecognized hypocrisy. Rhetoric becomes self-perverting—"a soune without any purpose," as Elyot has it (*Gouernour,* sig. F7v). Euphues has it all ways and no way, arguing first for the mind, then against coy ladies and for courtly lovers, and then, in still another reversal, in favor of women's reason. A lack of social grace is compounded with a blindness to social sophistry, and his argument becomes an assault until his emotions suddenly overtake his feigned eloquence. With his aposiopesis, we are bluntly reminded that the performing Euphues remains untrained *and* inexperienced.[18] His audience is not deceived. "Well Gentleman, aunswered *Lucilla,* in arguing of the shadow, we forgoe the substaunce" (sig. D3v; 1:201).

Such an abrupt halt would be a clear enough victory for Lucilla in a world free of sophistry and posturing. But "so often," G. Wilson Knight reminds us, "a seeming conclusion in Lyly turns into its opposite."[19] Lucilla cannot tell whether Euphues' emotion is real or feigned. The exaggerated lovesickness of Euphues is mirrored in the Petrarchanism of Lucilla's own troubled soliloquy about her feelings for Euphues immediately after his hasty departure (sigs. E2–E2v; 1:205). With both characters, love is a sickness of the soul. As a consequence, Lucilla borrows the language of contrarieties that until now has characterized only Euphues' rhetoric: "But," "Aye, but," "If," "Tush," "Wel, wel." She also borrows his argument that a man of good nature cannot be transformed, cannot be corrupted. In her recital of folly and wisdom, Lucilla dwells on foolish ignorance and unwise folly; she wins for herself similar abusive behavior by robbing Euphues of his issues and positions. But as she does so she also transforms the issue from one of nature versus nurture to one of concupiscence versus conscience. She informs the secular humanism of her inner debate by Christianity, following Eubulus. But she is not Eubulus; her thoughts move downward only. The imagery of Lucilla's self-counsel descends the Platonic ladder of love, showing her progressive loss of reason (sigs. E2v–E3; 1:205). Her trust of human nature is riddled with doubts, and her attempts to defer to fixed systems of classical and Renaissance thought likewise reduce them to mere rationalizations. Will overcomes principle, and her twisted rhetoric disrupts her powers of logic (sig. E3; 1:206). Convinced that infidelity to Philautus will warn Euphues of her fallen nature, Lucilla is unable to reason her way unaided to a solution to her dilemma (sigs. E3v–E4; 1:207). As the mirror of Euphues, Lucilla too figures for Lyly human nature devoid of humanist education: unrestrained, self-indulgent, foolish, and easily corruptible.

Lucilla's confusion is analogous to Euphues' "mad moode" (sig. E4v; 1:209)—his partial training in humanist doctrine gives him the means of argumentation without rational control (sigs. E4–E4v; 1:208). Euphues' incomplete sense of humanist rhetoric perverts rather than perfects nature. He also determines to dissemble (sig. F1; 1:209) and so "enherite the larᴶe of folly" (sig. F1; 1:210), discarding self-discipline and the trained beliefs of Athens to secure his right to inhabit Naples. Antipathetic to Eubulus and even to the higher love he once bore Philautus, Euphues now shares Lucilla's perspective and language. He turns sophist before Philautus. He equates rhetoric with truth in admitting he is in love, but uses rhetoric as artifice in pretending to love Livia (sig. F2; 1:212). In using Philautus as his "Shadow," Euphues shifts Lucilla's meaning of "insubstantial" and his own original meaning of "close companion" to another meaning then current, "blind" or "decoy."[20] Like Castiglione, then, Lyly establishes a sequence of voices that comment on each other: the factitious praise of Euphues, the calculated deceptions of Lucilla, the naive bewilderment of Philautus, the consuetudinal axioms of Eubulus, and the bemused tolerance of a clear-headed narrator. As in *Il Libro del Cortegiano,* none of these voices alone constitutes the story or embodies its meaning, for the signification lies in our response to judge their effect by comparisons and in the aggregate.

But *Euphues* is not simply a tale about a prodigal humanist who fails to heed lessons dictated to him by his elders; Lyly's fiction also examines acculturation as a means of nurturing wisdom, as in Gascoigne's *Adventures of Master F. J.* When we next meet Euphues, he has not only learned self-control but he is also transformed by a wonderfully supple and subtle *estilo culto,* which (like F. J.) he is too naive to employ properly. His speech is no longer a singular dissembling but a refined rhetoric by which he shows women to be vulnerable because of, rather than despite, their virtues (sig. G1v; 1:216). Whether consciously or not, Euphues' ardent praise of women (sigs. G2v–G3; 1:218) is composed of similes about destruction, his imagery persistently denying the premises he means to confirm through illustration. His insistence on his own love is so negatively put as to arouse as much suspicion as belief (sigs. G3–G3v; 1:219) and in the "wisdom" of her response, Lucilla matches his equivocation with her own (sig. G3; 1:219–20). As in her speeches to Philautus and Ferardo, Lucilla imitates rather than designs the fashion. Lyly thus uses two similar but not identical rhetorics to underline the fact that, for all her cleverness, Lucilla's fundamental candor makes her remarks a poor substitute for Euphues' denser, more ironic speech. In the geography of *Euphues,* Naples reduces life to instinct and imitation, whereas Athens (if we are to judge by Euphues as he matures) causes men to test, interpret, judge, and reconsider.

The artlessness of Lucilla's language—such as her slip of tongue when she confesses her "lust" rather than her "love" for Euphues (sig. E4; 1:207)—indicates her simplicity even in dissembling, and she is easily persuaded by her father, Ferardo, to admit her love for Euphues. Her biography, unlike his, is not of various kinds of education but of the various stages of her passion; she is schooled by her emotion rather than her intellect, bringing to a kind of completion the animal imagery that has accompanied, with persistent obbligato, her various examinations of human nature. Lucilla's increasingly candid character thus becomes her increasingly hopeless fate. "If Nature canne no waye resist the furye of affection: how shoulde it be stayed by wisedome?" (sig. I3; 1:231): her question to Ferardo echoes Euphues' to Eubulus. The central dilemma of humanism, it encircles both the substance and the presentation of *Euphues.*

We are thus encouraged to hear Euphues' unspoken question in Lucilla's plaintive self-defense, but Lucilla's relatively uneducated wit is limited to statements of love whereas Euphues enjoys the lively intellectual interchange of debate on a variety of issues. Lucilla understands only the formal declamation whereas Euphues, with a broader awareness and possessed of a growing sense of detachment and self-irony, enjoys conversations as *conversazione* (courtly performances) and as *controversiae* (disputations). Lucilla (and Philautus) speak to accomplish an end; Euphues speaks to perform, as well as to test responses and consequences. It is the difference between Naples and Athens, the humanist tour of experience examining the tenets of humanist rhetoric at first hand.[21] Euphues' self-education is to be compared, then, not with either Lucilla's passion or Eubulus's precepts but with Philautus's growth, which parallels Euphues' own.

Lucilla's rejection of Philautus at last prompts from him a speech that draws together the various threads of his learning: (*a*) that knowledge can be gained at Athens, (*b*) that experience must enlighten and ratify such learning, and (*c*) that some things will remain mysterious and so must be conveyed by equivocations that catch the paradoxes of truth and existence (sigs. I3v–I4; 1:232–33). Philautus's address is repeated in a letter to Euphues, the symmetry of his ideas caught in the symmetry of his style (sigs. I4–K1v; 1:233–35). But the letter is an act of self-vindication that awakens a reply in kind. And as they match words, so do their fates match. At his next visit to Lucilla, Euphues learns he too has been rejected for one Curio. The mirroring public rhetoric of his and Philautus's letters is now balanced by the private rhetoric of their anguished soliloquies and, at last, by their mutual reconciliation. Animal imagery is succeeded by a lexicon more elevated. Each will now become "a myrrour of Godlinesse hereafter . . . beeing purified in the styll of wisdome" (sig. I2; 1:242).

Words that once clothed actions now reveal them. But the reunion of wit and will that reunited Euphues and Philautus cannot align "*Naples* the nourisher of wantonnesse" and "the Philosophers in *Greece*" (sig. L1; 1:241). Instead, Euphues proposes, only "Philosophy, Phisick, Diuinitie, shal be my study" (sig. L1v; 1:241). He will balance the instruction and precepts of Eubulus with the study and investigations he plans to undertake in Athens, while Philautus remains in Naples. Yet both will correspond, for each will continue to teach the other his own particular perspective; "though their bodies were by distance of place seuered, yet the coniunction of their mindes should neither be seperated by ye length of time nor alienated by change of soyle" (sig. L4v; 1:246). Giving an appropriate value to both instruction and experience but precedence to neither, Lyly argues for wisdom *and* wit, the court forever conjunct with the university (sigs. L4–L4v; 1:245–46). The solution reminds us that the Greek word εὐφυής means not only "well-endowed" but also "well-*grown*," that is, whole, and symmetrical.[22] The narrative concludes with Lucilla's heedless fall, the prodigal-son story at the start of the work leading to the prodigal-daughter motif at its close.[23]

The opening half of *Euphues* centers on Euphues' experience in Naples,[24] his courtly affair a debased "Adventures of Master Euphues," but the second half is restricted to his precepts, composed but not enacted in Athens. "I coulde finde nothing either more fit to continue our friendshippe or of greater force to dissolue our folly," he writes to Philautus in the first of his letters, "then to write a remedy" (sig. M1; 1:246). In maintaining a balanced view of a broader humanism despite Ascham's recent strictures on travel, Lyly demonstrably returns to an earlier English humanism[25] in his epistles of precepts. The first two, a personal letter to Philautus and a general letter to the women of Italy, reintroduce the necessary coordination of private and public rhetorics, attesting to Euphues' growing wisdom. The personal letter, taken by Lyly directly from the *De Remedis Amoris* of Ovid, fuses classical allusions from Athens (sig. M2; 1:248) and proverbial lore current in Naples (sigs. M2–M3v; 1:249). But the moderation of his style conceals the immoderation of Euphues' counsel, for he preaches total abstinence from women (sig. M3v; 1:250) while his language slowly assumes a religious cast (sigs. M4–M4v; 1:251). Rather than fall victim to the folly of unreason, Euphues argues, Philautus should take up a learned profession such as law, medicine, or divinity, which will reinforce the natural, social, and philosophical orders subscribed to by Christian humanism. "The man beeing idle, the minde is apte to all vncleanenesse, the minde being voyde of exercise, the man is voyde of honestie" (sig. M4; 1:251). Finally, in advocating *self*-discipline, Euphŭes fully takes the place of Eubulus (sig. N1; 1:252–53); and, lest his plea for a life of newly found propriety be misinterpreted, Euphues warns against a solitary life (sig. N3v; 1:256). In the public letter, the same behavior is advocated for gentlewomen by drawing on other classical precedents and proverbs. Life and learning are thereby collated and both made properly educative; at their most axiomatic and euhemeristic, Euphues' twin letters sustain their apodictic force.

While these letters show a change in Euphues' perspective, the following pair, on education and faith, show a maturing of language, the tight symmetrical style easing into sentences of Ciceronian periodicity. Both are more abstract. "Euphues and his Ephoebus" (*ephēbos,* one arrived at puberty) is a paraphrase of the pseudo-Plutarch's *De Educatione Puerorum,* the first essay in the *Moralia,*[26] with additional passages from Plutarch's *De Garrulitate* and from Erasmus's *Colloquium Puerpera.* "Age alway ought to be a myrrour for youth," Euphues argues (sig. S1; 1:283): the home environment, the education of both mind and body culminating in philosophy, and the teaching of virtue to youth are his major issues (sigs. S1–S2; 1:283–84). But he also adds moral fervor, attacking dicing, dancing, fastidious clothes, idleness, drinking, and whoring (sig. S1; 1:284). Thus, in Euphues' letters, virtue and eloquence are inseparable (sig. S4; 1:288).[27] "Euphues and his Ephoebus" is in the form of a declamation; "Euphues and Atheos," taken partly from Cicero's *De Natura Deorum,* begins as a dialogue but soon becomes a sermon. The Christian humanism advocated for children now becomes that faith necessary to combat a world of sin, disbelief, and irreverence (sig. T4; 1:294). In a tour de force, Euphues' *inventio* becomes his *dispositio*: his thunderous language never fumbles, never repeats, its intensity maintained by incorporating large sections of Scripture. The zealous denunciation of sin and the affirmation of God complement the sweeter reasonableness of "Euphues and his Ephoebus," forming a minidisputation that reminds us of the complementary attitudes and styles of More-persona and Hythlodaye in *Utopia* 1 and 2. Even more deliberately, "Euphues and his Ephoebus" is Lyly's response to the debate between Eubulus and Euphues on nature and nurture, and "Euphues and Atheos" answers the debate between Euphues and Lucilla on concupiscence and conscience.

These two treatises on secular and sacred learning are the focus of the second half of *Euphues* as the debates with Eubulus and Lucilla were central to the first. "Euphues and his Ephoebus" and "Euphues and Atheos" are symmetrically flanked by the shorter letters to Philautus and to gentlewomen that precede them and to a balancing series of applications to various friends that follows. Euphues in Athens, then, is not so remote from life that he can no longer communicate wise advice: he knows how to translate classical and humanist precepts into letters that comfort Eubulus on the death of his daughter, Bontonio on his exile (an abridgment of Plutarch's *De Exilio*), Alcius on his discreditable behavior, and Livia on her sorrowful life. This second series closes with Euphues' promise of a pilgrimage to England with Philautus, a precise fusion of precept and experience, which, in the course of the fiction, has moved from the secular to the spiritual. *Euphues,* recognizing the inherent dangers of too much wit and witty sophistry—"He that seeketh the depth of knowledge: is as it were in a *Laborinth*" (sig. S4v; 1:289)—and advocating in its stead the proper use of language as signifier of behavior, thus reinforces through a balanced narrative and series of essays all the fundamental tenets of an English Christian humanism.

The overall movement from sophistry to spirituality in *Euphues* reminds us of Erasmus's *Encomium Moriae*, both in the idea of prodigality—catching up the contemporary humanist practice in such plays as *Acolastus, Misogonus, Nice Wanton,* and even Gascoigne's *Glasse of Gouernement,* all going back to Senecan models in the Tudor schoolroom plays of Plautus and Terence—and also in fixed resonances of Folly's autobiography. There are echoes of *Utopia,* too, in the careful balancing of Neapolitan activity followed by Athenian letters of precept, as the ills of an actual Europe are implicitly corrected or prevented by the theoretical premises and acts of Hythlodaye's newly discovered land, while Euphues himself recalls the callow F. J. Yet none of these striking resemblances is at first apparent to us (as they may have been to Lyly's first readers) because the symphonic arrangement of ideas and perspectives after Castiglione and the elaborately mannered and repetitive style after the Sicilian and Athenian rhetorics of Gorgias and Isocrates persistently obtrude. There is stylistic point to this, of course: Lyly means to set up through authorial control a pattern grounded in the humanist trust in order and reason against which the chaos of events and sophistic rhetoric is eventually defeated. There is also philosophic point: Lyly's attention to thoughtful and careful symmetry of phrases, clauses, sentences, and speeches as well as exempla, ideas, and debates, reinforced by the use of alliteration, assonance, and parallelism, introduces a whole new style of humanist poetics in order to stress the balancing of precept and event and the value of moderation to humanist thought. In Lyly style and significance can never be divorced: the style reveals the underlying claim to an orderly universe; the need for interpenetrating thought and deed—where word *becomes act* and is sufficient to do so—dictates style. Not to see this strategy whereby the presentation of the work is an ongoing dialectic with the events and ideas stated in it is seriously to misread *Euphues*.

We are told that Lyly means us to take him seriously, though not the characters themselves, at the start of *Euphues*: his attack on mannered language by using mannered language is far wittier and more intricate, say, than Lucian's parody, which Lyly may have had in mind.[28] "A foole hath intruded himselfe," Lyly writes in the dedicatory epistle to Sir William West, Lord De La Warr, "to discourse of wit" (sigs. A2v–A3; 1:180). Lyly invokes Erasmus's Folly, for his fool will also speak, according to the title page, of "the pleasantnesse of loue, and the happinesse he reapeth in age," and conclude with "the perfectnesse of Wisedome" (sig. A1; 1:177). Moreover, the story of *Euphues* is exemplary and educative because through fiction it attempts to portray truth.

> Alexander hauing a skar in his cheeke, held his finger vpō it, that Appelles might not paint it, Apelles painted him with his finger cleauing to his face, why quod Alexander, I laid my finger on my skarre bicause I would not haue thee see it, (yea said Apelles) and I drew it there bicause none els should perceiue it, for if thy finger had ben away, either thy skar would haue bene seene, or my art misliked: whereby I gather, that in all perfect workes, as well the fault as the face is to be showen. [Sig. A2; 1:179]

Such a choice for good art is neither strategic nor even voluntary but "the necessity of the history" (sig. A2v; 1:180).

What seems traditional on the surface, however, is a joke, for the classical precedent that is cited is one that Lyly, anticipating Euphues' method, has concocted for his own argument. There is no authority for this anecdote of Apelles. And, as it is untrue, so the particular "history" that is made to parallel it, while generally admonitory, is called into question. The implied duplicity is not one of substance only; it applies also to the discussion of style. The conditional "If" is our signal. "If these things be true, which experience tryeth, that a naked tale doth most truly set forth the naked truth, that wher the coūtenaunce is faire, ther neede no colours, that painting is meeter for ragged wals thē fine Marble, that veritie thē shineth most bright when she is in least brauery" (sig. A3; 1:181), then the tale of Euphues must be false, because the language that conveys it is thick with "colours." Lyly's opening letter repeatedly refuses to practice what it proposes, supplying instead an equivocation that must "recreate the *mind* of the curteous Reader" (sig. A3; 1:180; italics mine), leading us behind the work and beyond it. In addition, a second letter, addressed *"To the Gentlemen Readers,"* disavows any serious purpose and instead cites the ephemeral quality of all literature. The purpose of this second letter, communicated with levity, "is to challenge [the readers'] readiness to find and to know, to confront their predilection to see only what they fancy," Richard Haber tell us.[29] *Euphues* as parable of prodigality thus uses humanist forms, such as the anecdote, history, and epistle, to show the very relativity of such forms, just as the characters themselves have ambiguous names: Euphues means "well-endowed"—but it can also mean "naturally clever"; Philautus can mean "a love higher than the self" (that is, brotherly love) as it can also mean "self-love" or "self-regard." Such equivocating letters and names, patterned after the forematter of Gascoigne and, more recently, of George Pettie,[30] introduce a book of contrarieties in which Lyly forces the reader always to test the premises and observations behind what, on the surface, appears to be only another conduct book.[31] Rather than being what Jusserand calls the "king of the *précieux,*" Lyly displays an "extraordinarily nimble wit" and "a gift for the complex playing with words" that, while appearing captious, actually use the forms of declamation and disputation and a syntax of symmetry to raise fundamental issues because of the slipperiness of linguistic usage in his day.[32]

Still, *Euphues* is far more than a work of mere Lucianic teasing or a display of nimble wit—that belongs to the putative protagonist Euphues (by his very name) in his fallen state. Rather, Lyly is too keenly aware of the deep crevices of incongruity in humanist thought as a student of the New Learning who could not win himself a post at the university or court and as an heir to a rhetoric and system of thought which, making all things possible, guaranteed none of them as probable. He is wiser than Euphues, relying on aphorisms to dissuade Eubulus, or Lucilla, as she searches out commonplaces to persuade Ferardo. Lyly even "recognizes the complexity and contraditions and dramatic oppositions *within* the single personality," Knight observed some time ago, and he aligns these with "the baffling indecisiveness of all moral categories. So he starts with a concrete, often mythical or pseudo-historical, figure and lets his abstract thinking play round and into its growth. The ideas within his human delineation will be many and paradoxical."[33] Because of his infinite options and their unsettled principles, Lyly's characters talk at cross-purposes. They often say one thing and imply another or mean one thing and say another. They contradict themselves by referring to a contradictory world in their constant search for coherence and cohesion.[34] Their divided minds make for a divided speech and a divided thinking that is protracted by their intuitive understanding that words can conceal as well as convey meaning. As in Castiglione's work of eloquence, simulation prompts dissimulation. Highly patterned speech serves "both as barrier and protection," Madelon Gohlke tells us, "simultaneously aggravating and mitigating the problem to which it responds."[35] It masks Euphues' uncertainty, Philautus's anxiety, and Lucilla's shame. Indeed, "when the rhetoric collapses, as it does in the case of Lucilla after she deserts Euphues for Curio, so does any pretence of an idealized self."[36] In *Euphues,* Lyly argues that humanism tends to break down order by advocating multiple and antonomous sources at the same time such a process of thinking, speaking, and writing attempts to protect and preserve the humanism that fosters it. Lyly's characters face the same anxiety and bewilderment that Castiglione's do—but without the possibility of a workable sprezzatura.

Rather, Lyly's means for presenting so complicated a position is Erasmian: rhetorically, *Euphues* is a series of exercises in copia.[37] Reading Erasmus's *De Copia,* Joel B. Altman remarks,

> one can recapture momentarily the excitement that a man like John Lyly must have experienced in drawing together his own *silva,* with potential proofs gathered under such headings as "Beneficence," "Treachery," "Gratitude," "Fidelity." Just look at the matter that Erasmus suggests might be placed under the heading "Inconstancy": from the poets, *fabulae* about Mercury, that cunning disguiser; exempla of Proteus, Morpheus, and Circe; the personification Opportunity; anecdotes about the hero Ulysses, always adapting himself to circumstances; from natural history, *similitudines* of the circling moon and of the changing autumn sky; a *collocatio* of the ebbing and flowing sea; from moral philosophy, exempla of the whims of childhood, the fickleness of women, the uncertainty of the multitude; from the arts, the *descriptio* of a shifting weather vane and of delicately balanced scales; from ingenium, a *comparatio* of the inconstant mind of man and a glittering mirror that hangs in a busy forum reflecting the movements of the crowd below; from history, the elusive nature of Cataline and the inconstancy of the Greeks; from comedy, the uncertainty of the lover Phaedria; from tragedy, the varying moods of Phaedra. The list goes on and on.[38]

In stockpiling epithets (from such grammar school texts as Ioannes Ravisius Textor's *Specimen epithetorum*), classical tags and anecdotes (from Erasmus's *Adagia,* for instance), and references to the natural world (from Pliny the Elder's *Naturalis Historia*), Lyly's characters turn matter meant for illustration into the actual substance of their ideas and remarks. *Descriptions, exempla, sententiae, ethopoeiae,* and *loci communes* all serve as Aristotelian enthymemes, compacted syllogisms that, appearing as declaration or documentation, are actually perceived and employed as condensed arguments. In such a style, Richard Helgerson notes, "analytic wit allows no synthesizing wisdom" (*Elizabethan Prodigals,* p. 69); we can at best render local judgments.

And in this, as in nearly everything else, Lyly's roots are classical. Though his deliberate presentation of balanced ideas suggests both the sophist Protagoras (who argued that man is the measure of all things so that all judgments have equal weight and validity) and the skeptic Arcesilaus (who was the first to propose that because all positions had counterpositions the best man could do was suspend any final judgment), Lyly actually returns us once more to the Socratic principle of man's limited knowledge. His particular understanding of Socrates' awareness that he knows only that he does not know may be found in Plato's *Theaetetus*. This mature Platonic dialogue has much the same bearing on *Euphues* that the *Phaedrus* has on the *Utopia*. Here, in a companion piece to the *Sophist,* Plato's attack on sophistry as an attack on the validity of any instinct or opinion (161D–E) limns the self-centered arguments that Lyly uses to figure Naples, and Plato's attack on philosophers (such as the skeptics), who keep their heads in the clouds with ideas so abstract that they never confront the real problems that exist "in the city" (173E–174B), suggests Lyly's view of Athens where Euphues, for all his moral teaching, finds himself ill equipped to live among a more active community of men. Socrates argues that

> the philosopher does not even know that he does not know; for he does not keep aloof from them for the sake of gaining reputation, but really it is only his body that has its place and home in the city; his mind, considering all these things petty and of no account, disdains them and is borne in all directions, as Pindar says, "both below the earth," and measuring the surface of the earth, and "above the sky," studying the stars, and investigating the universal nature of every thing that is, each in its entirety, never lowering itself to anything close at hand. . . . Why, take the case of Thales, Theodorus. While he was studying the stars and looking upwards, he fell into a pit, and a neat, witty Thracian servant girl jeered at him, they say, because he was so eager to know the things in the sky that he could not see what was there before him at his very feet.[39]

For Plato as for Lyly, the soul and mind of man are like wax with stamped impressions that may change or even melt into one another (194C–195B). And such instincts, opinions, ideas, and impressions may all be undermined by orators, "for they persuade men by the art which they possess, not teaching them, but making them have whatever opinion they like" (201A). The *Theaetetus* teaches the value of considered individual judgment not as a means to solipsism but as a necessary measure of caution in the complex world of varying interpretation of various humanist texts.

Such an advanced and refined conceptualization of the connections between truth and language and such a complicated understanding of the functioning of words show how strikingly different Lyly's achievement in a humanist poetics is from other, lesser courtesy books with which *Euphues* is often compared, such as the *Galateo of Maister Iohn Della Casa,* translated by Robert Peterson of Lincoln's Inn in 1576, *"wherin vnder the person of an* old vnlearned man, instructing a youthe of his, he *hath talke of the maners and fashions it behoues* a man to vse or eschewe" (sig. B1), or *The ciuile Conuersation of M. Stephen Guazzo* (1586), translated by George Pettie (Books 1–3) and Bartholomew Young of Middle Temple (Book 4), where Pettie's chief emphasis is on appropriate and decorous conversation (sig. B7) with a rude dismissal of rhetoric, sophistry, and "speaking by contraries" (sigs. D4–D4v) and Young's contribution is an exemplary symposium on what is most like a woman and the virtues of praise. Rather, *Euphues* is directly aligned with Hoby's translation of *Il Cortegiano* (first published in 1561, but attracting little attention until the second edition of 1577, the year Lyly was composing *Euphues*),[40] and, before that, the impressive but now nearly forgotten dialogue *Il Moro* (*More*) (1556). Written in Italian by Ellis Heywood, the son of the leading dramatist of the More circle John Heywood, *Il Moro* combines the schoolroom and salon by transporting a symposium among courtiers to More's house in Chelsea. As in Castiglione, social intercourse soon gives rise to scholastic disputation with the host Thomas More as adjudicator. He is qualified for the role by being an ideal humanist.

> Ma il S. T. Moro si come quegli, che con allegrezza & prontezza ubbidiue alla uirtu, oltre ad ogni altro era faceto, & piaceuole molte, & trouandosi in compagnia, ilche ne l'hore de mangiare et altre non buone dallo studio, facea molto uolentieri, assai si dilettaua con acuna dubbiosa propositione di metterla in dispute di qualche cosa giouevole, in tutte le quali cosi facilmente sapeua scalzar il dritto, che ben sarebbe stato ritroso colui, a cui a pieno egli non hauesse sodis fatto.

> Sir Thomas More was one who obeyed virtue with joy and eagerness, and, when in the company of others, where he liked to be during the hours of dining and others unsuitable for study, he enjoyed turning a doubtful proposition into a useful debate. He knew so well how to make it yield truth that the antagonist whom More could not satisfy completely would have to be very obstinate.[41]

The following discussion echoes the life and works of More and Erasmus as well as *Il Cortegiano:* when Laurence argues (at confused length) for riches as the basis of happiness (sigs. B7–C4; 11–15),[42] Charles responds by employing More's own definitions of the covetous and liberal man, turning Laurence's ideas into the self-accusations of a fool pretending to wisdom while upholding seriously the idea of social responsibility (sigs. D3v–G1v;

21–26). Parallel to Euphues' double defense of a friend's proper devotion in *Euphues,*[43] Charles defends practical liberality before Laurence (sigs. D6v–E1v; 23–26) and theoretical liberality, in what Roger Lee Deakins calls the "debate-within-a-debate" (p. xxi), before Alexander. Charles's own proposition, that happiness derives from honor, parodies the examples of Erasmus's Folly.[44]

The second day, like the first, draws on traditional humanist sources for support—on Aristotle, Plutarch, Livy, Pliny, Ovid, Seneca, and the Greek Anthology—as well as on the more recent work of Boccaccio and John Heywood himself. Peter, arguing for love as the basis of happiness, invokes the spirit of Florentine Neoplatonism by urging the goodness of soul and the love of friends (sig. H3; 46). Noticing the startling absence of the love of God in Peter's argument, More suspends judgment for the first time in *Il Moro,* asking instead to hear the remaining declamations. Alexander argues that humanist reason defines knowledge as the greatest happiness (sigs. I8v–K2v; 58–59), Leonard proposes that everything provides happiness at one time or another (sigs. K3–K4; 59–60), and Paul claims that because happiness is infinite no finite means can guarantee it (sigs. K5–K7; 61–62).[45] This last argument is grievously pompous, setting the stage for More's subsequent reply. Although keenly aware of the limitations of language (sig. G3v; 40), More sets forth happiness as that contentment based on the reasoning of one's own needs followed by resting the mind and soul in the contemplation of God. More's position silently corrects and complements all the arguments preceding his, bringing the discussion to an end that is both intellectually and aesthetically satisfying. In addition, More has confirmed Charles's sense of the humanists' community, Peter's need to love, and Alexander's praise of reason, moving concerns of *Il Cortegiano* into closer proximity with the English Christian humanism the historic More had come to represent for Catholics like Heywood and Protestants like Lyly.

"In Heywood's dialogue," Deakins writes, "seriousness and lightness are held in perfect suspension, and this juxtaposition of opposed qualities creates the balance that emerges as More's most salient characteristic. More loves life, but he does not value it unduly" (p. xiii). For Ellis Heywood as for John Lyly, such balance incorporates both mind and body, thought and deed. "Et qui si tacque il S. T. Moro," Heywood concludes,

lasciando nelli animi di chi l'ascoltarono una grandissima ammiratione, per uedergli in che modo cō queste parole, a punto corrispodeva la uita di chi le proferiua.

And here More stopped, leaving a great admiration in the souls of those who listened to him when they saw how exactly his life corresponded to the words he spoke. [Sig. M2; 70]

Il Moro employs the triadic structure we have seen so common to humanist poetics by which both sides of a debate are reconciled, but it does so by earning the resolution through a severe testing of many of the principles on which humanist thought rests: Heywood and More win their way, as Lyly wishes his reader to do, weighing the strictly balanced halves of *Euphues,* to a *figura* of the perfect humanist within an academy of courtiers.[46]

Il Moro is a pioneering work of humanist fiction in England and the most important predecessor to Lyly, although it lacks the originality and complexity of both *Il Cortegiano* and *Euphues.* The other noteworthy imitation of Castiglione, Edmund Tilney's *A briefe and plesant discourse of duties in Mariage, called the Flower of Friendshippe* (1568), is a minor piece of fiction that nevertheless has a unique charm. The occasion reported is a symposium at the Lady Julia's house before two respected humanists, "*M. Ludouic Viues,* and an olde Gentleman called M. *Erasmus*" (sig. A4v), where Master Pedro di Luxan

wel remembred how *Boccace* & Countie *Baltizar* with others recoūted many proper deuises for exercise, both pleasant, & profitable, which, quoth he, were vsed in ye courts of Italie, and some much like to them, are practised at this day in the English court, wherein is not onely delectable, but pleasure ioyned with profite, and exercise of the wyt. [sig. A5]

The simplicity of Tilney's imitation is most appealing; the book is evenly divided between Master Pedro's instructive oration for husbands and the balancing advice for women by Lady Julia. Lord Pedro's opening remarks are Italianate—he questions whether qualities of beauty, wealth, virtue, or lineage make the best wife—but very soon he is concerned with other issues that (as in Gascoigne's later work) had come to be associated with the English Reformation—such issues as adultery, dicing, gaming, brawling, and drunkenness (sigs. B8v–C1). His concluding counsel, "the better to nourishe, and mayntayne thys *Flower*" of marriage (sig. C2v), is a fundamental tenet of humanism, a man's "education of his Children" (sig. C2v). Lord Pedro's plainspoken discussion of virtue conquers his earlier tendencies toward a more courtly presentation; and Lady Julia is likewise characterized by her rhetoric: it is florid, repetitive, and wandering. Only near the close of her confirmatio does she list a wife's requisite qualities (shamefastness, obedience, loyalty) and responsibilities (a well-governed home, skill at needlework, cooking): "thereby, she shall enlarge ye *Flower of Friendship* betwene hir & hir husband, whose face must be hir dayly looking glasse, wherein she ought to be always prying, to see whē he is merie, when sad, when content, and when discōtent, wherto she must alwayes frame hir owne countenance" (sig. E4v).[47] Her understanding of a married couple mirroring each other, as one half of Tilney's perfectly balanced work inversely images the other half, foreshadows Lyly's definition of the friendship between Euphues and Philautus (sig. D1v; 1:197), and it is difficult to believe that this work of humanist poetics, which turns conversation to declamatory modes of anatomizing virtue, written by the man who bested Lyly in their rivalry for the Mastership of the Revels, was unknown to him.

Heywood and Tilney illustrate the serious fictive tradition of humanist poetics initiated by Castiglione, but there was also at least one parody in Philibert de Vienne's *Le Philosophe de court* (Lyons, 1547; Paris, 1548), translated by George North and published in London three years before *Euphues*. Virtually unknown today,[48] North's Lucianic *Philosopher of the Court* (1575) is a wonderful spoof. "I would assaye to become a good Orator," North's Philibert says, "you by importunate meane, haue cōstrained me to become a Philosopher" (sig. B2). The hoax that follows is a parody of Cicero's *De Officiis* 1: "Our new and morall *Philosophie,*" Philibert continues, "may thus be defined: A certaine & sound iudgment, howe to liue according to the good grace and fashion of the Court" (sig. C5). Suitable performance rather than self-knowledge is for Philibert the end of true learning, and virtue is that which passes for fashion in the court's opinion.

The source for Philibert's encomium moriae is Lucian's *De Parasito* (The Parasite). Beginning with a sophistical confusion of the nature of good and evil (sig. C4v), *The Philosopher of the Court* is an increasingly expanded jest in which distended counsel and perverted terminology constitute the essential means. Much of the work is taken up with a confirmatio, for instance, which deflates the four classical virtues of wisdom (or prudence), justice, magnanimity, and temperance.[49] He writes of the first of these,

> Prudence ... consisteth in a skilful iudgement and knowledge of true things ... As of Musicke, the playing on the Lute, the Citterne, the Citrone, the Harpe, the Cornet, the Flute, the Virginals, the Viall, and other sweete musical instruments. Also to daunce all maner of daūces. .... The Arte to compose deuices, Posies, pleasant purposes, Songs, Sonets, and Baliats, or amorous Lamentacions, in prose, verse, or ryme, very pitifull and in Tragicall manner, as beseemes the languishing paine of a seruant beeing in displeasure, and euill rewarded of his mistres: Further, it is singular good, to haue some pretie sprinckled iudgement in the commō

places and practizes of all the liberall sciences, chopt vp in hotchpot togither, out of the whiche we may still help ourselues in talke, with apte deuises. . . . Also to haue store of histories, to passe the time meet for any company, and with the more assured cunning to couche our credite, it shall not be amisse to enterlace our discourses with certeine suddaine lyes and inuentions of oure owne forging. [Sigs. D5–D5v]

For the philosopher in Philibert's version of Urbino, the ideal of prudence allows moderation to degenerate into mediocrity, courtly behavior to be redefined as dissimulation, and courtly speech to become pompous humbug.[50]

Philibert next partitions justice. Distributive justice "is sayd to be the theater or place of humaine felowship," the courtier's liberality exercised best as a generosity "vnder the which all people are boūd & ioyned one with the other" (sig. E3). A salient characteristic of Thomas More's thought and More's characterization in *Il Moro* is thus undermined. And communicative justice is even more boldly demeaned as the ability to cheat and get away with it (sig. E6v). As for the remaining virtues "of the Auncientes" (sig. C7), courtly magnanimity is well-executed courage and anger; Cicero's love of family as the basis for noble generosity is now an assertive self-authority. "Abeunt studia in mores," he proposes; "Oure studies and affections are transformed into manners" (sig. G7v). Because courtiers must judge each other on the basis of bodily graces and gestures and by facial expressions, these are used to deceive men and to hide imperfections (sigs. G7v–G8). Courtly actions constitute one splendid masquerade. As a consequence, temperance must mean accommodation. "Temperance entreth our harts, & mollifieth all the parts of it, & cōstrayneth it not to talk euill, or be offended at any thing though the same be imperfect, in suche sorte, that partlye it dissembleth, and partlie it applyeth, and obeyeth to all these circumstances" (sig. H4v). Classical virtues are thus reformulated by Philibert, adjusted into finely tuned arrangements he calls honesty and "good Grace" (sigs. H5v–I6v). Philibert, like Erasmus and, on occasion, More, portrays a world upside-down, mocking Renaissance court philosophy by insinuating the need to set cockeyed perspective straight once more.

The wit of *The Philosopher of the Court,* like the wit of Euphues before Lucilla, is self-reflexive, for Philibert as a teacher is transformed into the greatest sophist of all. His own work amply qualifies him, for it is (in its casuistry) all form and no substance. In pursuit of deception, he attempts to deceive us. The parody of Castiglione is always surfacing, too, in his open praise of exemplary Italian courts, in the redefinition of sprezzatura as straightforward deception, and in the translation of dissimulation as the true meaning of *grazia*. By forsaking the debates of *Il Cortegiano* for a monologic declamation regarding courtly hypocrisy, Philibert undermines the motivations of courtly behavior and degrades courtly manners. Those who would serve the prince serve only themselves and in their hypocrisy register their own debasement. The high spirits that bubble through North's often pedestrian translation supply further proof that Philibert's outrageous exposé is meant to be the most extravagant of parodies. How appropriate that George North should dedicate such a sham mirror for courtiers to Christopher Hatton who, Sir John Perrot tells us, "came thither [to court] as a private Gentleman of the *Innes of Court* in a *Maske;* and for his activity, and person, which was tall, and proportionable, taken into [the queen's] favor."[51]

Yet, incredibly, North himself seems to have taken Philibert seriously. In his dedication to Hatton, "Captaine of the Queenes Maiesties *Garde, and Gentleman of hir* highnesse priuie Chamber" (sig. A2), North commends his translation as "both floures and fruite (not to supply the scarcetie, but to encrease the plentie and pleasaunte purposes) of Courtly Philosophie" (sig. A2v). He offers his treatise as a useful manual, testifying to it as another Englished Castiglione.

> Spread (I humbly praye) the gladsome beames of your fauourable and well liking cheere vpon it: so shall you render to the reader my Author much betterd, make him of other gentlemen Courtiers more accepted, my pen to further trauell encouraged, and my selfe in this enterprise most glad and pleased. [Sigs. A2v–A3]

Occasionally North tones down his original, and, less frequently, he omits uncommonly strong passages of irony. What remains is the sort of handbook Euphues and Lucilla might take seriously when they attempt to deceive each other for personal, lustful ends. Philibert, viewed unironically, sanctions the hypocrisy Euphues and Lucilla make characteristic of Naples, but seen satirically, Philibert's treatise exposes their foolishness and implies their downfall. Doubtless Lyly knew this satirical act of imitatio; surely he would understand its sly wit. For Philibert returns us, once more, to Lyly's initial image of wax.

> The Gentleman Courtyer is . . . plyant like waxe, redie to receyue any honest or frendly impression. For if it be needefull to laughe, hee reioyceth: If to be sad, he lowreth: If to be angry, he frowneth: If to feede, he eateth: If to faste, he pyneth. And to conclude, he is ready to doe whatsoeuer it be, according to the humors and complexions of his felowship and Courtly companie, althoughe his affections are cleane contrary. [Sigs. I4v–I5]

Given Philibert's broad irony, everything including humanism can bear the brunt of his satire. Thus Socrates "Himselfe doeth serue vs for example, for although he was euer like vnto himself, constant and not variable, and desirous not to be seene other than he seemed: yet was he the greatest dissembler in the worlde" (sig. H7v). The humanist at court is the new *un*wise fool, the early Folly redivivus. "If the meane be good," Philibus claims, "he that deceyueth his companion most cunningly and subtlely, is most wyse" (sig. H8). And the one who is truly foolish is the academic— the humanist scholar such as William or George Lily,

> oure maysters of Artes, who haue mouths to kisse, armes to embrace, and faces to countenance, & can do all this well: yet were it straunge to see one of them in his old girded gowne furred with white, his burnt pantofles, & his night cap of freese, to fall on dauncing & sporting amōg fayre Ladies. . . . neyther his wanton looke, or smiling cheare, his humble curtesie, nor lowe embracing, (though they would suffer it) would serue him amōg them. . . . And why so? Bicause those reuerēces are not wel pleased & beseeme not a man of iudgemente and knowledge, too please such companie. For if hee did, hee woulde bee otherwise apparelled, and muster in gallanter manner: hee woulde frame a courtlie countenance, . . . and vnderstand nothing but mery & gladsome purposes. And thus finely furnished with his little Page in place of his poore & ragged scholler, he might peraduenture bee welcome. [Sigs. C5v–C6]

Philibert reveals how bankrupt humanist counsel to the prince had become since More's eloquent plea in *Utopia* 1; *The Philosopher of the Court* finally—and convincingly, if we may take the humorless Harvey's reaction as typical[52]—displays the indifference many in John Lyly's generation had for works like *Il Moro* and the *Flower of Friendshippe,* their silent agreement on the severely limited utility of the humanist education once promulgated by William Lily and Erasmus.

Confronted with both the serious and the satirical work deriving from Castiglione, whose symmetrical style had once so cautiously and carefully balanced the real and the ideal at Urbino, Lyly is concerned, too, with the signification of word and simile and the possible duplicity of idea and image. Long sequences of *isocolon* and *parison* are deliberate strategies by which antitheses within a single grammatical structure insist on our *re*conception, through the act of triangulation, of a meaning that Lyly feels able only to imply; long stockpilings of similes often through their mere headiness of creation and exaggeration imply Lyly's strong if witty dubiety regarding their truth, their usefulness, their very significance. There is much of the high spirit of Lyly's inventive wit here, to be sure, but the very possibilities he takes up to employ or parody his grandfather's own basic grammar show us how vulnerable all words are for him.[53] Attracted to the very sounds and rhythms of English syntax, imaginative and playful to an astonishing degree, as a humanist Lyly was also deeply troubled by an ubiquitous sophistry. "Heere you may see Gentlemen, the falsehood in felowship, the fraude in friendshippe, the paynted sheath with the leaden daunger," he admonishes us in *Euphues,* "the faire wordes that make fooles faine" (sig. F4v; 1:215). The "singuler eloquence and braue composition" for which Webbe praises Lyly, then, are not merely the syntactic equivalencies for a humanist doctrine of moderation (as the art of triangulation always is with the humanist writer of fiction) but necessities demanded by the casuistry Lyly witnessed in the applications of his beloved humanism in his own time.

But Lyly's advocacy of humanism should not surprise us, for John Lyly, by family achievement and likely through family expectation, was *the* most conspicuous humanist of the third generation in England. "His family uniquely characterizes its time," Albert Feuillerat reminds us; "Apparently from modest background, by his single and absolute attachment to the cause of letters, he came to achieve the most enviable notoriety" ("La famille de Lyly est singulièrement caractéristique de son époque. . . . D'origine vraisemblablement très modeste, par son seul et absolu attachement à la cause des lettres, elle finit par atteindre à une notoriété des plus enviables.")[54] John Lyly's grandfather William Lily, godson of his namesake William Grocyn, was England's pioneer teacher of Greek, a central figure of the initial English humanist movement. Although the only image of Lily now extant is the stained-glass window in the southwest bay of the hall of Christ Church, Oxford, where he completes a sequence of windows portraying Linacre, Erasmus, Wolsey, More, Surrey, William Warham, and Colet, he arrived in Oxford before the founding of Christ Church, attending Magdalen College as his son and grandson were to do. There, in the company of Linacre, Grocyn (then Divinity Reader), Thomas Starkey, Cardinal Pole, and perhaps Colet, Lily steeped himself, like Eubulus, in "grammatical and poetical and other humane arts," not only for his own benefit but to prepare himself to be a teacher or grammar master in Magdalen.[55] When his course at Magdalen was completed, William Lily (again like Euphues) furthered his humanist education by taking the Grand Tour from 1488 to 1492, following the example of Grocyn. First he made a pilgrimage to Jerusalem, then an unusually dangerous journey; on his return he stopped at Rhodes to study Greek and at Rome and Venice to study Ciceronian Latin under Giovanni Sulpicio and Julius Pomponius Laetus Sabinus. Later, in Rome, Lily studied once more alongside Linacre as well as Colet, Warham, and Christopher

Bambridge; when in time they returned to England, the group expanded to include Thomas More. Lily probably taught More some Greek; they shared lodgings for a period at the Charterhouse; and they competed in translating Greek epigrams into Latin.

Lily's historic fame, however, rests on his post as Colet's first High Master of St. Paul's School, London, and on his grammar. The post of High Master called for the sort of man Roger Ascham would characterize in *The Scholemaster* (1570) as *euphues* (well-endowed)—he must be "whole in body, honest and virtuous, and learned in the good and clean Latin literature and also in Greek, if such may be gotten."[56] Lily's qualifications are verified by Polydore Virgil, who calls Lily "a man such as Horace speaks of *integer vitae scelerisque purus*," whole of life and pure of guilt.[57] Lily taught at St. Paul's from 1510 until his death from the plague in 1523. During that period he also wrote a syntax which, revised by Erasmus and combined with Colet's accidence, was published sometime before 1527. The purpose of the Lily–Colet text points, directly and pragmatically, to the training of John Lyly as a boy in Canterbury and of Euphues in Athens: grammar is viewed as secondary to literature, Latin being the language "wherin is conteyned a great treasorye of wysedome and knowledge."[58] The text is also—with deliberate resonances on the part of John Lyly—a source of *Euphues*. The moral *sententiae* that frame the fiction, introduced by Eubulus at the outset and Euphues at the close, are taken from those precepts labeled "Godly Lessons for Chyldren" that follow the eight parts of speech in the Lily–Colet grammar and so validate this early fruit of Tudor humanism. John Lyly employs such precepts as

> It is the fyrst poynte of wysedome, to knowe thy selfe.
> Feare of the Lorde, is the begynnyng of wysedome.
> There is no manne that synneth not.
> If we saye we be fautelesse we deceyue our selues, and truthe is not in us.
> Se not whā thou giuest, haue an eie whā thou takest.
> Pleasure is the bayte of myschiefes.[59]

This "great treasorye," soon known simply as "Lily's grammar," was required in all Tudor grammar schools by Henry VIII's royal proclamation of 1542; subsequent proclamations of Edward VI, Mary, and Elizabeth I made Lily's name—and so John Lyly's name, too—a household word.

But William Lily did not provide his grandson with the only humanist model he was expected to emulate. Lily was succeeded in the coveted post at St. Paul's School by his son-in-law, John Lyly's uncle John Ritwyse, whom Anthony à Wood calls the most distinguished grammarian of his day in England.[60] Ritwyse amended Lily's poem on the gender of nouns and added a vocabulary to it for succeeding generations of grammars; he was also the first English author of record to write a school play—his *Dido* was performed before Wolsey sometime between 1522 and 1528 and again before Elizabeth I in 1564.[61] Ritwyse was followed as High Master by William Lily's daughter Dionysia, whose marriage to the school's usher James Jacob produced for John Lyly aunts and uncles whose names, such as Scholastica and Polydore, are half-suggestive of Eubulus and Philautus. But members of the second Lily generation remained, despite their several noteworthy achievements, distinctly in the shadow of William Lily's reputation. William's eldest son George followed his father to Magdalen but went down without a degree; by 1534 he was with Cardinal Pole's learned household in Padua.[62] Later George Lily became a canon at Canterbury and the author of several learned books; he "inherited the thirst for learning," Morris W. Croll writes, "and under the protection of Reginald Pole built himself a reputation as antiquarian, historian, and geographer."[63] John Lyly's father, Peter, considerably less distinguished, was nevertheless in time awarded the living as prebendary and registrar at Canterbury under Elizabeth I's archbishop, Matthew Parker.

John Lyly's strongly humanist background, then, was something he could not have escaped even if he had wanted to. "Tous ces instincts—héritage de la race—avaient encore été fortifiés par le milieu où Lyly avait grandi," Feuillerat sums.

> Le maison du *Registrar* était certainement fréquentée par les dignitaires de l'archevêché, tous gens instruits et qui, en vertu de leur état, faisaient profession de savoir. Leurs manières, leur langage avient dû envelopper l'enfant de cette atmosphère chaude, câline et prenante, particulière aux gens d'église à quelque confession qu'ils appartiennent, et continuer l'oeuvre du sang.

> All these instincts—the inheritance of his stock—had been further fortified by the environment in which Lyly had grown up. The Registrar's house was certainly frequented by the dignitaries of the archbishopric, all of them educated men who by virtue of their condition made a show of their knowledge. Their style and language must have wrapped the child up in that warm atmosphere which is peculiar to church people of whatever creed, and have carried on the influence of his birth. [John Lyly, p. 21]

John Lyly was taught by his father, or a local tutor in Canterbury, or at the Queen's School connected with the cathedral—his background similar to that of Stephen Gosson and Christopher Marlowe, his contemporaries from neighboring wards of the city—and then, at the age of fifteen, he followed his grandfather and uncle to Magdalen College, Oxford. At university he doubtless heard John Rainolds, the Greek Reader at Corpus Christi, and notes from those lectures, which displayed to Lyly the features of *isocolon, paromoion,* and *parison* in which the symmetry of euphuism is grounded,[64] may also have led directly to parts of the orations in *Euphues* and *Euphues and his England,* while one or another *propositio* formulated for university sophisters at their disputations may have resulted, without much change, in the debates on nature and nurture, love and lust, which are incorporated into his fiction. Certainly the line between Oxford disputations and the debates in *Euphues* is a thin one. Here too Lyly renewed his acquaintance with the work of Plutarch and Pliny, Ovid and Cicero, on which his own books so heavily rely. After his Oxford degree he went a step farther to be incorporated M.A. at Cambridge, eventually signing his books (as Robert Greene was soon to do) *utriusque Academiae in artibus magister* (master of arts at both universities).

That Lyly continued to pursue a life of the mind after graduation is amply demonstrated by his request of William Cecil, Lord Burghley, to intercede in his behalf for a teaching post at Magdalen, "quo in eorum societatem te duce possim obrepere" ("so that under your auspices I may be quietly admitted as a fellow there"), pointing to his M.A. at Cambridge, and noting Magdalen, Oxford, as Burghley's old college.[65] Apparently he did not win the position: the next we hear of him he has settled in London at the Savoy, the residence of the earl of Oxford, Burghley's son-in-law. Other evidence suggests that he soon became part of that humanist household of Burghley's that, by 1580, most closely revived More's former residence at Chelsea.[66] "Here, even more than at Oxford," Croll contends, "Lyly must have felt the weight of his grandfather's name; and here he began his literary career, not as a dependent of courtiers, but as the successor of Ascham, to whom the task of carrying the discipline of humanism to a new generation had fallen as by natural choice" (*Style,* pp. 246–47). What is boldest in Lyly's fiction, then—and what forcefully demonstrates the importance of fiction as a *genre* to the Tudors—is that once we are reminded of his background we see how the insistent anatomization of the ideas and style of humanism constitute a critically astringent examination of the author's own roots: with Lyly humanist fiction for the first time openly approaches cultural autobiography.

The *donnée* for *Euphues* is taken from Ascham's major humanist treatise,[67] widely current when Lyly left Canterbury for Magdalen because it summed Ascham's practices with such pupils as the queen herself. This descendant of distinguished humanists himself turned to a leading humanist: *The Scholemaster* (1570) is the procatarctic cause, the immediate source, of Lyly's title. Following *Republic 5* (455B), Ascham declares *euphuia* to be the first quality of the mind. He defines it as that [which] is apte by goodnes of witte, and appliable by readiness of will, to learning, hauing all other qualities of the minde and partes of the bodie, that must an other day serue learning, not trobled, māgled, and halfed, but sounde, whole, full, & hable to do their office: as, a tong, not stamering, or ouer hardlie drawing forth wordes, but plaine, and redie to deliuer the meaning of the minde: a voice, not softe, weake, piping, womannishe, but audible, stronge, and manlike: a countenance, not werishe [sickly-looking] and crabbed, but faire and cumlie: a personage, not wretched and deformed, but taule and goodlie: for surelie, a cumlie countenance, with a goodlie stature, geueth credit to learning, and authoritie to the person. [Sigs. D3v–D4]

This is also the propositio of *Euphues* and the dispositio of Lyly's fiction. "In writing this booke," Ascham tells us in the preface, "I haue had earnest respecte to three speciall pointes, trothe of Religion, honestie in liuing, right order in learning" (sig. B4). Reversing the order (as the simplest form of creative reliance and the most obvious sort of homage), we have the precise arrangement of topics in *Euphues*.

Once we place this Senecan model alongside Lyly's fiction, correspondences appear not singly but in battalions. Ascham's summing of Aristotelian psychology resonates in Lyly's plot and characterization:

There be in man two speciall thinges: Mans will, mans mynde. Where will inclineth to goodnes, the mynde is bent to troth: Where will is caried from goodnes to vanitie, the mynde is sone drawne from troth to false opinion. And so, the readiest way to entangle the mynde with false doctrine, is first to intice the will to wanton liuyng. [Sig. (I3) misnumbered I2]

Enlarging on this elsewhere, Ascham's thought and style (combining Gorgian figure and Ciceronian periodicity) resemble those of Eubulus.

Moreouer commonlie, men, very quicke of witte, be also, verie light of conditions: and thereby, very readie of disposition, to be caried ouer quicklie, by any light cumpanie, to any riot and vnthriftines when they be yonge: and therfore seldome, either honest of life, or riche in liuing, when they be olde. [Sig. D1]

For Ascham—as Lyly knew—a Euphues is by nature and age especially susceptible.

From seauentene to seauen and twentie, that wise men shold carefullie see the steppes of yougthe surelie staide by good order, ih that most slipperie tyme: and speciallie in the Courte, a place moste dangerous for yougthe to liue in, without great grace, good regarde, and diligent looking to [Sigs. H2v–H3]

John Lyly was that age then too. Ascham's classical metaphors are also identical to those Lyly uses—"New wax is best for printyng: new claie, fittest for working: new shorne woll, aptest for sone and surest dying: new fresh flesh, for good and durable salting" (sig. E3)—and his amplification of pseudo-Plutarch is identical to Lyly's varying copia.

Additionally, the philosophy of *The Scholemaster,* as an epitome of the Tudor humanists' best thinking, suggests the *plot* of *Euphues.*

> If will, and witte, by farder age, be ouer allured frō innocencie, delited in vaine sightes, filed with foull taulke, crooked with wilfulnesse, hardned with stubburnesse, and let louse to disobedience, surelie it is hard with ientlenesse, but vnpossible with seuere crueltie, to call them backe to good frame, againe. For, where the one, perchance maie bend it, the other shall surelie breake it: and so in stead of some hope, leaue an assured desperation, and shamelesse contempt of all goodnesse, the fardest pointe in all mischief, as *Xenophon* doth most trewlie and most wittelie marke. [Sigs. E3–E3v]

The precept Roger Ascham derives from the *Cyropaedia* looks forward to Eublus's advice in Naples and the life of the student in Euphues' Athens. "Learning teacheth more in one yeare than experience in twentie: And learning teacheth safelie, when experience maketh mo miserable then wise" (sig. G2). Thus Ascham's position condenses the advice, too, of the later Euphues to Philautus in the letters of precept that balance the narrative of the first half of *Euphues.* For theory and experience here, despite Ascham's attacks on Italy, are symbiotic in *The Scholemaster* as they are in *Euphues.*

> Som other, hauing better nature, but lesse witte, (for ill commonlie, haue ouer moch witte) do not vtterlie dispraise learning, but they saie, that without learning, common experience, knowledge of all facions, and haunting all companies, shall worke in yougthe, both wisdome, and habilitie, to execute anie weightie affaire. Surelie long experience doth proffet moch, but moste, and almost onelie to him (if we meene honest affaires) that is diligently before instructed with preceptes of well doinge. For good precepts of learning, be the eyes of the minde, to looke wiselie before a man, which waie to go right, and which not. [Sig. G2]

This is the context for the well-known attack on things Italianate in *The Scholemaster;* and Ascham's dichotomy between old "speciallie honored" (sig. H3) Rome and a new Rome known for "sinne . . . lust and vanitie" (sig. H3v) is, in the singular time plane of narrative, transformed by Lyly into Athens and Naples. As Ascham advances two views of Italy and various English imitators, so he sees the Grand Tour as potentially help-ful—if Athenian principles are held to in Lyly's derivative metaphor.

And yet is not *Vlysses* commended, so much, nor so oft, in *Homere*, because he was πολύτροπος, that is, skilfull in many mēs maners and facions, as bicause he was πολυμῆτις, that is, wise in all purposes, & ware in all places: which wisedome and warenes will not serue neither a traueler, except *Pallas* be alwayes at his elbow, that is Gods speciall grace from heauen, to kepe him in Gods feare, in all his doynges, in all his ieorneye. [Sig. H4]

In *The Scholemaster,* too, the travel that tests the precepts of learning leads to a faith in things unseen and occasions for the grace of God.

Ascham's treatise stands in relation to *Euphues* as Plutarch's *Life of Lycurgus* stands to More's *Utopia;* it is a Senecan model. But More draws his poetics not from Plutarch but from Plato, and from the *Republic, Timaeus,* and *Critias* specifically, whereas Lyly's poetics is taken from Plutarch. We know he used "The Education of Children" for "Euphues and his Ephoebus"; it is likely he also knew Plutarch's companion essay, "How to Read Poetry," that follows it. There we find a defense of poetry that makes possible *Euphues* and so serves as its proegumenic, or more distant, cause. "Philosophers . . . for admonition and instruction, use examples taken from known facts," Plutarch advances; "but the poets, accomplish the same result by inventing actions of their own imagination, and by recounting mythical tales," or at least allegorical names.[68] In addition,

Poetry, inasmuch as it has an imitative basis, employs embellishment and glitter in dealing with the actions and characters that form its groundwork, yet it does not forsake the semblance of truth, since imitation depends upon plausibility for its allurement. This is the reason why the imitation that does not show an utter disregard of the truth brings out, along with the actions, indications of both vice and virtue commingled. . . . Now since this is so, let the young man, when we set him to reading poems, not be prepossessed with any such opinions about those good and great names, as, for instance, that the men were wise and honest, consummate kings, and their standards of all virtue and uprightness. For he will be greatly injured if he approves everything, and is in a state of wonderment over it, but resents nothing, refusing even to listen or accept the opinion of him who, on the contrary, censures persons that do and say [the opposite] things. . . . but rather let him cherish the belief that poetry is an imitation of character and lives, and of men who are not perfect or spotless or unassailable in all respects, but pervaded by emotions, false opinions, and sundry forms of ignorance, who yet through inborn goodness frequently change their ways for the better. For if the young man is so trained, and his understanding so framed, that he feels elation and a sympathetic enthusiasm over noble words and deeds, and an aversion and repugnance for the mean, such training will render his perusal of poetry harmless. [25B–26B]

Lyly's witty and playful manner, then, is part of the educative function of *Euphues;* we as readers are placed *in Euphues' position,* forced to pick our way among the alluring ideas and elaborate style to set apart once more commingled vice and virtue. The process of reading becomes its own downward (or upward) path to wisdom.

As the connective threads back through Ascham to Plutarch show, Lyly's mind is essentially interested in a humanist poetics. But it is no less essentially rhetorical in its concerns: as More with the syncretic mind of the creative humanist synthesizes both Plato and Plutarch, so Lyly's fiction has its antecedent poetics in the remarks of both Plutarch and Isocrates. The latter's high praise for rhetoric is central to one of his works best known to the Tudors, the oration "To Nicocles" where he remarks that "Through [speech] we educate the ignorant and appraise the wise; for the power to speak well is taken as the surest index of a sound understanding, and discourse which is true and lawful and just is the outward image of a good and faithful soul."[69] To illustrate this, Isocrates describes the sort of soliloquy that is crucial to Lyly's portrayal of Lucilla and Euphues.

> With this faculty we both contend against others on matters which are open to dispute and seek light for ourselves on things which are unknown; for the same arguments which we use in persuading others when we speak in public, we employ also when we deliberate in our own thoughts; and, while we call eloquent those who are able to speak before a crowd, we regard as sage those who most skilfully debate their problems in their own minds. And, if there is need to speak in brief summary of this power, we shall find that none of the things which are done with intelligence take place without the help of speech, but that in all our actions as well as in all our thoughts speech is our guide, and is most employed by those who have the most wisdom. [8–9]

Such passages are instructive, for they remind us that for the Tudors Isocrates was a humanist resource first because he was a philosopher and secondly because he was an eloquent rhetorician, his moving defense of both education and oratory in the *Antidosis* (especially 30 ff.) a vital and seminal text. William Baldwin is representative of Tudor understanding when he remarks in *A treatise of Morall Phylosophie* (1547) that Isocrates "was of suche fame for his learnĩg, namely for moral Philosophy, that he semed to many rather a god thã a man" ([1550 ed.] sig. H3v), and Richard Rainolde, in his *Foundacion of Rhetorike,* praises Isocrates as his one example of *chria,* using a Tudor commonplace about the early Greek sophist as part of his amplification:

The eloquēce of Isocrates was so famous, that Aristotle the chief
Philosopher, enuied his vertue & praise therin: Demosthenes also, who
emong the Grecians chieflie excelled, learned his eloquence, of the
Oracions whiche Isocrates wrote, to many mightie and puisaunt princes
and kinges, do shewe his wisedome, & copious eloquēce, as to Demonicus
the king to Nicoles, Euagoras, against Philip the king of the Macedoniās,
by his wisedome and counsaill, the Senate and vniuersal state of Athens was
ruled, & the commons and multitude thereby in euery part florished:
chieflie what counsaill, what wisedome, what learnyng might bee required,
in any man of high fame and excellencie: that same was aboundantly in
Isocrates. [Sig. E1][70]

Both Baldwin and Rainolde echo their master Cicero, whose praise of
Isocrates appears throughout the *Orator* and *De Oratore:* "magnus orator
et perfectus magister" (a great orator and an ideal teacher), Cicero calls
him in the *Brutus* (8.32).

Matter and manner thus interpenetrate in *Euphues:* torn and divided
speeches expose the torn and divided minds of Lyly's characters. And it is
in Isocrates that we see repeated the absolute inseparability of the search
for defining virtue and the best of all prose styles. The *propositio* in the
"hypothesis" of the work then attributed to Isocrates known as "To
Demonicus" is typical:

Only those who have travelled this road in life have been able in the true
sense to attain to virtue—that possession which is the grandest and the
most enduring in the world. For beauty is spent by time or withered by
disease; wealth ministers to vice rather than to nobility of soul, affording
means for indolent living and luring the young to pleasure; strength, in
company with wisdom, is , indeed, an advantage, but without wisdom it
harms more than it helps its possessors, and while it sets off the bodies of
those who cultivate it, yet it obscures the care of the soul. But virtue, when
it grows up with us in our hearts without alloy, ils the one possession which
abides with us in old age; it is better than riches and more serviceable than
high birth; it makes possible what is for others impossible; it supports with
fortitude that which is fearful to the multitude; and it considers sloth a
disgrace and toil of honour. This it is easy to learn from the labours of
Heracles and the exploits of Theseus, whose excellence of character has
impressed upon their exploits so clear a stamp of glory that not even endless
time can cast oblivion upon their achievements. [5–8][71]

The Isocratean "Demonicus" is full of the aphoristic phrases that remind
us of William Lily's grammar, and of *Euphues.*

Be fond not of violent mirth, nor harbour presumption of speech; for the
one is folly, the other madness. [15]

If you love knowledge, you will be a master of knowledge. What you have come to know, preserve by exercise; what you have not learned, seek to add to your knowledge; for it is as reprehensible to hear a profitable saying and not grasp it as to be offered a good gift by one's friends and not accept it. [18]

Guard more faithfully the secret which is confided to you than the money which is entrusted to your care; for good men ought to show that they hold their honour more trustworthy than an oath. Consider that you owe it to yourself no less to mistrust bad men than to put your trust in the good. [22]

Prove your friends by means of the misfortunes of life and of their fellowship in your perils; for as we try gold in the fire, so we come to know our friends when we are in misfortune. [25]

Cultivate the thoughts of an immortal by being lofty of soul, but of a mortal by enjoying in due measure the good things which you possess. [32]

Consider that nothing in human life is stable; for then you will not exult overmuch in prosperity, nor grieve overmuch in adversity. [42]

As secular wisdom of a high order that looks forward to later Roman stoicism, Isocrates' moral commentary is as unswerving in its commitment to wisdom and moderation as his thoughtful expression is without exception eloquent. "I hold that man to be wise who is able by his powers of conjecture to arrive generally at the best course," he sums, "and I hold that man to be a philosopher who occupies himself with the studies from which he will most quickly gain that kind of insight."[72]

Isocrates was also known to the Greeks and Tudors as the man who promoted and popularized the highly schematic prose style of Gorgias of Leontini—the self-consciously splendid style based in figures of balance and sound combined with a figure that brings together oppositions and builds verbal patterns from antitheses: in short, the syntactic patterns of *Euphues.* It is this deliberate style of eloquence that Cicero honors (*De Oratore* 2.22.94; *Orator* 13.40) and Quintilian has in mind when he remarks that Cicero's own prose style imitates Isocrates' (*Institutio Oratoria* 10.1.108). Cicero also pays considerable attention to placing and describing his master at *Orator* 52–53.

Gorgias autem avidior est generis eius et his festivitatibus—sic enim ipse censet—insolentius abutitur; quas Isocrates, cum tamen audivisset adulescens in Thessalia senem iam Gorgiam, moderatius temperavit. Quin etiam se ipse tantum quantum aetate procedebat—prope enim centum confecit annos—relaxarat a nimia necessitate numerorum, quod declarat in eo libro quem ad Philippum Macedonem scripsit, cum iam admodum esset senex; in quo dicit sese minus iam servire numeris quam solitus esset. Ita non modo superiores sed etiam se ipse correxerat.

But Gorgias is too fond of this style, and uses these "embroideries" (his own word for it) too boldly. All these Isocrates used with still greater restraint, in spite of the fact that he was a young man when he had studied with the aged Gorgias in Thessaly. Moreover, Isocrates himself as he grew older—he lived to be nearly a hundred—had gradually relaxed the extreme strictness of his rhythm, as he says in his address to Philip of Macedon, written in his ripe old age; in this he says that he was less attentive to rhythm than had been his custom. This indicates that he had corrected, not only his predecessors, but also himself. [176][73]

This care—combined with considerable sophistication—is what Isocrates himself continually advances. "It is my opinion," he writes in his *Panegyricus,* "that the study of oratory as well as the other arts would make the greatest advance if we should admire and honour, not those who make the first beginnings in their crafts, but those who are the most finished craftsmen in each, and not those who seek to speak on subjects on which no one has spoken before, but those who know how to speak as no one else could" (10).[74] For Isocrates as for Tudor grammar masters from William Lily onward, rhetoric was the center of the humane curriculum.

All intelligent people will agree with me that while many of those who have pursued philosophy have remained in private life, others, on the other hand, who have never taken lessons from any one of the sophists have become able orators and statesmen. For ability, whether in speech or in any other activity, is found in those who are well endowed by nature [*euphues*] and have been schooled by practical experience. Formal training makes such men more skilful and more resourceful in discovering the possibilities of a subject; for it teaches them to take from a readier source the topics which they otherwise hit upon in haphazard fashion. But it cannot fully fashion men who are without natural aptitude into good debaters or writers, although it is capable of leading them on to self-improvement and to a greater degree of intelligence on many subjects. ["Against the Sophists," 14–15][75]

The Gorgian rhetorical strategies subordinated to thought by Isocrates and imitated by Cicero were codified by Quintilian in his great books of style in the *Institutio.* This is especially true of the chapters that deal with amplification (8.4), *sententiae* (8.5), tropes (8.6), figures of thought (9.2), and figures of speech (9.3). Such use of patterned sound as the basis of an eloquent prose style is further conveyed to the Tudors through Thomas Wilson's *Arte of Rhetorique* (1553), where he pays considerable attention to *similiter desinens* and *similiter cadens,* while the *Ad Herennium,* which the Tudors took to be Cicero's, lends further authority to such figures, especially *isocolon, homoioptoton, homoioteleuton*, and *paronomasia* (4.20–22). It is this collocation of figures of thought *and* figures of speech that prompts John Hoskins to praise Lyly for his poetics of eloquence in *Directions for Speech and Style*.[76] It is also this sort of careful and elaborate writing that prompts Gabriel Harvey, in his annotations, to refer to Lyly's stylistic forebear who writes *The Scholemaster* as "Noster Isocrates," our Isocrates.[77] Wherever we turn, Ascham's humanist work seems to press in on Lyly's.

Once we understand this, however, it is the resilience of Lyly's mind, its restless inventiveness and its overall toughness, that most impresses us. One Senecan model is never enough for a wit as adept as his, and one object of reference never sufficiently imaginative. The more we read the works Lyly read alongside his grandfather's grammar, the more we realize how synthetic his mind is, how it builds by associations. Thus his poetic may be derived from Isocrates, but it also derives from Plutarch. Similarly, his Senecan original for the conceptualization of friendship embedded in the story of Euphues, Philautus, and Lucilla in which utility and pleasure ought to lead to goodness to be fruitful is from Aristotle's *Ethics*.

> There are accordingly three kinds of friendship, corresponding in number to the three lovable qualities; since a reciprocal affection, known to either party, can be based on each of the three, and when men love each other, they wish each other well in respect of the quality which is the ground of their friendship. Thus friends whose affection is based on utility do not love each other in themselves, but in so far as some benefit accrues to them from each other. And similarly with those whose friendship is based on pleasure: for instance, we enjoy the society of witty people not because of what they are in themselves, but because they are agreeable to us. . . . And therefore these friendships are based on an accident, since the friend is not loved for being what he is, but as affording some benefit or pleasure as the case may be. Consequently friendships of this kind are easily broken off, . . .
> The perfect form of friendship is that between the good, and those who resemble each other in virtue. For these friends wish each alike the other's good in respect of their goodness, and they are good in themselves; but it is those who wish the good of their friends for their friends' sake who are friends in the fullest sense, since they love each other for themselves and not accidentally.[78]

Lyly's plot, however, a sequel to the opening scene of *The Scholemaster*, realizes Cicero's *De Amicitia*, that grammar school chestnut for learning Ciceronian (and thereby Isocratean) style. There Cicero—at times following a Senecan model of his own in the witty, self-parodying Platonic dialogue *Lysias*—tells how friendships are formed:

> Quapropter a natura mihi videtur potius quam indigentia orta amicitia, applicatione magis animi cum quodam sensu amandi, quam cogitatione quantum illa res utilitatis esset habitura . . . si aliquem nacti sumus, cuius cum moribus et natura congruamus, quod in eo quasi lumen aliquod probitatis et virtutis perspicere videamur.

> Wherefore it seems to me that friendship springs rather from nature than from need, and from an inclination of the soul joined with a feeling of love rather than from calculation of how much profit the friendship is likely to afford . . . which arises when once we have met someone whose habits and character are congenial with our own; because in him we seem to behold, as it were, a sort of lamp of uprightness and virtue.[79]

And how they are fostered:

> Accedat huc suavitas quaedam oportet sermonum atque morum, haud-quaquam mediocre condimentum amicitiae. Tristitia autem et in omni re severitas habet illa quidem gravitatem, sed amicitia remissior esse debet et liberior et dulcior et ad omnem comitatem facilitatemque proclivior. . . . Firmamentum autem stabilitatis constantiaeque est eius quam in amicitia quaerimus fides est; nihil est enim stabile, quod infidum est.

> To this should be added a certain affability of speech and manner, which gives no mean flavour to friendship. While unvarying seriousness and gravity are indeed impressive, yet friendship ought to be more unrestrained, genial, and agreeable, and more inclined to be wholly courteous and urbane. . . . Now the support and stay of that unswerving constancy, which we look for in friendship, is loyalty; for nothing is constant that is disloyal. [18.66, 65]

And how they come to an abrupt end:

> Nulla est igitur excusatio peccati, si amici causa peccaveris; nam, cum conciliatrix amicitiae virtutis opinio fuerit, difficile est amicitiam manere, si a virtute defeceris.

> Therefore it is no justification whatever of your sin to have sinned in behalf of a friend; for, since his belief in your virtue induced the friendship, it is hard for that friendship to remain if you have forsaken virtue. [11.37]

Here sentiment in Cicero is echoed by plot in Lyly. But Cicero's essay states an ongoing set of instructions that is also—implicitly—meant to be insinuated by Lyly's referential fiction.

> Haec igitur prima lex amicitiae sanciatur, ut ab amicis honesta petamus, amicorum causa honesta faciamus, ne exspectemus quidem dum rogemur,

studium semper adsit, cunctatio absit, consilium verum dare audeamus libere, plurimum in amicitia amicorum bene suadentium valeat auctoritas, eaque et adhibeatur ad monendum non modo aperte, sed etiam acriter, si res postulabit, et adhibitae pareatur.

Therefore let this be ordained as the first law of friendship: Ask of friends only what is honourable; do for friends only what is honourable and without even waiting to be asked; let zeal be ever present, but hesitation absent; dare to give true advice with all frankness; in friendship let the influence of friends who are wise counsellors be paramount, and let that influence be employed in advising, not only with frankness, but, if the occasion demands, even with sternness, and let the advice be followed when given. [13.44]

The Ciceronian essay can therefore be seen as an epitome of *Euphues,* the series of ideas that the fiction tests. Words are made deeds. Ideas become actions. In turn *Euphues* honors and *realizes* the work of Ascham's "Master *Tully*" (*Scholemaster,* sig. S2) by dramatizing him.

That Lyly's intentions in *Euphues* were realized and understood by his contemporaries is evident in another work of humanist fiction, which in turn makes *Euphues* its model: Stephen Gosson's *Ephemerides of Phialo* (1579). Gosson too measures the efficacy of education by measuring it through the eloquence it is meant to teach. In Book 1, Phialo leaves his studies at Siena for the city of Ferara where he meets the courtier Philotimo; there, in what Walter R. Davis calls "The purest exemplar of the rhetorical mode" in fiction,[80] Phialo fails to heed Philotimo's warnings about courtly sophistry but instead rebukes and counsels his new friend in a formal oration.[81] In Book 2, "A Canuazado too *Courtiers*" (sigs. C7vff), Phialo again declaims, this time criticizing the courtier Jeraldi for studying Castiglione and, as an alternative, providing his own "patterne of a Courtier" (sig. D1v), which relies on the classical and scriptural precedents associated with the Tudor humanists.

> I woulde haue him too bee in spirite a *Cyrus,* in temperaunce, an *Ageselaus,* in witte a *Themistocles,* in experience a *Philip,* in boldenesse a *Brasidas,* in tongue a *Pericles,* in friendeshippe a *Ionathas,* in Wisedome a *Solomon;* exercised in armes, skilfull in Bookes, liberall in giftes, lowlie in Pompe, valiaunt in fighte, in Victorye mercifull; and too saie all at once, in his whole life a true Christian, that rather seeketh a Kingdome in Heauen, than a Scepter onearth, an immortall Crowne, than a vanishing wreath; the glorie of GOD, than his own prayse. [Sigs. D1v–D2]

This balance in his advice as in his syntax leads us to Gosson's portrait of an ideal man: he is "in birth a Prince, in life a Philosopher, in troubles a souldier, in peace a Scholer" (sig. D2v). Book 3 of Phialo's ephemerides, or daily occurrences, is a formal disputation praising and dispraising the courtesan; the debate is summed by Jeraldi, who gives the victory to Phialo.[82] Despite Phialo's effective speeches, however, Gosson is also aware of the problems of language, as he acknowledges in his prefatory epistle to Sidney.

> For such as haue tried the conclusion, knowe, that he which baiteth his hookes with medicinable drugges, catcheth the greatest store of fishe; yet are they not toothesome, nor good to bee brought vnto the table: And hee that tempers his speeche with art, smootheth his style with a double tongue, shall quickly haue infinite swarmes of freendes, but angle with poyson, and doe much hurt. [Sig. *4]

Gosson is also aware that a humanist poetics must educate men even as he fears man's imperfectibility (sigs. F6–F6v).

Euphues was published when Lyly was twenty-five; he published *Euphues and his England* (1580) as a counterstatement at the age of twenty-seven. "I was cōtent to set an other face to Euphues," he writes in the prefatory letter, "but yet iust behind the other, like the Image of Ianus" (sig. A2v; 2:4).[83] The description is just—from the dedications, which are similar in content and employ the same formularies,[84] to the concluding letters, which attempt to reassert coordination of life and learning (sig. L14; 2:228). Philautus's travel to England with Euphues, the temptation he receives in the presence of Camilla, and his reunion with Euphues are all in deliberate correlation to the earlier fiction, confirming and justifying the exemplary tales in this other half of the Janus image. Such a philosophical integrity of both works, leaning heavily on education from books and travel as the constituents of a virtuous and useful life, witnesses in its narrative plexus the clarity and strength of Lyly's outlook.

If the two works are similar in idea and purpose, they are nevertheless dissimilar in technique, perhaps because of a change in audience: the preface to the earlier work is addressed to gentlemen, that of the second (in a separate prefatory letter) to gentlewomen. Whereas *Euphues* unfolds in a sequence of debates that lend meaning through their reiteration of fundamental principles, *Euphues and his England* is a series of boxes within boxes, the stories of Callimachus, Fidus, and Philautus evoking in turn the need for instruction, self-discipline, and selfless love of principle.[85] Various levels of recollection, narration, and dramatization recall to us the many layers of fiction-as-truth in Gascoigne's *Adventures of Master F. J.* Precise Ramist dichotomies of language give way to less rigid syntactic arrangements while the clarity of subject grows cloudy as various narrative tales emphasize different elements of what is essentially the same story. The chain of being, to which *Euphues* pays repeated imagistic attention, is also displaced, significantly, by the imagery of the maze and the labyrinth (sig. H1; 2:52). Lyly means this deliberately. "Gentlemen and Gentlewomen," he interrupts, "it may seeme I have taken a newe course" (sig. H4; 2:57). The reason is clear, given the multiplication of characters meant to suggest the infinitude of worldly experience: "Euery one followeth his owne fancie." Not clearly defined debates but strings of topoi from the rhetorical handbooks supply Lyly with his fundamental material, as G. K. Hunter remarks:

> The narrative tends to move, somewhat jerkily, from one page of his commonplace book to another. We may give an outline of the topics drawn on for the opening section of *Euphues and his England:*
> (1) The incommodity of travel (13–14).
> (2) Carefulness versus Prodigality [Tale of Callimachus] (14–30).
> (3) Advice to travellers ⎫(31–32).
>   Description of Britain ⎭
> (4) The mystery of kingship (36–44).
> (5) Praise of the regiment of bees (44–46).
> (6) Expectation versus Experience (49–51).
> (7) The incommodity of love (52–53).
> (8) Wine—pro and contra (54–55).
> (9) The variousness of love (57).
> (10) Praise of beauty (59).
> (11) Wit in woman (60).
> In each of these cases we see Lyly drawing on a theme of Renaissance discourse; the attitude veers from page to page as he picks up now one set of attitudes, now another.[86]

Here Lyly finds, as Castiglione before him, that the court is the chief testing ground for precepts of the humanist schoolroom.

Public debate and private soliloquy at the English court show Lyly's canny psychological insight too as his characters, reaching out for solace rhetorically, reach for the wider realms of myth and proverb. Such speeches are subtly paired and, given the slight shades of difference that emerge within the distinguishing perspectives of different characters, take on once more the force of disputations on belief versus behavior. As in similar debates between More-persona and Hythlodaye in *Utopia* 1, Lyly as More invites us to detach ourselves so as to define the conflict and advance our own verdict.

> I haue not made Euphues to stand without legges, for that I want matter to make thē, but might to maintein them: so that I am enforced with the

olde painters, to colour my picture but to the middle, or as he that drew Ciclops, who in a little table made him to lye behinde an Oke, wher one might perceiue but a peece, yet cōceiue that al the rest lay behinde the tree, or as he that painted an horse in the riuer with half legges, leauing the pasternes for the viewer, to imagine as in the water. [Sig. A4; 2:6]

What *Euphues and his England* loses in grammatical density with its relaxation of strict *isocolon* and *parison* it gains conceptually. As narrative episodes multiply, Lyly's clever wit softens into warm human comedy and even farce.[87] Yet, dialectically, much is also explicitly at stake. Language itself is the issue, and with it all of human learning and writing that has been derived from it.

When *Adam* wooed there was no pollicie but playne dealing, no colours, but black & white. Affection was measured by faith, not by fancie: he was not curious, nor *Eue* cruel: he was not enamoured of hir beautie, nor she allured with his personage: and yet then was she the fairest woman in the world, & he the properest man. Since that tyme euery Louer hath put too a linke, and made of a Ring, a Chaine, and an odde Corner, and framed of a playne Alley, a crooked knot, and of *Venus* Temple, *Dedalus* Laborinth. [Sig. S3; 2:121]

In all ways, humanism must deal with and heal fallen men.

It is an astonishing and noticeable change—but it is also one we have seen before: like Folly's appeal to a kind of Holy Eucharist at the close of her speech or the chastening conclusion to *The Adventures of Master F. J.,* in *Euphues and his England* the initial *display of wit* common to both a poetics of wordplay and a poetics of eloquence is transformed into a sobering *commitment to values*. As a consequence, Lyly's more strenuous fiction undertakes to show the results of man's fall in a triad of cautionary tales by Callimachus, Fidus, and the active narration of Philautus, which reinforce each other and balance the moralistic, solitary, and (because he never learns how to rejoin those in an active life) unregenerate Euphues. In the first of these tales, Callimachus is meant to recall and build on the advice of Eubulus.

My good Sonne, thou art to receiue by my death, wealth, and by my counsell wisdome, and I would thou wert as willing to imprint the one in thy heart, as thou wilt be ready to beare the other in thy purse: To bee rich is the gift of Fortune, to be wise the grace of God. Haue more minde on thy bookes then thy bags, more desire of godlinesse then gold, greater affection to dye wel, then to liue wantonly [Sig. B2v; 2:15]

But his warning recalls, too, the younger Euphues:

> As the Cypresse tree, the more it is watered, the more it withereth, and the oftener it is lopped, the sooner it dyeth: so vnbrideled youth, the more it is also by graue aduice counselled, or due correction controlled, the sooner it falleth to confusion, hating all reasons that woulde bring it from folly, as that tree doth all remedies, that should make it fertile. [Sig. B2v; 2:15]

Such wisdom, then, needs confirmation in experience. Callimachus first rebels against this stingy inheritance, which substitutes piety for material fortune.

> Shal I then shew the duetie of a childe, when thou hast forgotten the Nature of a Father? . . . as the hearbe *Moly* hath a floure as white as snow, and a roote as blacke as incke, so age hath a white head shewing pietie but a blacke heart swellyng with mischiefe. . . . In steede of coyne, thou hast left me counsayle: O politique old man. Didst thou learne by experience, that an edge can be any thing worth if it haue nothing to cut. . . . Wisedome hath no Mint, Counsell is no coyner. He that in these dayes seeketh to get wealth by wit, with-out friends, is lyke vnto him, that thinketh to buye meate in the Market, for honestie with-out money, which thriueth on either side so well, that the one hath a wittie head, & an emptie pursse, the other a godly minde, and an emptie belly. [Sigs. B4–B4v; 2:18]

This time, however, such a sequence of premises is contained within a story and characterization at the outset of the fiction, as emblematic pro-positio.

Thus it is with considerable forewarning that Philautus—now in the company of Euphues as his tutor—makes his journey to England where they arrive at Lyly's native town of Canterbury, "an olde Citie, some-what decayed, yet beautifull to behold, most famous for a Cathedrall Church, the verye Maiestie where-of stroke them into a maze" (sig. E2v; 2:35–36). There they are hosted by the beekeeper Fidus, whose confirming monitory narratives remind us not of Pliny but of Aesop. Unlike Uncle Callimachus, however, Fidus leads an active, not a contemplative, life; already England is a place of corrective behavior, anticipating Philautus' final decision to remain actively in the English court rather than retire to study on a remote mountain with Euphues. "I am not so presise," Fidus tells the two young men,

> but that I esteme it as expedient in feates of armes and actiuitie, to employ the body, as in studie to wast the minde: yet so should the one be tempered with the other, as it might seeme as great a shame to be valiant and courtly with-out learning, as to be studious and bookish without valure. [Sig. G4; 2:50]

His cautionary tale, however, rather than setting forth one moral lesson after another as various propositio (as Uncle Callimachus does), limns the future experiences of Philautus, especially when he recalls his own inner debate concerning love in his earlier courtship of Iffida.

> *Fidus,* it standeth thee vppon eyther to winne thy loue, or to weane thy affections, which choyce is so hard, that thou canst not tell whether the victorie will be the greater in subduing thy selfe, or conquering hir.
> To loue and to liue well is wished of many, but incident to fewe. To liue and to loue well is incident to fewe, but indifferent to all. To loue without reason is an argument of lust, to liue with-out loue, a token of folly. The measure of loue is to haue no meane, the end to be euerlasting. [Sig. H1; 2:52]

His chopped logic and syntax are reminiscent of the fragmented thoughts of Lucilla and Euphues after their initial meeting; and Fidus falls in love with Iffida, who is already pledged to Thirsus. In contrast to both these tortured exempla, Euphues supplies more peaceful precepts empty of experience and, as a consequence, gives advice that Philautus will find irrelevant while furthering his own rapidly growing misogyny.

> It is likely then *Philautus* that the Foxe will let the Grapes hang for the Goose, or the English-man bequeath beautie to the *Italian?* No no *Philautus,* assure thy selfe, there is no *Venus* but she hath hir Temple, where on the one side *Vulcan* may knocke but *Mars* shall enter: no Sainte but hath her shrine, and he that cannot wynne with a *Pater Noster,* must offer a penny. [Sig. N2v; 2:87]

Once Euphues allows learning to intrude on life to the point that it replaces activity, his sourness grows past repair, and his advice (however humanistic in principle) lessens in authority.

This tough reexamination of humanism by Lyly, and his unblinkered judgment on its potential weakness, is also to be found in *The Scholemaster,* which remains, even here, one of his Senecan originals. "I wold wishe," Ascham writes,

> that, beside some good time, fitlie appointed, and constantlie kepte, to encrease by readinge, the knowledge of the tonges and learning, yong ientlemen shold vse, and delite in all Courtelie exercises, and Ientlemanlike pastimes. And good cause whie: For the self same noble Citie of Athenes, jiustlie commended of me before, did wiselie and vpon great consideration, appoint, the Muses, *Apollo,* and *Pallas,* to be patrones of learning to their yougthe. For the Muses, besides learning, were also Ladies of dauncinge, mirthe and minstrelsie: *Apollo,* was god of shooting, and Author of cunning playing vpō Instrumentes: *Pallas* also was Laidie mistres in warres.

Wherbie was nothing else ment, but that learninge shold be alwaise mingled, with honest mirthe, and cumlie exercises: and that warre also shold be gouerned by learning, and moderated by wisdom, as did well appeare in those Capitaines of *Athenes* named by me before, and also in *Scipio* & *Caesar,* the two Diamondes of Rome.

And *Pallas,* was no more feared, in weering *Aegida,* thā she was praised, for chosing *Oliua:* whereby shineth the glory of learning, which thus, was Gouernour & Mistres, in the noble Citie of *Athenes,* both of warre and peace. [Sig. G3v]

By taking Ascham's ideas into a fictional portrayal of the English court much as the actual Ascham had carried his lessons to the queen at Windsor, Lyly means to examine the potential autobiography of the humanist counselor to his prince.

The best dramatic scenes in *Euphues and his England* are at the English court where language, as in the opening books of *Il Cortegiano,* becomes play. Lyly's wit functions conceptually, for he employs Italian models for the English court even as he had used English humanist treatises for his earlier portrayal of Naples. Behind this second major work of Tudor fiction reliant on Italian sources are such romances as the *Asolani* and the opening of Boccaccio's *Decameron;* the *trattati d'amore* such as Ortensio Lando's *Questioni Amorose* (1552), the *Ragionamento d'Ulisse* (1552), and Giròlamo Bargagli's *Veglie Senesi* (1572); and stock Italian *dubbi d'amore* such as "Chi più facilmente si persuade esser amato, l'huomo o la donna," "Naturalmente chi e più constante, l'huomo o la donna," and "Se per magica si può flettere animo duro": "Who is more easily persuaded of being loved, a man or a woman?" "By nature who is more constant, a man or a woman?" "Whether a strong mind may be beant [changed] through magic."[88] Here fallen language is taken to the farthest remove from human need when all verbal endeavors become artificial rather than autochthonous; the very lack of sincerity and ability causes Euphues to forsake his friend and retire in disgust, more useless even than Uncle Callimachus. For here Lyly displays with deft parody all the familiar Italian stratagems—the masque where "vnder the colour of a daunce [lovers] discouer their whole desires" (sig. F4v; 2:103), the intricate formal steps of dance matched by complicated patterns of speech; the hand posies; the messages slipped into pomegranates and books by Petrarch—all with an energy or abandon that looks forward to Petruchio, Viola, and Rosalind.[89] So verbally debauched does Philautus temporarily become that he views love wholly as rhetoric (sig. Cc4v; 2:176). He turns even to the magic linguistic web of "sorcerie" (sig. F2; 2:113), a sign that he like Lucilla has temporarily lost the battle of mind over matter when discipline can no longer govern passion. But

England, unlike the Naples of *Euphues,* is providential, and Philautus is suddenly rescued, as we are, by the Italian magician Psellus. "Doe you thinke Gentleman," he sums, "that the minde being created of God, can be ruled by man, or that anye one canne moue the hart, but he that made the hart?" (sig. R3; 2:114). Psellus thus reiterates Callimachus's faith in man won by patience, Fidus's belief that men trust and accept the gods, and the initial English setting of Canterbury with its glorious cathedral. Euphues, judge of orations at the dinner party where all the lovers' tales are knit together and resolved, remains singularly alone and isolated, refusing to marry high humanist principles with the daily requirements of life. Philautus, on the other hand, learning to weave precept into experience, gives up Camilla, long pledged to Sirius (as Iffida was to Thirsus), and marries his little "violet" Fraunces: Philautus learns to be lowly wise. At plot's end, as elsewhere through commonplace prescriptions, Lyly returns us to those ideas most firmly subscribed to by the Tudor humanists: that wisdom is virtue, wit is inconstancy, and proper belief lies in perceiving (and contemplating) the Christian nature of man and the universe. The need for action and thought grounded in principle reasserts itself (cf. sigs. Ee1–Ff1; 2:185–90). We come, in *Euphues and his England,* to the ultimate Lylyan equipoise, the durable and necessary humanist stratagem in an imperfect and fallen world by which symmetry of style and thought is salvational: two letters concerning physical love exchanged between Philautus and Camilla give way to two other letters between Euphues and Philautus concerning love of a deeper and more lasting sort (sigs. Kk1v–L13v; 2:218–27). While struggling toward a language that can embody a reliable statement of virtue, the tentative conclusion of *Euphues and his England* searches for a humanist rhetoric to replace that which is fallen—and we are asked to search too.

This outlook is more startling, more significant, and more poignant than that which concludes *Euphues* because Lyly's second fiction seems purposively to embrace wider and more complex traditions of humanist fiction. Just as his slow unwinding toward a religious awareness evokes Erasmus, so the social setting of the English court is reminiscent of Castiglione (whose eloquence alone it matches). This involvement in a growing, conscious development of humanist fiction finds its closing references in a coda praising England that reminds us of Thomas More. Here, in an elaborate detail of geography, government, economy, and society supplied by William Harrison in his addition to Holinshed's *Chronicles* (1577), Lyly not only answers the false opening description borrowed from Caesar but responds point by point to Hythlodaye's overt and covert attacks on England in *Utopia* 1 and 2. Lyly's concluding encomium—this latter-day *encomium sapientiae,* which uses Harrison rather than parodying Plutarch's *Lycurgus*—is no appendix, no afterthought, however. Beyond mere narrative, where he interrupts the action to address his reader, Lyly makes this final declamation his *conceptual* conclusion. It ends with Elizabeth I as the mirror for mankind, her reflection in England the pattern for all Europe (sigs. F1 ff.; 2:190 ff.). Purposively too the account finishes on a tribute to her humanism:

> Hir Godly zeale to learning, with hir great skill, hath bene so manifestly approued, yt I cannot tel whether she deserue more honour for hir knowledge, or admiration for hir curtesie, who in great pompe, hath twice directed hir Progresse, vnto the Uniuersities, with no lesse ioye to the Students, then glory to hir State, where after long and solempne disputations in Law, Phisicke, and Diuinitie, not as one wearyed with Schollers arguments, but wedded to their Orations, when euery one feared to offend in length, she in hir owne person, with no lesse praise to hir Maiestie, than delyght to hir subiects, with a wise and learned conclusion, both gaue them thankes and put hir selfe to paynes. O noble patterne of a Princely minde.

And to her humanist rhetoric:

> Her wit so sharpe, that if I should repeat the apt aunsweres, the subtill questions, the fine speaches, the pithie sentences, which on the sodayne she hath vttered, they would rather breed admiratiō, than credite. [Sigs. Ii2v–Ii3; 2:213]

This living embodiment of the Senecan fourth cause is vital in a fallen world where our models remain otherwise indeterminate. Philautus, for instance, having lost Camilla, faces an uncertain future with Fraunces, while Euphues, despite his wise counsel—and also because of it—retreats to a nearly useless life "in the bottome of the Mountaine *Silixsedra*" (sig. L14; 2:228). Like Hythlodaye he withdraws, excluded, to an altogether fictional world (sig. L14; 2:228). Lyly thereby modifies the force of fiction before the living example of Elizabeth I and the need to transcend both book and individual to a life of principles. His fiction as fiction, while pointing the way, can only point, and he has his own reservations: perhaps, he tells us, *Euphues and his England* had "rather lye shut in a Ladyes casket, then open in a Schollers studie" (sig. *1v; 2:9). Keenly aware of eristics, Lyly assays to locate truth where he can by acknowledging that it exists not between hypothesis and verification, or even between affirmative and negative sides of debate. Rather, it is to be found in serious examination that transcends man as he transcends his thought and study. Here too Lyly found some comfort and direction in his mentor Isocrates. "It is well," Isocrates writes,

> that in all activities, and most of all in the art of speaking, credit is won, not by gifts of fortune, but by efforts of study, For men who have been gifted with eloquence by nature and by fortune, are governed in what they say by chance, and not by any standard of what is best, whereas those who have gained this power by the study of philosophy and by the exercise of reason never speak without weighing their words, and so are less often in error as to a course of action [*Antidosis* 292]

In the humanists' exercise of reason and in a poetics of such an inspired eloquence lies the true beginning of wisdom.

SIX

Omne Tulit Punctum Qui Miscuit Vtile Dulci:

Robert Greene's Fiction of Wonder

 JOHN LYLY'S *EUPHUES: THE ANATOMY OF WIT* AND *EU- PHUES AND HIS ENGLAND* SUPPLY WITTY AND MORAL COMMENTS ON MAN'S IMPERFECTIONS BY DEVEL- OPING A PARTICULAR POETICS OF eloquence, drawn from Isocrates, in narratives of prodigality; in this way, Lyly testifies to inhering Christian values wherever humanism is ramified: in the Italian cities, among scholars in the Greek university, or at the English court. The last concentrated fictive efforts of Robert Greene, the Tudors' most industrious man of letters—marked with the motto *Sero, sed serio* (Late, but sincere)—also follow this biblical patterning: *Greenes Neuer Too Late* (1590), *Francescos Fortunes* (1590), *Greenes Mourning Garment* (1590), and *Greenes Farewell to Follie* (1591) all trace the decline and repentance of their protagonists in forceful parables that, rather than the euphuism of his earlier work, show Greene's abiding indebtedness to Lyly. These are the tales we think of when we think of Robert Greene.[1] Such works of repentance seen as fictionalizations of Greene's own prodigal life are the commonly received view of his work, the view first promulgated by such contemporaries as John Dickenson in *Greene in Conceipt. New raised from his graue to write the Tragique Historie of faire Valeria of London* (1598).[2] But this understanding fails to explain Greene's ability to capture the imagination then and now, his perennial attractiveness for anyone who reads him. In fact, the source of Greene's power is radically *different* from Lyly's and new to humanist poetics: it stems from the lyricism of his eloquently marvelous and marvelously eloquent stories of transformation. Greene's humanist fiction is a fiction of wonder.

About this peculiarly affective and powerful poetics Greene seems always to have been aware. In the dedication of *Greenes Mourning Garment* to the earl of Cumberland, for instance, he remarks, "how I hope your Lordship will be glad with *Augustus Caesar,* to read the reformation of a second *Ouid*."[3] While this may reinforce the popular Tudor notion of Greene as a writer wholly concerned with the *Ars Amatoria* and the *Remedia Amoris*, it is the later Ovid that Greene means to invoke—the Ovid who reforms men as in the French *Ovide moralisé*, or the Latin *Metamorphosis Ovidiana moraltier ... explanatu* with its quadruple interpretings (*literaliter, naturaliter, historialiter, allegorice*). It is the Ovid who transforms human nature through the marvelous metamorphosis of understanding and will. Genuine and significant instruction, Greene tells the gentlemen scholars of both universities in the preface to *Greenes Mourning Garment*, comes at moments of amazement—of engaged mental activity suspended out of bafflement—which must then be comprehended and utilized by alert minds.

> *Sodain changes of mens affects craue great wonder, but little beliefe; and such as alter in a moment, win not credit in a moneth. These premisses (Gentlemen) driues me into a quandary, fearing I shall hardly insinuate into your fauours, with changing the titles of my Pamphlets, or make you beleeue the inward metamorphosis of my minde, by the exterior shew of my workes, seeing I haue euer professed my selfe Loues Philosopher.* [Sig. A4v; 9:122]

Nevertheless, this is what he intends. "*The inward metamorphosis of my minde*": Greene is not simply pointing a moral; he means also to prove that what effects great wonder can also effect worthwhile belief. In his transforming works, he dramatizes a transformation of human conception outwardly clothed in the transformation of human behavior, much as Ovid reveals changes in the human mind or condition through his metamorphoses of men and women into animals and trees. It is this specific latter-day, re-forming Ovid that Greene means to figure beneath the splendid rhetoric of his endless schemes and tropes. For in thought and in language Greene is repeatedly drawn to the marvelous as an educative way to explore man's imperfect and perfecting nature, his potential for moral self-fashioning. And his endlessly figuring rhetoric—the restless explorations of an inventive, enchanting, and boldly testing imagination—is what so seduces and holds us in the sheer joy of his improbable fictions.

In all these ways, *Greenes Mourning Garment* is a representative work. Here, beneath the countless embellishments of an ornamental narrative, the story of the wayward Philador who loses his fortune and becomes a swineherd is, in nearly all of its many details, Greene's wondrous own transformation of Gnaepheus's Latin humanist play *Ascolastus*.[4] But what changes Greene's special magic brings. When Philador meets a passionate gentleman on his return journey (the geography having its own pointed nexus of cartography, biography, and metaphysic) and gives him the precepts he received from his father (being wise now) as a shepherd might (being lowly now), his transformed action and attitude suggest the metamorphosis of *his* mind. And that he teaches by precept—first in a declamation (sigs. H1–H2; 9:193–96) and then by a gift of aphorisms suggestive of Ovid in their application of unnatural natural history—shows that his earlier transformation into a swineherd, out of physical and economic necessity, has brought about a further change into the role of teacher (following a declamatory soliloquy of self-assessment) so that he may undergo a last transformation in resuming his life as a son. The Ovidian metamorphosis of nature, Greene tells us, signifies a metamorphosis of thought every bit as much as it suggests a conversion of soul. To this decidedly Ovidian foundation, Greene adds the wonders of compatible Alexandrian romances. For their various conventions too—especially their final moments of reunion and reconciliation—are akin to both the goal of reformation advocated by Christian humanists and the means of worldly experience urged by humanist educators.

This fresh application of humanist rhetoric in *Greenes Mourning Garment,* moreover, serves its humanist thought. Philador is at first characterized by a wonderful sophistry, seen in the opening disputation with his father. But, later, such acts of sophistry are taken over by the three Siren-like sisters whose brothel is openly compared to the residence of Circe (sig. E3; 9:163), and as a witness to such abuse of language, Philador learns by brutal experience how to distinguish among rhetorics of various kinds. Thus his final declamations, to the passionate gentleman and to his father, echo the purified language of his soliloquy as a swineherd. This transformation, too, by which humanist rhetoric is salvaged after being subjected to the terms of romance within the leisure of fiction (like, say, the sophistic debate in Book 3 of Herodotus), is a distillation accomplished first and best for humanist poetics in Greene's special alembic. In a wondrous parallel development, Greene's initial premise of Fortune as that force which would "exceede Nature in excellence, as Nature had ouer-reacht her selfe in cunning" (sig. B2; 9:127) transfers a fundamental idea of the romance (which Ascham, for one, condemned) to the sphere of a conventional humanism. As if to make this too very plain, Greene has the young reprobate Philador pronounce his praise of travel as a kind of encomium moriae (sigs. B4–B4v; 9:133–34). But in Greene such wonder of new sights and new lands must also lead to the ultimate wonder of humility. Inevitably, this becomes Greene's final transformation of both the tenor and the vehicle of humanist fiction.

Still, Greene's changes in humanist fiction are not meant to replace or even to change the humanists' fundamental principles. Quite the opposite is the case. In transporting his explorations of man's educability and perfectibility to strange lands, Greene means to keep the concerns of Tudor humanism squarely before us. Indeed, in grafting the marvels of Ovid and of Alexandrian romance to the conservative moral tenets of humanism, Greene seems anxious from the first to declare his allegiance to the New Learning. His initial publication, *Mamillia* (written in 1580, published in 1583), composed when he was a graduate student at Clare Hall, Cambridge, is a patent reformulation of *Euphues* and its humanist ideas: *Mamillia* is

> *A Mirrour or looking*-glasse for the Ladies of Englande. Wherein is disciphered, howe Gentlemen vnder the perfect substaunce of pure loue, are oft inueigled with the *shadowe of lewde luste: and their firme* faith, brought a sleepe by fading fancie: vntil wit is ioyned with wisdome, doth awake it by the helpe of reason [Sig. A1; 2:3]

This simple story shows its humanist model at every step: Pharicles falls in love with Mamillia and then, enamored of Publia, leaves her, while Mamillia, chastened by the experience, seeks counsel from her father and nurse and learns the truth of their precepts through her own personal loss. Greene's pleasure in the art of imitating Lyly is seen in his joyful reversals of the sex of the chief characters—and in the whole chain of reversals that then follows—as John Clark Jordan noted some time ago.

> Corresponding to Euphues' departure from Athens, we have Mamillia's departure from the court to her father's house. . . . Euphues goes from home to gain worldly experience. Mamillia is away from home in the midst of temptations, and goes home in order to avoid them. When Euphues arrives in Naples, he is offered advice, which he haughtily rejects. Mamillia is offered advice, which she accepts and earnestly tries to follow. The reversal is carried, also, to the main characters. In *Euphues* there are two faithful male, and one faithless female, characters; in *Mamillia* there are two faithful female, and one faithless male, characters. Corresponding to the fact that Euphues met Lucilla through Philautus' introduction is the fact that it was Mamillia who introduced Pharicles to Publia. Corresponding to the quarrel between Euphues and Philautus when Euphues falls in love with Lucilla, there is the falling out between Mamillia and Publia when Pharicles and Publia fall in love. Corresponding to Euphues' secluding himself at Silexedra is Publia's entrance into a covent. And corresponding to Euphues' letters, are the letters of Mamillia to her friend, the Lady Modesta. This definite parallelism is sufficient to show what I mean in saying that *Mamillia* is planned upon *Euphues*. [*Robert Greene*, pp. 15–16]

Even the rhetoric in *Euphues* and *Mamillia* is similar, for the polysyndetic sentiments of Mamillia's and Pharicles' soliloquies, and Greene's celebratory comparison of the young lovers to Admetus and Alcestis, Portia and Cato, Cornelia and Gracchus (*Mamillia* 2 [1583], sig. B4; 2:157) suggests the essential harmony of the humanist community in which even those most estranged by emotion or most distanced by time are linked by the profound similarities of their nature. Like *Euphues,* too, *Mamillia* is equally concerned with nurture; the stories of the past are instructive, as Jacques is at pains to show in *Mamillia* 2 (sigs. N3 ff.; 2:282 ff.). As *Euphues* traces the decline of its hero, so *Mamillia* 1 describes the loss of Mamillia; and *Mamillia* 2, analogous to *Euphues and his England*, tells how Pharicles' sojourn as a pilgrim provides the regeneration necessary to reunite them. The resemblance of plot and attitude is encapsulated on the title page of *Mamillia* 2 as well: "WHEREIN WITH PERPETVAL fame the constancie of Gentlewomen is canonised, and the vniust blasphemies of womens supposed ficklenesse (breathed out by diuerse iniurious persons) by manifest examples clearly infringed" (sig. A1; 2:139).

The next year, 1584, Greene published *Morando*, this time openly imitating Castiglione's *Cortegiano. Morando* emphasizes the sapience and prudence that Greene relates elsewhere to Castiglione[5] in its courtly art of conversation: at Morando's grange house seven miles distant from Bononia several gentlemen solace a melancholy widow and her three daughters through instructive and diverting debates on the nature of love. The first debate, between Peratio and Lacena, concerns the country proverb that "Loue doth much but money doth all" (sig. 34v; 3:61); the second considers whether "to liue without loue is not to liue at all" (sig. D4; 3:84); and the third deals with the propositio that "women are more subiect vnto Loue then any other mortall creatures" (sig. F2v; 3:104). This "tritameron" on the nature of love in *Morando* 1 is continued in *Morando* 2 by the examination of love nurtured by an eloquence that can succeed through clever indirection, that can hinder by way of self-defensiveness, and that can disrupt love by quarreling. Entertaining narratives illustrative of love's nature and used to support the propositions of *Morando* 1 give way in *Morando* 2 to exempla of willed reason. Both halves of Greene's diptych, reassembled by Morando at the close of part 2, define finally the perfect lover, rather than the perfect courtier, through a perfected eloquence. Three years later, in *Euphues his censure to Philautus* (1587), Greene follows the model of *Il Cortegiano* even more closely as Ulysses, Helenus, Hector, and Achilles, in a courtly conversation at the Greek camp during a brief respite from the Trojan War, and later at Troy, help Priam as judge at their symposium to fashion the perfect soldier.[6] But this "SOPHO-MACHIA" (1634 ed., sig. A3; 6:155) proudly pronounces an extended and syncretic pedigree in the dedicatory epistle:

having by happ chaunced on some parte of *Ephues* counsell touching the perfection of a souldier, sent from *Silexedra* his melancholie cel to his friende *Philautus* new chosen generall of certaine forces, wherein under the shaddow of a philosophicall combat betweene *Hector* and *Achilles,* imitating *Tullies* orator, *Platoes* commonwealth, and *Baldessars* courtier, he aimeth at the exquisite portraiture of a perfect martialist, consisting (saith hee) in three principall pointes; wisedome to gouerne; fortitude to performe; liberalitie to incourage. [Sig. A2; 6:151–52]

In such apprentice works, Greene practices the humanist art of imitatio, careful that we see his originals even as he transforms them through the sea change of wonderful setting and wonderful rhetoric into something new and strange.[7]

Indeed, such imitations are natural enough for an innkeeper's son from Norwich who, if related to more prominent landowners in the West Riding of Yorkshire[8]—we know almost nothing of his life with certainty— nevertheless entered St. John's College, Cambridge, as a sizar on 26 November 1575 and was admitted to the B.A. there sometime in 1580; who may well have traveled extensively in Italy and Spain prior to that;[9] and who seems to have planned a career at Cambridge, transferring to Clare Hall for his M.A. while completing a second book (*Mamillia 2*, sig. A3; 2:143). Later he would proudly proclaim himself *academiae utriusque magister in artibus,* (master of arts at both universities) as a requisite condition of his authority.[10] Writing thirty-five books in little more than a decade, twenty of them novels or collections of stories, sometimes at the rate of two, three, or four volumes a year in a seamless palimpsestic canon, this "omnigatherum," as Gabriel Harvey spitefully labels him,[11] could (and would) repeat whole passages or pages of his source material or his own earlier work with ease, giving them continued and uneroded applicability.[12]

Greene acknowledges his firm foundation for this prodigious body of work in the tradition of Tudor humanism when he lists "Foure things [which] make a man wise. (1. Studie. (2. Experience. (3. Nightly consideration. (4. And immitation of the wise" in *The Royal Exchange* (sig. G1v; 7:298), reiterating through opposition those things most infelicitous, which include "He which is ignorant & wil not learne. And he which can instruct and will not teach" (sig. D3; 7:284). We can take him at his word, even in his fiction of wonder. Just as Ulysses, Helenus, Hector, and Achilles urge precepts of love, wisdom, fortitude, and liberality by applying them to stories about the faithless Maedina, the wise Queen Cimbriana, the brave Frontinus, and the magnanimous Roxander in *Euphues his censure to Philautus,* so other frame tales of Greene in the

1580s teach by coupling propositio and proof. In *Planetomachia* (1585), Venus and Saturn dispute the excesses of peevishness and carnal love. In *Penelopes Web* (1587), Penelope entertains her maidens with instructive stories to teach the virtues of obedience, chastity, and silence while awaiting the return of Ulysses. And in *Greenes Orpharion* (1589), Orpheus's account of the cruel Lidia and Arion's gentler narrative of the constant Argentina imply for us, between these extremes, their own harmonious mean.

Greene pays even greater homage to the Ciceronian humanism of his predecessors in humanist fiction in two of his most mature works—the *Ciceronis Amor* and *Gwydonius*. *Ciceronis Amor*. *Tvllies Loue* (1589) is, at first glance, a straightforward romance (similar to Elyot's tale of Titus and Gisippus and to *Euphues*) in which friends place their love for each other above the love for women even when one of them, wooing a woman for the other, finds that he is the one whom she desires. Greene understood how fundamentally congruent such a story is with the later philosophic essays by the historic Cicero on love, friendship, and even patriotism. Greene portrays Cicero as a shy but witty youth whose eloquent orations on love consistently place the highest premium on the love of friends and the love of country. This characterization of Cicero, about whom the Roman senators, Greene tells us, "had no other table talke but of [his] eloquence . . . , some commending his witte, other his study, some his vertues, but all his special gifts of nature" (sig. G3; 7:168), has its basis in Plutarch's life. But *Ciceronis Amor,* Greene writes to Lord Strange in his dedicatory epistle, is also an attempt to supplement Plutarch (sig. A2; 7:100), and in developing a romance, Greene finds it necessary to soften Plutarch's portrait of a determined and aggressive Terentia (*Life of Cicero*, 20.2, 29, 41) and a conspiratorial Lentulus.[13] Thus the opening disputation between these two on the wisdom of heterosexual love (sigs. C4–D3; 7:128–36) is considerably subdued by Cicero's own subsequent oration on the virtue of friendship.

> The auncient Greetians sweete *Lentulus* yt set downe principles of friendship, account for the secrete conuersing of friendes, and their mutuall participating eyther of priuate sorrows or concealed pleasures, the principall end of such professed amitie. Therefore did *Theseus* choose *Pirrithous, Orestes Pylades* & to that end, or else you wronge me, serues *Tullie* to his *Lentulus*. [Sig. E2; 7:143]

Such sentiments are also found in the *Moralia* of Plutarch. But Greene distinctively places these common humanist topoi in a rhetoric of Ciceronian periodicity, a rhetoric that deliberately replaces the Isocratean rhetoric of Lyly. *Ciceronis Amor* maintains a quiet equation between the power of love and the power of eloquence, humanist thought and humanist rhetoric, and Cicero's own love for Terentia, imitated in Lentulus's for her companion Favius, and the clown Fabius's (awakened by the power of love to self-education) for Cornelia. Indeed, as love captures each of the characters in turn, so each turns to an imitatio of Cicero, and each finds a maturing of character caught in a maturing of language that becomes more relaxed and more *poetic* as Greene's humanist fiction unfolds. In this quiet fashioning of Cicero and his imitators, there is a marvelous transformation of several particularized Roman citizens, but this is essentially a humanist fiction in which the poetics of wonder is not yet fully realized.

Ciceronis Amor is more subtle but not nearly so complicated as *Gwydonius. The Carde of Fancie* (1584). The title page locates this tale's basic debate structure—it is "a cruell Combat betweene Nature and necessitie" (sig. A2; 4:3)—but the actual title catches up further equivalencies and equivocations, much as the titles of *Encomium Moriae* and *Utopia* do: "carde" means "portrait" (of the developing humanist), "chart" or "compass" (of his progress) and "warning" or "lesson" (for the hero and for Greene's readers), while "fancie" suggests the love or infatuation of the mature Gwydonius, the will of the younger protagonist in the opening pages, and the imaginative ideal self for which, in the intermediate passages, he increasingly yearns.[14] This major "tragicall Comedie" (sig. K1v; 4:98) is twice the length of most of Greene's other fictions. In it he pushes the action far beyond Philautus's England, Euphues' Naples, or even Cicero's Rome, to the romantic and exotic environment of a Barnabe Rich or a Georgie Pettie[15]—to Mitelyne, Barutta, and Alexandria—and for the same reasons: to maintain distinct outlines of his humanist trope and to sustain man's perfectibility as a very real possibility.

At the outset Gwydonius, the son of Duke Clerophones, is like Euphues a young man of potentially good nature. "His personage indeede was so comely, his feature so well framed, each lim so perfectlye couched, his face so faire, and his countenance so amiable, as he seemed a heauenly creature in a mortall carcasse" (sig. B1v; 4:12–13)—yet he is betrayed by bad qualities of mind, by imperfect nurturing.

> But his minde was so blemished with detestable qualyties, and so spotted with the staine of voluptuousnesse, that he was not so much to be commended for the proportion of his bodie, as to be condempned for the imperfection of his minde. [Sig. B1v; 4:12–13]

As a consequence, Clerophontes agrees with his son that travel would be beneficial and would allow Gwydonius a refocused understanding of himself. The father's words of counsel are similar to those of Eubulus.

Be not wilfull in thy dooings that they count thee not witlesse, nor too rash, that they think thee not deuoyd of reason: be not too merrie that they count thee not immodest, nor too sober least they call thee sullen, but shew thy selfe to be an olde man for thy grauitie, and a young youth for thy actiuitie: so shal all men haue cause to praise thee for thy manners, and commend thee for thy modestie. Be not too curious *Guydonius,* that they deeme thee not proud, nor too curteous, least they call thee counterfaite. Be a friend to all, & a foe to none, and yet trust not without triall, nor commit any secret to a friendlye stranger, least in too much trust lye treason, and thou be forced by repentaunce to crie *Peccaui.* [Sig. B4v; 4:21–22]

But Greene's Gwydonius will be no duplicate of Euphues; and at this point the instruction of Clerophontes so diverges from that of his predecessor in Lyly that once more a wondrous reversal of humanist conventions is what alerts us in Greene's fiction. Clerophontes goes on to comment that

in my opinion, the fittest kind of life for a young Gentleman to take (who as yet hath not subdued the youthful conceiptes of fancie, nor made a conquest of his will by witte) is to spende his time in trauell, wherein he shall finde both pleasure and profite: yea, and buye that by experience, which otherwise with all the treasure in the world hee cannot purchase. For what chaungeth vanitie to vertue, staylesse wit to stayed wisedome, fonde fantasies to firme affections, but trauell: what represseth the rage of youth, and redresseth the witlesse furie of wanton yeares, but trauell: what tourneth a secure life to a carefull lyuing, what maketh the foolish wise, yea, what increaseth wit and augmenteth skill, but trauell: in so much that the same *Vlysses* wonne, was not by the tenne yeares hee lay at *Troy,* but by the time he spent in trauell. [Sigs. B3v–B4; 4:19]

Unlike Eubulus, who expected the worst before he had any confirmation of Euphues' faltering actions, the duke trusts his son until contradictory evidence proves he should not. Still, his farewell contains a certain sorrow that heightens the register of his advice.

Now *Gwydonius* that thou hast heard the aduertisement of a louing father, follow my aduice as a duetifull Childe, and the more to binde thee to perfourme my former preceptes, that this my counsaile be not drowned in obliuion, I giue thee this Ring of gold, wherein is written this sentence, *Praemonitus, Premunitus.* [Sig. C1; 4:22–23]

This opening scene, loosened syntactically from its model in Lyly but tightened dramatically through its specificity in person and place, introduces the entire scope of values and principles that will direct all the subsequent examples, anticipate the princess Castania in its edge of reprimand, and in its sharpened juxtaposition of good father and depraved son properly scheme a story built on sequential conflicts of mind, spirit, and body. Within the oration of this apparently exoteric scene, nothing is pointless.

Gwydonius confronts two environments: at Barutta, he is "a myrrour of immoderate lyfe" (sig. C1v; 4:24) and suffers bankruptcy and imprisonment. Later, "set . . . free from his Purgatorie" (sig. C3; 4:27) by a Senate that can find no evidence for charges brought against him, Gwydonius continues on to Alexandria, "pinched wyth pouertie and distressed with want, hauing no coyne left wherewith to coueruaile his expences, [where he] thought it his best course, if it were possible, to compasse the Dukes seruice" (sig. D1v; 4:34). As a lowly servant in the court of Duke Orlanio, "a Schoole of vertue to such as brideled their mindes with discreation, [but] a nurse of vice to those tender yeeres that measured theyr willes wyth witlesse affection" (sig. C3v; 4:29), Gwydonius metamorphoses his princely identity beneath a ragged cloak that reveals an inner sense of penance. But, having learned his father's lessons of virtue and self-discipline, Gwydonius must now study an appropriate language of eloquence, for he falls in love with the princess Castania. For her, proper behavior is more than virtuous conduct, it is also refined conversation. The requirements of humanist principles are now conveyed in a humanist style as dialogue and soliloquy replace narrative.

As Gwydonius's disguise denies his lineage, so now his speech must deny his disguise. His language, heightened, reflects his own sense of equivocation in its Isocratean structures and sounds, but with a Ciceronian absence of metaphor and allusion.

> Sith . . . my care proceedeth from your beautie, let my sore be cured by your bountie, sith the perfection of your person hath wrought my bane, let the effect of your courtesie procure my blisse, and reiect him not so rigorously, which respecteth you so reuerently. Loath him not so hatefully, which loueth you so heartely: nor repaie not his dutifull amitie, with such deadly enmitie. [Sigs. L2v–L3; 4:112–13]

Gwydonius's perseverance slowly wins Castania, while his hard-won self-discipline and his social behavior still demonstrate his heroic fortitude. Gwydonius develops into an idealized humanist portrait,

> who besides the beautie of his bodie, and the bountie of his minde whereat all *Alexandria* wondred, had by good gouernment and perfect practise, obtained such a dexteritie in all things, as in feates of armes no man more forward, in exercise none more actiue, in playe none more politicke, in *parle* none more pleasant, amongst his aunciens very wise, amongst the youthfull who more merrie. [Sig. G1; 4:64]

But it is his own father's invasion of Alexandria that gives him the chance to show that his physical reformation is equal to that of his mind and soul. At first paralyzed once more by his equivocal position as son of the invader Clerophontes and subject of the invaded Orlanio, Gwydonius tests his own precepts, and in a second disguise, as Orlanio's son Thersandro, he fights his own father and then, removing his disguise, defeats him in a duel. The reformed humanist, reborn in behavior, attitude, and principle now teaches his father, who had refused proper tribute to Alexandria and had led troops against that country. Gwydonius thus singlehandedly reunites the kingdoms of Mitelyne and Alexandria, marries Castania and so unites the royal families, and returns to his father's house heroically, restoring his own position as prince of Mitelyne. The utter incredibility of a son volunteering to enter the lists against his own father to support a rival kingdom is dissolved in our sheer amazement at the story itself, and in its commitment to revalidate the educability of man. Dysology functions merely as the occasion for redefining rectitude. While *Ciceronis Amor* pays homage to humanist fiction, *Gwydonius* boldly announces Greene's special fiction of wonder: this extraordinary conclusion, in which the son of Orlanio is transformed into the son of Clerophontes (or so it is presumed) and a son is found to be dueling his father for a foreign land in order to conquer his own country—there is no more stunning scene than this in the whole of Tudor fiction—is a moment so beset with wonder that it seems to shatter all the rational precepts of Clerophontes with which the fiction began. Before such strange and miraculous events, humanist precepts have little relevance. Yet the final marvel of Greene's fiction, of course, here and elsewhere, is that all the multiple transformations of fate, in the final analysis, confirm the tenets of humanist thought that he like the other Tudors had inherited from Erasmus and More, Elyot and Ascham.

Gwydonius, like other fictions of wonder by Robert Greene, has its chief Senecan model in Alexandrian fiction. The very wealth of fancy and imagination available through the antique models of Greek romance is developed with far greater depth and consistency by Greene, serving as a significant dimension to his unique and engaging poetics of eloquence. These romances—what Wallace A. Bacon has recognized as "the first Western novels in prose"[16]—grew in turn out of the Senecan *controversiae,* which invited rhetorical developments of extremely unlikely and even fantastic situations, opening the widest possible avenues to an orator's ingenuity: they too, from the Tudor perspective, had a respectable humanist pedigree. In an important study, Arthur Heiserman reminds us of the features of a prototypical Greek romance such as those on which Greene draws.

Its protagonists can be much more admirable, for their fidelity and courage, than the protagonists of comedies and even more admirable, or worthy of emulation, than those of epic and tragedy; but like comic characters, and unlike tragic ones, they are purely fictive, neither legendary nor historical. They suffer the direst threats to their lives and values, threats which the romance, unlike a comedy, can ask us to take seriously; but, as in a comedy, if not in a tragedy, they survive all these perils to live happily ever after. This kind of *erōtika pathēmata,* in which admirable characters survive the perils caused by love, fortune, and their own fidelity, became a most persistent form of Western literary art.[17]

Whatever Greene's immediate ends in the commerce of entertainment and instruction, these romances permitted him new directions for exploring the humanists' trust in man and allowed him as a writer of humanist fiction to explore the outer edges of man's possibilities with a wondrous *admiratio* while employing all the various resources of a humanist's imagination. The randomness of time and space, the tendency toward the exotic and the melodramatic, the rapidly shifting scenes, the interest in spectacular event and tableau, the extreme trials of virtue and the exaggerated dimensions of vice—all these features of Greek romance were attractive to writer and reader alike. They invited endless rhetorical embellishment. They also suggest to us how easily such pagan texts could be Christianized by the humanists: the Wheel of Fortune could become the secret ways of Providence. As one who enjoyed "a formidable contemporary reputation as a writer of romances," as Edwin Haviland Miller has it,[18] Greene could also put the romance to work as a kind of pagan sermon, the tribulations of his wandering and lost heroes another opportunity for self-analysis and repentance. Thus, on the one hand, Greene created a deliberate poetics of delight, which he defines in the epistle to the earl of Leicester that prefaces *Planetomachia* (1585): *"The minde wearied with weightie affaires, seeketh assoone to be recreated with some pithie conceipts, as with any deepe contemplations; & rather with sleight deuises to procure mirth, thē with sollemne shewes to foster melancholie"* (sig. *2v; 5:6). Greene's enchanting narratives never lie because they never affirm, as Sidney was then writing in his *Defence* (sig. G1; 102);[19] instead, they transport us beyond the recalcitrance and disorder of everyday life to allow us to witness and perhaps to emulate innocent and elevated prototypes. We learn through the distancing that allows wonder. On the other hand, Greene's repeated explorations in a humanist fiction that draws heavily on Greek romance allow him more serious examinations of man's changeability and the uncertainties and contingencies of life. The idea appears succinctly in the picture of Fortune that the penitent Arbasto keeps at his side.

The picture whiche thou seest heere, is the perfect counterfaite of her inconstant conditions, for she like the Polipe fishe, turneth hirselfe into the likenesse of euerie obiect, and with the Cameleon taketh hir whole delight in change, being sure in nothing but in this, that she is not sure. [*Arbasto, The Anatomie of Fortune* (1584), sig. B3: 3;184][20]

Confronting such mystery establishes an occasion for faith and supplies the conditions that permit moral interpretation. Like Arbasto, Greene understood the potential significations in romance.

Of those Greek romances accessible to Greene, there is no clear indication left to us that he was familiar with the *Argonautica* of Apollonius Rhodius, although the spectacle of Zetes and Calais, children of the North Wind (1), the inset story of Cyrene and the vision of Apollo (2), Jason's epideictic speech to Medea and her inner debate (3), and Medea's clever decoy and the miraculous escapes on the homeward journey (4) resemble several of the incidents and allusions in his own Tudor fiction of wonder. The case is far different with the *Clitophon and Leucippe* of Achilles Tatius (c. A.D. 172–94). Translated into Latin in 1544, into Italian in 1546, and into English in 1584, this story of faithful lovers who withstand torture, separation, deceit, presumed infidelity, and dangerous travel, and whose account provides an elaborate description of the garden at Tyre, the soliloquies of both hero and heroine, and the marvels described by an oracle, is characterized by Tatius himself as a series of adventures that "are really like fiction," "a whole swarm of stories."[21] Greene mines Tatius as his own special treasure,[22] being especially attracted to this Alexandrian model which supplies fictions that pretend to be reasoned accounts but are really fictions. And what a storehouse it is! The grand assortment includes an erotic painting of Europa (p. 7), a providential dream (p. 13), a marvelous battle on flooded land (p. 223), as well as frequent references to Fortune and wonderful retellings of the Ovidian stories of Procne (pp. 245–47), Pan (pp. 403–9), and Rhodopis (pp. 435–37). There is a minidisputation based on Pliny (pp. 103–5). "Precisely so far as Greene's work belongs to the literature of illusion, it is fed by the work of Achilles Tatius," Samuel Lee Wolff writes; "it is Achilles Tatius who affects him at the largest number of points, and is his first and latest love."[23] Wolff traces specific borrowings in *Arbasto, Gwydonius, Alcida, Neuer Too Late, Morando, Pandosto,* and *Philomela* (*Greek Romances*, pp. 376–408). But most important of all, Achilles Tatius seems to have been a rhetorician.[24] Clinias's superb attack on women (*Clitophon*, pp. 25–29), Clitophon's self-debate (p. 65), his endless prayer for Leucippe (p. 157), the disputation on sex at sea (pp. 269–71), Leucippe's letter (p. 277), and the formal declamation on anger (pp. 333–35) are all self-indulgent rhetorical extravaganzas. "Love is a fine master of rhetoric," Achilles Tatius writes (p. 301), but so is he; "As a rhetorician," Wolff tells us,

> he shares the Renaissance fondness for antithesis and paradox. His only method of characterization is an antithetical soliloquy, dialogue, or letter by his personages, or antithetical comment by himself. He is not, of course, interested in character, but such characterization as he does attempt resolves itself thus into an analysis of "conflicting emotions." The mania for antithesis vitiates his "psychology" by breaking up character into striving opposites. It vitiates both his style and the speech of his personages by turning both into a Euphuistic balancing of conceits and arguments. Wit and Will; Virtue and Fortune; Nature and Fortune; Nature and Necessity; Fancy and the Fates; Love and Destiny; Nature and Nurture; Desire and Despair; Beauty and Bounty; Beauty and Virtue; the Sore and the Salve; Outward Favor and Inward Valor; Reason and Passion; Bliss and Bale; Hand and Heart; Weal and Woe; Excellence, not Birth; Wit before Wealth; Mirth and Mourning; Love and Law;—these and a hundred other alliterative couples are forever see-sawing through his pages. [*Greek Romances*, pp. 376–77]

But we are not always aware of this, so entranced are we with the display and spectacle. Books 7 and 8 are special feasts of rhetoric in which all of the scraps remain. The court cases, fables, biographies, and explanations employed to conclude the confusing and arbitrary adventures of Clitophon and Leucippe are resolved in the final marvelous controversia of their trial in which the judicial protestations of their innocence are confirmed by the fabulous trials of the panpipes and the Styx (pp. 439, 441) and the oracle is realized in their marriage.

In 1577 Thomas Underdowne published his English translation of still another Alexandrian romance, Heliodorus's *Aethiopian Historie* (c. A.D. 250), which Greene also uses extensively, Wolff notes, in writing *Philomela, Planetomachia, Gwydonius, Ciceronis Amor, Pandosto,* and *Menaphon* (*Greek Romances,* pp. 408–32). In this lengthy tale of Chariclea (Glorious Grace) and Theagenes (Goddess-begotten), "the apogee of ancient romance,"[25] the narrative is deliberately scrambled. It begins *in media res* and, for the first half, proceeds with one story nestled within another. Unscrambled, the story derives from what seems a marvel: a black woman giving birth to a white girl because she was looking at a picture of Andromache at the moment of conception. Beyond that, there is the series of conventional unmaskings through the course of the romance by which characters continually shift relationships. Unraveling the situation is part of the joy of reading Heliodorus, as it must have attracted Greene, but the entanglements are more than narrative obstructions; they are part and

parcel of Heliodorus's epistemology as translated by the Tudor Underdowne. "Oh humaine estate moste vnstable, and full of al manner of
changes," the counselor Cnemon comments,[26] while Chariclea's mother
notes that "no man knoweth the vncertainety of fortune" (sig. G6; 108).
In the prophecies, dreams, and revelations that abound in their world,
catching them by surprise, disrupting their cautious plans, bringing about
improbable conjunctions of persons and events, the two young lovers cling
to each other despite the two apparent deaths of Chariclea, the physical
torture of Theagenes, and other events that continue, from time to time,
to separate them. Their loyalty and faith are finally rewarded in the
marvelous property of the Pantarbe, which prevents Chariclea from
burning, and the wonderful flooding of farmland by the Nile, which allows
Hydaspe to convey ships to Syene. The key juncture in the plot occurs when
Theagenes stages a marvelous abduction of Chariclea and the two travel
to Calasiris to rest their fate with Fortune (sigs. H2–H2v; 116); this
awareness that life is a union of active commitment and passive endurance
is what finally leads them to freedom and marriage. Chariclea glosses the
meaning of their adventures to Theagenes at their end. "GOD giueth vs
such successe wherein is more aduersitie harbored, then our outward
felicitie can counteruaile." she tells him (sig. N5; 197). Beyond the
continually embedded plots and the releasing commentary by the characters there is Underdowne's serial marginalia that rehearse Heliodorus's
philosophy as the Tudors received it: "Necessitas plus poscit quam pietas
solet. Seneca" (sig. D3v; 58); "Fortune is vncertaine" (sig. G6; 108); "No
estate is stable in this world" (sig. L2; 161); "Nothing is certaine in this
world" (sig. M3; 179). The persistent twistings and turnings of events, so
openly dependent on Fortune, nevertheless have their providential ordering, too; from a desperate *tableau vivant* of massacre and shipwreck, which
begins the romance, to the wedding and admission to priesthood at the
close, Heliodorus's romance firmly proceeds from savage chaos through the
marvels of paganism to the conditions of spirituality, a structure of
narrative analogous to that of theme, which Greene employs in the best of
his fictions, in *Gwydonius,* in *Perimedes,* and in *Pandosto.*

Also in 1587 Angel Day published his English translation of "Longus,"
which he titled *Daphnis and Chloe: Excellently describing the weight of
affection, the simplicitie of loue, the purport of honest meaning, the resolution
of men, and disposition of Fate* (originally A.D. 150–200). A contemporary
of Tatius, "Longus" was probably a sophist, to judge from his matter, style,
and language. J. M. Edmonds tells us that

> The use of set speeches for "stock" occasions (Lamo's lament for the
> ravaged garden, 4.8), of full-coloured descriptions of "repertory" scenes

(the description of the garden, 4.2), of soliloquies in which the speaker debates with himself (Gnatho's speech on Love, 4.17; Daphnis's soliloquy, 3.6), and the frequently observed tendency of the narrative to arrange itself as a string of episodes—these considerations, combined with others of an external nature . . . point clearly to the schools of rhetoric, where Hannibal, according to Juvenal, "became a declamation," and boys were taught to make speeches on imaginary themes.[27]

From "Longus" Greene received his most suitable environment for a fiction of wonder, the simplicities and marvels of pastoral that inform *Menaphon* and *Pandosto*. "Longus" 's marvelous romance of the babies of two members of the nobility discovered and reared by a shepherd and a goatherd, with its fresh and innocent tracing of their increasing physical attraction for each other, has some of the heavier machinery we have come to expect from the Alexandrian romance: treachery, war, cruelty, jealousy, and death. Day's translation, however—or, more precisely, adaptation—omits the more sensuous passages of self-discovery by Daphnis and Chloe as well as the war between the Mytilenaeans and the Methymnaeans; and it makes pastoral love rather than fortune and the seasonal cycle of birth and death rather than unexpected separation its central concerns, thus departing considerably from its late Greek original. All these changes are in accord with Greene's two pastoral romances, as Wolff has long since shown us (*Greek Romances*, pp. 432–40). Indeed, Day's description of Lamon's special garden (Book 4) has numerous affinities with Greene's own pastoral settings—

> The shew of this place was a thing of most excellent pleasure, as well of the scituation, prospects, plentie and varietie of deuises, as also for diuersitie of trees, and all kinds of fruits. To this had *Lamon* of all others a most speciall regard, wherein his carefull in-sight and continual trauaile had wrought so great perfection, as seemed to bee helde a thing rare and wonderfull. The trees hung yet laden with all kinde of fruites, plums, apples, peares, mirtes, granades, oringes, limons, figs, oliues, and twentie other pleasing conceits. Besides the number whereof, the order yet curiositie and braue disposition of euerie thing was such, as a man would haue thought it a paradise, and deeplie haue sorrowed to forethinke that the least spoile in the world should haue happened vnto it [Sig. N2v]

—just as his earlier discovery of Daphnis looks forward to Porrus's discovery of Fawnia in *Pandosto*:

> the heardsman wonderfully abashed, drew yet at the last more neere, & serching further, founde it was a male childe, well growen for his age, of beautie merueilous, and farre more richly attired, than beseemed any wayes the infelicitie of his fortune, abandoned so miserablie as he was, and laid

forth, to euerie common aduenture. The vesture wherin he was wrapped was a rich mantle of purple veluet, the compasse fastned about his necke with a brooch of gold, and by his side was layde a short fine sworde of most excellent workemanship, all curiously guilt, on the hiltes and the handle thereof, of the most precious yuorie. [Sigs. A1v–A2]

But Day also adds an even more freely adapted section in "The shepheards Hollidaie" (sigs. K1v–L2). Similarly liberated in good measure from Near Eastern settings he knew only by name, Greene turns to his own native Norfolk for the homely settings of his fiction of wonder. Day's translation lent Greene a sense of description and mood; "he used his pastoral," Wolff remarks, "not as an independent tale, but either as an ornament to some inclusive story or as a solvent for the complexities and a remedy for the troubles which afflict his personages in city or court" (*Greek Romances,* p. 368).

Greene seems to have found the overall design for *Pandosto* in still another Greek romance known only in Latin texts, the *Historia* of Apollonius of Tyre. Translated by Laurence Twine as *The Patterne of Painefull Adventures* and entered in the *Stationers' Register* in 1576,[28] this romance is about the division between a father and his abandoned daughter. The riddle of Antiochus, which Apollonius alone is able to answer, governs his fate because it first exiles him; in Greene this becomes a prophecy from Apollo, which Pandosto neither understands nor heeds. Twine tells us his fiction is one "Containing the most *excellent, pleasant and variable* Historie of the strange accidents that befell vnto Prince Apollonius, the *Lady Lucina his wife,* and Tharsia his daughter. *Wherein the vncertaintie* of this world, and the fickle state of mans life are liuely described" (sig. A1; 6:423). The unknown author was presumably a Greek sophist also,[29] and his narrative has all the trappings of Greek romance—a storm, a shipwreck, separation, pirates, attempts on the heroine's chastity, and a family reunion—but, as in Greene's *Pandosto,* the chief emphasis seems to be on portraying the protagonist. Apollonius is developed as clever, educated, generous, athletic, faithful, emotional, and just. What is more, he is primarily interested in his daughter's education, just as his role as schoolmaster opens the way for him to court Lucina; moreover, Tharsia is betrayed by the couple in whose charge she is left, as Porrus decides to betray Fawnia by disclaiming her. Greene's romance has nothing like the angelic vision that visits Apollonius; the *Historia* has nothing so pronounced and controlling as the passion of jealousy that sweeps over Pandosto in fits and starts. Instead of a sense of a mysterious providence, the *Historia* has only a sense of random destiny.

> But as there was neuer yet any thing certaine or permanent in this mortall
> life, but alwaies we be requited with sowre sauce to our sweete meate, and
> when wee thinke our selues surest in the top of ioy, then tilt wee downe
> soonest into the bottome of sorrow, so fared it now vnto these personages
> in the midst of their iollitie. [Sig. L2v; 6:477]

Such a fatalistic view by an intrusive narrator gives a special premium to
the wonder of discovery and reunion that concludes the *Historia*.
Apollonius finds his wife living and his daughter chaste, and his family is
reunited and returned again to Tyre. Yet the outcome—and the wonder—
is no greater than the reunion of Clerophontes and Gwydonius on the
battlefield at Alexandria and its effect on two dukedoms. And the single
marriage at the end of the *Historia* (and *Pandosto*) is doubled at the close
of *Gwydonius*; Greene often shares with the other major Tudor writers of
humanist fiction a restless inventiveness that turns to the sanctioning of
classical sources only to remake them.

Twine shades his presentation of the *Historia* to a Tudor audience with
numerous allusions to God. Greene seems to do likewise in *Planetomachia*.

> Let the learned iudge, whose deuine thoughts reache vp to the skies, and
> there with secret contemplation doth contemne the baze minds of such as
> with the Scarab Flye, delighteth only to liue in dung and mire.... Thrise
> vnhappy then wee he thought, who are not delighted with this sweete and
> pleasaunt contemplation, and whose minds are not moued with the
> wonderfull works of God and Nature. [Sig. A1v; 5:16–17]

But this is a rare moment in Greene. Usually the pregnant parallels
between the Greek sense of destiny and the faith of the Christian humanists
are only quietly insinuated; what is explicit is a more classical sense of
Fortune, such as the observation in *Orpharion* (1589) that "poore knights
haue their loues not in their own willes, but as Loue and Fortune pleaseth
to allot" (sig. D2v; 12:39); there "the influence of the starres" shapes our
lives (sig. D3; 12:41). It is precisely this sense of uncertainty, often coupled
with a fluid perspective on events, that so disorients and unstabilizes us in
Greene's fiction, that provides the incredible tale Arbasto tells of a whole
sequence of incredible reversals where the plot is the most wondrous thing,
or, in *Mamillia 2*, that brings us also to "haue great cause to muse and
maruel" when Mamillia suddenly appears before a court of magistrates to
plead the cause of Pharicles (sig. K1v; 2:244).

Still, Greene's understanding of fortune runs much deeper than the
chaotic events that cram the Greek romances might at first suggest. Beyond
plot, he seems to sense in these sources of wonder a faith in humanity and
a trust in its powers of thought, action, and endurance that is similar to the

view promulgated by the Tudor humanists. So we are not surprised that when he comes to define fortune at length, that apparently unpredictable side of life that admits both the terrible and the marvelous, he draws on the wisdom of the ancients that was stored ready to hand in such commonplace books as the one Peratio uses for his declamation in *Morando 2* (1587).

> *Aristotle* who by the sharpenes of his reason pearced into the depth of many physicall and supernaturall conclusions, long demaunded by his Scholler *Alexander* the great, what Fortune was: made this answere: That it is a casuall and accidentall cause in things, which being purposely done for some certaine end, haue no apparent cause of their falling out otherwise, so that a man may well say, that such a thing came to him by Fortune. [Sigs. H3–H3v; 3:128–29]

"Being purposely done for some certaine end": Greene's natural kinship with Greek romance stems also from his awareness that Greek plots of separation and suffering are ultimately plots of mystery and redemption: the suffering of Philomela, like the endurance of the exiled Dorothea in his late play *The Scottish Historie of Iames the fourth, slaine at Flodden* (published 1598), is not simply miraculous[30] but also exemplary, not simply entertaining but instructive too. The major period of Greene's humanist fiction is that in which he ascribes his books with the motto of an openly humanist poetics, *Omne tulit punctum, qui miscuit utile dulci* (He wins all the prizes who mingles the useful with the pleasant).

Like other Tudor humanists too, Greene recognizes that fiction is *sub specie rhetoricae*; the significance of his contribution to humanist poetics rests not only with his choice of a fiction of wonder drawn from Greek romance but with a rhetoric of wonder ultimately derived from Longinus. Although Greene may not have known the work of Longinus directly— there is now no recorded edition of it in England until 1636—Longinus lay behind a number of Italian treatises and rhetorics, and it is his understanding of the sublime as the end of art that most aptly describes what Greene attempts in the acts and monuments of wonder toward which his major fictions constantly move. The sublime, Longinus tells us,

> consists in a consummate excellence and distinction of language, and that this alone gave to the greatest poets and historians their pre-eminence and clothed them with everlasting fame. For the effect of genius is not to persuade the audience but rather to transport them out of themselves. Invariably what inspires wonder casts a spell upon us and is always superior to what is merely convincing and pleasing. For our convictions are usually under our own control, while such passages exercise an irresistible power of mastery and get the upper hand with every member of the audience.
>
> Again inventive skill and the due disposal and marshalling of facts do not

show themselves in one or two touches: they gradually emerge from the whole tissue of the composition, while, on the other hand, a well-timed flash of sublimity scatters everything before it like a bolt of lightning and reveals the full power of the speaker at a single stroke.[31]

Both oratory and poetry, according to Longinus, should not merely present ideas clearly, but aim to excite and enthrall (187.2–188.1) for "other qualities prove their possessors men, sublimity lifts them near the mighty mind of God" (36.1). Περὶ ὕψους, by the writer we call Longinus, the friend of Plotinus and the tutor to Porphyry—the work we call *On the Sublime*—was translated in two editions, by Robortello and Manutius, in 1544.[32] This treatise on an affective poetics was inspired by Plato, ever the fountainhead of humanist poetics, in his discussion of fantastic—or unreal, unrepresentative—art in *The Sophist*. There the Elean Stranger talks of

> another art which has to do with words, by virtue of which it is possible to bewitch the young through their ears with words only while they are still standing at a distance from the realities of truth, by exhibiting to them spoken images of all things, so as to make it seem that they are true and that the speaker is the wisest of all men in all things. [234C][33]

Attempting to rescue the wonder of fantastic art from charges of sophistry in the *Sophist*, Aristotle replies with a formalized *Poetics* that insists that plots be representational and events explicable. But he also maintains that pleasure is the true end of poetry (4.6), a pleasure that rests in the magnitude and arrangement of events (7.8–9) and with the reversal and discovery of what is unknown, what surprises by sudden recognition: tokens, memory, or inference (11.4; 16.1–9). "That the marvellous causes pleasure," he writes, "is shown by the fact that people always tell a piece of news with additions by way of being agreeable" (24.17);[34] Aristotle concludes that

> in general any "impossibility" may be defended by reference to the poetic effect or to the ideal or to current opinion. For poetic effect a convincing impossibility is preferable to that which is unconvincing though possible. It may be impossible that there should be such people as Zeuxis used to paint, but it would be better if there were; for the type should improve on the actual. [25.26–29]

Longinus also advocates the type that arouses *admiratio*, but for him pleasure is not so restricted as Aristotle would have it. He does not demand disclosure or revelation because the moments of pleasure are for Longinus of a different order than that of reason: "examples from poetry show a romantic exaggeration, far exceeding the limits of credibility" (15.8).

Pleasure occurs for Longinus at moments of wonder, when "Thoughts are luminous things, and words too," as T. R. Henn has it[35]—at moments of intense ecstasy that neither inform, guide, nor persuade us, but through transporting us become ends in themselves.

"There are," Longinus continues, "five genuine sources of the sublime in literature" (8.1).

> The first and most powerful is the command of full-blooded ideas—I have defined this in my book on Xenophon[36]—and the second is the inspiration of vehement emotion. These two constituents of the sublime are for the most part congenital. But the other three come partly of art, namely the proper construction of figures—these being probably of two kinds, figures of thought and figures of speech—and, over and above these, nobility of phrase, which again may be resolved into choice of words and the use of metaphor and poetic ornament. The fifth cause of grandeur, which embraces all those already mentioned, is the general effect of dignity and elevation. [182v.8]

Amplification by rhetorical figures is integral to this process so long as they are organic. "Figures seem to be natural allies of the sublime and to draw in turn marvellous reinforcement from the alliance," Longinus says (17.1); "they all serve to lend emotion and excitement to the style" (29.2). Much of *On the Sublime,* as a consequence, is given over to cataloguing the figures, discussing apostrophe, asyndeton, anaphora, diatyposis, inversion, periphrasis. Disposition is likewise important to sublimity: "Nothing is of greater service in giving grandeur," Longinus adds, "than the composition of the various members" (40.1). In practicing all these rhetorical means to a poetic end, he urges, as the later Tudor humanists do, the practice of imitatio.

> We too, then, when we are working at some passage that demands sublimity of thought and expression, should do well to form in our hearts the question, "How perchance would Homer have said this, how would Plato or Demosthenes have made it sublime or Thucydides in his history?" Emulation will bring those great characters before our eyes, and like pillars of fire they will lead our thoughts to the ideal standards of perfection. [14.1–2]

By such means, according to Longinian poetics, "we should still do our utmost to train our minds into sympathy with what is noble and, as it were, impregnate them again and again with lofty inspiration" (9.1).

Demetrius, a contemporary of Longinus and the author of a treatise *On Style,* also known to the Tudors, extends a Longinian sense of the wonderful by encasing it in an elevated and elegant style. "In fine," Demetrius tells us, "it is with language as with a lump of wax, out of which one man will mould a dog, another an ox, another a horse."[37] According to Demetrius, the elevated style has three concerns—thought, diction, and composition—and uses such figures as anthypallage, epanaphora, and anadiplosis; metaphor, simile, allegory (sparingly), onomatopoeia, and epiphonema. It is used for force and grace. The elegant style, on the other hand, has charm and vivacity and is often used in poetry. It also may employ such figures as anadiplosis and anaphora, but it will in addition make use of proverbs, fables, comparisons, and instances of hyperbole.[38]

It is precisely such elaboration and embellishment that Greene employs to such advantage in his translation of the Greek romances into a humanist fiction of wonder; and it is this that doubtless accounts for a good deal of his popularity during the period that Madeleine Doran has labeled "an age of eloquence."[39] Like the Alexandrians who "lingered to elaborate whatever pleased,"[40] many Elizabethans also came to regard the florid, middle style of Gorgias and Isocrates as normative.[41] Rhetorical copia became its own verbal act of wonder. So the full title of Thomas Wilson's handbook is *The Arte of Rhetorique, for the vse of all suche as are studious of Eloquence.* And Richard Rainolde's *Foundacion of Rhetorike,* following Aphthonius, argues that

> Nature it self beyng well framed, and afterward by arte and order of science, instructed and adorned, must be singularlie furthered, helped, and aided to all excellencie, to exquisite inuencion, and profounde knowledge ... as a Oratour to pleate with all facilitee, and copiouslie to dilate any matter or sentence. [Sig. A1]

He then defines rhetoric as that which

> in most ample and large maner, dilateth and setteth out small thynges or woordes, in soche sorte, with soche aboundaunce and plentousnes, bothe of woordes and wittie inuencion, with soche goodlie disposicion, in soche a infinite sourte, with soche plesauntnes of Oracion, that the moste stonie and hard hartes, can not but bee incensed, inflamed, and moued thereto. [Sig. A1v][42]

The process Rainolde describes echoes that advocated by the poetics of Aristotle and the rhetoric of Demetrius. It is in this sense that "artificial" and "curious," meaning "artfully made" or "elaborately wrought," were, for the Tudor humanists, approbative.[43] "Nihil enim est aliud eloquentia nisi copiose loquens sapientia," Cicero writes, echoing Demetrius; "eloquence is nothing else but wisdom speaking copiously."[44]

This wondrous act of copia through the employment of varying idea and expression to which Greene shows such favor is furthered in the various textbooks of the humanist schoolrooms. Greene extends his resources, for instance, by multiplying topics or finding-places for arguments, following such humanist texts as Aristotle's *Topica* (1–8) and Cicero's *Topica, De Oratore* (cf. 3:53.206–8), and *Orator* (13.40 ff.). Nearly half of the *Rhetorica ad C. Herennium* is devoted to style and to the figures of rhetoric. "In gravi consumetur oratio figura," the author of the *Ad Herennium* writes,

> si quae cuiusque rei poterunt ornatissima verba reperiri, sive propria sive extranea, ad unam quamque rem adcommodabuntur, et si graves sententiae quae in amplificatione et commiseratione tractantur eligentur, et si exornationes sententiarum aut verborum quae gravitatem habebunt, . . . adhibebuntur.

> A discourse will be composed in the Grand style if to each idea are applied the most ornate words that can be found for it, whether literal or figurative; if impressive thoughts are chosen, such as are used in Amplification and Appeal to Pity; and if we employ figures of thought and figures of diction which have grandeur.[45]

Quintilian carries the tradition forward. "Alia copia locuples, alia floribus laeta"; "copiousness may consist either in wealth of thought or luxuriance of language."[46] According to Quintilian,

> Ne causae quidem parum confert idem hic orationis ornatus. Nam, qui libenter audiunt, et magis attendunt et facilius credunt, plerumque ipsa delectatione capiuntur, nonnunquam admiratione auferuntur.

> Rhetorical ornament contributes not a little to the furtherance of our case as well. For when our audience find it a pleasure to listen, their attention and their readiness to believe what they hear are both alike increased, while they are generally filled with delight, and sometimes even transported by admiration. [8.3.5]

Much of Book 8 and the first three chapters of Book 9 of the *Institutio Oratoria* are given over to amplification, tropes, and figures.[47] Quintilian's way of varying the description of capturing a town (8.3.67–70)—taken over, as we have seen, by Erasmus in *De Copia*—is only one dramatic example of how a brutal and devastating event can nevertheless elicit wonder.

The widespread interest in a rhetoric of wonder by means of copious embellishment through figures of speech and thought that was promulgated among the Roman rhetoricians was warmly received by Tudor England—first through Stephen Hawes's *De Curia Sapiencie* (1480–81) but primarily through Erasmus's *De Utraque Verborum ac Rerum Copia,* a text he composed especially for St. Paul's School, London, and dedicated to Colet. The *De Copia* (1512) and later Joannes Susenbrotus's *Epitome troporum ac schematum et grammaticorum* (1540), derived from it, were well known to Greene and his readers. Book 1 of *De Copia* is a handy thesaurus of formulas for varying words compactly. Erasmus argues that brevity of phrase is a necessary foundation for multiple variations (chap. 6, sig. A6v), a point Longinus had made in *On the Sublime*. Erasmus's method, taken directly from Quintilian (3.56), is twofold—in metaphor and change of word form; and in aggregation, expansion, and amplification of argument (chap. 7, sigs. A6v–A7), or the multiplication of words and thoughts. In Book 2, Erasmus shows how to build a passage to extraordinary lengths, making use (as Greene does) of dreams and of fictitious narratives set within the argument. The most famous is his set of variations on the death of Socrates.[48]

The Latin texts of Erasmus and Susenbrotus led, in Greene's time, to other texts in English by those rhetoricians Sister Miriam Joseph terms the "figurists"[49]—Richard Sherry, Henry Peacham, George Puttenham, and Angel Day,[50] who compiled, in each of their volumes, a concordance of nearly 200 figures presumably in constant use.[51] Such relatively easy figures of words as anaphora, antistrophe, symploce, polyptoton, interpretatione or homoioteleuton; such easy figures of thought as parrhesia, diminutio, exergasia, exemplum, ethopoeia, and prosopopoeia; and even such difficult ornaments as antonomasia, metonymy, hyperbaton, catachresis, and antimetabole must have been endlessly enjoyable to those Elizabethans who popularized them. Thus Sherry in *A treatise of Schemes & Tropes very profytable for the better vnderstanding of good authors* (1550) praises the *Tabulae de Schematibus et Tropis* of Petrus Mosellanus because "no eloquente wryter maye be perceiued as he shulde be, wythoute the knowledge of them" (sig. A6v). Henry Peacham's *Garden of Eloquence* (1577, 1593) was written, he tells the bishop of London, because "wisedome doe requyre the lighte of Eloquence, and Eloquence the fertillity of Wysedome" (1577 ed., sig. A2v); and his further reasoning must have held special significance for a fiction writer like Greene.

> The Oratour may leade his hearers which way he list, and draw them to what affection he will: he may make them to be angry, to be pleased, to laugh, to weepe, and lament: to loue, to abhorre, and loath: to hope, to feare, to couet, to be satisfyed, to enuye, to haue pittye and compassion: to meruaile, to beleeue, to repent: and briefely to be moued with any affection that shall serue best for his purpose. By fygures he may make his speech as cleare as the noone day: or contrarywyse, as it were with cloudes and foggy mistes, he may couer it with darkenesse, he may stirre vp stormes, & troublesome tempestes, or contrariwyse, cause and procure, a quyet and sylent calmnesse, he may set forth any matter with a goodly perspecuitie,

and paynt out any person, deede, or thing, so cunninglye with these couloures, that it shall seeme rather a lyuely Image paynted in tables, then a reporte expressed with the tongue. [Sig. A3]

George Puttenham agrees with this position in his *Arte of English Poesie* (1589). Language, he sums, is never "so well appointed for all purposes of the excellent Poet, as when it is gallātly arrayed in all his colours which figure can set vpon it.[52] For Puttenham, as for other Tudors, rhetoric was primarily an art to dazzle and transport; in this sense, he writes, "Poets were also from the beginning the best perswaders and their eloquence the first Rethoricke of the world" (sig. C3v;8). The primary means of eloquence for Puttenham, as for Erasmus, is copiousness, creating art that "is not only an aide and coadiutor to nature in all her actions, but an alterer of them, and in some sort a surmounter of her skill, so as by meanes of it her owne effects shall appeare more beautifull or straunge and miraculous" (L11v; 303). In addition, "arte is as it were an encountrer and contrary to nature, producing effects neither like to hers, nor by participation with her operations, nor by imitation of her paternes, but makes things and produceth effects altogether strange and diuerse" (sig. L12; 304). So effectively does the use of a rhetoric of wonder transport perceptions, in fact, that Puttenham himself personifies and so makes fictively authentic and living such rhetorical figures as "the Ouer reacher, otherwise called the loud lyer," "the Rerewarder," and "the Middle marcher."[53] The early Tudor translators of Italian fiction point the way for Greene too: William Painter, in *The Palace of Pleasure* (1566), embellishes his stories with long introductory discourses, and Geffraie Fenton, in *Certaine Tragicall Discourses* (1567), amplifies his narratives with marginal glosses.

Given Greene's understanding of figural poetics, it is not surprising, then, that elegance and embellishment are what strike us first, and most lastingly, in his humanist fiction. "Like a musician," Edward Haviland Miller comments, "Greene endeavors to fill the ear with pleasant sound and to create an harmonious emotional effect.[54] In his richest composition, Greene's language of sound and thought is always on display. He can vary the same word, as in his verbal dancing with "compass" in Philomela's effect on the Shipmaster: "for he had almost forgot his Compasse, he was so farre out of compasse with thinking howe to compasse *Philomela*" (sig. G3; 11:173). But more customarily he varies a single idea, such as Philomela's definition of carnal love (sigs. C1v–C3; 11:128–33), Achilles' greeting of Prolixena in *Euphues his censure to Philautus* (sigs. B2v–B3; 6:160–61), the kinds of marriages listed by Penelope's nurse in *Penelopes Web* (sigs. B3v–C1; 5:158–62), or, at the beginning of that book, the elaborate way in which Greene tells us that a Ulysses tired of war wishes to go home (sig. B1; 5:149–50). Often, too, Greene strives as much for humor as for beauty, as in Venus's description of melancholy Saturnists in *Planetomachia* (sig. B4; 5:49) or Sephestia's elaborate mockery of the shepherd Menaphon's unshepherdlike embellishments of language. Greene's fictive poetics is not analytic like Lyly's but affective. His predispositions may have been greatly strengthened by the strong hold Ramus and his disciples held on Cambridge during Greene's days at St. John's and at Clare Hall—in 1588, the Ramist educator William Kempe advocates his master's desire to assign beautification and emotional effectiveness as the sole ends of rhetoric in *The Education of children*[55]—but familiarity with Greene's work and his own persistent references to Aristotle and Cicero make it much more likely that he (like his friend Nashe) was traditionalist, even anti-Ramist. In either event, what Greene himself claims to emphasize is not his matter but his manner: "I excuse my selfe with the answere that *Varro* made, when he offred *Ennius* workes to the Emperour," he says in his defense of *The Myrrovr of Modestie,* "I giue quoth he another mans picture, but freshlie flourished with mine owne coulours" (sig. * 4; 3.7–8). These "coulours" of the figurists are what give to Greene's fiction its permanently enchanting magic.

Such verbal magic is fully seen in the haunting and bittersweet melancholy that characterizes the reflective scenes of *Menaphon* (1589). Such a mood may at first seem at too great odds with an incredible plot, the conclusion of which so disgusted Edward Arber.

> The Story, judged by our modern tests, is full of glaring absurdities. That MELICERTUS should woo his long-lost wife, and not come to recognize her; and that PLEUSIDIPPUS should woo his own mother, and she not know him, is utterly contrary to probability, and the constitution of human nature.[56]

In *Menaphon* the style also seems unusually stiff and clogged for Greene. Walter R. Davis, who likes this work, comments that "Variety of style is always kept foremost in the reader's mind in *Menaphon,* chiefly because its characters are always so much concerned with style, constantly discover things through style, and so frequently comment on each other's style," and he goes on to give several examples *(Idea and Act,* pp. 173–74). What have been isolated in *Menaphon,* that is, are both kinds of wonder drawn from a figurist poetics—a story that depends on the suspension of reason to amaze and astonish, and a rhetoric that extends language by a dazzling display of figures of thought and speech. Both situation and style easily admit those marvelous incidents that Greene takes over from Alexandrian romance—the paradoxical oracle, exposure of the king's daughter, ship-wreck, false autobiographies, and betrothals without consummation from Heliodorus; the disdain of the lovers and contests of rhetoric from Achilles Tatius; the pastoral setting, ridicule of rustic manners, and abduction by pirates from Longus; and the hints of incest from Apollonius of Tyre.[57]

Despite this, *Menaphon* is a curiously moribund narrative, its pacing unusually relaxed, the fiction not so much dramatic as lyric. The framing prophecy, for instance,

> *When Lambes haue Lions for their surest guide,*
> *and Planets rest vpon th'arcadian hills:*
> *When swelling seas haue neither ebbe nor tide,*
> *When equall bankes the Ocean margine fills*
> [Sig. B1v; 6.34]

—predicts a cessation of all action: the story moves inexorably toward the stoppage of all life and time.[58] The action of the thin story line concords. Menaphon, watching the shipwreck of Sephestia, her baby, and an old man, sees

These three (as distressed wrackes) preserued by some further forepoynt-ing fate, coueted to clime the moūtaine, the better to vse the fauor of the Sunne, to drie their drenched apparaile; at least crawled vp where poor *Menaphon* lay close, and resting them vnder a bush, the old man did nothing but sende out sighes, and the woman ceased not from streaming foorth riuolets of teares, that hung on her cheekes like the droppes of pearled deaw vppon the riches of *Flora*. The poore babe was the touch-stone of his mothers passions; for when he smiled and lay laughing in hir lappe, were her heart neuer so deeply ouercharged with her present sorrowes; yet kissing the pretie infant, shee lightened out smiles from those cheekes, that were furrowed with continual sources of teares; but if he cried, then sighes as smokes, and sobbes as thundercracks, foreranne those showers, that with redoubled distresse distilled from her eyes. [Sig. B4; 6.42–43]

The three castaways form a *tableau vivant* in which activity loses significance by repetition (the old man's sighs), or one action is canceled out by another (the tears and smiles—with tear-stained cheeks—of Sephestia); in either event, the view of Menaphon is robbed of action, of life. Moreover, its influence spreads: the lovesick Menaphon soon assumes the same near-lifeless position (sigs. C4–C4v; 6.54–55) that is later assigned to life itself (sigs. D2v–D3; 6:63). As Pleusidippus appears before Erphilia and Agenor in their garden just after they have described him, as if realization rather than change were the most man could hope for (sig. G1v; 4:96), so the fiction ends in an intricate situation in which characters act to accomplish a state that already exists: Sephestia is married to Melicertus, Pleusidippus is pledged to Olympia, Menaphon becomes enamored of Pesana, and Doron marries Carmela. Never, as we reflect on this work of humanist wonder, was an alternative possible. For it is appreciation, not involvement, that Greene means to emphasize. This is true at every juncture; the working out of the oracle that seems to contain its own static reflections is done not dramatically but by the entrance of a *deus* (or *dea*) *ex machina,* an old woman who can only be astonishing to us, first appearing, without warning, to interrupt with an oration the one scene of tense action.

> Well, *Democles* commanded the deathsman to doo his deuoyre; who kneeling downe and crauing pardon, readie to giue *Melicertus* the fatall stroake, there stept out an olde woman attired like a Prophetesse, who cryed out; Villaine holde thy hand, thou wrongest the daughter of a King ... For know *Democles* this *Melicertus* is *Maximus,* twice betrothed to *Sephestia,* and Father to yong *Pleusidippus:* nowe therefore the Oracle fulfilled, is the happie time wherein *Arcadie* shall rest in peace. At this, the people gaue a great shout, and the olde woman vanisht. *Democles* as a man rauisht with an extasie of sodaine ioye, sate still, and stared on the face of *Sephestia* [Sigs. L1v–L2; 6:143–44]

"Rauisht with an extasie of sodaine ioye, sate still, and stared": Menaphon opens and closes with tableaux of static wonder that are explicit tributes to Greene's poetics, the whole wrapped in a style of elegance and elevation taken straight from the rhetoric of Demetrius,[59] transforming the art of narrative into prose poem or ballet. Thus it resembles the final battle of *Gwydonius* where revealed identities solve present dilemmas and restore the past.

Perimedes The Blacke-Smith (1588) is also representative of Greene's period of highest achievement in a poetics of wonder: a fiction about the dynamics of fiction, this work in Demetrius's elegant mode still retains its charm. Pronouncedly humanist in its educative aim—the title page calls it "A golden methode, how to vse *the minde in pleasant and pro*fitable exercise" (sig. A1; 7.3)—*Perimedes* is in addition an enchanting entertainment sufficient to draw old men from chimney corners and children from play. For in it "*is contained speciall principles fit for the* highest to imitate" (sig. A1; 7:3) in the stories the childless Perimedes and his wife tell each other, "sometime discoursing of what came first in their heads, with *Pro & cōtra,* as their naturall logick would graunt them leaue, other while with merie tales, honest, and tending to some good end without either lasciousnesse or scurilitie" (sig. B1v; 7:13). They drift from abstract precept to illustrative experience and back, with all the assurance and familiarity of vicarious repetition. The romances they share, fresh and new with each retelling, grace their lives (and ours) with romance, while their childlike credulity makes them, for us, durably appealing. There is, moreover, a purity in the precepts that Delia trots out that derives not so much from their idealism as from their potential usefulness: she supplies her husband with recipes for merry conceits, patience, content, hope, and heartsease. Perimedes, in his turn, applies proverbial wisdom to their situation, which in its very deprivation is rendered beautiful because it is the cause for fiction. For Perimedes and Delia, the virtues of their fictional nobility merely match their own inner worth and so mirror their own potential adventures, while the unpredictable whims of Fortune are ready at hand to explain why, in a world that should reward the virtuous, the blacksmith and his wife suffer a hard lot.

Perimedes The Blacke-Smith is thus a deliberate, delicate variant on the humanist art of imitation. Isolated in their humble cottage, Perimedes and Delia have a firm grasp on the wonders of Greek romance, stretching marvelously through time and space, as well as the wondrous possibilities of a figural rhetoric. The blacksmith invites his wife to associate herself with Mariana, the wife of Prestynes, lieutenant to the king of Tyre, who flees home when her land is invaded and her husband imprisoned. The initial separation is compounded when pirates make off with her nurse, her child, and her newly born baby, and a despot offers to take her to his land to live as the second lady of his court and sister to his wife. Such misfortunes are met by Mariana's steadfast hope and patience, just as Delia daily meets hers, while her life (unlike Delia's) unfolds at court. Years pass swiftly, and Mariana's son, grown and searching for his father, visits the despot, is identified, and, with the defeat of the tyrant who invaded Tyre, is reunited with his family and married to the despot's daughter. Although Delia rages on behalf of Mariana against Fortune, she shares the protagonist's eventual triumph. The next evening it is Delia's turn to tell a story, and she provides Perimedes with a briefer and less figured mirror of himself in the gentleman Alcimides who "although fauoured thus with sondrie good qualities ... liued poorely, and yet contentedly in meane estate" (sig. D4; 7:47). When he leaves the island of Lyppary to make his fortune so as to marry the more fortunate Constance, he is captured by pirates, and Constance, in sympathy and despair, tries to follow him to a watery grave. In this quiet narrative projection, Delia communicates her own loyalty to Perimedes, and his reply, on the third evening, is the best story of all, for he concludes their exercise in self-rendered, self-reflexive fantasy with the richly brocaded love story of Melissa and Bradamant, who from their initial meeting capture the spirit of Greek romance.

He heard a great rushing in the bushes, wherevpon desirous to see what it might be, he espyed *Melissa,* at whose sight he stood so amazed, as if with *Medusaes* head he had beene turned to a stone: the Lady as much agast, hauing a coosin of hirs with hir called *Angelica,* vttered not a word, but the Louers made mute with loue, stood as persons in a trance, til *Bradamant* discoursing his loues, and making open his priuie passions, fell downe at her feete, and craued mercie. [Sigs. G1v–G2; 6:78]

But his poverty prevents their courtship, and when Melissa is exiled with her tyrannical father to Libya, Bradamant follows her, establishing himself at that foreign court so as to win her hand. The lesson Perimedes draws from this tale commends both Delia and himself and sanctions their pastime: "Thou séest *Delia,*" he sums, "howe farre wit is preferred before wealth, and in what estimation the qualities of the mynde are in respect of worldly Possessions" (sig. G4; 7:84–85). These three exemplary tales, ostensibly about gluttony, gaming, and wealth, are transformed through the wonder of their substance and their telling into thoughts that savor of content, a kingdom of quiet minds by which Perimedes and Delia create a smaller Urbino from the conditions of character rather than from conditions of position and wealth.

Orpharion (1589) is an even more self-conscious fiction of wonder in its numerous levels of reality and artifice. The narrator tells us he was once caught in those "continual perturbations Fancy afforrdes to such as account beauty the principal end of their affects" (1599 ed., sig. A4; 12:9). Journeying in search of aid from Venus, he falls asleep and in his dream is transported to the very Temple of Jove where he learns, to his (and our) astonishment, that the process of love is like the process of fiction, of wonder. Venus,

knowing the olde verse to bee too true for her to disproue, *Quod latet ignotum est: ignoti nulla Cupido,* that what is secret from vs we neuer desire: to inueagle them with her charmes, she presents beautie excellent by nature, yet far more gorgious by arte: faire faces, smiling lookes, alluring gestures, sweet speeches, these are the baites that she layes to intrap. [Sig. B2;12:15]

Narrative leads here to dream, leading to an anatomy of art. But we are far from done: to instruct the narrator, Jove sends Mercury to Hades to fetch the ghosts of Orpheus and Arion to inform the narrator by further fictions (within the narrative within the dream within this work of fiction, and by ghosts). When he arrives, Orpheus is primarily concerned with the moral value of art—a point he makes by calling on wonders of unnatural natural history that seem to contradict Venus.

As the fish Ramera listning to the sound of the trumpet, is caught of the Fishers: as the Porcupine standeth staring at the glimmering of the Starres, and is ouertaken with dogges: as the Leopard looking at the Panthers painted skinne, is caught as a pray: so he which taketh too much delight to gaze vppon beautie, is oft times galled with greefe and misery: yea, his pleasure shall inferre such profite, and his good will such gaines, as if hee reapt the beautifull Apples of *Tantalus,* which are no sooner toucht, but they turne to ashes. . . . this (right mightie Gods) is my censure of beautie, that vnlesse ioyned with vertue, it is like the feathers of the Phenix, placed in the carkasse of a Crow: but where faith and feature are Relatiues, that beauty I call diuine and metaphisical, for because *gratior est pulchro veniens è corpore virtus.* [Sig. C1; 12:23–24]

Orpheus sets about to prove his point by telling the tale of Lidia—although "no tongue can expresse, nor imagination conceiue it" (sig. C1v; 12:26). The tale matches anything in Greene for its reversals and incredibilities, as the young Acestes courts Lidia, is rejected, joins enemy troops, defeats her father, changes sides to claim her, and then, imprisoned, dies by eating his own flesh. Arion, in song, in argument, and in a parallel narrative, finds this view of women and love too tragic; he prefers the constancy of Argentina who, like Acestes, is separated from her lover and imprisoned, her life at stake, until she finds a way (as Acestes does not) of escaping punishment by setting the king of Sicily to an impossible task (her own fiction within the fiction of Arion). Her projected sense of how King Marcion will respond—he wishes to eat before seeing her, having been starved for several days—confirms the efficacy of fiction for a woman whose initial difficulties were caused by her love for Philomenes, a man whose knowledge of love came from books, not experience. She overcomes the dangers of fiction, that is, by trusting to her own fiction. The schematic cross-references between these two tales of ghosts that Davis locates (*Idea and Act,* pp. 151–52) suggest that Greene means us to interpret both extremes of feminine behavior— treachery and constancy—as deficient and excessive, calling on us to supply a third, mediating view, much as two notes on the harp accompanying Arion make a harmonious chord when heard together. Surely this is a fundamental means of humanist poetics behind *Orpharion,* but beyond that is the poetics of wonder, not only in the improbable romance each poet relates but in the narrator's dream and, finally, in Greene's accomplishment, creating a fiction that dazzles us because it questions the efficacy of fiction while confirming the value of fiction by the very means of fiction.

With such works as *Gwydonius, Perimedes,* and *Orpharion,* Greene is the finest exponent of a fiction of wonder, but he is not the first or only Tudor representative of this kind of humanist fiction. *The Palace of*

Pleasure by William Painter seeks romantic settings for a teaching literature by going to Xenophon, Herodotus, Plutarch, Livy, and Roman historians as well as Boccaccio and Bandello (by way of Belleforest) for stories selected *"for example and imitacion right good and commendable"* ("To the Reader," sig. ¶¶2); *"Profitable they be in that they disclose what glorie, honor, and preferment ech man attayneth by good desert, what felicitie by honest attempts, what good successe, laudable enterprises doe bring to the coragious, what happy ioy and quiet state godly loue doth affect the imbracers of ye same"* (sig. ¶¶3v). His eighth novel, "Of a father that made suite, to haue his owne sonne putte to deathe" (sigs. F4–F4v), reveals with astonishing brevity the proverbial dimension Painter lends to romance. Painter's successor, George Pettie, in *A petite pallace of Pettie his pleasure* (1576), takes most of his eleven tales from Ovid, Livy, Hyginus, Plutarch, and Tacitus and, developing them through debates and soliloquies to a far greater extent than Greene in the later 1580s, also applies a limited variety of verbal ornaments.[60] The important link between these early humanist translators and the sort of romance that appealed to Greene is George Whetstone's "Rinaldo and Giletta," a discrete section of *The Rocke of Regard* (1578). In this "discourse" the secret courtly love affair of the two protagonists, a substitute message to Rinaldo by his rival Fitzaldo that nearly results in Rinaldo's suicide, and the eventual reunion of the lovers when Rinaldo discovers Fitzaldo's treachery and kills him in combat constitute Whetstone's adaptation of Gascoigne's *Adventures of Master F. J.* and Ariosto's story of Ariodant and Genevra,[61] which Whetstone tries to pass off as another translation from an anonymous Italian romance (sig. B4). Whetstone's awkward but sometimes dramatic farrago of rhetorical speeches and letters, his use of the romantic convention of coincidence, and his final reliance on Christian design,[62] for all its frequent infelicities, displays several of those ingredients that Greene employs so well.

Considerably superior to Whetstone's single fiction is much of the work of Barnabe Rich. Rich's first story (from Belleforest), the slaughter-ridden love affair of the lady of Chabry and her doctor Trolonio in the *Right Exelent and pleasaunt Dialogue, betwene Mercvry and an English Souldier* (1574; sigs. I3–L8v), is embroidered by a humanist dialogue on the role of the soldier (sigs. B3v ff.); exempla of classical soldiers and commanders (sigs. C1v ff.); and most marvelous of all, a set of murals in the castle of Mercury that displays giants, serpents, dragons, lions, and bulls; and war scenes at Thebes, Troy, Carthage, and—surprisingly—Turwin (sigs. A7v–B1). The collection of eight stories, some of them original, published in 1581 as *Riche his Farewell to Militarie profession,* is a demonstrable advance. The military life is prominent; best known is "Of Apolonius and Silla" (sigs. I1v–L4v), from Pettie and others and, in turn, the basis for Shakespeare's *Twelfth Night*. The finest story, however, is the first, "Sappho, Duke of Mantona" (sigs. C4–I1), for which Thomas Mabry Cranfill has traced "at least twenty-three sources."[63] This explicit tale of fortune is structured in nearly discrete episodes, alternating between sets of characters much the way Greene does, but, unlike Greene, Rich attempts to unify his work by making several episodes parallel. Thus the banishment of Sappho and his family is paired with the later banishment of his son Aurelianus; the jealousy of Sappho by the court at Mantona prepares us for his host's jealousy in Tarissa; the effectual kidnapping of Sappho's wife by his host foreshadows the actual kidnapping of his son; and Aurelianus's love for Valeria, daughter of the duke of Vasconya, anticipates Phylene's love for Arbanius, son of the duchess of Petrona. Such elaborate inner correspondences produce a strong sense of fate and so cause us—rightly, as things turn out—to sense larger and more patterned forces at work that, somehow, will reunite Sappho and his family in due time. The same need for parallelism is also evident in Rich's fourth tale, "Of Fineo and Fiamma" (sigs. O1v–P4), adapted from Cinthio, in which two young lovers are tied in boats, one as an exile, the other as a prisoner, before they are rejoined as servants to the king of Tunis who, impressed by their idealism, miraculously frees them and arranges for their wedding ceremony.

Rich's most ambitious humanist fiction—a narrative encomium moriae—is *The straunge and wonderfull aduentures of Dō Simonides,* written in two parts (1581; 1584). Book 1 opens when the Don's childhood friend Clarinda rejects his proposal of marriage because "I amongst so many," she tells him, "am least able to counsell you" (sig. C1). But no one is able to counsel Don Simonides. His first reaction is to leave his home. For this he is rewarded, in a hermit's costume, with a sequence of comic and tragic tales that are all exemplary (as with Greene's humanist fiction) and that attempt to teach him penance, constancy, contrition, humility, patience, and compassion—that is, they all focus on lessons peculiarly apt for a pilgrim—yet he fails to learn from any of them.[64] Even the varying of rhetorical forms fails to communicate sufficiently.[65] Rich warns his gentleman readers that Book 2 is reduplicative (sig. A4). Here the Don reaches Rome, the destination of his pilgrimage, but it has little effect. He hears a friar, a lawyer, and a soldier dispute the virtues of their professions and then rebuts each of them; on route to Naples he is given an exemplum of disappointed love in the deaths of Priscilla's suitors but ignores it; he rejects a sermon and a letter from Fredericke de Cieuta at Naples on the Don's foolish attitudes; he fails to complete the analogy between himself and the tale of Orienta and Fulvius told him by Corubus on his sea voyage to Athens; and, once there, finds humanist precepts washed ashore only puzzling although he studies them alongside Euphues. Even a letter to Euphues from Philautus comes to nothing. When Don Simonides returns to Seville he finds Clarinda, who had vowed to remain chaste forever, has married "an olde doating Citizen called *Baldio*" (sig. T4v). It is Rich's last joke on the would-be pilgrim who failed to learn wherever he went and who failed to achieve at home what he wanted most. Rich's unflagging inventiveness and stamina carry the art of varying a single idea in *Don Simonides* 1 and 2 to lengths unmatched by any other Tudor writer of humanist fiction, as Greene's Arbasto, *The Anatomie of Fortune* (1584), also about a hermit who suffers from unrequited love, which may be an adaptation of Rich's propositio, demonstrates.

Aside from Greene, then, the finest fiction of wonder is John Grange's *Golden Aphroditis: A pleasant discourse* (1577).[66] In a prefatory poem, W. S. commends the author for his "Eloquence and loftie style" (sig. B4),[67] but W. S. fails to point out what most distinguishes this unique work: its necessarily opaque, obscurantist manner, which Grange confesses to with the Latin tag *Alagere & non intelligere, nempe neglegire est* (sig. S4v). For the riddling *Golden Aphroditis*—the title itself juxtaposing a sense of the perfect and heavenly with that of the imperfect and carnal—is the sole Tudor fiction of anagogy, the story of the miraculous wedding of god and man. Here, in the action of *The Golden Aphroditis,* as well as in our act of reading it, those "*who wil the curnell of the nut must breake the shell*" (sig. I3v).

The chief characters in Grange's parable of spiritual salvation are the human N. O., awakened to religious awe by the metamorphosis of his cousin Hippomentes into a beast for having profaned Cybele's temple, and the maiden A. O. of Scyros, the semidivine daughter of Diana and Endimion.[68] N. O.'s higher longings—opposing his name—are figured in his sudden love for A. O. caused by the intervention of Cupid. A. O.'s dual nature in turn is figured in the name given her by Diana, for it signifies the divine Oracle of Apollo—significantly the god of wisdom and medicine— which announced her birth and Diana's first and last carnal act, her alpha and omega (sigs. C2; C3v). Although destined as lovers, N. O. and A. O. find their courtship a difficult one. As with most lovers in Greene's fiction, the total trust and surrender demanded by love is part of it, as well as the fear of "to muche credulitie and light beliefe" (sig. C2).[69] But, since N. O.'s eventual divinity is also at stake as well as A. O.'s own admission to the heavenly councils, their tense relationship must combine inner self-control with outward obeisance—and (a still greater obstacle) the use of mundane courtly love conventions to convey religious longings. *The Golden Aphroditis* is thus a story of the ritual of love as a rite of purification.

N. O meets this dual challenge by an open language of paradox. "I winke for feare, least my too much contemplation of thy wonderful beautie daze my greedy eyes," he tells his beloved, "for by proofe I fynd it not ouer easy to clyme the Egles nest, and thy great curtesie is a ready repulse to my rudenesse, yet beare with my blynking folly: for it is great good will that grauelleth me, and the feare of repulse maketh my heart to freese" (sig. Div). A. O. resorts to other conventions: as partly divine, she speaks to N. O. almost exclusively in enigmas; as partly human, she uses the courtly tradition of the challenging mission, sending N. O. to steal a jewel from the forehead of Venus herself to establish his dominance over physical love. Both witness to their love as true and untrue—"I with the sight of thee am rauisht" (sig. Fi)—because it makes the real appear ideal, a metamorphosis willed by N. O. and A. O. but not yet sanctioned by the gods. Only after several months of their courtship do they experience signs of divine approval. Although he is the most shadowy figure of all, I. I., in his appearance as N. O.'s rival, provides both lovers with a final test of virtue and constancy. Moreover, after their betrothal, N. O. visits the Garden of the Muses and finds the grass there "curiously carued and cut of eche side, adorned with pinnacles and pillers in māner of a fayre large bedsteede" (sig. L3).

A. O. pledges herself to N. O. at Christmas, and their wedding is celebrated at Easter in a three-tiered castle constructed by Diana. Representatives of all three levels of creation participate: in the uppermost banqueting hall made of jasper and marble Jupiter leads the festivity, Venus and Minerva once more sit beside each other, Apollo plays his harp, and Bacchus delivers drunken speeches; at the middle level, Neptune watches as the sirens sing like nightingales and the sea nymphs perform a ballet; and even in the lowest hall, Pluto and his subjects revel in watching the torments of Ixion and Tantalus. The marriage is thus a general act of reunion and the restoration of order at all levels of existence. This act of narrative reconciliation works aesthetically too, for it comments on the inset story of the farmer and the priest, which in a fabliau of selfish (literally cupid-inous) love reverses the story of the principal lovers. Thus *The Golden Aphroditis,* with its mystical overtones, aligns itself with the instructive tradition of humanist poetics. Grange compares his work, at the close, to the *Encomium Moriae,* which through "clokes of mery conceytes" likewise touches "euen the chiefest poyntes which pertayneth to mans saluation." For Erasmus "shewed no greater learnyng in any one booke of his penning, than he did in this" (sig. N4).

The Golden Aphroditis was, so far as we can now judge, a limited success, yet it discloses the joy that the third generation of English humanists took in the enigmatic, the riddling, and the apparently incredible (represented in Greene's fiction by wonderful emblems and divine oracles). Peacham, for example, has reservations about the effectiveness of the enigma as a trope of speech, but his joy in the enigma as a trope of writing is immediate and exuberant: "for when men fynde at last, by long consyderation, the meaning of some darcke riddle, they much delight and reioyce, that their capacity was able to compasse so hard a matter, and commende highly the deuysers wit" (sig. D2). It is clear from the ingenuity of the examples that Peacham subsequently provides (sig. D2v) that a source of the pleasure is in the creation or construction of the apparently marvelous but actually rational conundrum. This kind of pleasure, which Greene's fiction also provides, takes us very near to the initial impulse of fiction itself; for us, as for the Elizabethans, it is a fiction of wonder at its outermost limits.

Greene shares with several of these other Tudor writers of a fiction of wonder, most notably Painter and Pettie, an interest in the work of Boccaccio; according to Gabriel Harvey, everyone was reading Boccaccio among other Italian writers when Greene was at Cambridge;[70] earlier, Ascham, in *The Scholemaster,* claims that a tale by Boccaccio was often made more of than a story from the Bible (sig. I3). Giovanni Boccaccio was known as a distinguished Latin scholar attached for some time to the court of King Robert of Anjou at Naples and the author of the *De Casibus Virorum Illustrium,* the *De Montibus,* the *De Claris Mulieribus,* and, most helpfully, the *Genealogia Deorum Gentilium* with its fourfold means of interpreting the gods. But although this humanist came in time to prefer a life of scholarly retirement with occasional lectures and much writing, it is his body of works on love to which the Tudor writers of fiction most frequently turn. His *Amorous Fiammetta,* translated in 1587 by B. Giouano del M. Temp. (Bartholomew Yong), is full of the rhetorical lamentations of Fiammetta, who is forsaken throughout the work by "a propper yong Gentleman" of "yong and florishing age," Panphilus (sig. A4v). The *Ameto,* with its six stories of cardinal virtues told by nymphs, was a structural model—a clear Senecan original—for Greene. Boccaccio's monumental *commedia umana,* the *Decameron*—it opens with "Umana cosa è" (human it is)—written in retirement about another retirement at the Poggio Gherardi and the Villa Palmieri, is a treasurehouse of a hundred tales of love from which Greene took several, including the first and second tale of Perimedes and Delia in *Perimedes The Blacke-Smith* (*Decameron* 2.6, 5,2) and the transformation of Fabius in *Ciceronis Amor* (5.1).[71] It is indicative that Greene, drawn to this work of "copious and felicitous diction,"[72] chose, as Samuel Lee Wolff notes, those tales that especially resemble Greek romances[73] while avoiding the more erotic Boccaccio. The fictions of the *Decameron* have their own frame of reference in the devastating plague that struck Europe between 1346 and 1350—virtually incurable, highly contagious, random in its victims—which, comparable to the plague of fifth-century Athens described by Thucydides, could be as awesome, as whimsical, and as terrifying as the oracles and tempests that frequently begin Greene's fictions of wonder. Both writers like to open with quickly sketched narrative situations, the framework and the inset tale positing a dynamic dialectic from the start. At least as important as the *Decameron* was Boccaccio's *Filocolo* Englished by H. G. in 1567, the excessively long romance of Florio and Biancofiore, their separation by willful parents, and their final salvation by the miraculous intervention of Mars and Venus, for it makes many excursions into mythology and paraphrases extensively from Ovid's *Metamorphoses*. Most useful of all was H. G.'s English translation of *Filocolo 4* as *Thirteen Most Pleasant and Delectable Questions of Love* (1566, 1571, 1587) with its framework of a shipwreck, its setting of a garden for the posing of courtly questions concerning love, and two of the questions—the third, on valor, courtesy, and liberality, that is the basis for *Euphues his censure to Philautus,* and the sixth, on the virtue of silence, that is the basis for the third tale of *Penelopes Web*.[74]

Greene shares Boccaccio with other writers of the fiction of wonder; what sets him decisively apart is his additional use of Ovid: in many ways, his poetics is as much Ovidian as it is figurist. Indeed, the rhetorician Ovid—who studied under Porcius Latri of Corduba and Arellius Fuscus from Asia Minor and who was, the elder Seneca assures us, regarded as particularly adept at declamations—seems as important to Greene's fiction as Cicero and Quintilian with all of their schemes and tropes. As a "second *Ouid,*" Greene "euer professed my selfe Loues Philosopher" (*Greenes Mourning Garment,* sigs. A4–A4v; 9:121–22). He was much influenced by the *Heroides,* a collection of suasoriae and controversiae which, in the form of letters, draw the portraits of a faithful Penelope, a forgiving Briseis, a despairing Dido, or a complaining Phyllis, as well as debates of love between Helen and Paris, Hero and Leander and Acontius and Cydippe, among others. Greene takes many of his details of characterization from these letters as well as the Ovidian technique of varying stock themes and even standard rhetorical devices within the sharply circumscribed arena of love complaint. He may also have learned varying perspectives on love from Ovid's *Amores* as well as the *Ars Amatoria,* which he discusses at length in the first appended letter to *Mamillia* 2 (sig. L1v; 2:254).

These borrowings by Greene are formative but pervasive throughout his humanist fiction; his even greater reliance on Ovid's *Metamorphoses* is adulatory and explicit. The triumphantly rhetorical *Metamorphoses* is the longest classical exercise in the art of varying, a collection of epyllia that recount 250 tales of transformation, of instability, and of constant change,[75] favorite themes of much Latin neoteric poetry. The powerful drive toward narrative, the speed of the storytelling, the vivid pictorialism, the elliptical and syncopated development of plot, the highly selective use of detail are all features of the *Metamorphoses* that instructed Greene in his fictive art, while the basic use of the theme—showing the inner state of mind by the metamorphosis of outer form and the apparent superiority of fortune to the momentary will of individuals—Greene also borrows as a central concern of his fiction of wonder. Greene emulates the carefully balanced arguments in the *Metamorphoses* between such figures as Medea and Byblis, or Myrrha and Scylla, with their careful presentation of alternatives and their rhetorical questions and antitheses; the more elaborate debate between Ajax and Ulysses is the model for Greene's debate between Hector and Achilles. It is here, in fact, in *Metamorphoses* 13 (rather than with the Pythagorean theory outlined in *Metamorphoses* 15), that Greene's interest centers: in Ovid's most extended debate followed by the death speech of Polyxena, the mourning of Hecuba, and the marvelously complicated narrative of Polyphemus's courtship of Galatea enclosed by the tale of her love of Acis as told by Scylla when recounting the story of Glaucus's transformation to Aeneas.

Many of these numerous variations of narrative structure in Ovid appear in Greene. Scylla's tale to Aeneas resembles Arbasto's story to a company of people about the waywardness of Fortune; the daughters of Minyas passing time with stories as they spin is taken over as the frame for *Penelopes Web*; the contest of the Muses with the daughters of Pierus becomes the contest between Orpheus and Arion. But it is the philosophical implications of metamorphosis that strike Greene most tellingly and most lastingly. Through this singularly powerful notion in Ovid, John Barsley remarks,

> It is possible to see the poem as an escape from contemporary reality into a world of imagination and fantasy, where moral problems are dissolved by metamorphosis and human tragedy is similarly averted, but it is also possible to see it as a reflection of a world of uncertainties and arbitrary force, where the individual has no secure identity and no control over his own destiny. The element of lightness and fantasy in the poem is undeniable and needs no illustration, but the darker element should not be underestimated. . . . There is a good deal of undeserved human suffering,

which the metamorphosis endings do not ultimately cancel, physical sufferings in particular are sometimes described in almost sadistic detail. . . . The *melior natura* of the Creation story (1.21) is soon replaced by lustful or vengeful anthropomorphic gods and eventually by an impersonal system of endless change (15.176 ff.). The *Metamorphoses* is not in fact based on a coherent philosophical system.[76]

But it is splendidly arbitrary and random. Greene is never as brutal as, say, Ovid or Nashe in his own more wondrous scenes of slaughter (as in *Gwydonius*), but the pain of love and the fearful contingencies of life are everywhere in Greene's fiction. This is what Bernardino has in mind when he tells the countess Ferneze, "our yeres growen & budding forth a restles desire to plesure, which if we should cut off with a continuall remembrance of death, we should preuent time & metamorphose our selues by concert into a contrary shape" (*Farewell to Follie* [1591], sig. B3; 9:241; cf. Ovid, *Metamorphoses* 11.273 ff.). The potential danger of transformation—as in Maesia's conversion to a maid or Vadislaus's change to a beggar in the same story (sigs. D4, E3; 9:265, 274)—must carry the same anxiety if the story is to function dramatically at all, as we are reminded when we learn that Vadislaus "made a metamorphosis of a monarchie into flat gouernment of tyrannie" (sig. E3; 9:272); that Aristotle, according to Cosimo, defines love as "a metamorphosis of mens bodies and soules into contrarie shapes" (sig. G1v; 9:290); or that Semyramis is incapable of change (sigs. I3v–I4; 9:318–19). Rosamond's willful desire to become a pool like Echo or marble like Niobe, like Philador's actual transformation into a swineherd (*Greenes Mourning Garment* [sigs. D3v–G3v; 9:162–88]), is less serious only because it is less permanent. Ovid's "fascination with the incongruous," as Barsley has it (*Ovid*, p. 37), is a source of the fiction of wonder for Greene as it was for the Greek romancers. For they too transmitted the ideas and techniques of Ovid—seen in the flurry of miracles (such as the man of bronze) that concludes the *Argonautica*; the tapestry, the contest between Apollo and Daphne, and the tales of Procne and Pan in Achilles Tatius; the story of Echo and the final transformations of Daphnis and Chloe in "Longus"; and the conversions of Apollonius of Tyre from prince to hermit, Tharsia from princess to whore, and Lucina from queen to priestess in the Apollonius *Historia*. Transformation as a necessity of plot awakening a sense of miracle, as a physchological condition inducing fear, or a philosophical consideration addressing Fortune is, in its range of possibilities, at the center of Greene's poetics.[77] And, as with all writers of humanist poetics, Greene means his readers to keep the imitated patterns and ideas in mind as Greene uses them or diverges from them in this humanist fiction of imitatio.

Greene's basic text of Ovid was almost certainly *The .xv. Bookes of P. Ouidius Naso, entytuled Metamorphosis,* translated by Arthur Golding (1567), with its clear theme: "Al things doo chaunge. But nothing sure dooth perrish" (15.183).[78] From the Pythagorean portrayal of human beings eternally changing shape through the various ages of man (15.221–38) to the glorious transformation of Julius Caesar into a star at the close of this massive poem, Golding sees the power and possibility of metamorphosis. His own moral—not to say Puritan—Ovid is developed frequently in the epistle as he Christianizes the more obvious of Ovidian tales, seeing as Ovid does that the power of love and fate, told through the power of poetry, will grant him his own immortality (sig. a2; 404). Golding's own poetics, which Greene shares, is developed further in his preface.

> For as the Image portrayed out in simple whight and blacke
> (Though well proportiond, trew and faire) if comly colours lacke,
> Delyghteth not the eye so much, nor yet contentes the mynde
> So much as that that shadowed is with colours in his kynde:
> Even so a playne and naked tale of storie simply told
> (Although the matter bee in deede of valewe more than gold)
> Makes not the hearer so attent too print it in his hart,
> As when the thing is well declarde, with pleasant termes and art.
> All which the Poets knew right well: and for the greater grace,
> As Persian kings did never go abrode with open face,
> But with some lawne or silken skarf, for reuerence of theyr state:
> Euen so they following in their woorkes the selfsame trade and rate,
> Did under covert names and termes theyr doctrines so emplye,
> As that it is ryght darke and hard theyr meening to espye.
> But beeing found it is more sweete and makes the mynd more glad,
> Than if a man of tryed gold a treasure gayned had.
> For as the body hath his ioy in pleasant smelles and syghts:
> Euen so in knowledge and in artes the mynd as much delights.
> Wherof aboundant hoordes and heapes in Poets packed beene
> So hid that (sauing vntoo fewe) they are not too bee seen.
> And therfore whooso dooth attempt the Poets woorkes to reede,
> Must bring with him a stayed head and judgement too proceede.
> [Sig. A2v; 426]

Such rhetorical color and obscurity awaken pleasure—and pleasurable wonder—in Ovid, in Grange, and in Greene.

The word "metamorphosis," like the words "wonder" and "amaze" in their various lexical forms, appear throughout Greene's work, but "metamorphosis" is more dominant in the works from 1590 onward. One fiction, *Alcida,* is also titled *Greenes Metamorphosis* (written perhaps as early as

1588), "VVherein is discouered," the title page tells us,

> a pleasant transformation of bodies into sundrie shapes, *shewing that as vertues beautifie the mind, so vani*ties giue greater staines, than the perfection of any quality can rase out: *The Discourse confirmed with diuerse* merry and delightfull Histories: full of graue *Principles to content Age, and sawsed with pleasant* parlees, and witty answeres, to satisfie youth: profitable for both, and not offensiue to any. [1617 ed., sig. A2; 9:3]

This work is signed R. G. and bears the motto, "Omne tulit punctum, qui miscuit utile dulci." A friend, G. B. of Canterbury, writes a Latin poem honoring the work in imitation of Ovid, and an anonymous friend writes that

> Olim praeclaros scripsit *Chaucerus* ad Anglos,
> Aurea metra suis patrio sermone refundens:
> Post hunc *Gowerus*, post hunc sum carmina *Lydgate,*
> Postque alios alij sua metra dedere Britannis.
> Multis post annis, coniungens carmina prosis,
> Floruit *Ascamus, Chekus, Gascoynus,* & alter
> *Tullius* Anglorum nunc viuens *Lillius,* illum
> Consequitur *Grenus,* praeclarus vterque Poeta
> [Sig. B1v; 9:13]

—his place earned by his Ovidian poetics. These instructive tales of transformation are told to a shipwrecked narrator when he alone makes it to the shore of Taprobane—"the Ile seemed a sacred Eden, or Paradise: much like that faire England the flower of Europe, stored with the wealth of all the Westerne world" (sig. B2v; 9:17)—only to learn it is strange and wondrous, a place where

> *Mercurie* walked in the shape of a Country Swaine, *Apollo* kept *Midaes* sheep, and poore *Philemon* & *Bawcis* his wife, entertained *Iupiter* himselfe, supt him & lodged him: they honored an vnknowne ghest: he not vngratefull to so kinde an Oast, for hee turned their Cottage to a Temple, and made them Sacrificers at his Altars. [Sig. B3; 9:19]

The unusual, lonely, and sad old woman named Alcida who welcomes the weary stranger tells him, over the course of two days, of her three daughters. Representing pride, fickleness, and constancy, they were transformed by the gods for their various forms of selfishness into a marble monument, a chameleon bird, and a rosebush. As the old lady finishes the last of her stories of admonition about the defects and excesses of love—meaning the narrator (and us) to moderate such behavior—a ship appears miraculously, and from Alexandria, to rescue the narrator. As he leaves, "The poore Lady, seeing her selfe alone, fell to her wonted teares, which the gods taking pittie on, before my face turned to a fountaine" (sig. K3v; 9:112–13). As with Golding, wondrous tales in Greene are finally subjected to moral messages.

Greene's employment of the Alexandrian romance of wonder, the Demetrian sense of elegance, the figural rhetoric of dazzling display, and the Ovidian poetics of change as the one certain thing in life all come together in his masterpiece, *Pandosto. The Triumph of Time* (1588). This novel draws knowingly from Alexandrian romance, for *Pandosto* brilliantly joins scattered motifs from them all: the oracle and trial scene from Heliodorus as well as the rhetorical speeches and humor of Achilles Tatius, the pastoral atmosphere and respect for simplicity in "Longus," and the more psychologically valid development of the theme of incest, which through the riddle of Antiochus is the inciting incident and fundamental motif in the Apollonius *Historia*. *Pandosto* seems deliberately to sum Greene's work, too, bringing together the pastoral elements in *Menaphon,* the more didactic stories of an ideal woman like Marpesia (comparable to Bellaria) and Meribates (a less tragic Pandosto) from *Alcida,* as well as Fortune in *Arbasto,* transformations in *Ciceronis Amor,* and the plot and moment of wonder in *Gwydonius.* All blend here in the crucible of Greene's creativity, taking us now considerably beyond the Ciceronian poetics of Castiglione and the balanced Isocratean poetics of Lyly to a new, freer poetics of wonder all his own.

Pandosto claims at the first to be an honest, sometimes painful account of man's incontinence caught in an unrelenting anatomy of human jealousy.

> Among al the Passions wherewith humane mindes are perplexed, there is none that so galleth with restlesse despight, as ye infectious soare of Iealousie: for all other griefes are eyther to bee appeased with sensible perswasions, to be cured with wholesome counsel, to be relieued in want, or by tract of time to be worne out, (Iealousie only excepted) which is so sawsed with suspitious doubtes, and pinching mistrust, that whoso seekes by friendly counsaile to rase out this hellish passion, it foorthwith suspecteth that he geueth this aduise to couer his owne guiltinesse. [Sig. A3; 4:233–34)

Pandosto's agonizing inability to trust his childhood friend, his wife, or even his own sight and hearing makes him sharply discrepant to Bellaria, who is "by birth royall, learned by education, faire by nature, by vertues famous" (sig. A3; 4:234). Pandosto acts by instinct and feeling; the educated Bellaria acts through reason and self-discipline. Each is innocent of the other's fundamental nature, their marriage a tragic mismatch.

Pandosto. The Triumph of Time puts not only the king of Bohemia on trial but (through Bellaria) the efficacy of humanism, the potentiality for wonder, and even the quite possibly fatuous belief in the educability of man. It is as if Greene returns to unfinished observations, too, in his portrait of the tyrant Valdrako in Venus's tragedy in *Planetomachia* and the story of the obedient Barmenissa in *Penelopes Web* and places these two exemplary possibilities against the heightened, marvelous setting of the island Taprobane: not merely icastic but also fantastic art is scrutinized.

Greene's dispositio is such that like Pandosto we are initially puzzled by Bellaria's behavior toward Egistus:

> her countenance bewraied how her minde was affected towardes him: oftentimes comming her selfe into his bed chamber, to see that nothing should be amis to mislike him. This honest familiarity increased dayly more and more betwixt them; for *Bellaria,* nothing in *Egistus* a princely and bountifull minde, adorned with sundrie and excellent qualities, and *Egistus,* finding in her a vertuous and curteous disposition, there grew such a secret vniting of their affections, that the one could not well be without the company of the other. [Sig. A4; 4:237]

We too might suspect her motives if the objective narrative did not tell us otherwise. It is this behavior that first instills jealousy in Pandosto, and it is their failure to recognize his anger that allows them to continue with what are, for him, provocative actions. Only after his observations over a period of time have given him confirming evidence does his jealousy become so intense that he is unwilling and unable to believe the protestations of his friend, his wife, and his servant Franion, all of whom, he feels, might have good reason to feign innocence. His irrationality does not actually begin until he plans the treacherous murder of Egistus; only then does Greene label his enterprise "diuellish" (sig. B1; 4:240).

Franion's highly formal soliloquy in which he decides to leave Pandosto and join Egistus thus provides the kind of reasoned, balanced examination that the characters until now have failed to supply, and it looks forward to Bellaria's reasoned responses during her trial. Against their disciplined moderation, Pandosto's rage is too irrational for our continued sympathy— even when Egistus sails away from him at night, Franion betrays him, and Bellaria's pregnancy is revealed. For the facts bear at least two constructions, we see, and Pandosto is no longer able to withstand such possibilities, to withstand doubt or ambiguity. Jealousy warps human nature in Greene's view because it prevents the free interplay of reason and event: it cancels out the possibility of wonder. Pandosto's lying accusations bewray his own metamorphosis as they show him moving away from icastic reconstruction, in which he has matched his fears with witnessed events, to self-serving fictions that free him of any guilt or responsibility. Our own sense of wonder comes in suddenly witnessing the power of wonder to betray.

With such enormous change in Pandosto, only Bellaria struggles to reintroduce faith, trust, and the possibilities for wonder in her husband under the guise of agreeing to his premise of absolute justice. The psychology succeeds, for Pandosto is not only brought to see the truth when the oracle declares her innocence but, almost incredibly, he finds the wherewithal to confess his gross misjudgment before his own people. His shame is nearly as excessive as his rage had been (sig. C3; 4:261). It is truly a moment of *meraviglia*. But experience is too tardy in teaching him, for his son and wife have died, inexplicable victims of his folly. Only his peers prevent his own suicide as his hasty act of retributive justice; he must learn instead to live a life of penance.

Enlightenment therefore is hard-won in Bohemia; it comes naturally in Sicily. Greene's pastoral interlude in *Pandosto* is equally exemplary; but it instructs through a validated wonder, as in his earlier humanist fiction. In defining the sufficiency of a simple life, it lends substance to love and belief. The cruel illogicality of events in Bohemia is replaced by a purity of heart that quietly condemns any form of discontent: where men are satisfied, there can be no possibility of deception and distrust; because contentment eliminates ambition and change, Sicily also seems timeless. From the moment when the aging shepherd Porrus finds in Fawnia his lost sheep, but one which makes him rich with both gold and fatherhood, "maruailing how such a seely infant, which by the Mantle, and the Chayne, could not be but borne of Noble Parentage" (sig. C4v; 4:266), Sicily is also the place of joyous miracles rather than inexplicable fate (a matter of emphasis as well as perspective). The other miracles—Prince Dorastus's discovery of a princess in Fawnia ("he stoode in a maze" [sig. D3; 4:274]) and their mutual love when he is transformed into a shepherd—are quick to follow.

Dorastus's first soliloquy, a judicial oration, serves as a corrective to the first soliloquy of Pandosto. He argues for a trust in human nature, submission in behavior, and fortune as embodied in the virtues of the beloved.

> He that striueth against Loue, shooteth with them of *Scyrum* against the winde, and with the Cockeatrice pecketh against the steele. I will therefore obey, because I must obey. *Fawnia*, yea *Fawnia* shal be my fortune, in spight of fortune. The Gods aboue disdain not to loue womē beneath. Phoebus liked *Sibillia, Iupiter Io,* and why not I then *Fawnia,* one something inferiour to these in birth, but farre superior to them in beautie, borne to be a Shepheard, but worthy to be a Goddesse. [Sig. D4; 4:278]

Alliteration, antanagoge, antisagoge, contrarium, hypophora, isocolon, progressio, prosapodosis, effictio, ethopoeia: even short speeches in Sicily are laden with the ornamentation of a regenerated rhetoric. Incredibly, the presumed shepherd's daughter speaks an equally elevated language, although she must be persuaded to action, for she is adequately sustained by the pastoral existence.

> Sir (quoth she) beggers ought not to striue against fortune, nor to gaze after honour, least either their fall be greater, or they become blinde. I am borne to toile for the Court, not in the Court: my nature vnfit for their nurture: better liue then in meane degree, thun in high disdaine. [Sig. E1v; 4:283]

The growth of their miraculous love is, therefore, a surrender by each of them: Dorastus emblematically gives up his role as prince, and Fawnia gives up her simple life of the quiet mind (sig. E1v; 4:282).[79] Their surrender to each other will eventuate in a similar surrender of Egistus, Porrus, and Mopsa to their romance.

The flight of these two young lovers to Bohemia, with Porrus captive at their side, amends Fawnia's earlier exile from her homeland. Upon their arrival, wonder evokes wonder: "*Pandosto* amased at the singular perfection of *Fawnia*, stood halfe astonished, viewing her beauty, so that he had almost forgot himselfe what hee had to doe" (sig. F4; 4:303–4). But "Fortune is plumed with Times feathers, and how shee can minister strange causes to breede straunge effectes" (sig. D3; 4:274). The general view is that Greene seriously maculates his larger exemplum in Pandosto's unexplained reversion to lust for his disguised daughter and his impetuous arrest of Dorastus. But the difficulty lies chiefly in our failure to understand Greene's poetics, by which only the right virtuous kind of wonder arises from grandeur of thought. In a merely real world of likeness making, in icastic imitation where Pandosto lives, man's fundamental character is not easily changed. Pandosto has grieved for the loss of his wife and son; but he does not know his daughter is alive or that she has appeared in his court disguised as an Italian gentlewoman from Padua. The strong passion for women that can rise to jealousy now, after decades of deprivation, gives way to uncontrolled yearning. His incontinence remains, continuing to be, as Greene remarks earlier, "deuillish."

Pandosto also remains essentially unrepentant and unreconstructed because he has no one, as Fawnia and Dorastus have each other, to teach him. His loneliness makes him as perverse emotionally as the solitary Euphues, alone and unfulfilled in Silexedra, is perverse intellectually. One suffers from choler, the other from melancholy. When Fawnia resists

Pandosto's advances, when she becomes inflexible, his former anxiety and fear resurface, and he is reduced to "broyling at the heat of vnlawfull lust" (sig. G1v; 4:309). So strong are their passions—hers to principle, his to desire—and so fixed their deadlock of will that Greene's own narrative bursts into drama. This very explosion of rhetorical form (it happens nowhere else in Greene's fiction) suggests the energy with which he invests the scene.

PANDOSTO.

Fawnia, I know thou art not so vnwise in thy choice, as to refuse the offer of a King, nor so ingratefull as to dispise a good turne: thou art now in that place where I may commaunde, and yet thou seest I intreate: my power is such as I may compell by force, and yet I sue by prayers: Yeelde *Fawnia* thy loue to him which burneth in thy loue: *Meleagrus* [Dorastus] shall be set free, thy countrymen discharged, and thou both loued and honoured.

FAWNIA.

I see *Pandosto,* where lust ruleth it is a miserable thing to be a virgin, but know this, that I will alwaies preferre fame before life, and rather choose death then dishonour. [Sig. G2; 4:310–11]

Fawnia's language is Bellaria's, but the scene is in deliberate contrast to that of Bellaria's trial. There Pandosto did not plead, nor did he offer to let Egistus go, unaccused. The partial change of his character, wrought by grief rather than by principle, is given further evidence in his willingness to reconcile himself to his childhood friend and to free Dorastus. But his uninstructed nature is not strong enough to bear Fawnia's refusal of him, and he sentences her to death along with the servant Capnio and Porrus until Porrus, corresponding to the oracle from Apollo at the earlier trial, brings miracle to Bohemia by showing the tokens that discover the truth—by using those means that Aristotle said would produce pleasure and wonder in literature. By revelation Porrus resurrects Pandosto's daughter.

Fawnia's true identity may help to explain Pandosto's attraction for her; but his joy in her recovery is contagious.

Fawnia was not more ioyfull that she had found such a Father, then *Dorastus* was glad he should get such a wife. The Embassadors reioyced that their yong prince had made such a choice, that those Kingdomes which through enmitie had long time bin disseuered, should now through perpetual amitie be vnited and reconciled. The Citizens and subiects of *Bohemia* (hearing that the King had found againe his Daughter, which was supposed dead, ioyfull that there was an heire apparant to his Kingdome) made Bonfires and showes throughout the Cittie. The Courtiers and Knights appointed Justs and Turneis to signifie their willing mindes in gratifying the Kings hap. [Sig. G4; 4:316]

Pandosto learns from Porrus's announcement as he learned from the oracle at Delphi. But now as then the lesson comes too late to nurture him into a life of submission and content. Transported from Bohemia to the wonderful land of Sicily for his daughter's marriage, he kills himself. As we have come to understand the parallel trial scenes, his attempted suicide is no surprise; as we learn that his incontinent nature is not one to know content, so we appreciate his inability to find quietness of mind in the pastoral environment. A man too ready of passion, Pandosto is also too quick to judge, unable to alleviate his sense of guilt and unable to surrender to resurrection, to fortune, to *miracle*. His story confirms Greene's advocacy of a fiction of wonder by showing us what happens to those without the capacity to be truly amazed. In *Pandosto* Greene proposes a renewed need for exemplary humanist fiction and reveals a strong belief in the restoration of a humanist order while casting doubt on the educability and perfectibility of those men who are unable to be astonished, to be transported from the mundane world.

He does so in beautifully embellished language. "To vtter the mynde aptely, distinctly, and ornately, is a gyft geuen to very fewe," Richard Sherry writes in 1550 (sig. B2). Greene may have yarkt up pamphlets to keep himself in pickled herring and Rhenish wine; he may have pandered to public taste; he may even have written too much too fast. But for humanist poetics he not only forges a new fiction of wonder, finds ways to employ the ecstasy and grandeur of Aristotle and Demetrius, and senses the relevance of Ovidian transformation, but also finds through the means of Erasmian copia (taken from Cicero and Quintilian) fresh ways to strengthen and enfranchise the fictive imagination. Greene's work on a fiction of wonder left the humanist poetics of fiction permanently changed—itself transformed. If he was unlike other writers of humanist fiction in not directly serving the court, the army, or the university, his final statement that men might be amazed and transported—in short, inspired and elevated—means that he became, at the end, more and more aware of man as a fallen creature in need of the instruction provided by the humanists, using as models humanist texts, translations, and rhetoric.

One of his last works, *Greenes Vision* (1593), makes the need for this poetics of wonder clear. In a basic survey of the kinds of fiction open to him by 1590, Greene first forsakes the fabliaux and love stories of Chaucer on general grounds, and in the specific instance of the tale of Tomkins. Greene also dismisses the duller morals of Gower. Instead of either pure fiction or pure allegory, Greene seeks his final authority in the moderate Solomon. "Wisdome hath her dwelling with knowledge, and prudent counsaile is hir own," Solomon tells Greene: "with her is the fear of the Lord and the eschewing of il" (sig. H2v; 12:276–77). But Greene's first Senecan model was the more secular Ovid. As his career progressed, it was Golding's Ovid toward which Greene moved in deeper and deeper agreement. There the use of wonder to awaken, question, disturb, and transport remains, fleshed out with the embroiderings of a figurist rhetoric, while the clear fixed center holds the moral signification. "Gods, and fate, and fortune are the termes of heathennesse," Golding writes in his epistle,

> If men vsurp them in the sense that Paynims doo expresse.
> But if wee will reduce their sense too ryght of Christian law,
> Too signifie three other thyngs theis termes wee well may draw.
> By Gods wee vunderstand all such as God hath plaast in cheef
> Estate to punish sin, and for the godly folkes releef.
> By fate the order which is set and stablished in things
> By Gods eternall will and word, which in due season brings
> All matters too their falling out. Which falling out or end
> (Bicause our curious reason is too weake to comprehend
> The cause and order of the same, and dooth behold it fall
> Vnwares to vs) by name of chaunce or fortune wee it call.
> If any man will say theis things may better lerned bee
> Out of diuine philosophie or scripture, I agree
> That nothing may in worthinesse with holy writ compare.
> Howbeeit so farre foorth as things no whit impeachment are
> Too vertue and too godlynesse but furtherers of the same,
> I trust wee may them saufly use without desert of blame.
> [Sigs. B1–B1v, 14–15]

The repentance tracts of Greene's last years were written at the time he called himself a "second *Ouid*"; the conjunction is no accident. Nor is it coincidental that he quotes Solomon in *Greenes Vision,* the last of his fictions of a humanist poetics:

> Learning hath many braunches, and teacheth her Schollers many strange things, and yet my Sonne when thou hast waded the depth of hir knowledge, and sought into the secret of her bosome, thou shalt finde all thy labours to be vexation of minde and vanitie. Canst thou number and extract, as the cunning Arithmetician: or with Geometrie measure the ground, and leuell out the plaines by the excellencie of thine arte. Canst thou reach vnto the heauens with thy knowledge, and tell the course of the Starres, setting downe their aspects, oppositiues, times, and sextiles, and discourse of the influence of euery Star? canst thou with musick please thine eare, and with the meladie of hir Cordes make thy heart merrie? Canst thou tell the secrets of Philosophie, and like a cunning naturalist, discouer the hidden aphorismes of arte, and set out the nature and operation of all things? wel my sonne, say thou canst write of all these things, yet when thou dooest with a carefull insight, enter into the

consideration, what the end of all is, thou shalt finde the studie of them to bee vtter vexation of minde, and vanitie: and the fame that growes from such labours, to vanish awaye like smoake, or a vapour tossed with the winde: If then all be follie, seeke Wisedome, and shee will teach thee the feare of the Lord. . . . all knowledge except it, is mere follie! and there is no wisdome, but the knowledge of the law of the Lord. [Sigs. H3–H3v; 12:277–78,280]

It is Greene's greatest metamorphosis of all, this combination of Alexandrian fortune and antique ecstasy with Christian humanism. Such knowledge is the result of wonder and the acceptance of it. Imitatio leads to simple admiratio, and active employment ceases before a transported vision. Rhetoric no longer means verbal persuasion or manipulation; it means transfiguration. The antique sense of epiphany becomes, in the hands of Robert Greene, a whole new sense of art that, by inspiring the artist, inspires us. At such moments of epiphanic vision, artist, poet, poetry, and audience are made one and the incredible adventures of men as various as Gwydonius and Pandosto are made truly credible in a shower of wisdom and grace.

SEVEN

Primus inter pares: Sir Philip Sidney, the *Arcadia,*

and the Poetic Uses of Philosophy

 "IT IS SIGNIFICANT," C. S.
LEWIS WRITES REGARDING *THE
COUNTESSE OF PEMBROKES AR-
CADIA* BY SIR PHILIP SIDNEY (PUB-
LISHED 1593), WHICH HE LIKE OTHERS
CONSIDERS A HEROIC ROMANCE,
"that the whole story moves neither to a martial nor an amorous, but to a
forensic, climax; the great trial scene almost fills the fifth book."[1] This
splendid prose epic of Prince Pyrocles of Macedon, son of Euarchus, and his
cousin Musidorus, prince of Thessalia, their joint education, their Grand
Tour by way of tournaments, battles, and rebellions, and their courtships
in disguise of the Princess Pamela and her younger sister Philoclea doubles
the customary shipwrecks, reunions, and marriages we perpetually find in
Greene's more traditional fictions of wonder. The *Arcadia* is distinguished
by its new joint concern with philosophy and poetry: it is Sidney's own
particular contribution to a humanist poetics of fiction, his *totius vitae
imago,* and to this peculiar end it is also stubbornly, resolutely rhetorical.
The reason is supplied by Musidorus. "Words ennoble selfe nobility," he
sings, while disguised as the shepherd Dorus during a singing match in the
Second Eclogues (sig. T4; 409),[2] and this verbal realization of the
humanists' sense of man's dignity continually recurs in major scenes as well
as in their connective passages. "No one has really tasted the *Arcadia* who
does not remember the epistle of Philanax in Book I, Zelmane's speech to
the rebels in Book II, the discussions on beauty and on the existence of God
in Book III, or that on suicide in Book IV," Lewis adds, "not to mention
the maxims of law, government, morals, or psychology, which are scattered
on nearly every page" (*English Literature,* p. 335).

Given Sidney's "deep-seated instinct for form"—the phrase is Kenneth
Myrick's—these are serially arranged in a mounting narrative epitasis
firmly uniting philosophic substance with rhetorical disposition. We find
the use of humanist rhetoric most noticeably in Cecropia's two detailed

disputations, with Philoclea on pudency (3.5) and with Pamela on providence (3.10), but there are numerous others, such as the opening debate between Strephon and Claius on the significance of Urania (1.1) and that between Pyrocles and Musidorus on the life of honorable action (1.9). But such exercises in formal logic fused with deliberative rhetoric are confounded by incompleteness: the debate between Strephon and Claius is interrupted when the shepherds see a burning ship, that between Pyrocles and Musidorus when Kalander calls his guests to a stag hunt.[3] Such formal disputations nevertheless anticipate the later debates on the most commonplace humanist subjects—the active versus the contemplative life, reason versus love and passion, self-indulgence versus service—while the whole comes to its final conclusion in the greatest debate scene in all of Tudor literature, the joint trial of Pyrocles, Musidorus, Pamela, Philoclea, and Gynecia at the joint hands of a prosecuting Philanax and an adjudicating Euarchus.

They, too, are incomplete; even the trial is annulled when Basilius reappears. Scattered among such debates are also numerous interior monologues which, cast as declamations, are themselves inherent disputations: the self-anatomy of Erona (2.13; sigs. O1–O1v; 304–5), the stay against despair of the imprisoned Philoclea (3.14; sig. Bb3; 518), or Philanax's divided mind over Pyrocles' actions toward Basilius (4.5; sig. Nn1v; 748), to name only a few. But that these never stray far from the rooted impulses of omnific humanist thought is made manifest in Philoclea's formal declamation, from exordium to peroration, on the act of love as mankind's chief means of right *imitatio* (2.4; sig. K4; 239). It is the emphasis on *action* that, inevitably, gives inconclusiveness to the speeches of *Arcadia*: Musidorus pleads that "all is but lip-wisdome which wants experience" (1.18; sig. F4v; 170); Pyrocles claims that such "disputations are fitter for quiet schooles then my troubled braines, which are bent rather in deeds to performe then in wordes to defende" (1.12; sig. D6v; 136). If humanist philosophy subjected to the practices of humanist rhetoricians crowds out much of the possible action in *Arcadia* to formulate a narrative constructed of frustrated set pieces in accord with the other novels of humanist poetics of eloquence that have gone before it, it is because humanist rhetoric for Sidney steadfastly continues to serve, direct, and advise us (as readers) on judging actions. In his traceries of public and private lives, of reason against passion in civilizations as in love, Sidney composes a novel that progresses steadily toward a composite sense of an integrated and harmonious universe of character, thought, speech, and deed. It is a universe where, fundamentally, "The daungerous diuision of mens mindes, the ruinous renting of all estates" (5.1; sig. Pp1; 783) is, alone, what threatens the extinction of a landscape and society that is meant as the epitome of the humanist ideal, a nonsatiric Utopia. For the *Arcadia* is the work of a man noted for being "that exact image of quiet, and action," as Fulke Greville informs us, stemming from "the riches of the *Athenian* learning, wit, and industry."[4] An extraordinary fiction that saw at least seventeen editions before 1674—and remained England's best-selling novel into the eighteenth century—Sidney's *Arcadia* is the meridian of Tudor humanist fiction, magnificent and monumental, a catholicon of later Tudor poetics.

Acknowledging this, we are at once aware of its countless ties to other humanist fictions. Like the Silenus image that characterizes Erasmus, the *Arcadia* comes to us Janus-faced at the outset: it is both a "spider's web" of intricate idea and form, as Sidney promises in the dedicatory epistle to his sister, and, also there, a mere "idle worke" (sig. ¶3; 57), a trifle; elsewhere, still Erasmian, two singers debate it as a "pilgrimage" at the same time that it claims to be earthbound, with "*players pla'st to fill a filthy stage*" (2.13; sig. N4; 296). Other deliberate connections are embedded in the style. The transalliterations of Lyly frequently combine with the parallelism of ideas employed by Greene and the logical forward movement of perception we will find in Lodge, as in these closing lines of the opening chapter:

> the honest shepheards *Strephon* and *Claius* (who being themselues true friends did the more perfectly iudge the iustnesse of his sorrowe) aduise him that he should mitigate somewhat of his woe, since he had gotten an amendment in fortune, being come from assured persuasion of his death, to haue no cause to dispair of his life: as one that had lamented the deathe of his sheepe, should after know they were but strayed, would receiue pleasure though readily he knew not where to finde them. [Sig. A3; 68]

With Sidney as with his predecessors, such a formal rhetorical narrative is a natural as well as a necessary process of instruction; "a very good Orator," one of his characters remarks, "might haue a fayre fielde to vse eloquence in, if he did but onely repeate the lamentable, & truely affectionated speeches" (1.5; sig. B4; 91).

Yet, in pursuing his ideal of teaching the rectitude and perfectibility of man fostered by humanist belief, Sidney is not so naive as to insist on an incorruptible language. Far from it. Not only does human perception discover truth and witness to it; it is also liable to error and misjudgment. Strephon's and Claius's bewilderment and revisionary responses to the initial shipwreck illustrating "humane inhumanitie" (1.1; sig. A2v; 66) is one of the many equivalencies warning of the more obvious, more deadly serious, misperception of Dametas by Basilius (1.3; sigs. A6–A6v; 78). And just as the senses can be misled by betrayed instincts, determined predispositions, and infectious wills, so also can rhetoric—and for good purposes as well as bad—be contaminated. Such acts "disguisest our bodies, and disfigurest our mindes" (1.18; sig. F5; 174). Thus the admirable Kalander deceives the Helots by express sophistry; he and his men

> sent a cunning fellow, (so much the cunninger as that hee could maske it vnder rudenes) who with such a kinde of Rhetorike, as weeded out all flowers of Rhetorike, deliuered vnto the *Helots* assembled together, that they were countrie people of *Arcadia,* no lesse oppressed by their Lords, and no lesse desirous of liberty then they, and therfore had put themselues in the field, & had alreadie (besides a great number slain) taken nine or ten skore Gentlemē prisoners whō they had there well and fast chained. [1.6; sig. B5v; 95–96]

Other illustrations come quickly to mind. Musidorus achieves his disguise through a letter that betrays Manalcas (1.18; sig. F5v; 173); Plangus commits outright sophistry to conceal his youthful affair (2.15; sigs. O3v–O4; 313); Pampilius is "a resolute Orator" who abuses language "to justify his cruel falsehood" (2.18; sig. P5v; 337),[5] actually confusing Pyrocles, and us, for some time. Such open rhetorical malpractices call forth our own counterjudgments; Sidney, like Erasmus, More, and Gascoigne, invokes our dissent. As a varying technique, he turns frequently too to oxymoron and synoeciosis, uniting paradosical or competitive terms in a figurative rhetoric that embeds an implied judgment (for the implied reader) within the text just as Erasmus, More, and Lyly do. An obvious example of this is the well-known instance of Kalander's garden, which treats the topos of art and nature.

> The backside of the house was neither field, gardē, nor orchard; or rather it was both field garden, and orchard: for as soone as the descending of the stayres had deliuered them downe, they came into a place cunningly set with trees of the moste tast-pleasing fruites: but scarcelie they had taken that into their consideration, but that they were suddainely stept into a delicate greene, of each side of the greene a thicket, and behinde the thickets againe newe beddes of flowers, which beeing vnder the trees, the trees were to them a Pauilion, and they to the trees a mosaicall floore: so that it seemed that arte therein would needes be delightfull by counterfaiting his enemie error, and making order in confusion. [1.3; sig. A4v; 73]

This description of the garden surrounding "a naked *Venus* of white marble, wherein the grauer had vsed much cunning, that the naturall blewe veines of the marble were framed in fitte places, to set foorth the beautifull veines of her bodie" (1.3; sig. A4v; 74), follows the equally protreptic union of natural and spiritual lexicons in the description of the first shipwreck:

> amidst the precious thinges were a number of dead bodies, which likewise did not only testifie both elements violence, but that the chiefe violence was growen of humane inhumanitie: for their bodies were full of grisly wounds, and their bloud had (as it were) filled the wrinckles of the seas visage: which it seemed the sea woulde not wash away, that it might witnes it is not alwaies his fault, when wee condemne his crueltie. In summe, a defeate, where the conquered kept both field and spoile: a shipwrack without storm or ill footing: and a wast of fire in the midst of water. [1.3; sig. A2v; 66][6]

Here, as in the later, more visionary poetics of Vaughan, image and idea are inextricable, the places of memory made memorable places: "we find, that as our remembraunce came euer cloathed vnto vs in the forme of this place," Strephon posits at the fiction's start, "so this place giues newe heate to the feauer of our languishing remembrance" (1.1; sig. A1v; 62). Such Sidneyan procedures lead, with the pastoral and Petrarchan vocabularies, to a new set of triangulations, fresh yet decisively related to Erasmus's and Greene's dynamic of progressively transcendent thought and open conclusion:

> My sheepe are thoughts, which I both guide and serue:
> Their pasture is faire hilles of fruitlesse Loue:
> On barren sweetes they feede, and feeding sterue:
> I waile their lotte, but will not other proue.
> My sheepehooke is wanne hope, which all vpholdes:
> My weedes, Desire, cut out in endlesse foldes.
> What wooll my sheepe shall beare, whiles thus they liue,
> In you it is, you must the iudgment giue. [2.3; sig. K2; 232]

It is Sidney's tacit subscription to the tradition of humanist poetics.

Without doubt these glistering facets of a traditional humanism further provoked and promoted Sidney's nearly universal reputation as a stunning example of Machiavelli's *uomo singolare*: *Primus inter pares*, the greatest genius and noblest genius, as Sir William Temple puts it.[7] The innumerable eulogies heaped upon him at his untimely death are conveniently summed (and promulgated) by his mid-nineteenth-century translator Steuart A. Pears:

> He had a right to the very first place among the young noblemen of the day, from his many accomplishments, his person, his education, knowledge of languages, skill in music, in poetry, and in every kind of scientific attainment. His superiority, too, in all manly exercises, as a horseman and swordsman, was sure at that period to add greatly to his influence.[8]

The letter of Sidney's mentor Hubert Languet on 24 September 1580 confirms this.

> While we lived together, I so greatly admired the acuteness of your apprehension, young as you were, the soundness of your judgment, and your high and excellent spirit, that I had no doubt, if God granted you long life, your country would find no small assistance in dangers from your virtue; especially since I observed, in addition to those mental endowments, splendour of birth, majesty of person, the expectation of great wealth, the authority and influence of your relations in your country, and all those other things which are commonly called gifts of fortune.[9]

Yet, seen close up, such portraits of Sidney, various if fulsome, have depended mostly on the beholder's eye: so quick bright things come to confusion. For the boy who was an excellent musician and orator, sportsman and soldier, scholar and statesman, poet and critic, was also impetuous, extravagant, reckless, and arrogant.[10] As a model of polite learning, his outspoken response to the earl of Oxford as the leader of those at court opposed to Calvinism was strangely shortsighted, his testiness finally requiring a rebuke from the queen herself; his enterprise and ambition on the embassy to Germany ended in disaster when he attempted to unite rather than balance foreign powers; even the learning and classical political theory in *Arcadia* could give way to extended ceremonial tilting (Book 2) and crude comedy of a peculiarly aristocratic ruthlessness (Books 1, 4). More generally, there is a baffling and frustrating incongruity between the commonly accepted interpretation of Sidney as first Leicester's and then Walsingham's man at court who nevertheless is unable to see political issues with any complexity and subtlety and who is unable (or unwilling) to understand the queen's deliberate tactics of delay and compromise. The essential Sidney is a man of contradictions. He is called mature and highly serious, yet Languet is perpetually disturbed by his laziness and irresponsibility. He is praised for his charm and good looks, yet his manner could be erratic and his face was scarred by smallpox. He was most fervently engaged in the radical Protestant movement of his day—one of the major discussions in the *Arcadia* concerns the advocacy of the subaltern magistracy introduced by Huguenot political commentators (3.4; sig. X6v; 452)[11]—and yet there is good reason to believe that his yearning for peace and quiet and his extended visits to Wilton, which resulted in the *Arcadia,* were perhaps the most pleasant, as surely as they were the most restful, productive, and significant, periods of his brief life.[12] Yet he seems to have understood such contradictions in himself. His almost instinctive use of philosophy in his serious fiction, along with poetic images embedding such philosophy, modeling his life in retirement after Cicero's shows us how he attempted to confront and resolve them. In reading the *Arcadia,* he asks that we do too.

For, properly read, the *Arcadia* is not merely a tribute to humanism; it is also, through a newly forged humanist poetics, a considered reexamination of the precepts and practices advocated by Tudor humanists. Charles Lamb, among others, has noticed this, in his initial dismay at "a young man disguising himself in woman's attire, and passing himself off for a woman among women."[13] For Pyrocles' first significant decision is to locate his ideal not in a soldier or a statesman but in the picture of a woman (rather than the woman herself) with which he falls in love (1.12)—by all humanist standards the wrong choice. Sidney continues to insist on Pyrocles as a fallen hero in his manipulative speech to the Helot rebels (2.26) and in his percipient tendencies in the disputation on suicide (4.4), while the disputation over right rule between Basilius and Philanax— seemingly another humanist chestnut done up in traditional dress— concludes with the right ruler insisting on his irresponsible self-exile and the counselor assuming rule he does not wish to undertake (1.4). Such extensive experimentation with prosopopoeia—perhaps at first playful, another exercise in sprezzatura—is multiplied as Pyrocles becomes first Daiphantus and then Zelmane, as Musidorus becomes Palladius and then Dorus, and as Kalander (καλὸς ἀνήρ, the good man) disguises a whole army in order to defeat the Helot rebels by pragmatic deceit. Rather than using disguise to test desirable potential identities, the characters in *Arcadia* tend to lose themselves in their own fictions—the effect is similar to that of Folly or G. T.—as Sidney supplies us with a study in alterity that leads irrevocably toward a spreading, deepening tragedy of character and state.

This transforming characterization is not without design—we learn in 2.23 why the name of Zelmane adopted in 1.13 is chosen, as the generative oracle reacted to in 1.4 is revealed in 2.28 and the beasts loose in Arcadia in 1.19 and Clinias's rebellion in 2.27 are accounted for in 3.2—but the *effect* of confusion in the necessary triangulations of our reading is nevertheless sustained. Such deliberate confusion is meant to force us to question humanist ideas, too. The additional confusion of seemingly gratuitous characters and plots, such as the events involving Philoxenus and Philopenus (1.11) or Phalantus and Artesia (1.16, in the story of Amphialus), fashions an unquenchable complexity in a world where no order seems certain, no closure seems possible. Not simply the humanist's belief in reason but man's very capacity to understand is at stake here—as it is in More and Lyly. Nor is there any relief at the level of narrative perspective, for here the opening narrators are displaced by Musidorus, whose autobiography is first begun by him (2.6–10), then continued by members of his audience, Philoclea and Pamela, who have no way of knowing (2.13, 15), and finally by his cousin Pyrocles (2.18), while Philoclea, recounting the death of Tiridates at the hands of Pyrocles and Musidorus (2.13), needs to be confirmed by the actions of Queen Artaxia as reported by Pyrocles (2.19). Such episodic presentation is meant to raise fundamental issues of human epistemology while the presentation awakens us to the power, need, and limitations of rhetorical report and summary. Moreover, stories as humanist *hypo-theses* rather than *theses* are temporally fragmented, as when the episode of the imprisonment of Pyrocles and Musidorus by Andromana (2.20) and their escape as engineered by Palladius (2.21) interrupts the shifting evaluations of Pamphilus (2.18, 19, 22), or, more simply, the battles of Amphialus against the supporters of Basilius are juxtaposed to the duel of the clowns Dametas and Clinias (3.13), clearly a parody (and self-parody). However much such intricacies of narration and action may have amused courtiers and their ladies reading the novel aloud in their Elizabethan great houses, the dispositio of Sidney's narrative is such that we are asked not only to suspend our disbelief but continually to metamorphose our own values and standards of judgment. We can sympathize with Richard Helgerson when he observes that

> We begin on the side of civic humanism, pass through a stage of detached tolerance, and end excited by vicarious lust. We recognize the folly of Basilius's retirement and all along judge without hesitation his passion and Gynecia's, yet for every action of theirs that we firmly reject, we allow another quite like it of Pyrocles or Musidorus until principle is irrevocably lost in a maze of partiality.[14]

Our problem, Richard C. McCoy further notes, is "to attain perspective and poise" (*Sidney,* p. 22).

What is true in piecing together various portions of a single incident— not all of which join so neatly as some critics might have us believe— becomes more important when serious humanist principles are more explicitly examined. What are we to make, for instance, of Gynecia's apparently useful counsel to Basilius—

> it shall well become you so to gouerne your selfe, as you may be fit rather to direct me, then to be iudged of me; and rather to be a wise maister of me, then an vnskilfull pleader before me. Remember the wrong you haue done is not onely to me, but to your children, whome you had of mee: to your countrey, when they shall finde they are commaunded by him, that can not commaund his owne vndecent appetites: lastly to your selfe, since

with these paynes you do but build vp a house of shame to dwell in. [4.2; sig. Mm1; 727]

—when we realize that the advice to the ruler comes in a cave of darkness from a woman who neglects to mention her own recent intentions of adultery (and so the general depravity of them both)? If Gynecia's wisdom has an antecedent in placement and persona, it is in the wise foolishness of Erasmus's Folly, but here it is extended into clearly fictive narrative. In such a context, the uses of sophistry we have already noted take their natural place, while the immense complexities of the composite *Arcadia* in coming around to the definition of justice by Euarchus (5.6) that reaffirms the book's premise as set forth by Pyrocles (1.7)—well doing united with well knowing—are undermined when Musidorus manages to redefine the terms of the trial by shifting attention from the son's offenses to the father's responsibilities, much in the same way Quintilian urges the young lawyer facing probable defeat to shift the charges he is arguing from theft to sacrilege so as to win.[15] Given such sudden and basic changes in attitude, the characters of *Arcadia* are, when all is said and done, ambiguous simulacra, both material images in the grand designs of humanism and specious imitations of impossibly ideal or base forms of behaviors whose clay feet cast persistent doubts on the realization of those principles they are meant to embody. Like the studies of philosophy and history in Sidney's *Defence of Poesie,* these partial tales meant initially to lure children and old men need in addition our own continued reexaminations.

Possibly just because Sidney's argument in the *Arcadia* invites serious doubts, his contemporaries display a uniform anxiety to praise him for a securely traditional, if pleasurable, pedagogy in his support of humanist principles. Gabriel Harvey for one notes that "He that will Looue, let him learne to looue of him that will teach him to Liue, & furnish him with many pithy and effectuall instructions"; for such a person, the *Arcadia,* according to Harvey, "would enkindle a noble courage ... to euery excellent purpose."[16] For Fulke Greville, the "dead images" of the *Arcadia* "[shew] the judicious reader, how he may be nourished in the delicacy of his judgment";[17] he cites, among other exempla, the warning of the bad ruler whose self-chosen exile may result in "the conspiracies of ambitious subalternes" (sig. B6v). Even Milton, whose irritation at the presumed paganism of the *Arcadia* is notorious if now somewhat more understandable, found the *purpose* of Sidney's fiction to be instructive as he enters it in his *Commonplace Book.*[18] In the nineteenth century, Thomas Zouch is representative of most later critics, who uniformly find in the *Arcadia* "useful observations on life and manners ... sage lessons of morality, and judicious reflexions on government and policy."[19] For us, given the supremacy of a tradition of humanist poetics, such a chorus of assent must seem pleonistic. What amazes us instead is the huge sweep of Sidney's accomplishment, the comprehensiveness of his canvas. "Questions of government, education, law, and even theology, no less than building and gardening, are discussed with a philosophical seriousness which gives to the most fantastic incidents a certain air of reality," Julius Lloyd wrote some time back,[20] while C. S. Lewis notes that the *Arcadia* "gathers up what a whole generation wanted to say."[21]

True, Sidney seems to earn such commentary when he shows "how much good the harnes of education doth to the resistance of misery" (3.20; sig. Dd1v; 551) by defining right instruction as virtuous self-discipline fit to direct rather than judge (4.2; sig. Mm1; 727). He also presents throughout the *Arcadia* a sequence of exemplary and cautionary characters who, like the pictures in Kalander's house and like the incidents rehearsed in Book 2, instruct by inviting emulation or rejection. But in this also the aphetic capacity of Sidney's novel is astonishing. Philoclea's description of Dorus, for instance, could stand as the *bonum vir* of humanism—he exceeds "the beautifulnesse of his shape with the beautifulnesse of his minde, and the greatnesse of his estate with the greatnesse of his actes" (2.5; sig. K6v; 247). This recognition verifies Sidney's earlier description of Musidorus disguised as Palladius, this time as filtered through the perception of Kalander, as having

> a mind of most excellent composition (a pearcing wit quite voide of ostentation, high erected thoughts seated in a hart of courtesie, an eloquence as sweet in the vttering, as slowe to come to the vttering, a behavior so noble, as gaue a maiestie to aduersitie: and all in a man whose age could not be aboue one and twenty years. [1.2; sig. A4v; 73]

Similarly, Dorus describes Pyrocles for Pamela as "noble, as a long succession of roiall ancestors, famous, and famous for victories could make him: of shape most louely, and yet of minde more louely; valiaunt, curteous, wise" (2.6; sig. L2v; 252). The education of both princes, too, is ideal by humanist standards, precept transformed into practice and back again.

> By the good order of *Euarchus* (well perfourmed by his sister) they were so brought vp, that all that sparkes of vertue, which nature had kindled in them, were so blowne to giue forth their vttermost heate that iustly it may be affirmed, they enflamed the affections of all that knew them. For almost before they could perfectly speake, they began to receaue conceits not vnworthy of the best speakers: excellent deuises being vsed, to make euen their sports profitable; images of battailes and fortifications being then deliuered to their memory, which after, their stronger iudgments might dispense, the delight of tales being conuerted to the knowledge of all the

stories of worthy Princes, both to moue them to do nobly, and teach them
how to do nobly; the beautie of vertue still being set before their eyes, and
that taught them with far more diligent care, then Grammaticall rules,
their bodies exercised in all abilities, both of doing and suffring, and their
mindes acquainted by degrees with daungers; and in sum, all bent to the
making vp of princely minds: no seruile feare vsed towards them, nor any
other violent restraint, but still as to Princes: so that a habite of
commaunding was naturalized in them, and therefore the farther from
Tyrannie: Nature hauing done so much for them in nothing, as that it made
them Lords of truth, whereon all the other goods were builded. [2.7; sig. L4;
258–59]

So traditional and explicit a sequence of thought makes it obvious why both
the Tudors and subsequent critics have been quick to point to the
absoluteness of Sidney's humanist beliefs. But in doing this alone, they fail
to look at the inconsistencies of speech and act, of sentiment and proponent,
that are Sidney's more significant means of instruction. Indeed, the
archetypal humanist program of education for the two princes is augmented by the Grand Tour (2.3; sig. K1; 228), "whereas," Dorus reminds
Pyrocles, "you weare wont in all places you came, to giue your selfe
vehemently to the knowledge of those thinges which might better your
minde; to seeke the familiaritye of excellent men in learning and souldiery:
and lastly, to put all these thinges in practice both by continuall wise
proceedinge, and worthie enterprises, as occasion fell for them" (1.9; sig.
C4v; 110); in turn, Musidorus taught Pyrocles (2.18; sig. P4; 333). But
what they *give* themselves *to,* what they are asked to learn *from*, is a world
most commonly portraying lust, deceit, arrogance, and savagery. Their
own model through their enactment of life as trial is Pyrocles' father
Euarchus, whose chief distinction is to make "one place succede another in
the progresse of wisedome & vertue" (5.2; sig. Pp3; 789). It is this man,
with the perfection of his training, who is unable to negotiate either
fatherly love *or* princely justice. In *Arcadia,* the alternative to this engaged
ruler of narrow resources who acts as best he can is Basilius, the ruler of
narrow vision who hastens into retirement. His virtual imprisonment of his
daughters displays as excessive a protection of his children as Euarchus's is
deficient. The issue is compounded when Thomas Moffet tells us Euarchus
bears a startling resemblance to Sir Henry Sidney, Sir Philip's father.

Grandis enim erat Pater honore itidem vt virtute vir, domi consiliarius
prudentissimus, foris bellator optimus: Prorex tam moderate severus in
Hibernia, vt desiderari misericordiam non sineret: Gubernator tam miser-
icors in Wallia, vt etiam severus: tam misericore et severus vnique, vt
semper iustus.

For the father was a man exalted alike in honor and virtue, the most prudent of counselors at home and the best of warriors abroad; a lord deputy in Ireland so moderately severe that he would not suffer mercy to be wanting; a president of Wales so compassionate that he was also stern; everywhere so compassionate and stern that he was always just. [Fol. 19; 85–86][22]

When we get to identical encomia for Basilius and Amphialus, who at other junctures in the novel are even more clearly men of mistaken ideas and widely different from each other, we cannot miss Sidney's point: that we must evaluate characters and events beyond, not simply as circumscribed within, immediate contexts. The suffering of Gynecia and Cecropia—so tonally indistinct at times—confirms the point. While the plot of the *Arcadia* insists on the caution of Pyrocles and Musidorus, the disposition of the narrative demands like caution of us: reflective judgments, not initial perceptions, are—as always with the humanists—considerably more valid.

Nothing is easier than misconstruing Sidney's work by oversimplification, so complicated is it to read, so desirable does it make resolution, and so congruent is its surface with the traditional humanist education for which Sidney himself was apparently always widely known. Rehearsing the facts rather than the encomia explains our culpability to be misled. Born the same year at Penshurst as John Lyly was at Canterbury, Philip seems to have been from the start what his father called him—*lumen familiae suae* (the light of the family).[23] The boy's first years were spent in the same great house in Sussex where another famous English humanist, Humphrey, duke of Gloucester, once took residence and where from time to time Philip was in the company of Lady Cecil, Lady Bacon, and Lady Hoby, three of the most learned women of his mother's generation, with whom Lady Mary Sidney was especially good friends.[24] These years were filled too, perhaps inordinately, with studies. According to the early biographer Thomas Moffet, Philip was given at the age of seven a tutor as well as

Eius de studio studia Philippi erant omnia: imo quum parentum indulgentia ea discendi libertas concederetur, suo vt tempore et arbitratu scholam adiret: tamen calido vel potius ardente literarum studio conflagrans, maximam diei partem studijs insumpsit, vt vix ientaculo, merendae raro admodum vacaret: imo pro prandio saepe habuit et coena, scientias humaniores omneque disciplinarum genus imbibere. . . . [Et], vix decennis, Grammatices laude atque scientia cui cessit? paulo post de praeceptis Rhetoricis quem timuit? . . . Fluebat eius cubiculum eruditis epistolis: voluptatem illi magister et gaudium imperabat, quoties depromi aliquid ex antiquis acroamatis, vel hauriri nova iuberet. Ingenij, rationis, memoriae incudem noctes dies*que* perpetuis et contextis studijs exercuit, ad salutis aliquam iacturam: nec tamen propterea literas, valetudinis insidiatrices, mittere voluit.

entire liberty with regard to his learning, so that he might go to the schoolroom at his own time and by his own choice, yet, burning with a warm, or rather a fervid, zeal for letters, he spent the largest part of the day in studies, so that scarcely was he unoccupied at breakfast, and still more rarely at luncheon. Indeed, in place of lunch and dinner he used often to imbibe sciences, liberal arts, and every kind of discipline. . . . [And], when barely ten years old, to whom did he yield in reputation for and knowledge of grammar? A little later whom did he fear in the matter of rhetorical principles? . . . His bedroom overflowed with elegant epistles; the master commanded his delight and joy, so far as he assigned passages for recitation to be drawn from ancient writers, or modern lore to be devoured. Nights and days in ceaseless and related studies he worked upon the anvil of wit, reason, and memory, at some harm to his welfare; yet he did not wish on this account to give over literary studies, which lie in wait against health.[25]

In 1564, at the age of ten, Sidney entered Shrewsbury School where the headmaster was the distinguished humanist and Puritan Thomas Ashton,[26] until recently a fellow of St. John's College, Cambridge—and so a conduit to Sidney of the teachings of Ascham, Cheke, and Watson.[27] The school orders for Shrewsbury list the prescribed Latin and Greek texts then standard for the most part—Cicero, Caesar's *Commentaries,* Sallust, Livy, Vergil, Horace, Ovid, Terence, Isocrates, and Xenophon, as well as a book of dialogues taken by Ashton from Cicero and Vives—and Thomas Marshall's accounts record for us that Sidney purchased Ashton's text of *De Officiis* in his second year as well as a French grammar and "example-books for phrases and sentences in Latin and French,"and a copy of Calvin's catechism.[28] Indeed, the Puritan interests of Ashton and his assistants Atkys and Lawrence were not ignored. The boys at Shrewsbury were required to attend parish churches and to pay particular attention to the sermon while the customary morning and evening prayers, with the students "devoutly upon their knees," were said and sung daily. His schoolmate Fulke Greville recalls "His talk ever of knowledge and his very play tending to enrich his mind."[29] This somber attitude toward a straitened regimen was encouraged in Sidney by both his parents.[30]

During his second year at grammar school, Sidney visited Christ Church, Oxford, in the company of the rhetorician and statesman Thomas Wilson; there he saw the utility of didactic art in the Latin comedy *Marcus Geminus,* the Latin tragedy *Procne,* and two parts of *Palamon and Arcite* by Richard Edwardes, Master of the Children of the Chapel Royal.[31] Two years later he went up to Christ Church himself, to study under a succession of unusually fine but rigorous tutors: Thomas Thornton, later vice-chancellor of the university; Dr. Thomas Cooper, dean of Christ Church from 1566 and vice-chancellor of the university from 1567; and Nathaniel Baxter, later a poet and Puritan controversialist.[32] Sidney's extraordinarily fine talent for disputing is registered by Richard Carew:

> being a scholler in Oxford, of fourteene yeeres age, and three yeeres standing, vpon a wrong conceyued opinion touching my sufficiency, I was there called to dispute *ex tempore* (*impar congressus Achilli*) with the matchles Sir *Ph. Sidney,* in presence of the Earles, *Leycester, Warwick,* and diuers other great personages.[33]

At Oxford during a period of luminaries—other students included Richard Hakluyt, Walter Ralegh, Henry Savile, Thomas Bodley, Richard Hooker, Edmund Campion, Robert Parsons, and Richard Stanihurst as well as Lyly and Carew—Sidney nevertheless set himself apart, according to Moffet, for the scholarly company he kept.

> Nunquam ad templum, palaestram, scholasterium publicum (quo se frequens exercuit) prodire visus est, non illustris comitatu omnium doctorum.

> He was never seen going to church, to the exercise ground, or to the public assembly hall (where he frequently employed himself), except as distinguished among the company of all the learned men. [Fol. 12v; 75]

Sidney's own gift for eloquence, and his own love for it, are recorded in his motto —*Vix Ea Nostra Voco*—taken from Ovid's account of a Ulysses who honors his eloquence rather than his lineage.[34]

Such exemplary formal training was of course complemented by the Grand Tour. Traveling in the train of Lord Lincoln, the lord high admiral, in 1572 at the age of eighteen, Sidney went first to the court of Charles IX; in Paris he stayed with Sir Francis Walsingham, from the safety of whose house he saw with horror the atrocities of the St. Bartholomew's Day Massacre; then he went on to Frankfurt, Heidelberg, Vienna, Hungary, Italy, Poland, and Holland, meeting humanist scholars, inquiring into the affairs of the countries he toured, and making friends, which would later lead him to believe he could become the queen's international champion of Protestantism.[35] He knew well enough the educational purpose of his journey, for he later directs his brother to it in letters in which we find him intellectually inquisitive, seemingly insatiable.[36] His research also involved reading: he prepared himself for Hungary by studying Pietro Bizari's *Historia della Guerra Fatta in Ungheria*; in Venice he read Contarini's *La Republica e i Magistrati de Vinegia* and Ruscelli's *Imprese Illustri* as well as collections of letters by Paolo Manuzio. On his journey he also studied some astronomy in Venice, practiced horsemanship in Vienna, searched for Amyot's French translation of Plutarch's *Moralia,* became acquainted with Machiavelli's *Principe,* and continued his study of Greek. His correspondence with Languet, whom he met early on, is punctuated with references to his studies, especially to the pursuit of eloquence and the figures of rhetoric.[37] He also met men of learning, culture, and influence.[38]

Still he did not tire of learning. Returning to London, he lodged at Leicester House, home of his maternal uncle, where he was politically close to the court and geographically close to the Inns of Court; Moffet reports that he much preferred, however, to withdraw from the queen's retinue to "cum Academicis quibusdam in quocun*que* hospitio legeret aut disputaret"; "read and dispute somewhere in an inn with a few University men" (fol. 17; 83). Sir Henry's earlier fear (in 1569) that "he wylbe to mutch gyven to hys booke" is telling; he was able to read and speak French and Italian, Spanish, German, and some Greek.[39] He also conversed with Bruno and, along with Sir Edward Dyer, studied chemistry with John Dee; he discussed painting with the English miniaturist Nicholas Hilliard; and he made plans with Drake to sail to the New World. It is at this time that he writes to his brother Robert advising him to study standard humanist fare— Thucydides and Xenophon, Tacitus, Livy, and Plutarch—and to combine his study of poetry and oratory with history and military science, his work in music with practice at horsemanship.[40] (Stow records Sidney's final address to his troops on 6 July 1586 as an oration with this combination of humanist resources.)[41] What is clear in all this is not only the supreme quality of Sidney's education even by humanist standards but his insatiable intellect.

Whether Carew found Sidney difficult to defeat in their disputation at Christ Church or was embarrassed to debate Sidney before his opponents' own relatives is unclear; but Sidney's continuing interest in the figures of rhetoric, the study of logic, and the skills of the disputant must have shown him from early on, as it so patently displayed to the other writers of humanist fiction, the inherent lubricity of language. As we have seen, reliable rhetoric and deliberate sophistry both have significant place in *Arcadia,* but in this, as in much else, Sidney may have followed earlier writers, may have designed *Arcadia* in those thoughtful and playful moments at Wilton as a kind of *summa* of humanist poetics. For resemblances are myriad. The *Arcadia* has a number of affinities, for instance, with the *Utopia.* Both focus on the ruler's willed separation from other people and emphasize the need to counsel rulers wisely. Both books treat the education of the major characters through declamation, debate, and analysis. Furthermore, both show the peculiar power of locale on the characters: the primary description of Sidney's land, which is known "partly for the svveetnesse of the ayre, and other naturall benefites, but principally for the vvell tempered minds of the people" (1.3; sig. A5; 75), is strongly indebted to More. At the same time, *Arcadia* shares with *Euphues* a fundamental emphasis on the need to know. Anatomies of the self, such as that by Philoclea in 3.39, are indebted to the soliloquy and extended inner debate of Lucilla. So is the frequent use of contrasting antitheses that John F. Danby has noted.[42] Kalander's house (1.3) is contrasted to Basilius's lodge (1.13); Pamela's prayer (3.6) is correlated to the prayer of Musidorus (4.6); the sacrifice of their servants' lives for Pyrocles and Musidorus (2.7) anticipates Musidorus's self-sacrifice for his cousin (2.8).

But the humanist who stoutly proclaims that "I am no Pickepurse of an others wit"[43] also drew heavily on other contemporary works as well. "Truly I haue knowne men, that euen with reading *Amadis de gaule,* which God knoweth, wanteth much of a perfect *Poesie,* haue found their hearts moued to the exercise of courtesie, liberalitie, and especially courage," Sidney writes in the *Defence* (sig. E2; 92).[44] The long oral and written tradition of *Amadis,* influential in the sixteenth century through the four-volume Spanish narrative popularly assigned to Garci Ordoñez de Montalvo (Sargossa, 1508), was unknown to Sidney. Rather, all his borrowing—and it is substantial—comes from later additions to the French edition (1570–74). Here, in the disguise of Amadis as the Amazon Nereide (Book 8) and his attraction to Bazilique (which Sidney condenses to *Basilius,* Greek for "king") and in the disguise of Agesilan as the Amazon Daraïde (Book 11) who, shipwrecked on Galdap, is attracted both to King Galanides (who proposes marriage) and Queen Salderne (who proposes adultery), Sidney found the basis for Pyrocles' disguise as Zelmane and the complications of "her" attractiveness to both Gynecia and Basilius. Musidorus's disguise, similarly, may take its cue from the disguise of Florisel as a shepherd in *Amadis 9.* There are additional borrowings— Zelmane's address to the rebels (2.26) may have its original in Daraïde's address to an excited mob preparing to storm the chateau of Phoebus where they feel their queen and princess are endangered (*Amadis 12*) as the rebels seek to free their rulers in *Arcadia;* Daraïde's encounter with two women beating a naked knight tied to a tree (*Amadis 11*) may have been elaborated by Sidney to become the exemplary tale of Pamphilus (2.18); and Pyrocles' encounter (dressed as Amphialus) with Queen Helen of Corinth in her coach (1.10) seems to have been derived from parallel incidents in *Amadis 1, Amadis 9.27,* and *Amadis 9.49.* Doubtless the excitement and imagination of such a French romance must have appealed to Sidney, but so also must its encyclopedic character: we are closer to Sidney's habit of mind when we realize that the sprawling French *Amadis* is not only an exciting adventure story of shipwrecks and miracles, comic interludes and grotesque moments, but also a manual of war, a treatise on the art of love, a courtesy book with courtly and festive tournaments, and a book of the governor with its own catalogue of good and bad lovers, just as *Arcadia* is. Turning this into the form common to fictions of humanist poetics, and subtly Christianizing it, would have energized Sidney's imagination as well as his humanist and Protestant leanings. And it is equally noteworthy that the only English version then available to him reduced the romance to exemplary orations as speeches or letters, thus emphasizing the fundamentally *rhetorical* nature that is inherent even in the longer French narrative.[45]

Other contemporary sources for Sidney's *Arcadia* are listed by John Hoksins in the sixteenth-century manuscript that has come down to us as *Directions for Speech and Style*. "For the web, as it were, of his story," Hoskins notes, "he followed three: Heliodorus in Greek, Sannazarius' *Arcadia* in Italian, and *Diana* de Montemayor in Spanish."[46] If Sidney's poetics owes something to *Amadis,* it is also (like Greene) extensively indebted to Underdowne's translation of Heliodorus's *Aethiopian Historie.* Heliodorus begins with a startling scene, full of danger and destruction, a pirates' raid on shore instead of at sea, which is fraught with its own mysteries and paradoxes. Here as in the *Arcadia* disaster is juxtaposed, and with astonishing success, to the sublime and the visionary for the heroine Cariclea, source for Sidney's Urania. But Sidney alters details. In Heliodorus, the woman remains; she is armed; and she is actively searching for her lover Theagenes while spied upon by thieves. Comparing the two passages, it would seem Sidney worked by inversion. Here in this Alexandrian romance are Sidney's complications of plot, where the just are nearly executed until amazing discoveries (especially the relationships between the judging and the judged) are disclosed. In Heliodorus, Cariclea's father Hidaspes, like Euarchus, is willing to take the life of his own child to preserve justice. In Underdowne's translation, the *Aethiopian Historie* also moves to a forensic climax with Cariclea's passionate self-defense. But to no avail: "All the Oration of Hidaspes, declareth what is the dutie of a good kinge," Underdowne writes in the margin (sig. S5). In the *Arcadia*, the unmasking of Zelmane and Dorus condemns them; only the miraculous restoration of Basilius sets them free, an event that transcends human law. So too in Heliodorus: the fiery tests of chastity do not save Cariclea and Theagenes, but the miraculous birth of the white girl to black parents does.

Thus the question of how Gynecia could help kill her own husband is displaced by another; and both are answered. Gynecia meant only to put her husband to sleep; Cariclea's mother conceived her while looking on a picture of Andromeda. And as in the *Arcadia*, so in the *Aethiopian Historie*, miracles transform attitudes, become the last stage of learning. "Perhappes also they were sturred to vnderstande the truth by inspiration of the gods, whose will it was that this shoulde fall out wonderfully, as in a comedie" (sig. T5). Between these scenes, the wicked mother Arsace (7–8) was likely the model for Cecropia.

Yet these similarities do not constitute Sidney's chief instruction by the *Aethiopian Historie*, although this is what previous scholars tend to rehearse. For Heliodorus takes a noteworthy tangle of episodes about bloodthirsty pirates and thieves, ambushes and strange lands, burnings and poisonings, sudden deaths and widespread massacres and, without Sidney's vision of tragedy or sense of irony, nevertheless conceptually arranges and manages them. It is this stunning ability at technique—a true mastery of a seemingly artless poetics of complicated love and adventure—that Sidney admires, just as Greene did before him. Heliodorus was the first of the great romancers to interweave multiple plots; the first to invert chronology; the first to begin with an oracle and end with a prophecy; the first to open visually with a ghastly *tableau vivant*. Prophecy, magic, destiny, character, and human will are all—once we know enough—seen as correlative, in Heliodorus as in Sidney. There is the complicated and puzzling beginning, the emphasis on stage imagery through the long middle, and the slow, detailed denouement exploring the ethical, political, and romantic considerations that beset absolute justice before, swiftly, a reversal and revelation make all things right, surpassing law and reason. Such disposition—which awakens interest in causes by first revealing consequences and by reinforcing philosophic ideas through inset tales—is stated emphatically, moreover, in Jacques Amyot's enthusiastic proem to his translation of Heliodorus (Paris, 1547), an essay Sidney almost surely knew.[47]

It is clear that Heliodoran poetics supplies Sidney with a *form* (as it does Greene) just as the *Amadis* supplies incidents. But Hoskins notes other Senecan models as well. The most enchanting of them is Jorge de Montemayor's *Los siete libros de la Diana* (1559), Englished by Bartholomew Yong in 1583 at the request of a friend while Sidney was composing the *New Arcadia* and published in 1598 as *Diana of George of Montemayor* along with Alonso Perez's and Gaspar Gil Polo's continuations. Like Sidney, Yong was a declared humanist—his title page announces he had studied at Middle Temple—and his work resembles most nearly *Arcadia 2* in its collocation of several interlocking love stories architecturally arranged. The centerpiece of the work is Diana's temple, presided over by Felicia, which neatly divides several narratives of frustrated love from, in most instances, their happy conclusions. This temple first surprises us, just as it "suddenly appeered vnto their sight"; it is "vna gran casa de tā altos y soberuios edificios, que poniā gran contentamiento, a los que los mirauan" (sig. H5); "a stately Pallace, with so high and loftie turrets, that it filled them [the shepherds and shepherdesses] full of woonder and delight to behold it" (sig. H1v; 131–32).[48] Such a vision is sharply disjunctive with the sunny pastures and cool groves that characterize the two side panels of this tripartite romance. This general combination of the pastoral and the courtly is Montemayor's most significant legacy to Sidney, and the striking presentation shows that the power of civilization is the power of man's achievement through reason and judgment: the purpose is humanist and instructive. But while the court of *Diana* is essentially a court of love, firmly Neoplatonic in its orientation, the shape of the romance is, like so many works of humanist poetics, the shape of a treatise: in a fiction informed by Felicia and her marvelous temple, with its wondrous objects of visual instruction and its magic potions that lead to self-understanding, the emphasis of Montemayor is on the process of education. This too Sidney adopts in *Arcadia*; and it is as significant as the opening paragraphs which, in the technique of scene painting, has commonly been thought Sidney's only debt to *Diana* (if for the wrong reason). Montemayor's opening reads,

> Baxaua de las montañas de Leon el ouidado Sireno, a quien amor, la fortuna, el tiempo, tratauan de manera, q̄ del menor mal que en triste vidi padescia, no se esperaua menos que perdella. Ya no lloraua el desuenturado pastor, el mal que la ausencia prometia, ni los temores del oluido le importunaua: porque via cumplidas las prophecias de su recelo, tan en perjuyzio fuyo, que ya no tenia mas infortunios con que amenazaille. Pues llegando el pastor à los verdes y deleytosos prados, que el caudaloso rio Ezla con sus aguas va regando, le vino a la memoria el gran contentamiento de que en algun tiempo alli gozado auia: siendo tan Señor de su libertad, como entonces subjecto a quien sin causa lo tenia sepultado en las tinieblas de su oluido. [Sig. A4]

> Downe from the hils of *Leon* came forgotten *Syrenus,* whom loue, fortune, and time did so entreate, that by the least greefe, that he suffered in his sorrowfull life, he looked for no lesse then to loose the same. The vnfortunate Shepherd did not now bewaile the harme, which her absence did threaten him, and the feare of her forgetfulnes did not greatly trouble his minde, bicause he sawe all the prophecies of his suspicion so greatly to his preiudice accomplished, that now he thought he had no more misfortunes to menace

him. But the Shepherd comming to those greene and pleasant meades, which the great riuer *Ezla* watreth with his cristalline streames, the great felicitie and content came to his wandring thoughtes, which sometimes he had enioyed there, being then so absolute a Lord of his owne liberty, as now subiect to one, who had wrongfully entered him in darke oblivion. [Sig. A1; 10–11]

The emphasis here is not on the pastoral setting but on the disturbed state of mind caused by love and its consequent "darke obliuion." Frustration, anger, jealousy, and despair characterize the first three books of the *Diana,* captured in the tales of "Deceitfull *Ismenia*" (sig. B4; 36–37), who dresses as a woman so as to mingle with the shepherdesses but pretends to be a man, and emblematized in the appearance of "tres salvages, de estrona grandiza y fealdad"; "three monstrous and foule Savages" (sig. D11; sig. E1; 75), like those in Spenser, who suggest the total chaos of the lovesick mind. The world of *Diana* abounds at first with hopelessly tangled relationships that bring confusion, displacement, and genuine grief— Felismena's disguise makes her pander for her own beloved; evil magic apparently causes a father to murder his son; and even Diana's father forces her into an unwanted (and undesirable) marriage. In the initial episodes relating fractured personal relationships, Montemayor emphasizes that tragedy in love is directly related to deception and disguise: he lays the ground for his subsequent premise that harmony comes about by educated attitude. Oblivion, the point of the descent into the valley of the shadow that begins the *Diana,* is a perspective of the mind, which, enlightened by Felicia, can still achieve a happy and fortunate restoration.

Yet it is the characters who insist on their respective personal tragedies; and their griefs are often absurdly exaggerated. For Montemayor also teaches Sidney the value of an ironic wit. Thus one unusually complicated maze of affections is highlighted when Selvagia remarks that

que ni yo a Alanio, ni Alanio a Ysmenia, ne Ysmenia a el, no era possible tener mayor affection. Ved que estraño embuste de amor. Si por ventura Ysmenia yua al campo, Alanio tras ella, si Montano yua al ganado, Ysmenia tras el, si yo andaua al monte con mis ouejas, Montano tras mi. Si yo sabia que Alanio estaua en vn bosque donde solia repastar, alla me yua tras el. Era la mas nueua cosa del mundo oyr como dezia Alanio sospirando, ay Ysmenia: y como Ysmenia, dezia, ay Seluagia: y como Seluagia dezia ay Montano: y como Montano dezia, ay mi Alanio. [Sigs. C3v–C4]

it was not possible for me to beare greater affection to *Alanius,* nor *Alanius* to *Ismenia,* nor *Ismenia* to *Montanus,* nor *Montanus* to loue me more, then in very trueth he did. Beholde what a strange cousinage of loue: If *Ismenia* went by chaunce to the fielde, *Alanius* went after her; if *Montanus* went to his flockes, *Ismenia* after him; if I went to the hils with my sheepe, *Montanus* after me; if I knew that *Alanius* was in the wood, where he was wont to feede his flocks, thither I hied me after him. And it was the strangest thing in the world to heare how *Alanius* sighing saide, Ah my *Ismenia*; and how *Ismenia* said, Ah my *Montanus*; and how *Montanus* said, Ah my *Seluagia*; and how *Seluagia* saide, Ah my *Alanius*. [Sig. B6; 42]

Such authorial high spirits, reminiscent of equally comic moments in the *Arcadia* of Sidney (such as that in 1.19; sig. F6v; 177), result in celebratory passages of inflated rhetoric summed in Montanus's unwitting Erasmian observation that all lovers are fools (*Diana,* sig. C2; 47).

Montemayor's narrators with their multiple tales of unfulfilled loves joyously prepare us for the providential appearance of the temple of Diana. But these hyperbolic stories and soliloquies about unrequited emotions also have their serious side. For it is difficult at times to judge our own responses to these stories-within-stories: events change so radically and various perspectives are so disjointed that we have difficulty discerning one tale from another, and fiction from truth. This is especially so with Selvagia's account: it is dependent in part on her recollection, in part on her ignorance, in part on letters that give us some interpolation of facts, in part on the analogous "Song of the Nymph" (sigs. C6v–D1; 60–62), and in part on Syrenus's response (sigs. D1v–D2; 62–63) as someone deeply sympathetic and yet unable to understand others because of his own unfulfilled desires. This is a display of perspectives nestled within one another that Gascoigne would have envied. Even in the last third of the *Diana,* the locus of romantic reconciliation, there is a residual incompleteness. For the chief characters, Syrenus and Diana, remain separated because of their own miscalculations of each other and misunderstanding of facts; breaking off, Montemayor promises to complete the stories of Syrenus and Diana and of the Portuguese shepherds Danteus and Duarda "en la segunda parte deste libro" (sig. O12), "in the second part of this booke" (sig. O2v; 242), a part that never appeared. The continual interruptions of the first three books of *Diana,* like the final breaking off, lend to the work a permanent tentativeness which, alongside the firm lessons of Felicia and the host of reunions in the final three books, give to Montemayor's achievement an undeniable equivocation that also reminds us of Sidney's *Arcadia.* For we recall that the temple of Diana embodies not only tablets illustrating the values of love but also their antitype, "fierce *Mars,*" whose "Obeliske with maruellous art and skill" illustrates "proud squadrons of the Romaines on the one side, and the Carthaginian campe on the other side" (sig. H4; 139). Such mingled forces within the citadel of civilized values, like Montemayor's witty detachment, provide their own means for triangulation, insuring for the *Diana* as Sidney evokes for the *Arcadia* our participatory judgments.

Hoskins's third source for the *Arcadia* was the premier pastoral of the day, and it is natural—A. C. Hamilton thinks it "inevitable"[49]—that Sidney would turn to Jacopo Sannazaro's *Arcadia* for his pattern of landscape, mood, and event. It is true that the perfection of the climate of the earlier *Arcadia* and the remoteness of its landscape, as well as the plainness of its life and its emphasis on a refined artfulness even in rustic pastimes, gave Sidney an employable "foreconceit." But there is also about Sannazaro's work a sublime if limpid simplicity of attitude, a constancy of perspective and tone. Even the physical contests of shepherds, the memorial service about Massilia's tomb, and the raging river and frightful ravine share a certain distanced placement that renders them all equally artful, perfected, unreal. Thus the scene painting that opens Prosa 5 and scenes of action are related by the same distilled style:

> Era gia per lo tramontare del sole tutto l occidente sparso di mille vari eta di nuvoli: quali violati: quali cerulei alcuni sanguigni: altri tra giallo nero: & tali si rilucenti per la ripercussione de raggi: che di forbita a finissimo oro pareano. Per che essendosi le pastorelle di pari consentimento levate da sedere intorno ala chiari fontana: i duo amanti pusero fine ale loro canzoni.

> At the going down of the sun now all the west was scattered over with a thousand kinds of clouds, some violet, some dark blue, some crimson, others between yellow and black, and some so shining from the reflection of sunbeams that they seemed to be of the finest polished gold; so that as the shepherd maidens by common consent arose from sitting about the clear fountain, the two lovers made an end of their songs[50]

> Ma discesi nel piano: ei sasso si monti dopo le spalle lasciati (come ad ciascuno parve) novelli piaceri ad prendere rincominciammo. Hora provandone ad saltare: hora ad dardeggiare con ci pastorali bastoni: et hora leggerissimi ad correre per lespiegate campagne.

> But when we were got down onto the plain and the stony mountains were left behind us, we began again to take up new pleasures, as seemed good to each one; now making trial of ourselves in leaping, now in throwing contests with our shepherd's staves, and now in sprinting through the open fields [Sigs. C6v–C7; 56]

This sustained vision had its own quiet power for the sixteenth century, a power resulting in Hamilton's apercu that "Sannazaro's *Arcadia* is a work much greater than itself, as its extended use by later poets proves. Its significance for them lay in its potentiality."[51]

Still, it would be too partial to deduce from this that mood is all Sidney borrowed from his Italian original, for he must have found in Sannazaro, because we do, a fragility that is always threatened by the prescience of death. Prosa 1, for instance, opens with a description at least as ominous as it is inviting:

> Jace nella sommita de Parthenio non humile monte dela pastorale Arcadia un dilettevole piano: di ampiezza non molto spatioso poi che il sico del luogo nol consente. Ma di minuta & verdissima herbetta si ripieno che se le lascive pecorelle con gli avidi morsi non vi pascesseno: vi si potrebbe di ogni tempo ritrovare verdura.

> There lies on the summit of Parthenius, a not inconsiderable mountain of pastoral Arcadia, a pleasant plateau, not very spacious in extent, since the situation of the place does not permit it, but so filled with tiny and deep-green herbage that, if the wanton herds with their greedy nibbling did not pasture there, one could always find green grasses in that place. [Sig. A4; 30]

Here beside a fir tree "nato ad sustinere i pericoli del mare," "born to endure the perils of the deep" (sig. A4; 30), a "pitiable" Ergasto is unable to tend to his flocks, his thoughts clouded by "(ma meste) strigi & importune nottole," "sad screech owls and troublesome bats," and by "(ma solo) pruni & stecchi chel cor ledono," "thorns and splinters that lacerate the heart" (sig. A4v; 35, 32). His attitude is contagious. At first Montano discovers it when, in the singing contest that follows, he describes their surroundings in terms of "il lupo pien dinganni"; "the wolfe ... full of deceits" (sig. B1; 37). But later all the shepherds join in a celebration about the tomb of Ergasto's mother, dead one year that night. The holy temple too is marred by paintings above the entrance where "colli bellissimi & copiosi di alberi fronzuti & di mille varieta di fhora," "very beautiful and rich ... leafy trees and a thousand kinds of flowers" (sig. B4v; 42) are displaced by

> certe nymphe ignude le quali dietro un tronco di castagno stravano quasi mezze nascose: ridendo di un monotone: che per intendere ad rodere una ghirlanda di quercia: che dinanzi agliocchi gli pendea: non si ricordava di pascere la herbe: che dintorno gli stavano. In questo venivano quattro satyri con le corna in test: ei piedi caprini: per una macchia di lentischi pian piano per prenderle dopo le spalle ... Apollo biondissimo: il quale appoggiato ad un bastone di selvatica oliva: guardava gli armenti di Admeto ala riva di un fiume: [& per attentamente mirare duo forti tori che con le corna si urtavano:] non si aduedea del sagace Mercurio: che in habito pastorale: con una pelle di capra appicata sotto al sinestro humero: gli furava le vacche.

certain naked Nymphs who were standing, half-hidden as it were, behind
the trunk of a chestnut tree, laughing at a ram who because of being intent
on biting an oaken garland that was hanging before his eyes was forgetting
to crop the grasses that grew round about. Therewith four Satyrs with
horns on their heads and goatish feet were stealing very softly through a
thicket of mastic trees to seize them from behind [while beside them] fairest
Apollo who, leaning on a wild-olive staff, was guarding the herds of
Admetus on the bank of a river [is] unaware of clever Mercury who in
pastoral dress with a goatskin pinned up under his left shoulder was
stealing away his cows. [Prosa 3, sigs. B4v–B5v; 43]

At the very least, such passages suggest the *illusion* of a perfected landscape,
indicating that even Sannazaro was fundamentally equivocal about this
tiny space of land adopted from Polybius and Vergil.

For what distinguishes Sannazaro's work even more—and what Sidney
seems to have taken directly into his English *Arcadia* in the true spirit of
humanist imitatio—is the persistent pain of love as the substance of life.
Images suggesting this are basic to Sannazaro's plot, with shepherds
confessing their sorrows or attempting, without much success, to cheer
themselves up. And it appears again and again in particular images, such
as the beechen cup offered instead of a stag as the reward in a singing
contest, an image from Theocritus via Vergil. The cup

tiene nel suo mezzo di pinco il rubicondo Priapo che strettissimamente
abraccia una nympha: & ad mal grado di lei la vuol basciare. Onde quella
di ira accesa torcondo il volto indietro: con tutte sue forze intende ad
suicupparsi da lui: & con la manca mano gli squarcia il naso: con cl'altra
gli pela la folta barba. Et sonoui intorno ad costoro tre fianciulli ignudi &
pieni di vivacita mirabile: de quali luno con tutto il suo podere si sforza di
torre ad Priado la falce di mano: aprendoli puerilmente ad uno ad uno le
rustiche dite. Laltro con rabbiosi denti morbendoli la hirsuta gamba: fa
segnale al compagno che gli porga aita.

has painted about its middle the ruddy Priapus, who is most straitly
embracing a Nymph and is trying to kiss her against her will: kindled with
wrath at this, her face twisted away, with all her strength she is bent on
freeing herself from him, and with her left hand she is scratching his nose,
with the other she plucks his thickly-curling beard. Round about them are
three little boys, naked and full of wondrous liveliness, one of whom is
exerting himself with all his power to tear the reaping hook from Priapus's
hand, with puerile force opening one by one the gnarled fingers: another
with raging teeth biting his hairy leg makes a sign to his companion that
he should help him. [Sig. C4; 52]

In fact, although Sannazaro's work is customarily considered static, there is movement to its conceptual arrangement that finds grim parallel in the outbreak of civil war and the stockpiling deaths in Sidney's own *Arcadia*. The Italian *Arcadia* progresses from the relatively harmless and contained grief of Ergasto (Prosa 1) through the dance of death to castanets about the sepulchre of Androgeo in Prosa 5 to culminate in the narrow avoidance of Carino's suicidal leap from a cliff in Prosa 8. Sannazaro's intensifying juxtaposition of the shepherd's life of play and song to a narrowing focus on life as pain and death ends, at some length, with the celebration about Massilia's tomb on the first anniversary of her death, which is led by the grief-stricken only son.

Sannazaro's own appearance in Prosa 7 and subsequently as the frustrated Sincero—"sotto infelice prodigio di comete: di terremoto: di pestilentia: di sanguinose battaglie nato"; "born under the luckless omen of comets, or earthquake, pestilence, and bloody battles"—also suffers "si misera vita," "so wretched an existence" (sigs. E4; F1; 70, 72). Trailing his cold mistress "nele solitudini" to solitary places where even the animals are "inamorata," love-stricken self-projections, he is, at the close of the *Arcadia,* taken on a sad journey through the underworld, past the Fates, the "pitiable" Eurydice, and the head of a historical Pompeii in Prosa 12, to witness the death of his own unconsummated love. The epilogue displays the painful consequence, both for Sincero—"Ogni cosa si perde ogni speranza e mancata: ogni consolatione e morta"; "Everything is lost; all hope is vanished; every consolation is dead" (sig. N2; 153)—and for his poetry: "le nostre Muse sono extinte. secchi sono i nostri cauri. Ruinato e il nostro Parnaso. Le selve son tutte mutole"; "Our Muses are perished; withered are our laurels; ruined is our Parnassus; the woods are all become mute" (sig. N1v; 152). At the close, Sannazaro shows Sincero escaping Arcadia permanently, yet he remains haunted by its memories: like the indecisive singing contest between Ofelia and Elenco where Montano awards the victory to Apollo rather than to either disputant (Ecloga 9, Prosa 10), the climactic visit to the temple of Pan in Prosa 10, which is characterized by Pan's frustrating chase of Syrinx, or the funeral games for Messilia where the contestants cheat to win (Prosa 11), the earlier *Arcadia* ends inconclusively. Still, such an indeterminate ending follows naturally a work fundamentally grounded in the paradoxical recognition that even the remote land of idealized pastoral could concentrate on pain, loss, waste, and death—and this equivocation is not, in its import, lost on Sidney. Although the English *Arcadia* invests actions with ethical significance, ambiguity persists in Sidney too: his indebtedness to Sannazaro is far richer than Hoskins acknowledges—and perhaps different. Together with the *Amadis* and Heliodorus, Sannazaro with his felicitous mixture of poetry and prose serves as one of Sidney's chief Senecan models, but, in none of these instances, in ways accounted before.

The 1593 *Arcadia* transforms each of these models under the philosophic pressures that Sidney applies, making their narrative concerns and strategies propaedeutic to his astringent attempt to validate humanism in a more realistic, more imperfect world, and through a philosophic and poetic amalgam peculiarly his own. Thus Strephon's plaintive cry by which memory only calls to mind deprivation—"O my *Claius*, saide he, hither we are now come to pay the rent, for which we are so called vnto by ouer-busie Remembrance, Remembrance, restless Remembrance, which clayms not only this dutie of vs, but for it will haue vs forget our selues" (1.1; sig. A1; 61)—shows how a sense of loss can lead to awareness, guilt, penance, and self-abnegation. The fused classical and Christian commonplaces of humanism are confirmed in Strephon's further remark drawing its terms from humanist rhetoric: "But what is all this? truely no more, but as this place serued vs to thinke of those things, so those things serue as places to call to memorie more excellent matters" (1.1; sig. A1v; 63). Rhetorical topoi make men aware of the value of the places of memory; invention is both refuge and salvation. This ability to confront the loss of the present—as Pyrocles and Musidorus, Pamela and Philoclea, will all be called on to confront the depravity of their fellowmen—by using the past to chart a future, and even to assure its healing purpose, illustrates at the outset of *Arcadia* how for Sidney humanist philosophy and practice are inseparable. The need for such an ability to transcend the present moment is demonstrated again when Musidorus is found, hardly alive, and asks the two shepherds to rescue his cousin who still drifts aboard the wreckage of a sea bloodied by man's inhumanity. Their trust in their ability and the rightness of their cause temporarily lends these shepherds the courage of a hero such as Musidorus: they transcend their past and present activities in a daring rescue. When they fail, their hope turns Musidorus from suicide (1.1). This analysis of humanist epistemology, introduced so simply, takes on increasingly complex forms. Kalander, for instance, is able to be so compassionate a host to Musidorus that it is some time before his guest discerns that the father is really distraught over the capture of his son by the rebellious Helots (1.5); yet it is Kalander's ability to transcend his own grief that allows him to cure Musidorus and thus nurture a champion to free Clitophon (1.7). This is just another of many such instances. The obverse also occurs, as when Basilius's retreat from responsibility when consulting an oracle constricts his present behavior, weakens his people when he leaves them with a surrogate ruler, and virtually ends the liberty of his family (1.4). Again and again as *Arcadia* 1 unfolds, rhetoric is used to expose thought necessarily, for again and again actual events are *transformed*—the word is common in the *Arcadia* as in Greene's fiction—by thought and by imagination. Self-reflection can lead to self-aggrandizement (as with Dametas, 1.4), to self-justification (as with Basilius, 1.3), to self-realization (as with Kalander through his rational and artful cultivation of his garden, 1.2), or to self-abandonment (as in the disguises of Pyrocles and Musidorus, 1.12–14, 18). Just as humanist rhetoric can slip into sophistry, so humanist thought can slide into arrogance and self-delusion. In such a world of mutability where everything and everyone potentially are and are not what they first seem, men learn to adjust rapidly to shifting circumstances, as Basilius conforms to his pastoral retreat. In such a world, man learns to accept surprise and mystery, as Musidorus accepts the reappearance of Pyrocles as champion of the rebel Helots and his enemy on the battlefield. In such a world, man can easily be led to debase himself, as Pyrocles dressed as an Amazon, taking on a woman's costume and restricted behavior, is shown to do, although Sidney tempers this with wit and sympathy. Our increasingly complicated and multiple responses to *Arcadia* 1 stem, then, from Sidney's increasingly complex awareness of the virtues and shortcomings of the humanist's practice of self-fashioning, while his rhetoric, to accommodate this, moves more and more into wit, irony, and paradox. "O heauen and earth," Musidorus sums at one point,

> to what a passe are our mindes brought, that from the right line of vertue, are wryed to these crooked shifts? But o Loue, it is thou that doost it: thou changest name vpon name; thou disguisest our bodies, and disfigurest our minds. But indeed thou hast reason, for though the ways be foule, the iourneys end is most faire and honourable. [1.18; sigs. F4–F4v, 173–74]

It is the same justification Queen Helen uses when her romanticism takes her on a dangerous search for Amphialus (1.11), one that may ultimately lead to his recovery. It is the romanticism employed by her bastard brother Phalantus of Corinth whose excessive love for Artesia results in a pompous display of chivalric gallantry (1.15–17) that never leads anywhere at all. Only in their *corruption* of language are we given any firm index to the wisdom of their thoughts.

Arcadia 2 works backward chronologically to explain the present narrative situation, but it progresses forward epistemologically by charting the novel's fullest range of possibilities in the elevation or corruption of human nature. In Sidney's unflinching anatomy of man's imperfection, the suicidal sacrifice of the gentleman servants of Pyrocles and Musidorus to save their masters (2.7) is matched by the loyalty of Zelmane, daughter of Plexirtus (2.23). Yet all three fail to outweigh other events of pride, greed, and lust. Sidney refers to love in the initial sentences of *Arcadia* 2 as "the cup of poyson" (2.1; sig. H6v; 213) and this intoxication becomes contagious, not only in the growing lust of Gynecia (not yet tempered by guilt) but also in the stories of Plangus and Queen Erona (2.12, 29), of Erona and Antiphilus (2.13, 29), and of Pamphilus and Dido (2. 18–19) and Leucippe (2.22). Lust is here so firmly characterized by greed and pride that even the attempts of Anaxius to submit wrongdoing to a trial by combat are futile (2.19). Nor is love as a private concern its only destructive force; the public dimension of love takes on a persistent form of tyranny in *Arcadia* 2, the truncated attempt at democracy by the Helots in *Arcadia* 1 followed here by the arrogant domination of the king of Phrygia (2.8), the king of Pontus (2.9), and Plexirtus in his betrayal of both the king of Paphlagonia and his good son Leonatus (2.10, 22). So depraved is Plexirtus, in fact, that he tricks two brothers, Tydeus and Telenor, into killing each other (2.22), their deaths resulting somewhat later in the grief-stricken death of his daughter Zelmane (2.23). While the various stories of intrigue recounted by Musidorus, Philoclea, Pamela, and Pyrocles show the various relationships by blood and marriage that imply that the entire world of Greece and Macedonia, encircling Arcadia, is united in the common ties of depravity, humanist rhetoric is once again corrupted. Clinias's sophistic attempt to unseat Basilius brings private and public evil (for he would avenge Cecropia's hatred of her brother) inside Arcadia itself (2.27–28); he is defeated only when Pyrocles uses his own sophistry to calm the insurgents Clinias has stirred up (2.25). When we see how similar the speeches of Pyrocles and Clinias actually are, relying on flattery and special pleading, we come to realize how serious Sidney's disclosure of the depraved humanist has become.

This extensive condemnation of fallen human nature in *Arcadia* 2, showing its breadth and variety in a range of public and private acts concluding in tyranny, is given intensive examination in *Arcadia* 3 when a handful of persons confined to Cecropia's castle begin, in several ways, to prey on each other (3.5–6, 9–11). Their passions of power and lust take the forms of bribery (3.5), invitation (3.9), persuasion (3.10), threat (3.20), intimidation (3.22), and force as Cecropia and Amphialus try to impress their will on the luckless Philoclea (3.3, 9) and, that failing, on Pamela (3.10). Deceit characterizes Cecropia; when her craft fails in her direct approaches to the two women she has imprisoned, she attempts disguised executions that reveal and parody her essential helplessness (3.21–22). Her frenzied behavior leads to a reckless accidental death (3.24), yet her son's guilt-ridden complicity in her attempts to win Philoclea for him show his own susceptibility for self-abasement (3.19). Meantime, the captives, unable to transform their condition, transform their thoughts with a faith that guarantees a better existence after the patient suffering of their current earthly trials: "each thing being directed to an ende, and an end of preseruation: so proper effect of iudgment," Pamela tells Cecropia (3.10; sig. Z3; 491). She turns from disputation and soliloquy to prayer (3.6). Her faith along with Philoclea's, a major advancement over their simple trust in themselves in *Arcadia* 1 and 2, prepares them for their liberty at the hands of a resurrected Musidorus and Pyrocles, who appear in their own identities to lay siege to the castle from inside and out and so set free the prisoners. Yet the advancement through faith of Pamela, Philoclea, Pyrocles, and Musidorus, realizing the final (and justifying) end of humanist thought, comes at the heavy expense of the lives of Argalus and Parthenia, who are no match for Amphialus (3.12, 16), and Clinias and Amphialus, whose self-knowledge might, in time, have saved them. "He died as joyful as he left them sorrowful," we are told of Amphialus, "who had known him a mirror of courage and courtesy, of learning and arms; so that it seemed that Mars had begotten him upon one of the Muses" (3.32; 614). It is now the practice of self-sacrifice that allows certain men and women to be saved; a virtuous new self is discovered (not formulated) by losing the old self. Again, the certainty of principles revealed in a forceful and unwavering rhetoric, as in Pamela's firm response to Cecropia—"if his knowledge and power be infinite, then must needes his goodnesse and iustice march in the same ranke" (1.10 sig. Z3v; 492)—is Sidney's way of revealing this innermost growth and transformation of mind.

This Christian humanism toward which the major characters have been struggling throughout the first three books becomes an explicit *propositio* at the beginning of *Arcadia* 4. "The almighty wisdome euermore delighting to shew the world, that by vnlikeliest meanes greatest matters may come to conclusion: that humane reason may be the more humbled, and more willingly giue place to diuine prouidence" (4.1; sig. Kk4; 715) limns the education of Pamela and Philoclea, but what do we make of the others? At the close of *Arcadia* 3, Dorus dupes Dametas, Mopsa, and Miso with outrageous fictions so that he may be free to abduct Pamela; at the start of *Arcadia* 4, Pyrocles begins to plan his sophistic arguments to entice Gynecia and Basilius to reunite by persuading them to independent acts of adultery (4.2). While such motives are more understandable and more acceptable than Timautus's in his sophistic attempt to unseat Philanax (4.12), the language is surprisingly similar. Musidorus's unregenerated nature is further displayed in his enjoyment at mutilating the peasants who try to stop his abduction of Pamela.

> The first he ouertooke as he ran away, carying his head as farre before him,
> as those maner of runnings are wont to doe, with one blowe strake it so

cleane off, that it falling betwixt the hands, and the body falling vpon it, it made a shew as though the fellow had had great haste to gather vp his head againe. Another the speed he made to runne for the best game, bare him ful butt against a tree, so that tumbling backe with a brused face and a dreadfull expectation, *Musidorus* was straight vpon him: & parting with his sword one of his legs from him, left him to make a roring lametation that his morter-treading was marred for euer. A third finding his feet too slowe, aswell as his hands too weake, sodainly turned backe, beginning to open his lippes for mercie. But before he had well entred a rudely compiled oration, *Musidorus* blade was come betweene his iawes into his throat, and so the poore man rested there for euer with a verie euill mouth full of an answer. [4.6; sigs. Mm3v–Mm4; 754–55]

The elaborately witty and distancing rhetoric takes on its own sophistic overtones as if to diminish Musidorus's delight in butchery.

Such behavior sets Musidorus apart from those whose increasing sense of guilt causes them to witness recent events and their own culpabilities in a harsher and more honest light. For Basilius (4.2), Gynecia (4.3), and Pyrocles (4.4), their remembrance of things recently past brings release only through self-recrimination and self-punishment. Their places of memory, which resemble those of Strephon and Claius in outward grief, show a distinctly superior motivation. Rather than dwelling on their loss, they reform their intentions to correct the past. Places of memory result in more positive rhetorical invention, in more positive reformation of character. Finally, Musidorus, too, through his imprisonment with Pamela, learns the value of prayer.

> *Musidorus* looking vp to the starres, O mind of minds (said he) the liuing power of all things, which doest with al these eyes behold our euer varying actiōs, accept into thy fauorable eares this praier of mine: If I may any lōger hold out this dwelling on the earth which is called a life, grant me ability to deserue at this Ladies hands the grace she hath shewed vnto me, grant me wisdome to know her wisdome, and goodnesse so to encrease my loue of her goodnesse that all mine owne chosen desires, be to my selfe but second to her determinations. Whatsoeuer I be, let it be to her seruice, let me herein be satisfied, that for such infinite fauours of vertue, I haue some way wrought her satisfaction. But if my last time approcheth, and that I am no longer to be amongst mortall creatures, make yet my death serue her to some purpose, that hereafter she may not haue cause to repent herself that she bestowed so excellent a mind vpon *Musidorus.* [4.6; sig. Mm5; 758–59]

In its several hardships, life itself has taught Musidorus and the others, paradoxically through their limitations, how they may achieve their fullest humanity.

The dangerous division of men's minds, however, the ruinous renting of all estates, has now brought Arcadia to feel the pangs of uttermost peril, we are told at the outset of *Arcadia* 5. We come, at the end, dangerously near our own remembrance of the beginning when the blood of man's inhumanity stained the sea where Pyrocles clung to the mast of a ruined ship. What has changed is not the world—it remains dangerous if instructive—but the capacity of men to be educated. While Strephon and Claius took a certain delight in grieving, the leaders of Arcadia take little joy in punishing Pyrocles and Musidorus, now dressed in princely robes, and in preventing those marriages the princess Pamela and her sister Philoclea most desire. Although we can feel they have earned some pleasure and happiness, they seem frustrated even in this brief, final book. What is needed to overcome the vengeance sought by Philanax and the literal obedience to the law demanded by an impartial Euarchus is something beyond their joint belief in a society governed by a quid pro quo. They need something that contradicts or transcends "dead pitilesse lawes" (4.5; sig. Mm3; 752). Their amazement at Basilius's recovery, then, is not simply a matter of the marvelous but the validation of their hopes in an event that overcomes mere reason. Remembering back to an earlier, peaceful Arcadia, Basilius and Philanax, along with Euarchus, now realize the reinstitution of joy through a complete transformation of events. As Basilius's prophecy is literally validated by events, so too are the many themes introduced on the opening pages of *Arcadia* 1. Yet, if Sidney's fiction seems to have come full circle merely, we miss the point: the education of Pyrocles and Musidorus, Basilius and Gynecia, Pamela and Philoclea, Philanax and Dametas, has permanently changed them. Their grand new society, rhetorically nearly wordless in its joy, finally validates the humanist's belief in the capacity of man. Further confirmation, necessary to test this new order, however, lies beyond *Arcadia* 5; it lies, too, with us.

The *Arcadia,* then, in the disposition of events and ideas and in the multiple inventions subjected to figures of thought and speech, takes on, at the most general level of development, the form of a humanist treatise. It is a characteristic the *Arcadia* shares at a formal level with most works of humanist fiction—it is the basic form of the early English novel, and one that gains classical authority through such works as Xenophon's remarkable biography of Cyrus. The *Cyropaedia,* "the principal Greek text in the school curriculum at Shrewsbury,"[52] devotes Book 1 to declamations and disputations on right instruction and proper behavior; the remainder is given over to the fruits of an appropriate education. In certain orations, inset tales, and the use of wit there are other resemblances as well.[53] But we misconstrue the *Arcadia* if we locate Sidney's poetics, or, through them, his meaning, merely through the classical and contemporary works that teach him form and supply him incident. On the surface, it is true, there are direct and significant linkages with stories of heroic achievement that recall classical epic and chivalric adventure, just as there are indications of proper courtly behavior that show Sidney's interest in such earlier humanist works as *Il Libro del Cortegiano* and a fashionable wit that has occasional tonal resemblances to *Euphues*. There is a conclusion apparently similar to Greene's. These all relate to what Sidney calls poetry in his *Defence*. But Sidney's fundamental interest is not here. It lies elsewhere in the much more significant, if more abstract, concerns of philosophy—especially political philosophy taught by the ancients—which informs every incident in the composite *Arcadia* from the implied comparison of Basilius's irresponsible retreat to the country with Kalander's similar isolated refusal to deal with the causes of the Helots' rebellion *before* it erupts (and endangers his own son) to Euarchus's inability to make law conform with human needs and desires at the close. Beneath the gallantry, excitement, romance, and wit of its mere plot, the *Arcadia* is everywhere concerned with the dangers of monarchy and of oligarchy—in that, it is an indirect address to Elizabeth I and her privy council—as the restless mind of Sir Henry Sidney's son struggles to understand all the implications of the political government of a nation and the spiritual government of one's soul.

His self-proclaimed companion Fulke Greville recognized this in Sidney from the first, if we read him rightly. "In all these creatures of his making," Greville remarks pointedly,

> his intent, and scope was, to turn the barren Philosophy precepts into pregnant Images of life; and in them, first on the Monarch's part, lively to represent the growth, state, and declination of Princes, change of Government, and lawes: vicissitudes of sedition, faction, succession, confederacies, plantations, with all other errors, or alterations in publique affaires. Then again in the subjects case; the state of favor, disfavor, prosperitie, adversity, emulation, quarrell, undertaking, retiring, hospitality, travail, and all other moodes of private fortunes, or misfortunes. In which traverses (I know) his purpose was to limn out such exact pictures, of every posture in the minde, that any man being forced, in the straines of this life, to pass through any straights, or latitudes of good, or ill fortune, might (as in a glasse) see how to set a good countenance upon all the discountenances of adversitie, and a stay upon the exorbitant smilings of chance. [*Life,* sigs. B8–B8v; 15–16]

For Sidney, private and public matters are inevitably interrelated, cause and effect, effect and cause, and each event serves as an elenchus of man's citizenship as of his soul. So "that this representing of vertues, vices, humours, counsells, and actions of men in feigned, and unscandalous [that is, educational] Images," as Greville insists through painstaking repetition, "is an enabling of free-born spirits to the greatest affaires of States" (sigs. B1v–B2; 2–3): the most essential Senecan originals of the composite *Arcadia* are in the philosophical treatises of Aristotle and Plato and the late works of Cicero.[54] And it is precisely this infusion of classical philosophy into a Tudor fiction of eloquence that we find Sidney's greatest (and grandest) contribution to a humanist poetics.

If Sidney recalled (rather distantly) his study of Xenophon from his days at Shrewsbury, the chief contribution from his reading at Christ Church was the *Politics* and *Ethics* of Aristotle, to which he keeps returning. Aristotle was a Macedonian (like Euarchus and Pyrocles) who spent most of his life of learning and teaching in exile (like Pyrocles and Musidorus); and it is the systematic quality of his philosophy that seems to have appealed especially to Sidney and served him as ground text for the composite *Arcadia*, first suggested through these insinuating references of place. "Man is by nature a political animal," Aristotle argues in the *Politics* (1.1.9; 3.4.2),[55] one who is distinguished by reason and by reasoned speech and whose words indicate what is useful and harmful in society—that is, what is pragmatic—and what is right and wrong for individual and society—that is, what is moral (1). In all instances, then, rhetoric for Aristotle is hypotactic, in service to both state and individual, governor and governed, hero and courtier, shepherd and servant. It follows from these premises that "the city-state is prior in nature to the household" (1.1.11), but the two are correlative, signifying each other.

> Every state is as we see a sort of partnership, and every partnership is formed with a view to some good (since all the actions of all mankind are done with a view to what they think to be good). It is therefore evident that, while all partnerships aim at some good, the partnership that is the most supreme of all and includes all the others does so most of all, and aims at the most supreme of all goods; and this is the partnership entitled the state, the political association. [1.1.1]

Both marriages are to be informed and made "a unity by means of education" (2.2.10).

From *Politics* 1 and 2 stems much of the political theory of the *Arcadia*; from the more practical consequences in *Politics* 3 and 4 come many of the incidents. Starting with the premise that "a good ruler is virtuous and wise" (3.2.5), Aristotle argues at great length against the deviations from the ideal forms of government:

tyranny corresponding to kingship, oligarchy to aristocracy, and democracy to constitutional government; for tyranny is monarchy ruling in the interest of the monarch, oligarchy government in the interest of the rich, democracy in the interest of the poor, and none of these forms governs with regard to the profit of the community. [3.5.4]

Serially, these ideas are realized by Sidney in both versions of the *Arcadia* and account for much of the additional theory of right and wrong rule that by precept or action governs the additional album of rulers introduced in *New Arcadia* 2. In Aristotelian terms, Basilius is a tyrant, for his exile is self-indulgent—and that is precisely how Antiphilus defines him in the composite *Arcadia* (2.29; sigs. S3–S3v; 398). Another addition has Dorus describing to Pamela the origins and faults of oligarchies in his history of Macedon and in his analysis of the government Euarchus inherited before his sense of justice and law made it right again (2.6; sig. I1; 254–55). Tyranny is anatomized in his history of Phrygia (2.8), of Pontus (2.9), and of Paphlagonia (2.10), while the danger of democracy, for Sidney that many-headed hydra (2.26; sigs. R4v–R5v; 383, 385–86), is explained by Clinias (2.27; sigs. R6v–S1; 390–92), whose own rebellion, along with that of the Helots (1.5–7), transforms idea into circumstance, or "pregnant Images of life." Sidney further dramatizes Aristotle's long and elaborate discussion of the causes of political disorder in *Politics* 5 (2–6) in his characterization of the Paphlagonian king, a good ruler who is easily deceived (2.10), in Antiphilus as a bad ruler who is too easily flattered (2.29), in Artaxia who is too militaristic (2.29), and in Cecropia who is too selfish and greedy for power (3.5 ff.). Of all the bad rulers described in the *Politics,* the worst for Aristotle is just that which is realized in Basilius—"a monarch that exercises irresponsible rule" (4.8.3)—while the finest form of government for Aristotle is what in Sidney Euarchus is thought to aspire to: "the greatest good and good in the highest degree in the most authoritative of all," Aristotle sums, which is "justice" (3.7.1). And such praise seems suggestive of Sidney's closing scenes: "it is preferable for the law to rule rather than any one of the citizens, and according to this same principle, even if it be better for certain men to govern, they must be appointed as guardians of the laws and in subordination to them" (3.11.3).[56] Much as Plutarch's *Life of Lycurgus* directs our attention and conveys More's meaning through the satire of the *Utopia,* so Aristotle's *Politics* is meant to guide us through the *Arcadia,* helping us to comprehend, interpret, and judge characters and events, confirming events and their meaning in the *Arcadia* and, in turn, renewing through reapplication the wisdom of the *Politics.*

Moreover, politics and morality are by nature joined in Aristotle, as in

Sidney, so that all forms of government—but most especially monarchy—rely on men who exercise to know and who know in order to exercise. "How great dissipations monarchal governments are subject to," the subject of *Arcadia* 4.7, stems rather from "the discoursing sort of men than the active, being a matter more in imagination than practice" (sigs. Nn1–Nn1v; 766–67); it is a strong humanist statement that is also Sidney's personal plea for a position at court commensurate with his training and (by then) his growing association with leaders on the Continent. Less personal, but surely as indicative of Sidney's thought and design of the *Arcadia,* is his comment in the *Defence* that even pastorals "can shewe the miserie of people, vnder hard Lords and rauening soldiers," while "blessednesse is deriued, to them that lie lowest, from the goodnesse of them that sit highest" (sig. E3v; 94–95). Poetry and politics are inseparable for Sidney, as they were for his predecessor Thomas More, while his examination of Arcadia stands in the same instructive way that More's *Utopia* does, the Aristotelian counterpart to the more Platonic fiction at the start of Tudor humanist poetics.

Sidney's most overt political discussions are in *Arcadia* 2 and 5, whereas in the remaining three books of the composite work the problems of governing society remain just beneath the surface, subordinate to the problems of governing the self. Conceptually, this is no accident, for these remaining chapters are grounded in Aristotle's several *logoi,* or discourses, partly common to the *Eudemian Ethics,* which the Tudors knew as a single work: the magisterial *Nicomachean Ethics.* For the Tudor humanists, it was their chief philosophical source for the understanding of moderation, or *aretē,* virtue. It is here that Aristotle argues that will (or moral character) and passion (or appetite) are subject to reason, which, locating a floating mean between excess and deficiency, seeks moderation as the guaranteed way to *eudaimonia,* happiness, which is for Aristotle the proper end of conduct. When we succeed in this, our behavior takes on a new *energeia* (which in the *Defence* Sidney uses to identify the most successful poetry as well, sig. I3; 117). But for Aristotle the *Ethics* was a practical science, not a theoretical one, and he insists that it is joined to—is the counterpart to—his study in *Politics.* In this, Sidney realizes Aristotle better than any other Tudor humanist: the *Arcadia* means to secure that relationship. Indeed, nearly all of the nonpolitical (as well as some of the political) declamations and debates of the *Arcadia* stem directly from points made in the *Ethics* and, like them, aim to persuade us that personal and political behavior must nourish rather than impede each other. Where the characters of the *Arcadia* go astray is where they seek to divorce the two concerns. Not only do Basilius and Gynecia, for instance, allow

excessive passion and acts of will to overcome them; but their shortsighted-
ness in their pursuits of Pyrocles and Musidorus has serious political
implications that threaten the rule of Arcadia and invite the invasion of the
Helots and Cecropia. Cecropia, on the other hand, conceives politics too
narrowly, without the ethical component; it is her son, Amphialus, who
sees both the ethical and the political implications of his relationship with
Philoclea but whose behavior is never sufficiently moderated. The
chivalric duels that swell out in *Arcadia* 2 reveal his excessive desire to
display love rather than perform direct acts of love, his foolish and
inconsequent behavior made particularly evident by its juxtaposition to the
very real battles Pyrocles, Musidorus, and others have just recounted in
Arcadia 2 which were firmly directed toward political and ethical ends.

That Sidney had Aristotle's philosophical *argument* clearly in mind is
equally evident. Book 2 of the *Ethics* shows ethical responses to be a matter
of trained habit, *hexis*—literally, a matter of having or holding—that leads
to what we would call a "moral instinct." It is the sort of "conscience" that
guides Pamela and Philoclea. This too comes from a voluntary, deliberate
forechoice, *proairesis*—not unrelated to the discussion of the foreconceit in
the *Defence*—resulting from practice. In a fundamental way, the *Arcadia*
is, in its long educative process of Pyrocles and Musidorus (and, at the
conclusion, of Euarchus, Basilius, and Gynecia), the development of
proairesis through the accumulated actions that teach the will and the
appetite by constantly subjecting them to reasoned responses. Although for
Aristotle the will is free to behave as it wishes, reason nevertheless acts as
a voluntary *moral* control. Thus behavior is always connected to just those
virtues Sidney analyzes so carefully in *Arcadia*—magnanimity (specifically
assigned to Euarchus by Musidorus in 2.6 and 2.9, where it is associated
with Aristotelian magnificence), courage, wit, and modesty. Moreover,
Ethics 7 describes just those qualities that distinguish all the villains of
Arcadia—vanity, incontinence, obstinacy, irascibility, and inconsistency—
in its discussion of the weakness of will. In drawing on *Ethics* 7, Sidney pays
particular attention to *akrasia* (7.2), a man doing what he knows he should
not do, in his most moving portraits, those of Amphialus in *Arcadia* 3 and
of Gynecia in *Arcadia* 4 and 5. It is, in fact, the sense of *akrasia* that
Cecropia never achieves and is what sets her apart from the other
characters, although her initial intentions—to do her best for her son—are
not unlike the good intentions of the other major characters.

Wherever we turn in the *Arcadia,* the speeches that constitute much of
Sidney's fiction are grounded in one or more of the virtues discussed in the
Nicomachean Ethics, often implying their political ramifications as well.
Moreover, these set speeches, such as Helen's story (1.11), Gynecia's

tortured soliloquy (2.1), Philoclea's discovery of her love for Zelmane (2.4), Zelmane's apostrophe to the river Ladon (2.11), and Basilius's apostrophe to night (4.2), are so composed through a delightful rhetorical varying that we are caught up in the argument and are invited as readers to work out with the characters their own best responses for virtuous action. Occasionally such pieces of oratory have direct results, as when the steward's formal report enlists the aid of Musidorus in the battle against the Helots (1.5) or when the speeches of Palladius and Diaphantus settle that rebellion (1.6, 7). In such instances, we test our own reasoning. Even in those speeches meant to serve as humanist models—Pyrocles as the newly discovered Amazon to Musidorus (1.9), Dorus on Mopsa (2.2), or Dorus's letter to Pamela (2.5)—we are meant to ascertain the *moral* and *political* wisdom of the argument. Sidney's consistent style of embellishment—not merely that of periphrasis, which Hoskins praises so lavishly (*Directions*, pp. 46–50), but also his use of anadiplosis, anaphora, epizeuxis, ploce, prosonomasia, traductio, paroemia, and hyperbaton—is meant to be not luxurious elaboration but a basic means of personal redefinition of Aristotelian virtues in a way that constantly freshens them despite continuous reapplication. If we do not read the *Arcadia* in this basic sense of putting Aristotelian philosophy on trial and redeeming it, we misunderstand both Sidney's substance *and* his style.

The *Arcadia* pays its greatest respect to the *Nicomachean Ethics* by putting at the center of its concern the two chief subjects of Aristotle's treatise. The first (and last) to be treated in Sidney's study is justness, the subject of an independent essay by Aristotle that the Tudors knew as *Ethics* 5. There Aristotle is clear that justice is both a political and a moral concern that, appealing to an absolute concept, by necessity takes on relative form. He seems to limn Euarchus's predicament and the central questions raised in *Arcadia* 5 when he first defines justice: the just, he claims, "means that which is lawful and that which is equal or fair" (5.1.8)[57]—but legality and equity are not always the same thing, as Euarchus quickly realizes. Yet, *philosophically*, they *must* be.

> We saw that the law-breaker is unjust and the law-abiding man just. It is therefore clear that all lawful things are just in one sense of the word, for what is lawful is decided by legislature, and the several decisions of the legislature we call rules of justice. Now all the various pronouncements of the law aim either at the common interest of all, or at the interest of a ruling class determined either by excellence or in some other similar way; so that in one of its senses the term "just" is applied to anything that produces and preserves the happiness, or the component parts of the happiness, of the political community.

And the law prescribes certain conduct; the conduct of a brave man, for example not to desert one's post, not to run away, not to throw down one's arms; that of a temperate man, for example not to commit adultery or outrage; that of a gentle man, for example not to strike, not to speak evil; and so with actions exemplifying the rest of the virtues and vices, commanding these and forbidding those—rightly if the law has been rightly enacted, not so well if it has been made at random.

Justice then in this sense is perfect Virtue. [5.1.12–15]

It is clear that Aristotle wants justice somehow to coordinate law, custom, class, and suitable conduct while recognizing that these may be incongruous. None of them is so supreme that other considerations are made subordinate or irrelevant. The genus justice has several species— distributive (5.3.12), corrective (5.4.1), natural (5.7.1), legal (5.7.4), voluntary and involuntary (5.8.5); injustice, too, has many categories (5.2.6). That Euarchus refuses to admit conditions and circumstances that might mitigate against law in an (unrealistic) pure state suggests that his own behavior is finally immoral and unjust. This is confirmed by his notion of an absolute sentence similar in kind to the crime, for Aristotle is emphatic that reciprocity does not make the unjust just (5.5.2), does not right wrong. Aristotle's humane conclusion—"Men think that it is in their power to act unjustly, and therefore that it is easy to be just. But really this is not so" (5.9.14)—gives a further issue to Pyrocles, Musidorus, and Gynecia that Euarchus steadfastly refuses to admit. Yet, because justice is the most fundamental union of ethics and politics for Aristotle, it becomes the central subject for him, as it is the climactic subject for Sidney.

Enclosing the public concern of justice in *Arcadia* is the private concern of friendship. This is Aristotle's other independent concern in the *Ethics*—and it receives by far the most prominent treatment, taking up two of the ten books (8, 9). It is easy to see how the issue of friendship speaks to the private concerns in *Arcadia* 1–4, as Aristotle defines it. "Friends," he tells us, "we consider the greatest of external goods.

Also if it be more the mark of a friend to give than to receive benefits, and if beneficence is a function of the good man and virtue, and it is nobler to benefit friends than strangers, the good man will need friends as the objects of his beneficence. . . . Nobody would choose to have all possible good things on the condition that he must enjoy them alone; for man is a social being, and designed by nature to live with others; accordingly the happy man must have society, for he has everything that is naturally good. . . . Therefore a man ought also to share his friend's consciousness of his existence, and this is attained by their living together and by conversing and communicating their thoughts to each other; for this is the meaning of living together as applied to human rights, it does not mean merely feeding in the same place, as it does when applied to cattle. [9.9.2–10]

Sidney realizes this collocation of the private and public by making his heroes a prince and a potential ruler (Prince Pyrocles courts Philoclea; Musidorus courts Princess Pamela); their loves are necessarily rife with political implication. Such desires and intentions are for Aristotle governed by the intellect (*Ethics* 6), which works through prudence (*phronēsis*), as with Pyrocles and Musidorus, or intuition (*nous*), as with Philoclea, or wisdom (*sophia*), as with Pamela. Not only do the four major characters allow Sidney variations on justice and friendship through a fundamental chiasmus, but they also allow him to pursue the several ways Aristotle proposes for virtuous knowledge. And, whichever way we choose, he concludes in *Ethics* 10, we will proceed to the highest state of knowledge, the disinterested contemplation of truth, *theōria*.

> But if happiness consists in activity in accordance with virtue, it is reasonable that it should be activity in accordance with the highest virtue; and this will be the virtue of the best part of us. Whether then this be the intellect, or whatever else it be that is thought to rule and lead us by nature, and to have cognizance of what is noble and divine, either as being itself also actually divine, or as being relatively the divinest part of us [*nous*], it is the activity of this part of us in accordance with the virtue proper to it that will constitute perfect happiness; and it has been stated already that this activity is the activity of contemplation. [10.7.1]

Sidney works this out deliberately by proceeding from the soliloquies of Pyrocles and Musidorus in *Arcadia* 1, where contemplation seems to lead them to think of appetite, to the debates between Cecropia and Pamela and Philoclea in *Arcadia* 3, where the life of pure contemplation is defended by the daughters of Basilius, to *Arcadia* 5, where such a state is potentially possible given the chastening experience of the trial. Pure contemplation of the Deity or the divine is for Aristotle a temporary state because a moral life also means active political and social engagement (although this provides happiness in a secondary degree). It is the business of politics, Aristotle clearly implies, so to organize the state that as many citizens as possible may be trained and enabled to attain frequent periods of contemplation. The betrothal of Pyrocles and Philoclea and of Musidorus and Pamela signifies their ability to find *theoria* through each other while presaging for Macedonia and Arcadia a political rule conducive to contemplation for its citizens, one likely to be superior to the government now achieved by Euarchus and Basilius respectively. In sum, the *Arcadia,* in its primary attempt to fuse poetry with philosophy, is the finest example in humanist poetics of Aristotelianism fictively realized.

But Sidney was essentially a bookish man[58]—and the *Arcadia* is grounded in the same conflation of Aristotle and Plato that ideationally distinguishes his *Defence*. There is good reason to believe that Sidney owned the splendid three folio volumes of Plato as translated by Henri Stephanus in 1578;[59] it seems clear from Sidney's text, at any rate, that although Aristotle's work is his chief Senecan original in its masterful confluence of politics and ethics he also has in mind the various dialogic, mythopoeic, rhetorical, and political forces that P. Friëdlander finds employed in Plato's trilogy on society and good government—the *Republic,* the *Statesman,* and the *Laws.*[60] In these works Plato's position is congruent with Aristotle's but with a different emphasis. Plato's premise is that wise private and public behavior is directed by a conceptual knowledge of the good (*Republic* 7. 517B–C; *Laws* 5.727D–E). The means for learning the good Socrates discusses in his long examination of the education of the Guardians in the *Republic* (3–4, esp. 402D; cf. *Laws* 7.793 ff.). For Plato, learning is a matter of moving toward the ideal through the principle of imitatio. "Education," he tells us, "is the process of drawing and guiding children towards that principle which is pronounced right by the law and confirmed as truly right by the experience of the oldest and most just" (*Laws* 2.659D).[61] Such passages have a close bearing on the description of the education of Pyrocles and Musidorus (*Arcadia* 2.7; sigs. L2–L2v; 258–59). Socrates urges such training because of the natural imperfection of societies—like timocracy, oligarchy, democracy, and tyranny (*Republic* 8.544E ff.), the types lacking in virtue that appear as basic designs for Sidney's portrayal of Clinias and Timantus (548D ff.), Antiphalus and Gynecia (558D ff.), and Cecropia (571D). For Plato as for Aristotle, the tyrant (or corrupted monarch) is the least desirable man (576E ff.). "To sum up," Plato writes in the last of his works, "the life of bodily and spiritual virtue, as compared with that of vice, is not only more pleasant, but also exceeds greatly in nobility, rectitude, virtue and good fame, so that it causes the man who lives it to live ever so much more happily than he who lives the opposite life" (*Laws* 5.734D).

It follows logically, then, that men choose their own fates: Socrates' concluding myth of Er (*Republic* 10.614A ff.) shows how individual freedom operates in a world governed by forms and principles. "No divinity," he sums, "shall cast lots for you, but you shall choose your own destiny" (617E).[62] Consequently, Plato's Athenian Stranger likewise argues, everything may seem to be chance but is not.

ATHENIAN STRANGER. God controls all that is, and … Chance and Occasion co-operate with God in the control of all human affairs. It is, however, less harsh to admit that these two must be accompanied by a third factor, which is Art. For that the pilots' art should co-operate with Occasion—verily I, for one, should esteem that a great advantage. Is it not so?

CLINIAS. It is.

ATHENIAN STRANGER. Then we must grant that it is equally true in the other cases also, by parity of reasoning, including the case of legislation. When all the other conditions are present which a country needs to possess in the way of fortune if it is ever to be happily settled, then every such State needs to meet with a lawgiver who holds fast to truth.

[*Laws* 4.709B–C]

What explains the apparent discrepancy between the patterning of Order and God and the random events of life is the shaping direction of the exceptional individual as political ruler—hence the *Statesman* as the bridge between the *Republic* and the *Laws* in Plato's trilogy. In a key passage the Athenian Stranger likens the statesman to a doctor.

THE STRANGER. Let us suppose that a physician or a gymnastic trainer is going away and expects to be a long time absent from his patients or pupils; if he thinks they will not remember his instructions, he would want to write them down, would he not?

YOUNG SOCRATES. Yes.

THE STRANGER. What if he should come back again after a briefer absence than he expected? Would he not venture to substitute other rules for those written instructions if others happened to be better for his patients, because the winds or something else had, by act of God, changed unexpectedly from their usual course? Would he persist in the opinion that no one must transgress the old laws, neither he himself by enacting new ones nor his patient by venturing to do anything contrary to the written rules, under the conviction that these laws were medicinal and healthful and anything else was unhealthful and unscientific? If anything of that sort occurred in the realm of science and true art, would not any such regulations on any subject assuredly arouse the greatest ridicule?

YOUNG SOCRATES. Most assuredly.

THE STRANGER. But he who has made written or unwritten laws about the just and unjust, the honourable and disgraceful, the good and the bad for the herds of men that are tended in their several cities in accordance with the laws of the law-makers, is not to be permitted to give other laws contrary to those, if the scientific law-maker, or another like him, should come! Would not such a prohibition appear in truth as ridiculous as the other?

YOUNG SOCRATES. It certainly would.

[*Statesman* 295C–296A][63]

For Plato, wise leadership also employs flexibility and change—supporting what one knows or judges to be "noble and good" and loathing what one knows or judges to be "evil and unjust" (*Laws* 3.689A); it entails the continuing agreement of knowledge, opinion, or reason. All these in conjunction (or what Aristotle calls simply the legal and the just; law and equity) constitute the best kind of wisdom, *sophia* (*Laws* 3.689D). The lack of such accord is, conversely, the worst kind of ignorance, *amathia* (*Laws* 3.689A). *Sophia* in Plato is a matter of self-education transformed into self-mastery—and it is this process that is also the subject, the movement and development, of *Arcadia* 5. Plutarch carries forward his understanding of *politeia* as both statecraft and citizenship in the *Moralia*—in the *Praecepta Gerendae Reipublicae* and the fragmentary *De Unius in Republica Dominatione, Populari Statu, et Paucorum Imperio,* ultimately derived from the *Republic*. Sidney knew these, too, although it is not likely that he needed such confirmation of authority.

Sidney is not merely the only writer of humanist poetics to ground his fiction in Aristotelianism but also the only one to syncretize Aristotle and Cicero by using as still a third Senecan original the late Platonic works of the exiled Roman orator. Cicero's *De Re Publica,* for instance, the fragments that, modeled on the *Republic,* are meant through the figure of Scipio to transform Rome into the ideal state, also compares the various forms of government much as Aristotle does (1.27.43 ff.). "Quid est enim civitas nisi iuris societas?" Cicero asks: "For what is a State except an association or partnership in justice"? (1.32.49).[64] Much more important for Sidney is its sequel, the fragmentary *De Legibus,* arguably Cicero's most attractive dialogue. The *De Legibus* is at once more philosophical than its model, Plato's *Laws,* and more systematic than Aristotle's *Politics*. Cicero supplies the definitions of law that are put forward by Euarchus and by Pyrocles in *Arcadia* 5.

> Lex est ratio summa insita in natura, quae iubet ea, quae facienda sunt, prohibetque contraria. eadem ratio cum est in hominis mente confirmata et confecta, lex est. itaque arbitrantur prudentiam esse legem, cuius ea vis sit, ut recte facere iubeat, vetet delinquere.

> Law is the highest reason, implanted in Nature, which commands what ought to be done and forbids the opposite. This reason, when firmly fixed and fully developed in the human mind, is Law. And so they believe that Law is intelligence, whose natural function it is to command right conduct and forbid wrongdoing. [1.6.18–19; cf. 1.7.22–23][65]

Law comes for Cicero as for Plato to transcend men and human community.

> Legem neque hominum ingeniis excogitatam nec scitum aliquod esse populorum, sed aeternum quiddam, quod universum mundum regeret imperandi prohibendique sapientia.

Law is not a product of human thought, nor is it any enactment of peoples, but something eternal which rules the whole universe by its wisdom in command and prohibition. [2.4.8]

But man's reason, to reach the sense of divinity, must first pass through the sense of human community advocated by Aristotle in the *Politics* and *Ethics* and by Plato in the *Statesman*. To define that, Cicero turns to a discussion of friendship that owes much to *Ethics* 8 and 9.

Cum hanc benivolentiam tam late longeque diffusam vir sapiens in aliquem pari virtute praeditum contulerit, tum illud effici, quod quibusdam incredibile videatur, sit autem necessarium, ut nihilo sepse plus quam alterum diligat.

When a wise man shows toward another endowed with equal virtue the kind of benevolence which is so widely diffused among men, that will then have come to pass which, unbelievable as it seems to some, is after all the inevitable result—namely, that he loves himself no whit more than he loves another. [1.12.34]

Law, love, and utility lead to justice and virtue, Cicero writes (1.15. 42–43). As Quintus sums in the dialogue,

Certe ita res se habet, ut ex natura vivere summum bonum sit, id est vita modica et apta virtute perfrui aut naturam sequi et eius quasi lege vivere, id est nihil, quantum in ipso sit, praetermittere, quo minus ea, quae natura postulet, consequatur, quod inter haec velit virtute tamquam lege vivere.

It is undoubtedly true that to live in accordance with Nature is the highest good. That signifies the enjoyment of a life of due measure based upon virtue, or following Nature and living according to her law, if I may call it so; in other words, to spare no effort, so far as in us lies, to accomplish what Nature demands; among these demands being her wish that we live by virtue as our law. [1.21.56]

In his characteristically pragmatic codification of Greek philosophy, Cicero thus makes it clear why Sidney's fiction has two heroes, not one, so that love and friendship may function to add equity to law and to ground virtue and private concern in social and political associations.[66] It is the same systematic pragmatism that characterizes Cicero's remaking of the *Ethics,* his *De Officiis,* with its twin concerns of theoretical doctrine and practical rules (1.3.7). This treatise, concerned with morality, expediency, and their relationship, stems from the four cardinal virtues of Plato (wisdom, justice, fortitude, temperance) as set forth in *Ethics* 6–7.

Omne, quod est honestum, id quattuor partium oritur ex aliqua: aut enim in perspicientia veri sollertiaque versatur aut in hominum societate tuenda tribuendoque suum cuique et rerum contractarum fide aut in animi excelsi atque invicti magitudine ac robore aut in omnium, quae fiunt quaeque dicuntur, ordine et modo, in quo inest modestia et temperantia.

All that is morally right rises from some one of four sources: it is concerned either (1) with the full perception and intelligent development of the true; (2) with the conservation of organized society, with rendering to every man his due, and with the faithful discharge of obligations assumed or (3) with the greatness and strength of a noble and invincible spirit; or (4) with the orderliness and moderation of everything that is said and done, wherein consist temperance and self-control. [1.5.15][67]

All comes to rest, according to Cicero, with the ruler (as in *Arcadia* 5).

Est igitur proprium munus magistratus intellegere se genere personam civitatis debereque eius dignitatem et decus sustinere, servare leges, iura discribere, ea fidei suae commissa meminisse.

It is, then, peculiarly the place of a magistrate to bear in mind that he represents the state and that it is his duty to uphold its honour and its dignity, to enforce the law, to dispense to all their constitutional rights, and to remember that all this has been committed to him as a sacred trust. [1.34.124]

Sidney uses other works of Cicero, of course, such as the *De Natura Deorum*, where the Stoic Balbus is the original for Pamela's forthright position in *Arcadia* 3.10—although she stops short of declaring that the world and man are perfect and perfectly in accord,[68] perhaps because he sensed quite keenly the ideological cleavage between his pagan antecedents and his own Protestant beliefs. He may also have sensed, as his fellow Tudors did, that of all the pagans Cicero (with Vergil) seemed closest to the Christian understanding of God and man. At any rate, it is certain that only those ideas concerning politics and ethics that are validated in the late works of Cicero are those which, through him, Sidney searches out in Aristotle and Plato. We have long noted Sidney is often Ciceronian in style; what we have failed to recognize is how Ciceronian he also is in his thought.

And just how close that thought is to Christian ideas is illustrated by the work of Philip de Mornay, sieur du Plessis-Marly, Sidney's friend, whose *De la Vérité de la religion chrestienne* (Antwerp, 1581) Arthur Golding says Sidney began to translate.[69] Whether or not that was the case, it is surely a work Sidney knew. And many parts of this Protestant apologetics are relevant to *Arcadia*. A particularly important summary chapter is chapter 18, "That God is mans souerein welfare, and therefore that the cheef marke which man should ame at, is to returne againe vnto God" (sigs.

XIV–YI). Here Mornay urges man to exercise virtue, "The calmenesse of our affections" (sig. X7), in achieving policy, "the right vse of reason in the gouerning of worldly affaires" (sig. X7v), as the means to wisdom, "the beholding of God and of things belonging to GOD." He continues, "This requireth a man to lift vp himselfe aboue the world, and aboue himselfe; I meane that a man should retyre from all outward things into his owne soule, the Soule vnto her Mynd, and the Mynd vnto God" (sig. X8). "It remaineth then in the end, that wee must atteine to that by Fayth, which wee cannot atteyne vnto by Reason; that wee must mount vp by liuely beleef aboue our vnderstãding, vnto the things whereunto the eye of our mynd is not able to reach" (sig. X8v). The classical philosophers' state of divine or eternal virtue is for Mornay the equivalent of Providence, and although Sidney could not expect all humanists—even all Christian humanists—to know Mornay, he surely means to imply in the *Arcadia* that the pagan philosophy of Book 5 is in perfect accord with Christianity. As in the *Defence* where David's Psalms become an ideal model for poets, so in the *Arcadia* poetry transforms antique thought into *Christian humanism*.[70]

Classical models give Sidney organized thought; they are also his source for humanist rhetoric. Of the two, it is his ability at rhetoric that most impressed the other writers of his day. Peter Heylyn comments for many of them when he contends that the *Arcadia* "comprehendeth the vniuersall art of speaking,"[71] while Abraham Fraunce uses about eighty quotations from the unpublished *Arcadia* in his *Arcadian Rhetorike* (1588), giving Sidney pride of place just after Homer and Vergil. Hoskins's shorter *Directions* contains another 180. Whether or not they shared with Zelmane the "eloquence of amazement" because of a "long methodized oration" (3.22; sig. Dd4v; 561), they discovered as we do that the lasting power of the *Arcadia* is its power to persuade. To this end, rhetoric is examined and employed with an incredible variety and fertility. It is properly defined by Zelmane (2.26; sig. S2v; 386), analyzed by Philoclea (2.17; sig. P3; 330), and corrupted by the sophistry of Clinias (2.27; sigs. S3–S3v; 388–89). Dorus extends it to parody when he awards Mopsa "her tongue with victorie" as his ideal accolade (2.3; sig. K2; 232): the range of rhetoric in the *Arcadia* is immense. But all of it comes to rest, finally, in the best use of language, explained and practiced by Euarchus in his self-defense (5.8; sig. Ss1v; 842). There the rational use of language is surpassed only by the miracle of our "vnsearchable wisedomes" (5.8; sig. Ss2; 843).

Sidney's chief authority on rhetoric is Aristotle. He writes Languet that he wishes to learn more Greek so as to translate him; "I am utterly ashamed," he confesses, "to be following the stream, as Cicero says, and not go to the fountain head."[72] Hoskins fathomed this interest in Aristotle's *Rhetoric* rather than that of Ramus—as a Ramist divorcing technique from content, Fraunce has done Sidney a disservice[73]—and he did so without being told: "This was my opinion ever; and Sir Philip Sidney betrayed his knowledge in this book of Aristotle to me before ever I knew that he had translated any part of it. For I found the two first books Englished by him in the hands of the noble studious Henry Wotton."[74] Of modern commentators, Neil L. Rudenstine, in a long discussion of ornament and rhetoric in Sidney, repeatedly demonstrates that figures are inseparable from ideas, disposition from invention, but rather are intended to be functional. This explains Sidney's distaste for a Ciceronianism at Oxford that stressed figures of speech as too limited—"Qui dum verba sectantur, res ipsas negligunt," he writes to his brother, in his only complaint of the humanist curriculum at Christ Church[75]—because imitation of Cicero had been misconceived (as by Erasmus's Nosopomus and others like him) as staying with Ciceronian vocabulary, phrasing, and diction without adding the individual writer's own style and temperament, or the speaker's interests in *ethos* and *pathos*.[76] The deliberate pairing, in *Arcadia* 2.26–27, of the persuasions of Zelmane and Clinias as proper and sophistic, the one leading to reconciliation and the other to rebellion, is only one of the more obvious examples of how invention and disposition are always cemented in Sidney. Ben Jonson knew this, too. He remarks with customary aphorism and mordacity that "Sir *Philip Sidney* and Mr. *Hooker* (in different matter) grew great Masters of wit, and language; and in whom all vigour of Invention, and strength of judgment met. . . . And as it is fit to reade the best Authors to youth first, so let them be of the openest, and clearest. As *Livy* before *Salust, Sydney* before *Donne*."[77]

This development of humanist ideas (especially of politics and ethics) through Aristotelian and Ciceronian rhetoric based in figures of thought *rather than* figures of speech is evident everywhere in Sidney's writing and at every stage in his abbreviated career. It characterizes the debates and dialogues that, according to Jon S. Lawry, constitute nearly all of the narrative sections and eclogues of the *Old Arcadia*. The substance of *The Lady of May* "is a rustic parody of a scholastic debate," Katherine Duncan-Jones tells us, this particular entertainment relying more on rhetorical invention than on spectacle or music.[78] The same concentrated unity of invention and disposition is apparent in the letter to Alençon and in the defense of Sir Henry Sidney's administration in Ireland.[79] Even the sonnets of *Astrophil and Stella* (1590), Richard A. Lanham reminds us, "might be more clearly conceived as *progymnasmata*, . . . rhetorical efforts which press the failure of philosophy into service as the final, clinching argument."[80] Such works are of an imagination all compact: in all of them, idea and presentation are indivisible, Sidney's own work varying illustrations of the theory he sets forth in his *Defence of Poesie* (1595). There, with considerable wit,[81] Sidney states his rhetorically based poetics as a formal *responsio*,[82] which argues that art is based in a foreconceit or poetic image that functions as both a major and a minor premise, both precept and illustration: a double enthymeme. According to Sidney, such images, like the best rhetorical inventions, work to tease men and attract children, demonstrate ideas memorably, and so move an audience to virtuous action. Only such images make us *exercise* to know. "If *Oratio*, next to *Ratio*, Speech next to Reason, be the greatest gift bestowed vpon *Mortalitie*, that cannot bee praiselesse, which doth most polish that blessing of speech" (sig. F3v; 100). At the conclusion of the *Defense*, in the apparently digressive listing of poetic genres and in the apparently random commentary on particular poets, Sidney continues to unite both speech and reason, thought and presentation, as, earlier, he showed how poetry must be a marriage between two grotesque prosopo-poeiae—wandering Philosophy and record-bearing History—who, left alone, would remain woefully partial and inferior.

It is in this very carefully developed sense that Sidney's longest and most careful work, the *Arcadia*, is highly rhetorical, "a gladiatorial display of oratory which outshines anything achieved in English before and perhaps since," as Maurice Evans has it.[83] It is in this carefully developed sense that Sidney explores the possibilities of the double enthymeme such as Cicero sets out as his rhetorical program initially in *De Oratore* i.

> Quis enim aliud, in maxima discentium multitudine, summa magistro-rum copia, praestantissimis hominum ingeniis, infinita causarum varietate, amplissimis eloquentiae propositis praemiis, esse causae putet, nisi rei quamdam incredibilem magnitudinem, ac difficultatem? Est enim et scientia comprehendenda rerum plurimarum, sine qua verborum volubili-tas inanis atque irridenda est; et ipsa oratio conformanda, non solum electione, sed etiam constructione verborum; et omnes animorum motus, quos hominum generi rerum natura tribuit, penitus pernoscendi; quod omnis vis ratioque dicendi in eorum, qui audiunt, mentibus, aut sedandis, aut excitandis expromenda est. Accedat eodem oportet lepos quidam facetiaeque, et eruditio libero digna, celeritasque et brevitas et responden-di, et lacessendi, subtili venustate, atque urbanitate coniuncta. Tenenda praeterea est omnis antiquitas, exemplorumque vis; neque legum, aut iuris civilis scientia neglegenda est.

> For, where the number of students is very great, the supply of masters of the very best, the quality of natural ability outstanding, the variety of issues unlimited, the prizes open to eloquence exceedingly splendid, what else

could anyone think to be the cause, unless it be the really incredible vastness and difficulty of the subject? To begin with, a knowledge of very many matters must be grasped, without which oratory is but an empty and ridiculous swirl of verbiage: and the distinctive style has to be formed, not only by the choice of words, but also by the arrangement of the same; and all the mental emotions, with which nature has endowed the human race, are to be intimately understood, because it is in calming or kindling the feelings of the audience that the full power and science of oratory are to be brought into play. To this there should be added a certain humour, flashes of wit, the culture befitting a gentleman, and readiness and terseness alike in repelling and in delivering the attack, the whole being combined with a delicate charm and urbanity. Further, the complete history of the past and a store of precedents must be retained in the memory, nor may a knowledge of statute law and our national law in general be omitted. [1.5.16–18][84]

Only such a comprehensive vision could suggest such a massive anatomy of an entire culture as the *Arcadia* with its portrait of a civilization testifying throughout to the value of and need for human dignity. It remains unique, towering above the other Tudor fictions, in its imaginative power and sweep.

The means of conveying such a complex achievement is Sidney's understanding of the inherent complexity of the poetic image of a double enthymeme, connecting logic of thought with means of expression. "Est enim finitimus oratori poeta," Cicero writes; "the truth is that the poet is a very near kinsman of the orator" (*De Oratore* 1.16.70). *Ratio* and *oratio* are permanently forged. Maurice Evans seems to have this in mind when he shows how the scene in which Musidorus first discovers Pyrocles disguised as an Amazon (1.12) illustrates Sidney's poetics. "In essence," he writes, Sidney

depicts a brisk quarrel between the two in which they come as near to direct abuse of each other as their princely dignity will allow, until their normal feelings of love for each other reassert themselves and they embrace in tears. The progress of this quarrel from self-righteousness and evasion, to anger, to dismay and so to love again, is expressed by means of an elaborate verbal choreography which, beginning with long set addresses, develops into the opposition of formal stichomythia as feelings run higher, and subsides into a freer, more flowing rhetoric when the deeper emotions come into play. The leisurely formality of the treatment should not blind us to the precision with which Sidney delineates the range and development of the underlying emotions; and the passage, indeed, owes much of its humour as well as its peculiarly touching quality to the juxtaposition of highly formal rhetoric with all too human feelings. As the young men play their parts with the earnestness and ceremony of a duel, one is made conscious of the nature and tensions of civilization itself. [Introduction, p. 16]

Far more complex yet, the varying of Pyrocles and Musidorus as Diaphantus and Palladius, Dorus and Zalmane, and the Black Knight or Forsaken Knight and the Ill-Apparelled Knight grounds the *Arcadia* in a *fourfold* chiasmus. In addition, Sidney employs *gradatio* combined with *antithesis* at each point of his narrative to dig deeply into the psychology of private and public moments that display the cardinal virtues and the deadly sins, his figures of thought exploring with a kind of patience and comprehensiveness (as well as imagination and a poetry of sound) those systematic patterns of mind and consciousness on which humanist culture rests.[85] In this he is, as he confesses in the *Defence*, "a peece of a *Logician*" (sig. B1v; 73). The heavily Latinate syntax and the deliberate assortment of Ciceronian figures—such as the description of going to bed as "[making] their pillows weake proppes of their ouer loaden heades" (3.40; sig. Hh4v; 666) or phrasing a reprimand by periphrasis as in "couldst thou not aswel haue giuē me a determinate deniall, as to disguise thy first disguising, with a doble dissembling?" (5.3; sig. Pp6;799), which so mislead and distract twentieth-century commentators—are Sidney's way of heightening language and meaning in order to assign them significance and dignity well beyond the immediate narrative context. (The syntax, when we study it, is surprisingly Attic, unlike the more Asiatic language of Gorgias—and Lyly.) At the same time, Sidney declares and withholds meaning by such deployment of language, because he means deliberately to convey that poetry is a means, not an end; the end remains instruction and persuasion rather than appreciation or involvement merely. He wishes to awaken *thoughtful* pleasure: he wants us to work too. That is because words are for him powerful counters that can be played for good or bad ends. The crucial inset stories of the *Defence*—Menenius Agrippa stemming a Roman rebellion followed by Nathan the prophet leading the holy poet David back to himself and so to God, the two at the exact fulcrum of Sidney's argument and so the centerpiece of it (sigs. E2v–E3; 93–94)—reveal his own strategic use of style. And the more we read the *Arcadia*, the more we realize that here too *everything* has point.

Sidney's use of Ciceronian rhetoric is the use of such figures of thought as comparison, antithesis, simile, and personification rather than figures of diction (anaphora, isocolon, homoioteleuton). Clauses are often related to form syllogisms. Such employment of logic through rhetoric is a natural outgrowth of Sidney's understanding of poetic image. It is a conflation that is ultimately derived from Aristotle's *Poetics*, which, following the sort of reasoning basic to Aristotelian physics, insists on a narrative built from formal causes leading to recognizable effects. This process creates a pattern that inherently displays a rational order in both substance (or topic) and artifact. Such a poetics is particularly humanist, because it gives high respect to patterns conceived and practiced by the exercise of reason. As Sidney is at pains to follow the principles of Aristotelian poetics, he is equally concerned with Aristotelian rhetoric. His use of Aristotle can be seen especially well in his frequent attention to ethos, or the relationship between the speaker and his audience. Aristotle's definition comes in *Rhetoric* 1.2.3–6:

> Now the proofs furnished by the speech are of three kinds. The first depends upon the moral character of the speaker, the second upon putting the hearer into a certain frame of mind, the third upon the speech itself, in so far as it proves or seems to prove.
>
> The orator persuades by moral character when his speech is delivered in such a manner as to render him worthy of confidence. . . . It is not the case, as some writers of rhetorical treatises lay down in their "art," that the worth of the orator in no way contributes to his powers of persuasion; on the contrary, moral character, so to say, constitutes the most effective means of proof. The orator persuades by means of his hearers, when they are roused to emotion by his speech [*pathos*]. . . . Lastly persuasion is produced by the speech itself, when we establish the true or apparently true from the means of persuasion applicable to each individual subject.[86]

Ethos, then, works outward (in understanding the psychology of the audience) and inward (in learning how to project a particularly apt persona). Sidney shows his concern with ethos when he writes his father on 25 April 1578—

> So strangely and dyversely goes the cource of the worlde by the enterchanginge humors of those that governe it, that thoughe it be most noble to have allwayes one mynde and one constancy, yet can it not be allwaies directed to one pointe; but must needes sometymes alter his course, according to the force of others changes dryves it[87]

—and in his letters to the queen concerning Alençon and Sir Henry. Aristotle amplifies the subject of ethos considerably in *Rhetoric* 2.1.2–6—the portion Sidney translated and passed on to Wotton—and a number of other chapters in *Rhetoric 2* instruct the speaker on the manipulation of various emotions, such as anger (2.2, seen with Philanax in *Arcadia* 4), mildness (2.3, as in Cecropia's initial approaches to Philoclea in *Arcadia* 3), friendship (2.4, as with Pyrocles and Pamela in *Arcadia* 4), fear (2.5, as with Clinias and Dametas in *Arcadia* 3), shame (2.6, as employed in the portrayal of Gynecia in *Arcadia* 5), pity (2.8, as with Musidorus in *Arcadia* 5, Philoclea before Cecropia in *Arcadia* 3), indignation (2.9, as with Musidorus confronting Pyrocles in *Arcadia* 1), and envy (2.10, as in Gynecia before Zelmane in *Arcadia* 2). A detailed sense of time and audience, of both ethos and pathos, is shown by Dorus as he attempts to write Pamela (3.1; sig. X1v; 437) and by Philoclea when she faces a similar problem in addressing Pyrocles as Zelmane (2.17; sig. P3; 330), by Argalus in his challenge to Amphialus (3.12; sig. Aa4v; 503), and in Dametas's parallel but parodic challenge to Clinias (3.13; sig. Bb1v; 510). Similarly, accommodating language is employed by Musidorus in addressing the rustics who arrest him (4.6; sig. Nn5v; 761) and by Dametas in talking to Miso (4.1; sig. L15v; 722).

Ethos also characterizes Musidorus and Pyrocles. Musidorus is presented to us as older, more masculine and sensible, while Pyrocles is younger, more emotional and impressionable. Both have dignity and courage, but Musidorus's speeches emphasize military and political affairs, whereas Pyrocles is concerned with psychological conflicts. Because Musidorus is disguised as a shepherd, his design in wooing Pamela is to lay claim to nobility; moreover, she is, as his audience, wiser, more serious than her sister. Musidorus speaks to her of good government and the right education, of public chivalry, of friendship, of magnanimity and justice. Pyrocles, conversely, has the more gentle and beautiful Philoclea as his audience, although his disguise is one of an Amazon. Thus his concern is with ethical judgment and integrity, while his tales are tales about love. In all of his talk, he is at pains to show his own values are beyond question.[88]

What is true in characterization and dialogue is also true in narrative action. Zelmane's attempt to calm the rebels attacking Basilius's lodge (2.26) is particularly noteworthy. Her first step is to calm the angry mob, which she does by coupling her own courage with a show of disinterestedness; she argues that the mob must be after her, although there is no cause for that since they would not wish to attack the king himself. She flatters the rebels into listening to her because of her own knowledge of events inside the lodge. Once she has gained their attention, she works from particularities to generalities, as Aristotle says one should do in addressing intellectual inferiors; she shows them that, as they could not choose a single leader earlier, so they would have difficulty presently finding a champion to fight for them; rather, as their experience has shown them, they will have an easier and more successful life by allowing their rightful ruler to continue to govern them. This is the main body of Zelmane's speech, but in concluding she is careful to allow her listeners to save face; she points out that their intentions were honorable even if their estimation of the situation was wrong. Now that they understand Basilius's ability to govern, the same love of him that made them rise against him will cause them to withdraw. In this oration, she wins part of the crowd but not all. As a consequence, she invites those who remain loyal to the king to join her and protect him from the remainder of the hostile troops. Her rhetoric gives rise to action, and this action allows her rhetoric to succeed. Precept and need, the humanists' first premise, is thus realized by a rhetoric of ethos used for peaceful and wise ends.

Other applications of Aristotelian ethos have more selfish views in mind. Amphialus, for instance, in calling troops to support his attack on Basilius the better to win Philoclea, accommodates his speeches to further his rebellion by changing the rewards he offers various men in return for their support. "To his friends, friendlines; to the ambitious, great expectations; to the displeased, reuenge; to the greedie, spoile: wrapping their hopes with such cunning, as they rather seemed giuen ouer vnto them as partakers: then promises sprong of necessitie" (3.4; sig. X6v; 452). "I speake reason," Cecropia tells Philoclea, but she deliberately takes the girl's weaknesses into mind by using flattery—"match your matchlesse beautie with a matchlesse affection" (3.5; sig. Y2v; 458–59)—to praise marriage and to distract Philoclea from her chief objection, that she does not love Amphialus. Even in the great trial scene in Book 5, Philanax is forced to construct an argument for the prosecution because he has no evidence other than circumstantial that Pyrocles and Musidorus had any connection with the death of Basilius (whereas with Gynecia he has her confession). His sarcastic name-calling and his heightened description of the crime are therefore attempts to distract Euarchus and the Arcadians from the serious lack of evidence. His fabricated sense of others' guilt—he is distraught by his love for the "dead" king and his concern for the integrity of the position of king—is corrected for our sense of rhetoric by Euarchus, whose verdict based on the places of logic (by *relation,* for the princes as foreigners are not exempt from Arcadian law; by *effect,* because they no longer behave as princes; and by *final cause,* which is the seriousness of the crime) restores a sense of reason and judgment in a rhetorically charged environment.[89]

This anthology of accommodating rhetorics based in a firm understanding of Aristotelian ethos remains distinct, however, from the corruptions of sophistry in what constitutes Sidney's somewhat Lylyan anatomy of mischievous wit. Cecropia's debate with Philoclea is a case in point, for the more she talks, the more sophistic she becomes. In this, she is twinned with Artaxia, "to whom the eloquēce of hatred had giuen reuenge the face of delight" (2.29; sig. T1v; 402). Plangus's use of clever language—which Sidney openly condemns—causes him to lose Andromana (2.15; sig. O4; 313). Yet the finest portrait of sophistry in the Arcadia—and one of the finest in Tudor literature—is in the character of Plexirtus, the evil son of the Paphlagonian king.

> For certainely so had nature formed him, and the exercise of craft conformed him to all turninges of sleights, that though no man had lesse goodnes in his soule then he, no man could better find the places whence arguments might grow of goodnesse to another: though no man felt lesse pitie, no man could tel better how to stir pitie: no man more impudent to deny, where proofes were not manifest; no man more ready to confesse with a repenting manner of aggrauating his owne euill, where denial would but make the fault fowler. [2.10; sig. M5v; 281]

His own character is buried in the friendship he pretends toward his brother Leonatus, put on the throne by Pyrocles and Musidorus.

> Where what submission hee vsed, how cunningly in making greater the faulte he made the faultines the lesse, how articially he could set out the torments of his owne conscience, with the burdensome comber he had found of his ambitious desires, how finely seeming to desire nothing but death, as ashamed to liue, he begd life, in the refusing it, I am not cunning inough to be able to expresse: but so fell out of it, that though at first sight *Leonatus* saw him with no other eie, than as the murderer of his father; and anger already began to paint reuenge in many colours, ere long he had not onely gotten pitie, but pardon, and if not an excuse of the faulte past, yet an opinion of a future amendment: while the poore villains (chiefe ministers of his wickednes, now betraied by the author thereof,) were deliuered to many cruell sorts of death; he so handling it, that it rather seemed, hee had more come into the defence of an vnremediable mischiefe already committed, then that they had done it at first by his consent. [2.10; sig. M5v; 282]

Plexirtus's corruption of Aristotelian ethos for selfish ends resembles Cecropia's misuse of accommodating language, but their motives are different. Cecropia wishes an extended kingdom for her son and feels cheated by Basilius's late marriage, which dispossesses Amphialus; Plexirtus wishes gain only for himself. But, temporarily at least, both Philoclea and Leonatus listen, and Leonatus is fatally deceived. In this range of possibilities, clearly Sidney did not feel that Aristotelian ethos was in itself good or bad; it is good when Zelmane pacifies the rebels and Pamela argues for divine order; it is evil when it promotes suffering, suicide, and war. Humanist principles are therefore inseparable from a humanist rhetoric for Sidney, just as the rhetoric must be aligned to humanist belief and values: the *Arcadia* stands as a testimonial to the deep reserves of Sidney's humanist philosophy, a product of his restless search for the ways in which words can be made to function. To such ends, he employs the most challenging tropes, such as synoeciosis, syncrisis, and anatanagoge, made aurally appealing by a rhetoric of sound and rhythm based in polysyndeton, epanalepsis, and epizeuxis.[90] It is this sense of thought and language that Quintilian supports when he comments that Cicero proclaimed eloquence has its origin in wisdom and that the instructors of morals and of eloquence are identical (*Institutio Oratoria* 12.2.6).

In addition, Sidney's stylistics may also be Hermogenic. Johannes Sturm's edition of the Greek rhetorican Hermogenes of Tarsus—reckoned the single most important Greek rhetorician of imperial Rome and a rival to Cicero and Quintilian—was published in 1555–58; it was reprinted, with Latin translation and Latin commentary, in 1570–71 and could well have appealed to Sidney's love for (and study of) Greek. Hermogenes had a strong following in Tudor England, which we seem to have lost sight of—Elyot recommends rhetoric be taught "either in greke out of Hermogines / or of Quintilian in latine / begynnyng at the thirde boke" (*The Gouernour* 1.11; sig. E4), and Richard Rainolde, in his preface to *A booke called the Foundacion of Rhetorike* (1563), states that "No man is able to invente a more profitable waie and order, to instructe any one in the exquisite and absolute perfection, of wisedome and eloquence, then *Aphthonius, Quintilianus* and *Hermogenes*" (sig. A3v). Hermogenes' *Art of Rhetoric,* with its three books on status (topoi), invention, and style, was most useful to the Tudors for its elaboration on the seven ideas of style, including ethos as one of them. The other major ideas are clarity (purity, lucidity), grandeur, beauty, speed, verity, and gravity. Some twenty subcategories expand these stylistic concerns; grandeur, for example, is divided into asperity, vehemence, and vigor as styles for reproof or blame, and magnificence, splendor, and circumlocution for praise, while ethos involves simplicity (as with shepherds), sweetness (for fable), subtlety (for using such figures as metonymy, metaphor, and irony), and modesty (for ingratiating others). Grandeur—which Sturm translates as eloquence—is often reserved for heroic epic, as in the case of the *Arcadia.* While Aristotle gives a wide range of stances under the concept of ethos, Hermogenes allows a range of tonality, emphasizing decorum and introducing the concept of an "idea" of style that is similar to a Platonic Form—and to the idea of "foreconceit" that Sidney advocates in the *Defence.*

It is with some sense of rhetorical stylistics as this, seeming to conflate Plato (and Hermogenes), Aristotle, and Cicero, that Sidney fashioned the style for *Arcadia,* but he also guarantees logical form and progression to the substance of his thought through particular rhetorical *structures.* The very simplicity of his plan here is stunning: in *dispositio, Arcadia* 1 and 2 rest on declamation and epideictic oratory, emphasizing narrative and supplying direct speeches of praise and blame; *Arcadia* 3 moves into disputation and deliberative rhetoric, centering as it does on the verbal debates of Cecropia and her opponents, which are translated by Amphialus into the more active debates of his chivalric challenges and parodied by Dametas and Clinias; and *Arcadia* 4 and 5, concerned as they are with matters of wrong and right, guilt and innocence, center on forensic rhetoric. Invention is thus reinforced by formal rhetorical organization, which supplies its own *gradatio* through its tactical subtext. Quintilian, in fact, remarks that the most serious tasks of rhetoric involve the great powers of forensic rhetoric in its treatment of law (*Institutio* 2.4.33). Equally astonishing in its simplicity is the dispositio of *Arcadia* 5, which, dramatically and psychologically sound in its presentation of the trial of Pyrocles, Musidorus, and Gynecia, is Sidney's supreme tribute to Cicero. It follows as a precise Senecan model—*point by point*—the pseudo-Ciceronian *Ad Herennium*. Thus Philanax opens the trial with a direct accusation (*Ad Herennium* 1.6–8), proceeds to a perverted statement of facts (1.12–14), and then adduces his own legal proof (1.18–25). Pseudo-Cicero's secondary concerns at each step—such as dispositio, ethos, and pathos—are clues for us to measure Philanax's corruption of language and of forensic form. More significant yet— and in this we must recognize Sidney's model because we must judge Philanax by his precise departure from it—is the discussion of proof and refutation (1.18–25) where circumstantial (or conjectural), interpretive (or legal), and judgmental (or juridical) evidence are comparatively treated and weighed. When we recognize that Philanax has made conjectural evidence (or *questions* of fact, according to the *Ad Herennium*) into grounds for legal and juridical argument (transforming invention into actuality), we see how he has at once corrupted humanist ideas, logic, dialectic, and rhetoric. Pyrocles and Musidorus realize this, too; their attempts to defend Pamela, Philoclea, and themselves (and the women, in their letters, mean to defend them) force Philanax backward, for, working in reverse, they argue from wrong judgment through questions of interpretation and so return to fundamental questions of fact. That is, the accused prince and his cousin would purify perverted rhetoric by taking it back to its untainted source.

Philanax's prosecution is initially based on the ideas in *Ad Herennium* 1, and, because he must proceed with apparent logic, follows in order the concerns of this best-known of all Tudor rhetorical treatises.[91] Once challenged, Philanax finds additional ammunition in the directives of *Ad Herennium* 2: he supports the probability of affairs by comparison (Pyrocles dressed as a woman, for instance), signs ("her" costume), and presumptive proof ("her" continuing deceit), leading to subsequent action and, hence, confirmatory proof (*Ad Herennium* 2.3–12). Euarchus, in his turn, continues to follow the prosecution's model by making the case legal rather than juridical, thus having it rest on absolute interpretation of absolute law (2.13–18) rather than admitting the possibility of a contrary natural law and the need for equity (2.19–20). When they are read against their sources as Sidney intended, then, *both* Philanax and Euarchus are seen to corrupt the purpose, design, and language that they as civilized men *presume* to uphold. The point is not the distinction between the prosecutor and the judge but their *shared* corruption of humanist principles. This misconstruction of a Senecan original is Sidney's means to awaken our discontent, but his instruction is made pleasant by following Hermogenic decorum: in the patterned (if dramatic) trial scene, the formal speakers descend in rank from Euarchus and the protector Philanax, while the topics the defense chooses and their speeches *ascend* in importance: we are given Pyrocles on justice, followed by Gynecia on good and evil, Philoclea on chastity, and Pamela on eternal life. Such deliberate placement forces on us the discrepancy between station and status (or topos, in the Hermogenic sense) and again suggests the superior logic of the regenerated humanist. Logic and style are allied and fused once again. As for language, it is what Aristotle refers to in his *Rhetoric* as "compacted"; that is, it

> consists of periods, and by period I mean a sentence that has a beginning and end in itself and a magnitude that can be easily grasped. What is written in this style is pleasant and easy to learn, pleasant because it is the opposite of that which is unlimited, because the hearer at every moment thinks he is securing something for himself and that some conclusion has been reached; whereas it is unpleasant neither to foresee nor to get to the end of anything. It is easy to learn, because it can be easily retained in the memory. The reason is that the periodic style has number, which of all things is the easiest to remember; that explains why all learn verse with greater facility than prose, for it has number by which it can be measured. [3.9.3]

In each of these ways, the *Arcadia* is a profoundly *instructive* work, teaching us the way to private and public action that appeals to *memoria*; to our *own* places of memory, made important at the start of *Arcadia* 1; but the description of style, here in Aristotle, is the description of Sidney's Ciceronian (periodic) style. It is perhaps this rich conjunction of antique models and directives that produces the powerful effect that C. S. Lewis, for all his dislike of rhetoric, nevertheless so deeply feels. "Even at this distance," he says of Sidney, he "is dazzling" (*English Literature*, p. 324).

Yet, perhaps most dazzling of all, Plato's most incisive charge against poetry (and through Gosson the most damaging charge against poetry in Sidney's lifetime)—that its eroticism conquers reason (*Republic* 10.597D–608A)—is precisely the issue of the trial conducted by Euarchus. He argues that the passion of Pyrocles, Musidorus, and Gynecia has corrupted them and that their perversions should be punished by death; in Platonic terms, he means to demonstrate the need for a philosopher king.

> "The law ... declares that it is best to keep quiet as far as possible in calamity and not to chafe and repine. . . . [But] if you would reflect that . . . part of the soul that . . . in our own misfortunes was forcibly restrained, and that has hungered for tears and a good cry and satisfaction, because it is its nature to desire these things, [this] is the element in us that poets satisfy and delight." [*Republic* 10. 604B–606A]

In the *Republic,* Plato (like Euarchus) seeks refuge in what Sidney in the *Arcadia* terms "dead pitilesse lawes" (4.5; sig. Mm3; 752). But, as we have seen, the *Republic* is the first stage in Plato's trilogy of philosophic works on government. The second, the *Statesman,* transforms Euarchus's position, as essentially preliminary and wrong, when it argues that the ruler, not laws, must govern men—"it is clear that lawmaking belongs to the science of kingship; but the best thing is not that the laws be in power, but that the man who is wise and of kingly nature be ruler" (294A) because

> law could never, by determining exactly what is noblest and most just for one and all, enjoin upon them that which is best; for the differences of men and of actions and the fact that nothing, I may say, in human life is ever at rest, forbid any science whatsoever to promulgate any simple rule for everything and for all time. [294B]

Euarchus's skewed scale of values thus denies the Greek sense of justice, *dikaiosynēs,* as something *more* than legal—something *also ethical,* like our word "righteousness." By insisting on vengeance as the basis for law (5.7; sigs. Qq4–Qq5; 835–38), he denies that equity basic to Plato's last discussion in the *Laws.* Aristotle is in agreement, in the limitation of law (*Politics* 3.1286a; *Ethics* 5.1.13–15) and in the necessity for equity as well as justice (*Ethics* 5.1.9–11), while Cicero says essentially the same thing (*De Legibus* 1.12.33–34; 1.15.42; *De Officiis* 3.7.33). By limiting himself to law, Euarchus relies wholly on what is known. Conversely, by arguing what can be and should be—the common province of poetry and morality in the *Defence*—Pyrocles and Musidorus must argue from the known and the unknown, must work from logic and from trust and belief. They are prepared, then, as Euarchus and Philanax are not, for the wondrous miracle of Basilius's recovery, a resurrection that shatters mere case-hardened law. Euarchus, locating constancy in *self*-certainty and *human* knowledge only, has no capacity for such wonders whereas Pyrocles and Musidorus, transcending human limitation through love (as Gynecia, Pamela, and Philoclea transcend actuality through prayer and Basilius transcends it through prophecy) *are* prepared. In Basilius's transformation comes all the rest. This, too, takes us back to Plato—to the conclusion of the *Republic* with its myth of Er; to the ideal portrait of the statesman; and to the concept of the metamorphosing power of law, with a Nocturnal Synod set to govern its change. This conclusion to *Laws* (12.961 ff.) is parallel to the *Republic* and similar to the ending of *Arcadia*.

"I wish the orator to be a philosopher," Quintilian writes; "esse oratorem philosophum velim" (*Institutio* 12.2.6). It is *this* he has in mind when he describes the orator as a good man—*vir bonus dicendi peritus* (12.1.1). For the more homely Elyot, nearer in time and temperament to Sidney, this was called providence. "Providence," he writes, "is wherby a mā nat only foreseeth cōmoditie and incomoditie prosperitie and aduersitie but also consulteth & there with endeuoureth as well to repelle anoyaunce as to attaine and gette profite and aduantage"; it is grounded in prudence and foresight, but finally, he adds, "there is in prouidence suche an admiration and maiestie, that nat onely it is attributed to kinges and rulers but also to god creator of the worlde" (*Gouernour* 1.23; sigs. L5v–L6). It is such a sense of providence that concludes *Arcadia*. "Prouidēce," Mornay writes in the English translation of *De La Vérité de la religion chrestienne* (*A Woorke concerning the trewnesse of the Christian Religion*),

> is nothing els but a wise guyding of things to their end, and that euery reasonable mynd that woorketh, beginneth his worke for some end, and that God (as I haue said afore) the workemaister of all things, hath (or to say more truely) is the soureine mynd, equall to his owne power: doth it not follow that God in creating the worlde, did purpose an end? [Sig. L7v]

As a poet—or second maker, as he is defined in the *Defence*—Sidney turns the unexpected, incomplete, paradoxical conclusion of the *Arcadia* into an occasion for faith, transforms its irresolution into an opportunity for providence and grace where poetry, oratory, philosophy, and religion all meet. The faith that contains paradox, while sustaining it, is a faith of recovery, of ideal justice (as in the *Laws* and the *Ethics*), and of *art*. The *Arcadia completes* its thoughtful action on *open paradoxes,* as we have seen, but paradoxes more apparent than real—such as the trial when there is no crime—so that the concern with human justice is shifted into a concern for divine justice (our thoughts transcending our clayey beings) while, more mundanely, turning the act of reading into an act of self-cultivation, a self-civilizing through a reawakened sense of morality. The final incompleteness of the *Arcadia*, then, is the incompleteness endemic to faith in things not known or seen.

Sidney's *Arcadia,* this late, great masterpiece of humanist poetics, was translated into French, German, Dutch, and Italian long before any other Elizabethan works of literature were, and in England it underwent more editions in the seventeenth century than either Spenser's works or Shakespeare's. It also naturally attracted many latter-day imitations—new acts of imitatio, twice removed from classical roots. John Dickenson's *Arisbas* (1594) juxtaposes Timoclea's story of action against Arisbas's story of reflection to serve as mirrors of constancy once they are reunited in Arcadia, but the description of this ideal land is a much diminished version of Sidney's (sigs. E3–E3v). Dickenson's *The Shepheardes Complaint* (1596), again set in Arcadia, is a loose collection of tales of good and ill luck, which he sums as "the ineuitable lot of destiny" (sig. C3v). Gervase Markham's *English Arcadia I and II* (1607) is heavily influenced by Sidney's work; many of the scenes (such as the tournaments and trial) and many of the characters (such as the disguised prince and the shepherds who mourn the loss of their love at the outset) are in direct imitation, but glib and uninspired complications are self-indulgent, and the result is an unintentional parody of the original *Arcadia*. W. W. Greg and C. R. Baskervill have also traced a number of plays stemming from Sidney's fiction.[92] But none of these works—not even Beaumont and Fletcher's *Cupids Revenge* (1615) or Shirley's *Arcadia* (1632?)—has the intensity and high seriousness of the 1593 novel.

This is largely true because they lack the philosophic depth of Sidney's *Arcadia*, its deeply considered presentation on justice and friendship and its thoughtful working out of a poetics for humanist fiction. It is also true because, like the works of Erasmus, More, and Lyly, the *Arcadia* is also, at some deep level, autobiographical. The allusions to Wilton fair and to Languet (Eclogues 1, sig. H5v; 206; Eclogues 3, sig. K5v, 705) and the presence of the figure Philisides (Eclogues 3, sig. Kk5v; 705) as an anagrammatic projection only hint at the rich vein of fact buried within the fiction. The noble lineage of Musidorus, for instance, while not royal, is matched by Sidney's on his mother's, the Dudleys', side, as well as by the Sidney line, known for its deeds: Sir Philip's grandfather had commanded the victorious right wing at Flodden Field and Edward VI had died in Sir Henry Sidney's arms. The great Sussex estate of Penshurst, presented to the Sidneys by Henry VIII, has what is now thought to be the finest surviving fourteenth-century hall and magnificent gardens that, more than the property at Wilton, resemble Kalander's estate. Euarchus is the same age as Sir Henry Sidney was when Sidney first began the *Arcadia*. The battles and tournaments in *Arcadia* are similar to those Sidney experienced: his own participation and costume in the "Pageant of Beauty" before the queen at Whitsun 1581, as recalled by H. Goldwell in *A Briefe Declaration of the Shewes,* are a part of *Arcadia* 2 in embryo, the apparent hyperbole in the description of dress similar to Sidney's own outlay of £42.6s. for clothes to wear to the great Kenilworth entertainment of 1575.[93]

This rich brocade of life is transferred directly into the *Arcadia,* but there it conceals a desperate and even tragic life that nevertheless gives the fiction much of its haunting quality. As one of Elizabeth's most dutiful administrators, Sir Henry was never sufficiently valued or rewarded—Sir Edward Molyneux gives testimony to this[94]—and there is frequent concern in the *Arcadia* with the undervaluation of certain characters. Like Parthenia, Lady Mary Sidney was permanently scarred by smallpox while nursing the queen through an epidemic, while Sir Philip himself was facially scarred as well.[95] Nor was his life free of pain. Sidney had the misfortune to witness the St. Bartholomew's Day Massacre where up to 10,000 may have been killed, and he may have been forced to ride pillion to view Coligny's mangled body.[96] If so, this goes some way to explain the atrocities detailed in *Arcadia* with such sardonic bitterness. There was, finally, shocking poverty because the queen insisted on Sir Henry's services but could not (or would not) pay him commensurate wages. The begging letters of Sir Philip's mother, Lady Mary, tell of her straitened existence at court. She writes William Cecil, principal secretary, on 1 June 1570,

> The term [of court] ends on Wednesday, the progress begins shortly after. I shall be left in miserable state any way if it please not your honour to take care of me, for after the term once ends I shall want my friends' assistance in all my causes. . . . How . . . can [the queen] stick at so small a trifle as poor £ 22 a year for 12 years' service? Well, God knows to what end I only desire it.

To Sussex, the lord chamberlain, she writes on 1 February 1573,

> my chamber is very cold, and my own hangings very scant and nothing warm: myself rather a little recovered of great extremity of sickness than that I can either boast of hope of perfect health or dare adventure to lie in so cold a lodging without some further health.[97]

Given this serious discrepancy between the public glamour and private need of the Sidney family under Elizabeth I, we can understand Sir Philip's quick temper with Oxford on the tennis court or his passionate longing for a retreat with his sister at Wilton. It was not a matter of his constant recognition that he was squandering his enormous talents on courtly ceremonies that came to nothing but that in the ten short years between his schooling and his untimely death much that he sought was denied him: a position with his father in the government of Wales, a suit to be master of ordnance with the earl of Warwick,[98] ambassadorial positions for which he had cultivated friendships and had learned languages, even the possibility of refurbishing the family fortunes in a voyage to the New World with Drake. Instead, he was commanded to accompany the distasteful Alençon to Holland; he saw himself knighted by default; he found his lack of fortune prevented his marriage to the woman he loved and caused him to marry one he did not. Against such poor luck, he clings tenaciously to his reverence for Platonic and Aristotelian philosophy, his respect for Ciceronian rhetoric, and his vision of a brighter, better Arcadia, a land where moral justice can be realized and through equity the workings of providence discerned. There is, finally, a quiet urgency that goes into the composition of the *Arcadia* and its revisions.

Throughout the long struggle in life and art to improve if not perfect himself, Sidney holds to what Plato calls the necessary being of becoming (*Statesman*, 283D). The 1593 *Arcadia* focuses on "The almighty wisdome euermore delighting to shew the world, that by unlikeliest meanes greatest matters may come to conclusion: that humane reason may be the more humbled, and more willingly giue place to diuine prouidence" (4.1; sig. Kk5; 715). In the forthright inclusiveness of the *Arcadia,* which can be seen as "life's riddling text," as Margaret E. Dana has it,[99] Sidney keeps seizing opportunities, as Greville says in the biography of his friend, for "morall Images, and Examples,(as directing threds) to guide euery man through the confused *Labyrinth* of his own desires, and life" (*Life*, sig. P8; 223). Thus the novel opens with shepherds transcending their own abilities by contemplating Urania; it concludes by inviting all men to transcend the mundane world of law and causation by combining mere justice with an equity that in Christian terms clearly (and most significantly) becomes the Lord's justice tempered by Christ's mercy. Thus, like Lyly's, Sidney's fiction is one of eloquent reformation; like Greene's, it is about eloquent transformation too. Set against a life that cheated Sidney's every hope and bore down relentlessly on those around him, the *Arcadia* examines the cruelty and anguish of a corrupted world by projecting a splendid image of another existence where, philosophically informed and poetically conceived, art can still cultivate and learning still civilize. It is an extraordinary achievement, this willful act of humanist poetics that comes in the waning days of Tudor humanism when the realities of tyranny, war, and social and religious upheaval began to raise profound questions about the educability—much less the perfectibility—of man. The magnificence of the *Arcadia* is finally owed to the purpose and effort it awards—and to the significance it insists on—for a humanist poetics.

III

THE POETICS OF DOUBT AND DESPAIR

Presumption is our naturall and originall infirmitie.
Of all creatures, man is the most miserable and fraile, and
therewithall the proudest and disdainefullest. Who perceiveth and
seeth himselfe placed here, amidst the filth and
mire of the world, fast tide and nailed to the worst, most senceles,
and drooping part of the world, in the vilest corner
of the house, and farthest from heavens-coape, with those creatures,
that are the worst of the three conditions; and yet dareth
imaginarily place himselfe aboue the circle of the Moone, and reduce
heaven under his feete.
MONTAIGNE, translated by John Florio

EIGHT

Introduction

 THE SECOND MAJOR PERIOD OF TUDOR HUMANISM, FROM 1558 TO 1588, WAS A TIME OF REL-ATIVE COMPOSURE. IT WAS AN AGE WHEN ELIZABETH I ENCOURAGED LEARNING, AS HER FATHER HAD DONE in the days of Erasmus and More. This was a time when a developing nation, which was establishing a navy, trade with Europe, and colonies abroad, saw another dawn much as Erasmus had witnessed, one reinforced with the continual flourishing of grammar schools and the expansion of the universities of Oxford and Cambridge along with the Inns of Court in London. Although there were occasional rebellions in the unruly northern parts of the country, especially in Yorkshire and along the border country shared with Scotland, plots by Francis Throckmorton and the earl of Northumberland on the queen's life, the incarceration and eventual execution of Mary Stuart, and scattered beginnings of a Puritan movement opposing the Established Church codified in the brief Admonition to the Parliament of 1572, it was nevertheless, relatively speaking, a time of peace, expansion, and joy. State homilies upholding tradition and order read at weekly Sabbath services, proclamations and royal progresses, and the establishment of several myths about the wisdom and mercy of the Virgin Queen countered any signs or forces of instability.

But the serious threat of Spanish invasion in the Low Countries in 1585 and the planned Armada of 1588, as well as subsequent fears of Irish and Scottish insurgence, outbreaks of plague increasing in frequency and severity, and a spiraling economy, made the 1590s in England a very different time indeed. Heavy government expenses on defense and expansion meant that goods and services costing £100 in 1510 and £340 (with devalued silver) in the 1580s suddenly climbed to £381 in 1594, £515 in 1595, and £685 in 1597 before decreasing slightly around the turn of the century. International unrest interrupted the transportation of cloth goods, causing Flanders and Belgium to compete successfully with England for markets; thriving provincial market towns in the southwest and northeast of England where weaving had succeeded farming were soon areas of desperate poverty. Tin production declined disastrously with new competition from German and Bohemian producers. London dealers doubled the inflated prices requested by the Pewterers Company. Loan rates soared. French and Portuguese fishermen threatened the fishing and fish-packaging industries both in East Anglia and off the coasts of Iceland and North America. The newly poor, along with disbanded soldiers and unneeded sailors, and retainers and farmers out of work crowded the streets of London, in poor health and without money. Thus the 1590s—the period of the humanist fiction of Thomas Nashe and Thomas Lodge—is a decade marked by new constrictions of energy, faltering expectations, and growing doubts about the educability—and even the very nature—of man. For how could a writer insist on man's perfectibility when, all around him, man could no longer maintain even the shreds of his once glorious dignity?

The struggle we witness in Sidney, therefore, to envision a better civilization that would redeem a humanism founded to teach and destined to nurture—one that might permit the self-reflexive wit of John Lyly or the wondrous fabling of Robert Greene—gives way to the nervous, excoriating satires of a writer like Nashe. Ciceronian philosophy and periodicity of style are displaced in Nashe by jeremiads of denunciation; even his extravagant burlesques of the Ramist Gabriel Harvey, with their stern and provocative defenses of the Aristotelian rhetoric and logic that characterized the New Learning, take on a deeper need to protect that traditional body of classicism from the incursions of a diluted if stylish university curriculum by those less intelligent and less appreciative of their Greek and Roman heritage. In Lodge, who studied not at the Ramist-infected Cambridge but at the recusant Trinity College at Oxford, there is a deepening sense of man's darker nature; with the renewed Puritan emphasis, too, on man's depravity, Lodge's fiction is a series of more and more urgent attempts to counter such troubling ideas with a greater search for credible occasions of felicity. Indeed, of these two central writers in the waning days of humanism in England, and of humanist fiction, one becomes a preacher by default, the other an active recusant. Yet what must surely strike us now with a searing force is not just the urgency of their defenses of humanism but their ruthless honesty, particularly when confronting a new skepticism reinforced by a faltering faith as the Tudors approached the end of the century and, as many predicted, the end of the world. By making, at times, the autobiographical roots of their fictive efforts more visible, they not only draw on new and different models to preserve the humanist poetics of their predecessors but, in very real ways first suggested perhaps by the life of Sidney, become models themselves.

The Continental text that serves best as an index of the mood and concern of the 1590s, then, is neither the witty *Encomium Moriae* nor the eloquent *Il Libro del Cortegiano,* the one from the international fraternity of humanists and the other from the cultured courts of Italy. Instead it is an anonymous pamphlet from the destitute cities of Spain, the *Vida de Lazarillo de Tormes* (1554) by an unknown Spanish humanist writing in the tradition of Vives and More.[1] Englished by David Rowland as *The Pleasaunt Historie of Lazarillo de Tormes* (1574; reprinted in 1586, 1596), the fiction seems to take hold in England in the 1590s and well into the next century. For this *Historie* has neither the wit and wordplay nor the yearning for an ideal civilization that characterize its predecessors in Tudor fiction; indeed, it is in no way "pleasaunt" despite the printer's attempt to declare it so. Rather, as Javier Herrero writes, in Spain as in England, "Beneath the dreams of arcadia and chivalry a world was growing that was too frightening to be faced squarely."[2] What at first appears to be the random experiences of a rogue, therefore, becomes, in any sustained reading, what Herrero has called a carefully organized, carefully articulated study in "the anguish of the dispossessed" ("Renaissance Poverty," p. 876). "The *Lazarillo* is," he goes on, actually "the story of a starving family in sixteenth-century Spain, some of whose members are too weak to survive, no less succeed. Their effort to gain day-to-day sustenance meets with torture, exile, death" (p. 876).

Fiction as the anatomy of wit has now become the anatomy of the outcast. In the dying days of the century this must have been unavoidable. Pierre de l'Estoile reports of the Paris of 1596 that "the crowds in the streets were so great that one could not pass through; they are only masks and images of death, naked or clad in ragged robes";[3] a papal bull of Sixtus V published in 1587 points to beggars in Rome who "fill with their groans and cries not only public places and private houses, but the churches themselves; they roam like brute beasts, with no other care than the search for food."[4] Nor was England exempt. There is in the British Museum (Landsdowne MS 81 [60]) a letter from Edward Hext, a justice in Somersetshire, who writes plaintively to the privy council in 1596,

> I do not see howe it is possible for the poore Cuntryman to beare the burthens dewly laide uppon him, and the rapines of the Infynytt numbers of the wicked wandringe Idell people of the land, So as men are driven to watch their sheepefolds, ther pastures, ther woods, their Cornfilds, all things growing too too comon. Others there be (and I feare me imboldened by the wandringe people) that stick not to say boldlye they must not starve, they will not starve. And this yere there assembled lxxx in a Companye and tooke a whole Carteloade of Cheese from one drivinge it to a faire and dispersed it amongest them, for which some of them have indured longe imprisonment and fine by the Judgment of the good Lord Chief Justice att owr last Crismas Sessions; which may grow dangerous by the aide of suche

numbers as are abroade, especially in this time of dearthe, who no dowpt animate them to all contempte bothe of noblemen and gentlemen, continially Bussinge into there eares that the ritche men have gotten all into ther hands and will starve the poore.

Two years earlier, in 1594, the lord mayor of London, Sir John Spencer, wrote the same privy council about the greedy landlords around Kentish Street, Newington, and Southwark whose crowded tenements, which let rooms for "penny-rents," led to congestion, begging, and crime; Elizabethan London was providing the country with its first ghetto. Spencer estimates these beggars and rogues at 12,000 and asks for a meeting of the justices of Sussex and Surrey to take measures to keep them from crossing London Bridge into his city. Severe punishment and even mutilation did little to reduce crime when criminals had no choice, but the situation for all must have been intolerable: the humane and comprehensive Poor Law of 1598 commands that

> suche person shalbe taken, the Tythingman or Headborow being assisted therein with thadvise of the Minister and one other of that Parrish, be stripped naked from the middle upwardes and shall be openly whipped untill his or her body be bloudye, and shalbe forthwith sent from Parish to Parish by the Officers of every the same, the nexte streighte way to the Parish where he was borne.

The enraged outcries are those we have heard before—in Raphael Hythlodaye's excoriating condemnation of the class society promoted by capitalism, "a manifest conspirocie of rich men against poore men," Nashe calls it in *The Unfortunate Traueller* (sig. D4v)—but now there is no longer the temperate voice of a More-character to counter such claims and to urge the humanists' contending hopes through educated counsel and improved social legislation.

Such beggars and rogues as we find in Nashe's *Unfortunate Traueller,* then, and such cruel use of wealth and power as we find in Lodge's *Margarite of America,* are first embodied in the anonymous *Vida de Lazarillo de Tormes.* Lazarillo itself is the Spanish eponymy for the biblical Lazarus, a beggar, as Lazarillo could be in turn the model for Nashe's Jack Wilton, but his name carries a significant burden of insinuating references, most of them now lost on us but hardly lost to the first Spanish readers of the *Vida.* "Its several connotations combined to suggest the character's sense of misery, degradation, and powerlessness," Herrero tells us, adding,

> These are the most important meanings: (1) leper, derived probably from Lazarus, the patron saint of the lepers; the occurrence of the name in

Spanish is relatively late; (2) beggar, with a deeply religious connotation, since Lazarus is the name of the beggar in the biblical parable of the miser (Luke xvi.19–31); (3) the man resurrected by Jesus (John xi.1–5), Lazarus of Bethany, who during the Middle Ages was identified with the begger Lazarus; this misunderstanding gave an unusual dignity to this great archetype of human misery, welding the sense of poverty with the concepts of death and resurrection; (4) "brought to the point of death by hunger," a meaning reflected in the frequent use of the Spanish *lazerado* and *lazeria* and suggested by the false etymology that derived "Lázaro," from the Latin *lacerare*. The semantic complexity of the name would seem to fit a tragic character much better than a comic one, and in a highly ironic book like the *Lazarillo* its use points out the sad reality behind the comic treatment. ["Renaissance Poverty," pp. 879–80]

The victim of a decayed humanism—when the Spaniard Vives's essays on the dignity of man and the education of women no longer seem relevant—Lazarillo like Nashe's Jack Wilton and Lodge's Margarita searches vainly for signs of God's grace. But "From the confrontation between this helpless child and the horrifying forces that threaten him," Herrero sums, "the powerful irony of the book is born" (p. 876). For *Lazarillo* is about dis-ease; the epidemic from which Lazarillo suffers is poverty. The poor of Spain, like the poor elsewhere in Europe, the sixteenth-century Spanish canon Miguel Giginta writes in his *Tratado del remedio de pobres* (1579), are

> tan desventurados pobretos, que no han menester poco favor del señor para no morirse desesperados, o rabiando, de considerar que estando ellos pereciendo en tan varios extremos de miserias, gasten los ricos cristianos en edificios, aderezos, cocina, bestias, y ostras demasias, superfluamente. y que muriendo tantos pobres de frio. haya tantas gualdrapas y mantas para sus caballos, en buenas caballerizas, dejándoles e ellos en la calle.

> such unhappy wretches, that they need not a little of our Lord's help to avoid dying of despair or anger, seeing how they suffer all the extremes of misery, while the rich Christians spend their fortunes superfluously on palaces, jewels, banquets, animals, and other excesses; and, while so many of the poor die of cold, the rich keep their horses housed in comfortable stables, covered with beautiful trappings and blankets; the poor, meanwhile, are left in the streets.[5]

Such general commentary seems now, in retrospect, an exacting gloss on the *Vida*.

The *Pleasaunt Historie* is set in the same period as Nashe's *Unfortunate Traueller,* the fiction unfolding against actual historic events between 1510 and 1540, and it likewise traces the growing awareness in its narrator of a careless, selfish world, a world in which humanity seems essentially depraved.[6] Lazarillo is born in a flour mill, an *aceña,* on the river Tormes in Tejares, a small village near Salamanca. When he is eight, his father, a worker in the mill, is accused of stealing some wheat and confesses his guilt ("y confesó y no negó, y padesció persecución por la justicia"), surely, as Herrero has said, "a sardonic parody of the Gospel [since] 'he went ahead and confessed everything, and he suffered persecution for righteousness' sake'" ("Renaissance Poverty," p. 880). He is exiled and takes a job as a muleteer against the Moors, but he is killed during a military expedition to Gelves—he dies, as his wife will sardonically put it, for his faith. Lazarillo's widowed mother moves to Salamanca where she takes a job in a laundry; among her customers, again ironically, are some stableboys of the *comendador de la Magdalena,* an ecclesiastical nobleman; by one of them, a black slave, she has another child. Like her first husband, Zaire furnishes wood and also food by stealing from the fodder given the horses. "Not even the crumbs fallen from the rich man's table are given to them," Herrero tells us wryly, alluding to Christ's parable of the rich man; "when they try to live on what is left over from the *comendador's* horses, they are tortured and the family unit destroyed" (p. 881). They, like their biblical predecessors, are forced to flee the stable and are persecuted. Lazarillo's mother has no choice but to give her son to someone who can raise him. Unfortunately, she chooses (or in the world of this fiction is forced to choose) a man who is physically blind and spiritually mean.

Thus from the outset Lazarillo's personal epic journey through life is demeaning, much as Jack's and Margarite's journeys are, because his world lacks any sense of order or justice. At first Lazarillo manages to get along by playing tricks on others; his biography begins, misleadingly, as a jest book. But the jokes become serious, like the thefts of his father and stepfather. As Lazarillo manipulates his blind master's food bag and wine jug to his own advantage and learns to steal bread from the miserly priest—both desperate mockeries of the Holy Communion—he schools himself in corruption. His life realizes the words of the *ciego,* the blind man, when he batters the boy's head against a stone statue of a bull while remarking that in order to live one must have "one tricke more than the diuel him self" (sig. A8v). Such early instruction is not easily forgotten. The long middle section, analogous to Nashe's account of Jack's adventures with Surrey-character, is Lazarillo's description of his ritualistic life with the *escuidera* who appears devoutly religious by regularly attending Mass and being the last to leave. But this is all performance. His fine clothes belie the fact that he is an impoverished squire living in unfurnished rooms; his elaborate morning ritual of dressing for public view is likened by the author to a priest preparing himself elaborately for the Mass. Having run away from his first master and been dismissed by the second, Lazarillo is deserted by the third.[7] Now he is forced to be what his parents had attempted to avoid at all costs—a beggar. Canon Giginta tells us what this actually suggested for the Spanish readers of the *Vida*. In the streets, he says,

> Ahi verán mozuelas y mozuelos perdidos, flacos, dolientes, sarnosos, llagados, estropeados y enfermos de varias maneras viejos y no vejos, contan mal color los más, y mortecinas caras muchos, que a bien considerarlo parecen de los que pintan penando ... Sálganse otras mañanas a los hospitales las horas de recibir enfermos, y verán cuantos llegan ya tales de esas calles que pueden contarse por muertos en ellas; y cuantos se han de volver por falta de cama y comida y han de irse desolados a echarse por esos muladares, o caerse en el primer lugar que de desvalidos tropiezan, y morirse alli de aborrecidos, sin querer aguardar más remedio en vano.

> you will see lost boys and girls, thin, groaning, scabby, ulcered, crippled, ill in all kinds of ways, and old and younger men, with such poor color and many of deathly hue, that it seems that they are a picture of damned souls. . . . [L]et us go out in the morning to the hospitals at the time when they receive the sick and you will see how many arrive there from the streets that are already as good as dead; and how many must go back because there is neither bed nor food, and they must wander desolate until they throw themselves on some dung heap, or fall wherever they happen to faint, there to die in despair, abandoning all hope.[8]

What could seem an arbitrary set of adventures, then, is actually an escalating alienation: Lazarillo's youthful innocence and trust are replaced by disillusion and wariness.

In a deceptively easy and colloquial style, *The Pleasant Historie* thus traces the anatomy of a deprived boy attempting to survive with *honora* in a hostile, immoral world. When Lazarillo finally discovers that self-seeking is the basic way of life at all points of his society, he capitulates: the last we see of him, he is a servant to His Excellency, the archpriest of Saint Salvador, the highest churchman in a fiction crammed with satire of the Church—and, significantly, the lowly crier of wine. But he has paid a heavy price even for this. He has secured his job by marrying the archpriest's concubine, purchasing *honora*, clearly, at the cost of his soul. Lazarillo's open admission of this defeat, surrendering to a continuing state of hypocrisy, is chilling.

> God hath done more for mee, than I haue deserued, and I dare sweare by the holy sacrament, that shee is as honest a woman as any that dwelleth within the foure gates of *Toledo*: and hee that sayeth the contrarie, I will bestowe my life vpon him. So from thence foreward, they neuer durst moue any such matter vnto me, & I had peace allwayes in my house. [Sigs. H4v–H5]

The pressure to conform in order to exist results in the process of dehumanization, in a lasting decision to will self-ignorance. Like *The Unfortunate Traueller* of Nashe or Lodge's *Margarite of America,* the horror and pain of such a choice at the conclusion of *The Pleasaunt Historie of Lazarillo de Tormes* are papered over with a false sense of ceremony.

> This was the same yeere that our victorious Emperour entred into this noble citie of *Toledo,* wher his court was kept with great feastes and triumphes, as your mastership hath heard: finally, it was then that I was in my prosperitie, and in my chiefest time of good aduenture. [Sig. H5]⁹

The outward fortunes of Lazarillo commenting on those whom his parents served—a good marriage and useful service—cause him to will his own blindness. He becomes the counterpart of his own first master who bashed his head against the stone bull.

This self-imposed blindness is similar to that which allows Jack Wilton, as a soldier in the bloody army of Henry VIII, to masquerade the dangers and uncertainties of his life by refocusing it as a game of mumchance and, in the end, to rush toward the treacherous Field of the Cloth of Gold where, under ceremonial pretense of their own, the kings of England and France plot future slaughter. It is such self-blindness too that causes the more virtuous Margarite, in Lodge's novel, to return to her betrothed Arsadachus only to discover he has killed Diana and their child in a bloodbath and mutilated their corpses at his own wedding feast. Such stark images—Nashe will compare man attempting to survive in the late Tudor world to a roach stranded on dry land—are so graphic and so dreadful that they continue to press on our sensibilities. Such a vision is surely, deliberately, apocalyptic. In the case of *Lazarillo de Tormes,* though, especially when placed alongside the *Encomium Moriae* or *Il Cortegiano,* it can appear severely attenuated; without gaining the resonances and enrichment provided by drawing on the antique texts of humanism that had generated the great fiction of the period, this appears a much diminished thing. But we must be careful of such judgments; though *Lazarillo* seems to limit its focus to the social and economic conditions that surely give it birth, it is at great pains to associate events with the Church and with churchmen, so that layers of meaning and shades of judgment are constantly made from a biblical perspective. *Lazarillo* is meant to be a parable of a time without Christ—that is, a time when the vicar of Christ, too, is impotent. What *Lazarillo* has accomplished for humanist poetics, then, is the substitution of sacred for secular reference: it has its clear Senecan models, too. And it is just this lesson that Nashe and Lodge also mean to convey. Yet, also heirs of their humanist education and heirs too of a growing tradition of humanist fiction, they also seek new, correlative Greek and Roman texts as well. Nashe, for instance, finds in the writers of the Second Sophistic models who, like himself, would change satire into sermon, into lessons that his father might well preach in his Norfolk parish. The recusant Lodge could, in his turn, draw not only on the Holy Sacraments of the Roman Church but on the congenial and reassuring model of Seneca himself. Neither solution was ready at hand or, perhaps, any more permanent than Plato, Aristotle, Cicero, Ovid, and Heliodorus had been to their friends and predecessors. But the fictions of Nashe and Lodge remain some of the most significant achievements in the dark, grim age in which they were conceived, composed, and—cutting so close to the bone—too quickly forgotten. They not only reveal for us now the final treasures of Tudor humanist poetics; they also provide authoritative perspectives on the end of the era they initially yearned to celebrate.

NINE

"Gallant young *Iuuenall*": Thomas Nashe and

the Revival of the Second Sophistic

 THROUGHOUT THE VARIED WRITINGS OF HIS BRIEF CAREER, THOMAS NASHE'S WORKS LIKE THOSE OF HIS PREDECESSORS IN HUMANIST POETICS TAKE ON A TONE FROM CICERO THAT REMAINS more or less constant. But it is not, in Nashe's case, the Cicero of the *De Oratore* that informs *Il Libro del Cortegiano* with its portrayal of the ideal orator. Nor is it the *De Legibus* that, when we read the *Arcadia,* directs our thoughts to an ideal state where both justice and equity are practiced by statesmen and poets. Instead, it is—tellingly—the Cicero of *In Pisonem,* his invective against Lucius Calpurnius Piso,[1] a speech Erasmus and More may also have had in mind when fashioning their manipulative *prosopopoeiae* of Folly. This attack before the Roman senate in A.D. 55 against the father-in-law of Caesar, who had remained in power when Cicero was exiled for his part in exposing the Catilinarian conspiracy, is "a masterpiece of misrepresentation," as R. G. M. Nisbet has it.[2] Employing a calculated rhetoric by which he conveniently forgets some facts and exaggerates or misconstrues others, Cicero displays the sort of gusto that makes his speech a direct antecedent to Nashe's lightest works as well as his darkest ones, such as the late Tudor flyting with Gabriel Harvey. As with Nashe's *Haue with you to Saffron-walden* (1596), the *In Pisonem* is an encomium moriae, another praise of folly: at the start, when Cicero should trace Piso's lineage, what we get is this: "Obrepsisti ad honores errore hominum, commendatione fumosarum imaginum, quarum simile habes nihil praeter colorem"; "You crept into office by mistake, by the recommendation of your dingy family busts, with which you have no resemblance save colour" (1.1). But the quick joy Nashe takes in his attacks on his Puritan and Ramist antagonist from Cambridge is altogether missing in Cicero. Instead there is an overriding bitterness, punctuated by outbursts of uncontrolled abuse and violence that remind us of the other—and, in many ways, the more

revealing—side of Nashe, the Nashe of *Christs Teares over Jerusalem* (1593) and *The Unfortunate Traueller* (1594):

> Nam quod vobis iste tantum modo improbus, crudelis, olim furunculus, nunc vero etiam rapax, quod sordidus, quod contumax, quod superbus, quod fallax, quod perfidiosus, quod impudens, quod audax esse videtur, nihil scitote esse luxuriosius, nihil libidinosius, nihil posterius, nihil nequius.

> You may in the past have thought him merely dishonest, cruel, light-fingered; you may more recently have found him greedy, grovelling, headstrong, arrogant, deceitful, perfidious, shameless, impudent; but you may take it from me that he is the last word in voluptuousness, in licentiousness, in baseness, in villainy. [27.66]

This passionate excessiveness is echoed, in Nashe, in Christ's lament, in the analogous excoriation of a plague-stricken London, and in the final recriminating speeches of Esdras and Cutwolfe. The cause of such a similarity is not far to seek—it is in Cicero's and Nashe's shared, abrupt awareness of ideas, hopes, and loyalties irrevocably betrayed. It is seen here in a rhetoric of self-righteousness, a rhetoric of vengeance against injustice and immorality that Cicero and Nashe pursue as a necessary stay against defeat and despair. "*Lord,*" Nashe writes chorically elsewhere, "*haue mercy on vs.*"[3] In a Rome that forgets human liberty as it veers toward imperialism, in an England veering toward puritanism and parliamentarianism, the plans and principles of humanism forgotten or ignored, Cicero and Nashe cry out for coherence, for a restoration of man's reason and dignity.

We tend to forget this darker side of Nashe because it scrapes along our nerves too. Instead, we remember his remarkable way with words, his ability to keep his scorn before us as a remorseful joy. "There is a mountaine in *Cyrenaica* consecrated to the South-wind," he writes to the reader in his preface to *The Unfortunate Traueller,*

> which if it be toucht with a mans hand, there arise exceeding boystrous blastes, that tosse and turmoile the sands like waues of the Sea. As great a miracle was that in me is experienst, for let me but touch a peece of paper, there arise such stormes and tempestes about my eares as is admirable. Euen of sands and superficiall bubbles they will make hideous waues and dangerous quicke-sands. This is my last will and Testament: those that tosse at me, ile tosse at them againe if I can, always prouided it bee not a Tennice-play of Pots and Cups, like the Centaurs feast.

And then—abruptly for us—the real motive cracks the surface of this self-conscious poseur: "Diuinity is the ground-worke of my Booke, no more herein will I doe then shall haue his ground from Diuinity." And—the message revealed—it is half-covered in humor; "Farewell, Paules Church-yard, till I see thee next, which shall not be long" (sig. **3v; 2:186), leaving as a final image that outdoor pulpit alongside London's great cathedral where popular preachers of the Established Church concentrated on denouncing the sins of the land–or the graveyard: the equivocation grows dark and grim. "Nashe thinks in images," G. R. Hibbard sums acutely, speaking of *The Terrors of the Night*, his rambling discourse on dreams, apparitions—and fear—"but the thought, such as it is, is quite serious and orthodox."[4]

"Nashe thinks in images": it is the secret of his rhetorical power—and of his perennial attractiveness. Such images, A. K. Croston comments,

> are not elaborated: the mind is passed on from one to the next with an almost bewildering rapidity, concrete and abstract being mingled and juxtaposed in infinite variety, the only principle being the enlarging of the immediate impression. . . . The impression given by reading Nashe is that of an extremely alert mind always conscious of the medium of expression, playing on it as a complex instrument.[5]

This is a common—and understandable—impression. So, writes C. S. Lewis, Nashe is "the perfect literary showman, the juggler with words who can keep a crowd spell-bound by sheer virtuosity"; he is, Hibbard adds, "Essentially a clown and an exhibitionist."[6] They are responding to the accumulating similes and metaphors, the bundles of analogies that Nashe uses, putatively as entertainment, to con-struct his fictional essays and his essaylike fictions. But the similitude, as he knew from Aristotle (and more recently from Tudor rhetoricians like Peacham) has its more serious, protreptic, purposes at the same time. Puttenham instructs us in his *Garden of Eloquence* that "by thinking on the similitude, [the audience] is brought in mind straight way" (sig. Biv).

Thus in the exuberant preface to *The Unfortunate Traueller,* the "stormes and tempestes about my eares" are meant to hearken back to the flood that only Noah's family survived and forward to the Revelation of St. John. The "dangerous quicke-sands" imply similar references in Christ's parables and Paul's letters. Together they explain more clearly why "This is my last will and Testament." Alert after long years of humanist training to the potentialities of language and to the way words as well as ideas accordion out their meanings, Nashe is always aware of this underside of human corruption—and always implying it, even in his light rapier thrusts against so single an opponent as Gabriel Harvey. Facts too, like ideas and images, are metaphoric in Nashe: they contain meanings, true, but they also point to other meanings that are not always so explicit except when, as in "last will and Testament"—or in the song about plague in *Summers last will and Testament* (written 1592?)—reality intrudes, upsets the pleasant delusion of joy that has screened out any genuine agony, and turns the work inside-out and upside-down, exposing the deeper significance Nashe has been skirting all along.

This imprisoned vision, this mordant grief, often gives to Nashe's prose a nervous edge. He races from one idea to another, from one image to the next, because he cannot bear to stop and reveal all that he has seen. If he is, as Agnes C. Latham maintains, "an artist [of] caricature,"[7] then his is the same kind of exaggerated cartooning that characterizes that sequence of grotesque Old Testament bosses in the vaulted ceiling of the cathedral sanctuary at Norwich where Nashe spent a formative part of his life or, even more, the nightmarish bosses that decorate the vaulted walkways of those cloisters. There is something somberly fitting about the fact that Nashe's portraits—in *Pierce Penilesse* (1592), in *The Unfortunate Traueller,* and in *Haue with you to Saffron-walden*—take on the appearance of gargoyles. Although Lewis does not make this observation directly, it is, as we would expect, not far from his mind either. "Nearly all Nashe's comic images," he says, "are comic only if you see them in a flash and from exactly the right angle. Move a hair's breadth, dwell on them a second too long, and they become disturbing" (*English Literature,* p. 414). Living with this troubled, haunted perspective—one divided between a sharp view of the world stuffed with sin and a poetic that must make it palatable and yet urgently and unavoidably clear—Nashe must have felt uncomfortably close to someone like Juvenal, who also found *difficile est saturam non scribere* (it is difficult not to write satire).[8] Nashe's father—first apparently as the stipendiary curate for the living at Rollesby, Norfolk, then as rector at West Harling—may have suggested such apocalyptic warnings in his preaching. At any rate, through his humanist writing, Nashe would preach too.

It seems that this sense of mission—one that must have been underscored by his awareness of how alien life could be from the grand humanist thoughts conveyed at St. John's College, Cambridge—was felt very early by Nashe. "What I haue written," he tells Sir Charles Blount in the dedication to his first work, *The Anatomie of Absurditie* (published 1589),

> proceeded not from the penne of vain-glory but from the processe of that pensiuenes, which two Summers since ouertooke mee: whose obscured cause, best knowne to euerie name of curse, hath compelled my wit to wander abroad vnregarded in this *satyricall* disguise, & counsaild my content to dislodge his delight from traytors eyes. [Sig. ¶ 3; 1:15]

Nashe addresses Sir Charles regarding his "pensiuenes" in the year his mother died, and he wrote the pamphlet two years earlier, the year of his father's death. We do not know how they died; Nashe never tells us. Nor does he tell us that of his seven brothers and sisters five died within a day, a year, or three years of their births; his sister Rebecca died just past her tenth birthday; and his brother Israel, who alone outlived him, died a year after he did at the age of thirty-two. The likely cause of some or all of these deaths is the plague: Norfolk was the hardest hit by plague in epidemic after epidemic in the 1580s and 1590s—the hardest hit save London—and in Norwich, the queen's second city in size, one-third of the people (or 5,000 of them) were killed in the single plague year of 1579, the city never again reaching a population of much above 11,000 until well into the next century.[9] Whether this ignominious contamination drove Nashe away from East Anglia and so toward London or whether his instinctive desire to mock and scorn, to rail over his impecunity or the loss in learning and letters, are ways of avoiding a direct confrontation with his own desperately mortal and fragile self we can never know for certain; but it is a fact that the plague is the single most prominent image throughout his work.

His acerbity, then, breaking out from time to time through his extravagant gestures of speech and thought, is not surprising. When we add to his particular circumstances the more general concerns of the 1590s—a decade of widely fluctuating periods of inflation and depression, angry factions of Puritans and reformers, increasing threats from Spain, and the attempted poisoning of the aging queen within the walls of Whitehall itself—we can appreciate his rage, and his outrageousness. What is more surprising is his genuine ability to be playful—to take childish delight in endlessly inventing absurd names for someone like Harvey, such as Hibble de beane, Himpenhempen Slampamp, Hoppenny Hoe, Hankin Booby (*Haue with you,* sigs. G4v, I1v, K2v; 3:46, 54, 63). Yet he turns even this to advantage, too: humorlessness, he tells Harvey, is what characterizes his opponent and all Puritans (*Strange Newes* [1592], sig. L1v; 1:325). Such deft moments recede, however, except in the works addressed to Harvey; in the more serious ones—like *Christs Teares* and *The Unfortunate Traueller*—it is the sense of indignation that prevails. That is how his contemporaries saw him too. "His style was wittie, though it had some gall," Judicio says of a character based on Nashe in *The Return from Parnassus,* while Thomas Dekker thinks of him after his death "still haunted with the sharpe and *Satyricall spirit* that followd him heere vpon *earth*" and Michael Drayton sees the "Sharply *Satirick*" as "his being."[10] As for Nashe himself, he proclaims a model in Pietro Aretino, pointedly the satirist of a decadent and corrupt Italy under the Medicis. "We want an *Aretine* here among vs, that might strip these golden asses out of their gaye trappings, and after he had ridden them to death with rayling, leaue them on the dunghil for carion," Nashe argues in *Pierce Penilesse* (sig. I3v; 1:242); while in *Nashes Lenten Stuffe* (1599) he announces that "I most affect & striue to imitate *Aretines,* not caring for this demure soft *mediocre genus,* that is like water and wine mixt togither; but giue me pure wine of it self, & that begets good bloud, and heates the brain thorowly" (sig. A4v; 3:152). Indeed, Aretino as a *railleur extraordinaire*—Titian's *una terribile maraviglia*—"was the precedent Nashe needed," David C. McPherson writes, "a dashing, egocentric satirist writing in prose and in the vernacular about current events and people with outrageous hyperbole and sharp invective—a man who, exactly like Nashe, wrote religious tracts as readily as bawdry, fulsome dedications as readily as satire."[11] He also has the *unsettled* quality of Nashe, so that in a comedy like the *Cortigiana* the "fine stories" that the common people devour are on topics like

> la guerra del Turco in Ungheria, le prediche di Fra Martino, il Concilio, istorie, istorie. La cosa d'Inghilterra, la pompa del Papa e de l'Imperadore, la circumcision del Vaivoda, il sacco di Roma, l'assedio di Fiorenza, lo abboccamento di Marsilia con la conclusione, istorie, istorie.

> the Turkish war in Hungary, the sermons of Fra Martino [Luther], the Council [of Trent], stories, stories, the English affair [the divorce of Catherine of Aragon], the Pomp of the Pope and the Emperor, the Circumcision of the Vaivoda, the Sack of Rome, the Siege of Florence, the Conference of Marseilles with the conclusion; stories, stories. [1.4]

The series bears, at the start, a striking resemblance to the apparently random subjects of *The Unfortunate Traueller.*

It is just this satiric, apparently improvisational arbitrariness that describes *Pierce Penilesse,* Nashe's revealing portrait of London in the 1590s. This is a composite work written over "a considerable period," according to Ronald B. McKerrow (*Works,* 5:18), an anatomy of the prodigal in which Pierce decides to damn himself to the devil if only he is rescued from the sins of London and from his own poverty: he is a kind of comic, Everyman's Faust, a Tudor Lazarillo. The maieutic Pierce's Sodom contains all seven of the deadly sins, such as Greed:

> Famine, Lent, and dessolation, sit in Onyon skind iackets before the doore of his indurance, as a *Chorus* in the Tragedy of Hospitality, to tell hunger and pouertie thers no reliefe for them there: and in the inner part of this vgly habitation stands Greedinesse; prepared to deuoure all that enter, attyred in a Capouch of written parchment, buttond downe before

with Labels of wax, and lined with sheepes fels for warmenes: his Cappe furd with cats skins, after the Muscouie fashion, and all to be tasseld with Angle-hookes, in stead of Aglets, ready to catch hold of all those to whom he shewes any humblenes: for his breeches, they were made of the lists of broad cloaths, which he had by letters pattents assured him and his heyres, to the vtter ouerthrowe of Bowcases and Cushin makers, and bumbasted they were, like Beerebarrels, with statute Marchants and forfeitures. But of al, his shooes were the strangest, which, being nothing els but a couple of crab shels, were toothd at the tooes with two sharp sixpennie nailes, that digd vp euery dunghil they came by for gould, and snarld at the stones as he went in the street, because they were so common for men, women, and children to tread vpon, and he could not deuise how to wrest an odde fine out of any of them, [Sig. B1; 166–67]

To the poverty-stricken Pierce (and to Nashe) such property is galling. So is its misuse when Nashe (or the narrator) is introduced to it, in St. Paul's, by a Knight of the Post: "The next obiect that encounters my eyes, is some such obscure vpstart gallants, as without desert or seruice, are raised from the plough to be checkmate with Princes: and these I can no better compare than to creatures that are bred *Sine coitu*, as crickets in chimnies" (sig. B3v; 1:173). The chief of all sins, the sin of pride, even envelops Nashe's typical heroes, the men of learning:

> An other misery of Pride it is, when men that haue good parts, and beare the name of deepe scholers, cannot be content to participate one faith with all Christendome, but, because they will get a name to their vaineglory they will set their self-loue to studie to inuent new sects of singularitie, thinking to liue when they are dead, by hauing theyr sects called after their names, as *Donatists* of *Donatus*, *Arrians* of *Arrias*, and a number more new faith-founders, that haue made *England* the exchange of Innouations, and almost asmuch confusion of Religion in euery Quarter, as there was of tongues at the building of the Tower of *Babell*. Whence, a number that fetch the Articles of their Beleefe out of *Aristotle*, and thinke of heauen and hell as the Heathen Philosophers, take occasion to deride our Ecclesiasticall State, and all Ceremonies of Deuine worship, as bug-beares and scar-crowes, because (like *Herodes* souldiers) we diuide Christs garment amongst vs in so many peeces. [Sig. B3; 1:171–72]

But it is crucial if we are to understand Nashe to see how the abuse of learning is inextricable from the abuse of religion. Thus "the enemies of Poetrie" are both "babling Ballat-makers," the poets without learning, and the Puritans who "preach pure *Caluin*, or distill the iuice of a Commentary in a quarter Sermon" (sig. D3; 1:192).

This last passage comes at the precise center of *Pierce Penilesse*; it is the linchpin of Nashe's poetic satire-turned-sermon. He illustrates what he means by providing the work's only *true encomium*; and it is of a learned preacher. It is

> Siluer tongu'd *Smith,* whose well tun'd stile hath made thy death the generall teares of the Muses, queintlie couldst thou deuise heauenly Ditties to *Apolloes* Lute, and teach stately verse to trip it as smoothly as if *Ouid* and thou had but one soule. Hence alone did it proceed, that thou wert such a plausible pulpit man, that before thou entredst into the rough waies of Theologie, thou refinedst, preparedst, and purifidest thy minde with sweete Poetrie. If a simple mans censure may be admitted to speake in such an open Theater of opinions, I neuer saw aboundant reading better mixt with delight, or sentences which no man can challenge of prophane affectation sounding more melodious to the eare or piercing more deepe to the heart [Sig. D3v; 1:192–93]

Preaching is for Nashe the truest form of poetry as poetry is that which cleanses man's soul and rids the world of sin. With poetry there is purity, and with purity there is life everlasting: "What age will not praise immortal *Sir Phillip Sidney,*" he asks (sig. D3v; 1:193). It is not Sidney's poetry that is redeemed for Nashe but *Sidney himself.* Having offered us the basis for his sermonizing poetics, his propositio made scriptural text, he will not let us forget it. "Hell is nothing but error," he warns us; "none but fooles and Idiotes and Machanicall men, that haue no learning, shall be damned" (sigs. G1v; 1:218).

Pierce Penilesse is one of Nashe's major works; and it achieves that stature because its scattered observations come to cohere in our minds around the work's judging core that fuses learning and faith, wisdom and virtue. More than an anatomy of Tudor customs, it is one of the significant Tudor declarations of a humanist poetics. But Nashe's very first work, the youthful *Anatomie of Absurditie,* sets forth a similar poetics. In attacking "the abusiue enormities of these our times," Nashe locates them in those thoughts and writings that are empty of meaning because empty of virtue.

> It fareth nowe a daies with vnlearned Idiots as it doth with she Asses, who bring foorth all their life long; euen so these brainlesse Bussards, are euery quarter bigge wyth one Pamphlet or other. . . . Such and the very same are they that obtrude themselues vnto vs, as the Authors of eloquence and fountains of our finer phrases, when as they sette before vs nought but a confused masse of wordes without matter, a Chaos of sentences without any profitable sence, resembling drummes, which beeing emptie within, sound big without. Were it that any Morrall of greater moment, might be fished out of their fabulous follie, leauing theyr words, we would cleaue to

their meaning, pretermitting their painted shewe, we woulde pry into their propounded sence, but when as lust is the tractate of so many leaues, and loue passions the lauish dispence of so much paper, I must needes sende such idle wits to shrift to the vicar of S. Fooles, who in steede of a worser may be such a Gothamists ghostly Father. [Sigs. A1–A1v; 1:9–10]

The target here is not Greene, as commonly thought, whose humanist poetics of wonder is thoroughly grounded in a learning that his close friend Nashe, fellow Cambridge graduate, would have realized. What he is attacking are the lesser writers of romance—those like John Dickenson whose escapist works are bereft of any moral or intellectual significance. "They," Nashe says, "to no Common-wealth commoditie, tosse ouer their troubled imaginations to haue the praise of the learning which they lack" (sig. A2; 1:11), while their audience

vaunte reading when the sum of their diuinitie consists in twopennie Catichismes: and yet their ignoraunt zeale wyll presumptuously presse into the Presse, enquiring most curiouslie into euery corner of the Common wealth, correcting that sinne in others, wherwith they are corrupted themselues. [Sig. B3; 1:21]

Bad poetry leads to false piety: "Who made them so priuie to the secrets of the Almightie, that they should foretell the tokens of his wrath, or terminate the time of his vengeaunce?" (sig. B3v; 1:23). Fabricated learning and fabricated religion—not true poetry—are what Plato banished from his Republic and Augustine eliminated from the City of God (sig. B4v; 1:25). On the other hand, Nashe tells us, like Sidney he accounts

of Poetrie, as of a more hidden & diuine kinde of Philosophy, enwrapped in blinde Fables and darke stories, wherin the principles of more excellent Arts and morall precepts of manners, illustrated with diuers examples of other Kingdomes and Countries, are contained: for amongst the *Grecians* there were Poets, before there were any Philosophers, who embraced entirely the studie of wisedome, as *Cicero* testifieth in his *Tusculanes,* whereas he saith, that of all sorts of men, Poets are most ancient, who to the intent they might allure men with a greater longing to learning, haue folowed two things, sweetnes of verse, and variety of inuention, knowing that delight doth prick men forward to the attaining of knowledge. [Sigs. B4v–C1; 1:25]

The end of poetry and learning is the reformation of society and the salvation of the soul (sig. E1; 1:43). "*Socrates* who reduced Philosophy vnto the manners, sayd, that thys was the greatest wisedome, to distinguish good & eruill thinges" (sig. E3v; 1:47).

Since then the onely ende of knowledge ought to be to learne to liue well, let vs propound this vse and end vnto our selues, least after so many yeres paines, we misse of the marke whereat our parents in our education aymd. Turning ouer Histories, and reading the liues of excellent Orators and famous Philosophers, let vs with *Themistocles,* set before our eyes one of the excellentest to imitate, in whose example insisting, our industry may be doubled, to the adequation of his praise. [Sig. E3v; 1:48]

Nashe means to make humanist thought and humanist rhetoric instruct men by imitatio: we must learn from such a figure as Pierce to replace the Knights of the Post with Henry Smiths and Sir Philip Sidneys.

Pierce Penilesse has its Senecan models in Juvenal's first satire on the depraved state of Rome and the seventh satire on the decline of learning and the loss of preferment; the pageant *Summers last will and Testament,* another early work, finds its original in Juvenal's tenth satire, concerned with the coming of death and the final resolution that all things must be left in the hands of God and the eighth satire on legacy hunting. Here Nashe's subject is Summer confronting his own end as Autumn approaches, determining the significance of his life by inquiring of others and adjudicating among contenders for his goods. But, wherever he turns, the weakened old man is met by mockery. Ver, or Spring, is a self-indulgent spendthrift, whose self-defense is an encomium moriae on prodigality. Sol's boundless pride and lasciviousness blind him to his destructive powers of flood and drought, killing life through excess and deficiency. Orion can define himself only by praising the dog—but betrays himself by relying on the obvious sophistry of Sextus Empiricus. These self-serving responses to Summer's interrogation suggest a misuse of learning, a decay of rhetoric, and the dissolution of virtue. As *Pierce Penilesse* converts lively satire to a potent source for sermonizing, so *Summers last will* converts the spectacle of pageantry into a lament on mortality. The show, staged at the home of the bishop of Croydon where Nashe and others had fled when the plague struck London, is never far from this spreading disease—as in Summer's almost unbearably sad song *"Adieu, farewell earths bliss,"* which in its various verses details the chronology of death and burial while repeating in its chorus the phrase put on the doors of houses struck by the black death: *"Lord, haue mercy on vs"* (sigs. H1–H2; 3:282–84). The entertainment itself moves from the madcap morris dancers brought on by Ver through the empty brightness of Sol to the threat, as Autumn describes Winter, of ice and snow rotting life altogether (sig. G4; 3:280). When the satyrs and wood nymphs enter at the end to carry off Summer, their song has become a dirge.

> *Autumne hath all the Summers fruitefull treasure;*
> *Gone is our sport, fled is poore* Croydens *pleasure:*
> *Short dayes, sharpe dayes, long nights come on a pace,*
> *Ah, who shall hide vs from the Winters face?*
> *Colde dooth increase, the sicknesse will not cease,*
> *And here we lye, God knowes, with little ease:*
> *From winter, plague, & pestilence, good Lord, deliuer vs.*

Here too we suddenly move out of the confines of Croydon, startled to see the play, like *Pierce Penilesse*, is meant to be about *us*.

> *London dooth mourne, Lambith is quite forlorne,*
> *Trades cry, Woe worth that euer they were borne:*
> *The want of Terme is towne and Cities harme;*
> *Close chambers we do want, to keepe vs warme,*
> *Long banished must we liue from our friends:*
> *This lowe built house will bring vs to our ends.*
> *From winter, plague, & pestilence, good Lord, deliuer vs.*
> [Sig. I1v; 3:292]

The exile of the body to Croydon is likened to the soul's exile on earth from God: *Summers last will* has all the compacted, grieving, universal force of parable.

These three works—*Pierce Penilesse, An Anatomie of Absurditie*, and *Summers last will and Testament*—are all early, but they are among Nashe's most serious efforts. It is no coincidence that two of the three are modeled on satires of Juvenal, or that all of them deliberately employ humanist rhetoric, in its various forms, to promulgate humanist ideas. This open allegiance in *Summers last will* is especially clear, in its unique juxtaposition of colloquy, forensic oration, and disputation, its numerous appeals to antique mythology, and its blatant borrowings from writers like Sextus; but this is to be expected from a writer who tells the patron of his first work that he hopes "you will euery way censure of me in fauour, as one that dooth partake some parts of a Scholler" (sig. ¶4v; 1:8). It is, in fact, this poor boy from East Anglia, who probably never attended a grammar-school[12] yet managed to prepare himself for Cambridge, enter as a sizar in 1581 or 1582, and then become a scholar of the Lady Margaret Foundation, who, of all writers of humanist fiction, has left us the most stirring tribute to humanism. In a letter addressed "to the gentlemen stvdents of both vniuersities" prefacing Greene's *Menaphon* (1589), Nashe writes admiringly of Erasmus, of More, and of

> that most famous and fortunate Nurse of all learning, Saint *Iohns* in *Cambridge*, that at that time was a Vniuersity within it selfe, shining so

farre aboue all other houses, Halles, and hospitals whatsoeuer, that no Colledge in the Towne was able to compare with the tithe of her Students; hauing (as I haue heard graue men of credite report) moe Candles light in it, euery Winter morning before foure of the clocke, then the foure of the clocke bell gaue strokes; till she (I say) as a pittying mother, put to her helping hand, and sent, from her fruitfull wombe, sufficient Scholers, both to support her owne weale, as also to supply all other inferiour foundations defects, and namely, that royall erection of Trinity Colledge, which the Vniuersity Orator, in an Epistle to the Duke of Somerset, aptly termed *Colonia deducta* from the suburbs of Saint *Iohns*. In which extraordinary conception, *vno partu in rempublicam prodiere,* the Exchequer of eloquence, sir *Iohn Cheeke,* a man of men, supernaturally traded in all tongs, sir *Iohn Mason,* Doctor *Watson, Redman, Ascam, Grindall, Leuer, Pilkinton:* all which haue, either by their priuate readings, or publique workes repurged the errors of Arte, expelled from their puritie, and set before our eyes a more perfect methode of studie. [Sigs. A4v–B1; 3:317]

Herbert Marshall McLuhan, in an exhaustive study of Nashe's intellectual roots and development, also finds St. John's "the great bulwark of patristic and classical studies":[13] here is the source of the love of learning combined with the religious zeal (and the love of the Church Fathers) that distinguishes Nashe's work from that of other writers of humanist fiction. Here we find the humanist basis of his beliefs reinforced; here he learns the disputatious style; and here he comes to fear and despise the New Men epitomized by Gabriel Harvey—those Puritans and Ramists who became "particularly active in St. John's" during Nashe's time, as Hibbard reminds us (*Nashe*, p. 5), and who threatened to bring down in one massive rubble all the humanist foundations so carefully built by Ascham, Cheke, and their disciples of the recent past. Nashe's praise of Cambridge, then, is followed by his exposure of these false scholars.

But how ill their precepts haue prospered with our idle age, that leaue the fountaines of Sciences, to follow the riuers of Knowledge, their ouer-fraught studies with trifling compendiaries may testifie: for I know not how it commeth to passe, by the doting practise of our Diuinitie Dunces, that striue to make their pupills pulpit-men before they are reconciled to *Priscian*; but those yeares which should bee imployed in *Aristotle* are expired in Epitomies, and well too, they may haue so much Catechisme vacation, to rake vp a little refuse philosophy. [Sig. B1; 3:317–18]

It is the cruelest of ironies that this son of a rector of the Established Church who had come to study with the heirs of Erasmus found only those Puritans and Ramists who would dismiss his teachings. But, if Nashe was bitterly disappointed, he stuck by his convictions; he took no part in Reformist learning.

Instead, he went to London where he aligned himself with such patrons as Archbishop Whitgift, Bishop Richard Bancroft, and, eventually, George Carey, son of the first Lord Hunsdon and captain-general of the Isle of Wight (where, in exile, Nashe was his most productive). All of them were members of the Establishment, and of the Established Church. And his writing, for all its wild abandon in style, its energy, its wit, was serious business to him. When Harvey accuses him of leading a wanton life in London, he replies scornfully, in *Strange Newes,*

> For the order of my life, it is as ciuil as a ciuil orenge; I lurke in no corners, but conuerse in a house of credit, as well gouerned as any Colledge, where there bee more rare quallified men and selected good Schollers than in any Noblemans house that I knowe in England. [Sig. L4; 1:329]

Nashe may be referring here to Croydon, "a little academy" of poor scholars, according to Sir George Paule, Archbishop Whitgift's comptroller;[14] "Undoubtedly," Michael Ayrton comments, "Nashe must also have spent much of his time at his books for his writings display a wide if indiscriminate reading, a sound knowledge of Latin and Greek."[15] Indeed, they are of many kinds, these sources: Ovid, Vergil, Horace; theologians from Augustine and Athanasius to Tyndale and Erasmus; Continental writers like La Primaudaye and Castiglione; Spenser, Marlowe, and Lyly; Watson, Warner, and Sir John Davies. In *The Anatomie of Absvrditie,* McKerrow notes, Nashe draws on Brian Melbancke, Greene, Ascham, Macrobius, Ovid, Elyot, and Agrippa (*Works,* 5:117–19); in *Pierce Penilesse,* on Pictorius, Sextus, and perhaps Justus Lipsius (5:120); in *Summers last will,* on Horace and Terence (5:122). Although few of his classical sources go much beyond the readings at the university, he never stops using them—in fact, he parades them with such energy and showmanship that we are constantly aware how eager, how urgent, he is in his desire to advocate humanism even in the years that begin to register its sharp decline. This is true not only with the pagan but with the patristic writing. "With teares be it spoken," he says in his epistle dedicatory to *Haue with you to Saffron-walden,*

> too few such lowly Parsons & Preachers we haue, who, laying aside all worldly encumbrances, & plesant cõuersing with Saint *Austen, Ierome, Chrisostome,* wilbe content to read a Lecture, as he hath done, *de laca caprina,* (almost as slender a cast subiect as a Catts smelling haires,) or trauerse the subtile distinctions twixt short cut and long taile. [Sigs. A4v–B1; 3:8]

His scorn of Harvey is part and parcel with his accusation in *Christs Teares* that the coming of puritanism has meant the end of humanism at St. John's.

Nashe's advocacy of classical and patristic learning—and his own clear sense of rhetorical form in satire and diatribe—has its origin in the revival of the Second Sophistic at Cambridge, as McLuhan painstakingly traces it.[16] We owe our initial understanding of the Second Sophistic to Philostratus, who uses this concept in his *Lives of the Sophists* to describe the beginnings of a rhetorical movement involving both secular Roman writers and Church Fathers that arose in the first century and continued as late as the fourth, culminating in the work of Augustine. (Philostratus's own history ends around the year 200.) He characterizes the movement, of which he was a part, as analogous to the First Sophistic, centered in Protagoras in the fifth century B.C. "We must regard [this] ancient sophistic art," he writes,

> as philosophic rhetoric. For it discusses the themes that philosophers treat of, but whereas they, by their method of questioning, set snares for knowledge, and advance step by step as they confirm the minor points of their investigations, but assert that they have still no sure knowledge, the sophist of the old school assumes a knowledge of that whereof he speaks.[17]

The exemplar of this style of self-assertion and self-certainty for Philostratus is the sophist Gorgias.

> For he set an example to the sophists with his virile and energetic style, his daring and unusual expressions, his inspired impressiveness, and his use of the grand style for great themes; and also with his habit of breaking off his clauses and making sudden transitions, by which devices a speech gains in sweetness and sublimity; and he also clothed his style with poetic words for the sake of ornament and dignity. That he also improvised with the greatest facility I have [already] stated. [492]

In no sense, then, was the rhetoric of the First Sophistic divorced from eloquence—or from philosophy; rather, it was a high rhetoric that insured the propagation of civilized values. This is also true of the Second Sophistic. "The commonest themes of the great sophists of the empire," remarks George A. Kennedy,

> were the cultural values of Greek civilization and their manifestation in the Roman Empire. The sophists were like fashionable preachers who encouraged belief in inherited values of religion and morality in the most polished and elegant form, and they contributed significantly to the stability of a society whose major goal was preservation of the status quo in the face of barbarian attack and new religious movements.[18]

This being so, it is plain enough why Nashe thought their techniques so

318 · THE POETICS OF DOUBT AND DESPAIR

useful in preserving humanist learning and in attacking the New Barbarians like Harvey.

The Second Sophistic took cultural ideas from all branches of study and delighted in embellishing them, as Joseph Marshall Campbell reminds us; to this end, the Rev. Thomas E. Ameringer notes, there was a close imitation of such Attic masters as Demosthenes, Isocrates, Thucydides, Herodotus, Xenophon, and Plato.[19] "Distinct threads of the Second Asiatic style," Campbell adds, also "lead back to the old sophistic prose. It is not that the rhetors of Asia deliberately chose certain of the earlier sophists as models, but these Asiatics were pressed by their own predispositions into the display of passionate pathos and fantastic grandness."[20] The orators of the Second Sophistic—now turned writers—found their own texts in Cicero's *Brutus* 286 or in Dionysius of Halicarnassus's *De Compositione Verborum* 18, or in his critical essays on Demosthenes and Thucydides. Dionysius's description of the writing of Thucydides seems particularly helpful in assessing Nashe.

> In his choice of words he preferred those which were metaphorical, obscure, archaic and outlandish to those which were common and familiar to his contemporaries. In the construction of both shorter and longer clauses he chose the arrangements which were dignified, severe, compact, and firm-footed, and those which jarred the ear by the clashing of inconsonant letters rather than those which were melodious, smooth, polished and free from any conflict of sound. To figures of speech, in which he was especially eager to outstrip his predecessors, he devoted particular attention. . . . The ostentatious figures of speech are also to be found in his work in no small number—I mean those parallelisms in length and sound, word-play and antithesis, which were excessively used by Gorgias of Leontini, by Polus and Lycymnius and their followers. . . . I may summarise the instruments, so to speak, of Thucydides's style as follows: there are four—artificiality of vocabulary, variety of figures, harshness of word-order, rapidity of significance.[21]

Thucydides, moreover, weds important matter to such a style with high seriousness.

A major form that developed in this style during the Second Sophistic was the diatribe, a form that becomes increasingly important in Nashe's work. Derived ultimately from passages in Plato where Socrates abandons dialectic for a debate with a feigned antagonist, in later Alexandrian times it was developed for declamations by writing speeches as *logomachiae* in which the author and a feigned party dispute *as if* speaking in dialogue. "In the emptiness of the times," according to Campbell, "it took to moralizing; pouncing upon the follies of men, reprehending them or ridiculing them."[22]

Such a form lent itself naturally to satire; and McLuhan notes that Lucian—the satirist translated by Erasmus and More and admired by Rabelais and Aretino—was "one of the most interesting links between this mode of florid prose with its satirical intention, as it was cultivated in the [Second Sophistic] and as it was cultivated by St. Chrysostom and St. Basil, for example, in the fourth century" ("Place of Thomas Nashe," p. 410). Nashe seems to have known this connection—in the Lucianic spirit on which he seems to comment when citing More's *Utopia* in *The Unfortunate Traueller* and his use of "strange worlds" in that fiction, and in his other satires with a Lucianic spirit: *Pierce Penilesse,* the second part of *Christs Teares, Strange Newes, Haue with you,* and the extravagantly fantastic *Lenten Stuffe.*

Surely Nashe was aware of another link as well: that the Second Sophistic had a profound influence on Christian writing in the early period of the Church. "The Second Sophistic," Kennedy sums in his history of classical rhetoric,

> in fact influenced Christianity as early as the second century. In the fourth century, when Christianity had become the official religion of the empire, both the emperors and the orators who celebrated their virtues were usually Christians, and a Christian sophistry was created by Fathers of the Church like Gregory of Nazianzus in the form of panegyrical sermons for the great feasts of the Christian year or for funerals. Gregory and Basil the Great, both trained in the schools of sophists, are their artistic equals in oratory. This tradition of Christian sophistry remains strong throughout the Byzantine period in the East. It can be found in the western Middle Ages as well, but in a more subdued form, and it was embraced with enthusiasm by the humanists of the Renaissance both as a way of ingratiating an orator or writer with the rich or powerful and for the sheer joy of unrestrained artistic expression. [*Classical Rhetoric*, p. 39]

Satire as well as panegyric could instruct Christian values, as we see in the works of Tertullian and Lactantius. But the Fathers did not need to depend on rhetorical models among the pagan sophists; there were more than enough in the Holy Bible itself, in those scourges of God among the Old Testament writers (to whom Jack Wilton compares himself) who wrote speeches in the form of covenants (as Cutwolfe delivers) or as prophecy (as the English earl in *The Unfortunate Traueller*), or in the New Testament with Christ's many parables (such as the one Nashe uses as his text for *Christs Teares),* or the more informal spontaneous exhortations or fables (as in *Lenten Stuffe*). The prosopopoeia of Christ in *Christs Teares* has its antecedent in the prosopopoeia of Wisdom. The New Testament word for "preach" is *kērussō,* proclaim (Mark 13:10): much as

Nashe implies in *Strange Newes* and *Haue with you* (as well as other works), the truth stands for itself. It need not be "argued" or "proven" because once stated it is so obviously so. Loosely organized proclamations thus were called *homiliai* (Greek for "conversations")—a patristic form taken over directly in the homilies printed for preachers to read weekly in the Established Church of Edward VI and Elizabeth I. Other sermon forms were developed by these Church Fathers: the preaching by exegesis, or hermeneutics; by the systematic partitioning and analysis of a text (becoming especially elaborate under Origen); and by the panegyric as developed by Eusebius.

We do not now know what Church Fathers were studied at St. John's in Nashe's day, although some seem to have been a part of the study there. So Nashe's allusion to St. John Chrysostom, for instance, may be just that; but the eloquence of John of the Golden Mouth, as he was called, often rests on an easy colloquialism, similar to that effected by Nashe. In his homily on St. Babylas, for example, his style is considerably more restrained than that of Nashe, but the illustrations and occasional phrasing are not dissimilar.

> For when Julian who surpassed all in impiety, ascended the imperial throne, and grasped the despotic sceptre, straightway he lifted up his hands against the God who created him, and ignored his benefactor, and looking from the earth beneath to the heavens, howled after the manner of mad dogs, who alike bay at those who do not feed them and those who do feed them. But he rather was mad with a more savage madness than theirs. For they indeed turn from, and hate their friends and strangers alike. But this man used to fawn upon demons, strangers to his salvation, and used to worship them with every mode of worship. . . . O wretched and miserable man! as it was impossible to destroy the heaven and to quench the sun, and to shake and cast down the foundations of the earth, and those things Christ foretold, thus saying; "Heaven and earth shall pass away, but my words shall not pass away."[23]

Even closer in tone and rhythms is Chrysostom's descant on "evil" which resembles Nashe's employment of "stones" and "gathering" in *Christs Teares*. It is in one of Chrysostom's several homilies on demons.

> There is then evil, which is really evil; fornication, adultery, covetousness, and the countless dreadful things, which are worthy of the utmost reproach and punishment. Again there is evil, which rather is not evil, but is called so, famine, pestilence, death, disease, and others of a like kind. For these would not be evils. On this account I said they are called so only. Why then? Because, were they evils, they would not have become the sources of good to us, chastening our pride, goading our sloth, and leading us on to

zeal, making us more attentive. . . . He *calls* this evil therefore which chastens them.[24]

St. John Chrysostom was equally adept at exegesis, as his homilies on Romans 6:5 and 7:14 make clear;[25] but perhaps the most impressive Church Father at this form of writing was St. Basil in the *Hexaemeron*, nine homilies on the opening chapters of Genesis. Even Augustine's *Confessions,* which McKerrow finds to be a source of *Christs Teares* (*Works*, 5.124) and which Nashe alludes to frequently, closes with a long allegorical exegesis on the creation of the world as told in Genesis as evidence of his conversion by way of the rhetoric of Cicero and Ambrose (11–13). It is helpful to remember, too, that that homiletic form as well as the exegetical, developing the rhetorical possibilities inherent in a single theme or situation, is not unlike the satiric method of Juvenal—a point George A. Kennedy also makes.[26]

G. R. Owst shows in some detail how these practices of the Second Sophistic, fusing pagan and patristic rhetoric, were conveyed to the Renaissance:[27] here too is straightforward exposition and paraphrase as well as the use of anecdote, fable, legend, and marvel. Thomistic categories and subcategories were familiar, as instructed in the *Tractatus de forma Sermonum*:

> Predicatio est thematis assumpcio, ejusdemque thematis divisio, thematis subdivisio, concordantiarum congrua citacio, et auctoritatum adductarum clara et devota explanacio.

> Preaching involves the taking up of a Theme, the division of the same theme, the sub-division of the theme, the appropriate citing of concordant points, and the clear and devout explanation of the Authorities brought forward.[28]

Indeed, "There are many," one preacher notes at the close of the thirteenth century,

> who, when they come to sermon, . . . do not care what the preacher says; but only how he says it. And if the sermon be well "rhymed," if the theme be well "divided," if the brother discourses well, if he pursues his argument well, if he "harmonizes" well, they say: "How well that brother preached!" "What a fine sermon he made!" That is all they look for in the sermon, nor do they attend to what he says.[29]

Sermons were distinctive not for organization alone but for elaborate wordplay—repetition, punning, even the use of acrostics.[30] *The Practise of Preaching* by Hyperius of Marburg, Englished by John Ludham in 1577, advocates the same support for the legacy of the Second Sophistic.

Whatsoever thinge is profitable to teach perspicuously, or also to moue and perswade withall, all that shall the Preacher purchase to himselfe as most requisite and necessary furniture. Therefore let him know, that argumentations tripartite, quinquepartite, Euthymemata: also Schemes and Tropes: further the crafte of amplifying and mouing of affections, and finally whatsoever else of this order is taught of the Rhetoritians, masters of well speakinge, also appertayne and belonge unto him.[31]

There is a published sermon of John Fisher (1509) which is a long tropological exegesis on Psalm 116, including a prosopopoeia of Martha addressing Jesus, and an exegesis on Matthew 5 (1532), which reminds us of *Summers last will:*

The Ioyes of this worlde, be lyke myd somer games & Chrystmas games or playes. The Courte of kynge Edwarde, the Courte of kynge Rycharde, & the courte of the kynge, that how is ded where be they now? all they were but counterfeyt ymages and dysgusynge for a tyme / it was but a playe for a tyme. But the courte of heuyn is alway stable in one poynte / where the offycers chaung neuer. There is the true noblenesse, the sure honour, the very glory. [Sig. E1v]

Other Tudor sermons that show this love of division are the funeral sermon for the emperor Ferdinand by Edmund Grindal, bishop of London, on Matthew 24:44; Richard Hooker's sermon on pride based on Habakkuk 2:4; and one by Thomas Playfere on Luke 23:28[32] Playfere can make frequent use of patristic citation; J. W. Blench notes that in one sermon alone he refers to Theophylact, Jerome, Alcuin, Augustine, Clement, Prosper, Synesius, Gregory, Fulgosus, Fulgentius, John Damascene, Arnobius, Bernard, Cassianus, Lactantius, Ignatius, Prudentius, Anselm, Irenaeus, Epiphanius, and Optatus[33]—surely the Fathers during the Tudor period were not the exclusive property of the Roman Church alone.

Still, for the ornate Tudor preaching that derived from the Second Sophistic, Lancelot Andrewes remains perhaps the primary example—"by little and little I was drawne on to bee an Auditor of his," Nashe confesses in *Haue with you,* "since when, whensoeuer I heard him, I thought it was but hard and scant allowance that was giu'n him, in comparison of the incomparable gifts that were in him" (sigs. Q4v–R1; 3:107). The "incomparable gifts" that Nashe admires, Andrewes's ability at "dissecting his text as a scholar and a linguist," as Florence Higham has it, and to "take a word and shake it, like a dog with a bone,"[34] can be seen in his frequent use of the image of conduit pipes[35] or, like Nashe, the development of Christ's tears as the blood and sweat of the body on the Cross,[36] or in his division of the lesson on Hebrews 2:16 given as the Nativity Sermon on Christmas Day 1605:

And, what is the *seed of Abraham,* but, as *Abraham* himselfe is? And what is *Abraham?* Let him answere himselfe; *I am dust and ashes.* What is the *seede of Abraham?* Let one answere, in the persons of all the rest; *Dicens putrudini &c. saying rottennesse, thou art my mother and to the wormes, ye are my brethren.*

   1. They are *spirits*; Now, what are we, what is the *seed of Abraham? Flesh.* And what is the very harvest of this *seede* of *flesh?* what, but *corruption,* and *rottennesse,* and *wormes:* There is the substance of our bodies.

   2. They, (Angels) *glorious spirits:* We, vile bodies (beare with it, it is the *Holy Ghoste* owne terme: *Who shall change our vile bodies.*) And not only base and *vile,* but *filthy and vncleane: ex immundo conceptum semine, conceiued of vncleane seede:* There is the *metall.* And, the moulde is no better: the *wombe,* wherein we weare conceiued *vile, base, filthy,* and *vncleane.* There, is our *qualitie.*

   3. They, *heauenly Spirits, Angells of heauen:* that is, their *place* of abode, is in *heauen* aboue. Ours is heere below, in the dust; *inter pulices, & culices, tineas, aranese, & vermes;* Our place is heere among *fleas and flies, mothes and spiders, and crawling wormes.* There, is our place of dwelling. [Sig. B2]

This use of diacope (as with "*seed*") is Nashe's primary patterning in the first part of *Christs Teares*; the uses of aetiologia, anthypophora, and anacephalaeosis are also typical.

   And what of "Siluer tongu'd *Smith*"? He is even closer in style to Nashe, with his simple diction and imagery—

like a lark, that falls to the ground sooner than she mounted up: at first she retires as it were by steps, but when she cometh nearer the ground, she falls down with a jump: so we decline at first, & waver lower and lower till we be almost at the worst, and then we run headlong, as though we were sent post to hell[37]

—and his wit—

When one told *Socrates,* that he would very fain go to Olympus, but he feared that he should not be able to endure the pains: *Socrates* answered him, I know that thou usest to walk every day between thy meals, which walk continue forward in thy ways to Olympus, and within 5. or 6. daies thou shalt come thither. How easy was this: & yet he saw it not. . . . If men did bend themselves as much to do good, as they beat their brains to do evil, they might go to heaven with less trouble than they go to hell[38]

—or in the employment of diallage, directing his syntax as it does Nashe's—

In Paradise we might live or dye: in the world we live and must dye: in Heaven we shall live and not dye. Before sin nothing could change us; now every thing doth change us: for when winter comes we are cold, when age comes we are withered, when sickness comes we are weak, to shew that when death comes we shall dye. The clothes which we wear upon our backs, the Sun which sets over our heads, the Graves which lye under our feet, the meat which goes into our mouths, cry unto us, that we shall wear, and fade and dye, like the Fishes and fowls and Beasts, which even now were living in their elements, and now are dead in our dishes. Every thing, every day suffers some eclipse, and nothing stands in a stay, but one Creature calls to another, let us leave the World. Our fathers summoned us, and we shall summon our children to the Grave; first we wax old, then we wax dry, then we wax weak, then we wax sick, and so we melt away by drops; at last as we carried others, so others carry us unto the Grave; this is the last bed which every man shall sleep in: we must return to our mother's womb.[39]

There are also extant a number of Smith's sermons which are exegetical—such as those on Psalms 82:6–7 (*The Magistrates Scripture* [1590]), on Romans 13:14 (*The Wedding Garment* [1591]), on 1 Timothy 6:6 (*The Benefite of Contentation* [1591]), on Job 8:5–7 (*The Sinfull Mans Search: Or Seeking of God* [1592]), and on Luke 10:39–42 (*Maries Choice* [1592]). Smith's lesson, common to Andrewes and underlying much of Nashe's work, is that he holds, as Mitchell says of Andrewes, that

the relation of the preacher both to the learning of the past and to the active affairs of his own day was conditioned by his attitude to a theological conception of the Universe, the attitude which led to his regarding all things *sub specie aeternitatis*; from this viewpoint nothing employed could be considered merely ridiculous, for the juxtaposition that invited laughter, incidentally revealed the highest truth, and the impossible itself became the credible, being, as Tertullian assured men, to be believed, *quia impossibile est*. [*Pulpit Oratory*, p. 149]

Christianity itself could often be seen as a religion of paradox and incredibilities.

Nashe proclaims his allegiance to those sophists and Church Fathers who joined in the Second Sophistic by arguing for an ornamental high rhetoric as the most effective means of conveying (and rendering memorable) the most important truths. "Amongst all the ornaments of Artes," he declares in *The Anatomie of Absurditie*,

Rhethorick is to be but in highest reputation, without the which all the rest are naked, and she onely garnished: yet some there be who woulde seperate Arts from Eloquence, whose censures we oppugne, because it abhorres from common experience. Who doth not know y^t in all tongues taske eloquence is odious if it be affected, and that attention is altogether wanting, where it is reiected. A man may baule till his voice be hoarse, exhort with teares till his tongue ake and his eyes be drie, repeate that hee woulde perswade, till his stalenes dooth secretlie call for a Cloake bagge, and yet moue no more then if he had been all that while mute, if his speech be not seasoned with eloquence, and adorned with elocutions assistance. [Sigs. E2–E2v; 1:45]

Writers, then, need *both* art *and* eloquence, a "pregnant dexterity of wit, and manifold varietie of inuention," as he puts it in the preface to *Menaphon* (sig. B3v; 3:323).

To say that form in Nashe, therefore, is decidedly different from that of his predecessors in humanist fiction is true enough; but to argue, as many have, that he is formless is demonstrably wrong. The two pamphlets he wrote in his quarrel with Harvey, for instance, *Strange Newes* and *Have with you to Saffron-walden* are, as Lewis observes (*English Literature*, p. 412) following McKerrow (*Works*, 5:88), an imitatio of previous humanist quarrels, such as the one between Poggio Bracciolini and Francesco Filelfo and Laurentius Valla, as well as probable models from the Second Sophistic. By mocking Harvey's attacks as poor texts for exegesis, Nashe's inexhaustible wit points up how bad they are as Scripture and how little deserving they are of belief. At the same time, drawing on the sophists' use of philosophic rhetoric, he forces Harvey, in his replies, to betray his own Ramist separation of meaning and manner—as well as the Puritans' desire to forsake traditional Church forms of rhetoric. It is for this reason, then, that *Strange Newes* begins,

Heere beginneth the first Epistle
and first Booke of *Orator Gabriell to the Cati-*
linaries or Phillippicks.
Wherein is diuulged, *that venum is venum and will in-*
fect, that that which is done cannot (de facto) *be*
vndone, that fauour is a curteous Reader,
and G. H. your thankfull debter,

followed by "A Comment vpon the Text" (sig. C1; 1:267). It is only in terms of a traditional orthodox exegesis, stemming from Cicero's *Phillipics*, his orations against Catiline or Piso, or Tertullian's against the pagans, that we can appreciate what Nashe is doing with each idea Harvey raises—parodying it, varying it, fabling it. The grand joke of *Strange Newes*—and it deliberately comes early—is Nashe's invitation to Harvey to reply to him in a similar tropological method, which, as a Puritan and Ramist, he is unable to do.

Giue an instance, if thou canst for thy life, wherin in any leafe of *Pierce Penilesse* I had so much as halfe a sillables relation to thee, or offred one iot of indignitie to thy Father, more than naming the greatest dignitie he hath, when for varietie of Epithites, I calde thy brother *the sonne of a Ropemaker*.

We shall haue a good sonne of you anone, if you be ashamd of your fathers occupation: ah, thou wilt nere thriue, that are beholding to a trade, and canst not abide to heare of it.

Thou dost liue by the gallows, & wouldst not haue a shooe to put on thy foot, if thy father had no traffike with the hangman. Had I a Ropemaker to my father, & somebody had cast it in my teeth, I would foorthwith haue writ in praise of Ropemakers, & prou'd it by soũd sillogistry to be one of the 7. liberal sciences. [Sig. C2v; 1:269–70]

Harvey is trapped. To underline this, Nashe taunts Harvey about his father—all but forcing him to respond exegetically. In turn, he calls attention to his own father, a preacher of the Established Church—and a professional like Nashe at *orthodox* exegesis, right thinking and right saying.

Haue with you to Saffron-walden is even more inventive: another exegesis in which the ideas come thick and threefold. Nashe claims to write a colloquy in imitation of William Bullein's *Dialogue against the Fever Pestilence* (1564) (sig. D1v; 3:20)—the joke here is that Harvey's writing is pestilent; that (for Nashe) it is contagious; that it threatens to become epidemic. As if to eliminate the plague by a kind of rhetorical overkill, Nashe provides his three-way exegesis: a judicial oration against Harvey's statements, using only Harvey's lexicon and rhythms but in an orthodox setting; an exegesis by way of a mock biography (or ridiculous saint's life) that tends to parse the source of the text rather than the text itself; and finally a traditional exegesis of Harvey's counterattack in much the same way Ambrose and Lactantius reply to their accusers. And the challenge is out again: "Let *Gabriel* verefie anie one thing so against mee, and not thinke to carrie it away with hys *generall extenuatings, ironicall amplications, and declamatorie exclamations*" (sig. T1v; 3:122); that is, let him dismiss the ornamental rhetoric of the Puritans and practice that of the Established Church. And, as an even greater joke on Harvey, there is the recognition that he already has without even knowing it: "Nay, he himselfe hath purloyned something from mee, and mended his hand in confuting by fifteen parts, by following my presidents" (sig. V3; 3:132). Harvey has joined the devil's camp—and damned himself. It is Harvey pictured as Cicero's *insanus orator* (*De Oratore* 3.14.55–56; *Brutus* 233–34). To paraphrase Stanley Wells, in these two satires of Harvey, "Imagination quickens exegesis into art."[40]

Still it is *Christs Teares over Jerusalem* that is Nashe's fullest tribute to the Second Sophistic. With its textual basis in Matthew 23:37; its *prosopopoeia* of Christ (sigs. B1 ff.; 2:21 ff.); its verbal litany on "stones" (sigs. B2v; 2:24 ff.), "gather" (sigs. B4; 2:27 ff.), and "hen" (sig. D1v; 2:37 ff.); its structural *comparatio* of Jerusalem and London (as Henry Smith compares a lark and man or, more broadly, as the preacher Barrow of Pembroke Hall, Cambridge, compared his situation with that of Paul in Corinth, according to John Manningham's *Diary*); the exemplary portrait of Jerome as a corrective to the sins of others (sig. T4; 2:146); and the final exhortation and prayer (sigs. Z3–Z4; 2:173–75), this is Nashe's "elaborate sermon in the patristic manner," as McLuhan has it ("Place of Thomas Nashe," p. 387). In fact, it follows closely the dictates of Augustine in the *De Doctrina Christiana* 4.4. According to Augustine,

> It is the duty, then, of the interpreter and teacher of Holy Scripture, the defender of the true faith, and the opponent of error, both to teach what is right and to refute what is wrong, and in the performance of this task to conciliate the hostile, to rouse the careless, and to tell the ignorant both what is occurring at present and what is probable in the future. . . . If the hearers need teaching, the matter treated of must be fully made known by means of narrative. On the other hand, to clear up points that are doubtful requires reasoning, and the exhibition of proofs. If, however, the hearers require to be roused rather than instructed, in order that they may be diligent to do what they already know, and to bring their feelings into harmony with the truths they admit, greater rigour of speech is needed. Here entreaties and reproaches, exhortations and upbraidings, and all the other means of rousing the emotions are necessary.[41]

Although Nashe's sources are Peter Morwyn's translation of the *History of the Latter Times of the Jews' Commonweal* by Josephus (1565) and John Stockwood's 1584 sermon on the subject (McKerrow, *Works*, 4:213; Hibbard, *Nashe*, pp. 124–25), this is merely Nashe's matter for amplification; the Senecan model, which he would expect many of his readers to recognize, is the story of St. Stephen the Martyr on whose feast day (26 December) Nashe's text (Matt. 23:37) was read as the gospel lesson. It is the martyrdom of St. Stephen—like Nashe here a source of Pauline theology and a follower of Christ whose message linked Mosaic institutions with the progressive revelation of the Christian faith—whose story we are to recall. In the Book of Common Prayer the service for the Feast of St. Stephen links his life to the power of rhetoric in the second gospel lesson (John 1:1)—a theme Nashe picks up in his discussion of the need for special rhetoric in sermons—while the collect resembles Nashe's closing lines:

> Grant, O lord, that in all our sufferings here upon earth for the testimony of thy truth, we may steadfastly look up to heaven, and by faith behold the

glory that shall be revealed; and, being filled with the Holy Ghost, may learn to love and bless our persecutors by the example of thy first Martyr.

It is little wonder that J. B. Steane finds in *Christs Teares* "a feeling for prose rhythms which is closely akin to that of the Authorized Version, and which is beautiful."[42] Nashe also means to suggest the biblical book of Lamentations, the various passages in Jeremiah that are apposite, and, perhaps, such patristic writings as Chrysostom's exhortation to Theodore, which begins,

> "Oh! that my head were water, and mine eyes a fountain of tears!" it is seasonable for me to utter these words now, yea much more than for the prophet in his time. For although I am not about to mourn over many cities, or whole nations, yet shall I mourn over a soul which is of equal value with many such nations, yea even more precious. For if one man who does the will of God is better than ten thousand transgressors, then thou wast formerly better than ten thousand Jews. Wherefore no one would now blame me if I were to compose more lamentations than those which are contained in the prophet, and to utter complaints yet more vehement. For it is not the overthrow of a city which I mourn, nor the captivity of wicked men, but the desolation of a sacred soul, the destruction and effacement of a Christ-bearing temple.[43]

But Nashe knows the sermon tradition and the tradition of the Second Sophistic well enough to know that men will not accept the Word unadorned. He writes in *Christs Teares,*

> If you count it prophane to arte-enamel your speech to empeirce, and make a conscience to sweeten your tunes to catch soules, Religion (through you) shal reape infamy. Men are men, and with those thinges must bee mooued, that men wont to be mooued. They must haue a little Sugar mixt with their soure Pylls of reproofe; the hookes must be pleasantly baited that they bite at. Those that hang forth theyr hookes and no bayte, may well enough entangle them in the weeds, (enwrap themselues in contentions,) but neuer winne one soule. Turne ouer the auncient Fathers, and marke howe sweete and honny-some they are in the mouth, and how musicall & melodious in the eare. No Orator was euer more pleasingly perswasiue then humble Saint *Augustine*. . . . Logique, Rethorique, History, Phylosophy, Musique, Poetry, all are the handmaides of Diuinitie. Shee can neuer be curiously drest or exquisitely accomplisht, if any one of these be wanting. (Sigs. Q3–Q3v, Q4; 2:124, 126]

In the revised preface (1594) to this sermon he adds that "For the prophanesse of my eloquence, so they may tearme the eloquence of Sainct *Austen, Ierome, Chryssotom,* prophane, since none of them but takes vnto him farre more liberty of Tropes, Figures, and Metaphors, and alleadging Heathen examples and Histories" (sig. **2v; 2:183). In adapting the means and ends of the Second Sophistic to Tudor pamphleteering, Nashe found one last way to preserve humanist thought and humanist rhetoric by means of a poetics that, fashioned at the beginning of his career, admitted readily that the brutal facts of existence are comprehensible and useful only when they are subjected to the vision of events as *sub specie aeternitatis* under God.

Structurally, of course, *The Unfortunate Traueller,* Nashe's major fiction and one of the most significant latter-day works of humanist poetics, is, like its predecessors, in the form of an exegesis. It takes its text from *Christs Teares:* "Trauel & care for wealth, riches, and honor, is but care & trauel for trauel and care" (sig. L3; 2:88–89). This fictive survey of human achievement during the Tudor years stretches over a broad terrain—Thérouanne, Hampton Court, Marignano, Münster, Middleborough, Rotterdam, Wittenberg, Venice, Florence, Rome, Bologna, and Ardres and Guines—and it purposely scrambles the chronology of real events—the battles of Thérouanne (1513) and Marignano (1515), the Anabaptist uprising at Münster (1534) conflated with the battle of Frankenhausen (1525),[44] the sweating sickness in London (1517), Luther's debate with Carlstadt at Wittenberg (1519), the publications of the *Encomium Moriae* (1509) and the *Utopia (*1516), and the meeting at the Field of the Cloth of Gold (1520)—to see if by such hermeneutics some deeper pattern emerges. Having submitted the depravity of London to allegorical and tropological exegesis in *Pierce Penilesse* and to an extended *comparatio* in *Christs Teares,* it is as if he now wishes to broaden his canvas while still locating a kind of eternal signification, some sort of providential ordering, for the jumble of life. Such, he has already told us in *Pierce Penilesse,* is the peculiar challenge of poetry and the function of the poet.

> Gentles, it is not your lay Chronigraphers, that write of nothing but of Mayors and Sheriefs, and the deare yeere, and the great Frost, that can endowe your names with neuer dated glory: for they want the wings of choise words to fly to heauen, which we haue: they cannot sweeten a discourse, or wrest admiration from men reading, as we can, reporting the meanest accident. Poetry is the hunny of all flowers, the quintessence of all Sciences, the Marrowe of Witte, and the very Phrase of Angels. [Sig. D4; 1:194]

Drama illustrates how this can be accomplished.

> Nay, what if I prooue Playes to be no extreame; but a rare exercise of vertue? First, for the subiect of them (for the most part) it is borrowed out

of our English Chronicles, wherein our forefathers valiant acts (that haue
line long buried in rustie brasse and worme-eaten bookes) are reuiued, and
they themselues raised from the Graue of Obliuion, and brought to pleade
their aged Honours in open presence: than which, what can be a sharper
reproofe to these degenerate effeminiate dayes of ours. [Sig. F3; 1:212]

In fact, the authorities of the Second Sophistic had urged just such a
practice. "Historia vero temporum, lux veritatis, vita memoriae, magistra
vitae, nuntia vetustatis, qua voce alia, nisi oratoris, immortalitati commen-
datur?" Cicero instructs; "as History, which bears witness to the passing of
the ages, sheds light upon reality, gives life to recollection and guidance to
human existence, and brings tidings of ancient days, whose voice, but the
orator's can entrust her to immortality?" (*De Oratore* 2.9.36).[45]

Cicero is even willing, on occasion, to admit the fabulous, as in the cases
of Herodotus and Theopompus (*De Legibus* 1.1.5), while Thucydides is
willing to give new meanings to words (*History* 3.82). There is some
reason to think that Nashe had these theories, or the antique practices of
them, in mind during the composition of *The Unfortunate Traueller*, for
certain passages in the historical works of two writers most admired during
the period of the Second Sophistic—Thucydides and Livy—seem exemplars, perhaps Senecan models of passages in Nashe's fiction. There is
Thucydides' description of the Athenian battle led by Nicias, for instance
(7.84–85), while Livy's account of the war with Hannibal in which heroes
are made to embody the virtues of the Second Sophistic—dignity, public
service, reason, self-discipline—seems even closer to *The Unfortunate
Traueller*. In an elevated, Gorgian style of amplitude (Tacitus thought
Livy the most eloquent of the Roman historians), Livy provides chilling
pictures of human suffering. Here is his representation of a Roman defeat
at the hands of Carthaginians.

Postero die, ubi primum inluxit, ad spolia legenda foedamque etiam
hostibus spectandam stragem insistunt. Iacebant tot Romanorum milia,
pedites passim equitesque, ut quem cuique fors aut pugna iunxerat aut fuga.
Adsurgentes quidam ex strage media cruenti, quos stricta matutino frigore
excitaverant volnera, ab hoste oppressi sunt; quosdam et iacentes vivos
succisis feminibus poplitibusque invenerunt, nudantes cervicem iugulum-
que et reliquum sanguinem iubentes haurire; inventi quidam sunt mersis in
effossam terram capitibus, quos sibi ipsos fecisse foveas obruentesque ora
superiecta humo interclusisse spiritum apparebat. Praecipue convertit
omnes subtractus Numida mortuo superincubanti Romano vivus naso
auribusque laceratis, cum ille, manibus ad capiendum telum inutilibus, in
rabiem ira versa laniando dentibus hostem exspirasset.

The morning after, as soon as it was light, they pressed forward to collect the spoil and to gaze on a carnage that was ghastly even to enemies. There lay those thousands upon thousands of Romans, foot and horse indiscriminately mingled, as chance had brought them together in the battle or the rout. Here and there amidst the slain there started up a gory figure whose wounds had begun to throb with the chill of dawn, and was cut down by his enemies; some were discovered lying there alive, with thighs and tendons slashed, baring their necks and throats and bidding their conquerors drain the remnant of their blood. Others were found with their heads buried in holes dug in the ground. They had apparently made these pits for themselves, and heaping the dirt over their faces shut off their breath. But what most drew the attention of all beholders was a Numidian who was dragged out alive from under a dead Roman, but with mutilated nose and ears; for the Roman, unable to hold a weapon in his hands, had expired in a frenzy of rage, while rending the other with his teeth. [22.51.5–9][46]

Livy also provides his own picture of plague.

Accessit et ab pestilentia commune malum quod facile utrorumque animos averteret a belli consiliis. Nam tempore autumni et locis natura gravibus, multo tamen magis extra urbem quam in urbe, intoleranda vis aestus per utraque castra omnium ferme corpora movit. Ac primo temporis ac loci vitio et aegri erant et moriebantur; postea curatio ipsa et contactus aegrorum volgabat morbos, ut aut neglecti desertique qui incidissent morerentur, aut adsidentis curantisque eadem vi morbi repletos secum traherent, cotidianaque funera et mors ob oculos esset et undique dies noctesque ploratus audirentur. Postremo ita adsuetudine mali efferaverant animos ut non modo lacrimis iustoque conploratu prosequerentur mortuos, sed ne efferrent quidem aut sepelirent, iacerentque strata exanima corpora in conspectu similem mortem exspectantium, mortuique aegros, aegri validos cum metu, tum tabe ac pestifero odore corporum conficerent; et ut ferro potius morerentur, quidam invadebant soli hostium stationes.

And in addition pestilence brought to both sides a calamity which forthwith diverted the attention of the two armies from strategy. For owing to the autumn season and places naturally unhealthy, unendurable heat affected the health of nearly all the men in both camps, but much more outside the city than within. And at first they sickened and died owing to the season and their position. Later the mere care of the ill and contagion spread the disease, so that those who had fallen ill died neglected and abandoned, or else they carried off with them those who sat by them and those who nursed, having caught the same malignant disease. And so every day funerals and death were before their eyes, wailings were heard on all sides day and night. Finally, from habituation to misery they had so lost their humane feelings that, so far from escorting the dead with tears and the wailing that was their due, they did not even carry them out and bury them; and dead bodies lay strewn about before the eyes of men awaiting a like death, and the dead seriously affected the ill, the ill the sound, not only through fear, but also by putrefaction and the pestilent odour of corpses. And some, to die by the sword instead, dashed into the outposts of the enemy single-handed. [25.26.7–11).[47]

Finally, Nashe's Heraclide may mean for us to recall the desperate pleading and death of Livy's Heraclia (24.26).

Nashe's *Unfortunate Traueller* bares Livy's human savagery without the compensation of Livy's grand style. Instead, the real world of sixteenth-century Europe impinges nearly everywhere, its pressures undeniably disrupting the ornate rhetoric the Church Fathers had used to fortify and heighten the passion of their learning and sermonizing. The chiliastic world of the Tudor humanists, with its community of educable, perfectible, and even on occasion inspired men, is now imaged in the silly disputations and the mindless parrotings of Cicero. And Nashe's own parable, of a millennial society at Münster, is a tormented jungle of human ignorance and butchery, its dreaming cobbler hero a foolish believer and therefore a dangerous man, and the sermon to which it impels Nashe, for once breaking through his patently allographic narrator Jack Wilton, exposes a hope sternly chastened and the dismay and terror of incalculable loss. *The Unfortunate Traueller* is, therefore, a sharp and significant allotropy in humanist fiction; and its newly fashioned poetics stemming from fused classical and patristic roots is a desperate search for a properly urgent entelechy of the world as a humanist's hell. Against such dire needs, earlier forms of humanist poetics—the verbal games of More or Gascoigne that are exuberant and fearless, the remote providential fantasies of Greene, and the poetic philosophizing of Sidney—seem too distant and so unarguably irrelevant. None of them, Nashe implies in *The Unfortunate Traueller,* admits the seriousness of the endangered beliefs, humanist and Christian, at stake. Thus his own emergent skepticism, as McKerrow's statistics verify (*Works,* 4: 252 ff.), is firmly grounded in Cornelius Agrippa's *Of the vanitie and vncertaintie of Artes and Sciences,* translated by James Sanford in 1569. It is there that Agrippa poses the first fundamental challenge to the Second Sophistic, contending that

> there is nothing more noysome, nor more hurtefull to the Publike weale, then Learninge and Sciences.... al Sciences are nothing els, but the ordinaunces and opinions of men, so noysome as profitable, so pestilent as holsome, so ill as good, in no parte perfect, but doubtful and full of errour and contention.... *Rhetoricke* is nothing els, but an Arte of perswadinge and mouinge the affections, with subtile Eloquence, with exquisite colourings of woordes, and with a false likelihoode of the truth doth allure

the mindes of the simple, and leadeth them into the prison of erroure, seekinge to subuerte the sence of the truthe. [Sigs. C1, F3–F3v]

"In fine," Agrippa sums, "there was no state of common wealthe, whiche hath not in times paste bene turned vpside downe by this Arte." "None hath escaped vnhurte with the vice of Eloquence" (sig. F3). It is this striking image of the orderly world of humanism suddenly and violently set loose, disordered and disarrayed by historical circumstance and accident, that is so disturbing to the organic composition of a fictive perspective—that, in the acute observation of John Carey, so "dis-concerts."[48] For Nashe is keenly suspicious of unified thought or of any normative practice of language before the sheer *randomness* of life. His ardent prose hammers at the confinements of a traditional syntax[49] and forges strange compound words and neologisms to intensify the starkness of life, for, as he tells young pages in his preface to *The Unfortunate Traueller,* existence is merely a game of mumchance. Life, he means, is the reading of false (or loaded) dice thrown on the closed cover of the Acts and Monuments of life, denying the providential outlook that the Church Fathers proclaimed (sigs. A2–A2v; 2:207–8) and that he tries, manfully, scornfully, to recover. Merely to be alive, he concludes in the preface, is to be unfortunate: that is his powerful, vaticinal theme.

Such a fear for the threatened values of humanism is not what we first see in his fiction, nor was it, apparently, Nashe's original intention. For he begins his novel in precisely those ways we have been tracing throughout our study of humanist poetics, aligning it with older humanist works. His dedicatory epistle to Wriothesley, earl of Southampton, means to identify this book's Silenus, for Nashe addresses him as his "Ingenuous honorable Lord" (sig. A2; 2:201)—that is, variously *ingenious* or *ingenuous*, the newest wise fool.[50] To this paradoxical patron, Nashe offers a paradoxical work, a "phantasticall Treatise" in which he nevertheless promises "some reasonable conueyance of historie." It is a letter following a custom known to "methodicall antiquity," which introduces a work of "a cleane different vaine." Such statements are not antithetical; but they are not congruent either: the wit comes in seeing how, as coupling ideas, they just miss firm jointure. The delicious quality of these potential equivocations is more fully realized in Nashe's diffidence about dedications in general, to which all this opens out. As with the multiple perspectives in the prefatory letters to *The Adventures of Master F. J.* we find, cheek by jowl, Nashe appearing to beg outrageously—yet in the end with explicit irony "A new brain, a new wit, a new stile, a new soule will I get mee, to canonize your name to posteritie, if in this my first attempt I be not taxed of presumption"—and, just as forcefully, presuming cocky self-righteousness: "Of your gracious fauor I

despaire not, for I am not altogether Fames out-cast" (sig. A2v; 2:202).
The tone here is also distinctively Rabelaisian. Nashe knew his Rabelais;[51]
and as R. G. Howarth remarks, "in his boisterous satire, his wild fancy, his
command of odd language," we too make the connection.[52] Nashe's version
of Rabelais's "Prologe," moreover, presents to us Jack Wilton as Nashe's
own version of Panurge (Greek *panourgos*, or knave), a rascal whose
journey across Europe will, in its course, test his cunning, challenge his
ideas, and transform his confidence and self-reliance into doubt, terror, and
despair before confronting him with the ultimate mysteries of existence. As
if to guarantee the similarity, Jack Wilton also tells us his story, poxy
boozers that we are, from an alehouse: "soft let me drinke before I go anie
further" (sig. A3; 2:209). Nashe's "prince of . . . purses" (sig. A3v; 2:210)
is, before the soldiers of Henry VIII as Panurge before the giants, the
epitome of learning and cleverness, "sole king of the cans and blacke iackes,
prince of the pigmeis" (sig. A3; 2:209).

Jack's narrative proper begins, then, as a nearly harmless rogue's
progress. The cutpurse turned confidence man relies solely on the
inventiveness and exuberance of his rhetoric to create out of nothing a local
habitation and a name: noting the pride of the cider merchant serving
Henry's troops, he swindles from him, on the grounds of a single speech,
enough refreshment for the whole camp (sigs. B1– B1v; 2:215). Jack's use
of colloquial language and unnatural natural history through darting
allusion; the pretense of friendship and the stern lesson in morality; the
assumption of authority by mere bravado and the conclusion by way of
self-fulfilling prophecy—it is all a dazzling display of classical oration with
an energy that is characteristic of Nashe. "But I haue done a thousand
better iests, if they had been bookt in order as they were begotten," Jack
boasts (sig. B2; 2:217). And then, without pause (or embarrassment), he
is off again, reporting with verve the trick he played on a captain who had
the ill luck to beat him at dice even when Jack's own dice were loaded.
Through a forensic speech Jack persuades the captain to spy on the enemy,
a mission of nearly certain death. In its various appeals to classical
allusions, to proverbs, to history, and to myth, in its use of periphrasis,
homoeoprophoron, and sententiae, in its audacious and fanciful rhetoric,
the oration might have come directly from the Second Sophistic. It is Jack's
most wonderful creation of all.

> Perhaps (quoth I) you may haue some fewe greasie Cauailiers that will
> seeke to disswade you from it; and they will not sticke to stand on their
> three halfe penny honour, swearing and staring that a man were better be
> a hangman than an Intelligencer, and call him a sneaking Eauesdropper,
> a scraping hedgecreeper, and a piperly pickethanke; but you must not be

discouraged by their talke, for the most part of these beggarly contemners of wit, are huge burlybond Butchers like *Aiax,* good for nothing but to strike right downe blowes on a wedge with a cleauing beetle, or stand hammering all day vpon barres of yron. The whelpes of a Beare neuer growe but sleeping, and these Beare-wards hauing bigge lims shall be preferd though they doo nothing. You haue read stories, (Ile be sworne he neuer lookt in booke in his life) howe many of the Romaine worthies were there that haue gone as Spialls into their Enemies Campe? *Vlysses, Nestor, Diomed,* went as spies together in the night into the Tents of *Rhaesus,* and intercepted *Dolon* the spie of the Troians: neuer any discredited the trade of Intelligencers but *Iudas,* and he hanged himselfe. Danger will put wit into any man. . . . I see in your face, that you wer born with the swallow to feed flying, to get much tresure and honor by trauell. None so fit as you for so important an enterprise: our vulgar polititians are but flies swimming on the streame of subtiltie superficially in comparison of your singularitie, their blinde narrow eyes cannot pierce into the profundity of hypocrisie, you alone with *Palamed,* can pry into *Vlysses* mad counterfeting, you can discerne *Achilles* from a chamber maide, though he be deckt with his spindle and distaffe: as *Ioue* dining with *Licaon* could not bee beguiled with humane flesh drest like meate, so no humane braine may goe beyond you, none beguile you, you gull all, all feare you, loue you, stoup to you. Therefore good sir be ruld by me, stoup your fortune so low, as to bequeath your selfe wholy to this business. [Sigs. B3–B3v; 2:220–22]

The expropriation of Ovid and Pliny, the use of puns, ambiguity, and irony, the fast switching of exempla, is the work of a master; not until the spectacle has subsided and a more mundane narrative resumed do we realize, if we realize at all, what Nashe has done with those humanist techniques employed in the icastic and fantastic fiction of More, Lyly, and Sidney. Nashe has consigned them to jest and to prank.

In this, he would seem to pattern himself after his early patron Robert Greene, whose latter-day "cony-catching" pamphlets witness events as a "play at mum-chaunce, or decoy" (*A Notable Discouery of Coosnage* [1591], sig. C3; 169),[53] rhetorically oriented encomia moriae that use humanist forms of rhetoric both to teach us and to gull us concerning the activities and techniques of the underworld. Either way, Greene confronts a threatening world, making us his conies, tricked into buying and studying his exposés convinced they are factual rather than easy (and meretricious) entertainment. At a deeper stratum, at the level where morality is no longer a theme but part of the subject matter, Greene's divided purpose is more urgent. Before a world spun awry, he is unable to remain didactic. It is a danger Nashe shares. The joke Jack Wilton plays on the cider merchant turns him into a pitiful creature who "fell hee on his knees, wrong his handes, and I thinke on my conscience, wepte out all the syder that he had dronke in a weeke before" (sig. A4v; 2:213): viewed from subsequent events, he is the first character in *The Unfortunate Traueller* to suffer from the sweating sickness, that slow demolishing of humanity.[54] Other grim possibilities also shadow these earlier, lighter moments of Nashe's work. For we learn that Jack's motive is never fun; it is always revenge. (In this he looks forward to Esdras and Cutwolfe.) The consequences of such acts of revenge are finally never comic; they are often painful. And with Jack's own whipping—"Then was I pitifully whipt for my holiday lye, though they made themselues merrie with it manie a Winters euening after" (sig. B1v; 2:216)—we are introduced to the first in a series of self-induced punishments that will increase, climaxing in the horrible execution of Cutwolfe. "In the meane time," Jack confesses, "*I liue in hope to scape the rope*" (Sig. B4; 2:222).

At first, then, Jack undermines order from within, but as his travels continue he finds the outer world even more chaotic—and more alien. He attempts to search the past for counsel, returning to the time of Henry VIII, at the first dawn of humanism. Jack recalls distinctly that at Rotterdam

> we met with aged learnings chiefe ornament, that abundant and super-ingenious clarke *Erasmus,* as also with merrie Sir *Thomas Moore* our Countriman. . . . what talke, what conference wee had then, it were here superfluous to rehearse, but this I can assure you, *Erasmus* in all his speeches seemed so much to mislike the indiscretion of Princes in preferring of parasite and fooles, that he decreed with himselfe to swim with the stream, and write a booke forthwith in commendation of follie. Quick witted Sir *Thomas Moore* traueld in a cleane contrarie prouince, for he seeing most common-wealths corrupted by ill custome, & that principalities were nothing but great piracies, which, gotten by violence and murther, were maintained by priuate vndermining and bloudshed, that in the cheefest flourishing kingdomes there was no equall or well deuided weale one with a nother, but a manifest conspiracie of rich men against poore men, procuring their owne vnlawfull commodites vnder the name and interest of the common-wealth: hee concluded with himselfe to lay downe a perfect plot of a common-wealth or gouernment, which he would intitle his *Vtopia* [Sig. D4v; 2:245–46]

The past for Jack, as for Nashe, supplies no model and offers little hope, even at its brightest moments. The discontent of Erasmus and More with the corrupted societies they continually study finally corrupts them as well: Jack subsequently tells us that More comes to believe in the magical powers of Agrippa, as author of *De occulto philosophia,*[55] asking him to see "the whole destructiō of Troy in a dreame" (sig. E3v; 2:253), while Erasmus requested to see *Tully* in that same grace and maiestie he pleaded his oration *pro Roscio Amerino*. Affirming that til in person he beheld his importunitie in pleading, hee woulde in no wise bee perswaded that anie man coulde carrie awaye a manifest case with rethorike so strangely. To *Erasmus* petition he easily condescended, & willing the doctors at such an houre to hold their conuocation, and euery one to keepe him in his place without mouing: at the time prefixed in entered *Tullie,* ascended his pleading place, and declaimed verbatim the forenamed oration, but with such astonishing amazement, with such feruent exaltation of spirit, with such soule-stirring iestures, that all his auditours were readie to install his guiltie client for a God. [Sig. E3; 2:252]

What this passage clearly conveys is that Jack is making the Grand Tour of humanist education only to find (as Sidney never did), that the world is now decayed and corrupt—the journey an infernal trip through Hell—where even the best of the humanists are reduced to magic and wizardry to confirm their beliefs. The distrust of Erasmus and his need to prove continually Cicero's effectiveness is a strong challenge even to the teachings of the Second Sophistic.

Jack's key visit to Erasmus and More is bounded by two significant passages—the murderous rebellion at Münster and the self-indulgent scholasticism practiced at Wittenberg—but it has no influence on either of them. Both, then, indicate that, even in their own day, the best of the humanists could not save a world run mad with its own schismatic causes. A source for Nashe's account of the battle of Münster is an actual history, the humanist Languet's *Cronicles,* which notes for 1534 how

The Anabaptistes caused great trouble and rufflyng in the north partes of Germanie, and at the citee Monstrere, chusyng to theyr kyng one Iohn a Leyde, exercised muche crueltee, expellynge other out of the citee, that would not condescende to theyr belefe. This Iohn a Leyde, in token that he had both heauenly and erthly power, gaue to his garde greene and blew, and had for his armes the figure of the worlde rounde with a sworde thrust through it. He maried hym selfe .xv. wyfes, and ordeined that other shuld haue as many as thei listed, and all other thinges to be common amongest theim.

The bishop of Monstre, by the ayde of other princis, besieged the citee against the rebellious Anabaptistes fiftene or sixtene monethes. In whiche tyme the stubburne and frowarde people susteined so great scarcitee, and hunger, that they beying aliue, were like dead corses, and did eate commonly dogges, cattes, mise, with other vile beastes, and sethyng hydes, leather, and olde showes [shoes], dyd poune the same, and made bread therof. After longe siege the citee was wonne, spoyled, and destroyed with greate crueltiee and slaughter of that wicked people. [1549 ed., sig. 4B2v]

Another of Nashe's references, the *Famovse Cronicle of oure time, called Sleidanes Commentaries,* Englished by John Davis (1560), gives an even fuller account (sigs. Aa1–3B5). For Sleidanus, the Anabaptist tyranny brooked no disbelievers: "they tyed them vnto trees, or pillers, and shotte them in with dagges, theyr highe prophet greatly commendinge them & wylling them that would do God pleasure to shoote first: howbeit others were otherwise murthered" (sig. Aa5). The shock and anger of Lanquet and of Sleidanus's earlier description of atrocities well up in Jack Wilton's protracted denunciation of the Anabaptists, which has all the righteous scorn of a Jeremiah:

> nothing but stearne reuenge in their eares, made them so eager, that their handes had no leasure to aske counsell of their effeminate eyes, their swordes, theyr pikes, their bills, their bowes, their caleeuers slew, empierced, knockt downe, shot through, and ouerthrew as manie men euerie minute of the battell, as there falls eares of corne before the sythe at one blow: yet all their weapons so slaying, empiercing, knocking downe, shooting through, ouer-throwing, dissouleioyned not halfe so manie, as the hailing thunder of the great Ordinance: so ordinarie at euerie foot-step was the imbrument of yron in bloud, that one could hardly discern heads from bullets, or clottred haire from mangled flesh hung with goare. [Sig. D2v; 2:240–41]

Jack (or Nashe, interrupting his maieutic narrator) thus startles us by comparing the age of humanism to the age of Nero (sig. D1; 2:236) and these religious rebels to the Cynics (sig. D1; 2:237). Like Cardinal Wolsey, John of Leiden incites his own end: "Qui in suas poenas ingeniosus erat" (sig. D1v; 2:238). The larger rebellion also reminds Jack of the apocalypse: "But I pray you, ... Doth not Christ say, that before the Latter day the Sunne shall be turned into darknesse, and the Moone into bloud?" (sig. C4v; 2:235). His outrage is against the reality of human nature that permits such slaughter, antagonistic to the religious beliefs promulgated by the humanists and by the Church Fathers: "When Christ said, *the kingdome of heauen must suffer violence,*" Jack says, as nascent exegete,

> he meant not the violence of long babling praiers, nor the violence of tedious inuectiue Sermons without wit, but the violence of faith, the violence of good works, the violence of patient suffering. The ignorant snatch the kingdome of heauen to themselues with greedines, when we with all our learning sinke into hell. [Sig. C4; 2:234]

"When we with all our learning sinke into hell": *pace* humanist and patristic thought, men for Jack refuse to respect tradition; they no longer pay homage to the orderly world of reason. "They will digest no grapes of great Bishoprikes forsooth, because they cannot tell how to come by them, they must shape their cotes, good mean according to their cloath and doe as they say, not as they wold" (sig. D1v; 2:238). Moreover, "Church robbers in these dayes haue made a den of theeues": the relatively inconsequential game of mumchance, the opening image of *The Unfortunate Traueller,* now becomes a wicked "casting [of] lots for Church liuinges, as the souldiers cast lottes for Christes garments" (sig. D1v; 2:238). To this hostile denunciation of the Anabaptists' New Jerusalem, Nashe brings all the scorn of a disillusioned humanist who sees in the ruthless, maniacal John of Leiden the exploitation of a suffering humanity for his own private passions, and in his obliteration of hierarchy and degree for communism, in his denial of self-restraint in his numerous marriages, an infernal misreading of the *Utopia,* a total undermining of those values most cherished by the humanist tradition: order, tolerance, and open debate.[56]

In seeing the awful consequences of fallen humanity—its corruption and irrationality—Jack (and we) naturally seeks the cause. The Münster tyranny puts new weight on Erasmus's attempts to portray folly and More's argument for Utopia in the very next scene; and their relative failure anticipates the final scene of the series—the fatuous scholasticism Jack encounters in the following episode. Wittenberg presents Jack with a spectacle of pseudo-humanists whose talk renders them totally unproductive. He first hears the university orator welcome the duke of Saxony with an inflated speech that "was all by patch & by peecemeale stolne out of *Tully,* and he must pardon them, though in emptying their phrase bookes the world emptied his intrailes" (sig. E1; 2:246). He watches the sycophantic students, crying their flattery "mightily in their gibrige, lyke a companie of beggers" (sig. E1; 2:247). He sees an academic production of *Acolastus* "so filthily acted, so leathernly set forth, as would haue moued laughter in Heraclitus. . . . The onely thing they did well, was the prodigall childs hunger, most of their schollers being hungerly kept" (sig. E2; 2:249–50). He witnesses the disputation between Luther and Carlstadt in which gesture replaces language altogether, a technique subsequently parodied by seven other "Grosse plodders . . . that had some learning and reading, but no wit to make vse of it" (sig. D2v; 2:251). Such disappointing fruits of humanist education serve, however, as background for Nashe's finest prosopographia, that of

A bursten belly inkhorne orator called *Vander[h]ulke,* [who] they pickt out to present . . . an oration, one that had a sulpherous big swolne large face, like a Saracen, eyes lyke two kentish oysters, a mouth that opened as wide euery time he spake, as one of those old knit trap doores, a beard as though it had ben made of a birds neast pluckt in peeces, which consisteth of strawe, haire, and durt mixt together. He was apparelled in blacke leather new licoured, & a short gowne without anie gathering in the backe, faced before and behinde with a boistrous beare skin, and a red night-cap on his head. [Sigs. E1–E1v; 2:247–48]

His welcoming speech to the duke of Saxony shows where the energies of humanism were being misdirected, and how foolish they were when aped.

Welcome to Witenberg: welcome sayd I, O orificall rethorike wipe they euerlasting mouth, and affoord me a more Indian metaphor than that for the braue princely bloud of a Saxon. Oratorie vncaske the bard hutch of thy complements, and with the triumphantest troupe in thy treasurie doe trewage vnto him. What impotent speech with his eight partes may not specifie this vnestimable gift holding his peace, shall as it were (with teares I speak it) do wherby as it may seeme or appeare, to manifest or declare, and yet it is, and yet it is not, and yet it may be a diminitiue oblation meritorious to your high pusillanimitie and indignitie. Why should I goe gadding and fisgigging after firking flantado emfibologies, wit is wit, and good will is good will. With all the wit I haue, I here, according to the premises, offer vp vnto you the cities generall good will, which is a gilded Can, in manner and forme folowing, for you, and the heirs of your bodie lawfully begotten, to drinke healths in. [Sig. E1v; 2:248]

Vanderhulke's enthusiastic misapplications of the standard rhetorical handbooks—his absurd use of paradox, climax, parenthesis, anaphora, apostrophe, periodicity, and alliteration—might be, like the debate of gestures, something out of Rabelais: abandoned, exaggerated burlesque. But, following the visits to the Anabaptists and to Erasmus and More, the anticlimax is almost unbearably sad. The portrait of More here is foreshortened to a handful of lines, squeezed out by Jack's obsessive account of the fatuity of Vanderhulke. What is more dismaying, Luther's presence in the same farrago of observations betokens a nascent Protestant rebel like John of Leiden and shows us the environment from which he sprang. It is nothing like the Rome and the Byzantium of the Second Sophistic, when the Greek Church Fathers took over learning from their Greek and Roman predecessors. "The ignorant snatch the kingdome of heauen to themselues with greedines, when we with all our learning sinke into hell" (sig. C4; 2:234). Together the panels of Münster, Rotterdam, and Wittenberg constitute a triptych on humanism gone badly wrong, beginning with the disastrous consequences and tracking these back to certain possible causes in the longest and most emphatic passage in the first half of *The Unfortunate Traueller*.

Nashe's early and extended concern with the fundamental need for humanist learning and his despair over the depraved condition of its thought and rhetoric reveal other Senecan models that are barely contained in this splintering fiction: the humanists' Grand Tour and the Protestants' pilgrimage are both corrupted here.[57] So wretched has man's condition become that standard humanist treatises like Jerome Turler's *Traveiler* (1575), with its similar title, now look hopelessly naive. Turler argues traditionally that

> Experience is the greatest parte of humane wisedome, and the same is increased by traueil: I suppose there is no man will deney, but that a mā may become the wiser by traueiling. . . .
> The commoditie and profit of traueiling is dispersed throughout and in all things of the world, and there is no humane action or trade to be founde, but it may bee bettered and holpen by traueil. [Sigs. A3, C4v]

A kind of easy assurance that only good can come of such travel is frequent in letters of the period too. Even Aretino proposes the traditional view.

> Non è dubbio, che fino a i principi douerebbono per vn'tempo cacciare i figli al guadagno del pane altrui; la discrettione, il senno, i costumi, le virtù, e la riputationi seminate ne i compi del mondo, sono vsufrutti di qualunche peregrina per l'vniuerso; e per giunta de gli acquisti, che la forte propone a chi si diletta di vagare ne i siti de quella, e di questa ragione l'huomo nobilita lo essere, e rimbellisce la sembianza, tal che ritorna d'onde si partì con vna gentilezza strana, e con vna arte nuoua: e perche in ciascun gesto suo si scorge la degnità de la creanza è da ognuno guardato, e da tutti reuerito non altrimenti.

> Without doubt, even princes should send their children away for a while to earn their bread elsewhere. Wisdom, judgement, courtesy, virtue and fame are sown in the fields of the world and are harvested by those who journey abroad. As well as the acquisitions that come his way, the man who likes to wander from one part of the world to another thereby both improves his outward appearance and ennobles his soul; and so he returns whence he came with unwonted courtesy and new knowledge. And since his every gesture reveals the excellence of his breeding, he is respected and admired by all.[58]

The belief in the Grand Tour as the final, profitable stage of a young man's studies and preparation for life was, in fact, Italian in origin. But Nashe, schooled by the disciples of Roger Ascham of St. John's College, Cambridge, knew otherwise; and for Jack Wilton the world is initially fascinating, mainly antagonistic, and ultimately mysterious and threatening.

A somewhat closer model for *The Unfortunate Traueller* is *The .xi. Bookes of the Golden Asse, Conteininge the Metamorphosie of Lucius*

Apuleius, a collection of Milesian tales, Menippean and Varronian satires that depict episodic rogues' escapades in a ramshackle structure that resembles *The Unfortunate Traueller:* "At ego tibi sermone Milesio varias fabulas conseram auresque tuas benivolas lepido susurro permulceam," Apuleius begins; "In this Milesian tale I shall string together diverse stories, and delight your kindly ears with a pleasant history."[59] The translation from Latin by William Adlington first published in 1566, a fiction Nashe knew from the beginning of his career,[60] omits this preface. But the text closely resembles Nashe's fiction in its brilliant medley of reality and romance, of wit and pathos, of fantasy and observation, all conveyed in a florid rhetoric studded with neologisms in a way the Second Sophistic enjoyed. The main tale of Lucius, an Erasmian story of a wise fool that is both mock seriousness and serious mockery, is also very much to the point. *The Golden Asse* begins as a jest book characterized by an exuberance for life, experimentation with language, improvised spontaneity, and structural loose ends. But once Lucius's travels as an ass begin, the book grows increasingly savage. Like Jack, Lucius suffers a rude mental and spiritual awakening in the process of graduated victimization. His fragmented adventures also teach him the open lust and greed, moral and sexual perversion, treachery, torture, and butchery that characterize human nature. There is the mutilation of Socrates, whose heart is pulled out by Meroe through a sword wound in his throat (1), the loss of Thelyphron's ear and nose (2), and the thief's loss of his arm when it is cut off by his fellow conspirators so as to free him and save them all (4). Common to the wild dervish of episodes is this singular emphasis on man's cruelty—in the vicious behavior of the robbers, the sadistic boy, the catamite priests, and the baker's wife—that is woefully imbalanced by the kindness awarded Lucius by the nurseryman and Thiasus. Life only disillusions. "I gaue great thākes to my Assy fourme," Lucius tells us; "in yt by yt meane I had seene the experiēce of many thinges, and was become more wise (notwithstāding the great misery and labour which I dayly susteined)" (sigs. Aa4v–Bb1), and the priest agrees: "Neither did thy noble lignage, thy dignitie, neither thy doctrine any thing peruaile" (sig. Ii1). In Books 4–6 (placed correspondingly to the Münster-Rotterdam-Wittenberg section in Nashe) Apuleius tells the nearly independent story of Cupid and Psyche—an episode often detached in the Renaissance and circulated widely as fable, romance, or allegory—in which the prototypes for human behavior are located in Psyche's betrayal of Cupid and in the goddess's bribery for Paris. The descent into human purgatory in *The Golden Asse* ends in joy as Lucius is at last transformed back to a man, climbing the chain of being toward a final religious conversion to Isis. But there is no such compensatory good fortune at the conclusion of *The Unfortunate Traueller*: a sure measure of Nashe's own despair.

That *The Unfortunate Traueller* means to portray the Grand Tour gone sour there can be no doubt. "The long dissertation of 'the banished earl,' " which Steane finds "central" (Introduction, p. 33), corresponds precisely in length and tone to the earlier denunciation of the Anabaptists (although Jack is now the object of concern), the Eubulus-like earl supplying precepts that are the deliberate counterpart to the earlier action in the Münster-Rotterdam-Wittenberg section of the work.[61] "Thus he examined and schoold me," Jack recalls (sig. I3v; 2:297). The earl draws on classical wisdom as, earlier, Jack had turned to Scripture. He compares Jack to Icarus and cites Epicharmus: yet "Beleeue nothing, trust no man" (sig. I4; 2:298). The earl's *propositio* sums compactly his speech, alluding to the Spaniard Esdras and the Italian Bartol, to Apuleius, and to the chief threat to humanism imaged in John of Leiden's despotism (sigs. I3v–I4; 2:297).[62] In the *confirmatio*, the advice is more confined, and patently humanist.

> *Non formosus erat, sed erat facundus Vlysses: Vlysses* the long Traueller was not amiable, but eloquent. Some alledge, they trauell to learne wit, but I am of this opinion, that as it is not possible for anie man to learne the Art of Memorie, whereof *Tully, Quintillian, Seneca,* and *Hermannus Buschius* haue written so manie Bookes, except hee haue a naturall memorie before, so is it not possible for anie man to attain anie great wit by trauell, except he haue the grounds of it rooted in him before. That wit which is thereby to be perfected or made staid, is nothing but *Experientia longa malorum*, the experience of manie euils. [Sig. I4v; 2:299]

This speech alone rises above the many scenes of the second half of *The Unfortunate Traueller* that, as David Kaula points out, "comprise a vision strongly suggestive of the traditional iconographic images of Hell, images such as those of Brueghel and Bosch, which surrealistically intensify the weak and sinful condition of humanity by depicting it in terms of physical anguish and grotesque deformity.[63]

Death and decay likewise seem present everywhere. Even "the banished earl," Nashe's sardonic portrait of the outdated humanist, sounds a startling, awesome death knell. "Get thee home, my yong lad," he tells Jack, having preserved him from hanging, "lay thy bones peaceably in the sepulcher of thy fathers, waxe olde in ouerlooking thy grounds, be at hand to close the eyes of thy kinred" (sigs. K1v–K2; 2:303): he saves Jack from one death only to confront him with many more. And such an open analogy indicates those more implicit. Jack's self-proclaimed scourging of evil reminds us of the motives that, earlier in Jack's fiction, so drive the Anabaptists, where beliefs are also corrupted by baser motives of personal revenge, as Madelon S. Gohlke has remarked.[64] John of Leiden's narrow escape, in fact, anticipates Jack Wilton's. Jack's "life," as Nashe's subtitle clearly announces, is the chief, the *only,* subject of the novel because each event to which he is witness or in which he is participant not ony affects him but reflects him—and helps us to define that life, from his spiritual condition to his mental condition to his physical vulnerability as the novel proceeds. As man becomes corrupted or victimized, then, the novel preaches revenge (notably against Marignano and Münster but by analogy against Thérouanne, Hampton Court, Wittenberg, and Venice as well). And in the conclusion at Rome, in a series of events that will involve the wicked greed of Zacharie and the wicked lust of Juliana with the papacy itself, the relationship is intensified. Indeed, it becomes total when Cutwolfe usurps divine order and so assures his own damnation, as Gohlke also argues (p. 405), This is Jack's last and decisive lesson before his return to the English army at the fiction's close.

At such a "re-turning," this "life" concludes. For the banished earl's speech, grounded in the patristic commentary popularized by the Second Sophistic, makes this the central issue of the novel's title passage.

> The first traueller was *Cain,* and he was called a vagabond runnagate on the face of the earth. Trauaile (like the trauaile wherein smithes put wilde horses when they shoo them) is good for nothing but to tame and bring men vnder.
>
> God had no greater curse to lay vpon the *Israelites,* than by leading them out of their owne countrey to liue as slaues in a strange land. That which was their curse, we Englishmen count our chiefe blessednes; hee is no bodie that hath not traueld: wee had rather liue as slaues in another land, croutch and cap, and be seruile to euerie ielous Italians and proud Spaniards humor, where we may neither speak, looke, nor doo anie thing, but what pleaseth them, than liue as freemen and Lords in our owne Countrey.
>
> He that is a traueller must haue the backe of an asse to beare all, a tung like the taile of a dog to flatter all, the mouth of a hogge to eate what is set before him, the eare of a merchant to heare all and say nothing: and if this be not the highest step of thraldome, there is no libertie or freedome.
>
> It is but a milde kinde of subiection to be the seruant of one master at once: but when thou hast a thousand thousand masters, as the veriest botcher, tinker, or cobler freeborne will dominere ouer a forreiner, and thinke to bee his better or master in companie; then shalt thou finde there is no such hell as to leaue thy fathers house (thy naturall habitation) to liue in the land of bondage. [Sigs. I3v–I4; 2:297–98]

Travel is now likened to primal sin—and in a fiction that severely tries humanist thought. Lyly's sense of travel as education, Greene's sense of travel as providing occasions, Sidney's sense of wonder, and of travel as a test, are all fundamentally challenged. To this too Gohlke testifies. "The episode involving the English earl," she writes, "draws together the narrative and thematic concerns of the tale in a way which suggests that wit inevitably participates in the pattern of pride and punishment, which in turn structures life as a series of inescapable misfortunes" (p. 406). Wisdom is a matter of humility, not pride; of accepting, not searching; indeed, our destinies will be, by work's end, pronouncedly *un*searchable. The antithesis—constant travel, constant travail, constant *exposure*—only brings about, from the blood of Thérouanne and the sickness in London onward, a sense of contingency and tragedy that clearly presage the Last Judgment.

Such hideous events with their images threatening us at so many turns in *The Unfortunate Traueller* are more comprehensible when we realize that during the book's composition London was caught in yet another swift, merciless, and irresistible epidemic of plague. It must have seemed endless to men like Nashe, a visitation not unlike that described so powerfully in the opening pages of Boccaccio's *Decameron* (which bears striking similarities),[65] for 149 died in London during the week of 17 July, 666 died (454 from the plague) the week of 24 July, and 1,603 (1,130 from the plague) the week of 5 August [66]—all portents of the damnation of man and the Last Judgment for many. Predictably, then, the city was flooded with pamphlets and sermons of the kind Nashe's father must have familiarized him with in plague-ridden Norfolk.[67] In *The Poore Mans Iewell,* for example, reissued at the start of the sickness in 1592, Thomas Brasbridge claims:

> I could not go out of mine house, either at the fore, or backe doores, neither on the right hand, nor on the left: but I must needs haue passed by an infected house, next, or very neere adioining vnto mine owne. Yea both I, and my wife had schollers that fell sicke at our feet. [Sig. A2v]

The preacher William Cupper, in *Certaine Sermons* (1592), blamed man's obvious mortality on his own corruption. "We cannot flie so fast, but that the Lord is able to ouertake vs" (sig. F8v). And Anthony Anderson, in *An Approved Medicine against the deserued Plague* (1593), offers an extended prayer: "O Lord heare vs, and heale vs, . . . for our head Citie is sicke, her Sister Cities grone vnder this burden, their neighbor people are turned to their earth, and no part is free, from the noysome pestilence" (sig. B1v).

Nashe fled London—first to Archbishop Whitgift's palace at Croydon in 1592, then to Lord Carey's home on the Isle of Wight in 1593.[68] But the plague remains, in the form of a liturgical lament in *Christs Teares* and in Nashe's best poem, *"Adieu, farewell earths blisse"* in *Summers last will:*

> Beauty is but a flowre,
> Which wrinckles will deuoure,
> Brightnesse falls from the ayre,
> Queenes haue died yong, and faire,
> Dust hath closde Helens eye,
> I am sick, I must dye,
>   *"Lord, haue mercy on vs"*
> [Sig. H1v; 3:283]

This dirge for all humanity is sharply controlled in its brief and powerful lines, but even so the shift from third person to first person singular is abrupt and painful; it is even more startling when the last line shifts to first person plural, includes *us* in the choric word of its litany. Such motifs also erupt into open description when, in *The Unfortunate Traueller,* Jack reaches Rome.

> So it fel out, that it being a vehement hot summer when I was a soiourner there, there entered such a hotspurd plague as hath not bin heard of: why it was but a word and a blowe, Lord haue mercie vpon vs and he was gone. Within three quarters of a yeere in that one citie there died of it a hundred thousand, looke in *Lanquets* chronicle and you shall finde it. . . . All daye and all night long carre-men did nothing but go vp and downe the streets with their carts and cry, Haue you anie dead bodies to bury and had many times out of one house their whole loding: one graue was the sepulchre of seuen score, one bed with the alter wheron whole families were offered. . . . Some dide sitting at their meate, others as they were asking counsell of the phisition for theyr friends. I sawe at the house where I was hosted a maide bring her master warme broth for to comfort him, and shee sinke downe dead her selfe ere he had halfe eate it up. [Sigs. H3v–H4; 2:286–87][69]

This plague is analogous to the sweating sickness of 1517 that Nashe uses to introduce England in the work—and it is the first scene to strike the book's major key.[70] We are fortunate too in being able to measure Nashe's troubled vision by comparing his likely sources. Languet records simply,

> 1517. Many dyed in England of the sweating sickenesse and especially about London. [Sig. 3Z2v]

There is also Holinshed.

> This maladie was so cruell, that it killed some within three houres, some within two houres, some merrie at dinner, and dead at supper. [1598 ed., 3:262]

Finally, Nashe knew John Stow.

> About the feast of Lammas began the sweating sicknes, of the which many men died sodainly in the beginning thereof, and this plague continued till Michelmas, many died thereof in the Court, as the Lord *Clinton,* the Lord *Grey* of Wilton, and many other knights and gentlemen, by reason of which contagious sicknes, Michelmas terme was adiorned. After this to wit in the winter was a great death of pestilence almost ouer all England in euery town more or lesse, wherfore the K. kept himself with small company about him, willing to haue no resort to the court for feare of infection. [1592 *Annales,* sig. 3K1]⁷¹

Next to such relatively straightforward accounts, Nashe's graphic description is intense and grotesque—concentrated, visual, pained, and twice as long.

> Felt makers and Furriers, what the one with the hot steame of their wooll new taken out of the pan, and the other with the contagious heat of their slaughter budge and connie-skinnes, died more thicke than of the pestelence: I haue seene an old woman at that season hauing three chins, wipe them all away one after another, as they melted to water, and left hir selfe nothing of a mouth but an vpper chap. Looke how in May or the heat of Summer we lay butter in water for feare it should melt away, so then were men faine to wet their clothes in water as Diers doo, and hide themselues in Welles from the heat of the Sunne. . . . Mazons paid nothing for haire to mixe their lyme, nor Glouers to stuffe their balls with, for then they had it for nothing, it dropped off mens heads and beards faster than anie Barber could shaue it. . . . I heard where they dyde vp all in one Familie, and not a mothers childe escapde, insomuch as they had but an Irish rugge lockt vp in a presse, and not laid vpon anie bed neither, if those that were sicke of this maladie slept of it, they neuer wakde more. . . . This Mortalitie first began amongst old men, for they taking a pride to haue their breasts loose basted with tedious beards, kept their houses so hot with their hayry excrements, that not so much but their verie walls sweat out salt-peeter with the smothering perplexitie: nay a number of them had meruailous hot breaths, which sticking in the briers of their bushie beards, could not choose, but (as close aire long imprisoned) ingender corruption. [Sigs. C2–C2v; 2:229–30]

There are several starts at humor, but the wit is macabre and a laugh sticks in the throat. Little wonder: among the humanists of the first generation, this epidemic had even disturbed Erasmus and frightened More.

> Sic necesse fuit prioribus praesentes addere, quibus constare tibi ratio possit, simul vti quid nunc agatur apud nos intelligas: qui si vnquam alias, nunc maxime in maerore et periculo versamur, multis vndique morientibus,

omnibus fere qui Oxoniae, qui Cantabrigiae, qui Londini sunt, intra pauces dies decumbentibus, amissis plurimis optimis atque honestissimis amicis.

"We are in the greatest sorrow and danger. Multitudes are dying all round us . . . and we have lost many of our best and most honoured friends," More writes on 19 August[72]—and their protegé Ammonius died of it within eight hours. So did Colet. The figure left with only an upper chap is named in *Christs Teares* (sig. H4; 2:69)—he is Death; but the iconograph is clear from the start. And what is presented here is an aggregate of ugly deaths; it is a vision of Hell.

We can understand, then, Jack's hasty departure from an infected England: "Take breath how they would, I vowd to tarrie no longer among them" (sig. C3; 2:231). (It is a forceful parallel that his other abrupt departure is from Luther and Carlstadt [sig. E2v; 2:250]; by the end of the novel, his *normal* behavior is flight.) Before this awful epidemic, Jack's only experience with death has been the siege of Thérouanne—and then he was far away, on the outskirts (sig. A3; 2:209), and he can laugh off the battles: "I folowed the court or the camp, or the campe and the court, when *Turwin* lost her maidenhead, and opened her gates to more than *Iane Trosse* did" (sig. A3; 2:209).[73] Yet even here—in presumed moments of mirth—there is violation. Now, running from England, Jack enters the larger world of the humanists, one Nashe will transform into a panorama of horror.

First, Jack is drawn to the French rout of the Swiss at Marignano, an engagement that "[shattered] their military reputation," as J. J. Scarisbrick has it.[74] Again Nashe enlarges on what is most terrible in it.

> I saw a wonderfull spectacle of blood-shed on both sides, here vnweeldie *Switzers* wallowing in their gore, like an Oxe in his dung, there the sprightly *French* sprawling and turning on the stained grasse, like a Roach new taken out of the streame: all the ground was strewed as thicke with Battle-axes, as the Carpenters yard with chips, the Plaine appeared like a quagmyre, ouerspred as it was with trampled dead bodies. [Sig. C3; 2:231]

After Marignano there is Münster, after that Rotterdam and Wittenberg— all the countries important to the Northern Renaissance as prelude to Italy: to Venice, Rome, and Bologna. Each Italian city has its own wretched example of inhumanity, too, and its own way of undermining Jack's safety.[75] Venice is imaged under the management of Tabitha the Temptress, who deals in the commerce of human flesh. With her accomplice Petro de camp Frego, "a notable practitioner in the pollicie of baudrie" (sig. E4v; 2:255), Tabitha's whorehouse is made as sacred as a church (sig. E4v; 2:255); that she attempts to trade Jack for Surrey (or "Surrey" for "Jack") so that they wind up negotiating *themselves* by her treacherous and deathly calculations (and that their commerce is in counterfeit money, none of them innocent) only emphasizes the general perversion and social decay.

In Rome, the plague is associated with the Spaniard Esdras of Granada,[76] "a notable Bandetto, authorised by the pope," who with an accomplice ravages homes and women (sig. H4; 2:287). Now violation increases geometrically; the vision here is the vision of Tertullian in the *De Spectaculis*—and of St. John's Revelation. But Nashe does not let us escape into generalities. He describes in detail Esdras's most violent act, the rape of Heraclide, which Jack spies from his own bedroom.

> Dismissing her haire from his fingers, and pinnioning her elbowes therwithall, she strugled, she wrested, but all was in vaine. . . . On the hard boords he threw her, and vsed his knee as an yron ramme to beat ope the two leaued gate of her chastitite. Her husbands dead bodie he made a pillow to his abhomination. [Sigs. I1v–12; 2:292]

Like Livy's descriptions of violation and assault, Nashe captures the full event: Heraclide's death speech, her irrational attempts to understand what is happening to her; driving her to mental and physical collapse and suicide (sigs. I2–I3; 2:293–95). Jack is mistakenly arrested for Heraclide's death, barely escapes hanging, falls into Zadock's cellar, and is sold by him to Zacharie to be sliced up for anatomical lessons—a new roach out of his element and on display. Again he is saved—this time by the pope's own mistress, Juliana, who wishes to use his body, too, to satisfy her insatiable lust.[77] Sins and horrors compound. One day, while Juliana obscenely prepares herself "like an angel" (sig. L3v; 2:317) for the solemn St. Peter's Day processional, we are met with the execution of Zadock (sigs. L2v–L3; 2:315–16). Once more graphic detail seems obsessive, until we recall the similar pictorialism in the writings of Tertullian and Lactantius: the alliance with the Church Fathers could, in Nashe's day, not be plainer. We have lost his points of reference, but the Tudors would not have done so. Against such a vision of torture, even the martyrdom of St. Stephen, which inspired *Christs Teares,* seems very tame.

Yet the worst is still to come. Fleeing to Bologna, Jack arrives in time to see the execution of Cutwolfe. Zadock was tortured and killed because he was a Jew; Cutwolfe is killed because (for good enough reason) he slew the villain Bartol. But in Nashe's world motives do not matter; only cruelty does. Of Cutwolfe's executioner Jack says,

> old excellent he was at a bone-ach. At the first chop with his wood-knife would he fish for a mans heart, and fetch it out as easily as a plum from the

bottome of a porredge pot. He would cracke neckes as fast as a cooke cracks egges: a fidler cannot turne his pin so soone as he would turne a man of the ladder: brauely did he drum on this *Cutwolfes* bones, not breaking them outright, but like a sadler knocking in of tackes, iarring on them quaueringly with his hammer a great while together. No ioint about him but with a hatchet he had for the nones he disioynted halfe, and then with boyling lead souldered vp the wounds from bleeding: his tongue he puld out, least he should blaspheme in his torment: venimous stinging wormes hee thrust into his eares to keep his head rauingly occupied: with cankers scruzed to peeces hee rubd his mouth and his gums: no lim of his but was lingeringly splinterd in shiuvers. In this horror left they him on the wheele as in hell: where yet liuing he might beholde his flesh legacied amongst the foulnes of the aire. [Sigs. M3v–M4; 2:327][78]

Next to Lyly's wittier, metaphorical use of anatomizing, Nashe's literal description is now morally bankrupt. It is Jack's last adventure and the end of his Grand Tour utterly corrupted by fallen man.[79]

Humanist belief in man fails Nashe; but he tries desperately to hold on to humanist poetry. Against the atrocities of Jack's journey he arranges selected examples of art. The most important, amidst the orchards, fish ponds, and roof gardens of Rome so open to later violation, is "a summer banketting house belonging to a merchaunt, that was the meruaile of the world, & could not be matcht except God should make another paradise" (sig. H2v; 2:282). The golden world of art here produces a second nature, such as Sidney prescribes in his *Defence*.

It was builte round of greene marble, like a Theater with-out, within there was a heauen and earth comprehended both vnder one roofe, the heauen was a cleere ouerhanging vault of christall, wherein the Sunne and Moone, and each visible Starre had his true similitude, shine, scituation, and motion, and, by what enwrapped arte I cannot conceiue, these spheares in their proper orbes obserued their circular wheelings and turnings, making a certaine kinde of soft angelical murmering musicke in their often windings & going about, which musick the philosophers say in the true heauen by reason of the grosenes of our senses, we are not capable of. [Sig. H2v; 2:282–83]

Animate life is also paradisiacal, and in biblical terms: "the Wolfe glad to let the Lambe lye vpon hym to keepe him warme, the Lyon suffering the Asse to cast hys legge ouer him.... Serpents were as harmlesse to mankinde" (sig. H3; 2:284). But Jack (and Nashe) is not easily fooled; he has seen too much and now knows too much. Perfect art is perfect on earth because it is unnatural. It is artificial and mechanical.

The flore was painted with the beautifullest flouers that euer mans eie admired. ... Other trees that bare no fruit, were set in iust order. ... On the wel clothed boughs of this conspiracie of pine trees against the resembled Sun beames, were pearcht as many sortes of shrill breasted birdes ... Who though there were bodies without soules, and sweete resembled substances without sense, yet by the mathematicall experimentes of long siluer pipes secretlye inrinded in the intrailes of the boughs whereon they sate, and vndiscerneablie conuaid vnder their bellies into their small throats sloaping, they whistled and freely carold theyr naturall field note. [Sig. H2v; 2:283]

The irony of the metalworks reaches out to expose the whole contrivance. It is the height of pride, and of sin, this mechanical Paradise that would improve God's providential plan. It is no coincidence that Jack finds it in Rome, home of the papacy; or that it is all style and no substance, the religious equivalent of Puritan sermonizing and Ramist rhetoric; or that it returns us to Adam and Eve—and Cain and Abel. Here the failings of both humanist and patristic learning meet:[80] earthly Paradise is envisioned as another act of cony-catching.

The art of the summer banqueting house fails to respond sufficiently to the corrupted life in the natural world outside it, but Jack's praise of the poet Surrey seems at once a more serious and a more permanent possibility. The poet's work is eternal, from Jack's perspective a pure alternative to the mundane and the mechanical.

Destinie neuer defames hir selfe but when shee lets an excellent Poet die, if there bee anie sparke of Adams Paradized perfection yet imbred vp in the breastes of mortall men, certainelie God hath bestowed that his perfectest image on Poets. None come so neere to God in wit, none more contemne the world, *vatis auarus non temere est animus,* sayth *Horace, versus amat, hoc studet vnum,* Seldome haue you seene anie Poet possessed with auarice, only verses he loues, nothing else he delights in: and as they contemne the world, so contrarilie of the mechanicall world are none more contemned. Despised they are of the worlde, because they are not of the world: their thoughts are exalted aboue the worlde of ignorance and all earthly conceits. [Sig. D3; 2:242]

Sidney's conception of poetry lies directly behind this passage; and Nashe may have in mind the specific judgment in Sidney's *Defence of Poesie* that there are "in the Earle of *Surreis Lirickes,* manie thinges tasting of a Noble birth, and worthie of a Noble minde" (sig. H3v; 112).[81] It is the Surrey of the perfected English Latinity, as in his uncompleted translation of Vergil, with the formality of phrase, control of dignified diction, and rhetorically arranged passages—what Thomas Warton sees as elegant and precise[82] and what Nashe must have seen as an exemplar of the Ciceronian (and Gorgian) standards for the Second Sophistic. Then Surrey speaks, not as this classicist or in the arresting tone of the elegy to Wyatt—"W. resteth here, that quick could neuer rest"[83]—but as a flatulent Petrarchist.

> Thou knowst statelie *Geraldine*. . . . Her high exalted sunne beames haue set the Phenix neast of my breast on fire, and I my selfe haue brought Arabian spiceries of sweet passions and praises to furnish out the funerall flame of my follie. Those who were condemned to be smothered to death by sincking down into the softe bottome of an high built bedde of Roses, neuer dide so sweet a death as I shoulde die, if hir Rose coloured disdaine were my deathes-man. [Sig. D3v; 2:243]

The empty artifice of Surrey-character's pronouncements here have little in common with the careful, sweetened transliterations of the actual Surrey's best Petrarchan sonnets; they remind us instead of Gascoigne's callow F. J.; and here Surrey-character's imaginary and indulgent descriptions of death are obscene, coming just subsequent to the battle of Münster as they do. Again Nashe conveys irony through juxtaposition; and again Jack, trusting the world, is betrayed by it. The Surrey-character's fatuous love of Diamante in prison that follows (for he pretends that she is the nobly born Geraldine) anticipates a transformation he cannot make work—as the banqueting house does not work in the end—and his failure is especially acute when, later, Jack will transform Diamante by making her his wife and struggling to improve her fortunes.

The Surrey-character's fantastic chivalric tournament defending Geraldine's honor at her birthplace Florence occurs at the center of *The Unfortunate Traueller*. It is the fiction's longest single episode, incorporating its single longest description, and its placement is crucial: at the book's fulcrum, it balances the Münster-Rotterdam-Wittenberg episodes preceding it and the Venice-Rome-Bologna episodes that follow. Once again the focus is on art, on the past, and on those traditions that Europe, before its present bankruptcy of values, most honored. It is not mere artifice this time but distended and protracted parody. Surrey-character's helmet transformed into a watering pot to feed his impresa as it is fed in turn by his tears, his horse tricked out like an ostrich, turn him into a clown and his battles into a kind of Renaissance circus. Worse yet, Surrey's helmet, and those of his opponents, are more mechanical contrivances. All the poetry is gone. So is all real energy and emotion. The tournament at Florence is blighted; it is out of time and place, bringing no vital meaning (or salvation) to Jack Wilton's fallen world. The significance of Surrey is clear: as his poetry is flatulent conventionalism—show without substance, of tags from others, and therefore Ramist—so the tournaments are ineffectual events, like pagan services, like Puritanism. Similar to the banqueting house in the context of Jack Wilton's needs and of Nashe's world, they are blasphemous. They lack learning and belief in orthodox faith, which alone assure relevance. As a consequence, it is easy for us to see why Jack rather than Surrey-character wins Diamante ("My master beate the bush and kepte a coyle and a pratling, but I caught the birde" [sig. F3v; 2:263]) and why, once medieval society and Petrarchan poetry are shown as no longer pertinent to a humanism in its life struggle against present avarice, lust, and greed, Surrey-character abruptly leaves for England and is not heard of again (sig. H1; 2:279). For Nashe, Surrey is here a tragic buffoon: the most elegant of the Tudor poets under Henry—and therefore the most representative of the eloquence that anticipates a need for the Second Sophistic—is no longer adequate for the times of Elizabeth I.

Some shred of hope remains in Aretino. Nashe's praise of him, for his persistent revelations about the hidden ugliness of human nature, interrupts Jack's narration.

> His sight pearst like lightning into the entrailes of all abuses. This I must needes saie, that most of his learning hee got by hearing the lectures at Florence. It is sufficient that learning he had, and a conceit exceeding all learning, to quintescence euerie thing which hee heard. He was no timerous seruile flatterer of the commonwealth wherein he liued, his tongue & his inuention were foreborne, what they thought they would confidently vtter. Princes hee spard not, that in the least point transgrest. His lyfe he contemned in comparison of the libertie of speech. [Sig. F4; 2:265]

This master of invective, "one of the wittiest knaues that euer God made" (sig. F3v; 2:264), frees Jack and Diamante from a Venetian prison: his exercise of liberty is not in words only. But Aretino's portrait too is maculated. There were ominous rumblings in Jack's tribute: the lessons taken from Florence rather than antiquity, the lack of selectivity in his work, the carelessness of it. Aretino's reputation was mixed even for Harvey, who provides us with the common Elizabethan estimate: "Aretines glory, to be himself: to speake, & write like himself: to imitate none, but him selfe & euer to maintaine his owne singularity," Harvey scribbles in his *Marginalia*, suggesting the undisciplined indulgence of extreme pride, the refusal to seek Senecan originals.[84] It is this excess that Nashe scores too in the closing sentences of his digression through the mockery of imitatio—the practice Aretino eschews.

> *Aretine* as long as the world liues shalt thou liue. *Tully, Virgil, Ouid, Seneca,* were neuer such ornamentes to Italy as thou hast bin. I neuer thought of Italy more religiously than England till I heard of thee. Peace

to thy Ghost, and yet me thinkes so indefinite a spirit should haue no peace or intermission of paines, but be penning ditties to the archangels in another world. Puritans, spue forth the venome of your dull inuentions. A toade swels with thicke troubled poison, you swell with poisonous perturbations, your malice hath not a cleere dram of anie inspired disposition. [Sig. F4v; 2:266]

Such remarks, says McPherson, are "reminiscent of Aretino's own habitually hyperbolic praises of the minor noblemen whom he plied for gifts" ("Aretino," p. 1555). But Nashe's final image is most unsettling. Aretino's lack of human sentiment makes his work publicly destructive. It is also suicidal. He has no capacity to mourn, as Nashe so clearly does; he feels no real loss. Such criticism may seem precipitant until we realize that Jack too has introduced Aretino not as an expert satirist but as "chiefe Inquisiter to the colledge of curtizens" (sig. F3v; 2:264). He is not Aretino the satirist but the obscene Aretino who wrote poems to illustrate the scandalous and pornographic positions of love (the *modus sexualis*) drawn by Guilio Romano, and the author of the outspoken *Ragionamenti,* three dialogues concerning the promiscuity of nuns, wives, and courtesans in the cinquecento. Here his task, seen frontally, is demeaning. And although he is analogous to the banished earl in his single act of freeing Jack, he shows no open friendship (as Surrey-character does), gives no counsel (such as the earl offers), but leaves Jack and Diamante alone to face his Italy. It is as if he is setting up new possibilities for self-indulgent, fruitless scorn. As Aretino's scattershot invective ultimately provides Nashe with no sound or coherent model in *The Unfortunate Traueller,* so his chief function in the plot is to leave Jack and his courtesan once more randomly vulnerable.

The brief but forceful passage on Aretino shows us just what, besides the overwhelming failures of humanism, barely contains Nashe's own powerful style, his attempts to join flashes of grotesquerie and violence into an exegesis that speaks to his time. That exegesis relentlessly centers on Jack's mounting hopelessness and terror. Once the naive jester who "was ordained Gods scourge" (sig. C1; 2:226), Jack grows increasingly to be the world's victim. As one who at first refrained fastidiously from describing the punishment even of the cider merchant, his narrative ends crammed with details of torture. Jack's Grand Tour dis-orients. It takes him, and us, *away* from the orthodox lessons of Cicero and the Church. The more Jack witnesses, the more lonely, isolated, and vulnerable he becomes. Events and people betray him. Goodness is illusory. Love is debased into the commerce of courtesans. The search for encyclopedic humanist knowledge or inspiration leads only to "the halfe liuing ... mixt with squeazed carcases long putrifide" (sig. C3; 2:231): a portrait of the doomed and damned. With

Jack we move beyond human deceit to religious persecution at Münster and social and political vengeance and injustice throughout Italy. The very structures of Church and state are rotten at their foundations. Moreover, in his struggle to remain detached as an observer, satirist, and narrator, Jack finds that even he is subject to Petro de camp Frego's pistol and to prison, his life subject to the carvings of medical students. Our only description of Jack comes as Doctor Zacharie looks him over as a specimen for the laboratory. He is, says the anatomist, "of the age of eighteene, of stature tall, straight limd, of as cleare a complection as any Painters fancie can imagine" (sig. K2v; 2:304), but this too is a willed deception: later "he caused me to be stript naked, to feele and grope whether each lim wer sound & skin not infected" (sig. K2v; 2:305). The doctor does not know if his subject is healthy—and he has suspicions. This last demeaning act of the body bared—a bitter parody next to the betrothal scene in *Utopia*—leads to Jack's own nightmarish self-examinations; freed from danger of the plague, he is now a victim of his own sweating sickness.

> O the colde sweating cares which I conceiued after I knewe I should be cut like a French summer dublet. . . . Not a drop of sweate trickled downe my breast and my sides, but I dreamt it was a smooth edgd razer tenderly slicing down my breast and sides. If anie knockt at doore, I supposd it was the Bedle of surgeons hal come for me. In the night I dreamd of nothing but phlebotomie, bloudie fluxes, incarnatiues, running vlcers. I durst not let out a wheale for feare through it I should bleede to death. [Sigs. K2v–K3; 2:305]

The view is eschatological; "the words," Alexander B. Grosart claims, "run on wheels, and the wheels burn in their course."[85] The passage is a natural match to the murder of Esdras, before which Jack later stands transfixed in the last great scene of *The Unfortunate Traueller,* a scene that is more than eschatological, is apocalyptic. Cutwolfe describes Esdras's death before he is savagely executed himself; he speaks stretched on his own wheel.

> The veyne in his left hand that is deriued from the hart with no faint blow he pierst, & with the full bloud that flowed from it, writ a full obligation of his soule to the deuill. . . . I bad him ope his mouth and gape wide. He did so . . . therewith made I no more ado, but shot him full into the throat with my pistoll. . . . Reuenge is the glorie of armes, & the highest performance of valure, reuenge is whatsoeuer we call law or iustice. The farther we wade in reuenge the neerer come we to ye throne of the almightie. [Sig. M3v; 2:326]

The sweat and the pistol, like the earlier roaches and carpenter's chips, are images "boiling up from a dark void."[86] *The Unfortunate Traueller,* contemporary with pamphlets on the plague, is contemporary too with books on the promised horrors of the world's end, such as M. Francis Junius's *Briefe and Learned Commentarie Vpon the Reuelation of Saint Iohn* (1592) and John Napier's *Plaine Discouery of the whole Reuelation of Saint John* (1593).[87]

Jack's final, fearful insecurity leads to his one understanding: "Vnsearchable is the booke of our destinies" (sig. M4; 2:327). He knows the book of life is terrifying, but unrevealed. He knows only that he does not know. In fact, his world has prompted some rough approximations of justice—Esdras, Bartol, Zadock, and Cutwolfe are punished although Tabitha, Petro, Juliana, and Zacharie remain free—but his own wheel of fortune is circular. "And so as my storie began with the king at *Turnay* and *Turwin,* I thinke meete here to end it with the king at *Ardes* and *Guines*" (sig. M4; 2:328). His life (as we have it) opens and closes in celebration of warfare in the midst of military power and glory. At one point he had left it—then he went from the sweating sickness to the plague, to moral, social, and political epidemics. Now he chooses, in the company of his betrothed courtesan, to return to "the terror of the world" (sig. A3; 2:209). Nashe's last wicked irony—and it must not escape us—is that Jack rushes off to the Field of the Cloth of Gold to witness the same chivalric spectacles he had scorned at Florence and, as Nashe knew several decades past the event, to the deliberate dissimulation of peace already rotting as the French and English lay new schemes to betray each other.[88] With memories of Henry's face-saving siege of Thérouanne and Tournai, he joins the king at a display disguising treachery, a new and wicked artistic maneuver, its pageantry analogous to the papal procession in Rome. Jack's prodigality—however sympathetic in the long run, however compassionate in the short—is thus without sign of providence.

Next to the stark, bleak vision shared by *The Unfortunate Traueller* or even *The Pleasaunt Historie of Lazarillo de Tormes,* other contemporary works pale. *The Miseries of Mavillia* by Nicholas Breton (1584?), the journey of "the most vnfortunate Ladie, that euer liued" (title page), has as the protagonist-narrator a woman so full of self-pity that she fails to grieve over a boy who accidentally dies protecting her, while the loss of her estates to a shepherdess and her husband drives her to thoughts of suicide. *Piers Plainness* by Henry Chettle (1595) owes a good deal both to the *Lazarillo* and to Nashe, not least the sense of its own appeal as fiction—"it were a story to tell, and were it worth the telling I would describe it in a Story" (sig. B2v)—but Piers's misfortunes, as he passes from one master up the social scale to another, exposing the corruption in all the orders of a hierarchical system, serve to realign people so that they redeem themselves and each other: the form of *Piers Plainness* is the form of romance.

In fact, *The Unfortunate Traueller* has little connection with works of the Tudor period—except chronicle histories, sermons, and *The Pleasaunt Historie of Lazarillo de Tormes*—because Nashe draws his fictive poetics, as he draws his poetics generally, from the Second Sophistic. He is especially indebted to the satire of that period. The Lucianic spirit, for instance, that Nashe holds in common with Erasmus, More, and Rabelais, reminds us that *A True Story* by Lucian, that adventurous journey combining comic exaggeration and fantasy with historical personages, is a distant Senecan model for *The Unfortunate Traueller,* while Lucian's statement of his own poetics, in *The Dead Come to Life; or, The Fisherman,* helps to explain the basis of Nashe's scorn:

> I am a bluff-hater, cheat-hater, liar-hater, vanity-hater, and hate all that sort of scoundrels, who are very numerous, as you know. . . . However, I am very well up in the opposite calling, too: I mean the one with love for a base; for I am a truth-lover, a beauty-lover, a simplicity-lover, and a lover of all else that is kindred to love. But there are very few who deserve to have this calling practised upon them, while those who come under the other and are closer akin to hatefulness number untold thousands. So the chances are by this time I have lost my skill in the one calling for lack of practice, but have become very expert in the other (20).[89]

For some of his portraits, Lucian reaches back—as Nashe does through him—to Theophrastus, whose compacted, pungent *Characters,* with their peculiar combination of broad strokes and specific details, serve as models for the portrayals of individual types in *Pierce Penilesse,* the biography of Harvey in *Haue with you to Saffron-walden,* and the descriptions of Vanderhulke, John of Leiden, Esdras, and the courtiers who take up Surrey-character's challenge in *The Unfortunate Traueller.*

As for Roman fiction of the Second Sophistic, Nashe's work most resembles that of Petronius, whom Tacitus commends for his extravagant style, his self-abandonment, and his native simplicity (*Annales* 16.18). Renaissance editions of the *Satyricon*—derived perhaps from Latin *satura,* a plate filled with different kinds of food, a ramshackle medley of treats much like the apparent formlessness of *The Unfortunate Traueller*—began appearing as early as 1565 in fragments: there were a half-dozen editions by the time of Nashe's novel, although all were without the long *Cena Trimalchionis,* not discovered until the following century. Nashe shares none of Petronius's delight in outright obscenity (the travels of Encolpius, or "The Crotch," are brought about by his flight from the wrath of Priapus, the lord of lust), but both works reveal deep misgivings about their societies through a variety of characters who appear briefly to expose themselves more through their talk than through their actions. The two central characters in Petronius, the young man Encolpius, who seeks to complete his education by roaming through the known world, and the older poet Eumolpus, who has a displaced confidence in his own genius and who frequently indulges in composing or reciting his own poetry, are clearly ancestors of Jack and of Surrey-character. Eumolpus finds his model in Lucan, but throughout the *Satyricon*—even in the murder of Lycurgus and the quarrel over the booty sewn into a coat—Encolpius and his friends see themselves able, through wit, to face the threatening world by envisioning their pranks as heroic adventures. They have the same self-assurance Jack Wilton has as he makes his way toward Italy, the same cockiness and swiftness to satirize and mock, the same joy of living without any thought or plan for the future. But sheer vitality is all they ever have. Aside from the refining of language, there is little change in their attitudes or in their knowledge; for them, too, the Grand Tour does not come to much. The *Satyricon* has a good deal of the swagger of Nashe, but none of the real horror.

Thus Petronius is useful in understanding the first half of Nashe's chief fiction by seeing how Nashe implies sources to his fellow humanist readers and then diverges from them. Once Jack reaches Rome, it is clear that Nashe's model among the satirists of the Second Sophistic is not Petronius but Juvenal. All the depravity and corruption Jack Wilton finds in Italy are imaged in Juvenal's satires. They are caricatured in his first, programmatic satire (cf. 1.22–30) and elaborated, with increasing scorn, through the next four. It is here, William S. Anderson writes, that we find best the "portrait of a totally corrupt, chaotic, and disintegrating Rome,"[90] and it is here that we find the precise model for Nashe's particular combination of indignation (*facit indignatio versum*, 1.79) and hyperbole. This is the comparison Nashe's friends made too, applying with insight their understanding of humanist texts. Robert Greene calls Nashe "*young Iuuenvall*, that byting Satyrist" in his *Greenes Groatsworth of Wit* of 1592 (sig. F1); in the *Palladis Tamia* of 1598, Francis Meres sees him as "gallant young *Iuuenall*" (sig. Oo6). They have much in common. Juvenal "is a realist of the realists," G. G. Ramsay reminds us; "he grapples with the real things of life, and derives all his inspiration from the doings of the men and women of his own day."[91] Like Petronius, Juvenal's first satire opens with a parody of florid rhetoric that reminds us of the earlier Vanderhulke, but he quickly proceeds to more serious vices—to the greedy men like Zacharie, the courtesans like Tabitha and Juliana, and the thieves like Esdras and toadies like Bartol.

Similarly to Nashe, Juvenal writes out of personal obsessions, angered especially by anyone who would disrupt the social order—anyone who is ambitious, avaricious, or exploitative (1.87–109). He rails against the success of the ignorant and the untalented, scornful of those who are blind to his own worth or who have robbed him of his own just deserts. He is appalled by the effects of social and political mobility based on bribery and influence, of a world populated by all sorts of fools: decadent aristocrats, extended creditors, braggart politicians, hypocrites and thieves, even ravishers and murderers (3.21ff.; cf. 6, on women). "His introductory Satire," Peter Green tells us,

> with its forgers, gigolos, informers and crooked advocates, is a threnody on the theme of collapsing social values, on the impotence of the old middle classes when confronted by a ruthless, unprincipled, and commercially talented opposition. . . . Juvenal flays upper-class shortcomings all the harder because he sees his world in peril; his terror of social change made him treat infringements of accepted manners or conventions on a par with gross major crimes.[92]

Here there is also much room for Nashe's perennial cry of poverty. Juvenal is as embittered as Nashe by a state in which poets are always at the command and mercy of stupid or condescending patrons who know little and care little about the value of poetry (3.71–78); much of Nashe's work, too, displays an obsession with the ingratitude or insufficient respect of others (cf. 3.81–85) next to the success of pedantic or silly poets (like Harvey).

Moral degeneration can be measured exactly in Juvenal, as in Nashe, in the decline of rhetoric.

> Fidimus eloquio? Ciceroni nemo ducentos nunc dederit nummos, nisi fulserit anulus ingens.

> Trust in eloquence, indeed? Why, no one would give Cicero himself two hundred pence nowadays unless a huge ring were blazing on his finger. [7.139–40][93]

Such things mock Roman *virtù* for Juvenal and corrupt the basic *humanitas* that is its very foundation—*nobilitas sola est atque unica virtus* (virtue is the one and only nobility). "What we hear from Juvenal," Green sums, "is the cri de coeur of a doomed class" (Introduction, p. 35)—like the moral middle class to which Nashe belongs.

It is not only a congenial attitude and a common subject matter but a realizable technique that Nashe locates in Juvenal. The *Satires* are a series of rapid, nearly independent portraits of persons and acts, random and swift, in accretive bundles. The development is imagistic rather than logical; the organizing force is one of attitude rather than form. Like Nashe, Juvenal avoids abstractions, letting the overpowering details add up to their own generalizations. Once he has begun, there is a kind of neurotic compulsion to write about sin and poverty born of his powerful love and hatred of mankind, a sort of infuriated and infuriating despair. Juvenal, like Petronius, nevertheless harnesses his energies in a kind of truncated epic of his own making, consistently aiming for a Ciceronian grand style, constituted, as Inez Gertrude Scott has shown in considerable detail, on *copia* and *vis,* embellishment and passion.[94] Despite his rage—or perhaps because of it, aimed as it is to encourage eloquence—Juvenal writes in that elaborate Latin common to Cicero and St. John Chrysostom, to Persius and Basil. His work like theirs is studded with apostrophe, asyndeton, anaphora, hyperbaton, periphrasis, metaphor, metonymy, antonomasia, and ellipsis.[95] Such figures of thought, when saddled with Juvenal's scorn, make the power of his *Satires* undeniable; given also his deeply rooted, unshakable moral convictions, he singlehandedly, among the writers of the Second Sophistic, turns satire to the end of sermonizing. It is easy now to see why the Church Fathers were so drawn to the pagan Juvenal: Tertullian learns from him, for instance, and Lactantius quotes him.[96] It is easy to see too why Nashe, the son of the rector of West Harling, underappreciated and underpaid, found there the common spirit that would direct his own work. Like Nashe, Juvenal holds readers, as Gilbert Highet sums, "as he stammers with eagerness or grows hoarse with rage; they have discounted the exaggerations thrown out in his excitement; when he becomes incoherent mixing up mild misdemeanours with hideous crimes, they have realized that in a spoiled society a moralist cannot always distinguish."[97] And at times (as in Satire 3), when Juvenal's stark vision of the immoderate and immoral becomes overpowering, crowding him out of Rome and out of his poem, we see signs of that savage despair that also comes to characterize Nashe at his most powerful, and *The Unfortunate Traueller.*

It is Juvenal, too, who is the Senecan original of Nashe's last work, *Lenten Stuffe.* Juvenal's fourth satire opens with an appeal to the Muses; it continues with a mock-epic skit on the turbot, a fish so mythologically large and valuable that it takes a meeting of the emperor's council to determine what to do with it; and it stresses the epic journey of the fisherman with elaborate hyperbole. Nashe's *Lenten Stuffe,* too, is a lighthearted extravaganza on the foibles of man. In this final exegetical work, Nashe also returns to the beginning of humanist fiction, employing a mock epideictic oration like Erasmus and incorporating chronicle history like More.[98] *Lenten Stuffe* is a tribute to Great Yarmouth, where Nashe was seeking sanctuary at the time, and to its impressive fishing industry, so vital to Nashe's native East Anglia. He claims to be writing the pamphlet during April, during the spawning season of his subject. He draws his title jestingly from two sources: first from Gabriel Harvey's *Pierces Supererogation* (1593), where he is held up unflatteringly as a railing satirist and his work is thought to be "but lenten stuffe," likened to "old pickle herring". Secondly, Nashe derives his title from an anonymous pamphlet, *The Trimming of Thomas Nashe* (1597), which jokingly asks for favor because it is a product of Lent (sig. A2). The same high spirits continue in the work itself where he composes not one but two parodic encomia (of Great Yarmouth and of red herring) and where he so tangles his presentation that the propositio concerns the two, the partitio concerns the fish, and the ancestral tracing (out of place) concerns the romance of Hero and Leander. It is, as J. B. Steane says, "a virtuoso piece, *allegro con brio*" (Introduction, p. 42).

But the very choice of his classical model for *Lenten Stuffe* suggests that Nashe no more than Juvenal was able to reconcile himself—however temporarily—to the wickedness and wretchedness around him. Almost all of Nashe's learning had come from his days at Cambridge and from the pagan and patristic writers of the Second Sophistic, but the knowledge they had led him to was that of the savagery of his fellowman. Struggling to apply their methods of exegesis to his world in order to convey to his fellowmen their madness and their folly, in works that reach from the burlesque to the invective, he could neither correct their bad manners nor share sufficiently his horror at primal sin. Even in the dark, brutal, despairing fiction of *The Unfortunate Traueller*, where he contributed to humanist poetics one of its most powerful and enduring works, he seems not to have succeeded for long. For unlike several other works of humanist fiction—*Euphues, Pandosto*, the *Arcadia*—it seems never to have been popular, or reprinted again after two rapid editions in 1594. Doubtless so frank and honest a fiction was cold comfort to his fellow Londoners. For even as Nashe finished the book, Barrow, Greenwood, and Penry, three Puritans Separatists, were accused of sedition. The Catholic traitor Sir William Stanley (Lodge's boyhood companion) was known to be planning an invasion for the Catholics. Henry Young and others were coining money for unreasonable purposes in Sir Griffin Markham's chambers. Riots were threatened against foreign merchants resident in London, and Dr. Julius Caesar and his fellow commissioners were conducting a house-to-house search for seditious papers. Kyd was found in possession of atheistical documents, and Marlowe was slain in a Deptford tavern. And, around Marlowe, there were others dying: in the half decade before *The*

Unfortunate Traueller the Tudors suffered the loss of Leicester (1588); Sir Walter Mildmay, one of the queen's oldest and most respected ministers (1589); Warwick and Walsingham (both 1590); and Sir Christopher Hatton (1591). Burghley, the principal secretary, was, like the old queen, visibly aging. There were threats of war from Spain, of invasion from Ireland, and of unrest from France and the Low Countries. Frequent tracts argued the coming end of the world. In the midst of all this, Nashe contributed his one humanist fiction, in a prose that is tough and luminous, a prose of radical disengagement. It can make us shudder, this work of corpses on land and roaches out of the stream, because all its images finally cluster about an eschatological vision that heralds the death knell of humanist culture and humanist civilization despite Nashe's desperate attempt to make them current. In this unquiet prose of an unquiet mind, Nashe foreshortens the whole humanist era, from the England of Henry VIII to that of Elizabeth I, and demands that we tie together its fragmented segments. When he cites a commonplace tag out of Horace to begin *The Unfortunate Traueller*—"Coelum petimus stultitia"; "we seek the heavens in our stupidity" (*Odes* 1.3.38)—his best response is a question: "which of vs al is not a sinner?" (sig A3; 2:209). Little wonder, given this blanket condemnation of his society, that his body of work was called in (as destructive satire) to be destroyed by authorities. Still, in a way, it survived even that, given the stubborn resiliency of Nashe's own undistorted views: his ardent, urgent poetics of doubt and despair may well have challenged Thomas Lodge, whose humanist fiction, written through the same period of desperation, tries to answer Nashe's disappointment and scorn with an abiding trust in felicity in the darkening twilight days of humanist poetics.

TEN

O vita! misero longa, foelici brevis:

Thomas Lodge's Struggle for Felicity

 WHAT IS MOST DISTINCTIVE AND FORCEFUL ABOUT THE METEORIC CAREER OF THOMAS NASHE IS HIS BRIEF, BRILLIANT RAGE AGAINST THE DYING OF THE LIGHT; IN CONTRAST, THE LONG and seemingly endless struggle of Thomas Lodge—the other important writer of Tudor humanist fiction in the 1590s—is that of a man who refuses to lose hope in felicity. Equally anxious about the depravity of man and equally aware that the luxury of a poetics of eloquence under Elizabeth I was a possibility no longer open to him, Lodge seeks for new ways to validate the dignity of man and new kinds of instructive humanist fiction subsequent to the Spanish invasion of England. Even more, we can chart his life now by his unending attempt to restore learning not *only* to fiction but to criticism, poetry, drama, and philosophy: in Lodge as in Nashe, the attempt to rescue humanist poetics reaches out to embrace all forms. In locating a number of new resources to revitalize his own work, both from Greek and Roman history and from the Bible and the Roman Church, he sustained humanist poetics in an age of attrition, emerging as the last significant practitioner of Tudor humanist poetics in an age increasingly characterized by doubt and despair.

Perhaps he could endure because, at the start of his life, events seemed auspicious. Lodge was born in 1558, the year Elizabeth I ascended the throne, to a family long prosperous and influential. Edward Andrews Tenney writes that

> His pedigree shows that his father and his father's grandfather were knights; that his grandmother had a coat of arms in her own right, with a gentleman for her first husband and a knight for her second; that the family had produced lord mayors for London twice, sheriffs thrice, and aldermen for scores of years; that his uncle by marriage was Sir Thomas Chamberlain, governor of the Merchant Adventurers and sometime ambassador to

Spain; and lastly, that the great Grocers' Guild could hardly boast of more affluent and substantial members.[1]

Lodge's paternal grandfather, Thomas Littleton, moreover, was a justice of the common bench whose *Tenures* was a standard Elizabethan legal text at the Inns of Court; his father was a founder of the Muscovy Company in 1555 and lord mayor of London in 1562. For one from such a background, young Thomas Lodge received the proper training. As a boy, he lived in Derby House in Cannon Row, London, where he was companion to William, son of Henry Stanley, fourth earl of Derby. One of the greater families under Elizabeth, the Stanleys must have provided young Thomas with excellent training in languages, music, and gentlemanly skills—in the rudiments of a traditional humanist education. They were also a notable Catholic family who probably fostered in him his deep and abiding moral sense; his ties to them in later life, at any rate, were enduring.[2] In 1571, two years after Spenser, Thomas Lodge entered Merchant Taylors' School where he was taught by Richard Mulcaster; in 1573 he matriculated at Trinity College, Oxford. Extant records show that he underwent a rigorous four years there studying Latin and Greek, rhetoric and dialectic, taking prescribed lessons in Euclid, Porphyry, Plato, Aristotle, Agricola, and Joannes Caesarius; Valerius Maximus, Suetonius, Florus, Pliny, Livy, Cicero, Vergil, Horace, Lucan, Juvenal, Terence, and Plautus; Politian, Laurentius Vallensis, and Aulus Gellius.[3] He was admitted to the B.A. on 8 July 1577 and may then have gone on his own Grand Tour, to France and Spain, before his final determination during Lent 1578 after which, on 26 April, he joined his brother William at Lincoln's Inn. Through all these years he seems especially appreciative of "*Studious bookes*" as "*the true ritches of the minde,*" as he writes to Thomas Smith.[4] He also believed in "*the aduancement of Letters*"[5] as the basis for imitatio, for "what children [like men] apprehend," he tells us in *A fig for Momus* (1595), "The same they like, they follow and commend" (sig. E2; 3:35).

What sets Lodge's acts of humanist imitatio decisively apart from his predecessors, however, is its deliberately reiterative concern with virtuous action in this world as preparation for the beatitudes of the next. Such concern is vital, Lodge tells us in his description of the seven ages of man in *A Margarite of America* (1596), because

> An infant first from nurces teat he sucketh
> With nutriment corruption of his nature:
> And from the roote of endlesse errour plucketh
> That taste of sinne that waites on euery creature,
> And as his sinewes firme his sinne increaseth,

And but till death his sorrow neuer ceaseth.
[Sig. B3; 3.9]

Such a conception of original sin and of man's depraved state gives special emphasis to Lodge's repeated concern for "*the benefites of heauenly felicitie in the* life to come," as he puts it in his dedication to *Robert, second Duke of Normandy* of 1591 (sig. A4; 2:3), to his wishes for "affluence on earth, and felicitie in heauen" in his dedication of *Margarite* (sig. A4; 3:3), and to his wish for "*increase* of Worship in this life, and eternall bl[e]ssing in the life to come" in the dedication of *The Life and Death of william Long beard* (1593), a fiction set "Whilst all the world was in vprore, and schismes reigned in the Church, when God by prodigious signes, theatened pestilent plagues" (sigs. ¶4, A1; 2:3,5). As his career progresses, Lodge's concern with virtue and religion deepens, while his search for a suitable humanist poetics of felicity grows more urgent.

This latter-day testimonial to the need for humanist learning and its application is evident in the first work Lodge published, an unlicensed pamphlet written "in hudder mudder," according to Stephen Gosson,[6] in defense of poetry and drama (1580?). Lodge's basic argument is a moral one—that art should communicate allegorically:

> vnder the person of *Aeneas* in *Virgil* the practice of a dilligent captaine is discribed vnder ye shadow of byrds, beastes and trees, the follies of the world were disiphered, you know not, that the creation is signified in the Image of *Prometheus,* the fall of pryde in the person of *Narcissus,* these are toyes because they sauor of wisedome which you want. [Sigs. A2–A2v; 1:3–4]

Lodge finds his support in a collocation of authorities that anticipates the syncretic turn of his humanist poetics. He draws on humanists— "*Erasmus* will make that the path waye [to] knowledge which you disprayse" (sig. A3v; 1:6)—and on classical authors:

> *Seneca* sayth that the studdie of Poets, is to make childrē ready to the vnderstanding of wisedom, and yt our auncients did teache *artes Eleutherias i. liberales,* because the instructed childrē by the instrumēt of knowledg in time became *homines liberi. i. Philosophye.* . . . *Strabo* calleth poetry, *primam sapientiam. Cicero* in his firste of hys Tusculans attributeth ye inuencion of philosophy, to poets. [Sigs. A4, B3v; 1:7,22]

but he also adds a new emphasis by citing biblical and patristic authorities, much as Nashe later will:

> ask *Iosephus,* and he wil tel you that Esay, Iob and Salomon, voutsafed poetical practises, for (if *Origen* and he fault) not theyre verse was

Hexameter, and pentameter. Enquire of *Cassiodorus,* he will say that all the beginning of Poetrye proceeded from the Scripture. *Paulinus* tho the byshop of *Nolanum* yet voutsafe the name of a Poet, and *Ambrose* tho he be a patriarke in *mediolanū* loueth versifing *Beda* shameth not ye science that shamelesse *Gosson* misliketh. reade ouer *Lactantius,* his proofe is by poetry. & Paul voutsafeth to ouerlooke *Epimenides* let the Apostle preach at Athens he disdaineth not of *Aratus* authorite. it is a pretye sentence yet not so prety as pithy. *Poeta na scitur orator fit* as who should say, Poetrye commeth from aboue from a heauenly seate of a glorious God vnto an excellent creature man, an orator is but made by exercise. [Sig. A7; 1:13]

This astonishing farrago of references—some startling, many ill-digested—is in good measure from a treatise by Badius Ascensius,[7] as Lodge himself admits (sig. A7v; 1:14), but they are all cemented by the forcefulness of Lodge's prose and the evident commitment he has to a poetry informed by a decidedly Christian humanism. The argument comes to rest at last on the invulnerability of Horace's *Ars Poetica* as Lodge receives it:

> The holy spokesman of the Gods
> With heaue[n]ly Orpheus hight;
> Did driue sauage men from wods.
> And made them liue aright
> [Sigs. Bl–Blv; 1:18]

Though not insisting that all poets are holy men, Lodge does argue that poetry is a heavenly gift meant to instruct (in holy thoughts) through a pleasure that is not in itself *un*holy. This critical patchwork, hastily written and hastily printed, has come down to us in tatters, without title page, but it is nevertheless persuasive because Lodge understands that Stephen Gosson, to whom he is replying, aims his criticism not only at the abuse of poetry but, more seriously, at the corruptible nature of man. By transferring the act of writing poetry to holy inspiration, Lodge finds an early means to preserve a humanist poetics that is at once literary, philosophical, and *religious.*

Perhaps the single most salient fact about Lodge's defense of poetry and drama is that it blends the attitudes of Derby House and Merchant Taylors' School in a rhetoric common to Oxford disputations and the moot trials at Lincoln's Inn in a way that releases the powerful appropriateness of all of Lodge's resources. From 1580 onward, his literary tactics are, more or less openly, as philosophical as poetic. Something as apparently remote and innocuous as the sonnet cycle *Phillis* (1593), for example, comes to rest on a related sentiment: "I praise hir honny-sweet[e] eloquence, / Which from the fountaine of true wisdome floweth" (sig. D3v; 2:26). *Scillaes*

Metamorphosis (1589), clearly meant as a tribute to the Ovidian poetics of Greene, transcends Greene in a passage following the embellishment of the story of Glaucus and Scylla:

> He thanks his God, and sighes their cursed doomb
> That fondly wealth in surfetting bestowes:
>   And with Saint *Hierom* saith, *The Desert is*
>   *A paradise of solace, ioy, and blis.*
> Father of light, thou maker of the heauen,
> From whom my being well, and being springs:
> Bring to effect this my desired steauen,
> That I may leaue the thought of worldly things:
>   Then in my troubles will I blesse the time,
>   My Muse vouchsafde me such a luckie rime.
> [Sig. E2; 1:39]

Both collections of poetry serve as elaborate but telling prolegomena to *A fig for Momus*. Here the pagan god of criticism and mockery is metamorphosed into another, more transcendent god as the poem ends: "As I will leaue the world, and come and liue with thee," Philides remarks (sig. C3v; 3:22); Eglon replies,

> So doing thou art wise, who from the world doth part,
> Begins to trauell on to true felicitie.
> [Sig. C4; 3:23]

"To trauell on to true felicitie" is the theme that binds together all the disparate works of this Momus; thus in a discourse on dreams (Epistle 2; sig. E4ff.), the poet turns at Apollo's request to a narrative about Albertus Magnus with its own, more Christian moral ("Farre and more working is his heau'nly power, / In sending holy spirits euery howre" [sig. Flv; 3:42]), while advice to his fellow poet Michael Drayton (Epistle 5) turns from the counsel of Augustine and Jerome to the Old Testament:

> Oh let that holy flame, that heauenly light,
> That led old *Abrahams* race in darkesome night:
> Oh let that star, which shining neuer ceast
> To guide the Sages of balme-breathing East,
> Conduct thy Muse vnto that loftie pitch,
> Which may thy style with praises more enritch.
> [Sig. H3; 3:61]

This need for new wine in old bottles, thematic too in Eclogue 1 (sigs. B4v, C2; 3:16, 19), leads to his concluding, plainspoken advice to his brother in Epistle 4: "Spend praiers on God" (sig. H1v; 3:58).

A humanist poetics of felicity that is forged so carefully and consistently through his extant poetry is also the basis for Lodge's reappraisal of humanist fiction. His early concern that humanist principles be *necessarily* coupled with virtuous action is apparent in his first fiction, *An Alarum against Vsurers* (1584). Initially, *An Alarum* seems to be an odd collection of juvenile imitatio of deliberative declamation, Alexandrian romance, and allegorical satire, but a thoughtful reading shows us the work's essential unity: the exhortation and pastoral serve as humanist precept and illustration, while the concluding poem serves to reconcile the dialectic by partaking simultaneously of both. Lodge thus gives us a new kind of triadic art in which each of the three parts, separately and together, responds to the Latin motto on the title page of this and other works by Lodge: *O Vita! misero longa, foelici breuis* (sig. A1; 1:1). The opening oration concerns an archetypal usurer and a prodigal; but it is set, in Lodge's transforming rhetoric, in a cosmology significantly redolent of Ecclesiasticus.

> No maruell though the wise man accompted all things vnder the sun vain, since the chéefest creatures be mortall: and no wonder though the world runne at randon, since iniquitie in these later dayes hath the vpper hand. The alteration of states if they be lookt into, and the ouerthrow of houses, if they be but easely laid in open viewe, what eye would not shed teares to sée things so transitorie? and what wisedome woulde not indeauour to dissolue the inconuenience? [Sig. B1; 1:13]

This tale, constructed by a circumstantial reality that is remarkable for a fiction of its time, begins in the form of a parable. Lest we miss a point relatively new to humanist fiction, an early summary passage underscores it.

> The young Gentleman, vnacquainted with such like discourses [from a usurer], counting all golde that glysters, and him a faithfull frend that hath a flattering tongue, opens all his minde to this subtill vnderminer, who so wringeth him at last, that there is no secrete corner in the poore Gentlemans heart, but he knoweth it: after that, framing his behauiour to the nature of the youth, if he be sad, sober: if youthly, riotous: if lasciuious, wanton: he laboureth so much, that at last the birde is caught in the pit-fall, and perceiuing the vaine of the youth, he promiseth him some reliefe by his meanes: the Gentleman thinking he hath God almightie by the héele, holdes the Diuell by the toe, and by this meanes, is brought to vtter wracke and ruine. [Sig. B2v; 1:16]

The story is at once an exercise in *figural* art. This account, which Lodge insists is "no counterfait, but the true image of a rebellious sonne, and the rewarde of contempt of parents" (sig. C4v; 1:28), correlates with Lodge's own autobiography, especially when the unnamed boy's father comments that béeing by mée brought to the Innes of Court, a place of abode for our English Gentrie, and the onely nurserie of true lerning, I finde thy nature quite altered, and where thou first shuldest haue learnt law, thou art become lawlesse. [Sig. B4v; 1:20]

Even this early—a decade and a half before *A Margarite of America*—the nursery contaminates; and man's nature is depraved. Lodge's lengthy *effiguration* serves as an *exordium;* in the *narratio* of his rhetorical presentation other examples, more remote, are drawn from earlier epochs (sig. E1v; 1:38). This narrative of youthful prodigality at the hands of a usurer, a glancing tribute to Lyly, gains significance for Lodge because of its coincident religious significations.

Natures giftes are to be vsed by direction: he had learning, but hee applied it ill: he hadde knowledge, but hée blinded it with selfe opinion. All graces whatsoeuer, all ornaments what so they be, either giuen vs by our fore-parent, or grafted in vs by experience, are in themselues as nothing: vnlesse they be ordered by the power of the most highest. [Sig. C4; 1:27]

Then, breaking with Lyly and Greene but reminiscent of Sidney, Lodge writes not of reformation but of *redemption;* "the eye fixed on heauenlye contemplations, gazeth not on earthlye beautie" (sig. F2v; 1:48). Striking through the boundaries of narrative and parable, Lodge warns his reader rather than invites his judgment. If he fails to turn his thoughts upward, Lodge admonishes,

sodainly shal the wrath and curse of the Lord fall vpon you, and (without speedie repentaunce) he will consume you in a moment. O turne speedely vnto the Lord, and put not off from daie to daie, least his wrath be hot against you, and he make you pertakers of the plagues of *Chore* and *Abriam*. [Sig. F3v; 1:50]

The urgency of the message fragments the medium.

If Lyly serves Lodge as a point of departure for the first part of his apprenticeship in a humanist poetics of fiction, so something like Greene's stories of wonder serves him as the form in the next section—adding to the borrowing from *Euphues*—"The Delectable *Historie of Forbonius and Prisceria*" (sigs. G1–K4v; 1:53–84), "which being begun with so wonderfull causes, must needes finish with a miraculous effect" (sig. G3; 1:57). The romance is an example of antitheton: as the feckless, unnamed youth of the first part shows a wayward nature on his downward path to wisdom, Forbonius, as respondent force, shows self-discipline and faith from the start; and as exempla and allusions interrupt the opening declamation in the first parable of *An Alarum,* so now formal speeches and soliloquies—

brief orations—interrupt the narrative. Forbonius's love for Prisceria is
forbidden by her father Solduvius because of an old family feud. The
deliberation over their forced estrangement is first presented by Prisceria,
who in her own mini-disputation arranges the arguments on both sides in
an extended *isocolon:*

> Thou louest *Forbonius,* and why? for his vertue: yet thy father hateth him
> vpon olde grudges, with whom when rancour preuayleth, what may be
> more lookt for, then contempt and denyall? But *Forbonius* seeketh
> *Priscerias* fauor, and *Solduuius* friendship: but *Prisceria* cannot enioy
> *Forbonius,* without Solduuius fauor. But *Forbonius* will by happie marriage
> conclude all mallice, but thy father hauing an envious mind, will haue a
> suspitious eare. Alas why imagine I wonders in my fancy, hoping that those
> destenies (which inthralled my affection) wil subiect my fathers resolutions:
> since neither reason alloweth me any probabilitie to worke vpon, neither
> hath *Forbonius* any motion as I sée to compasse ought. [Sig. G3; 1:57]

But as in the first part, Forbonius's response moves away from the rhetoric
of Lyly and toward the newly fashioning rhetoric of Lodge.

> I glorie in the benefit of my martirdome, since a certain inward hope
> assureth me, that diuine beautie cannot be sequestered from iust pittie, nor
> a tried seruice in loue, requited with a disdainfull hate. [Sig. G3v; 1:58]

Finding no natural way to court Prisceria, Forbonius goes to the
Gymnosophist Appollonius, who preaches a sermon of patience (sigs.
G4v–Hl; 1.60–61), while the impatient Solduvius, suspecting the lovers,
sends Prisceria to a country house. Help comes to those who learn patience,
however, and Forbonius, disguising himself as a shepherd rather than
relying on the Gymnosophist's magic, wins Prisceria by singing of Corinna
and Corulus, clearly fictional versions of themselves. But he is caught by
Solduvius and imprisoned. Now, again, an act of forced humility leads to
still more self-understanding. Faith should ally itself with reason, not with
masquerade, and he approaches Solduvius directly with the art of formal
persuasion.

> Although enraged rancour hath made thée passe the limits of honour, (O
> *Solduuius*) yet passe not so farre in thy resolutions, as to staine the dignitie
> of thy person, with the martyrdome of a guiltlesse Gentleman. If I did hate
> thy daughter, that lyttle enuye that grewe by my Fathers displeasure, might
> by reason grow to déepe and rooted mallice, but when I loue *Prisceria,* why
> shoulde I bée contempned of *Solduuius*? It should seeme that loue was not
> accompted lothsome among the gods, when as prefixing a punishment to all
> escapes, they prescribe an honour to this: chiefly concluding it to be a vertue:

wherevppon thou must conclude, that eyther thou contemnest the decrées of the Gods, or measurest all thinges by thine owne mallice. [Sigs. K3v–K4; 1:82–83]

The clue to Lodge's meaning lies in this union of forensic humanist rhetoric with the power of faith and love. Solduvius relents, and the couple are married. "Forbonius and Prisceria," then, is a second, more subtle, parable about prodigal men—but a parable nonetheless.

The clue to the meaning of *An Alarum* lies in this juxtaposition of the two stories—one circumstantial, the other marvelous. (Lodge will repeat this formula in *Rosalynde* where pastoral romance in Arden realizes the precepts of Sir John of Bordeaux.) The risk is that, in transporting his readers to a land reminiscent of Alexandrian romance, Lodge may seem to forgo his parabolic intention. He encloses this fiction of wonder, then, with the facts of experience. The concluding part of *An Alarum* is a poem entitled "Trvths Com*plaint ouer England*" (sig. L1; 1:85), spoken by Melpomine who is self-exiled from England, once "the seate ... / Of Paradise" (sig. L1v; 1:86) when "learning was the Loadstone of the land" (sig. L2; 1:87), because the court has become a place of pride, ambition, injustice, and greed, reaching out to affect all walks of life. England is now a land of both usury and wrath: the metaphor of Forbonius and Prisceria is thus made as factual as the account of excessive moneylending. "Beléeue me Countrimen this thing is true" (sig. L4; 1:91). Deliberately echoing the speech of the usurer that opened *An Alarum,* Melpomine acknowledges that

> Iustice sore I feare by powre is led,
>   The poore may crie, and gladly creepe to crosse,
> The rich with wealth, though wealthie now are fed,
>   The simple man now onely beares the losse,
>   The Lawier he the golden crownes doth tosse,
> And now hath fées at will with cap and knée,
> And each man cries, good sir come plead for me.
> [Sigs. L3v–L4; 1:90–91]

But this poem, as this work of humanist poetics, also means to travel the road to felicity. Melpomine is still capable of holy visions that inspire her and are meant to inspire us.

> O blessed time, when zeale with bended knées,
> Gan blesse the heauens, that bent their powres diuine,
> The English hearts to wisedome to encline.
> [Sig. L4; 1:91]

Quietly but firmly, *An Alarum against Vsurers* is Everyman's guide along the pathway to salvation.

Lodge's second work of humanist fiction, *Rosalynde. Euphues golden legacie* (1590), was his most successful,[8] and it is still his best known; it is arguably in many ways too—in plot, in characterization, and in sheer *tone*—one of the best of all Tudor works of humanist poetics, the accomplishment of "a writer of very remarkable gifts," as J. J. Jusserand has it, "at his best."[9] It is also a striking, if more subdued, formulation of Lodge's developing poetics of felicity. Substantial honor is still paid to Lyly as the initiator of a Tudor humanist poetics—

> *Heere Gentlemen may you see in* Euphues golden Legacie, *that such as neglect their fathers precepts, incur much preiudice, that diuision in Nature as it is a blemish in nurture, so tis a breach of good fortunes: that vertue is not measured by birth but by action: that yonger brethren though inferiour in yeares, yet may bee superiour to honours: that concord is the sweetest conclusion, and amity betwixt brothers more forceable than fortune* [Sig. P4; 1:139][10]

—but here the emphasis has clearly shifted to the *vertue* of *action*, which is aligned through the careful management of ideas with *good fortunes, Nature,* and *nurture.* Thus active virtue, as these sentences unwind their meaning, is what makes fortune good.[11] Lodge's summary of his position thus treats Lyly's thesis as hypothesis; with great tact, he disrupts Lyly's circumscribed and cyclic patterning of events while freeing his own rhetoric (in agreement with his thought) from Lyly's balanced equivalencies. Lodge eliminates the juggled phrases and clauses of a self-reflexive irony because meaning for him is not plurisignificant. And unlike Shakespeare's adaptation, which has a circling geographical pattern, Lodge does not return us to Bordeaux: his fiction, like his plot, is progressive.

But it is not the title page alone of *Rosalynde* that alerts us to the fact that Lodge sees his fiction more as a correction than a continuation of his model. As if searching out the inherent possibilities for a witnessing Christianity in the humanist forms of rhetoric, most speeches in *Rosalynde*—again consciously like those in *Euphues, Pandosto,* and the *Arcadia*—are cast in the forms of declamation or disputation. Yet the whole cast and tone have changed. It follows that the opening speech of the dying Sir John of Bordeaux, containing *both* the position of Euphues and that of Eubulus, is delivered in a language that struggles to free itself from the euphuism of Lyly and Greene and the Ciceronianism of Sidney. "I will bequeath you infallible precepts that shall leade you vnto vertue," he says by way of propositio, and then, in the partitio, provides a surprising last will and testament.

> First therefore vnto thée SALADYNE the eldest, and therefore the chiefest piller of my house, wherein should be ingrauen as well the excellence of thy fathers qualities, as the essentiall forme of his proportion, to thée I giue fouretéene ploughlands, with all my Mannor houses and richest plate. Next vnto FERNANDYNE I bequeath twelue ploughlands. But vnto ROSADER the yongest I giue my Horse, My Armour, and my Launce, with sixteene ploughlands: for if the inward thoughts be discouered by outward shadowes, ROSADER will excéed you all in bountie and honour. [Sigs. B1v–B2; 1:10–11]

What begins as conventional bequest is overturned by denying the tradition of primogeniture. Sir John knows this—"*But* vnto ROSADER"—and he justifies it by "inward thoughts" (apparently superior to those of Saladyne and Fernandyne), which can only be proven by virtuous action ("discouered by outward shadowes") that will confirm Sir John's deathbed wisdom. This is decidedly *not* the wisdom of the ancients, by which the eldest son would have the greatest share of land if not all of it, and therefore departs from that body of knowledge and tradition on which Lyly, Greene, and even Sidney ground their humanist fictions. It relies, rather, on faith in the youngest son. His precepts of virtue mean just that: he will reward virtue governed by his trust in things unseen. At the same time, he sets a course of action for all three heirs—Rosader's obligation is to exonerate this break with tradition through superior outward shadows, while Saladyne and Fernandyne will necessarily learn virtuous behavior through self-containment, through agreeing to more limited inheritances. By this new division of goods, then, Sir John requires that even the one who receives the most is committed to a life of virtue, and all three are required to accept a relative division of goods that insures lessons of humility. Legally, this innovative legacy has the power of a deathbed bequest before three witnesses; morally, it asks the sons to follow the wishes (and by extension, the footsteps) of the father. Thus there is a clear model, an exemplar. Sir John's very next point is precisely this—"Let mine honour be the glasse of your actions, and the fame of my vertues the Loadstarre to direct the course of your pilgrimage" (sig. B2; 1:11)—while the language is deliberately religious. Life as "pilgrimage" is a life governed by "inward thoughts," which, given a living model in Rosader, will result in "outward shadowes" of both "bountie and honour." Material wealth is defined, then, by moral virtue. Because self-advancement is therefore measured by the self's growing virtue, its pilgrimage toward self-perfection (or bliss), a lack of ambition is the underside of its effective growth. Sir John now makes that point too.

> Climbe not my sonnes; aspiring pride is a vapour that ascendeth hie, but soone turneth to a smoake: they which stare at the Starres, stumble vppon stones; and such as gaze at the Sunne (vnlesse they bee Eagle eyed) fall blinde. [Sig. B2; 1:11]

Subsequent analogies are classical, out of Pliny and Ovid, and so reminiscent of Lyly and Greene; it was not Lodge's way to reprimand or rebel against his predecessors in humanist fiction, for they were the models on which he built his own poetics of felicity, but, true to the inner tenor of his mind—perhaps a consequence of Derby House or the personality of Mulcaster or the Catholic environment of Trinity College, Oxford—his task was to amend their work with his own.

One of Lodge's most attractive characteristics—it is there in the rawness of his defense before Gosson and in his anatomy of usury—is his clear-sighted awareness of the situation in which he has placed his ideas and characters. Sir John is dying; and his counsel may be wisdom, but it might just as well be senility. The awareness of such a possibility—Sidney has this talent, too—is not with Lodge, as it is with Sidney, meant to leave the issue open to our best judgments. The rational structure of Sir John's last speech guarantees his logic. Because all of life is for him a pilgrimage, cut to the eternal pattern that makes sense and confirms faith, this too is an object lesson Sir John receives from a beneficent God—*his* legacy, which he passes on in turn.

> In my fall see & marke my sonnes the follie of man, that being dust climbeth with BRIARES to reach at the Heauens, and readie euerie minute to dye, yet hopeth for an age of pleasures. Oh mans life is like lighning that is but a flash, and the longest date of his yeares but as a bauens blaze. Seeing then man is so mortall, bée carefull that thy life bée vertuous, that thy death may be full of admirable honours; so shalt thou challenge fame to bee thy fautor, and put obliuion to exile with thine honorable actions. [Sig. B3; 1:13]

Even in death, he is now the source of their imitatio; it follows, then, that the special wisdom of the elderly and the vision of truth granted the dying allow even his last, weakened act to take on a higher understanding of verity. His death, rather than releasing his sons from obligations, only sets more clearly for them the path they are to tread. Nancy R. Lindheim's helpful assessment of the slackened rhetoric in *Rosalynde*,[12] which is so apparent in the scenes in Arden, has its basis here, in Sir John's speech, where his union of nature and nurture resolves the dramatic antithesis that was the source of Lyly's and Sidney's verbal tensions. Life as pilgrimage causes them to harmonize, and the long confirmatio of Sir John's speech—where he draws lessons from his principles in the areas of politics and romance, anticipating the fraternal struggle of power between Saladyne and Rosader and the courtship of the two sons with Ganimede/Rosalynde and Aliena/Alinda—is, as a necessary consequence, merely the acting out of his precepts in a way that confirms his view of life as a series of acts eternally foreordained so as to lead men (and women) through the performance of virtue to a vision of things beyond this life.

It may be fanciful to suggest that Fernandyne, with his pitiful inheritance, finds a preordained way to joy through a life of secluded study, taking Sir John's precepts to their farthest reaches of application and realizing his inheritance in a way Sir John also foresees. It may be fanciful because Fernandyne's life of contemplation is discussed more fully in another work Lodge wrote that same year (*Catharos*) and because that concern is not apparent here. It is the life of Euphues subsequent to Lyly's fictions and so raises few or no problems. What is important is the discovery of how virtue, patience, and faith may be learned in the active life—the problems Lyly sets in *Euphues* and in *Euphues and his England*. That much *is* clear in *Rosalynde* as Euphues' *golden* legacy in the first significant question after Sir John's death and in the first significant debate. Saladyne understandably wishes to claim for himself the largest patrimony, which by birthright he feels is properly his, yet he hesitates to act against the will and (perhaps less consciously) the wisdom of his father. For him virtue and filial loyalty assume common identity, as Sir John knew they would. Thus virtue calls his pride to account and admonishes him:

> were thy fathers precepts breathed into the winde? hast thou so soone forgottē his principles? did he not warne thee from coueting without honor, and climing without vertue? did hee not forbid thee to aime at any action that should not be honourable? and what will bee more preiudiciall to thy credit, than the carelesse ruine of thy brothers welfare? [Sig. B4v; 1:16]

His memories of his father must be denied if his ambition is to be satisfied:

> What though thy Father at his death talked of many friuolous matters, ... shal his words be axioms, and his talke be so authentical, that thou wilt (to obserue them) preiudice thy selfe? ... What man thy Father is dead, and hee can neither helpe thy fortunes, nor measure thy actions: therefore burie his words with his carkasse, and bee wise for thy selfe. [Sig. B4v; 1:16]

Immorality is conceived by Saladyne solely in terms of disobedience. For Lodge, of course, this rightly has its biblical echoes.

Such an equation helps us explain why in so careful a work Rosader's doubts arise in the way that they do:

> Ah quoth he to himselfe (nature working these effectuall passions) why should I that am a Gentleman borne, passe my time in such vnnaturall drudgerie? were it not better either in *Paris* to become a scholler, or in the court a courtier, or in the field a souldier, than to liue a foote boy to my own brother: nature hath lent me wit to cōceiue, but my brother denied me arte to contemplate: I haue strength to performe any honorable exployte, but no libertie to accomplish my vertuous indeuours: those good partes that God hath bestowed vpon me, the enuie of my brother dooth smother in obscuritie: the harder is my fortune, and the more his frowardnesse. [Sig. C1; 1:17]

And it explains why Rosader's rebellion against Saladyne seems to come so suddenly[13]—it is because after suffering Saladyne's harsh will for three years Rosader realizes his behavior is not the act of humility Sir John suggested in his view of life as a pilgrimage but, rather, submission to a pride that is "contrarie to the testament of his father" (sig. C1; 1:17). Rosader's growing resentment turns into an outburst of righteous indignation at a significant point—when his eldest brother says, mockingly, "is your heart on your halfe penie, or are you saying a Dirge for your fathers soule?" (sig. C1v; 1:18)—and Saladyne saves himself before the superior moral (and physical) force of Rosader by remarking, again pointedly, that bloody revenge would only "staine the vertue of olde Sir IOHN of *Bourdeaux*" (sig. C2; 1; 19). Calling on the moral testament of their father, Saladyne asks them both to honor his testament by obeying the glass of his virtue; the understanding that prompts this act of reconciliation indicates his own inner capacity for amendment and redemption. Before such a moment of self-realization by Saladyne, Rosader withdraws.

But temporary reconciliation should not be confused with resolution. Neither brother has yet learned sufficiently how to bring will into line with understanding, "outward shadowe" into concord with "inward thought." Saladyne's tendency toward pride leads him to contract a wrestler to kill his younger brother; Rosader's tendency toward irascibility leads him to thoughts and acts of rebellion. Rosader needs the calming influence of old Adam Spencer, who not only feeds him but helps him to escape physical (and, given Lodge's figural art, spiritual) imprisonment, accompanying Rosader on his pilgrimage to the more gracious (and hence instructive) environment of Arden. Saladyne needs the treachery of a proud Torismond; then he voluntarily makes the same choice, seeking refuge and renewal in Arden. But at this point, too, Lodge transforms the humanist poetics he has inherited. Arden is not a land of wonder merely, as we might find in

Greene, or an inner refuge free from the cares of the outer world. Arden's environment is closer to Providence than Bordeaux and allows a certain additional margin of freedom—Gerismond can (temporarily) pretend to be Robin Hood; Rosalynde will play Ganimede and Rosader a lovesick swain; Phoebe and Montanus will parody them all with their stiffly artificial Petrarchisms—but they cannot, in the end, escape themselves. For beneath such deceptive differences—deceptive for those avoiding the moral obligations of life—there are striking similarities. The usurpation of Bordeaux invites new forms of open treachery unnatural to that country as the rule of Gerismond in Arden initiates a courtliness unnatural to the woods. The very real complicity to murder that awakens deathly instincts in the Norman wrestler corresponds to the deathly instincts of the lion in Arden. The starvation of Rosader in Bordeaux is followed by Adam's starvation in Arden. We know that no woods combines lemon and pine trees; it is an illusion that discloses the folly and foolishness of those in love. Selfish dreams betray the facts of God's world. By the same token, the distinctions we make at first between Bordeaux and Arden as the traditional microcosm and heterocosm of romance—Bordeaux (like Lyly's Naples) a country of conflict, artifice, pride, and chaos; Arden (like Lyly's Athens) a land of unity, naturalness, humility, and harmony—are more apparent than real, *our* wishes, perhaps, as disciples of Lyly and Greene and fallen readers of romance. What Lodge's lovers come to realize through the extended embellishments and variations of a rhetoric of courtship is what we come to realize in the process of reading: the physical imprisonment of Rosader and Saladyne in Bordeaux prefigures—is less subtle than but not different from—the emotional imprisonment in Arden. The lovers, like Gerismond and his men, are captured by self-desire, by forsaking their natural obligations. (That the complicated relationships in Arden involving Rosader, Saladyne, and Phoebe are worked out as variations of a triple chiasmus is surely a comment on *Gwydonius* and *Arcadia*.) But Saladyne's inner conflict over obligation in Bordeaux, like Rosader's inner conflict on meeting Saladyne to choose over land (sig. D3; 1:29), provides the pattern for the matured behavior in Arden. Rosader must choose to save or sacrifice Saladyne to the lion; Phoebe must learn to settle for Montanus; most difficult of all, Rosalynde must learn a way to end the unrestrained liberty and self-indulgence of them all by relinquishing her disguise permanently. What all of them must learn is the lesson of surrender. That lesson, too, was taught by Sir John as he surrendered his spirit to God, his earthly remains to his heirs.

That the lands of Bordeaux and Arden have inescapable resemblances is something that Lodge is at pains to make clear. The names of their respective usurping rulers (Torismond, Gerismond) are, for instance, interchangeable, as Alinda (renamed Aliena) or Rosalynde (playing Rosalynde) seem in some recess of awareness to acknowledge. The flowered speeches of love in Arden accord with the more stilted self-debates of each of the four lovers in Bordeaux, aligning the allusions to a heroic age of the past with bestial imagery, the twin temptations away from a life of obligation that finds its original rhetorical and epistemological pattern, too, in Sir John's deathbed speech.[14] Paralleling environments intersect parallel plots: both Rosader and Rosalynde lose their fathers, fall in love, and are exiled to Arden; both Saladyne and Alinda feel the need to choose the same recourse voluntarily. In Arden all four find, in the instructive postures of Phoebe and Montanus, the need to discover truth from inward thoughts, not outward shows. Outward shows may become absurd. But inward thoughts reveal all men and women similar. "We haue two bodies," Alinda says of herself and Rosalynde, "but one soule" (sig. D4; 1:31). Such an inward thought frees the lovers from self-posturing and allows each of them to lose himself or herself in caring for another. They find themselves by losing themselves.

The art of suggestive distillation that characterizes *Rosalynde,* then, is the art suggesting the means for felicity. Speech after speech confirms this, confirms Sir John's hypo-thesis. Here, for example, is Rosader before Ganimede.

> O shepheard (quoth ROSADER) knewest thou her personage graced with the excellence of all perfection, beeing a harbour wherein the Graces shroude their vertues: thou wouldst not breathe out such blasphemie against the beauteous ROSALYNDE. She is a Diamond, bright but not hard, yet of most chast operation: a pearle so orient, that it can be stained with no blemish: a rose without prickles, and a Princesse absolute aswell in beautie, as in vertue. But I, vnhappie I, haue let mine eye soare with the Eagle against so bright a Sunne, that I am quite blinde; I haue with APOLLO enamoured my selfe of a DAPHNE, not (as shee) disdainfull, but farre more chast than DAPHNE; I haue with IXION laide my loue on IUNO, and shall (I feare) embrace nought but a clowde. Ah shepheard, I haue reacht at a star, my desires haue mounted aboue my degree, & my thoughts aboue my fortunes. I being a peasant haue ventred to gaze on a Princesse, whose honors are too high to vouchsafe such base loues. [Sig. H4; 1:63]

Conventional humanist imagery strains to transcend, inspired by a pearl of great price. Life as a pilgrimage also suggests that the intersecting parallel movements develop. As Lodge's story matures, so do the characters, their rhetorics transforming with them: the starched retardation of the lexicon employed by Phoebe and Montanus is meant to make this evident. Here, in a later scene and with a more restrained rhetoric, is Saladyne, speaking to his brother whom he does not yet recognize.

> I kept ROSADER as a slaue. . . . The Gods not able to suffer such impietie vnreuenged, so wrought, that the King pickt a causeles quarrell against me, in hope to haue my lands, and so hath exiled me out of *France* for euer. Thus, thus sir, am I the most miserable of all men, as hauing a blemish in my thoughts for the wrongs I proffered ROSADER, and a touche in my state to be throwen from my proper possessions by iniustice. Passionate thus with manie griefes, in penaunce of my former follies, I goe thus pilgrime like to seeke out my Brother, that I may reconcile my selfe to him in all submission, and afterward wend to the holy Land, to ende my yeares in as manie vertues, as I haue spent my youth in wicked vanities. [Sig. L4v; 1:88]

The inciting event was the loss of land; but the important concern is the loss of a brother, of brotherhood. In *Rosalynde,* a whole survey of humanist rhetorics in the various riches of Ciceronian, Ovidian, and Petrarchan vocabularies transcends their customary limitations. In their delivery, statement leads to testament, hope to trust; self-defense becomes self-analysis and, then, self-realization. In their forms, declamations and disputations (in the inner debates) grow outward, become conversational, and then slip past conventional arrangement (dispositio) altogether. Traditional expressions peel away, and we are left to watch the transforming power of love as openly religious, the miraculous salvation of Rosader from the hands of a wrestler who has just killed two stronger franklins prophesying Saladyne's conversion and Rosalynde's ability to be resurrected from Ganimede.[15]

Rosalynde's rebirth, turning magical promise into miraculous presence, and metamorphosing a holiday into a holy day—a holy rite—recalls the humanist fiction of wonder by Greene. In Lodge's hands, however, such events are never mundane but rather figural, as the language here becomes openly Christian at the last. Rosalynde, we are told, is a figure of "grace," and the effect of her reappearance on others is also that of conversion.

> *Gerismond* seeing his daughter, rose from his seat & fel vpon her necke, vttering the passions of his ioy in watry plaints driuen into such an extasie of content, that hee could not vtter one word. At this sight . . . *Rosader* was both amazed & ioyfull. [Sig. R3v; 1:134]

"An ecstasy of content; both amazed and joyful": these are conventional religious paradoxes arising like the phoenix from what at first appeared a more conventional humanist fiction. Rosalynde's relinquishment, too, is constructed to position itself as a rebirth: she unites father and daughter (and so family) and three pairs of lovers (and so marriages). As with the more holy Resurrection, this too renews by healing ruptures. But it is not Christ whom Lodge names: wishing instead to show the power of humanist poetics to transform through Christian instruction and imitatio, he uses its more customary image of "phoenix." This is choric: Sir John was the first "Phenix" for Lodge (sig. B1v; 1:10); Montanus is recast as the "Phoenix" (sigs E4–F1; 1:40–41); the word is finally applied to Rosalynde (sig. H3; 1:61). Her inner resources for transforming herself allow her to transform them, allow the others to learn to transform themselves. All dichotomies disappear—the familial, political, social, and class conflicts; the antitheses between court and country, envy and love, ambition and sacrifice, art and nature, idea and act. The multiple and divisive are made One.

Taught by Rosalynde to look beyond and behind events, we can see how carefully Lodge has implied, too, that the events of the Old Testament prophesy the New and are transformed into them. The story of Saladyne and Rosader, for instance, hews closely to that of Cain and Abel.

> But vnto Kain and to his offring he had no regarde: wherefore Kain was exceding wroth, & his countenance fel downe.
>
> Then the Lord said vnto Kain, Why art thou wroth? and why is thy countenence cast downe?
>
> If thou do wel, shalt thou not be accepted? and if thou doest not well, sinne lieth at the dore: also vnto thee his desire *shal be subiect,* and thou shalt rule ouer him.
>
> Then Kain spake to Habel his brother. And when they were in the field, Kain rose vp against Habel his brother, and slew him.
>
> Then the Lord said vnto Kain, Where is Habel thy brother? Who answered, I cā not tel. Am I my brothers keper?
>
> Againe he said, What hast thou done? the voyce of thy brothers blood cryeth vnto me from the grounde.
>
> Now therefore thou art cursed from the earth, which hath opened her mouth to receiue thy brothers blood from thine hand. [Gen. 4:4–11]

This text is from the Geneva Bible, where an annotation to the seventh verse refers specifically to the paradox when event counters principle—in this case, too, the principle of primogeniture: "The dignitie of ye first borne is giuen to Kain ouer Habel." This rupture of brotherhood, which lays the foundation for Christ's great commandment, is redeemed in the spiritual fraternity urged in Galatians.

> For brethren, ye haue bene called vnto libertie: onely vse not your libertie as an occasion vnto the flesh, but by loue serue one another.
>
> For all the Law is fulfilled in one worde, which is this, Thou shalt loue thy neighbour as thy self.

If ye byte & deuoure one another, take hede lest ye be consumed one of another.

Then I say, walke in the Spirit, and ye shal not fulfil the lustes of the flesh. [Gal. 5:13–16]

This alignment of humanist fiction with scriptural text shows how a deep impulse of Lodge's art was anagogic;[16] the story of Rosader's struggle with Saladyne, his conventional courtship with Ganimede, and his final union suggest likewise Augustine's three ages of history—*ante legem, sub lege,* and *sub gratia,* the states of nature, law, and grace (*Of the Trinity* 4.4).

Put in terms of a more conventional Tudor humanism, Lodge leads his characters (and us) through various stages of preparation to that final, revelatory juncture where the quantitative concerns from logic, which concentrates on the abstract, general, flexible, impersonal, and the qualitative concerns of rhetoric, which employs things that are substantial, particular, applicable, and causistic, locate the sources of fiction. In Rome, Seneca Rhetor recalls the examples for *imitatio* of such jointures in *suasoriae* and *controversiae*. Put another way—Sidney's way in the *Defence*—the source of Lodge's fiction of felicity is the fusion of philosophy and history. Exploring this *qualitas* of fiction in a seminal and essential study, Wesley Trimpi writes that

conceptual activities all "estimate" a *particular* thing or state in relation to a qualitative norm of "due" measure, to which it owes its very existence, by taking into account the circumstances in which it moves or exists. Each estimation must change with the temporal progress of its object toward its given realization or completion. This is particularly true of the concept of καιρός, which denotes the precise proportion in which a thing ought to occur in order for it to fulfil its purpose. For the poet, it connotes the principle in accordance with which he should "lay out" his materials most advantageously with regard to his intention and to their importance. The dynamic and individual nature of the objects of qualitative measurement elucidates further Quintilian's preference for the *status qualitatis* over the *coniecturalis*. The latter asks only whether a thing happened. Its "material" is static, fixed (or absent) in history, in which the arguments it seeks are bound (*argumenta ex materia sumit*).[17]

The detractors to such an art form—beginning with Gosson, who refused to see any significance behind the literal image of poetry, the actual character in drama—argue that a story is just (and only) what it pretends to be. Lodge's answer in *Rosalynde* is more advanced in subtlety but essentially no different in kind than what he proposed in his 1580 treatise. Allegory has merely been advanced into anagogy while keeping the trappings of a more traditional humanist fiction practiced by Lyly, Greene, and others. Such a position as Lodge's is necessary to explain the use of the hermaphrodite by Plato in the *Symposium* or the use of the cave in the *Republic* or, for that matter, his use of Socrates in any of the Socratic dialogues. Cicero takes up the same issue in his *De Officiis* (3.9.39), where he defends Socrates' story of Gyges' magical ring. Here, in Trimpi's analysis,

> Cicero is defending Plato's use of the *fabula* of Gyges' ring against certain "philosophers" who criticized it on the grounds that the story was pure fiction (*fictam et commenticiam*). He responds that they miss the significance of this ring and fail to see what it illustrates (*vis huius aemuli et huius exempli*) if they are unwilling to understand the hypothetical nature of the fiction. They refuse to see the meaning of "if possible" (*id si posset*) and the fact that no one ever claimed such a ring could exist. The "assumption" of its existence serves to bring out clearly whether those willing to entertain it might seek what only favored their self-interest (*quod expediat*) or might flee all that is dishonorable (*omnia turpia per se ipsa fugienda*). This fable, then, might be an imitation of one of the models (*exemplis*) offered by nature and truth, an imaginary "sketch" (*umbra et imaginibus,* as opposed to a complete statue, *expressam effigiem*) that we must work from in the absence of an ideal portrait of justice. The word *vis* denotes not only the formal character of the example but the force of its significance in terms of what should be sought or avoided (*expetendum aut fugiendum*). [P. 34]

We would find no Forest of Arden if we were to tramp the borders of Bordeaux in search of it—that is Lodge's point—but there are, potentially, Ardens wherever we are—that is also Lodge's point. The fiction of true *qualitas* moves beyond its particularities to incorporate the widest set of meanings and the fullest set of applications. (In that it resembles the parables in the Scriptures.) Cicero comes to what is in effect a similar position in his defense of the poet, the *Pro Archia Poeta*: "Etenim omnes artes, quae ad humanitatem pertinent, habent quoddam commune vinculum et quasi cognatione quadam inter se continentur"; "Indeed, the subtle bond of a mutual relationship links together all arts which have any bearing upon the common life of mankind" (1.2).[18]

We would miss Lodge's actual *dispositio* in *Rosalynde,* however, as well as much of his subsequent struggle to found a poetics of felicity, if we should stop after having gone even this far. For Lodge, as for the scriptural Jesus, the power of fiction is that it confronts experience directly. Having brought us, along with his characters, to a realization of grace—and how it can inspire life and transform it into a successful pilgrimage—in *Rosalynde,* Lodge returns us to more pressing events (and dangers) in the quotidian, fallen world, just as the New Testament takes up the history after the

Resurrection because we remain lodged in our own clayey beings. We move openly, that is, to the events that have always been just to the edge of Lodge's narrative, the battles against the usurper Torismond. Felicity must be renewed in virtuous action. Lodge thus encloses the moment of transcendence in the needs of every day, as he did in the *Alarum against Vsurers;* Christian reflection and belief exist in the continuing trials of personal, familial, social, and political existence.

Lodge's understanding of "virtuous action" also has its humanist roots in Plato. There is a sense, of course, in which Socrates seems naively to believe that the clearing of the mind through the tough questions of the philosopher is sufficient to bring about moral reformation—hence such well-known dicta as "Virtue is knowledge" and "No one does wrong willfully." But there are dialogues of Plato that take up this problem with greater and more sustained energy, where virtue, or *aretē,* is defined as man's "good judgement in his own affairs, showing how best to order his own home; and in the affairs of his city, showing how he may have most influence on public affairs both in speech and in action" (*Protagoras,* 318E–319A).[19] *Aretē* is also measured by action. The *Protagoras* examines the same questions posed at the start of *Rosalynde*—how can a good man have both good and evil children (326E ff.)—but Plato's discussion is inconclusive. He returns to the knotty problems of defining and understanding the nature of evil in his sequel, the *Meno.* At the close of this Platonic dialogue, Socrates sums the argument.

> If through all this discussion our queries and statements have been correct, virtue is found to be neither natural nor taught, but is imparted to us by a divine dispensation without understanding in those who receive it, unless there should be somebody among the statesmen capable of making a statesman of another. And if there should be any such, he might fairly be said to be among the living what Homer says Teiresias was among the dead—"He alone has comprehension; the rest are flitting shades." In the same way he on earth, in respect of virtue, will be a real substance among shadows. [99E–100A][20]

Virtue is understood by act or by an agent of grace such as Rosalynde or by one teaching another, as Sir John instructs his sons. But even "the certainty of this," Socrates continues, "we shall only know when, before asking in what way virtue comes to mankind, we set about inquiring what virtue is, in and by itself" (100B), when life is an exploration—or a pilgrimage. And Plato also emphasizes Lodge's final point: that despite the desires of a Rosalynde or a Rosader, the world still contains its Torismonds. He moves from a discussion of the *qualitas* of *aretē* in the *Protagoras* and *Meno* to a less immediately hopeful sense of its *quantitas* in the *Republic,* where he admits they are still far from a world where the philosopher is acknowledged king.

> "Unless," said I, "either philosophers become kings in our states or those whom we now call our kings and rulers take to the pursuit of philosophy seriously and adequately, and there is a conjunction of these two things, political power and philosophic intelligence, while the motley horde of the natures who at present pursue either apart from the other are compulsorily excluded, there can be no cessation of troubles, dear Glaucon, for our states, nor, I fancy, the human race either. Nor, until this happens, will this constitution which we have been expounding in theory ever be put into practice within the limits of possibility and see the light of the sun." [5, 473C–E][21]

What is needed is the conjunction we find in the resurrection of Rosalynde, the special *qualitas* of fiction as Lodge means it. This in turn inspires. "Then," Socrates continues before Glaucon,

> "it was the nature of the real lover of knowledge to strive emulously for true being and that he would not linger over the many particulars that are opined to be real, but would hold on his way, and the edge of his passion would not be blunted nor would his desire fail till he came into touch with the nature of each thing in itself by that part of his soul to which it belongs to lay hold on that kind of reality—the part akin to it, namely—and through that approaching it, and consorting with reality really, he would beget intelligence and truth, attain to knowledge and truly live and grow, and so find surcease from his travail of soul, but not before." [6, 490A–B]

The *De Officiis* of Cicero shows the humanists' other primary authority in exacting agreement on the matters of virtuous action as, specifically, service. *Virtutis enim laus omnis in actione consistit:* the whole glory of virtue is in action (1.6.19), but action as Plato and Lodge define it, through service and through the giving up of oneself to others in order to define the self.

> Quoniam, ut praeclare scriptum est a Platone, non nobis solum nati sumus ortusque nostri partem patria vindicat, partem amici, atque, ut placet Stoicis, quae in terris gignantur, ad usum hominum omnia creari, homines autem hominum causa esse generatos, ut ipsi inter se aliis alii prodesse possent, in hoc naturam debemus ducem sequi, communes utilitates in medium afferre mutatione officiorum, dando accipiendo, tum artibus, tum opera, tum facultatibus devincire hominum inter homines societatem. . . . Etenim cognitio contemplatioque naturae manca quodam modo atque incohata sit, si nulla actio rerum consequatur.

> Since, as Plato has admirably expressed it, we are not born for ourselves

alone, but our country claims a share of our being, and our friends a share; and since, as the Stoics hold, everything that the earth produces is created for man's use; and as men, too, are born for the sake of men, that they may be able mutually to help one another; in this direction we ought to follow Nature as our guide, to contribute to the general good by an interchange of acts of kindness, but giving and receiving, and thus by our skill, our industry, and our talents to cement human society more closely together, man to man. . . . service is better than mere theoretical knowledge, for the study and knowledge of the universe would somehow be lame and defective, were no practical results to follow. [1.7.22; 1.43.153][22]

True greatness of spirit, Cicero tells us, consists of morally good deeds, admired and sought after despite any accidents of fortune [1.19.65, 20.66).

But the realm of idea, of *quantitas,* is often divorced from action, from *qualitas;* and the experiences of man's depravity that Plato witnessed shook his beliefs in the possibilities of *aretē,* much as the corrupt behavior of man would come increasingly to challenge Lodge. In his poignant seventh letter, Plato recounts the death of his beloved Socrates and his sudden understanding

When . . . I considered . . . the type of men who were administering the affairs of State, with their laws too and their customs, the more I considered them and the more I advanced in years myself, the more difficult appeared to me the task of managing affairs of State rightly. [325D][23]

Nevertheless, his commitment to virtue in action is so strong that when the promising young ruler Dion seeks his counsel, Plato agrees to advise him because "if we were ever to attempt to realize our theories concerning laws and government, now was the time to undertake it" (328B–C). But all his endeavors are "scattered . . . to the winds" (337D), for experience teaches him irrevocably that virtuous intention and example are, in his world, not enough.

In dealing with the unrighteous, a righteous man who is sober and sound of mind will never be wholly deceived concerning the souls of such men; yet it would not, perhaps, be surprising if he were to share the fate of a good pilot, who, though he certainly would not fail to notice the oncoming of a storm, yet might fail to realize its extraordinary and unexpected violence, and in consequence of that failure might be forcibly overwhelmed. And Dion's downfall was, in fact, due to the same cause; for while he most certainly did not fail to notice that those who brought him down were evil men, yet he did fail to realize to what a pitch of folly they had come, and of depravity also and voracious greed; and thereby he was brought down and lies fallen, enveloping Sicily in immeasurable woe. [351D–E]

To his despair, Plato learns bitterly the lesson Socrates tells more jocularly in the fable of the ship's crew where each would be captain, robbing the ship of any possibility of firm guidance (*Republic,* 6.488A–489A). Cicero's *Epistulae ad Familiares* is likewise full of disillusioned references to the practices of men—in the many letters to Lentulus Spinther (1) and to his wife Terentia (14); in his plea to Brutus to free Rome from despotic rule (11.5.2); and, in the *Epistulae ad Brutum,* when he asserts that "non ratio, non modus, non lex, non mos, non officium valet, non iudicium, non existimatio civium, non posteritatis verecundia"; "reason, moderation, legality, tradition, loyalty carry no weight; trained judgement, public opinion, respect for posterity go for nothing" (18.3).[24] Among the Tudors, Ascham in *The Scholemaster* sees the same abhorrent behavior in the learned of his time who are without religion, without felicity:

> they geuing themselues vp to vanitie, shakinge of the motions of Grace, driuing from them the feare of God, and running headlong into all sinne, first, lustelie contemne God, then scornefullie mocke his worde, and also spitefullie hate and hurte all well willers thereof. [Sig. I4]

Like the willful and wrongheaded readers of *Rosalynde,* they "counte as Fables, the holie misteries of Christian Religion" (sig. I4).

If Shakespeare's *As You Like It* is any indication, most of Lodge's readers suffered from such kind of misprision, in one form or another. Or so Lodge must have felt, for he spent the next quarter-century—the major part of his writing career—more openly condemning sin and praising virtue in action, searching still further for a more reliably successful humanist poetics of felicity. It signals the second clear stage in his work. *Catharos* (1591), published a year after *Rosalynde,* takes as its Senecan model Lucian's cynical philosopher Diogenes, exposing human nature from the cocoonlike safety of his tub. In a world notable for sin (sig. B1; 2:5), he agrees to advise the magistrate Philoplutos and his friend the philosopher Cosmosophos (sigs. B1v–B2; 2.6–7). To the ruler he remarks,

> First therefore, (*Philoplutos,* since thou art made a Maiestrate) sée thou diligently intend the seruice of the Gods, drawe thy decrees from their diuine motions: so shall thy people more voluntarily accept them, & thou with better conscience publish them. And (as a special rule) learne this second lesson, *Medice, cura teipsum:* pull the beame out of thine owne eye, then helpe thy brother: reforme thy faultes, then punish others folly. For men in authoritie are eyes of estate, according to whose life, euerie priuate man applieth his manner of life; so that the Poet said truly, *Regis ad exemplum totus componitur orbis.* [Sigs. B3v–B4; 2:10–11]

The wisdom offered Cosmosophos is even more explicit, if strange coming from a Cynic philosopher:

> heare you me, those men that are called to the seruice of the Gods, must haue vpright hearts, neither selfe will nor worldly promotion must withdraw them, *What profiteth a man to winne the whole world, and to loose his owne soule?* Such as are teachers of the simple sort must be as starres in darke nightes, lampes in blinde walkes. What profiteth it the talent to be hidden or what is gold vnlesse it byde the tryall? Those that haue care of soules, must be carelesse of the worlde, careles of wealth: and if danger threaten their flocke, they ought rather to suffer death, than to sée them seduced. [Sig. D2v; 2:24]

Such *theses* are applied to all the estates of man, through precept and fable, but the concentration is on usury and lechery, reapplying some passages from *An Alarum against Vsurers. Catharos* "is another example of Lodge's lifelong desire to lead the world into the paths of righteousness by means of pure satire or by exhortation," N. Burton Paradise sums.[25]

Catharos transfers the imitatio of Lucian's spirit (and that of the traditional Diogenes) to the exhortative structure of the Protestant sermon; in *Wits Miserie, and the Worlds Madnesse* (1596) the *Encomium Moriae* of Erasmus is Lodge's Senecan original. It begins where Erasmus ends, in the drunkenness of man and his tipsy, uncontrolled confession, metamorphosing the awareness of depravity shared by those primary humanist authorities, Plato and Cicero, with the apparently jocular, seemingly reckless, but sternly moral prose style that Nashe was also by this time perfecting. *Wits Miserie* portrays a world thickly populated with devils—where *Catharos* had been content to attack two deadly sins in a forensic oration, *Wits Miserie* catalogues all seven; but Lodge, still fashioning a particular poetics of felicity, draws heavily on scriptural and patristic learning. His encomium moriae finds additional patterns in the seven sins of the Apocalypse and in the sevenfold structure outlined by Augustine in his treatise *Of the Trinity* (4.4). In his initial *narratio,* Lodge schemes his work so that we cannot miss the antique texts of Plato and Cicero renewed by received Christian belief.

> When that old serpent the deuill (who with his tayle, drew vnto him the third part of the starres, and with his seuen heads and ten hornes, combated with *Michael* and his Angels) was ouercome: knowing (like a wily foxe as hée is) that his power was limited by a greater, and himselfe restrained by the mighty: yet willing to become Gods Ape (whome in enuie hée could not ouercome) hée sent out seuen deuils to draw the world to capitall sinne, as God had appointed seuen capitall Angels (who continually minister before

him) to infuse vertues into men, and reduce soules to his ser[u]ice. And as the seuen good are *Michael, Gabriel, Raphael, Vriel, Euchudiel, Barchiel,* and *Salthiel:* So of Sathans ministers, *Leuiathan* is the first, that tempteth with Pride; *Mammon* the second, that attempteth by Auarice; *Asmodeus* the third, that seduceth by Lecherie: *Beelzebub* the fourth, that inticeth to Enuie; *Baalberith* the fift, that prouoketh to Ire: *Beelphogor* the sixt, that mooueth Gluttony: *Astaroth* the seuenth, that induceth Sloth and Idlenes.

These seuen capitall sinnes sent out into the world, wanted no allurements to bewitch the eie; no oratory, to seduce the ear; no subtilty, to affect the sences: so that finally, seazing on the hearts of men, and wedded to their thoughts, they haue brought foorth many and pernicious children, to the generall mischiefe of all nature. Some like Centaures, begotten of clouds, (as *Ambition:*) some like Serpents, nourished in corrupt dunghils, (as *Sensualitie:*) some like vapors, raised vp to be consumed, (as *Flattery.*) Generally all so dangerous, that as rust deuoureth the iron, and the moth the garment, so do these sinnes our soules. [Sig. B1v; 4:8]

But even this compendium is not complex enough; his human anatomy of breeding sin produces a generous progeny that turns his categories into a moral organon to complete the more scientific organon of Aristotle.

Both *Catharos* and *Wits Miserie* are decided attempts, then, to marry humanist tradition to Christian strictures; in their combined portraits of fallen men, they lend more urgency to the precepts Sir John gives us at the opening of *Rosalynde* and confirm the view of the world as Hell that we find in Nashe's *Unfortunate Traueller*. Earlier, Lodge had attempted the same sort of moral allegation by way of drama. The *Wovnds of Ciuill VVar* (written between 1586 and 1589; published in 1594)[26] is Lodge's study of the naked power and machinations of ruthless leaders and of their delight in the savagery of war and bloodshed derived ultimately from Appian's *Civil Wars* (1.7–8) and Plutarch's *Life of Sulla* (3; 11 ff.) and *Life of Marius* (especially 33 ff.), three overlapping Greek histories of Rome that hesitate in finding anything to praise in their narratives of the butchery by Roman leaders. Lodge's immediate source is North's English translation of Appian (1578);[27] this alone provides a softening touch to Sulla's death, which in *The Wovnds of Ciuill VVar* gives the play the shape of the sermon Lodge wants. Appian's morality is insinuated in his outrage; but Plutarch's more openly didactic framework, in Sir Thomas North's 1579 translation, would clearly have been more to Lodge's taste. Here the early modest behavior of Marius aiming to win the consulship, his religious sacrifices before battle, and—throughout Plutarch's account—his belief in omens of good and bad fortune all prepare us for his final defeat at the hands of Sulla. This sense of Roman history as parable, easily translated into a story of the rewards of good and evil, may have caused Lodge to be attracted to

Plutarch; surely it was an early stage of his defining a poetics of felicity. A second play published under Lodge's name, *A Looking Glasse, for London and Englande,* was written in collaboration with Greene, probably around 1586.[28] Conceptually, the play is more of a piece with Lodge's poetics than with Greene's—the title tells us the play is meant allegorically, the story combines the Old Testament with a knowledge of Rasni of Nineveh taken from Josephus,[29] and the language of Rasni, dressed in sackcloth and ashes, is tonally closer to Lodge:

> *Rasni.* My soule is buried in the hell of thoughts,
> Ah *Aluida,* I looke on thée with shame.
> My Lords on sodeine fixe their eyes on ground,
> As if dismayd to looke vpon the heauens.
> Hence *Magi,* who haue flattered me in sinne.
> [Sig. H3v; 4.60]

The opening scenes in Nineveh, moreover, limning an anatomy of the seven deadly sins, the dramatic use of omens (reminiscent of the *Life of Marius*), and the presence of Hosea who, like Sir John of Bordeaux, hangs over the sons of London to exhort them to repent the sins of their fathers, all display Lodge's steady emphasis on man's fallen state. There is little cause, then, to wonder that the play, printed in 1598, was thought at the first to be wholly by Lodge.

For, by then, it was also clearly established—with his fictions of Robert, duke of Normandy, and William Longbeard, for example—that his humanist poetics of felicity naturally sought historical analogues: of all the Tudor writers of humanist fiction, Lodge is their chief historiographer. For him the use of Josephus's history of the Jews was as useful and illuminating a starting place as Plutarch's lives of noble Greeks and Romans or Appian's Roman history. In this practice, Lodge had much classical authority. "Est enim proxima poetis et quodammodo carmen solutum, et scribitur ad narrandum," Quintilian observes; "For [history] had a certain affinity to poetry and may be regarded as a kind of prose poem, while it is written for the purpose of narrative" (*Institutio Oratoria* 10.1.31).[30] Tudor pedigrees were also plentiful; George Puttenham, for one, writes pointedly that

> the Poesie historicall is of all other next the diuine most honorable and worthy, as well for the common benefit as for the speciall comfort euery man receiueth by it. No one thing in the world with more delectation reuiuing our spirits then to behold as it were in a glasse the liuely image of our deare forefathers, their noble and vertuous maner of life, with other things autentike. . . . Therefore the good and exemplarie things and actions of the former ages, were reserued only to the historicall reportes of wise and

graue men. . . . These historical men neuerthelesse vsed not the matter so precisely to wish that al they wrote should be accounted true, for that was not needefull nor expedient to the purpose, namely to be vsed either for example or for pleasure: considering that many times it is seene a fained matter or altogether fabulous, besides that it maketh more mirth than any other, works no lesse good conclusions for example then the most true and veritable. [*Arte of English Poesie,* sigs. F4–F4v]

Lodge clearly shared such sentiments. In a personal letter dated 22 November 1609 and only recently rediscovered by Joseph Houppert, the childless Lodge writes a "foster" son William Trumbull concerning his view on history.

I will briefly inform you in my mind how you make the use of your reading to your best profit in your kind. In reading history first choose the most approved—either Romans or others. And observe in them first that time wherein they wrote, the Princes under whom they served, the style wherein they write, their uprightness in judgment, their error in flattery, their disembling with times, their affections in religion, and as near as you may, begin with the most ancient. Then draw to yourself a book of common places wherein observe in every year the action and person of the Prince, the secret designs of his counselors, the rise or fall either of obscure or noble, the revolts or pacifications in religion, the rebellions, their causes and ends and so forth. And yielding each of these a due place under a fit title (not forgetting another book for quick and argute sentences, sayings and answer) and undoubtedly being furnished with this method, and prosecuting this course, you shall hoard up such a treasure for your memory, by this order (which as Plato saith is *memoriae custos*) that by yourself you shall readily reckon up the annals of time, unbowel the vicissitudes of ages, yea make yourself able to satisfy yourself or any man in any occurrent that is past. The use thereof these times and your occasions will easily teach you to find out.[31]

Indeed, history is the *only* kind of reading Lodge recommends.

Lodge's use of history here is traditional—both as a means of study and as a functioning pattern for humanist fiction where antique and Christian learning function correlatively. His counsel agrees with the Greek historian Polybius. "Had previous chroniclers neglected to speak in praise of History in general," Polybius writes,

it might perhaps have been necessary for me to recommend everyone to choose for study and welcome such treatises as the present, since there is no more ready corrective of conduct than knowledge of the past. But all historians, one may say without exception, and in no half-hearted manner, . . . have impressed on us that the soundest education and training for a life of active politics is the study of History, and that the surest and indeed the only method of learning how to bear bravely the vicissitudes of fortune, is to recall the calamities of others. [1.1.1][32]

Later he returns to the uses of history, adding,

> there are two ways by which all men can reform themselves, the one through their own mischances, the other through those of others, and of these the former is the more impressive, but the latter the less hurtful. Therefore we should never choose the first method if we can help it, as it corrects by means of great pain and peril, but ever pursue the other, since by it we can discern what is best without suffering hurt. Reflecting on this we should regard as the best discipline for actual life the experience that accrues from serious history; for this alone makes us, without inflicting any harm on us, the most competent judges of what is best at every time and in every circumstance. [1.35.7–10]

Doubtless it is the combination of painless reformation combined with a present guarding self-discipline or "virtue in action" that appealed to Lodge; moreover, history, too, confronted directly the image of fallen man that had so hounded Plato and Cicero. By placing man's acts of corruption in a safely remote past or in a remote *fiction* (as Nashe apparently could not do), Lodge (like Polybius) posits a more promising present; and when this failed, he could use the lessons dictated by historians for his own direction and, through fiction, plan for a better future.

Polybius was a set text at Trinity College, Oxford; Livy was the set text at the Merchant Taylors' School. Livy, for Tacitus *eloquentiae ac fidei praeclarus in primis,* a splendid stylist and a serious historian (*Annales* 4.34.3), also defended history as instructive, adding specifically its application through imitatio, as of a Senecan model.

> Hoc illud est praecipue in cognitione rerum salubre ac frugiferum, omnis te exempli documenta in inlustri posita monumento intueri; inde tibi tuaeque rei publicae quod imitere capias, inde foedum inceptu, foedum exitu, quod vites.

> What chiefly makes the study of history wholesome and profitable is this, that you behold the lessons of every kind of experience set forth as on a conspicuous monument; from these you may choose for yourself and for your own state what to imitate, from these mark for avoidance what is shameful in the conception and shameful in the result. [1. pref. 10–11][33]

Livy's *Ab Urbe Condita,* annalistic in form, displays a sturdy idealism and a remarkable range of tolerance which admits, again and again, passionate accounts of the deeds of noble men. Pentad after pentad stresses moral attributes and patriotic service: strategic reading for grammar school boys. But, for tussling with Latin syntax, they must have learned at some cost of Livy's elegant, even elaborate style—"cum in narrando mirae iucunditatis clarissimique candoris," as Quintilian puts it, "tum in contionibus supra quam enarrari potest eloquentem"; "a wonderful charm and transparency in narrative, while his speeches are eloquent beyond description" (10.1.101). It is a fine style that Lodge imitates in long stretches of *Robert,* as it is a style imitated by Dio Cassius (*Roman History,* 1.2), another set text. Such histories as these—along with the intense personal drama of Caesar's commentaries and the epic history of Lucan (where the use of omens is caught in Marlowe's contemporary translation)—seem to have taught Lodge those skills in rhetoric that are most useful to a poetics grounded in historiography: hypotyposis, pragmatographia, prosopopoeia, topographia, topothesia, chronographia.

Only such a poetics can account for the anthology of *"manie famoue pirats,"* which is tacked to the end of Lodge's next work of humanist fiction, *The Life and Death of william Long beard, the most famous and witty English Traitor, borne in the Citty of London,* published in 1593 (sigs. E1v–E3; 2:38–42), as well as the other accumulated moments or catalogues from history, some meant to awaken admiratio (such as Valasca, sigs. G1v–G4v; 2:54–60), others inviting condemnation (such as Rodorigo, sigs. H2v–H3; 2:64–65); together with the biography of William, they constitute "a glasse for all sorts to looke into" (sig. E1; 2:37). William's history itself is meant to demonstrate the abuse of history—the whole of *William Long beard* is developed by inversion. The evil signs at William's birth (sig. A1; 2:5), his failure to heed his brother's blasphemy at his public execution (sig. A2; 2:7), and his friendship with a depraved abbot (sigs. A2–A2v; 2:7–8) anticipate the following of ruffians attracted to his leadership by his misuse of rhetoric: with "honie spéech, he so animated the multitude, that like a second *Hercules* he drew them by the eares thorow the honie of his eloquence" (sig. A3; 2:9). William uses his ill-begotten talent to practice usury and to parody preachers with his own infernal sermons:

> the prouerbe is true among vs nowadaies.
> ### Homo homini Demon.
> We liue as we should know no lack, we flourishe as if we feare no fall, we purchase as if life could not perish: to win the world we make shipwracke of our soules. [Sig. B2; 2:15]

Demonic acts match demonic words: he "began . . . animating the baser sort against the better: so that the Nobilitie put vp much iniurie at his hands, the clergie were badlie vsed by him, and the officers of the cittie highlie offended" (sig. B2v; 2:16). His inexcusable behavior and unspeakable crimes cause London to rise against him, and he flees, with a carpenter's axe in his hand as a weapon, "into Bow church, not for his sanctuarie, but for a bulwarke of his safetie" (sig. D1; 2:29). Thus "That church which was sacred to praiers, was now made a den of rebels" (sig. D1v; 2:30) until the king's officers arrest and execute him. Brought to public death like his brother, William's final blasphemy is the misuse of history itself.

> But you will saie, I haue animated subiects against their prince. I confesse it, but vnder a milder title; I haue councelled them to compasse libertie, which (if nature might be equall iudge betwéene vs) I knowe should not be so hainouslie misconstred. [Sig. D2v; 2:32]

He turns his life into a historic object lesson for high treason. Such bad faith betrays the ignorant and innocent even after his death.

> There were manie superstitious women, who in their deuotion were wont to pray to him, and after his death digged vp the ground about the gallowes trée, affirming that manie had beene healed of sundrie sicknesses by the touch thereof. All this their idolatrous constructions at first began by reason of a priest, a néere alie to *William,* who openlie preached, that by vertue of a chaine wherewith *William* was bound, during the time of his imprisonment, ther were diuers men healed of hot feauers, the bloud that fell from him at such time as he was quartered, they cléerelie scraped vp, leauing nothing that could yéeld any memorie of him, either vnsought or vngotten: But at last the Archbishop of Canterburie remedied all these thinges, who firste accursed the Priest that brought vp the fables, and after that caused the place to be watched, where-through such idolatrie ceased, and the people were no more seduced. [Sigs. D3v–D4; 2:34–35]

Lodge emphasizes the moral: clearly he was attracted to the life of William just *because* he was reprobate—as if the subdued evil in *Rosalynde* failed to communicate sufficiently and he was determined to paint depravity in its ugliest colors. Behind the history is the intensely felt need for felicity still. And bliss is once more the final subject for Lodge; he concludes the story of William Longbeard with some "spirituall hymnes and songs" (sigs. D4–D4v; 2:35–36) to correct the way to damnation by describing the path to salvation. As a humanist historiographer, Lodge follows Caesar in this—*William Long beard,* like Caesar's various commentaries, seems one long *apologia pro vita sua*—while using the rhetorical speeches popularized by Appian, Polybius, and Livy.

If nothing else, a coarse and hasty humanist fiction like *William Long beard* seems to have taught Lodge that the most apt form of historiography, given the educated humanist's tendency for imitatio and the untrained reader's interest in heroes, was neither chronicle nor annal but biography. There is a clear direction for a humanist poetics in moral historical biography in the Statutes of Merchant Taylors' School derived by Colet and Erasmus from Quintilian (*Institutio Oratoria* 2.4.20–21). The study of historical biography is used to teach encomia, invective, and the collection and use of *florilegia* (2.4.21–22). The chief biographer used as a set text at Trinity was Suetonius, whose history of the twelve Caesars developed an understanding of history as the story of its leaders. Suetonius's dispassionate, astringent style is at variance with his rapid and dramatic narrative— more akin to Lodge—but his choice of writing history as *eidologie,* or classified accounts, rather than *chronologie,* narrative accounts, taken over from the Peripatetics, is clearly the model for the several additional sketches appended to the history of William Longbeard. Suetonius's formulaic pattern for lives, moreover—the subject's family and early life, his public career, his physical appearance, his private life—is the model for the dispositio of the chronicle material on William himself. Suetonius was fascinated by more colorful vices and more dramatic misdeeds, perhaps suggesting to Lodge that he could carry this to an extreme in his *dyscomium* of William and so make his point.

The chief difficulty with Suetonius for us (and doubtless for Lodge too) is that he makes no moral discriminations, no critical judgments. For that very reason, Plutarch was for Lodge a more important resource. Like Suetonius, Plutarch centers on epideictic rhetoric; unlike Suetonius, Plutarch's *Lives* take a decidedly moral shape—for him, *bion graphein* (to write a life) means to tell a story, his *viri illustres* diverting as well as instructive narratives. The choice is an important one, for Plutarch developed his own deliberate poetics, which he sets forth at the beginning of his *Life of Theseus*. In the 1579 translation by Sir Thomas North, doubtless the one Lodge knew, Plutarch writes that

> Like as historiographers describing the world (frende Sossius Senecio) doe of purpose referre to the vttermost partes of their mappes the farre distant regions whereof they be ignoraunt, with this note: these contries are by meanes of sandes and drowthes vnnauigable, rude, full of venimous beastes, *Scythian* ise, and frosen seas. . . . Wherein I would wishe that the inuentions of Poets, and the traditions of fabulous antiquitie, would suffer them selues to be purged and reduced to the forme of a true and historicall reporte: but when they square too much from likelyhode, and can not be made credible, the readers will of curtesie take in good parte that, which

I could with most probability wryte of such antiquities. [Sigs. A1–A1v; 1:29–30]

Plutarch is plainly drawing on the remarks of Strabo, as his analogy to geography makes evident; and Strabo's own comments on this point are pertinent.

> Now the aim of history is truth, as when in the Catalogue of Ships the poet [Homer] mentions the topographical peculiarities of each place, saying of one city that it is "rocky," of another that it is "on the uttermost border," of another that it is the "haunt of doves," and of still another that it is "by the sea"; the aim of rhetorical composition is vividness, as when Homer introduces men fighting; the aim of myth is to please and to excite amazement. But to invent a story outright is neither plausible nor like Homer; for everybody agrees that the poetry of Homer is a philosophic production. [*Geography* 1.2.17]

Poetry for Plutarch—as for Strabo—lies somewhere between truth and myth; here "History is *terra cognita*," Wesley Trimpi sums, "fiction *incognita*, which must be rendered probable in order to pass for history" ("Quality of Fiction," p. 48; cf. pp. 80–81 rep. *Muses*, p. 292). Both Plutarch and Strabo go back to a common source in Plato's *Statesman*, that is, and to his practice in the *Republic*.

That this particular Plutarchan poetics was not merely an expedient theory for the *Lives* is shown by the way Plutarch develops the same position, in greater detail still, in his essay "How to Study Poetry":

> "truth, because it is what actually happens, does not deviate from its course, even though the end be unpleasant; whereas fiction, being a verbal fabrication, very readily follows a roundabout route, and turns aside from the painful to what is more pleasant. For not metre nor figure of speech nor loftiness of diction nor aptness of metaphor nor unity of composition has so much allurement and charm, as a clever interweaving of fabulous narrative. But, just as in pictures, colour is more stimulating than line-drawing because it is life-like, and creates an illusion, so in poetry falsehood combined with plausibility is more striking, and gives more satisfaction, than the work which is elaborate in metre and diction, but devoid of myth and fiction." [*Moralia*, 16B–C][34]

It is here that we also find explicit Plutarch's desire to shape his work to teach virtue—and, as Lodge is quick to note, virtuous action.

> Whenever we find any edifying sentiment neatly expressed in the poets we ought to foster and amplify it by means of proofs and testimonies from the philosophers, at the same time crediting these with the discovery. For this is right and useful, and our faith gains an added strength and dignity

whenever the doctrines of Pythagoras and of Plato are in agreement with
what is spoken on the stage or sung to the lyre or studied at school, and
when the precepts of Chilon and of Bias lead to the same conclusions as our
children's readings in poetry. [*Moralia,* 35F]

He carries this same theory directly into the *Lives*.

For like as the eye is most delited with the lightest and freshest cullers: euen
so we must geue our mindes vnto those sightes, which by looking vpon them
doe drawe profit and pleasure vnto vs. For such effects doth vertue bring:
that either to heare or reade them, they doe printe in our hartes an earnest
loue and desire to followe them. [Sig. O6; 2:1–2]

So the *Life of Pericles*. The same ideas are raised again in the *Life of Aratus*,
where he argues that "in joyning their owne [parents'] vertues, of their
auncesters, they do increase their glorie, as inheriting their vertuous life, as
challenging their disent by blood" (sig. 6H1; 6:241). By this, Plutarch
means not simply blood ancestry but cultural ancestry, for the noble Greeks
and Romans he limns are common ancestors to him and to his readers. In
the *Life of Alexander* he explains why this history may take on the form of
fabula:

I do not declare al things at large, but briefly touch diuers, chiefly in those
their noblest acts & most worthy of memory. For they must remember, that
my intent is not to write histories, but only liues. For, the noblest deedes
doe not alwayes shew mens vertues and vices, but oftētimes a light
occasion, a word, or some sporte makes mens naturall dispositions and
maners appeare more plaine. [Sig. 3P1v; 4:298]

Such concerns are especially acute in the distant, semimythic lives of
Theseus and Romulus. This provides another basis for his insistent
morality and thereby further instructs Lodge.

Thus you heare howe neere *Fabius Pictor* and *Diocles Perparethian* doe
agree in reciting the storie, who was the first in mine opinion that wrote
the foundation of the cittie of *Rome:* howbeit there are that thincke they
are all but fables & tales deuised of pleasure. But me thincks for all that,
they are not altogether to be reiected or discredited, if we will consider
fortunes straunge effects vpon times, and of the greatnes also of the
Romaine empire: which had neuer atchieued to her present possessed
power & authoritie, if the goddes had not frō the beginning bene workers
of the same, & if there had not also bene some straūge cause, and
wonderfull foundation. [*Life of Romulus,* sig. C1; 1:78]

Amyot, in his preface to the French translation of 1559, also speaks of the
Vies as "*an orderly register of notable things sayd, done, or happened in tyme*

past, to mainteyne the continuall remembraunce of them, and to serve for the instruction of them to come," as North has it (sig. A4v; 1:8), while North urges the use of the *Lives* by means of imitatio in his dedicatory letter to Queen Elizabeth—"If they haue done this for glorye, what shoulde we doe for religion? If they haue done this without hope of heauen, what should we doe that looke for immortalitie?" (sig. *2v; 1:4–5)—and amplifies the point in his general preface:

> there is no prophane studye better then Plutarke. All other learning is priuate, fitter for Vniuersities then cities, fuller of contemplacion than experience, more commēdable in the students them selues, than profitable vnto others. Whereas stories are fit for euery place, reache to all persons, serue for all tymes, teache the liuing, reuiue the dead, so farre excelling all other bookes, as it is better to see learning in noble mens liues, than to reade it in Philosophers writings. [Sig. *3; 1.7]

North's translation is wonderfully faithful to Plutarch in showing how great heroes, prone to compromise, fight and die for their ideals. Wherever he can, Plutarch hews to facts and their meanings, eschewing the totally imaginary (as Lodge does in his biography of William Longbeard). Yet Plutarch means to show an essential unity between the Greek culture that is his national heritage and the Roman culture dominant in his own lifetime. Like Plutarch, Lodge argues too—in his biographies, his historical treatises such as *Wits Miserie,* and his philosophical tracts such as *Catharos*—that certain lives may not be worth living but that there are always things worth dying for. We see Lodge borrowing specifically from Plutarch, too, wherever we turn: his sense of William as seductive yet treacherous, eloquent but churlish, is modeled on Plutarch's Alcibiades, as his rebellion may be modeled on that of Aratus or Cinna, his catalogues of pirates and famous men following the *Life of Sertorius*. "Mostly," writes George Wyndham, Plutarch "is absorbed in presenting his heroes as they fought and as they fell; in unfolding, in scene after scene, his *theatrum* of stirring life and majestical death."[35] Like Plutarch, Lodge combines character delineation with the artistry of a detachable *significatio,* as Plutarch supplies to his *Life of Lycurgus*: "he thought the felicitie of a cittie, as of a priuate man, consisted chiefly in the exercise of vertue, and the vnitie of the inhabitants thereof" (sig. F3; 1:162).

Despite such a considerable reliance on Plutarchan poetics, though, Lodge never really affects the conversational, digressive style of Plutarch, just as he never imitates the Isocratean, Demetrian, or Ciceronian rhetoric of Lyly, Greene, and Sidney. Lodge's rhetoric is not drawn from the Second Sophistic, either, as Nashe's is, but the very reverse: it is Tacitean. Lodge's willingness to dismiss finally the elaborate language of Phoebe and Montanus, as well as the courtly language of Rosalynde and Rosader, anticipates the straighforward, even aggressive posture of the style used for *William Long beard*. Not that all variety is eliminated in its Spartan qualities—Ascham says of writing history (with Tacitus in mind) in his *Discourse . . . of the affaires and state of Germany* (1570?) that "The stile must be alwayes playne and open: yet sometime higher and lower as matters do ryse and fall" (sig. A4). But Tacitus's compacted style was not easy. "For Tacitus I may say without partialitie," A. B. writes the reader in prefacing his 1591 translation of Tacitus's *Historiae* by Henry Savile, "that hee hath writen the most matter with best conceyt in the fewest wordes of anie Historiographer ancient or moderne. But he is harde" (sig. ¶3). Such a distinctive style stems directly from Tacitus's own sense of history, and of writing history:

> quod praecipuum munus annalium reor ne virtutes sileantur utque pravis dictis factisque ex posteritate et infamia metus sit.

> my conception of the first duty of history [is] to ensure that merit shall not lack its record and to hold before the vicious word and deed the terrors of posterity and infamy. [*Annales* 3.65][36]

It is with an attitude such as this that the *Annales* and *Historiae* shape his epic theme of the failure of liberty in its struggles against tyranny; with ideas controlling his highly dramatic accounts, such figures as Nero, Agrippina, and Seneca loom large in the foreground while others recede, his overall perspective pitting the evils of someone like Tiberius rather too simply against the virtues of someone like Germanicus. Even in those scenes most stunningly drawn—the death of Agrippina (*Annales* 14.1–8) or the burning of Rome (*Annales* 15.38)—Tacitus relies for their effectiveness on the more trenchant, epigrammatic passages that carry the weight, or *gravitas,* of his thought. The Stoic passivity of Marcus Lepidus (*Annales* 4.20) or Seneca himself (*Annales* 13.2) has the reserve the Tudors found characteristic.

Lodge may have found his most useful Tacitean model in the *Agricola,* translated by Savile in 1591, two years before *William Long beard*. This Roman *laudatio funebris*—a *memoria virtutis* that is something more than merely a rhetorical panegyric—alternates layers of biography and history in presenting Tacitus's father-in-law as the Roman pontifex of Britain, highlighting his youthful education in the liberal arts (4), his military apprenticeship (5), and his rule through a combination of fear and clemency (20). Especially helpful to the author of *William Long beard* may have been the account of rebellion (28) and Agricola's address to his troops (30–34); especially appealing to the scholar Lodge would be the portrait of Agricola as an advocate of peace and quiet (21). Tacitus's "short, brusque, and lapidary" style, as Herbert W. Benario has it,[37] with its intensity, economy, insinuation, and boldness, relies on relatively few rhetorical figures—on parallelism, variation, alliteration, and chiasmus. Plutarch understood the manner of this style, thought it Spartan, and so effects it in the apophthegms in his *Life of Lycurgus* (sigs. R4v ff.; 1:136 ff.). Lodge himself comes to have some misgivings about the laconic style because of its apparent omissions, he tells us in his preface to the *Workes of Seneca* (1620)—but in the emerging second phase of his humanist fiction of felicity, in which he found it necessary to stress man's fallen condition more successfully than he had managed in *Rosalynde,* the forcefulness of Tacitean rhetoric has its merits.

Lodge's next humanist fiction of felicity, *A Margarite of America* (1596)[38] was composed on the disastrous voyage with Cavendish, "whose memorie if I repent not, I lament not" (sig. A4v; 3:4). Lodge claims to have discovered his history of Arsadachus and Margarita among the Catholic holdings in the New World—"in the librarie of the Iesuits in *Sanctum* [was] this historie in the Spanish tong" (sig. A4v; 3.4)—but, within the form of a humanist narrative, his rendering uncovers a fresh and awful sense of human cruelty and mutilation. Human warfare disturbs the peacefulness of nature as the work opens: "both the armies (awaked by the harmonie of the birds, that recorded their melody in euery bush), began to arme them in their tents, & speedily visit their trenches" (sig. B1; 3:5). Then suddenly, miraculously, the war between Protomachus and Artosogon, the rulers of Mosco and Cusco, is halted by the Erasmian counsel of the aged Arsinous, speaking to the folly of war and the massacre of the innocents (sig. B1v; 3:6).

> If for couetousnes ye hunt after conquests, how vaine are you, labouring like mad men to lay more straw on your houses to burn them, and cast more water on the sea to drowne it? Couetousnes is an affection that hath no end, an extreame that hath no meane, a profit full of preiudice. . . . subdue these errors in your selues for your subiects sakes: and sith *Protomachus* hath one daughter, and no more to inherit *Mosco,* and *Artosogon* one sonne and heire to suceede in the Empire of *Cusco;* let both these be ioyned together in happie matrimonie: so shall the cause of this different be quicklie decided, your selfe may roote out your ingrafted errors, your subiects enioy their desired peace, and finally, your Children shal haue greater cause to praise their fathers foresight, then to repent hereafter their vniust furie. [Sig. B2; 3:7]

Arsinous's proposal, couched in the philosophical precepts of humanism put to practical use, brings reconciliation and celebration; and Protomachus takes his daughter to visit the old man. His castle is an emblematic self-extension, a fortress of humanism. Although it is geographically sensual, as Strabo might have it—

> scituate by a gratious and siluer floting riuer, inuironed with curious planted trees to minister shade, and sweete smelling floures, to recreate the sences; besides the curious knots, the daintie gardin plots, the rich tapestrie, the royal attendance. [Sig. B2v; 3:8]

—the order and self-sufficiency are arranged to display humanist *sententiae* that are Tacitean in form and effect (such as "*Illis est grauis fortuna quibus est repentina*" [sig. B3; 3:9]) while his black ebony bed, encased with rubies, diamonds, and carbuncles, supplies an allegorical poem, *Humanae Miseriae discursus,* which develops the seven ages of man as a history grounded in original sin: the fiction's hypothesis (sig. B3; 3:9).

Such unnoticed precepts at the home of a peacemaker suggest the fragility of human intention while introducing a Christian, if not a Catholic, dimension to the fiction—and raising once more the question of felicity. The more secular counterpart is Artosogon's parting counsel to his son Arsadachus, prince of Cusco, counsel that seems deliberately to echo the advice that Sir John of Bordeaux gave to *his* sons.

> Thou art borne a Prince, which being a benefit sent from heauen, is likewise an estate, subiect to all vnhappinesse; for, whereas much durt is, thither come many carrions; where high fortunes; many flatterers, where the huge cedar growes, the thistle springeth, where the foorde is deepest, the fish are plentiest; and whereas soueraigntie is, there are many seducers. . . . In your counsailes, beware of too much affection: and in your actions be not too prowd; for the one will proue your little regard of conscience; the other the corruption of your nature. [Sigs. C3–C3v; 3:17–18]

His call derives from a Christian humanism. But the prince on whose marriage the settlement depends is by nature depraved. For such nature, precepts like these have little effect:

> euen so his lewd thoughts aimed at nothing, but wickednesse were the euident signes of his sinister behauiour: for being well shaped by nature, there was not any man more estranged from nurture; so that it was to be feared, that he should sooner want matter to execute his dishonest mind vpon, then a dishonest mind to execute any lewd matter: for among the traine appointed by his father to attend him, he took no delight but in those who were most lasciuious, who ministring the occasions, bred in him an earnest desire to do ill. [Sig. C4; 3:19]

Against such inner dry rot Lodge poises the ideal trust of Protomachus's daughter, the "pearl" Margarita. But virtue before such corruption is, in the fallen world of original sin, starkly inadequate. Arsadachus is encouraged by his countrymen Brasidas and Capaneus, and by the prince Thebion, countryman of Margarita "who had *Macheuils* prince in his bosome to giue instance," to "worke treasons" (sig. C4v; 3:20) in his pretense of love and courtship. Led to evil counselors concerning his betrothal, Arsadachus is also directed by his own baser instincts in loving Arsinous's daughter Philenia despite her engagement to Minecius. When she rejects his advances, he ambushes the couple on their wedding night, causing both their deaths—"*Minecius* lacking blood, *Philenia* breath, both of them entangled arme in arme, fell downe dead, leauing the memorie of their vertues to be eternized in all ages" (sig. E1v; 3:30). Thus, while he rides splendid to tournament defending Margarita's honor or banters deftly at courtly symposia on love where Margarita appears as the wise and chaste Diana (sig. G1; 3:45), his Machiavellian duplicity—reminiscent of an Alcibiades—parodies the chivalric tournaments in *Arcadia* and the courtly debates of *Il Libro del Cortegiano*. All we have come to trust ourselves for the endurance and well-being of Christian humanism—the precepts of an Artosogon, the exemplary behavior of a Margarita, the redeeming environment of a just and peaceful kingdom like Mosco—do not touch the fact of fall in *A Margarite of America*. Even the lion that had proven friendly to Saladyne, bringing about his reconciliation with Rosader in *Rosalynde,* will here kill and mangle Fawnia while preserving the chaste Margarita, her mistress.

Having returned home, Arsadachus's lust seeks a second, false Diana in the daughter of Argias, duke of Moravia; together they plan a secret marriage, thus destroying any basis for peace between Cusco and Mosco. The aging Artosogon, incensed at this treason, calls Argias before him,

> and without either hearing his excuses, or regard of his intreaties, presently caused him to be torne in peeces at the tailes of foure wilde horses, then casting his mangled members into a litter, hee sent them to *Diana* in a present, vowing to serue her in the same sawce her father had tasted, that durst so insolently aduenture to espouse with the sole heire of his empire. [Sig. K1v; 3:70]

His solace in imitating Thyestes rather than Christ, Caligula rather than Augustus, underscores the failure of a humanism he condemns further still in his second oration—truncated, staccato, Tacitean—canceling the effect of the elaborate precepts he had trusted earlier.

> Well did I hope that thy courage in armes, thy comelinesse in person, thy knowledge in letters were vertues enow to yeelde me hope, and subdue thy follies: but now I say and say againe, I affirme and affiirme againe, I sweare and sweare againe, that if men which are adorned with natural gifts do want requisit vertues, such haue a knife in their hands wherewith they do strike & wound themselues. [Sig. K2v; 3:72]

Such sententious remarks prove true. Arsadachus, like an imperial tyrant in Tacitus,

> was resolued in his villany without any reply (as if scorning the old man) caused his tong by a minister to be cut out, then commaunded his right hand to be strooke off, wherewith he had signed the writ of *Argias* death: afterwards apparelling him in a fooles coate, and fetching a vehement laughter, he spake thus: *Cuscans,* wonder not, it is no seueritie I shew, but iustice; for it is as lawfull for me to forget I am a sonne, as for him to forget he is a father, his tongue hath wronged me, and I am reuenged on his tongue, his hand hath signed to the death of my deere *Argias,* and it hath payed the penaltie: and since the old man doateth, I haue apparelled him according to his propertie and impatience, wishing all those that loue their liues, not to crosse mee in my reuenges, nor assist him in his sinister practises. [Sigs. K2v–K3; 3:72–73]

Even in his affair with Diana, this once glamorous knight is reduced to writing Petrarchan poetry that is marked by images of chill and death and a sense of defeated purpose (sigs. K4, L1, L1v; 3:75, 77, 78).

Through most of this harrowing course of events, the fiction retains some hope of virtuous action and felicity in the loyalty of Margarita, who gives Arsadachus a possible remedy for his corrupted nature:

> she was pacified by *Arsinous,* who told hir that the nature of the medicine which he gaue her, was such, that if *Arsadachus* were constant to her, it would increase his affection; if false, it would procure madnesse. [Sig. M2v; 3:88]

Despite the motto on original sin hanging on his bedpost, Arsinous seems oblivious to the possible damage such a potion might do; on her way to retrieve her missing fiance, Margarita ignores the omen of Fawnia's sudden death. We do not. We are prepared in every way for Arsadachus to go mad when he opens the box—but we may still be unprepared for the massacre that ensues. First, Arsadachus turns to Brasidas and with his cup "tooke him such a mighty blow on the head that he pashed out all his braines" (sig. M2; 3:87). He turns to his bride Diana and "with the caruing knife he slit vp the poore innocent ladies bodie, spreading her entrailes about the pallace floore, and seizing on her heart, hee tare it in peeces with his tyrannous teeth" (sig. M2; 3:87), and, having destroyed their wedding feast, he searches out his bastard son by her and "tooke it by the legges, battering out the braines thereof against the walles, in such sort as the beholders were amazed to see him; this done he flung it on the ground among the dead members of his mother" (sig. M2; 3:87). The horror here is as great as anything in Nashe: no one is safe in this frenzied bloodbath. Margarita arrives and, sensing his madness because of infidelity, she accuses him of murder, and he kills her too with his rapier (sig. M2v; 3:88). Then, fleeing to his chamber with a wild, tormented *confessio* he takes his own life.

Humanist rhetoric in *A Margarite of America,* writes C. S. Lewis,

> is raised to quite a new power. Far from being a mere external decoration, it becomes in the best passages at once an ironic contrast to, and a subtle expression of, the pride and passion of the speakers. If the book is not realistic, it is real; the compulsive imagination of a larger, brighter, bitterer, more dangerous world than ours.[39]

And even here, in the end, Lodge is able to sweep bare a tiny space for a regenerating humanism. Arsinous, "resoluing to spend the residue of his dayes in studies" (sig. F4; 3:43), makes one final speech to the Cuscans and is rewarded with rule of the land by a conquering Protomachus. In addition, he memorializes the tomb of his daughter Philenia and his son-in-law Minecius with an epitaph in keeping with Polybius's sense of the uses of the past. The verse, significantly, moves from classical to Christian humanism.

> Vertue is dead, and here she is enshrined,
>   Within two lifelesse bodies late deceased:
> Beautie is dead, and here is faith assigned
>   To weepe her wracke, who when these dide first ceased.
>   Pitie was dead when tyranny first slew them,
> And heauen inioies their soules, tho earth doth rew them.
> [Sig. E2; 3:31]

But the best is reserved for Margarita, whose epitaph transforms her into sainthood: "A blessed soule from earthly prison losed, / Ye happie heuens hath faith to you conuaide" (sig. N1; 3:93). In the awkward simplicity of his verses, combining faith in another life with trust in this one, all things fall away before the eternal verities of a humanism raised up by religion. The conclusion does not seem so much false or conventional or theatrical as terribly *earned*.

Besides some of the work of Nashe, only one other humanist fiction comes close to this portrayal of depravity in *A Margarite of America:* William Warner's *Pan His Syrinx* (1584; rev. 1597, the year following

Margarite). It is the story of Arbaces, separated from his family at the outset and reunited with them at the close. This frame surrounds seven portraits of man's corruptibility, due, says Warner, to the new age of gold which, following the Flood, is actually an age of greed.

> It is a worlde to note the wondrous alteration of all thinges, euen of late dayes, for omitting to speake of the time before the generall deluge, I will onely glaunce at the superfluitie of this our present age.
> It hath bene, yea within the time of my rememberaunce, that men thought themselues more sure, in their wilde Caues, then now safe in their walled Castles, better contēting themselues with the vnforced fruitfulnesse of the earth, then now satisfied with their fruitlesse compounds enforced by art. The simplicitie of nature prescribed of Ambition absolute law, but ouermuch curiositie now subuerteth both law and nature. What speake I of part? when it is manifest that no sooner golde and siluer the Ambassadors from hell, had insinuated themselues into the hartes of men, but that a generall subuertion was made of all. [Sigs. B3v–B4; 18–19][40]

Like *Margarite,* the central narrative begins with war, murder, and mass suicide (sig. D1; 29); Arbaces' escape (the first episode) is followed by the stories of six other case studies of the iron age. "Thetis" (sigs. D2v–F3v; 33–51) discovers "hanging smooke-dryed three quarters of a man" (sig. D3; 34) and tells of an adulteress punished by enforced cannibalism of her paramour; "Belopares" (sigs. F4–I1; 53–72) tells of a ship's crew that subsists by eating one another. "Calamus quartus," titled "Pheone" (sigs. I1v–M1; 73–98) is a romantic interlude, yet even here, in the loveliest of the tales, inhumanity remains Warner's obsessive theme: when a father and son vie for the same woman, the father "commaunded ... that *Crisippus* should be forthwith bound, and his heart (a present for *Marpissa*) ... carued from out his body" (sig. L3; 94). Clearly an initial shipwreck early in the novel is meant to stand for the subsequent series of shipwrecked souls.

The pastoral "Deipyrus," "Calamus quintus" (sigs. M1v–O2; 99–116), derived from Longus, tells about the king's nephew, who falls into a wolf trap but is saved by the king, while in "Aphrodite" (sigs. O2v–R1v; 117–40), Atys and Abynados are imprisoned by the tyrant Mazeres and escape to punish him at the cost of the lives of their friend Tymetes and his betrothed Aphrodite, who commits suicide. The last enclosed calamity, "Opheltes" (sigs. R2–T3v; 141–61), is Warner's retelling of the prodigal son. This rightly schemes the conclusion when all seven stories, like the pipes of Pan's syrinx, become harmonious. Then the dispossessed queen of Medes, Dricilla, takes the fire from the battlefield, which opens the work and transforms it into the light of learning.

I founde you without Gods, without Religion, without Lawes, or Gouernment, naked, wild, brutish, & beast-like, feeding on Roots, harbouring in Bushes, fearefull of your own shadowes, and to discribe you in a word, Monsters wrapped in man-like habbites: but in these through mine industry you haue now Reformatiō, & were it not that prouender doth pricke you, and fulnesse make you foolish, only you, might be said an happie people: and that, ywis, not somuch in respect the naturall pleasure, and plentie of this your popilous Iland (through a terrestiall Paradise) as in that mine experience and plat-forme hath warned you, and might haue armed you frō the Incursions of these Tyrants, the cōmon Skourge to all people. [Sig. U3v; 170–71]

Warner's final perspective is therefore much more hopeful than Lodge's.

For farther than the relentless portrait of depravity in *Margarite* Lodge's searching poetics for felicity could not go: he is no Nashe, no Juvenalian. He turned instead, in a third phase, toward the Catholicism of his youth as an answer, toward his own growing commitment to recusancy. But these phases of his work are not discrete. His first fiction with a decided Catholic orientation warns us of this. Earlier than the *Margarite,* it is *The Famous, true and historicall life of* Robert, *second Duke* of *Normandy, surnamed for his montrous birth and behauiour,* Robin *the Dieull* (1591). This history from "the *Norman* antiquaries" (sig. C1v; 2:14) combines historical data with a new kind of historical biography, that of the saint's life. Set around 750, the work derives from common legend and numerous folk tales, two of which were published in England by Wynkyn de Worde.[41] The story opens when the duchess Editha, increasingly anxious about her barrenness, one day enters a lovely countryside where

beating her amiable breasts with bitter strokes, . . . finally shee burst out into this small outrage. Well you heauens, since you neglect me, I respect you not, if God vouchsafe me no sonne, the Deuill send me one, so, though my woomb be wretched in bearing, yet happely I shall escape the scandale of vnfruitfulnes. [Sig. B3; 2:9]

In this blasphemous desire, she is overheard by her husband Aubert who reprimands her: "the Creature must not warre with the Creator, nor expostulate vnkindnesse with God" (sig. B3; 2:9). But her subjunctive appeal becomes her fate, her punishment. When Robert is born, "the heauens intimating some prodigious sequell, were afflicted with continuall thunders, the earth shooke as if amazed at Nature, the lightnings flashed with great furie" (sig. B4; 2:11)—like "the straunge & wonderfull signes that were sayd to be seene before *Caesars* death" in Plutarch's *Life* (sig. 3V6v; 5:64)—and the baby is delivered beyond the custome of nature with all his teeth, according to the opinion of the Historiographers, [and] was inchaunted, for instead of drawing nutriment from his Nurse, hee bit off her nipples, and being kissed in the cradle by the Ladie of *Sansernes,* hee bit off her nose. [Sigs. B4–B4v; 2:11–12]

Duchess Editha attempts to forestall further demonic behavior by spiritual and humanist training, seeking "a man of good life and great learning, who might instruct him in the feare of GOD" (sig. B4v; 2:12). But all her attempts fail.

As he matures, this conceivably comic child becomes as cruel and vicious as the depraved Arsadachus. He poisons the "rare" son of his tutor, explaining, "Master . . . I haue but put in practise that which you haue taught me in precept, and since I find you a man of such credite, I will boldly write vnder your lesson *probatum est*" (sig. C1; 2:13), then cuts his master's throat, "smilingly concluding his impietie in this sort. *Ille mihi feriendus aper*" (sig. C1v; 2:14). The duchess now urges repentence, her language transformed from her earlier moment of cursing.

If my secret complaints (thou sinfull yong man) had not more effect to mittigate the heauens, than to mooue thee, I would drie them vp and defie thee, but since they are pitious and respect prayers, I will weepe for thee to winne them to thee, in hope they will be as fauourable in mercie, as I am forward in moane. [Sig. C2v; 2:16]

But in his fallen state nothing will discipline or guide him. On the eve of his knighthood when he is at vigil in the Abbey of St. Peter's in Rouen (now called St. Owen's, the historian Lodge informs us), he enters a nunnery, calls for the nuns to disrobe, and ravishes the most beautiful (sig. C3; 2:8); at the ceremony itself, he draws his sword and very nearly kills his father. Later, banished to his own distant castle, Robert gathers together a gang of men in a life of continuing savagery, riot, debauchery, butchery, and mutilation. Like that of all wicked men, his wrath is drawn particularly to the virtuous; his behavior matches the atrocities in Plutarch's *Life of Sylla.* In one representative episode, he attacks his newly married neighbor, the lord of Beaumont, and

in the presence of his new espoused Bride (who being bound, could no wayes assist hym but with her couragious comforts) hee caused his limmes peecemeale to bee chopped off, and twixt euery torment, continually laboured eyther to perswade the Ladie to loue, or her husband to commaund her to lust. But the young Gentleman feeling the torments insufferable, and fearing his toongs default, bit off the same, depriuing the cruell rauisher the means of further hope, and his Wife occasion of hazarding her honour. Which when the tyrannous Prince perceyued, he increased his cruelties: in midst of which extremitie fayre *Emine* (for so was the Ladie called) cryed out in this sort to her husband: Ah *Bedmond,* the Conquest is welny finished, and loosing thy lyfe, thou hast purchased thy immortalitie. Be bolde noble young man, the deuine spirit shall florish, when this earthly drosse shall vanish: and though wee are separated on earth, we shall be vnited in the heauen. [Sigs. D2–D2v; 2:23–24]

Again, it is the language of religion that Robert cannot abide, as he could not abide the vigil or the nunnery on the eve of his more secular ceremony. Now, turning to Emine, "seeing no meanes possible to accomplish his loose and vnbridled lust, he sheathed his sword in her entralls, who mildly giuing vp the ghost, suffered her death with more then manly courage" (sig. D2v; 2:24).

But such demonic pride feeding on itself is insatiable. Robert oversteps all bounds when he kills one of his country's young peers on a hunt and returns the mangled body to his father; 4,000 rebel against Robert and with Duke Aubert's blessing. The duke of Constance—although the title is willfully ignored by Robert—wounds him in battle and, suddenly alone and without a horse, Robert senses his vulnerability.

Lifting vp his eyes to heauen, he beheld the Moone performing her course, the Starres ministring their dueties, and by their celestiall beautie began with himselfe to imagine the beautie of their maker, then called he to remembrance the olde rudiments of his master, as touching the essence and power of God, the wonderfull workmanship of the heauens, the beautifull order of the spheares, the strange creation of man, the influence of the celestiall bodies in these inferiour parts, and considered that all thinges were made by a determinate and inuiolable lawe limitted by prescript of Nature, and that if in the earthly compact of man the imperfection and griefe of one member afflicted the whole compact, much more a contrarie-tie in the powers both of soule and bodie threatned a confusion. . . . Hereupon began he to meditate on the nature of sinne, the causes of sinne, and the effects of sinne, and him thought that a voyce sounded in his eare, *the reward of sinne is death.* [Sig. E1v; 2:30]

His conversion is immediate, showing how he has harbored the earlier speeches of Duchess Editha, his tutor, and Emine in the deeper parts of his being. Robert no longer feels alone, and God's universe of order and plentitude provides him with a hermit who for the next seven days instructs him in the lessons of a spiritual faith. Thus armed, dressed in a hair shirt, Robert makes his pilgrimage on foot to Rome, no longer able to be frightened by a lion or a storm or seduced by a hamadryad in the Wood of Temptation.

Robert's fall and spiritual rebirth come at the exact center of Lodge's history, its pattern similar to Plutarch's *Life of Themistocles,* for example, where the portrait of a man of courage is transformed at midpoint to a study in patience. The second portion of Robert's life is as filled with incident as the first. His contrition before the pope is Catholic in its orientation while (synthetically) it also makes of him an Erasmian wise fool as he takes the position of court clown. He consigns himself to an additional seven years of penance, sleeping on a bed of straw with the dog belowstairs and willingly seeking the joys of humble service. Virtuous action proves the new disposition of his mind and spirit. When the Antichrist in the person of Behenzar, sultan of Babylon, falls in love with the picture of the mute daughter of the Roman emperor—a new Emine—and invades the citadels of Rome to take her, it is Robert, disguised as a soldier, who defeats him. But, to do so, Robert must forsake his plan of penance; his compromise is not to reveal his identity. In Lodge's instructive historiography, Robert as devil is displaced by the sultan, who now deceitfully claims the hand of the emperor's daughter; the mute woman, however, as counterpart to the foolish Robert, reveals his heroism at her marriage rites to the sultan when she is suddenly awarded the gift of speech. Her sudden rebirth prefaces Robert's rebirth as prince of Normandy—and it declares the sultan to be the new fool (sig. L1v; 2:78). The sultan's awareness of his own guilt gives the pope and emperor the occasion for mercy: they free Robert and permit him to return to his own people.

Now only Duchess Editha remains to learn mercy, and her biography in the second half of Lodge's narrative of salvation resembles Robert's in the first half. When Duke Aubert hears a false report of his son's death, he too dies, grief-stricken, leaving his lands to a trusted peer named Villiers. But greed soon overcomes Villiers, who seizes all the duke's holdings and imprisons Editha, accusing her of poisoning her husband. In solitary confinement, the duchess looks out on nature and, like her son before her, meditates on God's creation and her subversion of her own soul (sig. L3; 2:81). Robert, hearing of his mother's distress, defeats Villiers's knight in a combat of lances. The scene may be meant to recall Gwydonius fighting for his adopted country; but there he was battling his father, while here a son fights to save his mother's life. The difference is crucial—that was romance, and this is testament. "God neuer faileth those who put their trust in his mercie," the duchess vows to herself in her close prison (sig. L3v; 2:82); when Robert arrives, her faith is confirmed: "I know I am innocent; for my Champion, I haue not sought him, but God hath sent him" (sig. M1v; 2:86). Robert begs forgiveness from his mother and executes the rebels. "All the whole people applauded his righteous iudgement, and iustice was orderly executed, whilest each one meruailed at his excellencie and wisedome" (sigs. M2v–M3; 2:88–89), and the emperor bestows Robert his daughter, no longer mute, in marriage.

Given the dimensions and density of Lodge's first spiritual history, the moral he draws in this work seems surprisingly tame, even disappointing: "Here may the dispayring father finde hope in his sonnes vntowardnesse," he tells his gentlemen readers, "and the vntoward soone take example to please his dispayring father" (sig. M3v; 2:90). But, once again, implications count most in reading Lodge. By explicitly linking his history of Robert with the prodigal son stories of Lyly and Greene, he has returned them to the religious context from which they have been disjoined; by emphasizing the validity of parable, he has restored the original meanings to "father" and "son." Classical and secular history—of someone like William Long-beard or Arsadachus—narrates a linear life of a man as a citizen whose fortunes affect society at large and whose life serves as a model for our own participation in civilization. Spiritual history radically alters perspective. Events do not matter at all; the state of the soul counts for everything. Thus there is no need in *Robert, second Duke of Normandy* to hold Robert to account at the end for the murder of Beaumont or Constance; but there is every need to punish Duchess Editha—who killed no one—until she too has learned from experience the act and significance of contrition. Robert's conversion is no more sudden than the Incarnation itself, but his slow, subsequent pilgrimage complements and executes that vital moment. Lodge writes in *Robert* about pilgrimage and felicity—the same concerns he has in *Rosalynde*—but the religiosity is more open in this later phase of his poetics of faith.

This same period of Lodge's thought and work also produces the treatise *The Divel coniured* (1596). It is Lodge's mature *Defense of Poesie*, setting forth a new kind of imitatio for the Tudor humanist:

> it is a law among your sects, for eloquence, to follow *Cicero,* for excellence, *Demosthenes,* for Philosophie, *Plato* and *Aristotle,* for the Mathematicks, *Euclide:* What then letteth me (O *Metrodorus*) to imitate Christ? whose life is a law to mine & whose abstinence a lesson to instruct me? [Sig. B2v; 3:10]

The spokesman is Anthony, a "vertuous and solitarie Hermit . . . who forsaking his possessions, which were great, and renouncing the world as vaine, made the poore rich by his liberalitie, and his soule happie by his charitie" (sig. B1; 3:7). He directs us "with the immoued eie" of our minds to "behold God in faith" (sig. B1v; 3:8). To make plain his message in this, Lodge's most philosophic writing, Anthony preaches in turn to the three

estates of man who are distracted from God by their interest in Hell, the
natural heavens, and earthly affairs. To the first, the magician, he says,

> Thou séest now the vanitie, scope, and issue, of this bodie of curiositie, here
> is nothing in it but deceit; nothing, but blasphemie; no meanes, but wicked:
> flie it therefore, and be rather glad that thou knowest how bad it is, then
> sorrie, to haue forsaken that which is preiudiciall to thy soule.
> [Sig. F2; 3:41]

To the astrologer, who worships nature and fortune, he cautions (out of
Gregory),

> God forbid (saith he) that any Christian man should beléeue that there
> were any fate, or destenie. For God that made and fashioned man of naught,
> rules, gouerneth, and ordereth his life according to his deserts; and his
> righteousnes and mercie: and to be short, man was not made for the stars, but
> the stars for him. [Sigs. G3–G3v; 3:51–52]

Finally, he counsels the prince that he seek wisdom, justice, and discipline
from within (sig. K1v ff.; 3:72 ff.). Lodge's prose here is at its most
Tacitean—intertwined, dense, obscure—but his purpose and plan are
clearly set forth in his preface to guide his readers. "*Here,*" he writes,

> *shall you find that which* Aristotle *requireth in euery science, probabilitie in
> argument, and demonstration and truth in the end: here shal you find the
> stile varieng according to the matter, the matter sutable to the stile, and all
> of these aimed to profit.* [Sig. A4; 3:3]

In Lodge's *Novum Organum,* displacing the more earthbound *Wits
Miserie* in this third phase of a poetics of felicity, the First Cause and Final
Cause are both God. As a consequence, "Tota hominem, & non distractum,
*for there is as much lost in slighting ouer, as won by perusing warelie; if the
title make you suspect, compare it with the matter, it will answer you*" (sig.
A4; 3:3). "It will answer you": in the new works of this recusant humanist,
the wit and paradox, the ambiguities and equivalencies of earlier Tudor
writers of humanist fiction have gone; and only Truth remains.[42] The
schoolmaster John Brinsley advocates this too in *Lvdvs Literarivs* (1612)
when he writes that all scholars must be "trained vp in Gods true Religion
and in grace; without which all the other learning is meerely vaine, or to
increase a greater condemnation. This one alone doth make them truely
blessed, and sanctifie all other their studies" (sig. Kk3).

Yet how is a writer to make this point under Elizabeth I if he is, unlike
the Protestant Brinsley, a Catholic recusant? Clearly the question plagued
Lodge and presses in on the shape of his poetics, making the successive
phases of his work more and more insistently religious—it is religion,

Tenney maintains, that "excited his imagination, and moved him to compose much of his best prose and poetry" (*Lodge,* p. 104). Hindsight suggests Lodge sought support in the small, closeted groups of Catholics who settled pockets of the north and the suburbs of London during Elizabeth's reign, as they had Trinity College, Oxford, in Lodge's time there;[43] later, when Lodge chose to study medicine, he went abroad to Avignon, to a school located near the papal palace. His own library contained a number of Catholic books, while his sources, Richard Helgerson notes, reflect "a medieval and Counter-Reformation sensibility."[44] In addition, the Bodleian Library owns a manuscript of *Doctrina Christaā na linguoa Brosilica,* an elementary textbook of Catholic doctrine designed for missionaries, that is signed "Ex dono Thomae Lodge D. M. Oxoniensis qui sua manu e Brasilia deduxit"—like a souvenir of the Cavendish voyage when he also brought back a copy of *The Flowers of Lodowicke of Granada,* which he translated and published in 1601.

There is no clear indication of precisely when Lodge joined the Roman Church—throughout his career he dedicated books to Catholic patrons such as the countess of Derby, the countess of Cumberland, and the Hare family, and he published books with his Catholic brother-in-law Edward White—but it is reasonable to assume he was a communicant by 1596 or 1597, when he left for Avignon, or 1604, when he married a Catholic widow, Mrs. Jane Albridge (or Aldred), a former dependent of Sir Francis Walsingham and an especially active recusant. Fifteen ninety-six is the year of his most singularly Catholic work, *Prosopopeia Containing the Teares of the holy, blessed, and sanctified* Marie, *the Mother of GOD,* an extended meditation—N. Burton Paradise calls it "an intense religious rhapsody" (*Lodge,* p. 125)—on Luke 2:35: "*And moreouer, the swoord shall pearce thy soule, that the thoughts of many hearts may be opened*" (sig. A2; 3:3). In focusing on the agony of the Mater Dolorosa, Lodge contends, we may find the sweet pains of ecstasy:

> In meditating with Marie, you shall finde Iesus: in knowing Christs sufferance, you shall be inflamed in his loue: in hearing his wordes, you shal partake his wisdome, which who inioieth, leaueth the world as transitorie, and seeketh after heauen for immortalitie. Heereon Augustine exclaimeth, Vnhappie is he that knoweth all things, & knoweth thee not: blessed is he that knoweth thee to despise all things. [Sigs. A6v–A7; 3:12–13]

The force of an impassioned religious rhetoric comes in passages of *antistasis* and *diacope* such as this fervent concentration on "cross":

> O crosse, the image of mortification, the tree of redemption, the bond of peace, the seal of the couenant, I will crosse mine armes to imbrace thee.

Crosse, all my ioyes to containe thee, I will be a crosse to mine owne soule, if it seeke thee not, and count euerie comfort a crosse, that is not crost by thee. [Sig. G5v; 3:106]

The pitch of the language goes far beyond manipulated cleverness, as the use of prosopopoeia here, a basic rhetorical stratagem for the writing of history, has been transferred to a wholly new setting—and a wholly new purpose.

In both the *Prosopopeia* and *The Divel Coniured* Lodge frequently cites Ambrose, Gregory, Lactantius, and other patristic writers; but it is clear that his favorite, and the one he knows best, is Augustine. The *Confessions* lurk somewhere behind *Robert, second Duke of Normandy,* but Augustine's progressive growth toward God, from the theft of pears (2.4) through the use of Cicero (3.4), the alliance with the Manicheans (5.3), and the study of Ambrose (5.13), the Platonists (7.9), and the Scriptures (7.21), is so commonplace that there is no sure way of telling. Such a spiritual biography, however, is closer than the medieval hagiographies to Lodge's sense of moral lives. But the later works of Lodge, which imply a Catholic poetics, trace their origin to the *Civitas Dei*, in its figuring personal narratives that are simultaneously anagogical in meaning. Robert's story as that of prince and of devil is an extension, in individual terms, of the theory behind Augustine's two cities, that of man and that of God.

Fecerunt itaque civitates duas amores duo, terrenam scilicet amor sui usque ad contemptum Dei, caelestem vero amor Dei usque ad contemptum sui. Denique illa in se ipsa, haec in Domino gloriatur. Illa enim quaerit ab hominibus gloriam, huic autem Deus conscientiae testis maxima est gloria. . . . Scriptum est itaque de Cain quod condiderit civitatem; Abel autem tamquam peregrinus non condidit. Superna est enim sanctorum civitas, quamvis hic pariat cives, in quibus peregrinatur donec regni eius tempus adveniat, cum congregatura est omnes in suis corporibus resurgentes, quando eis promissum dabitur regnum, ubi cum suo principe, rege saeculorum, sine ullo temporis fine regnabunt.

The two cities then were created by two kinds of love: the earthly city by a love of self carried even to the point of contempt for God, the heavenly city by a love of God carried even to the point of contempt for self. Consequently, the earthly city glories in itself while the other glories in the Lord. For the former seeks glory from men, but the latter finds its greatest glory in God, the witness of our conscience. . . . Thus we read in Scripture that Cain founded a city, but Abel, being a sojourner, founded none. For the city of the saints is above, though it brings forth citizens here below, in whose persons it sojourns as an alien until the time of its kingdom shall come. On that day it will assemble them all as they rise again in their bodies, and they will receive their promised kingdom, where with their Prince who is king of the ages, they will reign for all eternity. [14.28; 15:1][45]

Given Augustine's example from Genesis, it is just possible that this notion, too, was behind the composition of Lodge's *Rosalynde,* as well as a natural extension of the allegorical significance he had proposed for art to Stephen Gosson in 1580, a decade before.

In exploring the possibilities of Catholicism—its beliefs *and* its rituals— for a poetics of felicity, *Robert, second Duke of Normandy* nonetheless holds strongly to the forms and strategies of Greek and Roman historiography. But *Evphves Shadow, The Battaile of the Sences. Wherein youthfull folly is set downe in his right figure, and vaine fancies are prooued to produce many offences* (1592), written a year later, is arguably Lodge's single most representative work and one unusually significant in seeing the later transformation of Tudor humanist poetics. Although it begins in Lodge's customary manner, by openly imitating humanist predecessors, his emerging Catholic poetics transforms them all. *Evphves Shadow* opens by *"limming out vnder the figure of* Philamis, *the fortunes of* Euphues" (sig. A4v; 2:8) when he arrives at "that pompious cittie of *Passan.*" There

> did *Philamis* make his staye, inuited therevnto by the salubritie of aire, and the sumptuousnesse of the buildings, finding there both courtlye companions to conuerse withall, and comlie ladies to disport withall, it was woonderfull to see, how insteed of Philosophie, he subdued fancie, reposing his worldly felicitie in prodigalitie and fashions. [Sig. B1v; 2:10]

The suggestion of Lyly could not be fuller. Philamis is counseled by the elderly Athenor, who resembles Eubulus, before befriending Philamour (Philautus) and becoming enamored of Philamour's betrothed, the proud but unapproachable Harpaste (Lucilla). Although Harpaste will not respond warmly to his letters or to his conversation, Philamis is given another means to woo her when, one day at a country house (Lodge's model now *Il Libro del Cortegiano*), he is made king for the friendly symposium of courtly conversation. He is asked to address his own situation—"*Whether it bee better to deserue and haue no friendship, or offend and finde fauour*" (sig. C4v; 2:24)—as F. J. is in Gascoigne's humanist fiction, but debate—words rather than action—is interrupted by the sudden appearance of Claetia, dressed in mourning and carrying a lamp and a sword. Claetia transfers us, swiftly, to Green's humanist fiction of wonder, while her tale of chivalric exploit recalls Sidney's *Arcadia.* She too has suffered from vowing much and giving little. When the handsome Rabinus sought her favor, she assigned him impossible tasks, which he accomplished; thus her last request was for him to rid the world of something she cannot abide—himself. Even this does not daunt his love; in a chariot of rich ebony, carved with figures representing triumphs and meant to be his hearse, he comes before her and "with a sharpe Raser, he soddainly cut all his vaines," dying in the Roman fashion described by Suetonius and Plutarch (sig. F3v; 2:46). Later, he appears to her in a vision, showing her his bloody wounds, and from fear, grief, and shame she now extinguishes her lamp and kills herself, as a Roman might, with her sword (sig. F4; 2:47).

But in this world dominated by social manners—where man as Lodge sees him remains degenerate—no one learns; even the use of humanist disputation and the presentation of precept and example have no effect. Eurinome still rejects Philamis; in addition, Harpaste rejects Philamour for Philamis; and, hearing this, Philamour attacks his friend. Philamis flees for his life to the country where he meets the shepherd Clorius. With his departure, Eurinome dies of grief, and Philamour, sick with shame, goes in search of him. Philamour is attacked by pirates but found and nursed back to health by the same Clorius, while the older shepherd Celio (whose name means "heaven") counsels him by suggesting he visit the hermit Calimander, whose magic once transformed lambs into heifers to aid another gentleman in meeting the demands of his beloved. Philamour travels to see Calimander and finds Philamis in disguise: their spiritual reunion supplies a miracle that causes a second miracle, providing Harpaste with omens to marry Philamour. "Things attained with long labour (Gentlemen),," Harpaste tells the people of Passan, "at the last breede most delight, and when the tryall is past, the truthe is more accepted" (sig. L3; 2:85).

The tight, Lyly-like rhetoric of the first scenes of *Euphues Shadow* opens into Ciceronian period with the imitation of Castiglione and Sidney and, once again, into a looser and more reverential diction in the pastoral and romantic landscape that recalls Greene. But all have been openly concerned with felicity, and each style, as Lodge sheds it, is used to speak to Christian doctrine. The movement is toward religious thought and contemplation—with virtue in action as suitable preparation. We are not surprised, then, when Lodge brings the work to a satisfying conclusion in his own style, centered on his own concerns; in place of Euphues' "cooling Carde for Philautus," we are given *"the Deafe mans Dialogue,"* a letter sent by Philamis to Philamour that recalls a dialogue between the master Celio (who is, Walter R. Davis notes, deaf to the things of this world)[46] and the disciple Philamis. This letter, meant as a critique of humanism, is Lodge's catechism. In it, Celio first shows his pupil that the subjects of the humanist trivium and quadrivium must rise to holy purpose. He says, in part,

I condemne [Arithmetic and Mathematics] not as vnnecessary, but would teach and traine thee in studies more necessary: numeration teacheth thee howe to count thy sheepe, but not how to amend thy sinnes. . . . Geometry lerneth thee how to mesure thy fields, but not maister thy fancies: what profiteth thee to know an aker of land, & not the anchor of life? [Sig. L4; 2:87–88]

Slowly, clearly, humanism is metamorphosed into Christian teachings on the road to felicity: "lyfe is a pilgrimage *Philamis,* a shadow of ioy, a glasse of infyrmitie, the pathway to death. . . . see thou that there is [in] no worldly felicitie, true felicity" (sig. M1; 2:89–90). Thus the word "shadow" is transformed from Lyly's meaning (companion) and Lodge's own earlier meaning (Philamis as a kind of Euphues) to something altogether more wonderful and significant, and a decided realization of Augustinian poetics:

> *Celio.* . . . the good in shewe is this vertuous vniting of life and learning, which taken by it selfe is a sollace, and compared with GOD, is but a shadowe, the true felicitie is to know God, the fained is that which was *Platoes Idea, Aristotles summum bonum,* the *Stoikes Virtues*: the Epicures, sensuall felicitie: the one the inuention of man: the other an inspiration from God. [Sigs. M2–M2v; 2:91–92]

Persistently, deliberately, but not altogether imperceptibly, the examples from pagan historical writing once revered by the Erasmian humanists, Lodge especially—"*Brutus* who hauing murthered *Caesar,* slew himselfe miserably with his owne sword. *Carundius Tirius,* who hauing made a Bedlam lawe, endured a bloudie end" (sig. M3v; 2:94)—are subordinated to a rhetoric of spiritual delight—

> oh theyr horror, oh theyr miserie, oh that men can be so peruerse, and God so propitious, who calleth all, and will succour sinners, who wil ease the heauy laden, comfort the comfortlesse, giue Manna euen to the murmurers: oh whither am I carryed with these contemplations? into what Oceans of delight? [Sigs. M2v–M3; 2:92–93]

—and then, finally, glide into patristic appeal—

> For *S. Augustine* saith: As the loue of God is the well of vertue: so is the loue of the world the wel of vices. Come vnto me (saith Christ) all such as are laden, & I will ease you. *Bernard* saith, the perfect seruaunt of Christ loueth nothing but him. . . . Heare *Hierome*: The power of the Deuill is of no force beeing resisted by a strong faith: And *Augustine,* who saith: That the Deuill can deceiue no man, except he confidently put his trust in him. Hast thou sinned through contention with thy brother, amend thy selfe:

Learne of *Paule* to the *Galathians* the sixth chap. Let euery one (saith he) among you beare the burthen of another [Sig. M4v; 2:96]

—coming back, at the last, to the final, transcendent theme of *Rosalynde*. At the end of *Evphves Shadow,* humanism itself recedes before such dazzling glories.

Celio shows how his ideas lead beyond humanist learning, beyond prodigal experience, and beyond even the most searching humanist rhetoric of disputation and symposium. His is "Not trifling Philosophie, but true: learne to know thy selfe how weake thou art: learne to know thy life how wretched: learne to know thy death how certaine: thou shalt then finde, that al things in this earth are the fruites of error: that heauen is the hauen of felicitie, death the harbour of worldlye miserye" (sig. L4v; 2:88). Plato's conjunction of the *quantitas* and *qualitas* of classical rhetoric has been submerged into the revelations of Augustine. While Lyly's Euphues was seen last at the bottom of the Mountain of Silexedra, content in his humanist contemplation there, Philamis is already climbing Mount Purgatory. That Lodge's final vision breaks free at last from all his models of humanist poetics is clearly demonstrated in the final action by which this teaching fiction circles back to its beginning: Philamis also writes Athenor, now banished from his country, telling this ideal humanist of his one last lesson: exile itself is a *felix culpa,* a shadow of the soul's temporary exile from Heaven to earth (sigs. N3v–N4v; 2:102–4).[47]

As *Rosalynde* is the culmination of Lodge's poetics of felicity as virtue in action, and *A Margarite of America* culminates his fiction on fallen man, so *Evphves Shadow* is the culmination of his fiction of Christian apologetics. Doubtless his increasingly open recusant actions made things difficult for him for, in 1596, he stopped publishing fiction altogether; and in 1598 he went to Avignon to pursue a degree in medicine (later to be acknowledged with a medical degree from Oxford). Through this long stretch of time, when he converted his own virtue in action into tending the poor, the sick, and the needy, he did not stop writing, however. Instead, his persistent humanist poetics of felicity entered a fourth and final stage, which produced, in 1602, a remarkable folio volume translating from Latin and French into English all the extant works of Josephus. In the life and work of this early Pharisee, Lodge triumphantly discovered a new way of combining his interests in the morally instructive powers of humanism, of history, and of God's divine will in the narrative of His chosen people. In translating Josephus's *Lamentable and Tragicall History of the Wars and Vtter Rvine of the Iewes,* Lodge conveys the experience of a Jewish captain at Galilee during the invasion of the Romans who was involved in the battles he describes: and there is much brilliant writing in his descriptions of the rout of the Roman legion of Cestius in the pass of Bethhoron, the burning of the temple, and the Jewish attacks on the Roman camp on the Mount of Olives.[48] Josephus serves Lodge as a new kind of historical exemplum, one participant in *sacred* history. What makes his history important is not merely its involvement in God's plan but the puzzling features of it (what we fail to get in Plutarch), especially Josephus's transfer of loyalty at the exact midpoint of his life when, on the defeat of the Jews at Jotapata (July A.D. 67) after a forty-seven day siege, he swore allegiance to Rome and returned to the emperor's palace to spend his remaining thirty years. Historians still do not know how to explain this strange act. Josephus attempts to account for it in the *Wars* in a variety of ways, which Lodge captures in some of his best Tacitean prose. Josephus tells of the eve of the final battle, for instance. As Lodge translates it,

> *Nicanor* ceased not to intreat him: and he perceiuing how his enemies began to waxe angry, and calling to mind the dreames he had in the night, wherein God foretold him of all the Iewes calamities, & what should betide the Roman Princes (for he could interpret dreames, and whatsoeuer God obscurely shewed, being instructed in the holy bookes of the Prophets, and himselfe a Priest as his parents were.) So at that time being as it were filled with the Spirit of God, and recording the dreames and horrible visions which he saw in his sleepe, hee prayed secretly to God after this manner; O Creator (quoth hee) seeing that it pleaseth thee to ruinate the nation of the Iewes, and that all good fortune is gone vnto the Romans, and that thou hast chosen my soule to foretell future euents, I yeeld vnto the Romanes to saue my life, protesting that I meane not to goe to them to play the traytor vnto my countrey, but as thy minister; and hauing thus spoken, yeelded himselfe vnto *Nicanor*. [1632 ed., sigs. 3P5v–3P6; 3.8]

This may have been Josephus's understanding of his actions, but the Jews did not share it.

> They all mourned for *Ioseph* thirty daies, and hired many musicians to sing funerall songs for him. At last, truth discouered it selfe, and the true newes of the destruction of Iotapata with the accidents there: also how *Ioseph* was not slaine, but liued with the Romans, and that the Romans honoured him with more than a captiue could expect. Then the Iewes began as much to hate him now liuing, as before they mourned for him when they supposed him dead. [Sig. 3Q1v; 3.10]

There is no indication of how Lodge—the born Protestant who had turned against the Tudor's state religion in midlife himself—interpreted Josephus's behavior, but we can understand his strong sense of affinity.

Josephus's more monumental work, which Lodge transcribes as *The Most Ancient History of the Iewes: Written by Ioseph the Sonne of Matthias*—the *Antiquities*—is in twenty books: ten are drawn almost exclusively from Scripture and extend to the exile (omitting such embarrassing incidents as the golden calf and the breaking of the Tablets), and the second ten bring the history through the life of Christ, making some Plutarchan parallels between Hiram and Solomon, Herod the Great and Agrippa. Josephus is a syncretic writer, and his second ten books rely not only on Scripture but on Nicolaus of Damascus, Dionysius of Halicarnassus, Polybius, and Strabo. It is here, in his long, painstakingly accurate translation, that Lodge finds models for humanist *imitatio* that he could never have created himself in his fictions. There is, for instance, the antitype in Herod:

> *Herod* spending lauishly much and many summes of money, both at home and abroad, hearing the *Hircanus* who raigned before him, opened *Dauids* Sepulchre, and tooke out of it three thousand talents of siluer, and that there was left yet farre more, able to defray any great charges whatsoeuer, he long time purposed to doe the like. And at this time in the night season accompanied onely with his most trusty friends, being very wary that none of the people should know of it, he entred into the Sepulchre: but he found no money there, as *Hircanus* did; but he tooke from thence a great company of precious attires and ornaments of gold; whereby he was enticed to make a more diligent search: and he sent two of his company for the nonce into the inner part of the Sepulcher, where the bodies of *Salomon* and *Dauid* were intombed; who were there lost, and as it is reported, fire came out of those secret places and consumed them. Whereat *Herod* being terrified, departed out of it. . . .
>
> After the Sepulchre was thus violated, *Herods* house began to decay, whether reuenge lighting vpon that part which was already scarce sound, or whether by meere chance such calamity at that time befell him, as might iustly be thought the reward of impiety. [Sig. 2Q2; 16.11]

In the margin Lodge sums: "Herod lost two of his men in Dauids Sepulchre. Nicholaus the historiographer reproued." There were also more edifying tales. One of the passages now thought spurious is Josephus's account of Christ; but it was not thought spurious in the Renaissance and must then have given greater credentials to Josephus and to Lodge (sig. 2T5v; 18.13). There is also the killing of John the Baptist.

> And whereas it came to passe that diuers flocked and followed him to heare his doctrine, *Herod* feared lest his subiects allured by his doctrine and perswasions should be drawne to reuolt. For it seemed that they would subscribe in all things to his aduice; he therefore thought it better to

preuent a mischiefe by putting him to death, then to expect some sudden commotion, which he might afterwards repent. [Sigs. 2V1v–2V2; 18.7]

In such stories as that of Herod, such sermonettes as that on John the Baptist, and in reports on such inspiring figures as Jesus, Lodge finds an ideal way to pursue his religious interests in a means approximating the form and force of humanist history and fiction, a new kind of humanist poetics that bears some resemblance to the life of translations to which Erasmus devoted himself at the beginning of the century. "For as life, so History (the Image of life) is fraught with pleasure, and displeasure," Lodge writes in his preface, "and onely in the vse of life, the wisedome of life consisteth" (1632 ed., sig. ¶3; 4:26–27). And to Charles, Lord Howard and baron of Effingham, to whom the volume is dedicated, Lodge writes at some length about the value of history and the purpose of his translation of Josephus. He asks Lord Howard to

> so let the zeale, magnanimity, and admirable constancy which euery where affronteth you in this Booke (and rauisheth the best mindes from the boundlesse troubles of this world, and draweth them into the contemplation of true perfection) so settle your honourable loue and affection to emulate the same, that as for glory in Armes; so for preseruing and protecting Artes, you may outstrip your competitors, and amaze too curious expectation. [1602 ed., sig. ¶2; 4:22]

Lodge has not lost faith in a humanist poetics of felicity based in history, but he gives us now a new reason; in this work "God [is] the Historiographer" (1602 ed., sig. ¶3; 4:26).

Lodge's translation of Josephus was highly respected by the Tudors and Stuarts, who surely understood how it extended the precepts and practices of humanism in a troubled decade; it is highly respected today. Lodge did not sacrifice his round of daily toil to execute it, however; there is considerable evidence that he was doctor to many of the recusant families in London at the same time. This other act of faith suggests a dogged courage; but it did not prevent difficulties. On 7 August 1611, he was called before a court at High Holborn to be examined for an oath of allegiance but was dismissed until further notice; on 1 June 1618, he was summoned to court again for nonattendance at "church, chapel or any usual place of Common Prayer."[49] In 1604 he had even been denied the right to practice medicine in London and had sought exile in Belgium where he found a temporary Catholic practice. Yet through the troubled first decades of the new century Dr. Lodge's faith in literature endured. "You have, with one pen," he wrote young William Trumbull, now at court, on 7 October 1613, occasion to please and displease many. Be curious in the use thereof. It is a little instrument of great things and as it hath gotten some men fame, so oft times harmeth it good men's credit. Use it like an asp's sting to the wicked and a comfortable medicine to the virtuous for by it men will judge their disposition and judgment and our indiscretion doth by no means sooner betray ourselves than in our writing.[50]

His writing betrays him too, of course, revealing felicity as the thrust it seems always to take—felicity as it forms and cultivates the mind, orders life, and guides action. With this, Lodge moves through a sense of philanthropic service to an increasing sense of philotheism toward the adoration of God.

In many of these ways, his life and mind parallel Seneca's; and it is not at all surprising that it is in this philosopher—whose faith and serenity carried him through the intrigues and slaughters during the reigns of Tiberius, Caligula, Claudius, and Nero and so make him an exemplary figure in the *Annales* of Tacitus—that Lodge found a final, splendid occasion for his humanist poetics of felicity. It is Seneca as the great subject for humanist imitatio to whom Lodge, in the end, is drawn: Lodge's final Senecan original is Seneca himself, with his fine epigrammatic style. Translating Seneca was an act several Catholic Fathers had accomplished before Lodge—Jerome, Lactantius, Augustine—while for Tertullian Seneca was *saepe noster,* often one of us. But Lodge's Seneca is also an antique philosopher whom the humanists indisputably had admired in England since Erasmus had produced his own edition of Seneca in 1515. Elizabeth I, Sir John Harington writes, did also "much admire Seneca's wholesome advisings."[51] Lodge's translation is not from the original, but from the intermediary edition of the Belgian humanist Justus Lipsius, first published in 1604; Lodge also translates Lipsius's life of Seneca, and his epitomes of all the letters and essays, what Francis Bacon calls the "disperced Meditacions."[52] Lodge declares for us his reasons for studying and translating Seneca in the most passionate preface he ever wrote.

I made choice of this author, whose life was a pattern of continence, whose doctrine a detection and correction of vanities, and whose death a certaine instance of constancy. Would God Christians would endeuour to practise his good precepts, to reform their owne in seeing his errours; and perceiuing so great light of learning from a Pagans pen, ayme at the true light of deuotion and pietie, which becommeth Christians. Learne in him these good lessons, and commit them to memory. That to be truely vertuous is to be happy, to subdue passion is to be truely a man, to contemne fortune is to conquer her, to foresee and vnmaske miseries in their greatest terrors is to lessen them, to liue well is to be vertuous, and to die well is the way to eternitie. [1614 ed., sig. b5v; 4:39]

For the qualities Seneca inculcates—courage, endurance, self-control, self-reliance, moral conduct and just dealing, simple habits, reason, obedience to the state[53]—are those advocated by the Tudor state and by Tudor humanists stretching back through Ascham and Elyot to More and Erasmus. Lodge, moreover, catches the Senecan paradox, advising tranquillity of soul and peace of mind while writing with "an urgency, an anxiety to raise the moral tone of mankind," as Anna Lydia Motto puts it; "his *Dialogues* reveal incessant quarrel and debate that seek to foster reform."[54] Seneca's use of analogy, too, is in obvious concert with Dr. Lodge.

> The same affection hath a Wise man towards all men, as the Physition hath towards his sick Patients, who disdaineth not to handle their priuities, if they haue neede of remedy, nor to see their vrines and excrements, nor to heare the outrages which feare maketh them to vtter. The wise knoweth that all these . . . are sicke and diseased. ["Of the Constancie of a Wise Man," sig. Ll4v]

Like Lodge too, Seneca frequently cites antique authorities—Cicero, Ovid, Livy;[55] like Lodge, his style is compacted with *sententiae,* exploiting such figures as antithesis, alliteration, homoioteleuton, apposition, asyndeton, and oxymoron—the renowned *style coupé.*

Seneca's prose writings, as Lodge's, are yoked by the metaphor of journey—of life as a pilgrimage. "We ascend from this life to the other" (*Epistulae Morales ad Lucilium* 21; sig. S6); "this is it that Philosophie promiseth me, to make me like to God" (48; sig. Y3v). "Are not we more foolish then children that feare at noone dayes?" Seneca asks; "Whatsoeuer is for our good, our good God and Father hath layd by vs. . . . Wee haue cause to complaine of none other but our selues" (110; sig. 2Q4). Yet for all his emphasis on the state of the individual disposition of soul and mind, Seneca maintains an active commitment to human society, as Lodge does. "Neither can any man liue happily who onely respecteth himselfe, who conuerteth all things to his owne profits: Thou must liue vnto another, if thou wilt liue vnto thy selfe" (48; sig. Y3). And Seneca allows Lodge to put to special use his lifelong commitment to the instructive quality of human history still seen, at the end, as anagogic.

> A great and generous thing is mans mind, it endureth not to be circumscribed by any limits, but those which are common to him with God. First of all, he acknowledgeth not himselfe to be naturally bred in any region or land whatsoeuer, as in *Ephesus* or *Alexandria,* or in any other country of the greatest extent, or most peopled. All whatsoeuer is inuironed

by the compasse of heauen is his countrey, that is to say, his round, composed of Seas and Lands mixed together, within which the extent of the ayre separateth and vniteth things celestiall and terrestriall, in which so many gods disposed in due order are intentiue to execute their commissions: secondly, he endureth not to be circumscribed by yeres: all yeres (saith he) are mine, no age is locked vp to great wits, there is no time thorow which humane thought hath not pierced. [102; sig. Cc5]

Lodge's whole life had been a voyage, or a series of them—literally, to the New World; socially, to landholdings he finally inherited from his brother despite family quarrels, especially with his father in his younger years; politically and religiously, to Rome. Yet this journey—this pilgrimage—was, in its scattered fragments, all of a piece; and in finding peace in the voyages of the imagination he found in Seneca a poetics that went beyond even Plutarch and Tacitus, Plato and Cicero, in its usefulness to him and in its verdict on his writings. These latter-day works are immensely important, as they are immensely urgent, in extending and interpreting the special concerns of his earlier, better-remembered fiction—his *Rosalynde* and his *Margarite of America*.

Still, his writings were not yet quite at an end: there remained *A Treatise of the Plague* (1603), his translation of *A Learned Summary Upon the famous Poeme of William of Saluste Lord of Bartas* (1621), and a book of prescriptions for Lady Ann, countess dowager of Arundel, *The Poore Mans Talentt* (1623), which he completed after he was too ill to deliver it to her personally (4:3). All were "My presents," as he puts it in *A Fig for Momus,* "riches of my mind" (sig. H1; 3:57). With his beloved Stoic authors, Lodge grew, as Isabel Rivers reminds us the Stoics also grew, "to concentrate less on the definition of the wise man and more on the stages by which the ordinary man could become wise. The forms of Roman Stoic literature—epistle, consolation, handbook, meditation—reflect this concern with the individual case."[56] "Of the life of man the duration is but a point, its substance streaming away, its perception dim, the fabric of the entire body prone to decay, and the soul a vortex, and fortune incalculable, and fame uncertain," Marcus Aurelius writes (*Meditations* 2.17).[57] Considerably closer in time, the Italian humanist Boccaccio set the way for a Tudor humanist such as Lodge; we can see, he writes, that *le vestigie dello Spirito santo* (the ancient poets imitate the footprints of the Holy Spirit).[58] And Lodge could make his own phrases, too. "Now at last," he writes in the preface to *Prosopopeia,*

after I haue wounded the world with too much surfet of vanitie, I maye bee by the true Helizeus, cleansed from the leprosie of my lewd lines, & beeing washed in the Iordan of grace, imploy my labour to the comfort of the faithfull. [Sig. A7; 3:13]

In 1625, when one of England's worst plagues struck London, Lodge stayed to treat the sick and dying; the plague killed him too, as it likely, at an earlier time, killed Nashe; and like Nashe he was buried somewhere, now unknown, in an open grave.

"Substance streaming away": in his persistent search for a viable humanist poetics in which the Erasmian image of man as moral, educable, and finally perfectible could be tested and affirmed, Thomas Lodge examined more possibilities and tried more avenues of approach than any other prose writer attempting a humanist poetics. He was fortified by antique texts and by Holy Scripture like Nashe, yet in the end, confronting directly the problems of human depravity, his resources from secular and sacred history, like Nashe's from the period of the Second Sophistic, proved inadequate. At two periods—around 1592 and again in late 1596—he seems nearly defeated. That he survived was due more to his dogged devotion to history, his inventive use of different texts, and his new concerns with Catholicism, than to his ability to regenerate an Erasmian humanism. For a brief period of time, Lodge was able to wash humanist poetics in the Jordan of grace. But it is significant that, in the end, Josephus led him back to war and to the defeat of the Jews by the barbarians from Rome while Seneca took him to the bloodiest reigns of the Empire recounted by Tacitus. They signal a gnawing doubt that even Thomas Lodge could no longer master. Humanist poetics, like humanism itself, was in its twilight years.

L'infinito vniuerso et Mondi: The Development

of a Posthumanist Poetics

The Element of Fire is quite put out, the Aire is but Water rarified,
the Earth is found to moue, and is no more the Center
of the Vniuerse, is turned into a Magnes; Starres are not fixed, but swimme
in etheriall Spaces, Cometes are mounted aboue the Planetes; Some
affirme there is another World of men and sensitiue Creatures,
with Cities and Palaces in the Moone; the Sunne is lost, for, it is but a
Light made of the conjunction of manie shining Bodies together, a
Clift in the lowest Heauens, through which the Rayes of
the highest defuse themselues, is obserued to haue Spots; Thus, Sciences, by
the diuerse Motiones of this Globe of the Braine of Man, are become
Opiniones, nay, Errores and leaue the Imagination in a thousand
Labyrinthes. What is all wee knowe compared with
what wee knowe not?

WILLIAM DRUMMOND OF HAWTHORNDEN

 OSTENSIBLY THIS STUDY OF HUMANIST POETICS, IN TRAC-ING GENERAL AND SPECIFIC RE-SOURCES OF TUDOR WRITERS OF HUMANIST FICTION, HAS BEEN ABOUT THE REFERENTIAL READINGS THEY designed[1]—meaning, for them, rested in a collaboration between the author and the reader in which the reader is always, in an ongoing process, required to judge the text in two dialectical ways: (*a*) by reading the Tudor text against its Senecan model or original (the famous fourth cause for classical poetry) in order to note meaning by convergence and divergence; and (*b*) by reading the text outward against his own experience. This was, from the start, a difficult balancing act—one in which Folly can be foolish or wise and *Utopia* is a land both icastic and fantastic—but it was worth pursuing because the humanists spoke out of and directed their remarks toward a common culture. This was a culture in which straightforward, analogous, or even ingenious methods of

fiction—borrowed from the celebrated techne of humanist rhetoric—would always serve to promulgate, even at the farthest reaches of exploration, the values of order, dignity, discipline, and moral virtue that author and reader were expected to share. *Hypo-theses* as the basis for fiction could center on a protagonist as naive as F. J. or spin tales as wondrous as those of Robert Greene and still serve as testaments to the worth of an antique culture because both fantastic art and icastic art (despite Plato's fears) were sufficiently *like* the truth to make the message clear. Fiction, in this way, extended the humanist schoolroom across the educated commonwealth; it served as a series of exempla; fashioning tales from principles, it also fashioned readers by means of the tales.

If the formal properties of the presentations—most easily seen in Lyly but shared by all writers of humanist fiction—were far enough from life itself to allow them to teach rather than to reify life's experiences, they were still meant to *interact* with life. Humanist fiction was never disinterested; as Stephen Orgel has pointed out for some time, their acts of narrative constituted a vital part of the reality of the time; "Acts of the mind are [nevertheless] real acts."[2] "Nothing spoke for itself; every action implied a rhetoric,"[3] and every rhetorical and literary work implied thought and action. My own earlier studies of political documents and state reports, where what is "fact" (or presented as authentic) is often fabrication and propaganda, and of rogue books, where fiction deliberately masquerades as fact,[4] demonstrate that from other quarters, too, the Tudors were supplying a printed culture where our cleaner, neater divisions of fiction and fact were unknown and remain largely inappropriate. Both played back and forth intertextually, so that there is some real difficulty (then and now), as Louis Adrian Montrose shows so convincingly, in locating where fiction is used for its own sake and where strategies used to assume power or to maintain a show of loyalty employ the means and conventions thought the province of poets.[5] Working toward a "cultural poetics" from the other direction, from the individual outward, Stephen Greenblatt's concept of "self-fashioning," in which individuals continually battle between what they conceive as "authority" and what "alien,"[6] like Richard Helgerson's helpful application in the cases of certain poets who would declare themselves laureate,[7] demonstrates further how a culture stemming from humanist rhetoric inherited a sense of dialectic and disputation that became ingrained not only as a habit of mind but as a directive of action.

But, once a rhetorical culture raises such questions and suggests such courses of action, what results, as Jonathan V. Crewe and Jonathan Goldberg have illuminated so well, is (in Crewe's words) "a profound irresolution about the nature of 'reality.' "[8] From the start, the humanists were aware of such a Pandora's box: "So many men, so many minds" remains one of the most memorable Erasmian proverbs. Beneath their wordplay, lending depth to their eloquence and leading in time to doubt, is the awareness of the major writers of humanist fiction that their own acts of poetry, outgrowths of controversiae, led their readers back to literary and rhetorical roots in Roman laws that were in the end irreconcilable—and that, in the course of history, allowed persuasion to take the place of truth even at the heart of the judicial system. That double image of the Silenus box, introduced by Plato and reintroduced by Erasmus, comes to haunt all of the humanist fiction we have been examining. Folly is the product of a lovely nymph—and of the god of wealth; her father was a drunkard, yet when she wishes to drink (at the end of her encomium) it is to drink *communally,* and there is a deliberate sense of the holy about it. G. T. is always praising F. J., but he is always undermining him, too, and he is himself a reification of Folly, more naive than he knows (or cares to admit). Raphael Hythlodaye likewise speaks irrationally and naively at times, yet the vision that inspires and *compels* him to talk is one we are meant to share—one that *engages* More-character for all of his dubiety at the end. Such forces, that is, as the foolish-wise Folly or Hythlodaye / More or G. T. / F. J. are not type and antitype so much as different emphases, constitutive parts of humanist concerns. We have only to place Philibert de Vienne's vision of a corrupt court alongside Castiglione's Urbino to see how Philibert is merely flushing out what Castiglione has only barely concealed; and Philibert's satire would not work at all if it did not have the countertext of *Il Libro del Cortegiano* alongside it, much as we would be hard put to fathom the conclusion of Folly's *declamatio* with no knowledge of the Eucharist, or More's satire in the *Utopia* without Plato's *Republic* and Plutarch's *Life of Lycurgus* to appeal to. William B. Worthen has recently pointed out that an *actor* could be defined for Tudor audiences as someone who enacted a person, representing him, doing as he would; but it could also draw on *hypocrite,* the Greek word for actor, which meant creating, deceiving, being something *else.*[9] Humanist fiction we have seen functioning in the same way: it is *something made* or com-posed of common places, *topoi,* Senecan originals; but it is also *something made up.*

Surely Lyly senses just this as the core of the dynamics of fiction when *Euphues* is presented in such a way that it balances both Castiglione and Philibert, or positions similar to theirs, in its constituent debates and disputations and in the delicate but vital symmetry of its style, its very grammar. No one—not Sidney, not Nashe, not Erasmus or More—is keener than Lyly in seeing the inherent properties of language and, behind them, the possibilities of the mind's workings. But it led him well past the Silenus as his sense of the dynamics of rhetoric and of fiction; the very malleability of self-presentation (and of self-fashioning) led him to the motif of the wax. Impressions, and creations, might be myriad—and what dazzles us can also be difficult and treacherous. Underdowne senses this in the earlier Alexandrian romances when he marks in the margin of his Heliodorus, "Oh humayne estate most unstable, and full of all manner of chaunges"; it is just such flux that causes Greene, in the romances to which he was profoundly (and also necessarily) drawn, to seek his Senecan original in a writer (and thinker) like Ovid. It is just possible, Greene urges on us, that truth is metamorphic, not merely metaphoric; that, indeed, one initiates the other, at least in poetics. Nashe—a colleague and friend to Greene—takes this up in another way, the way of the extemporal writer: "give me the man whose extemporall veine in any humour will excell our greatest Art-maisters deliberate thoughts; whose inuentions, quicker then his eye, will challenge the prowdest Rhetoritian to the contention of like perfection with like expedition" (sig. A2v; 3:312). Crewe's comment on this passage is apposite: "In enacting a shift from university wit to 'humour' as the foundation of rhetorical performance, Nashe reestablishes a vital connection between speech and being, substituting an impulsive expressiveness for premeditated effects" (*Unredeemed Rhetoric,* p. 29). It is this "impulsive expressiveness" that is his surface rhetoric, much like Lyly's use of *isocolon* or *paramoion,* to call attention to itself, of course; but it calls attention too, as we have seen, to the exemplars of the Second Sophistic from which it takes its vision and its stunning energetic force. Nashe is a good example in this of showing that what can be exhilarating—what can seem endless fecundity and joy—can also, without so much as a whisper, become terrifying as well. Lyly also anticipates this: "He that seeketh the depth of knowledge: is as it were in a *Laborinth,*" he says in *Euphues* (sig. S4v; 1:289).

THE DANGER, then, is one of intellectual chaos in which no grounds for meaning or significance (literally, no *significatio*) would remain. Humanist fiction could not function if references were numberless; that is why the Senecan models are always, to their educated readers, so consistent, so *evident*. Put another way, that is why Lyly can *risk* raising the image of wax or the idea of a conceptual labyrinth—because he knows that his own fiction functions as dialectic and that such a function is familiar, one could say commonplace, to his readers too: it is, to borrow modern critical terminology, their chief literary competency. Such was second nature to an audience raised on controversiae and disputations, where the Silenus could become a symbol for a whole culture. It is just such an inside-outside dialectic that, flexible enough, could be stretched to accommodate the many boxes within boxes of perspective that More uses, in his prefatory letters, to set the *Utopia* or Gascoigne *F. J.* or Lyly *Euphues*—or that allows Nashe to see, in the prefatory letter to *The Unfortunate Traueller,* the actual *convergence* (with the pages of his book / the pages at court) such traditional antonyms as ingenuity and ingenuousness.

In a provocative essay on intention in Sidney's *Arcadia,* Annabel M. Patterson applies these criteria to Sidney. She points to the apparent inconsistency—what we know is a deliberate basic dialectic—in his own remarks about his humanist fiction.

> They are, firstly, Sidney's mention of an unspecified "toyful book" or "books" in an October 1580 letter to his brother; secondly, an undated letter to his sister, entrusting her with the manuscript of an "idle worke ... done onelie for you, onely to you," a work whose "chiefe safetie, shalbe the not walking abroad" [a startling admission to which we shall return]. This letter was published by Fulke Greville as a preface to the *New Arcadia* in 1590. It suggests a recreative exercise, a pastime, intended at most for a small private audience. ... Thirdly, there is the preface to the 1593 composite text, which sets the problem of intention squarely before the audience, without making any gestures towards solving it: "though they finde not here what might be expected, they may finde neverthelesse as much as was intended, the conclusion, not the perfection of Arcadia: and that no further then the Authors own writings, or knowen determinations could direct. Whereof who sees not the reason, must consider there may be a reason which he sees not." This certainly sounds suspiciously like intentional mystification.[10]

What we would suspect, from the tradition of humanist fiction we have been tracing, is that the deliberate mystification is here only to insure the reader's conspiracy in unlocking the significance of the other two opposing ideas: that the work is a trifle or toy, on the one hand, and/or that it is something sufficiently significant that it should not be permitted, even accidentally, to fall into the wrong hands. Either may seem wrongheaded. How could a work so long and so ambitious be merely a toy? Conversely, what in this long testing of humanist learning and exemplary experience could be so liable to misreading, so potentially dangerous? I think that not only are these interesting questions about the *Arcadia,* which Patterson's sharp conjunction of dissimilar remarks makes so evident; I think these are *vital* questions about the *Arcadia.* Indeed, I think, in the age of humanist thought, humanist rhetoric, and eristics, that this is precisely the question Sidney is setting for his readers throughout.

That the problem is not unsolvable even now is shown by Patterson's willingness to expose the dialectic and her attempt to resolve it. Her understanding begins with Sidney's *Defence,* where he gives the standard Tudor reading of Vergilian pastoral:

is the poore pipe disdained, which somtimes out of *Maeliboeus* mouth, can shewe the miserie of people, vnder hard Lords and rauening souldiers? And again by *Titerus,* what blessednesse is deriued, to them that lie lowest, from the goodnesse of them that sit highest? Sometimes vnder the prettie tales of woolues and sheepe, can enclude the whole considerations of wrong doing and patience. [Sigs. E3v–E4; *Miscellaneous Prose,* pp. 94–95]

She says of this passage that

It is easy to assume that [it] could have very little bearing on a work as generically complex as the *Arcadia* with its romantic and epic interfiliations; but the pastoral theory of the *Defence* is, if one looks at it carefully, a good deal more complex than it seems.

The passage from the *Defence* is, in fact, distinctly cunning, both syntactically and semantically. It contains a condensed argument about the relationship between literature and socio-political experience. If you live "under hard lords or ravening soldiers" you may have to communicate "under the pretty tales of wolves and sheep." The prepositional symmetry ("under . . . under") supports the propositional irony of defining pastoral as the genre in which writers "lie lowest" in more senses than one. The central allusion is, of course, to Virgil's first eclogue, in which the sad shepherd, Meliboeus, converses for a moment before heading out into exile with his more fortunate neighbor Tityrus. Tityrus was almost always read, in the Renaissance, as a figure for Virgil himself. The historical context of the poem was the last phase of the civil war and the expropriation of farm lands in Italy by Octavius, who wished to reward his own soldiers and punish those who had supported Brutus and Cassius. Virgil's point was, or was traditionally seen to be, that the expropriated farmers were innocent victims, and that Virgil was only with the greatest caution exercising his responsibility as a writer, by indicating the severity of Octavius' policy. The dominance of the first eclogue over the entire Virgilian text as a whole had the effect, also, of measuring the other pastoral subjects, song contest, and especially love complaint, by those larger standards of responsibility; something that Sidney's contemporary, George Puttenham, felt his audience needed to remember: "the poet devised the Eglogue . . . not of purpose to counterfait or represent the rusticall manner of loves and communication; but under the vaile of homely persons, and in rude speeches to insinuate and glaunce at greater matters, and such as perchance had not bene safe to have disclosed in any other sort, which may be perceived in the Eglogues of Virgill, in which are treated by figure matters of greater importance then the loves of Titirus and Corydon." The connection between this theory and the *Arcadia* is made at the point where Sidney describes Arcadian mores. This point is differently located in the *Old* and *New* versions of the text. In the *Old Arcadia,* the description immediately precedes the First Eclogues, the first group of poems that interrupts the romantic narrative of Basilius and his daughters. "The manner of the Arcadian shepherds," Sidney wrote, "was to pass their time," either in music or sports: "But, of all other things, they did especially delight in eclogues, wherein sometimes they would contend for a prize of well singing, sometimes lament the unhappy pursuit of their affections. Sometimes, again, under hidden forms utter such matters as otherwise were not fit for their delivery." In the *New Arcadia* [and the composite text of 1593, which we have already studied], this passage was moved back to the opening description by Kalander of the unhappy state of affairs in Arcadia. The context is the news that Basilius has abandoned his responsibilities and gone into retreat on his country estate. The last phrase of the relocated passage was, moreover, significantly altered. Instead of "under hidden forms utter such matters as otherwise were not fit for their delivery," Sidney wrote, "under hidden forms utter such matters, as otherwise they durst not deale with." By making the textual alteration, Sidney removed the possibility that he might have been referring merely to a theory of pastoral decorum, in which any kind of high subject or deep thought was out of bounds. By relocating the passage, he placed it in a context that was already, in Kalander's account, critical of Basilius, so that the theory of "hidden forms" was connected to the problem of political expression, when a ruler is at fault. Further, to glance back at the passage from the *Defence* is to see that the crucial phrase, "under hidden forms," is an extension of the series "under hard lords" and "under the pretty tales"; while an intentional connection between the two passages is further assumed by the "sometimes . . . sometimes" formula in both. ["Under Pretty Tales," pp. 7–8 rep. *Censorship,* pp. 28–30]

This revision of such a crucial sign attached to a key *propositio* or hypo-thesis of the *Arcadia* will show why Greville thought it safe enough to leave the potentially dangerous phrase warning about the "safetie" of leaving the book lying around in the 1590 *Old Arcadia,* but the countess of Pembroke (with or without Greville's consent) thought it better to remove it in the composite 1593 text where it is clear that Basilius stands for Basilius but also for the ruler who relies too much on his principal counselor Philanax—not unlike a Virgin Queen who absents herself on glorious progresses while the principal secretary is left in charge at Whitehall. That *would* be too dangerous to have passing abroad. As for the passage the countess did leave—"who sees not the reason, must consider there may be a reason which he sees not"—it is a conundrum the way the *Encomium Moriae* and *Utopia* are and, what is more, by now so traditional to humanist poetics as to be passed over as mere convention. But of course it is not that, or at least not merely that, as the remarks in the *New Arcadia* about Basilius quickly demonstrate. There is a reason why, in rewriting the *Arcadia,* Sidney chose not only to keep but through Kalander to emphasize Basilius's absence from the court. What Sidney was making was a point crucial to his understanding of right government and misgovernment, out of Aristotle and Plato, to be sure, but what is more out of his own experience. (He was, after all, the most knowledgeable on court affairs in the circles at Penshurst and Wilton.) But if the *New Arcadia* was so important to him, why then abandon its revision? Because, no matter how complicated the anthology of rulers in *Arcadia* 2 and the "captivity episode" of *Arcadia* 3 made the work, they did not (witness the inept but workable seam by Hugh Sanford) undermine or repudiate the conclusion of the *Old Arcadia*. In fact, they lead more directly—and *more openly* (that is the point of the pointed replacement and revision)—to the bad rule of Euarchus. He was, we remember, the "savior," or so Philanax thought, because he was just and because he believed in the absoluteness of law. But, as we have also seen, it is law without equity, justice without mercy. The whole of *Arcadia,* from its exile of Basilius through its tyrannies and its oligarchies to its conclusion in *Arcadia* 5, is meant to invite good rule from Pyrocles and Musidorus for a land that enjoys no good rule from the outset, either because it is governed by the subaltern Philanax or because its criminals are judged by the alien Euarchus, neither of them the right ruler in title or in deed. So much we have seen in our earlier discussion. What Patterson points to, however, is the "relationship between literature and socio-political experience," and what Sidney is clearly saying is not only that Elizabeth is often an absentee ruler but that her government is inflexible and unwilling to admit exceptions (or new blood, like Sir Philip Sidney, to the corridors of power). Further implicated here, I think, and an argument I am making elsewhere given its complications,[11] is that an alternative hieriarchy of government, enhanced and highlighted for Tudor subjects, was the expansion of a court system that was assigned to deal with equity, or exceptions to the law, despite Elizabeth's lack of support. The impetus for this countersystem of justice was from the Calvinists (read Leicester, Walsingham, *and Sidney*), who demanded an examination of individual conscience and circumstance against the intransigence of Tudor law. But since Sidney, with his Calvinist leanings, would be associated with such a position, he apparently chose not to—and did not need to—complete rewriting *Arcadia*. The warning with its new placement in the *New Arcadia* is enough. It is to *distract* from this intention, but surely not to *detract* from the value meant for either *Old Arcadia* or *New,* that Sidney, and later his friend and sister, could keep referring to the work as a "toy" or a "trifle"; it is like pretending pastoral sheep are only, and merely, pastoral sheep. (This is, of course, a significant example in humanist fiction of what Greenblatt would call "subversive," because it so clearly pits the authority against the alien in Sidney's conception of, and writing of, the *Arcadia*.)[12]

Sidney thus uses the referential art of humanist poetics in choosing the pastoral and then employing it in the way that Vergil would. Earlier he had done this, as Orgel has so acutely seen, in *The Lady of May,* where he shrouds his own abilities and expectations not in a lowly shepherd but in an engaged forester so as to plead his case before the queen when seeming not to do so at all.[13] Yet such an understanding of poetry stems from the antique learning of the humanists in a tradition that extends back past Vergil, back in fact to Plato's *Republic,* which dominated Tudor theories of poetry and remains a main source—an identified source—of Sidney's own *Defence.* In *Republic* 3 Socrates distinguishes between two ways of rendering speech which he calls *diegesis* and *mimesis.* In the first of these, the poet is himself the speaker (as in Sidney's *Defence*) and never attempts to suggest that anyone else is addressing the audience (although here Sidney plays the part of a put-upon courtier asked to defend poor poetry unwillingly but resignedly). In *mimesis,* on the other hand, the poet tries to *create the illusion* that someone else is really speaking (as in *Astrophil and Stella* or, more complexly, in the *Arcadia*) through characterization (*prosopopoeia*) and place (*prosographia*), as in Pyrocles in Arcadia, although we know they are only rhetorical figures and we know the author is still creating them and, if less directly, still addressing us. It is just the blurring of this distinction (what later comes to be revered as a willing suspension of disbelief) that causes Plato—and in a way who can blame him in his sophistic culture?—to distrust poets and poetry by the time of *Republic* 10. Sidney knows this, of course: when he answers Gosson's charges that Plato banished poets (*Republic* 10), he says that cannot be for Plato was himself too good a poet (and he means: look at *Republic* 3). So distrustful is Plato, in fact, that by the time he comes to write the *Ion* he says that poets are mad, because they are unable to differentiate diegesis and mimesis (the point made about Sir by Ronald Harwood in the recent play *The Dresser*). Sidney's allusions to "toys," "trifles," and "idle works," then, are emphatic signals that he as author is disengaged enough from his work to know what it seems to say and what it does say—or, like the Silenus, what it looks like on the outside (a pastoral fiction) and what it actually is on the inside (an anatomy of Tudor government, with a critical perspective).

This is also the central position Sidney wishes to reinforce by illustration in the *partitio* of the *Defence*—for we remember he turns explicitly to Aristotle, who had attempted to answer Plato in his *Poetics* by restoring mimesis and diegesis as quite separate acts with quite different effects (according to Aristotle, diegesis exercises the mind, mimesis empties the audience of intermediate, blocking emotions of pity and terror to permit understanding on a visceral or emotional level). Aristotle is willing to admit both diegesis and mimesis because he is willing to admit both poetry and rhetoric, something the philosopher Socrates, fearing the sophists, is unable to do. But Sidney agrees with Aristotle in admitting both, as he tells us by *using* both. The *Defence* is most memorable, perhaps, because it is inhabited by two of Sidney's most splendid grotesques—clear instances of prosopopoeiae who remain *distinct* (because of their grotesquerie) from the put-upon poet-author (who is charming and normal). One grotesque is the (individual, particularizing) historian, "loaden with old Mouse-eaten Records, authorising himselfe for the most part vpon other Histories, whose greatest authorities are built vppon the notable foundations Heresay, hauing much ado to accord differing writers, & to pick truth out of partiality: better acquainted with a 1000. yeres ago, thē with the present age" (sig. C4: *Miscellaneous Prose,* p. 83). The other grotesques are the group of moral philosophers (numerous because they are always universalizing): "I see [them] comming towards me, with a sullain grauitie, as though they could not abide vice by day-light, rudely cloathed, for to witnesse outwardly their contempt of outward things, with bookes in their hands against glorie, whereto they set their names: sophistically speaking against subtiltie, and angry with any man in whom they see the foule fault of anger" (sig. C4; p. 83). Both, in the drama of the fiction of the *Defence,* are locked in battle, in eternal disputation; both, in the theory of the *Defence,* are images of the mind—one pictorial, the other conceptual. Their irreconciliation prompts Poetry to enter as adjudicator, to make sense of their debate and to draw from it useful lessons. But in the fiction within the *Defence* Poetry is never seen as History and Moral Philosophy are—we do not even know the gender of Poetry—because Poetry is never grotesque, never restricts or exaggerates the truth. It is clear from this "story" that neither History nor Moral Philosophy can work alone—that is, neither the present prosopopoeiae nor the informing antique text from classical philosophy—but that both need the poet. Both, that is, need Sidney. Both, that is, need humanist fiction (or a humanist poetics), which gives meaning to history by means of antique texts and renders such texts no longer antique by making them live once again in history. The use of a witty persona of Sidney in the *Defence* is to keep this function squarely before us: the essay begins with Sidney conversing with his Italian teacher of horsemanship; it ends with him wittily conversing with *us.* Between, he supplies a theory of poetic mimetic. The conjunction of the two make him a poet, a writer of humanist poetics. It also allows him to maintain a dialectic in his fiction—the *Arcadia* as a Silenus box—forwarding a tradition explicitly commented on by Erasmus, More, Gascoigne, and Lyly.

Commented on by them, that is to say, because it is not new. Neither is this obverse reading we have been giving humanist texts in the last few pages—or what could be called a subversive reading. It is endemic to a poetic openly allied with rhetoric, as Aristotle knew (and as Plato feared). But all the Tudor rhetoricians, knowing their antique philosophers and their antique poets too, knew that. So Thomas Wilson, in *The Arte of Rhetorique* (1553), can write of invention as "The findyng out of apte matter" (sig. a3v)—"apt" being the sort of encoding Sidney accomplishes with his portrait of Basilius and his characterization of Euarchus. Or take Richard Rainolde, who defines Aphthonian fable, in his *Foundacion of Rhetorike* (1563), as "a forged tale, cōtaining in it by the colour of a lie, a matter of truthe" (sig. A2). Surely this too is what Lyly means when, in the narrator's (his?) voice, the voice of *diegesis,* he comments in *Euphues* that "although yron the more it is vsed the brighter it is, yet siluer with much wearing doth wast to nothing" (sig. C4; 1:195), while his prosopopoeia Lucilla echoes him dramatically and dialectically, that is, mimetically: "in arguing of the shadow, we forgoe the substaunce" (sig. D3v; 1:201).

This *distinction,* then, represented by the Silenus box, which Patterson finds in the Tudor understanding of Vergil and which Sidney develops out of Plato and Aristotle as well, functions throughout the period of humanist poetics—and is "subversive" only as that poetics itself, given its two-sidedness, must be by nature subversive. Ralph Robynson sees it when he changes the title page of *Utopia* from "of the Godly gouernment" (1551 ed., sig. G5) to "of the politike gouernement" (1556 ed., sig. G5v), choosing to emphasize the point. Nashe does it, not only in the bitterness with which he compares More's "common-wealth" to his portrait of "piracies" (*Unfortunate Traueller,* sig. D4v; 2:245) but when the directness of his vision makes clear the analogy between the criminality and butchery of Esdras and Cutwolfe in Italy and the savagery and butchery at Turwin and Thérouanne (and only slightly concealed at Ardres and Guines). Even Lodge's *Rosalynde* opens, as we have seen, by upsetting primogeniture because moral character should somehow be made to challenge lawbound rules of inheritance when equity requires exceptions. Whether this double-edged basis of humanist poetics is realized through protagonist and deuteragonist (such as Rosader and Saladyne) or through protagonist and environment (as with Jack Wilton on his humanist's Grand Tour), it is this conflict that the poet, announcing in narrative voice or authorial voice or implying through comparison with other texts, uses to convey his meaning. (It is also the basic dynamics of fiction, thus the beginning of the English novel.) One of the grand accomplishments of humanist poetics, then, is to present both sides of a question—to admit both reality and fiction, to invite us to consider its own subversive side, as it were. Arising from an age of eristics, a rhetorical culture of opposition and competition, it turned that situation into one of "peirastics," of inquiring after truth, by converting the judge at the disputation, like the author of a fiction, into the interpreter of meaning *and* the reader of the text.

THE COMPLICIT relationship between author and reader, fostered in humanist poetics with the use of antique models and antique theories of poetry, realized anew in a theory such as Sidney advances in his *Defence* or Wilson in his *Rhetorique* and practiced in fictive prosopopoeiae such as those employed by Erasmus and More, Gascoigne and Lyly, functions securely because of known, shared, predictable values that both maker and consumer bring to the commonly shared texts. Just as readers of Tudor fiction could come to expect what authors would do, rhetorically and poetically, so they could locate the meaning of the fablings, so authors could rely on readers to penetrate the surfaces of their fictions. Tudor humanist writers taught Ciceronian philosophy and rhetoric by themselves imitating Cicero. But (to return to Greenblatt) when self-fashioning ceased to be a construction of previous beliefs and attitudes (what we might call activated topoi) and was used, defensively, to cover over the void where there was no meaning *except* in the self-construct, then humanist poetics could not function, because it lost all means of referentiality on which it was so elaborately, playfully, eloquently, instructively, usefully, *necessarily* built.

In this respect, it is a supreme irony of literary history that the Roman authority that most inspired humanism, and so became the chief Roman progenitor of a humanist poetics, also initiated its demise. The *De Natura Deorum* is a far different Ciceronian treatise from those that, dealing with the ideal orator and ideal state or the compromising practices of the rhetorician necessary to allow the state to function, had awakened in English humanists an abiding trust. In the *De Natura Deorum* Cicero, in the voice of Cotta, extends the newly defined doubt he has over the several names of one god to the very bases of civilization and especially, therefore, to that faculty of reason on which the humanists had placed so much emphasis.

Sentit domus unius cuiusque, sentit forum, sentit curia campus socii provinciae, ut quem ad modum ratione recte fiat sic ratione peccetur, alterumque et a paucis et raro, alterum et saepe et a plurimis, ut satius fuerit nullam omnino nobis a dis inmortalibus datam esse rationem quam tanta cum pernicie datam.

Our private homes; the law-courts, the senate, the hustings; our allies, our provinces—all have cause to know that just as right actions may be guided by reason, so also may wrong ones, and that whereas few men do the former, and on rare occasions so very many do the latter, and frequently; so that it would have been better if the immortal gods had not bestowed.

upon us any reasoning faculty at all than that they should have bestowed it with such mischievous results. [3.27.69][14]

Worse yet, these gods have allowed unaccountable events—the exiling of Publius Rutilius, for instance, a man of impeccable honor and of consummate learning, and the death of the beloved Socrates—while permitting evil men such as the brigand Harpalus, who praises them, to live (3.32.80–34.83). This New Philosophy of the New Academy is for Cicero a logical extension of his understanding of rhetoric as able to construct (self-fashion, despite the truth or over the void) the best, because most potentially victorious, law case. But for the humanists it calls all in doubt; it does not merely displace but destroys the learning—for the humanists, their New Learning—of the Old Academy and the teachings of Socrates and the writings of Plato.

Once raised, Cicero does not let the matter rest. In his *Academica,* a protreptic analysis of the New Skepticism cast as a dialogue like More's *Utopia* but now avowedly fictional ("quod numquam locuti sumus," pref. 1–2), Cicero casts himself as the champion of these teachings of the New Academy: diegesis and mimesis coincide. Introducing his case by way of Varro, he traces uncertainty back to the fountainhead of Socrates and Plato, as Erasmus and More do, but he substitutes high seriousness for their wit and love of paradox.

> Hic in omnibus fere sermonibus qui ab iis qui illum audierunt perscripti varie copioseque sunt ita disputat ut nihil adfirmet ipse, refellat alios, nihil se scire dicat nisi id ipsum, eoque praestare ceteris quod illi quae nesciant scire se putent, ipse se nihil scire, id unum sciat, ob eamque rem se arbitrari ab Apolline omnium sapientissimum esse dictum quod haec esset una omnis sapientia, non arbitrari se scire quod nesciat.

> The method of discussion pursued by Socrates in almost all the dialogues so diversely and so fully recorded by his hearers is to affirm nothing himself but to refute others, to assert that he knows nothing except the fact of his own ignorance, and that he surpassed all other people in that they think they know things that they do not know but he himself thinks he knows nothing, and that he believed this to have been the reason why Apollo declared him to be the wisest of all men, because all wisdom consists solely in not thinking that you know what you do not know. [1.4.16][15]

The fragmentary *Academica* 1 that the later Tudors came to know concludes with what remains an authoritative encapsulation of this New Learning of the Greeks and Romans (1.12.44–46). Cicero goes on in Book 2 in his own person to put forth what were apparently already the shibboleths of the New Skepticism that had by then gained sufficient historical and logical force to convince even him: I believe what I say, Cicero tells us; "ea sentire quae dicerem" (2.20.65). He begins by citing instances of our biological shortcomings. From where he is standing, Cicero claims, he can see Catulus's place at Cumae but not his villa at Pompeii, although there is nothing to obstruct his view, and this despite other men who have been said to see as far as twenty-five miles and some birds that see even farther (2.25.80). Moreover, even our recording senses are often unreliable. A distant ship appears to be at anchor but is actually moving (2.25.81). There may be nothing larger than the sun, yet it appears to be merely a foot in diameter, and Epicurus has argued it may even be somewhat smaller than it looks (2.26.82). It is not simply that man's senses are untrustworthy and therefore his judgment may be faulty but that *man is no longer even the measure:* Cicero's skepticism strikes at the roots of humanist thought. Cicero moves on from the unreliability of man's senses to the invalidity of logic or dialectic, thus directly challenging the Tudor practices at university.

> Nempe fundamentum dialecticae est quidquid enuntiatur (id autem appellant ἀξίωμα, quod est quasi effatum) aut verum esse aut falsum; quid igitur? haec vera an falsa sunt: "Si te mentiri dicis idque verum dicis, mentiris?" Haec scilicet inexplicabilia esse dictis, quod est odiosius quam illa quae nos non comprehensa et non percepta dicimus.... Quo modo igitur hoc conclusum esse iudicas: "Si dicis nunc lucere et verum dicis, lucet; dicis autem nunc lucere et erum dicis; lucet igitur?" Probatis certe genus et rectissime conclusum dicitis, itaque in docendo eum primum concludendi modum traditis. Aut quidquid igitur eodem modo concluditur probabitis aut ars ista nulla est.

> Clearly it is a fundamental principle of dialectic that every statement (termed by them *axiōma,* that is, a "proposition") is either true or false; what then? is this a true proposition or a false one—"If you say that you are lying and say it truly, you lie?" Your school of course says that these problems are "insoluble," which is more vexatious than the things termed by us "not grasped" and "not perceived." ... What judgement do you pass on the procedure of the following syllogism—"If you say that it is light now and speak the truth, it is light; but you do say that it is light now and speak the truth; therefore it is light?" Your school undoubtedly approve this class of syllogism and say that it is completely valid, and accordingly it is the first mode of proof that you give in your lectures. Either therefore you will approve of every syllogism in the same mode, or that science of yours is no good. [2.29.95–30.96]

Not content thus to challenge the Old Academy of Socrates and Plato, Cicero goes on to challenge Aristotelian thought by arranging his argument along the three main divisions advocated by the Peripatetics—physics and ethics follow hard on this examination of logic. The sea now looks purple under the west wind, he notes, but the wise man will not assent to this perception, for he will know it has previously appeared blue, may tomorrow

appear gray, and under sunlight become a shimmering white (2.33.105).
We do not know our universe (the Tudor macrocosm) because we do not
know our selves (the Tudor microcosm); ethics has also been a matter of
disputed perception and judgment. Aristo proved in practice what Zeno
argued in theory, that nothing is good except virtue; others hold the end of
goodness is pleasure; Carneades insisted the chief good was that recom-
mended by nature, and the Stoics, claiming that all sins are equal, aroused
violent disagreement from Antiochus (2.42.130–43.133). In light of such
various but comparably demonstrable theories, in the study of morality as
in the study of dialectic and biology, the best that man can honestly
advance is what is probable, for nothing remains clear and nothing remains
certain. Nothing is even *preferential*.

Tudor poets everywhere draw on the *De Natura Deorum* as a storehouse
of allusions to the gods, as do the sixteenth-century authors of Continental
and English emblem books, but they blink the radical attack on the
possibilities of man and his learning; they do not disturb the foundation of
humanist thought and humanist poetics. When Erasmus comes to tackle
the implications of this in the *Encomium Moriae,* for instance, in his
abbreviated but celebrated comments on the philosophers of his day—

> Quam vero suaviter delirant, cum innumerabiles aedificant mundos, dum
> Solem, dum Lunam, Stellas, Orbes, tamquam pollice filove metiuntur, dum
> Fulminum, Ventorum, Eclipsium ac caeterarum inexplicabilium rerum
> causus reddunt, nihil usquam haesitantes, perinde quasi naturae rerum
> architectrici fuerint a secretis, quasive e Deorum consilio nobis advenerint:
> quos interim Natura cum suis conjecturis, magnifice ridet. Nam nihil apud
> illos esse comperti, vel illud satis magnum est argumentum, quod singulis
> de rebus inexplicabilis inter ipsos est digladiatio. Ii cum nihil omnino
> sciant, tamen omnia se scire profitentur.

> how sweetely doe they raue in theyr owne opinion: whan constauntly they
> affirme there be worlds innumerable? Or whan they take vpon theim to
> measure the sonne, the moone, the planets and theyr conpasses, as it were
> by *vnchemease, or drawne with a sine:* Or whan they expounde the causes
> of thunder, of wyndes, of eclipses, and suche other inexplicable thyngs,
> nothyng doubtyng, as if they had crepte into natures bosome, or were of
> counsaile with the Godds. And yet dooeth nature lowdely laughe theim to
> scorne, with all theyr coniectures: coniectures I saie, and no certaine
> knowlage, whiche appereth by this, that one secte of theim agreeth not
> with an other, but rather contendeth togethers vpon euery little thing. And
> yet these men, who in deede know nothing, wil take vpon them to know
> all thyngs[16]

—he avoids the challenge to humanist learning by implying that the errors
arise in the derivative and shallow wranglings of the Scholastics who
intervened between the ancients and the men of the Renaissance New

Learning. Moreover, he places such dyslogistic opinion at a distinct remove, in the mouth of Folly. But such willed ignorance could not persist for long; by 1543 Copernicus is writing to Pope Paul III in his dedication to *De Revolvtionibvs Orbium coelestium* that it was precisely Cicero's *Academica,* followed by readings in Plutarch—"Ac reperi quidem apud Ciceronem primum, Nicetum sensisse terram moueri. Postea & apud Pluatarchum inueni quosdam alios in ea fuisse opinione, cuius uerba, ut sint omnibus obuia" (sig. iiii[17]—that alerted him to the possibility that the earth itself was in orbit. It was this antique learning that inaugurated his heliocentric theory of the universe, eventually heralding for the later Tudors a world sharply opposed to that propagated by the philosophic faith and deductive logic of humanism.

The *Hypotyposes* of Sextus Empiricus had an even more profound effect on later Tudor humanism. This comprehensive and authoritative outline of Pyrrhonistic thought—still "the best and most complete presentation of ancient Scepticism that has been preserved to modern times," as Mary Mills Patrick once put it[18]—was translated into Latin in 1562 and again with the whole corpus of Sextus in Paris in 1569. It profoundly influenced Montaigne and his distant cousin Francisco Sanchez. If the earlier Rabelais could mock the Pyrrhonist Trouillogan (3.15–16), the later Nashe actually paraphrases Sextus.[19] Little wonder he and the learned Thomas Lodge turned to the more secure faith of Christianity—and of Seneca—to maintain what humanist beliefs could still be retrieved. Beginning with the principle of *akatalepsia,* or the lack of certain knowledge concerning the inner nature of things, Sextus proposes the withholding of assent or dissent (*epoche*), preserving instead *isostheneia,* or equipollence, a balancing of arguments on both sides of the question. This, he advocates, leads us not only to an openness to further discovery and understanding but also to a quietude of mind. The consequent formulas for the Skeptics are two: "Omnia sunt incomprēsibilia" and "Nihil defino" (sig. ii4); "All things are non-apprehensible" and "I determine nothing" (1.29.211). Sextus's work follows closely the outline and presentation of Cicero's *Academica,* but his virtue is systematic detail; he is the great codifier of classical Skepticism. Thus Book 1 classifies examples of the unreliability of the senses into ten tropes of *epoche*—those based on differences in animals; in men; among the five senses; circumstances; position, distance, and place; mixtures; the quantity and constitution of objects; relations; frequence or rarity of occurrence; and cultural relativity in systems, customs, laws, mythical beliefs, and dogmatic opinions (1.14.47–152). In addition, every matter of inquiry admits to an additional five modes developed by later Skeptics and examined in chapter 15; these are based on discrepancy, on regression ad infinitum, on relativity, on hypothesis, and on circular reasoning, or what became for the New Academy fallacious methods of reasoning.

To give due credit to the northern and Tudor humanists, they tried to offset such potential shortcomings (taking their cue from Aristotelian logic rather than Sextus's skepticism) by enlarging the sphere of argumentation to include such conceptualizations as analogy and deduction could provide them. But Sextus had already faced that challenge: from the outset, logic is his chief concern, the detailed attack on Aristotelian dialectic the very heart of his *Outline*. A disjunctive proposition, he claims, denies the validity of signs in syllogisms, for they are either apparent and therefore unnecessary or nonevident and therefore unworkable (2.11.127–28). Sextus further demonstrates—and quite rightly—that the deductive logic of the Aristotelian syllogism "proves" nothing, since the conclusion is already embedded in one or both of the premises (2.14): "Coagmentatio itaque ex sumptionibus & conclusione, non est demonstratio" (sig. oo2); "the argument which deduces what is non-evident by means of pre-evident premises is indiscoverable" (2.13.169).[20] Conversely, induction is a faulty method because the possibility of a single exception in any definable group requires that every instance be examined in the category being analyzed, and such scrutiny renders the induction redundant (2.14.195–96). Further, a full review of particulars is impossible, because particulars are by nature infinite and indefinite (sig. pp1; 2.15.204). Certain knowledge is as undiscoverable for Sextus in physics as it is through dialectic, as his further disjunctive arguments show (3.5–12). His treatment of ethics is abbreviated (3.23), but this may be due to the fact that cultural relativity, which denies the absolute truth of any single ethical proposition (his basic argument), was previously discussed and illustrated as the tenth trope in Book 1 (the skeptical belief advanced in our own day by Michel Foucault and Clifford Geertz).

By thus eliminating any precise and ascertainable body of knowledge, Sextus removes the possibility for precisely those absolute premises—such as the centrality and perfectibility of man, his educability and his transformation—upon which Tudor humanists erected an entire philosophy. It removes as well any possibility for exemplary models upon which Tudor humanists had constructed an entire system of education by means of imitation—and a humanist poetics for fiction. Sextus anticipates just this latter situation. In 3.28 he argues that there is no matter to be taught, for falsehood should not be taught and truth, as the entire Skeptic philosophy demonstrates, is unobtainable and unknowable. He further argues, in 3.29, that there can be no such thing as a teacher and a learner; it is absurd, he says, for an expert to teach an expert or a nonexpert to teach a nonexpert, or a nonexpert an expert, and, seeing that teaching one truth does not make a nonexpert expert, there is no means by which a nonexpert can be made expert (259–63).[21] Given such an undermining of humanist belief—the humanists' faith in man's reason and their trust in his abilities— is it any wonder that the *Academica* was one Ciceronian text that the humanists chose *not* to translate, as they chose to neglect the whole corpus of Sextus?

AS TUDOR humanist writers had found Continental models at earlier stages of their development of a poetics of fiction—in the work of Erasmus, Castiglione, and the anonymous author of the *Vida de Lazarillo de Tormes*—so the end of a viable humanist poetics was first measured by someone not under the rule of Elizabeth I: Montaigne is the first to recognize the impact on humanism of the New Skepticism and the New Science and to admit it into his own work. The golden retirement from the life of battle to the life of meditation that he planned in his decisive retreat to the country family estate and to the brick-floored rooms of his tower was as illusory and as effectually short-lived as the pleasure garden Jack Wilton finds in Rome. Montaigne significantly wrote no fiction. Instead, he wrote essays, literally *trials* of thought, examining the aphorisms of all the ancients he could lay hands on through the creative divergences he calls the art of *marqueterie*—essays marked by their awkward angularities of thought and awkward joints of style, where ideas jostle, contradict, even invalidate one another. Montaigne's first line of reasoning for this tentative form, this unfinished form, is the later Cicero, the Cicero, as we might expect, of the *Academica*. As Montaigne puts it, in John Florio's Englishing,

> It is not peradventure without reason, that we ascribe the facilitie of beleeving, and easines of perswasion, vnto simplicitie and ignorance: For, me seemeth to have learnt heretofore, that beliefe was, as it were an impression conceived in our minde, and according as the same was found either more soft, or of lesse resistance, it was easier to imprint any thing therein. *Vt necesse est lancem in libra ponderibus impositis deprimi: sic animum perspicuis cedere* [CIC. Acad. Qu. iv]. *As it is necessarie a scale must goe downe the ballance when weights are put into it, so must a minde yeelde to things that are manifest.* [Sig. I2; 1:221; 132].[22]

Meanwhile, to his study, Montaigne added rafters on which he had inscribed as mottoes quotations from the first book of Sextus's *Hypotyposes* that challenge the uniform validity of any humanist principle. "There is no reason which is not opposed by an equal reason"; "It may be and it may not be"; "Guiding ourselves by customs, and by the senses"; "I determine nothing"; "I do not comprehend things, I suspend judgment, I examine": such reminders from Sextus indict the power of learning as the power of resolution and final comprehension. In his darker moments, Montaigne's mounting anxieties remind us most of Nashe and Lodge on the corruptibility of man, as we peel away, as we inevitably must, the careful layers of Montaigne's carved, concealing revisions.

"The Apologie for Raimond Sebonde," by far the bulkiest portion of the 1580 *Essais* and still the longest of his works in the later editions, is Montaigne's own catholicon of the New Skepticism, the new New Learning; and it suitably displaces Sidney's *Defence* as the basic treatise for a *post*humanist poetics. Frequently passages from the *Hypotyposes* flash from the "Apologie," as Sextus moves into the center of Montaigne's life and thought.

> The senses are to some more obscure and dimme, and to some more open and quicke. We receive things differently, according as they are, and seeme vnto vs. Things being then so vncertaine, and full of controversie, it is no longer a wonder if it be told vs, that we may avouch snow to seeme white vnto us; but to affirme that it is in essence and in truth, we cannot warrant our selves: which foundation being so shaken, all the Science in the world must necessarily goe to wracke. What? doe our senses themselves hinder one another? To the sight a picture seemeth to be raised aloft, and in the handling flat: Shall we say that muske is pleasing or no, which comforteth our smelling and offendeth our taste? There are Herbs and Ointments, which to some parts of the body are good, and to othersome hurtfull. Honie is pleasing to the taste, but vnpleasing to the sight. [Sigs. Gg6v–Hh1; 2:396–97; 452–53).[23]

Consequently, as Barbara C. Bowen notes, the "Apologie" and other of Montaigne's essays are marked syntactically by repetitive uses of *mais* and *au contraire*.[24]

> He that should fardle-vp a bundle or huddle of the fooleries of mans wisdome, might recount wonders. I willingly assemble some (as a shew or patterne) by some meanes or byase, no lesse profitable then the most moderate instructions. Let vs by that judge, what we are to esteem of man, of his sense & of his reason; since in these great men, & who have raised mans sufficiencie so high, there are found so grose errors, & so apparant defects. As for me, I would rather believe, that they have thus casually treated learning, even as a sporting childes baby, and have sported themselves with reason, as of a vaine & frivolous instrument, setting forth all sorts of inventions, devices & fantasies, somtimes more outstretched, & somtimes more loose. The same *Plato,* who defineth man like vnto a Capon, saith elsewhere in *Socrates,* that in good sooth, he knoweth not what man is; and that of al parts of the world, there is none so hard to be known. By this variety of conceits & instability of opinions, they (as it were) leade vs closely by the hand to this resolution of their irresolution. [Sig. Ee2v; 2:314–15; 408][25]

The best Montaigne can settle for is a world characterized by flux: "My historie must be fitted to the present. I may soone change, not onelie fortune, but intention. It is a counter-roule of diuers and variable accidents, and irresolute imaginations, and sometimes contrarie: whether it be that my selfe am other, or that I apprehend subiects, by other circumstances and considerations" ("Of Repenting," sig. Ss5; 2.21–22; 611).[26] This shift from a humanist poetics to a posthumanist poetics is subtle yet profound: with the intervention of the *Academica* and the *Hypotyposes,* writers test the uncertainty of the New Skepticism rather than the efficacy of humanist thought and education. In such an intellectual environment, it is plain enough why an impatient Nashe turns to such self-defensive scorn after reading Sextus or why the more tolerant but equally anxious Lodge seeks refuge in Catholicism and in simply translating, without further comment, the sacred history of Josephus and the calming philosophy of Seneca.

We do not know precisely when English humanists first read Montaigne's 1580 *Essais*—perhaps many of them did not until Florio's translation of the larger *oeuvre* in 1603, when the first of the Stuarts ascended the throne—but the spirit of the New Skepticism that informs Montaigne also informs the fierce driving energies of Giordano Bruno, who spent two years at Elizabethan Oxford and in London beginning in 1583: Sidney apparently met him at the London house of Fulke Greville during the last stages of writing the *New Arcadia*, and Nashe may well have heard him lecture at Cambridge a decade before *The Unfortunate Traueller.* Felipi Bruno had been renamed Giordano in 1572 during his novitiate with the Dominican order, but already his inquiring mind had made him apostate: he used the monastery privy to hide his contraband copies of Erasmus's translations of the Church Fathers. More important than studying ways in which the New Learning could reinterpret Scripture, however, was Bruno's childhood expedition with his parents to Mount Vesuvius, which, from his home at the volcano's base, had always been for him the boundary of existence, a large barren wall that constituted the end of his world. As he approached the volcano, he remembered vividly all his years, he found it covered with life—with elms and oaks interwoven with richly laden vines; looking backward at his father's house now at the foot of the diminished hill Cicala, he saw that the tiny building had replaced Vesuvius on the horizon. "Bruno learnt with surprise," Alois Riehl sums, "that our eyes deceive us: he saw that as we advance we always carry the centre of our horizon with us: and the thought took root in his mind that Nature everywhere is one and the same, and distance alone alters the appearance of things."[27] This appalling discovery—the *Academica* and *Hypotyposes* realized immediately and personally—was for Bruno irrepressible. Leaving the Dominicans, he read Nicholas of Cusa, Thomas Digges, and Copernicus; and from his original premise of man as autogenous— Antoinette Mann Paterson, following Einstein, calls him "the father of relativity"[28]—he developed his notion of infinity, an idea that with singular force implodes humanist thought and the basis for a humanist poetics. Publicly defining and defending his radically new belief by asserting innumerable solar systems at a traditional Oxford disputation in June 1583, Bruno demolished this humanist ritual for debate and inquiry too, ruined the celebratory occasion, and was permanently exiled from his post at Oxford to the home of the French ambassador de Mauvissière in London.

But intellectual fall-out from this extraordinary epistemological revolution is both immediate in Stuart England and long-lasting. Francis Bacon for one echoes both Sextus and Bruno in Aphorism 1 of the *Novum Organon* (1620): "Man, being the servant and interpreter of Nature, can do and understand so much and so much only as he has observed in fact or in thought of the course of nature: beyond this he neither knows anything nor can do anything" (sig. E2). The apposite commentary is from the scientist William Harvey, who professes "both to learn and to teach anatomy, not from books, but from dissections; not from the positions of philosophers, but from the fabric of nature."[29] The consequence for a new posthumanist poetics is seen in Descartes, who redefines for posthumanist poetics the image of the wax.

> Sumamus exempli causā hanc ceram; nuperrime ex fauis fuit educta, nondum amisit omnem saporem sui mellis, nonnihil retinet odoris florum ex quibus collecta est, eius calor, figura, magnitudo, manifesta sunt: dura est, frigida est, facile tangitur, ac si articulo ferias, emittet sonum; omnia denique illi adsunt quae requiri videntur vt corpus aliquod possit quam distinctissmē cognosci. Sed ecce, dum loquor, igni admouetur, saporis reliquiae purgantur, odor expirat, color mutatur, figura tollitur, crescit magnitudo, fit liquida, fit calida, vix tangi potest, nec iam si pulses emittet sonum: remanétne adhuc eadem cera? remanere fatendum est, nemo negat, nemo aliter putat. Quid erat igitur in eâ quod tam distincte comprehenditur? certe nihil eorum quae sensibus attingebam, nam quae cunque sub gustum, vel odoratum vel visum, vel tactum, vel auditum veniebant, mutata iam sunt, remanet cera.

> Let us take, for example, this piece of wax which has just been taken from the hive; it has not yet lost the sweetness of the honey it contained; it still retains something of the smell of the flowers from which it was gathered; its colour, shape and size are apparent; it is hard, cold, it is tangible; and if you tap it, it will emit a sound. So, all the things by which a body can be known distinctly are to be found together in this one.

But, as I am speaking it is placed near a flame: what remained of its taste is dispelled, the smell disappears, its colour changes, it loses its shape, it grows bigger, becomes liquid, warms up, one can hardly touch it, and although one taps it, it will no longer make any sound. Does the same wax remain after this change? One must admit that it does remain, and no one can deny it. What, then, was it that I knew in this piece of wax with such distinctness? Certainly it could be nothing of all the things which I perceived by means of the senses, for everything which fell under taste, smell, sight, touch or hearing, is changed, and yet the same wax remains.[30]

As a practitioner of humanist poetics, Lyly had used the malleability and multiplicity of meaning in the nature of wax to limn a metaphor for man, following Plutarch, to focus our attention on the potentiality of human nature. With Descartes, human perception is refocused on the natural properties of the wax itself. Man only initiates the discussion by using his perceptions and recording his observations, knowing only that he can never fully know. *Then he disappears from the center of attention.* It is the wax which, in its shifting forms, remains.

AS WE CAN date the start of humanist poetics with the statutes of St. Paul's School, London, in 1512, so we can date the beginning of a posthumanist poetics with the 1540 publication of the first summary of Copernican astronomy, the *Narratio prima* of Rheticus. It is an astonishing and memorable decade, the 1540s, witnessing new foundations for astronomy, anatomy, and physics, and a wealth of scientific books of seminal, signal importance: Biringuccio's *De la pirotechnia* (1540) on metallurgy, chemistry, and technology; Gesner's *Historia plantarum* (1541) on systematic botany; Fernel's *De naturali parte medicinae* (1542) on human psychology; Fuch's *De historia stirpium* (also 1542) on a systematic medical botany; the work of Copernicus, Vesalius, Archimedes, and Euclid in 1543; Mattioli's *On Dioscorides* (1544) on medical botany; Turner's *Avium praeoipuarum* (also 1544) on ornithology; Cardano's *Artis Magnae* (1545) on algebra; Paré's *La method . . .* (also 1545), a practical treatment of gunshot wounds; Medina's *Arte de navegar* (also 1545) on nautical science; Agricola's *De ortu et causis* (1546) on metallography and fossils; Fracastoro's *De contagione* (also 1546) on hygiene; Mercator's *De ratione magnetis* (also 1546) on compass navigation; Fernel's *De abditis rerum causis* (1548) on physiological medicine; and Paracelsus's *Wundt und Leibartznei* (1549) on medical chemistry. But such works—like the rise of Skepticism—seemed not to take hold in England until more than a half-century later, until the publication of *The Twoo Bookes of Francis Bacon: Of the proficience and aduancement of Learning, diuine and humane* (1605).

Bacon's compendious mind and syncretic thinking fuse empirical observation with philosophical reasoning. Together they give strong support to the new New Learning. They also frontally attack the finest authors of a humanist poetics.

> Foure causes concurring, the admiration of ancient Authors, the hate of the Schoole men, the exact studie of Languages: and the efficacie of Preaching did bring in an affectionate studie of eloquence, and copie of speech, which then began to flourish. This grew speedily to an excesse: for men began to hunt more after wordes, than matter, and more after choiseness of the Phrase, and the round and cleane composition of the sentence, and the sweet falling of the clauses, and the varying and illustration of their workes with tropes and figures: then after the weight of matter, worth of subiect, soundnesse of argument, life of inuention, or depth of iudgement. . . . Then did *Car* of *Cambridge,* and *Ascham* with their Lectures and Writings, almost deifie *Cicero* and *Demosthenes,* and allure, all young men that were studius vnto that delicate and pollished kinde of learning. . . . It seemes to me that *Pigmalions* frenzie is a good embleme or portraiture of this vanitie: for wordes are but the Images of matter, and except they haue life of reason and inuention: to fall in loue with them, is all one, as to fall in loue with a Picture. [Book 1 (1605 ed.), sigs. E3–E4]

In Book 2, Bacon defines "poesie" more succinctly and more scornfully as "a part of Learning in measure of words for the most part restrained: but in all other points extreamely licensed: and doth truly referre to the Imagination: which beeing not tyed to the Lawes of Matter; may at pleasure ioyne that which Nature hath seuered: & seuer that which Nature hath ioyned, and so make vnlawfull Matches & diuorses of things" (sig. Ee1v). To this posthumanist denunciation of poesie Bacon contributes a clarified and more objective posthumanist denunciation of rhetoric. He exposes prejudicial idols of the mind resulting from individual or communal astigmatism (Aphorisms 41–44, *Novum Organon,* sigs. F3–F4). And he attacks contagious "distempers of learning," of which he names three in the *Advancement of Learning*: fantastical learning, which deceitfully imposes the authority of past wisdom on unsuspecting and credulous students (as, he might suggest misleadingly, Erasmus does); contentious learning, which cloaks a lack of substance with an "infinite agitation of wit" (Book 1, sig. D4v) and lets style substitute for idea (as, he might argue, Lyly practices); and delicate learning, which concentrates entirely on eloquence and copia (as he might find in Greene). In all of the strictures, Bacon enhances observation and objects at the cost of fine language and dismisses fiction (with one or two exceptions) for the major posthumanist forms: treatise and essay. He would (in all ways, it seems) leave off his earlier political works for his imitatio of Montaigne.

WE CAN PERHAPS understand posthumanist poetics more clearly by recalling two among its very few fictions. It is no coincidence that both of them are deliberate *departures from* works of humanist fiction we have already studied in some detail. Bacon's *Nova Atlantis* (written 1614–17; revised for publication c. 1623; published 1627), for instance, is—deliberately—a posthumanist *Utopia*. It clearly seems most indebted to an early exercise in rhetoric, to Bacon's mock orations for a series of mock counselors to a mock monarch written for the Christmas revels at Gray's Inn in 1594. In this oration for a youthful masque, Salomon's House is anticipated in the speech of the second counselor, who advises a study of philosophy with four foundations. The first is "the collecting of a most perfect and general library, wherein whatsoever the wit of man hath heretofore commited to books of worth be they ancient or modern, printed or manuscript, European or other parts, of one or other language, may be made contributory to your wisdom." But this learning is to be coordinated and modified by three other kinds. The second is a garden with a collection of all plants for study, as well as all rare beasts and birds and two lakes, one of salt water and one of fresh water, "in small compass a model of universal nature made private." The third is "a goodly huge cabinet, wherein whatsoever the hand of many by exquisite art or engine hath made rare in stuff, form or motion; whatsoever singularly chance and the shuffle of things hath produced; whatsoever Nature hath wrought in things that want life and may be kept; shall be sorted and included"; and the fourth is "such a stillhouse, so furnished with mills, instruments, furnaces, and vessels, as may be a palace fit for a philosopher's stone" with sufficient experimentation.[31] Here is a society based more in things than in ideas; in the later New Atlantis, too, the geometrical society Hythlodaye describes as based wholly on human reason is made into a land of scientific inventions that bases its existence on discovery. Induction replaces the humanists' use of analogy and deduction. New Atlantis with its busy experimentations chokes out all else: in the lower regions men conserve bodies for coagulation, induration, and refrigeration; in the upper regions they build structures where they witness meteors, snow, hail, rain, and lightning. "*Habemus etiam* Pomaria, *et* Hortos, *amplos, et varios,*" a Christian priest (Hythlodaye's successor) tells the visiting Englishmen (counterparts to More-character and Peter Giles),

> *Habemus etiam* Pomaria, *et* Hortos, *amplos, et varios; In quibus, non tam Nobis cordi est, Pulchritudo Ambulatorum et similium, quam varietas Terre, et Soli, diversis* Arboribus *et* Herbis *proprii. Aliqui autem corum,* Arboribus *et* Baccis *consiti sunt, ad Potuum, complura Genera conficienda, praeter Vineas. In his etiam Experimenta facimus, Insitionum, et Ino-*

culationum.... Arbores etiam et Plantas *grandiores efficimus, quam pro Natura sua; Et Fructus earum majores et suaviores; Atque Sapore, Odore, Colore, et Figura.*

We have also large and various *Orchards* and *Gardens,* wherein we do not so much respect Beauty, as variety of ground and soyl, proper for divers *Trees* and *Herbs*; and some very spacious, where *Trees* and *Berries* are set, whereof we make divers kinds of Drinks, besides the *Vineyards.* In these we practise likewise all conclusions of *Grafting* and *Inoculating....* We make them also (by *Art* much greater than their *nature,* and their *Fruit* greater and sweeter, and of different *taste, smell, colour,* and *figure.*) [32]

Openly "implicit in Bacon's vision of a new learning," then, "was an alteration in the conception of the learned man," as J. C. Davis has it. [33] He is a man whose sole ascertainable knowledge is what can be *observed* and *controlled*. But this is the scientist Bacon, the rhetorical idol slayer; the moral philosopher Bacon knows also that the knowledge earned by science is a form of power and that power in New Atlantis is insufficiently supervised. It is Davis's proper contention, then, that Bacon did not simply leave the *Nova Atlantis* unfinished; it is closer to the truth to say that he *could* not finish it. He could not finish it, that is, not because (as with the humanists) he wished to avoid closure so that his readers could collaborate with him through a sympathetic validation of his *hypotheses* but because, drawing on no antique or contemporary model except to destroy the usefulness of that model, he found himself in a moral and philosophic bind. As Davis comments,

Trapped in the exigencies of the utopian mode, Bacon exposes at once the problem and the impossibility of a scientific utopia. If science is to progress to the achieving of all things possible, minds, and to some extent actions, must be free of censorship and control. But scientific knowledge is power. It can, as Bacon knew, alter the material conditions of society and hence the structure of society itself. If we trust the scientist not only to pursue knowledge but to exercise his resultant power over society in a benevolent and enlightened way, then why may we not trust all men, particularly those not exposed to the temptations of scientific power? Why may we not, in other words, visualise a scientific perfect moral commonwealth? If, like the utopian, we cannot trust human nature, in scientists as well as others, how are we to have control without inhibiting freedom of enquiry? Bacon's failure to complete an ideal-society vision—his inability to assume either the automatic integrity of the scientist or to accept the stifling of free enquiry—is a great failure because it raises these still-unresolved issues at the moment of the conception of modern science. [*Utopia*, p. 137]

New Atlantis permits a religiosity—it was even a land founded by miraculous Pillars of Light and the delivery of scriptural books in a chest—but it is a faith that is wholly awarded to science. Indeed, "The identification of scientific truth with use and therefore with charity, with power and therefore with pity, is fundamental to Bacon's conception of true learning," Moody E. Prior writes; "Bacon often leaves the impression that the career of science is something of a religion in its selflessness and sense of dedication, and he at times spoke of the future scientists as though they were a priesthood."[34] The subject of science and the emphasis on induction in *Nova Atlantis* are decidedly posthumanist; the spare, stripped style and the absence of either declamation or disputation as the controlling form for this treatise likewise realize Bacon's theory of a purified, simplified, and more direct language.

Bruno's earlier *La Cena de la ceneri (Ash Wednesday Supper,* 1584), is a posthumanist redaction of *Il Libro del Cortegiano.* In a fanciful re-creation of a conversation at the London home of Fulke Greville that seems never to have taken place—it was more likely at de Mauvissière's—Bruno provides us with his modern-day court of Urbino. The table, like the salon at Urbino, is presided over by the finest of them all, Sir Philip Sidney, flanked by excessive pedants like Prudenzio and foppish triflers like Frulla. But there is a vital change in the basic configuration: the scientist, not the courtier, is the chief subject; the hero is not Bembo but Copernicus; and the final ascent is not climbing the Ladder of Love but contemplating the vast spaces of an infinite universe. The mood, moreover, while still self-aggrandizing (on the Nolan's part here, rather than on all of them), is no longer nostalgic, backward-looking; it is propagandistic and equally forward-looking. Bruno as the Nolan wishes to show, after the debacle at Oxford, that he does indeed know Copernican theory and that this, congruent with his own more private hermetic thought, renders Aristotelian physics and Ptolemaic cosmology irrevelant for all time. The dispositio of *La Cena,* like that of *Il Cortegiano,* is recursive as well as linear: the arguments interlock so that the attacks on Aristotle and the Peripatetic school are necessary components to the defense of Copernicus and Bruno. The title of *La Cena* puns, like *Utopia;* it refers to Christ's communion with friends—and a supper of ashes. And Bruno's *proemiale epistolá,* the prefatory letter to Sidney, is meant to remind us of the *Encomium Moriae* in its reference to the Sileni. But the doubleness of the Sileni suggests, as Bruno reworks the metaphor, not that the inside contents—or inside knowledge—will counter first impressions but that the Silenus box is always both outside and inside and that his catalogues of variants, in connection with the Sileni, are meant to be inclusive. It is totality, not contrariety, he is after. The use of Erasmus is revisionary.

Opposites do not cancel each other or reach *epoche* but merely become part of an infinite number of possibilities, microcosmic analogies to the infinite skies, and infinite worlds, of the macrocosm he describes in Dialogo terzo.

The five dialogues proper carry forward this transformation. Dialogo primo opens with an apparently humorous appeal to the Muses, suitable antecedent to the epic journey of pratfalls Bruno will make in Dialogo secondo to reach Greville's house. Once again the movement is from punning on liquor (as the drink at a banquet, at a communion, and as wine of the gods and godly insight) through the antobiographical reference to the goddess of memory, the art with which Bruno was associated at Oxford, to the harmony of the spheres implying the new harmony discovered by Copernicus and congruent with Hermes Trismegistus, another central subject of *La Cena*. Copernican mathematics is only a shadow of the Hermetic mysteries (Ideas) as this small dinner party is only a pretense for the truths Bruno will divulge insofar as the Muses help him find a suitable language. All humor disappears in Dialogo terzo with the introduction of Copernicus as a man of genius; we move from encomium to a discussion of his philosophy, for he alone saw the new dawn that brings men out of the cave of darkness into the light of the new New Learning. As the Nolan transforms Copernicus from man to metaphor, so we too are meant to be transformed by this philosopher-scientist. There is an attack, in Dialogo quarto, on English grammarians, whose concentration on eloquence has kept the attention of wise men averted from the greater and more significant truths, and an attack in Dialogo quinto on the errors of sense following the ideas of the New Academy. In the end, transformation becomes not merely method but theme. The Nolan frees his listeners from their limitations of sense and the confinements of past learning under Aristotle and Ptolemy and prepares them for the new truths of Copernicus and Hermes: they in turn are to see the world infinite in its reaches and its possibilities. This is the new dawn Bruno sees coming.

In abandoning the curriculum of the Old Academy (and of Oxford), then, Bruno like Bacon leads us from a humanist poetics to a posthumanist poetics. He moves from rhetorical art to scientific investigation, from witty paradox to philosophic speculation. The subject shifts too, from man—the measure for the humanists—to the universe and its vast stretches to infinity. The style changes also, from the balanced disputation, explicit or implicit, to the treatise which, moving inductively, gathers up facts to substantiate a hypothesis that remains in the end problematic (not simply incomplete). Instead of ending with the humanist practice of imitatio with which he seems to begin, Bruno as the Nolan moves inductively to arrive at a mystical sense of a grand but *in*comprehensible world.

It is important to note that the inconclusiveness of the fictions of Bacon and Bruno are fundamentally dissimilar from the kind of openness we witness in the *Encomium Moriae* or the *Utopia, Euphues* or the *Arcadia.* Those works refused final closure because the implicit disputation, between text and reader, between antique model and newly realized fictional particularity (as poetic *hypo-thesis),* demanded the active collusion of the reader. Bacon and Bruno really wish to *demonstrate to* the reader, not invite the reader to *collaborate with* them. But, unable to make full sense of the world around them, just as the Defense of Poetry in Montaigne's "Apologie" was unable to arrive at any certainties, Bacon stops in midwork, Bruno drifts off into Hermetic musings. For Bacon key questions at key junctures could not be faced: he does not tell us, for instance, how the government of New Atlantis works (although Hythlodaye had been detailed in his earlier discussion of this in *Utopia* and based his critique before More-character in Antwerp on it). Nor can Bacon portray in any detail the daily operation of Salomon's House. Atlantis and Salomon's House are simply *there;* givens. But they are only superficially described. They are incompletely realized. Bruno, too, faces a logical and philosophical impasse before the Copernican world he would have his listeners come to understand as well as appreciate, and his trailing off into mysticism at the close of *La Cena* is not the forging of a new poetics for fiction but a necessary consequence of positing something like poetry in a world that reaches beyond the capacity of the poet to envision. Indeed, the world of *fact alone*—the world of Bacon and of Copernicus—is, as Sidney knew all too clearly in his *Defence,* a world of History without Moral Philosophy—and *without* Poetry. It is, in its way, not only incomplete but grotesque. For an artist that must surely have been the case: it is instructive that neither Bacon nor Bruno—nor, before them, with his essays, Montaigne—ever wrote a successful *fiction.*

THE NEW INTELLECTUAL climate, therefore, at the start of the seventeenth century is no longer congenial to humanist poetics and humanist fiction. It no longer supports hypothetical examinations of a potentially perfectible man cultivated and civilized by a potentially Utopian society from fixed, antique models, the once-revered Senecan originals. For if men's senses can no longer be trusted, then surely men's hopes and dreams cannot be taken seriously; if observations show only change, antique models become irrelevant, devoid of any use as a repository of meaning and significance. If we cannot tell whether a distant ship is moving or not when we look at the ship, what confidence can we place in a fixed vision of England as Arden or Arcadia? The audience that *humanist* poetics had appealed to, the *traditional* audience on which it had necessarily *depended,* is irrevocably gone. As a consequence, as the work of Nashe and Lodge suggests, much intellectual effort turned from a trust in man to a new reliance on the providence of God. What new fiction is forged in the century ahead—apart from latter-day, lesser imitations of the great works of humanist fiction under the Tudors—is a fiction grounded in Puritan doctrine and its dream of a Promised Land, leading in time to such work as *Pilgrim's Progress* and even, in greater time, to the moral fiction of Swift, Defoe, and Richardson. As for the textualization of culture and the historicization of texts that Montrose finds as the fundamental dynamics of poetics throughout the English Renaissance, that found outlets in other forms—in the open satire of journalism or bourgeois drama or, at court, in masque and spectacle where, Stephen Orgel writes in *The Illusion of Power,* the initial impulse of the humanists to cloak criticism within the folds of fictions might continue to conceal and reveal, to dis-tract and to in-struct, in a dynamics of performance on the stage where the text is brought to life without the necessary intervention of antique reference. There, he tells us, under James I and VI and under Charles I, the illusion of power rests on the power of illusion, and the basic analogy is not to the past but to the cosmology of the present world. Rather than bringing Plato or Plutarch into fiction, this later age brings the theater and the globe into conjunction, so that the minutest act finds its real, and greater, relevance only in the larger, actual world of a never-ceasing present.

This is quite unlike the earlier age of Pico and Ficino and Thomas More. That earlier age was the time when Erasmus cried in ecstasy to see humanism herald a new dawn and when the wonderfully confident Spaniard humanist Juan Luis Vives, who tutored the children of Henry VIII, wrote his brief, sprightly "fable of man," as he calls it, in which a man ascending to Heaven and meeting an angel cannot determine—nor can the angel—who is who. Vives is having fun with Pico della Mirandola's portrayal of man ascending a kind of Jacob's ladder whenever he chooses, the subject of his *Oration on the Dignity of Man,* but this jeu d'esprit functions because behind the witty paradox is belief that man can, in fact, aspire to Heaven through the exercise of right reason and faith, that earthbound observations need not curtail equally valuable flights of vision and imagination where out-ward travel coexists with in-sight in poetry. There is no contrary world to prevent him and no uncertainty to rob him of hope and trust. It is the environment that developed a humanist poetics and fostered wonderfully vital, exploratory humanist fiction that would flourish from the *Utopia* of More to Lodge's *Margarite of America,* for if the novel suddenly rose at all, it rose under the Tudors. Sharply disjunctive is the quotation from the sixteenth-century Italian philosopher Julius Caesar Scaliger, which Sir Thomas Browne finds most congenial for the title page of his examination of popular learning, the *Pseudodoxia Epidemica, Vulgar Errors* (1646): "Ex Libris colligere quae prodiderunt Auctores longè est periculosissimum: Rerum ipsarum cognitio vera, è rebus ipsis est"; "To cull from books what authors have reported is exceedingly dangerous; true knowledge of things themselves is out of the things themselves." Browne would replace Plato with Montaigne as his authority. What Montaigne pioneers in the 1580 *Essais,* as the founder of a posthumanist poetics, is a new aesthetics in which the act of seeing replaces the replenishment of belief. The 1580 *Essais* is the first important text to transform the old movement of receiving wisdom to a new movement of seeking it anew, as a *tabula rasa.* When John Florio in 1603 finally brings all of Montaigne's essays into the humanist eloquence of his English vernacular, he ironically prepares the way not for the continuation of the Tudor grammar school but for the foundation of the Royal Society. Another new age has dawned, wherein lie quite different occasions for other readings.

INTRODUCTION

1. *Opvs Epistolarvm Des. Erasmi Roterodami,* ed. P. S. Allen (Oxford, 1910), 2:487 (hereafter cited as *EE*); trans. Myron P. Gilmore, *The World of Humanism, 1453–1517* (New York, 1952), p. 260.

2. Frederick B. Artz, *Renaissance Humanism, 1300–1550* (Kent, Ohio, 1966), p. 87.

3. Cicero, *Academica* 1.4.15. trans. H. Rackham, Loeb Classical Library (Cambridge, Mass., 1933, 1979).

4. Paul Oskar Kristeller, *Renaissance Thought and Its Sources,* ed. Michael Mooney (New York, 1979), p. 170.

5. Sears Jayne, *John Colet and Marsilio Ficino* (Oxford, 1963), pp. 5 et passim.

6. Kristeller, *Renaissance Thought,* pp. 174–75.

7. Pomponazzi, *Tractatus de immortalitate animae,* ed. Gianfranco Morra (Bologna, 1954), pp. 184–204; cf. Ernst Cassirer et al., eds., *The Renaissance Philosophy of Man* (Chicago, 1948), pp. 353–63.

8. Richard Mulcaster, *The First Part of the Elementarie* (1582); first editions are cited in the text unless otherwise specified.

9. Philip Sidney, *Defence of Poesie* (1595 Ponsonby quarto), sig. F3v; *Miscellaneous Prose of Sir Philip Sidney,* ed. Katherine Duncan-Jones and Jan Van Dorsten (Oxford, 1973), p. 100.

10. Quoted in T. W. Baldwin, *William Shakspere's Small Latine & Lesse Greeke* (Champaign, Ill., 1944), 1:412.

11. This summary is from J. Howard Brown, *Elizabethan Schooldays* (Oxford, 1933), p. 78.

12. Donald Lemen Clark, *Rhetoric in Greco-Roman Education* (New York, 1957), p. 212.

13. Quintilian, *Institutio Oratoria,* trans. H. E. Butler, Loeb Classical Library (Cambridge, Mass., 1922, 1968); cf. *Rhetorica ad Herennium* 1.1.1.

14. Thomas Nashe, *The Anatomie of Absvrditie* (1589), sig. E3v; *The Works of Thomas Nashe,* ed. Ronald B. McKerrow (Oxford, 1904), 1:48.

15. Cf. Thomas H. Cain, *Praise in "The Faerie Queene"* (Lincoln, Neb., 1978), p. 11.

16. Erasmus's *Colloquia* were required to be taught by the statutes of the grammar schools at Cuckfield by 1529, East Retford by 1552, Winchester and Rivington by 1564, Bangor by 1568, and Durham and Harrow by 1590, and there were other popular texts as well: Vives's *Exercitatio Linguae Latinae* (1532) early and the *Colloquies* of Maturin Cordier or Corderius (in use by the 1570s at Westminster) late, while the dialogues of Castalion's *Colloquia Sacra* (1545) provided religious instruction.

17. Records of such play performances dating from 1520–30 exist for St. Paul's and Eton and from 1570–80 for Westminster and Merchant Taylors; several plays were also performed at court before Elizabeth I by grammar school pupils. Nor were such occasions confined to London; Shrewsbury was justly famous for its school productions, sometimes drawing an audience of upward of 2,000. In this context, it is not surprising to learn that a few schoolmasters such as Nicholas Udall of Eton and Richard Mulcaster of St. Paul's wrote their own plays; what is surprising is that not more of them did. The converse is also true: such plays as John Heywood's *Mery play betwene Iohan Iohan the husbande / Tyb his wyfe / & syr Jhān the preest* (1533) are essentially dramatized disputations as is his *Play of the Wether* (1533).

18. This seventeenth-century handlist includes many works in rhetoric and poetry: Cicero's *Officiorum Libre* I (c. 1481), *Epistolarum familiarum* (1475), *Opera omnia* (1534), and *Le pistole ad Attico* (1555); Aeschylus, *Tragediae VII* (1557); Aesop (1501, 1570); Aristophanes' *Comoediae novem cum commentariis antiquis* (1547); Demosthenes (1570); Isocrates (1593); Juvenal (1490?); Lucan's *Opera* (1563); Ovid's *Opera* (1497, 1549); and Sophocles' *Tragoediae septem, cum interpretationibus* (1522); as well as Thomas Cooper's *Thesaurus* (1565), Thomas Elyot's dictionary (1538) and Cooper's revision (1552); Erasmus's *Omnium Operum* (1516) and Thomas Chaloner's translation of *Encomium Moriae* (1549); Thomas More's *Omnia Latina opera* (1566), *Works written in English* (1557), and *Eutopia* (Venice, 1548); Vives's *Opera* (1555); Bruno's *Il gl'heroici furori* (1585); and Sidney's *Arcadia* (1622).

19. "He shall teach rhetoric the first year, dialectic the second and third. In the fourth year he should add philosophy" ("Primus annus rhetoricam docebit: secunda et tertius dialecticam. Quartus adjungat philosophiam")—so the university statutes of 1570. Indeed, whatever the subject under study, college lectures at both Cambridge and Oxford were meant to supply the undergraduate "with topics, arguments, and syllogisms he could use in both college and university disputations." Craig R. Thompson writes (*Universities in Tudor England,* [Washington, D. C., 1959], p. 19).

20. Proven ability at disputations, along with attendance at lectures and other disputations, constituted the basic requirement for graduation. Andrew Clark has described them for us in some detail in the *Registrum Universitatis Oxon:*

"The first set of disputations came in, or after, the ninth Term, when the student was expected 'respondere in parvisis' (parviso, parvisiis), a disputation in grammatical and logical subjects.

"The 'quaestiones' or subjects of disputations were three in number, and had to be handed in to a Master of the Schools a week previous to the day of disputation. They had further to be affixed to the doors of the schools with the names and college of the disputants at 8 a.m. on the morning of the day of disputation, and to remain there throughout the day.

"The disputants were (1) 'scholares' who had already gone through the disputations, but who were doing it 'pro termino'; (2) 'scholares' who were doing it as an exercise for the degree (called responding 'pro forma').

"Three disputed at one time, one as a 'respondent' two as 'opponents.' A student doing it 'pro forma' was required (a) 'semel opponere,' (b) 'semel ab hora prima ad horam tertiam respondere.'

"The presidents and supervisors were Regent Masters, called in their exercise of this office 'Magistri Scholarum.' They soon became fixed deputies, four in number, selected by the proctors from the regents to serve for a year.

"These disputations took place on every Monday, Wednesday, and Friday in Term. The disputants assembled at S. Mary's, and from thence were conducted by the yeoman bedell of Arts to the schools of Arts, where the disputations were held.

"At the end of each day's disputations those who had been disputing 'pro forma' were created 'sophistae generales' (or briefly 'generales'), a sort of quasi-degree 'in logicalibus et grammaticalibus.' " (*Register of the University of Oxford* [Oxford, 1887], 2:21–22.)

Disputations for third- and fourth-year students dealt with questions in philosophy, while those for more advanced students concerned topics related to their professional faculties.

21. Thompson, *Universities in Tudor England*, pp. 21–22.

22. *An Elizabethan in 1582: The Diary of Richard Madox, Fellow of All Souls*, trans. and ed. Elizabeth Story Donno (London, 1976), pp. 73–74.

23. But this was not always the case; following Ascham in *The Scholemaster* (1570), Jerome Turler in *The Traveiler* (1575) lists a number of stereotypes, often ill-founded, of Germans, French, Spaniards, and Italians (sigs. D4v–D5v).

24. Cf. Aristotle, *Rhetoric* 2.1.3.

25. Thomas Wilson in *The Arte of Rhetorique* (1553), locating deceitful means of argumentation and false conclusions for some sixty pages, lays much of it at Quintilian's doorstep. He notes that Quintilian claims such sophistry is necessary in a world of wise and good lawyers but evil or ignorant judges.

26. Walter J. Ong, *Rhetoric, Romance, and Technology* (Ithaca, N.Y., 1971), pp. 65, 66.

27. William T. Costello, S. J., *The Scholastic Curriculum at Early Seventeenth-Century Cambridge* (Cambridge, Mass., 1958), p. 20.

28. Margaret Hastings, *The Court of Common Pleas in Fifteenth-Century England* (Ithaca, N.Y., 1947), p. 66. The course of study, however, was unchanged throughout the Tudor period.

29. Cf. *Ad Herennium* 1.8.13; Quintilian, *Institutio Oratoria* 2.4.2.

30. Clark, *Rhetoric*, p. 230.

31. An even larger number of *suasoriae* are noted by Philostratus in his *Lives of the Sophists*.

32. Cicero, *Brutus,* trans. G. L. Hendrickson, Loeb Classical Library (Cambridge, Mass., 1939, 1962).

33. Eugene M. Waith, *The Pattern of Tragicomedy in Beaumont and Fletcher* (New Haven, Conn., 1952), p. 172.

34. Wesley Trimpi, "The Ancient Hypothesis of Fiction: An Essay on the

Origins of Literary Theory," *Traditio* 27:12; rep. *Muses of One Mind* (Princeton, 1983), p. 15.

35. Richard A. Lanham, *The Motives of Eloquence: Literary Rhetoric in the Renaissance* (New Haven, Conn., 1976), p. 4.

36. Aristotle, *De Sophisticis Elenchis,* trans. E. S. Forster, Loeb Classical Library (Cambridge, Mass., 1955).

37. Sextus Empiricus, *Against the Professors,* trans. R. G. Bury, Loeb Classical Library (Cambridge, Mass., 1949, 1971), 2.46–47.

38. Trans. Bury (Cambridge, Mass., 1933), 3.110–11. Plutarch also often expresses impatience with the sophists. See *Praecepta gerendu reipublicae,* 802E, 815B; *Life of Lucullus,* 3.4; *Life of Cicero* 51.1; *Life of Lycurgus* 9.5; and *Life of Pompeius* 77.3.

39. Plato, *Gorgias,* trans. W. R. M. Lamb, Loeb Classical Library (Cambridge, Mass., 1925, 1975).

40. Isocrates, *Against the Sophists,* trans. George Norlin, Loeb Classical Library (Cambridge, Mass., 1929), 1,9.

41. Plato, *The Sophist,* trans. Harold North Fowler, Loeb Classical Library (Cambridge, Mass., 1921, 1952).

42. There are important surveys of these works in Baxter Hathaway, *The Age of Criticism: The Late Renaissance in Italy* (Ithaca, N.Y., 1962), pp. 13–16, 350–51, 390–91; Bernard Weinberg, *A History of Literary Criticism in the Italian Renaissance,* 2 vols. (Chicago, 1961), 2:636–46; and Erwin Panofsky, *Idea* (Berlin, 1924), pp. 96–98, n. 144 (trans. Joseph J. S. Peake [Columbia, S.C., 1968], p. 215, n. 51). I am also indebted to conversations with Katherine Duncan-Jones and D. H. Craig.

43. *EE* 1:545; see also William Ringler, Introduction to John Rainolds, *Oratio in Laudem Artis Poeticae* (Princeton, N.J., 1940), p. 20. Cf. E.K.'s rhetorical glossses to *The Shepheardes Calender* (1579).

44. Lanham, *Motives,* p. 7.

45. Seneca, *Epistulae Morales,* trans. Richard Gummere, Loeb Classical Library (Cambridge, Mass., 1920), Letter 90.46.

46. Trans. Gummere, 1925.

47. Trimpi, "Ancient Hypothesis," p. 2.

48. Hanna H. Gray, "Renaissance Humanism: The Pursuit of Eloquence," *Journal of the History of Ideas* 24:506.

49. F. M. Cornford, "Mathematics and Dialectic in the *Republic* VI-VII," *Mind* 41:42–43.

CHAPTER I

1. A. J. Krailsheimer, *The Continental Renaissance,* 1500–1600 (Harmondsworth, 1971), p. 361.

2. Johan Huizinga, *Erasmus of Rotterdam,* trans F. Hopman (London, 1952), p. 70.

3. 1595 Ponsonby quarto, sigs. F3–F3v; *Miscellaneous Prose,* ed. Duncan-Jones and Van Dorsten, p. 100.

4. *The Works of John Milton,* ed. Frank A. Patterson (New York, 1936), 12:220.

5. Margaret Mann Phillips, *Erasmus and the Northern Renaissance* (London, 1949), p. 13.

6. Huizinga, *Erasmus,* p. 4.

7. These works and others are discussed by Genevieve Stenger in *"The Praise of Folly* and Its *Parerga," Medievalia et Humanistica,* 2:97–117.

8. *Desderii Erasmi Roterodami Opera Omnia* (Lvgduni Batavorum; London, 1703 [hereafter cited as *LB*]), 4:406C–D; trans. Thomas Chaloner (1549), sig. Aɪv.

9. Folly understands logic, however, for she later claims to argue "Docebo autem non Crocodilitis, aut Sortis ceratinis, aut aliis id genus Dialecticorum argutiis" (*LB* 4:420A); "neither with *Barbara,* nor *Celarent,* nor any suche *Dialectical* quaynt subtilties" (sig. C4v).

10. "She is a woman with a woman's varying moods, now confidential, now aloof, sometimes amused, often furious, ready to break her ironic vein to coax or plead, or to pursue some tangential thought" (Sr. Geraldine Thompson, *Under Pretext of Praise: Satiric Mode in Erasmus' Fiction* [Toronto, 1973], p. 54).

11. This is further confounded by the Girardus Listrius commentary to the *Encomium Moriae,* a standard addition from the 1515 Basel edition onward, which is also partly Erasmus's own work. See J. Austin Gavin and Thomas M. Walsh, "The *Praise of Folly* in Context: The Commentary of Girardus Listrius," *Renaissance Quarterly* 24:193–209.

12. The Panegyric for Philip, archbishop of Austria and duke of Burgundy, declaimed at the royal castle in Brussels on 5 January 1504; George Faludy, *Erasmus (New York,* 1970), cites Erasmus's complaint about doing it (p. 97).

13. Hoyt Hopewell Hudson, *The Praise of Folly by Desiderius Erasmus* (Princeton, N.J., 1941), pp. 129–42; Walter Kaiser, *Praisers of Folly* (Cambridge, Mass., 1963), pp. 35–50. See also Ephraim Emerton, *Desiderius Erasmus of Rotterdam* (New York, 1900), p. 159; Huizinga, *Erasmus,* p. 69; and Thompson, *Pretext,* pp. 53, 57, 57n., who advances a new tripartite structural arrangement (pp. 57–83).

14. More later appears as a character in *Encomium Moriae;* see Richard S. Sylvester, "The Problem of Unity in *The Praise of Folly," English Literary Renaissance* 6 (1976):133n.

15. Paul Oskar Kristeller maintains this genealogy is patterned (at least in part) after that of love in Plato's *Symposium.* See "Erasmus from an Italian Perspective," *Renaissance Quarterly* 23:11. His view of further borrowing in the Platonic ecstasy at the close of the *Encomium* (p. 11) is correctly modified by Clarence H. Miller, "Some Medieval Elements and Structural Unity in Erasmus' *The Praise of Folly," Renaissance Quarterly* 27:510.

16. Other companions are Self-love, Adulation, and Delicacy and her nurses Drunkenness and Rudeness.

17. Love as the *vinculum Mundi,* the binding force of society, is from Plotinus; Panurge parodies this in the *Tiers Livre* of Rabelais by making debt the binding force (3.3).

18. Craig R. Thompson, Introduction to *Translations of Lucian,* in *The Complete Works of St. Thomas More* (New Haven, Conn., 1974), 3:1, p. xxxv.

19. Plato, *Symposium,* 215A–B. The Silenus of Alcibiades is also the subject of one of Erasmus's *Adagia* of 1515. See Margaret Mann Phillips, *The "Adages" of Erasmus* (Cambridge, 1964), pp. 269–96; Scriptures are likened to the Silenus in the *Enchiridion.* Lynda Gregorian Christian sees the Silenus as the sole thematic and structural principle of the *Encomium* in "The Metamorphoses of Erasmus' 'Folly,' " *Journal of the History of Ideas* 32:289–94.

20. This is the same technique Erasmus used with his critics, including Dorp—to vary between accepting Folly as his spokesperson and denying her because she is true folly.

21. Huizinga (*Erasmus,* pp. 74–75) finds two intertwined themes, and, later in the oration, he finds Folly dancing the tightrope of sophistry.

22. But James D. Tracy notes the criticism of rhetoric is "weak . . . in comparison [to that] aimed at dialectic or even grammar" (*Erasmus: The Growth of a Mind* [Geneva, 1972], p. 121).

23. It is no accident that "Good lorde" (sigs. N2v et passim.) is Folly's favorite expletive.

24. Ernst Robert Curtius, *European Literature and the Latin Middle Ages,* trans. Willard R. Trask (New York, 1953), pp. 138 ff. Curtius argues that Erasmus's source may be Lucian, *Menippus or Necromantia* in *Lucian,* trans. A. M. Harmon, Loeb Classical Library (Cambridge, Mass., 1925), 4:99–101. Here, Leonard Dean finds, "The debunking is so thorough that there is no positive ground left to stand on" (in Kathleen Williams, ed., *Twentieth Century Interpretations of "The Praise of Folly"* [Englewood Cliffs, N.J., 1969], p. 52.

25. The fictional Folly's simplistic judgment is otherwise, of course. "It was thei that raued, and had more nede than thou of *Elleborus* to purge theim, who toke in hand to driue and expell out of the, so pleasaunt, and happie a madnesse, in stede of a great disease, as thei toke it" (sig. G4v).

26. This may be a fictional reference to the bullfights in Siena and the Vatican courtyard, which so offended Erasmus during his Italian journey in 1506–9, as the attack on Church institutions may result from his research then in Roman libraries. See Tracy, *Erasmus,* p. 116.

27. Folly also refers to "my friends" Erasmus's *Adagia* on sigs. P 4v, Q4v.

28. James D. Tracy develops a similar theory concerning Erasmus's critique of medieval religion and of comtemporary education; see "Erasmus the Humanist," in Richard L. De Molen, ed., *Erasmus of Rotterdam: A Quincentennial Symposium* (New York, 1971), p. 44. Prior to the *Encomium Moriae,* Erasmus and More translated some of Lucian together.

29. *EE* 1:273–74; trans. F. M. Nichols (London, 1901–18), 1:226.

30. Marjorie O' Rourke Boyle suggests that Erasmus had earlier borrowed the

setting of the *Phaedrus* for his *Antibarbari* (*Christening Pagan Mysteries* [Toronto, 1981], p. 23).

31. Plato, *Phaedrus,* trans. Harold North Fowler, Loeb Classical Library (Cambridge, Mass., 1914, 1977); Fowler has "simply a superhuman wonder as regards discourses" (p. 459), but the translation of Walter Hamilton for the Penguin Classics text (Harmondsworth, 1973), is perhaps closer in spirit to Chaloner: "'Your passion for rhetoric, Phaedrus, is superhuman, simply amazing'" (p. 43). Subsequent references are therefore to both translations.

32. That is, Erasmus here Christianizes a text as he urges the *rhetor* to do in the *Antibarbari* (and the later *Ciceronianus*), and manages so well himself in the *Enchiridion.*

33. Boyle also argues (*Pagan Mysteries,* chap. 2) the importance of the *Republic* to the *Encomium Moriae.*

CHAPTER 2

1. *EE* 4:21, and n.27. cf. J. H. Hexter, who uses literally More's letter to Peter Giles in his reconstruction of the composition of *Utopia* in *More's "Utopia": The Biography of an Idea* (Princeton, N.J., 1952), pp. 15–29, and in "The Composition of Utopia," in *The Complete Works of St. Thomas More* (New Haven, 1965), 4:xv–xxiii (hereafter cited as *CW*), although as I shall argue later there may be some reason to doubt the truth of much of this letter.

2. So André Prévost, *Thomas More, 1477–1535, et la crise de la pensée européenne* (Lille, 1969), p. 84; cf. R. J. Schoeck, "'A Nursery of Correct and Useful Institutions': On Reading More's *Utopia* as Dialogue," *Moreana* 22:26.

3. Direct linkages between the *Encomium* and the *Utopia* are frequent. Cf. the title page of the 1515 Froben edition of the *Encomium* ("non minus eruditis quam festivis") with the title page of the 1516 *Utopia* ("nec minus salutaris quam festivus"). Or we might compare details within the works: Folly is born on one of the "insulae fortunatae," a land that figures Utopia; the title of *Utopia* may come from Lucian, whose works More and Erasmus studied together. In "Philosophies for Sale," Lucian writes, "Buyer. And what is the gist of your wisdom? Academic. My ideas; I mean the patterns of existing things: for of everything that you behold, the earth, with all that is upon it, the sky, the sea, invisible images exist outside the universe. Buyer. Where do they exist? Academic. Nowhere; for if they were anywhere, they would not be" ("Philosophies for Sale," 18 trans. A. M. Harmon, Loeb Classical Library [New York, 1915]).

4. More, *Utopia,* p. 48; sigs. B2v–B3; pp. 14–15. This and subsequent references to the text cite (1) the Basel edition of March 1518, determined the best copy-text (incorporating More's final wishes) and ed. Edward J. Surtz, S.J., *CW* 4:1–253; (2) the 1551 translation by Raphe Robynson, the first in England and the one best known to the Elizabethans; (3) the modernized text of Robynson in the accessible Everyman series (London, 1974).

5. Robbin S. Johnson, More's "Utopia": Ideal and Illusion (New Haven, Conn., 1969), p. 49.

6. Cf. Ovid, Metamorphoses 1.89–111; Plato, Republic 3–6; Acts 4:31–35.

7. Thus "Hythlodaeus is introduced to us as one whose sailing 'has not been like that of Palinurus [Aeneas' pilot who fell asleep and plunged into the sea] but that of Ulysses or, rather, of Plato,' so the reach of the reader's reaction is to countries of the mind; we all become voyagers, risking the journey away from home and the fixed points of the past, moving out of eye-sight of the old landfalls" (Schoeck, "Reading More's Utopia,"p. 26). Yet, as we shall see, the inherent disputation (as distinct from the "Dialogue of Counsel" in Utopia 1) of Utopia provides a contrary argument for nearly every proposition openly advanced in it. So, four pages later, Hythlodaye says, "Et certe sic est natura comparatum, ut sua cuique inuenta blandiantur"; "And verily it is naturally geuen to all men to esteame their own inuentyons best" (56; sig. C1; 20; my italics).

8. George B. Parks, "More's Utopia and Geography," Journal of English and Germanic Philology 37:224–36, discusses Waldseemüller's book and by consulting Renaissance geographies plots Hytholodaye's route, locating Utopia as Tasmania. Edward J. Surtz sees Erasmus generally and specifically reflected in Hythlodaye's learning, travel, and 1487 visit to England in "Sources, Parallels, and Influences: Supplementary to the Yale Utopia," Moreana 9:8.

9. Robert M. Adams, Preface to his translation of Utopia (New York, 1975), p. vii.

10. In a fine new translation by Daniel J. Donno (Berkeley, Calif., 1981).

11. Richard S. Sylvester, " 'SI HYTHLODAEO CREDIMUS': Vision and Revision in Thomas More's Utopia," Soundings 51:282. Sylvester thinks Hythlodaye "begins to lose control of his tale," symbolically enough, in his mental journey concerning Utopian travel (p. 288).

12. W. S. Campbell, More's Utopia and His Social Teaching (London, 1930), p. 48.

13. Alan F. Nagel, "Lies and the Limitable Inane: Contradiction in More's Utopia," Renaissance Quarterly 26:175–76, has independently made the same observation, as has Heiserman, "Satire," p. 171. Nagel adds, "More's first sentence of the Utopia thus seems to duplicate the self-contradiction of the island's name. By speaking of a mathematical impossibility he denies place and existence to Utopia" (p. 177).

14. See Heiserman, "Satire," p. 171.

15. For precise distribution of the manuscripts, see Elizabeth Frances Rogers, ed., St. Thomas More: Selected Letters (New Haven, 1961), pp. 73, 76, 80–82, 84–85, 87, 89–90.

16. H. G. Wells, Introduction to Utopia (New York, 1935), quoted in Ligeia Gallagher, ed., More's "Utopia" and Its Critics (Chicago, 1964), p. v.

17. J. Churton Collins, Introduction to Sir Thomas More's Utopia (Oxford, 1904, 1930), p. xviii.

18. Another joke: Hythlodaye praises Utopia because he claims it has few laws, yet what follows in Utopia 2 is a nearly endless recollection by him of Utopian

laws and regulations that are not to be broken under any circumstances. See J. W. Barnes, "Irony and the English Apprehension of Renewal," *Queen's Quarterly* 73:368; H. W. Donner, *Introduction to Utopia* (London, 1945), p. 63. For a contemporary comment on Utopian antilegalism, see Budé's letter to Lupset, printed in 1518 and later editions, in *CW* 4:6–9.

19. There are other etymological clues (and jokes). Harry Berger, Jr., has shared with me an unpublished essay in which he notes, "The worthy protophylarch knows that *au fond* he is a *tranibor* (*tranēs* + *boros,* 'plainly or distinctly gluttonous'); perhaps the revered phylarch whose culinary blandishments have helped render the household meal obsolete dreams at night that his powers ascend from his *syphograncy,* the venerable pig-sty or 'foul rag-and-bone shop of the heart.' Their older names and natures persist in the reformed language."

20. So A. W. Reed, "Sir Thomas More," in F. J. C. Hearnshaw, ed., *The Social and Political Ideas of Some Great Thinkers of the Renaissance and the Reformation* (London, 1925, 1949), pp. 137–40. See also Gerhard Ritter, *The Corrupting Influence of Power,* 6th ed., trans. F. W. Pick (Hadleigh, Essex, 1952), pp. 70–89, for a view of the insidious Utopian use of power within a society that is ostensibly moral and irenic.

21. A humanist joke derived from the Foundation Myth in Plato's *Republic* in which iron is related to the basest of men and women (415C). A good portion of the irony in *Utopia,* in fact, rests on passing allusions to Plato, for which see Arthur Barker, *The Political Thought of Plato and Aristotle* (London, 1959), pp. 526–29; Edward J. Surtz, S.J., *The Praise of Pleasure* (Cambridge, Mass., 1957), and *The Praise of Wisdom* (Chicago, 1957); and the annotations to Utopia in *CW* 4:267–570. In addition to Plato, the references to gold may intend to call to mind the Ethopians' use of gold in Heliodorus 4.

22. Pp. 168–69; Lewis may overextend the argument by calling the *Utopia* "a holiday work . . . which starts many hares and kills none" (p. 169) (C. S. Lewis, *English Literature in the Sixteenth Century, Excluding Drama* [Oxford, 1954], pp. 167–71).

23. Dominic Baker-Smith, *Thomas More and Plato's Voyage,* Inaugural Lecture at University College, Cardiff, on 1 June 1978 (Cardiff, 1978), p. 10.

24. John Traugott, "A Voyage to Nowhere with Thomas More and Jonathan Swift: *Utopia* and *The Voyage to the Houyhnhnms,*" *Sewanee Review* 69:545.

25. Amaurote seems to be an exception (116; sig. H1v; 59). Ernst Cassirer, *The Platonic Renaissance in England,* trans. James P. Pettegrove (Austin, Tex., 1953), pp. 109–10, sees a similarity here to Plato's *Philebus,* then recently published with a commentary by Ficino, in which (as Traugott puts it) "the life of unconscious pleasure is the life of an oyster" ("Voyage to Nowhere," p. 546). Michael J. B. Allen has recently translated Ficino's commentary on the *Philebus* (Berkeley, Calif., 1975).

26. Robbin S. Johnson, "The Argument for Reform in More's *Utopia,*" *Moreana* 31–32:131, 131 n. 35 "In spite of More's seeming reasonableness his ideal state was highly artificial," the historian J. D. Mackie writes; "in spite of

his liberalism, it was really a managed state whose people were not free" (*The Earlier Tudors,* 1485–1558 [Oxford, 1952, 1978], p. 263).

27. *OE* 1: Further observations may be found in the annotations in *CW* 4:384–93.

28. And, beyond that, to the process I have described as triangulation. Cf. Edward J. Surtz: "Hythlodaeus tries to force his hearers or readers into the necessity of choice between snow-white communism and black-sheep private ownership. The thinking audience knows that there exists a third alternative which is being neglected or ignored, perhaps deliberately and which takes into account both man's weakness and man's strength" ("*Utopia* is a Work of Literary Art," in *CW* 4:cxlii).

29. An important recent essay on More's art of dialogue here and elsewhere is Germain Marc'hadour's "Here I Sit: Thomas More's Genius for Dialogue," in Damian Grace and Brian Byron, eds., *Thomas More: Essays on the Icon* (Melbourne, 1980), pp. 9–42.

30. Sylvester, " 'SI HYTHLODAEO CREDIMUS,' " p. 275.

31. J. A. Picton et al., "Sir Thomas More's Utopia," *Notes and Queries,* 7th ser. 5:101–2, 229–31, 371; R. J. Schoeck, "Levels of Word-Play and Figurative Signification in More's 'Utopia,' " *Notes and Queries,* n.s. 1:512.

32. *CW* 4:10–11. More first called his work *Nusquama* rather than *Utopia,* from the Latin word for Nowhere for which Sylvester has conjectured some further significance. "For a group of men who habitually wrote and spoke Latin, the effect of More's shift to Greek was to distance the entire concept of his new country that did not, as its name insisted, really exist" (" 'Si Hythlodaeo Credimus,' " p. 273) and, further, to reinforce amusingly Hythlodaye's confession that he knew Greek (hence the possibility of *the good place*) better than Latin. Somewhat more remote etymologies may be found in Paul A. Sawada, "Toward the Definition of *Utopia,*" *Moreana* 31–32:135–46, and Ward Allen, "Speculations on St. Thomas More's Use of Hesychius," *Philological Quarterly* 46:165, 165 n. 44.

33. Heiserman, "Satire," p. 166; see also Elizabeth McCutcheon, "Thomas More, Raphael Hythlodaeus, and the Angel Raphael," *Studies in English Literature* 9:21–38, a a wide-ranging study that sees Hythlodaye as an altogether serious guide.

34. For some of these ideas, I am indebted to the late Frank Sullivan. Cf. Heiserman, "Satire," p. 166; McCutcheon, "Thomas More," pp. 23ff. Hans Ulrich Seeber sees Raphael as both physician and scourge of Satan in "Hythloday as Preacher and a Possible Debt to Macrobius," *Moreana* 31–32:71–86. Robert M. Adams translates the name even more comprehensively as "A fantastic trilingual pun [which] could make the whole name mean 'God heals [Hebrew *Raphael*] through the nonsense [Greek, *huthlos*] of God [Latin, *dei*]' " (*Utopia,* p. 6n). This would make his name the exact equivalent of Folly. More may have been reminded of Raphael from wall paintings of the Book of Tobias in St. Stephen's Chapel at Westminster Palace executed in the fourteenth century (the remains of which are on permanent display at the British Museum, London).

Other names are also ironic (for which see the translation of Paul Turner [Harmondsworth, 1965]): the capital of Utopia is Amaurote (spectral city or mirage) situated on the river Anyder (waterless river); the neighbors of the Utopians are the Alaopolites (townsmen without a town), the Achorians (people without a city), and the Polyerites (people of much nonsense). Their poet laureate is Anemolius (braggart), and their governing officers are named syphogrants (men of old wrinkled skin) and tranibores (plain gluttons). See Warren W. Wooden, "Thomas More and Lucian: A Study in Satiric Influence and Technique," [University of Mississippi] *Studies in English* 13:43–57, and the annotations in *CW* 4.

35. Cf. Johnson, "Argument for Reform," p. 134.

36. Quoted in James McConica, *Thomas More: A Short Biography* (London, 1977), p. 1.

37. William Roper, *The Lyfe of Sir Thomas Moore, knighte,* ed. Elsie Vaughan Hitchcock, Early English Text Society, no. 197 (London, 1935), p. 6.

38. R. W. Chambers, *Thomas More* (Ann Arbor, Mich., 1958, 1965), p. 18.

39. Quoted by Robert C. Elliott, "The Shape of Utopia," *ELH* 30:325.

40. Thomas Stapleton, *Vita Thomae Mori,* in *Tres Thomae* (1588), sig. K7; trans. Philip E. Hallett, *The Life and Illustrious Martyrdom of Sir Thomas More* (London, 1928), p. 132. For an example of More's jesting, see *The Diary of John Manningham of the Middle Temple,* 1602–1603, ed. Robert Parker Sorlien (Hanover, N.H., 1976), pp. 73–74.

41. Seneca, *Epistulae Morales ad Lucilium,* trans. Richard M. Gummere, Loeb Classical Library (Cambridge, Mass., 1917).

42. Robin Campbell, Introduction to *Seneca: Letters from a Stoic* (Harmondsworth, 1969, 1979), pp. 22–23.

43. Scholars now question Seneca's authorship of the *Octavia,* but the Tudor humanists never did. Citations in the text are from the Loeb edition, trans. Frank Justus Miller (Cambridge, Mass., 1917, 1961).

44. See John Crossett, "More and Seneca," *Philological Quarterly* 40:577–80, where Crossett makes these and other pertinent observations.

45. More, *Correspondence,* ed. Elizabeth Frances Rogers (Princeton, 1947), pp. 22–24.

46. Stapleton, *Vita Thomae Mori,* sig. B5; Hallett, *Life,* p. 15; Erasmus to Hutten, July 1519, *EE* 2:12–23.

47. Thompson, Introduction to *CW* 3:1, p. xviii. A good general introduction to the broader background for More, and its wider implications, is Hugh Trevor-Roper, "The Intellectual World of Sir Thomas More," *American Scholar* 48:22–32.

48. See the Introduction to *Utopia* by Surtz in *CW* 4, pp. cliv–clv et passim; and Lina Berger, "Thomas Morus and Plato: ein Beitrag zur Geschichte des Humanismus," *Zeitschrift für die gesamte Staatswissenschaft* 35:187–216, 405–83.

49. The third part of the sequel, the *Hermocrates,* apparently meant to bring Athenian history to the present, was (so far we can now judge) never written.

In dealing more and more with reality—as if the *Republic* were receding further and further from possibility—Plato left the *Critias* for the even more practical *Laws,* which he did not live to complete.

50. Plato, *Timaeus,* trans. R. G. Bury, Loeb Classical Library (Cambridge, Mass., 1929, 1961).

51. Humanist readers of *Utopia* who knew of this progression might speculate on the subject of the next day's discussion in Antwerp. Here the joke is on Hythlodaye.

52. In his letter to More, in *CW* 4:34–35.

53. Plutarch, *Life of Lycurgus,* trans. Bernadotte Perrin, Loeb Classical Library (Cambridge, Mass., 1914, 1967).

54. Cicero, *De Finibus,* trans. H. Rackham, Loeb Classical Library (Cambridge, Mass., 1914, 1961).

55. More to Ruthall, trans. Craig R. Thompson, in *CW* 3:1, 2–3.

56. T. S. Dorsch, "Sir Thomas More and Lucian: An Interpretation of *Utopia,*" *Archiv für Das Studium der Neueren Sprachen und Literaturen* 203:348. 203:348.

57. Lucian, *Menippus,* trans. A. M. Harmon, Loeb Classical Library (Cambridge, Mass., 1925).

58. John Hayes, Foreward to J. B. Trapp and Hubertus Schulte Herbrüggen, *"The King's Good Servant": Sir Thomas More,* 1477 / 8–1535 (London, 1978), p. 6.

59. Raphael initially represents light (enlightenment) and reason in *Utopia* but, like Folly, his characterization is transformed. His irrational insistence on the superiority of Utopia to Europe in the closing movements of *Utopia* 2 clearly means to bewray his pride, the fault he had charged the most serious of the Europeans in *Utopia* 1. Although McCutcheon sees Hythlodaye's role as guide and doctor to be an essentially serious one, she also observes "an extraordinarily ironic reversal, as the guide is guided, the enlightener led into the dark. [In having More-persona lead Hythlodaye from the garden] More is dramatically inverting the gesture which was St. Raphael's, who held the young Tobias by the hand as he guided him safely on his journey" ("Thomas More," p. 37). What has happened—quite literally and before our eyes—is that in *Utopia* 2 (as in *Utopia* 1 as a mirroring passage), for Erasmus, the other "characters," and us, Hythlodaye has become an orator of his own "praise of folly"—and as a foolish praiser—without his apparently knowing it.

60. See Edward Surtz, S.J., "Aspects of More's Latin Style in *Utopia,*" *Studies in the Renaissance* 14:95–109. In rhetorical figures, More uses asyndeton, polysyndeton, syzeugmenon and epanalepsis; in figures of sound, alliteration, assonance, paronomasia (which Lyly will also use heavily), parechesis, homioteleuton, homoioptoton (pp. 102–3). Surtz also traces interrogation, obtestation, and preterition (pp. 104–5) and various means of amplification (pp. 105–7). Richard Pace emphasizes More's mastery of language; see Surtz, "Richard Pace's Sketch of Thomas More," *Journal of English and Germanic Philology* 57:36–50.

61. This point is elaborated by Sylvester, " 'SI HYTHLODAEO CREDIMUS,' " pp. 284–85.

62. It is instructive to place beside Hythlodaye's account the anonymous *Relation, or Rather a True Account, of the Island of England* by a Venetian ambassador in 1500. See the modern edition translated by Charlotte Augusta Sneyd for the Camden Society, vol. 37 (London, 1847), esp. pp. 10, 19, 23–24, 34. On theft, see John O'Hagan, Introduction to *Utopia* (London, 1910, 1937), p. xix; on enclosures (about which there are presently conflicting accounts), see Joan Thirsk, *Tudor Enclosures* (London, 1958). The opposing viewpoint is given by Surtz, *Utopia,* in *Selected Works* (New Haven, Conn., 1964), p. 24n.

63. Hythlodaye may know Greek and take Aristotle on his voyage, but he seems not to understand Aristotle's comments on private possessions (*Politics* 1260*b*36–1264*b*25). See Thomas I. White, "Aristotle and *Utopia,*" *Renaissance Quarterly* 29:635–75.

64. In tribute to Erasmus, More proposes a more proper answer in a wise fool who argues that vagabonds might be more humanely cared for in monasteries or nunneries—more exactly anticipating the communism of Book 2—because he recognizes that the economy cannot support them (82; sig. E2v; 37). See Johnson, "Argument for Reform," p. 130. Robert C. Elliott, in *The Shape of Utopia* (Chicago, 1970), points out that this incident is an adaptation of Horace, *Satires* 1.7 (pp. 33–34).

65. More usually answers such questions implicitly; he is not in Utopia because he is not a native and was not allowed to remain.

66. For gardens before More's time, see A. Bartlett Giamatti, *The Earthly Paradise and the Renaissance Epic* (Princeton, N.J., 1966), pp. 11–86.

67. The joke is sharper when we recall that More was in Flanders to reopen wool exports for London merchants as he began *Utopia*. Rather than insist on attacking enclosures, he might note the then current English legislation against engrossing, forestalling, and enclosing. See David M. Bevington, "The Dialogue in *Utopia*: Two Sides to the Question," *Studies in Philology* 58:503.

68. Note the sly double meaning in the phrase describing Giles.

69. Harry Berger, Jr., "The Renaissance Imagination: Second World and Green World," *Centennial Review* 9:61. More's defense of the art of accommodation in political counsel in *Utopia* 1 is perceptively examined by J. C. Davis, "More, Morton, and the Politics of Accommodation," *Journal of British Studies* 9, 2:27–49.

70. Hythlodaye finds princes as much at fault as their sychophantic advisers: "both the rauen and the ape thincke their owne yong ones fayrest" (56; sig. C1; 20–21). But clearly this is meant as another jest, since elsewhere Hythlodaye had already praised Cardinal Morton, and as an adviser to Henry VII who had listened to him. See Wooden, "More and Lucian," pp. 49–50.

71. The jest continues; when More comes to the description of the bridge in *Utopia* 2 to which he refers here (118; sig. H2v; 59–60), he gives neither length. He might have stopped worrying—since in the text he gives no length at all.

72. Reference to "the latine tong" is another joke: *Utopia* was written and published in Latin.

73. G. K. Chesterton, rep. in *Moreana* 42:66.

74. Bevington, "Dialogue in *Utopia*," p. 497.

75. They are discussed in greater detail by Dana G. McKinnon, "The Marginal Glosses in More's *Utopia*: The Character of the Commentator," *Renaissance Papers* 1970:11–19. For the effect of the glosses on the fictionality of *Utopia*, see Joel B. Altman, *The Tudor Play of Mind* (Berkeley, Calif., 1978), pp. 81–82.

76. The term is taken from M. H. Abrams, *The Mirror and the Lamp* (New York, 1953), p. 35.

77. John Ruskin, *Letters,* ed. E. T. Cook and Alexander Wedderburn (London, 1909), 2:12.

78. *EE* 2:414; trans. Rogers, *St. Thomas More: Selected Letters,* p. 85.

CHAPTER 3

1. Merritt Lawliss, *Elizabethan Prose Fiction* (New York, 1967), p. 646.

2. George Gascoigne, *The Adventures of Master F. J.,* in *A Hundreth Sundry Flowres* (1573), sig. D1v (rep. Scholar Press [Menston, Yorkshire, 1970]). The text has also been edited by C. T. Prouty, as *George Gascoigne's 'A Hundreth Sundrie Flowres',* University of Missouri Studies, vol. 17 No. 2 (Columbia, 1942), where this poem is on p. 64. Subsequent references are to these texts.

3. So Leicester Bradner twice in "Point of View in George Gascoigne's Fiction," *Studies in Short Fiction* 3:18,22.

4. Robert P. Adams, "Gascoigne's *Master F. J.* as Original Fiction," *PMLA* 73:326.

5. E. K., "November eclogue" (1579), sig. M4. In his *Discourse of English Poetrie* (1586), William Webbe also notes Gascoigne was "a wytty Gentleman" (sig. C3v).

6. Gascoigne probably reveals his own humanist training in *The Glass of Gouernement* (1575) when he dramatizes the use of poetry for the rhetorical end of *memoria*. There the *rhetor* Gnomaticus tells his students, "to the ende that you shall the better imprint [your lessons] in your memorie, beholde, I haue put them briefly in wryting as a memoriall, and here I deliuer the same vnto you, to be put in verse euerie one by himself and in sundrie deuice, that you may therein take the greater delight, for of all other Artes *Poetrie* giueth greatest assistaunce vnto memorie, since the verie terminations and ceasures doe (as it were) serue for places of memorie, and helpe the mynde with delight to carie burthens, which else would seeme more grieuous: and though it might percase seeme vnto you, that I do in maner ouèrlode you with lessons and enterprises, yet shall you herein rather find comforte or recreation, than any encomberance: let me nowe see who can shewe himself the pleasantest Poet, in handeling therof" (sig. F4; *Works,* ed. John W. Cunliffe [Cambridge, 1910], 2:47–48). Linda Bradley Salamon traces possible relationships between Gascoigne's play and the humanist treatises of Elyot and Ascham in "A Face in *The Glasse:* Gascoigne's *Glasse of Gouernement* Re-examined," *Studies in Philology* 71:47–71.

7. B. M. Ward's edition (London, 1926) makes the greatest claim for the fiction as thinly disguised biography and autobiography; for studies showing the fictional basis of Gascoigne's narrative, see Adams, "Gascoigne's *Master F. J.*," pp. 315–26; Fredson Thayer Bowers, "Notes on Gascoigne's *A Hundreth Sundrie Flowres* and *The Posies*," *Harvard Studies and Notes in Philology and Literature* 16:13–35; and Leicester Bradner, "The First English Novel: A Study of George Gascoigne's *Adventures of Master F. J.*," *PMLA* 45:543–52.

8. Frank B. Fieler, "The Adventures Passed by Master F. J.," *Studies in Short Fiction* 1:31.

9. M. R. Rohr Philmus, "Gascoigne's Fable of the Artist as a Young Man," *Journal of English and Germanic Philology* 73:18.

10. Ibid., p. 23.

11. This proverb, from Erasmus's *Adagia* (114A), seems to be a favorite with Gascoigne; cf. *Iocasta*, in *A Hundreth Sundry Flowres*, sig. G1v; *Works*, ed. Cunliffe, 1:271; *Glasse of Gouernement*, sig. D4; 2:34.

12. Walter R. Davis, *Idea and Act in Elizabethan Fiction* (Princeton, N.J., 1969), p. 107.

13. The term is reviewed in Robert Scholes and Robert Kellogg, *The Nature of Narrative* (New York, 1966), pp. 264–65.

14. Alfred Aunderau, *George Gascoignes "The Adventures of Master F. J."* (Bern, 1966), p. 138.

15. Lawlis, *Elizabethan Prose Fiction*, p. 646.

16. Thomas Goddard Bergin, *The Sonnets of Petrarch* (Verona, 1965), p. vii.

17. Petrarch, *Rerum vulgarium fragmenta*, ed. and trans. Robert M. Durling (Cambridge, Mass., 1976).

18. Thomas Goddard Bergin, Introduction to *The Rhymes of Francesco Petrarca* (London, 1954), p. vi.

19. Petrarch, *De Rebus Familiaribus et Variae*, ed. Fracassetti (1859), 19.17; quoted in J. H. Whitfield, *Petrarch and the Renascence* (Oxford, 1943), p. 29.

20. Plato, *Symposium*, 180B; trans W. R. M. Lamb, Loeb Classical Library (Cambridge, Mass., 1925, 1975).

21. Lynette F. McGrath, "George Gascoigne's Moral Satire: The Didactic Use of Convention in *The Adventures Passed by Master F. J.*," *Journal of English and Germanic Philology* 70:442.

22. Ronald C. Johnson, *George Gascoigne* (New York, 1972), p. 128.

23. William J. Kennedy, *Rhetorical Norms in Renaissance Literature* (New Haven, Conn., 1978), p. 20.

24. Ovid, *Metamorphoses* 3. 370–78, trans. Frank Justus Miller, Loeb Classical Library (London, 1916).

25. Juvenal, Satire 10, lines 2–4, 9–10; trans. G. G. Ramsay, Loeb Classical Library (Cambridge, Mass., 1918).

26. Richard A. Lanham, "Narrative Structure in Gascoigne's *F. J.*," *Studies in Short Fiction* 4:47.

27. The first to cite such possible "sources" was Bradner, "First English Novel," p. 5.

28. Adams ("Gascoigne's *Master F. J.,*" p. 318) has counted 26 lines of the completed work assigned to Elinor or "SHE" and 420 lines to F. J. The bulk of the work—1848 lines or 80 percent—"is prose, either signed by G. T. or in context plainly by him."

29. Adams notes (ibid., p. 317) that the first page of *The Adventures* reads, "A Discourse of the Adventures *passed by Master F. J.* H. W. to the Reader," calling into some doubt a work that has passed through several hands, while Bradner, in "First English Novel," pp. 544–45, first noted that "the introductory epistles of 'H. W.' and 'G. T.' make it plain" that Gascoigne is the actual author of the work assigned to various other sets of initials.

30. Bowers has argued ("Notes," pp. 16–17,17 ff.) that A. B. is also imaginary; his work follows that of W. W. Greg, who claims in "A Hundreth Sundry Flowres," *Library* 4th Series, 7:274, n. 2, that "there was no printer with these initials working at the time."

31. This joke is compounded when H. D. and H. K. of the first edition are fictionally expanded to "Hercule Donaty" and "Haniball de Cosmis" (sig. O4v; 1:403).

32. In 1576 George Pettie employs the same bewildering array of *paragena* for *Pettie His Pallace of Pleasure:* (1) R. B.'s letter to gentlewomen explaining his decision to publish Pettie's romances for their pith and pleasure; (2) Pettie to R. B., loaning his wanton trifles but asking that they not be printed; (3) the printer to all readers explaining they are now presentable because of his tactful omissions. For a discussion, see William Nelson, *Fact or Fiction: The Dilemma of the Renaissance Storyteller* (Cambridge, Mass., 1973), p. 58.

33. Penelope Scambly Schott, "The Narrative Stance in '*The Adventures of Master F. J.*': Gascoigne as Critic of His Own Poems," *Renaissance Quarterley* 29:370.

34. Charles W. Smith, "Structural and Thematic Unity in Gascoigne's *The Adventures of Master F. J.,*" *Papers on Language and Literature* 2:102.

35. Gascoigne, *Noble Arte of Venerie* (1576), sigs. A3v–A4; see Charles and Ruth Prouty, "George Gascoigne, *The Noble Arte of Venerie,* and Queen Elizabeth at Kenilworth," in *Joseph Quincy Adams: Memorial Studies,* ed. James G. McManaway, Giles E. Dawson, and Edwin E. Willoughby (Washington, D.C., 1948), pp. 639–64.

36. Gabriel Harvey, *Marginalia,* ed. G. C. Moore Smith (Stratford, 1913), p. 166; also quoted in Charles Prouty, *George Gascoigne,* p. 278.

37. Thomas B. Stroup and H. Ward Jackson, "Gascoigne's *Steele Glas* and 'The Bidding of the Bedes,'" *Studies in Philology* 58:53.

38. William Baldwin, *Beware the Cat* (1570); there is a modern edition by William P. Holden ed., Connecticut College Monograph no. 8 (New London, 1963). Subsequent references are to the 1570 edition and Holden's text.

39. Stephen Gresham, "William Baldwin: Literary Voice of the Reign of Edward VI," *Huntington Library Quarterly* 44:114.

CHAPTER 4

1. Wayne A. Rebhorn, *Courtly Performances: Masking and Festivity in Castiglione's "Book of the Courtier"* (Detroit, 1978), p. 20.

2. First printed in 1576.

3. George Bull, Introduction to the Penguin text (Harmondsworth, 1967), p. 13.

4. The work is entitled *The School of Athens;* Lawrence V. Ryan is representative of modern scholars in calling Castiglione primarily the disciple of these two philosophers. See Ryan, "Book Four of Castiglione's *Courtier*: Climax or Afterthought?" *Studies in the Renaissance* 19:169.

5. Cicero, *De Oratore* 2.20.85, trans. E. W. Sutton and H. Rackham, Loeb Classical Library (Cambridge, Mass., 1942, 1959).

6. Quoted and translated in Daniel Javitch, *Poetry and Courtliness in Renaissance England* (Princeton, N.J., 1978), p. 22n. Remensis's comments come in his preface to Francis I, in *In Omnes De Arte Rhetorica M. Tul. Ciceronis Libros Doctissimorum Vivorum Commentaria.*

7. Cicero, *Orator* 1.3–4, trans. H. M. Hubbell, Loeb Classical Library (Cambridge, Mass., 1939, 1962).

8. Quintilian, *Institutio Oratorio* 12.10.78; the translation is a paraphrase of Butler's text.

9. For a detailed study of the manuscript changes and their import, see Ryan, "Book Four." J. R. Woodhouse, *Baldesar Castiglione: A Reassessment of "The Courtier"* (Edinburgh, 1978), chap. 6, makes a number of applications of Aristotelian doctrine to *Cortegiano* 4; see also Alfred D. Menut, "Castiglione and the *Nicomachean Ethics*," *PMLA* 58:309–21.

CHAPTER 5

1. See, for instance, Castiglione, *Il Libro del Cortegiano* 2.34, 3.70, 2.64, et passim.

2. The texts are the Italian Aldine text of 1528, sig. g3v; ed. Ettore Bonora (Milan, 1972), 2:64; trans. Sir Thomas Hoby (London, 1561), sig. U2; (rep. London, 1975), p. 154.

3. Morris W. Croll, *Style, Rhetoric, and Rhythm,* ed. J. Max Patrick et al. (Princeton, N.J., 1966), p. 245.

4. Richard Helgerson makes the same observation in *The Elizabethan Prodigals* (Berkeley, Calif., 1976), p. 60.

5. The figures are supplied by G. K. Hunter in *John Lyly: The Humanist as Courtier* (London, 1962), p. 72.

6. G. K. Hunter, *Lyly and Peele* (London, 1968), p. 17.

7. Lyly, *Euphues*: Textual references are to the 1579 quarto, and to *The Complete Works of John Lyly,* ed. R. Warwick Bond (Oxford, 1902, 1973).

8. Lawlis, *Elizabethan Prose Fiction,* pp. 118, 114.

9. "There is no escaping the realities of the actual world in *Euphues,*" David Lloyd Stevenson comments in *The Love-Game Comedy* (New York, 1946), p. 148, while A. Feuillerat, in *John Lyly: Contribution à l'histoire de la Renaissance en Angleterre* (Cambridge, 1910), refers to "l'influence dégradante de l'atmosphère" (p. 61) and Hunter to "a saraband of deceptions" (*Lyly and Peele,* p. 28).

10. The commonplace also begins Guevara's *Diall of Princes* as translated by T[homas] North in 1568, often cited as a source of humanist writing in the last part of the sixteenth century. See sig. *4.

11. As, for example, Joseph W. Houppert, *John Lyly* (Boston, 1975), p. 27. Eubulus's realistic allusions to such Romans relates to Lyly's application of Apelles in his dedicatory epistle to *Euphues,* while the situations Eubulus describes accurately predict the remaining events of the work. His speech functions in various ways—none so simplistically as critics have maintained.

12. This commonplace is also found in Don Anthony of Guevara, *Diall of Princes,* trans. Thomas North (1557), sig. a3v. In *Love's Labours Lost,* the Shakespearean play that most echoes *Euphues,* Rosaline may be describing a character like Lyly's intended portrait of Euphues in her portrayal of Berowne (2.1.69 ff.).

13. Walter N. King, in "John Lyly and Elizabethan Rhetoric," *Studies in Philology* 52:156–57, also sees Euphues' argument as one designed by the Ciceronian topics, using humanist rhetoric to satirize humanist rhetoric as sophistical. Still another rhetorical reading of *Euphues* is that of William G. Crane, *Wit and Rhetoric in the Renaissance* (New York, 1937), pp. 194–202.

14. Richard Haber, "The English Renaissance Novella and Hawthorne's *The Scarlet Letter:* Toward a Theory of Fiction" (Diss., University of Massachusetts, Amherst, 1976), p. 58.

15. Lyly may have remembered this dichotomy from Ascham; see sig. H3.

16. "It is a goodly vertue in any one man, at a sodain, to vtter wittely and ingeniouslie, the secrete and hid wisedome of his mynde," Richard Rainolde writes in the *Foundacion of Rhetorike* (sig. O1v). As illustrations for his prescriptive rhetoric, he includes both civil and contemplative questions, which adumbrate later arguments by Philautus and Euphues, respectively, but display nothing so raw as Euphues argues at this early juncture.

17. See Lyly, *Endimion* 2.2.

18. *Euphues* at this point exactly reverses the decorous and proper conversation in *Galateo,* John Della Casa's treatise of courtly manners which, translated into English in 1576, may have been consulted by Lyly. The old man in *Galateo* combines precept and deed and is apparently well heeded: "I haue determined (such is the Loue I beare thee) to shewe all the daungerous straights thou must passe: For my experience maketh me feare, yt walking that way thou mayst easily eyther fall, or by some meanes or other go astray. To the end thou maiest once, taughte both by my instructions and experience, be able to keepe the right waye, aswell for the helthe of thy Soule, as the commendation and prayse of the

Honourable and Noble house thou doest come of" (sig. B1). "The wordes you shall vse, must haue no double vnderstanding, but simple" (sig. L2v).

19. G. Wilson Knight, "Lyly," *Review of English Studies* 15:153.

20. Haber adds ("English Renaissance Novella," p. 91) that "It is possible to view this narrative detail, presented at such a significant point in the plot, as allegorically suggesting the dissolution of Humanistic knowledge, its commercialization and movement into a vehicle of human self-conceit and self-aggrandizement."

21. Davis notes that "Euphues and Lucilla present contrasting examples of the influence of will on wit, or of nurture on nature. While he discovers who he really is by playing out what he is not, she finds out her real nature by exploring it mimetically. Therefore, we see how the role she adopts and her realization of her true nature in that role both *grow* in the process of the action" (*Idea and Act*, p. 117).

22. James Winny adds that "The intricate lace border framing the title-page of *Euphues*, and the formal lay-out of the advertisement it encloses, are a rudimentary expression of this feeling for patterned symmetry" (Introduction to *The Descent of Euphues* [Cambridge, 1957], p. x).

23. The observation is Houppert's (*John Lyly*, p. 35).

24. In portraying Euphues' descent, Lyly's residual narrative is also rhetorically oriented, keeping to the advice of Thomas Wilson in his *Arte of Rhetorique*: "But when the persone shalbe touched, and not the matter, we must seke els where, and gather these places together. i. The name. ii. The maner of liuyng. iii. Of what house he is, of what countre and of what yeres. iiii. The wealthe of the man. v. His behauiour or daily enuryng with thynges. vi. What nature he hath. vii. Whereunto he is moste geuen. viii. What he purposeth frō tyme to tyme. ix. What he hath doen heretofore. x. What hath befaulne vnto hym heretofore. xi. What he hath confessed, or what he hath to saie for hymself" (sig. q2).

25. R. W. Dent has discovered a short poem by Lyly published in 1588, which schemes in miniature the patterned structure of *Euphues*, moving from precept through experience to a return to the wisdom of books; see "John Lyly in 1588," *English Language Notes* 7:9–11.

26. Since the edition of Daniel Wyttenbach (Oxford, 1795), pp. 29–64, *The Education of Children* is no longer attributed to Plutarch. Lyly doubtless found the essay attractive because it opens with frank recognition of differences in natural endowments in order to argue the need for instructing children, because it attacks low pay of teachers, and because it advocates the study of philosophy as the final stage of learning.

27. Lyly's Christianizing of Plutarch foreshadows those proverbs soon to decorate the title page of William Kempe's *Education of children in learning* (1588): "The rod and correction giue wisedome, but a child set at libertie maketh his mother ashamed"; "Foolishness is tied in the heart of a child, but the rod of discipline shall driue it away." Kempe's treatise is based on "Euphues and his Ephoebus" (sigs. U2–T1v; 1:260–88).

28. "You ask, my boy, how you can get to be a public speaker, and be held to

personify the sublime and glorious name of sophist," Lucian remarks at the opening of "A Professor of Public Speaking"; "life, you say, is not worth living, unless when you speak you can clothe yourself in such a mantle of eloquence that you will be irresistible and invincible, that you will be admired and stared at by everyone, counting among the Greeks as a highly desirable treat for their ears" (trans. A. M. Harmon, Loeb Classical Library [London, 1925]).

29. So Haber, "English Renaissance Novella," pp. 43–44, 46.

30. See chap. 3, n. 32, herein.

31. Many previous readers have rather too quickly associated *Euphues* with the prodigal-son story or with the tale of friendship of Titus and Gysippus (Boccaccio 10.8), retold by Thomas Elyot in *The Boke Named the Gouernour* 2.12. But the point of such allusions by Lyly is to point out both similarity and dissimilarity, just as his similes show inconsistency as well as consistency. He means to alert us by modifying those sources he seems to employ. For the prodigal son, see *Acolastus* (1540); Samuel Lee Wolff, "The Humanist as Man of Letters: John Lyly," *Sewanee Review* 31:8–35; Hunter, *John Lyly,* pp. 49 ff.; Helgerson, *Elizabethan Prodigals,* chap. 4. For Titus and Gysippus, see Clement Tyson Goode, "Sir Thomas Elyot's *Titus and Gysippus,*" *Modern Language Notes* 37:2, 9–11; Percy Waldron Long, "From *Troilus* to *Euphues,*" in *Anniversary Papers [for] George Lyman Kittredge* (Boston, 1913), pp. 367–71; and John Hazel Smith, "Sempronia, John Lyly, and John Foxe's Comedy of *Titus and Gesippus,*" *Philological Quarterly* 48:554–61.

32. J. J. Jusserand, *The English Novel in the Time of Shakespeare,* trans. Elizabeth Lee, new ed. Philip Brockbank (London, 1966), p. 105; Hardin Craig, *The Literature of the English Renaissance,* 1485–1660 (New York, 1962), p. 137; Robert Ashley and Edwin M. Moseley, *Elizabeth Fiction* (New York, 1960), p. 85.

33. Knight, "Lyly," p. 150; he is speaking particularly of Lyly's plays, but the comments apply equally well to the same style used in the prose fiction.

34. This point is acutely developed by Jonas A. Barish in "The Prose Style of John Lyly," *ELH* 23:14–35.

35. Madelon Gohlke, "Reading *Euphues,*" *Criticism* 19:110.

36. Ibid.

37. Northrop Frye could easily cite *The Anatomy of Wit* when he defines the anatomy as a highly complicated intellectual exercise, usually satiric, which is structured around a series of variations on a single theme (*Anatomy of Criticism: Four Essays* [Princeton, N.J., 1957], p. 312).

38. Altman, *The Tudor Play of Mind,* p. 205.

39. Plato, *Theaetetus,* trans. Harold North Fowler, Loeb Classical Library (Cambridge, Mass., 1921, 1967), 173E–174A. Sidney uses the same example in his *Defense of Poesie* (sig. C3v; *Miscellaneous Prose,* p. 82).

40. Ascham complains that *The Courtier* was little read at the English court despite Hoby's fine translation. A third edition appeared in 1588, and Bartholomew Clerke's Latin translation was printed in 1571, 1577, and 1585.

41. Ellis Heywood, *Il Moro d'Heli seo Heivodo Inglese,* trans. Roger Lee Deakins (Cambridge, Mass., 1972), p. 4. The portrait of More also shows him as the protomartyr and saint. "Come ueggiamo fare a molti, i quali con troppa spia ceuolezza, due mali ne fanno seguire, l'un', che di se stessi mostrano un non so che di, costretta voluntà, l'altro, che i piu impefetti spauentano, dando loró a uedere, che la virtù, non come si ragiona, di fuora solamente, ma etiando di dentro tenga dello spiacevole"; "[he did not have that] stiff reserve or misanthropy that we see in many people whose disdain brings about two evils: first, they plainly show just how hard it is for them to restrain their wills; and, second, they deter others who conclude that virtue must be just as unpleasant on the inside as it appears from the outside" (sig. A6v; 4).

42. More's response is wryly humorous: "Credemo d'auanzo, rispose il S. T. M., se ui sete studiato nella retorica di Cicerone, che n'habbiate letto piu presto il libro d'Inuentione, che quello di Partitione"; " 'We take for granted,' said More, 'that, if you studied the rhetorical works of Cicero you read the book *De inventione* with greater readiness than *De partitione'* " (sig. I8v; 57).

43. Dramatically, in narrative encounters with Philautus (sigs. D1v–D2; 1:198–99), and later, in a letter to him (sigs. M1–M4; 1:246–57).

44. Sig. D6v; p. 28.

45. At one point Paul draws on More's own unfinished treatise, *Four Last Things,* making More another character within the story—a box within a box we find also in Erasmus, More, and Gascoigne.

46. Deakins further comments, "The More of *Il Moro* not only speaks well of happiness, but also leads a happy life. He has enough wealth to be able to put his house at the disposal of his friends; he has the honor of his friends, who revere him as the wisest of their circle; he has love, that 'affinity of souls' that unites human beings in the most trustworthy of all bonds; and the fact that he has true knowledge is the burden of the entire dialogue. More in *Il Moro* is 'a speaking picture' of a man who has realized perfection in the active life as Lord Chancellor and is now about to achieve perfect realization of the contemplative life by confronting the vision of God" (in Heywood, *Il Moro,* pp. ix–x).

47. Lady Julia recounts the story of a woman who makes up a bed of the mistress of her adulterous husband so as to bring about his repentance and reformation, the exact reversal of the story of the slips in *The Adventures of Master F. J.,* which may have been a source; if so, it measures the difference between Gascoigne's largely humanist and Tilney's largely Reformist fictions.

48. The only published studies are C. A. Mayer, "L'Honnête Homme; Molière, and Philibert de Vienne's *Philosophe de Court,*" *Modern Language Review* 46:196–217; Pauline M. Smith, *The Anti-Courtier Trend in Sixteenth Century French Literature* (Geneva, 1966), esp. pp. 98–151; and Daniel Javitch, "*The Philosopher of the Court:* A French Satire Misunderstood," *Comparative Literature* 23:97–124.

49. "What is striking about [Philibert's] book," Javitch notes, "which appeared in an age when classical wisdom was revered, is its defiance, even rejection, of

classical authority" ("*Philosopher*," p. 98). Perhaps this is an early work in a growing line of treatises on the inadequacies of humanism.

50. "If I durst speake of Orators, who suppose of thēselues to haue double iudgements in al maner of sciences, for one litle word that they would perfectly to be vnderstand and eloquently vtter, being of small consequence, will trauell so far about for it, that some of them are neuer able to come to their matter againe" (sig. D8).

51. Quoted in Robert Naunton, *Fragmenta Regalia* (1641), sig. D4v, ed. John S. Cerovski (Washington, D.C., 1985), p. 67.

52. "And nowe of late forsoothe to helpe countenaunce owte the matter they have gotten Philibertes Philosopher of the Courte, the Italian Archebysshoppies brave Galatro, Castiglioes fine Cortegiano, Bengalassoes Civil Instructions to his Newphewe Seignor Princisa Ganzar, Guatzoes newe Discourses of curteous behavior, Jouios and Rassellis Emblemes in Italian, Paradines, in Frenche, Plutarche in Frenche, Frontines Stratagemes, Polyenes Stratagemes, Polonica, Apodemica, Guigiandine, Philipp de Comines, and I knowe not howe many owtlandishe braveryes besides of the same stampe" (*Letter-Book of Gabriel Harvey*, ed. E. J. L. Scott [London, 1884], pp. 78–79).

53. Cf. the scholboy's Latin tags in *Campaspe* 2.2.66–67 and allusions in *Endimion* (3.3.16–19; *Mother Bombie* 3.2.14; and *The Woman in the Moon* 5.1.140. Donald Edge traces a line in *Endimion* (3.3.38–40) to Lily's *Carmen de Moribus* "The Source of Some Latin Lines in John Lyly's 'Endimion' " (*Notes and Queries* 218[n.s. 20] [1973]: 453). Many of Lyly's mythological plots are traceable to classical sources or to humanist recapitulations of them, as the Midas story can be found in Erasmus (*Opera Omnia* [Lvgduni Batarowm; London, 1703], 2:138C–F).

54. Feuillerat, *John Lyly*, p. 3.

55. R. S. Stanier, *Magdalen School* (Oxford, 1940), p. 22. See also Hunter, *John Lyly*, pp. 17–25.

56. Quoted in Hunter, *John Lyly*, p. 19.

57. Polydore Virgil, in *History of England* (London: Camden Society, 1950), 3d ser. 74 (whole number 242), 147n.

58. "To the Reader," *A Shorte Introdvction of Grammar* 1549 ed., sig. A2. The first extant edition is 1527; the dates of earlier editions, read out of existence, are now unknown.

59. The important phenomenon of Lily's precepts is that they are nearly all negative; they profess man as fallen, and in need of education.

60. Hunter, *John Lyly*, pp. 25–26.

61. The evidence is a note in the hand of the antiquarian scholar Edmond Malone (1741–1812) in the Bodleian copy of *Euphues*. The play has also been assigned to Dionysia Lily; see Feuillerat, *John Lyly*, p. 11; Hunter, *John Lyly*, p. 26.

62. Hunter recites these facts, p. 26. Ellis Heywood's *Il Moro* is dedicated to Pole.

63. Croll, *Style,* p. 245. See also Anthony à Wood, *Athenae Oxonienses,* 1, sigs. G4v–H1, cols. 96–97.

64. The case is convincingly made by William Ringler, "The Immediate Source of Euphuism," *PMLA* 53:678–86.

65. The full text of Lyly's letter to Burghley is given, with translation, in Bond, ed., *Complete Works,* 1:13–14.

66. Hunter also traces a possible connection of the Burghley and Lyly families through marriage (*John Lyly,* p. 46).

67. *The Scholemaster* is "a work very much in the tradition of William Lily and pious pedagogy in England" (ibid., p. 49).

68. Plutarch, *Moralia* 20C, trans. Frank Cole Babbitt, Loeb Classical Library (Cambridge, Mass., 1927, 1969).

69. Isocrates, "To Nicocles" 7, trans. George Norlin, Loeb Classical Library (Cambridge, Mass., 1928, 1980).

70. The *chreia,* with its opposing speeches ascending from the negative exemplum to the positive to the exemplary, is fundamentally the *rhetorical* format of *Euphues*: Euphues moves from his foolish speech to Lucilla to a truer speech to himself to an exemplary speech in attempting, at the close, to instruct Philautus. Given Lyly's admiration for Isocrates, it is tempting to think that it was Rainolde's Aphthonian handbook to rhetoric that gave him the idea of using this particular form.

71. Isocrates, *To Demonicus,* trans. George Norlin, Loeb Classical Library (Cambridge, Mass., 1928, 1980).

72. Isocrates, *Antidosis* 271, trans. George Norlin, Loeb Classical Library (Cambridge, Mass., 1929, 1968).

73. Cicero, *Orator,* trans. Hubbell.

74. Isocrates, *Panegyricus,* trans. George Norlin, Loeb Classical Library (Cambridge, Mass., 1928, 1980).

75. Isocrates, "Against the Sophists," trans. Norlin.

76. John Hoskins, *Directions for Speech and Style,* ed. Hoyt H. Hudson (Princeton, N.J. 1935), p. 16.

77. Harvey, *Marginalia,* ed. Smith, p. 127.

78. Aristotle, *Nicomachean Ethics* 8.3.1–6, trans. H. Rackham, Loeb Classical Library (London, 1926, 1975).

79. Cicero, *De Amicitia,* 8.27, trans. William Armistead Falconer, Loeb Classical Library (Cambridge, Mass., 1923, 1979).

80. Davis, *Idea and Act,* p. 122.

81. William Ringler provides a close rhetorical analysis of the *Ephemerides* (or daily occurrences) in *Stephen Gosson* (Princeton, N.J., 1942), pp. 85 ff.

82. The courtesan Polyphine, like Lucilla, praises pleasure by means of sophistry: "Rhethorike, Logike, Philosophie, Musicke, all Artes, all Sciences, are referred too this, that they might profite, and bring vs pleasure. Howe triumpheth the Oratour, when he seeth the Client deliuered by his tongue? . . . The beasts of the earth, the fishes of the Sea, the foules of the ayre, the Sunne, the Moone, the

course of the Starres, the foure Elementes, the whole worlde was made for our vse, & this vse is the roote of al our pleasure: Our speach is giuen vs too increace acquaintance" (sigs. H4–H4v). Phialo's echoes of Euphues come in his references to God: "you are not your owne, but his that framed you; yf you be not your owne, deny your selfe; yf you be Gods, flie vnto him; cast of ye wanton desires of this life, seeke for not pleasure in these dayes, if you wish to auoid torment in the worlde too come" (sig. K5v). On Gosson's humanist rather than Reformist outlook, see Ringler, *Stephen Gosson,* p. 80, and Arthur F. Kinney, *Markets of Bawdrie* (Salzburg, 1974), pp. 28–37.

83. References are to the 1580 quarto and to Bond, ed., *Complete Works.*

84. See Hunter, *John Lyly,* p. 68.

85. Callimachus's rebellion retrospectively mirrors Euphues, and both serve as lamps for Philautus; even the more remote Uncle Callimachus is a variant of the same theme. Fidus too is a concentrated reprise of *Euphues* embedded in the later and longer book, his beehive an emblem of *proprietas* (as both *property* and *propriety*). Euphues, Philautus, Euphues (again), and Camilla are all variations, too, on the Eubulus, Euphues, Philautus, and Lucilla pattern, respectively, in *Euphues.* Yet we are also meant to note changes: Fidus's usefulness in retirement corrects Callimachus's reclusive life, just as Iffida's faithfulness (she is the female counterpart of Fidus) suggests the right alternative for Lucilla. Yet, in all these analogies (for *Euphues and his England* has a symphonic structure rather than the linear structure of *Euphues*), the style is more relaxed and the tone lighter; Euphues' recounting of Callimachus is so boring that Philautus cannot stay awake, while Fidus, in telling his tales, drones on like his bees. Davis (*Idea and Act,* p. 132) makes similar claims.

86. Hunter, *John Lyly,* p. 67.

87. So, at one point, Euphues continues to lecture Philautus while he is sick at a porthole of the ship on their voyage to England.

88. The best discussion of Lyly's relationship with Italian work is still Violet M. Jeffery, *John Lyly and the Italian Renaissance* (Paris, 1929).

89. Sig. P4; 2:103. The elevated classical allusions used in these debased parodies of the *questione di amore* are repetitive—to Lais, Atalanta, Helen, Venus, Vesta; Ulysses, Apelles, Alexander, Zeuxis, Lycurgus. So are proverbial references to iron, lodestone, fire, arrows, wasps, toads, serpents, and lapwings. Rather than demonstrate Lyly's imitations—for most of the joke is that they are all lifted directly from Erasmus's *Adagia;* they circumscribe the humorous limitations of his characters. Their lives are puzzling and a-maz-ing because their restricted verbal knowledge, like the physical labyrinth, admits so many meanings. For Lyly's ability at soliloquy, see sigs. N2v–N3; 2:88.

CHAPTER 6

1. This view is developed by Helgerson in *Elizabethan Prodigals,* chap. 5. The standard study of Greene's life and work remains René Pruvost, *Robert Greene et ses romans (1558–1592): Contribution a l'histoire de la Renaissance en Angleterre*

(Paris, 1938), but see also John Clark Jordan, *Robert Greene* (New York, 1915, 1965), chap. 3, and the useful biographical and critical conjectures in a dissertation by Brenda E. Richardson, "Studies in Related Aspects of the Life and Thought of Robert Greene, with Particular Reference to the Material of His Prose Pamphlets" (Oxford, 1976).

2. Dickenson sums his story on sigs. I3v–I4: "Thus (Gentlemen) haue you heard briefly related [the] Tragique issue of *Giraldos* wooing in age, and *Valerias* wantonnesse in youth: Had I intituled this discourse, *A looking Glasse,* the Metaphor had not been wholly immateriall: for herein may all sortes of readers note sundry points of weight: husbandes, the daunger of too much doting: wiues in her fall, the end of lustfull follie: parents, the mightie perill of soothing their children in check-free licentiousnesse: children, the fruit of disobedience and vndutifull demeanour: rash proceeders, the great difference of good and bad counsell, of honest and dishonest companie: with the danger of not imbracing the one, and not shunning the other: and that the rather, sith the force of companie, hath in the effecting of either such exceeding force, according to the Italian prouerbe, *Dimmi con chi tu vai, & sagrò quel che fai, Ictus piscator sapit,* but if wee account him wise, which being once hurt, doth shunne a second hazard: how much more iustly may wee commend their wisdome, who beeing not hurt at all, but learning heedfulnes at others costes, gouerne warily themselues by noting the issue of their indiscretion: which fore-sight and good fortune I wish vnto you all."

3. 1614 ed., sig. A4; 9:121. All references are to the first edition of Greene's works unless otherwise noted and to *The Life and Complete Works in Prose and Verse of Robert Greene, M.A.,* Huth Library, 15 vols. (privately printed, 1881–86).

4. Jordan makes this comparison in detail (*Robert Greene,* pp. 54–59).

5. Greene, *The Royal Exchange* (1590), sig. C1v; 7:253. *The Royal Exchange* is a fairly faithful translation of Orazio Rinaldi, *Dottrina della virtu, et fuga de' vitii* (Padua, 1585), to which Greene added a number of glossarial remarks such as the one on Castiglione. See Charles Speroni, *The Aphorisms of Orazio Rinaldi, Robert Greene, and Lucas Gracian Dantisco,* University of California Publications in Modern Philology 88 (Berkeley, 1968).

6. Davis's epitome of this work in *Idea and Act,* p. 149, is especially useful; despite the ostensible purpose of the fiction, each illustrative story incorporates all three virtues. But see also Samuel Lee Wolff, "Robert Greene and the Italian Renaissance," *Englische Studien* 37:326–28.

7. Greene's slighter works, such as *The Myrrovr of Modestie* (1584), an extended exercise in varying on the biblical story of Susanna and the Elders, and *Cornucopia* or *The Royal Exchange* n. 5 above, a sort of humanist commonplace book which incorporates entries on dignity (sig. D2v; 7:263), eloquence (sig. D4; 7:271), and perfection (sig. E3; 7:279), sanction the dominant force of humanist thought and rhetoric. Even the brief *Debate Betweene Follie and Loue* appended to *Gwydonius* (1584), claimed by Greene to be translated out of the French, relies on variation and a decidedly Erasmian portrait of Folly.

8. Most scholars have thought Greene to be the son of a saddler; in these biographical references, I am using the new research conducted by Brenda Richardson.

9. See *The Repentance of Robert Greene,* a dubious work (no sig.; 12:172).

10. See, for example, the title page of *Philomela. The Lady Fitzvvaters Nightingale* (1592), sig. A2; 11:107. Phoebe Sheavyn was materially helpful in biographical studies of Greene by first noting his appeals to sixteen different patrons in seventeen works in *The Literary Profession in the Elizabethan Age* rev. J. W. Saunders (rep. Manchester, 1967), p. 24; many of these Richardson traces to the West Riding. The most judicious use of materials in the reconstruction of Greene's life is still Thomas H. Dickinson in his Introduction to *Robert Greene* in the Mermaid Series (London, n.d.), pp. ix–xxiv; the most detailed analysis of his college experience is Johnstone Parr, "Robert Greene and His Classmates at Cambridge," *PMLA* 77:536–43.

11. Harvey, *Fowre Letters,* sigs. D1–D1v; ed. G. B. Harrison (London, 1922; rep. Edinburgh, 1966), p. 40.

12. Most scholars have disparaged Greene's extensive borrowing—and even his self-borrowing. See, for instance, H. C. Hart, "Robert Greene's Prose Works," *Notes and Queries* 4 (1905): 1–5, 81–84, 162–64, 224–27, 483–85; 5 (1906): 84–85, 202–4, 343–44, 424–25, 442–45, 463–65, 484–87, and 504–6; Roselle Gould Goree, "Concerning Repetitions in Greene's Romances," *Philological Quarterly* 3 (1924): 69–75; and C. J. Vincent, "Further Repetitions in the Works of Robert Greene," *Philological Quarterly* 18 (1939): 73–77. The prefatory essay on astrology in *Planetomachia* is an unannounced rendering of Lucian; see Johnstone Parr, "Sources of the Astrological Prefaces in Robert Greene's *Planetomachia,*" *Studies in Philology* 46 (1949): 400–10, but Greene draws as well on Pliny (Stanley Wells, "Greene and Pliny," *Notes and Queries* 206 [n.s. 8][1961]: 422–24), his classmate Thomas Bowes's translation of Primaudaye and Joannis Joviani Pontano (Parr, "Greene and His Classmates"), Plutarch (John W. Velz, "Robert Greene and Philip of Macedon (ccviii. 348)," *Notes and Queries* 210, 12 [1965]: 195), Pettie's Guazzo (John Leon Lievsay, "Robert Greene, Master of Arts, and 'Mayster Steeven Guazzo'," *Studies in Philology* 36 [1939]: 577–96), Henry Wotton (John S. Weld, "Some Problems of Euphuistic Narrative: Robert Greene and Henry Wotton," *Studies in Philology* 45 [1948]: 165–71), and Philip Melanchthon's Ptolemy (Don Cameron Allen, "Science and Invention in Greene's Prose, " *PMLA* 53 [1938]: 1007–18) as well. Normand Sanders finds more than seventy borrowings from Primaudaye (as translated by Bowes in 1586) in *Greenes Farewell to Follie* (1591) (see "Robert Greene's Way with a Source," *Notes and Queries* 212 [n.s. 14], [1967]: 89–91), but his greatest reliance seems to have been on *Pettie's Petite Pallace of Pettie His Pleasure* (1576), a collection of euphuistic romances also used by Lyly; see Vincent, "Pettie and Greene," *Modern Language Notes* 54 (1939): 105–11. That Greene's classical allusions were often second hand, implying a certain lack of industry, may be borne out by Parr's discovery that in *ordo senioritatis* of the baccalaureate class of 1580, Greene ranked 38 in St. John's class of 41 and 115 in the university class

540). Greene was not made a fellow of any Cambridge college, apparently dashing his hopes for a career at the university, was not admitted to the Inns of Court, and was not advanced to any benefice.

13. Plutarch actually writes of three men named Lentulus in the *Life of Cicero,* none of whom resembles Greene's character: the conspirator (17–18), the ally of Pompey (33, 38), and his son-in-law Tullia (41). Greene also takes several place-names from this source.

14. Cf. Davis's discussion of the double meaning of "fancy" in *Idea and Act,* p. 142.

15. In Rich's "Sappho, Duke of Mantona" (*Riche his Farewell to Militarie profession* [1581]), an unknown gentleman attains a position at court but is prevented from loving the duke's daughter until his origin is revealed; in the tale of "Admetus and Alcestis" in Pettie's *Petite Pallace* the lovers are children of two hostile rulers. Both Rich and Pettie also drew on Greek romances and *novelle.*

16. Wallace A. Bacon, Introduction to *William Warner's Syrinx; or, a Sevenfold History* (Evanston, Ill., 1950), p. xiv.

17. Arthur Heiserman, *The Novel before the Novel* (Chicago, 1977), pp. 5–6.

18. Edwin Haviland Miller, Introduction to *Ciceronis Amor: "Tullies Love" (1589) and "A Quip for an Upstart Courtier" (1592)* (Gainesville, Fla., 1954), p. 5.

19. Ponsonby quarto; *Miscellaneous Prose,* ed. Duncan-Jones and Van Dorsten. The dimension of magic and enchantment is also prevalent in Greene's drama, most notably in *Alphonsus,* with the marvelous descent of Venus and the nine Muses, the conjuring of Medea (3.950–79) and the priest of Mahomet (4.1258–88, 1320–40), and Amurack's dream (3.990–1035). Melissa uses enchantment to cure Orlando (*Orlando Furioso,* lines 1240–1310), and in *Friar Bacon and Friar Bungay* there is Bacon's brazen head (238–380) and magic perspective glass (1880–1965) as well as a contest of magic between Bungay and Vandermast (1170–1339) and Bacon's final mystical prophecy (2233–52).

20. A fuller account of man's changeability couched in a traditional humanist lexicon is found in the opening of "Tereus and Porgne," a source for George Pettie's *Petite Pallace.*

21. Achilles Tatius, *Clitophon and Leucippe,* trans. S. Gaselee, Loeb Classical Library (New York, 1918), p. 11.

22. Joseph De Perott identifies the Italian text as Greene's source; see "Robert Greene and the Italian Translation of *Achilles Tatius,*" *Modern Language Notes* 29 (1914): 63.

23. Samuel Lee Wolff, *The Greek Romances in Elizabethan Prose Fiction* (New York, 1912), pp. 408, 376.

24. "The scholiast Thomas Magister calls him an orator, and he may well have been an advocate: his general style is redolent of the rhetoricians, and the lawsuit towards the end of the romance betrays a practiced hand in the speeches on both sides" (Gaselee, in Tatius, *Clitophon,* p. viii).

25. Heiserman, *Novel,* p. 186.

26. Heliodorus, *Aethiopian Historie,* (1577), sig. L2; Underdowne, in *The Tudor Translations,* ed. W. E. Henley (London, 1895), p. 161. Subsequent references are to these texts.

27. J. M. Edmonds, Introduction to the Loeb edition of "Longus" (Cambridge, 1916, 1962), pp. xii, xi.

28. The first extant edition is from 1594(?), but there must have been earlier copies, nearer to the date in the *Stationers' Register.* A convenient modern text is that of Geoffrey Bullough in *Narrative and Dramatic Sources of Shakespeare* (London, 1966), 6:423–82. Subsequent references are to these two texts.

29. So Elizabeth Hazelton Haight, *More Essays on Greek Romances* (New York, 1945), p. 157.

30. Sir Bartram claims as much for Dorothea's salvation from a projected assassination: "When I read (now marke the power of God) / I found this warrant seald among the rest, / To kill your grace, whom God long keep, aliue. / Thus in effect, by wonder are you saued, / Trifle not then, but seeke a speadie flight, / God will conduct your steppes, and shield the right" ([3.3.62–67], sig. F4; 13:272).

31. 1.4; trans. W. Hamilton Fyfe, Loeb Classical Library (New York, 1927), p. 125. Subsequent references are to this text.

32. There was also the *Commentarius in Longinum* attributed to Franciscus Portus (c. 1570).

33. Plato, *Sophist,* trans. Fowler.

34. Aristotle, *Poetics,* trans. W. Hamilton Fyfe, Loeb Classical Library (New York, 1927).

35. T. R. Henn, *Longinus and English Criticism* (Cambridge, 1934), p. 12.

36. Not extant.

37. 244v.296; trans. W. Rhys Roberts.

38. This summary in part paraphrases the very useful introduction by Roberts to the Cambridge University Press edition of Demetrius, *On Style* (1902), pp. 33–34.

39. Madeleine Doran, *Endeavors of Art: A Study of Form in Elizabethan Drama* (Madison, Wisc., 1954), p. 25, but see chap. 2 generally. In *The Royal Exchange,* eloquence is defined as "Boldnesse. Understanding. Delight. And use" (sig. D4; 7:271).

40. Wolff, *Greek Romances,* p. 3.

41. Walter F. Staton, Jr., "The Characters of Style in Elizabethan Prose," *Journal of English and Germanic Philology* 57:197–207.

42. Doran (*Endeavors of Art,* p. 24) cites Pierre Charron's *De la Sagesse:* "Eloquence is not only a purity, and elegancy of speech, a discreet choice of words properly applied, ended in a true and a just fall, but it must likewise be full of ornaments, graces, motions" (Charron, *Of Wisdom,* 3.43, trans. Samson Lennard [1670 ed.; 1st ed., c. 1606–12], p. 523).

43. See Geoffrey Tillotson's helpful "Elizabethan Decoration," in *Essays in Criticism and Research* (Cambridge, 1942), esp. pp. 7, 10, 13.

44. Cicero, *De Partitiones oratoria,* trans. H. Rackham, Loeb Classical Library (Cambridge, Mass., 1942, 1960), 23.79.

45. *Ad Herennium* 4.8.11, trans. Harry Caplan, Loeb Classical Library (Cambridge, Mass., 1954, 1968).

46. Quintilian, *Institutio Oratoria* 8.3.87–88, trans. Butler.

47. "Sic igitur dicet ille, quem expetimus, ut verset saepe multis modis eadem et in una re haereat in eademque commoretur sententia"; "Our ideal orator then will speak in such a manner that he will cast the same thought into a number of different forms, will dwell on one point and linger over the same idea" (9.1.41). Quintilian takes expression to extreme lengths: "Conceditur enim amplius dicere, quia dici, quantum est, non potest, meliusque ultra quam citra stat oratio"; "For we are allowed to amplify, when the magnitude of the facts passes all words, and in such circumstances our language will be more effective if it goes beyond the truth than if it falls short of it" (8.6.76).

48. *Collected Works of Erasmus,* trans. Craig R. Thompson (Toronto, 1978), 24:639–41.

49. Sr. Miriam Joseph, *Shakespeare's Use of the Arts of Lanugage* (New York, 1947), p. 14. Sr. Miriam Joseph's study of Tudor rhetoric, pp. 3–40, 291–399, is still useful. An indispensable reference work for schemes and tropes is Richard A. Lanham, *A Handlist of Rhetorical Terms* (Berkeley, Calif., 1969).

50. Sherry, *A treatise of Schemes and Tropes* (1550) and *A Treatise of the Figures of Grammer and Rhetorike* (1555); Peacham, *The Garden of Eloquence* (1577; rev. and aug. 1593); Puttenham, *The Arte of English Poesie* (1589); Day, *The English Secretorie* (1586; rev. 1592, with a long section on figures added). Also, Leonard Cox, *The Art or crafte of Rhetoryke* (1532 ed., sig. A6), borrows classical places to vary the sevenfold form of oration and disputation. Day applies figures to elaborate his theory and practice of letter writing (1595 ed., sig. C1).

51. The explosion in the number of figures urged by the Tudor handbooks is graphically displayed by a chart in Joseph, *Shakespeare's Use of Language,* p. 35.

52. Puttenham, *Arte,* sig. S4v; ed. Gladys Doidge Willcock and Alice Walker (Cambridge, 1936), p. 159. Subsequent references are to these two texts.

53. Willcock and Walker, Introduction to Puttenham, *Arte,* p. lxxxii. John Hoskins's *Directions for Speech and Style,* although not published during the Elizabethan period, was also meant as a handbook for a young gentleman of the Inns of Court and deals primarily with varying and amplification; see the edition by Hoyt H. Hudson (Princeton, N.J., 1935).

54. Miller is speaking particularly of *Ciceronis Amor,* adding, "That [Greene] thought of his romance in musical terms is apparent in his preface" (Introduction to *Ciceronis Amor,* p. 6).

55. The student, Kempe writes, "shall followe the tropes and figures in the first part of Rhetorike. . . . he must obserue in authors all the vse of the Artes, as not only the words and phrases, not only the examples of the arguments; but also . . . euery trope, euery figure, aswell of words as of sentences" (sigs. G2v–G3).

56. Edward Arber, Introduction to Greene, *Menaphon* (London, n.d.), p. xvi.

57. See Wolff, *The Greek Romances,* pp. 444–45. The incidents Greene may have borrowed from his contempoaries—royalty disguised as shepherds and, meeting, failing to recognize each other (from William Warner's *Albion's England,* 4.20), and father and son wooing the wife and mother (from Sidney's *Arcadia*)—are also moments of unusual wonder. See Jordan, pp. 40–41.

58. In this and some following remarks, I am indebted to Richardson's dissertation, "Studies in Related Aspects of the Life and Thought of Robert Greene."

59. So Dorothy Schuchman McCoy can write of the content of *Menaphon* that "unlike Sidney's [*Arcadia*], it does not seriously attempt to comment upon real situations" (*Tradition and Convention: A Study of Periphrasis in English Pastoral Poetry from* 1557–1715 [The Hague, 1965], p. 176).

60. Herbert Hartman, in his edition of *A Petite Pallace* (London, 1938), lists and illustrates them in detail. He finds in Pettie alliteration, anagram, antithesis, annomination, assonance, consonance, repetition, and single and double rhyme among the *schemata verborum* and among the ornaments, anecdotes, illusions, myths, proverbs, and unnatural natural history, as well as a nascent interest in isocolon (pp. xxix–xxxii).

61. First noted by Charles T. Prouty in *Studies in Honor of A. H. R. Fairchild,* ed. Prouty, University of Missouri Studies 21, no. 1 (Columbia, 1946), p. 136. The best recent study (which I have seen in manuscript) is by Paul A. Scanlon of the University of Botswana, Lesotho, and Swaziland.

62. The references come, almost incidentally, in the central scene of the final battle: "Remorse of conscience anothing weakeneth *Fitzaldo,* but *Rinaldos* honest cause doubleth his strength, so that the longer he fought, the fearer he was, and yet *Fitzaldo* valiantly mainteines his dishonest quarrell. But what doth might auaile when God assistes the right" (sig. D7). Earlier, the plot has made two decisive turns on coincidence: Giletta prevents Rinaldo's suicide when overhearing him (sig. D2v), and Rinaldo (disguised as a hermit) saves Rosina and challenges Fitzaldo when he overhears hired assassins about to kill her (sig. D5v).

63. Thomas Mabry Cranfill, "Barnaby Rich's 'Sappho' and *The Weakest Goeth to the Wall,*" *University of Texas Studies in English,* 1945–46, p. 163. In the introduction to his facsimile edition of *Rich's Farewell to Military Profession: 1581* (Austin, Tex., 1959), Cranfill shows that Rich, like Painter and Pettie, took all of his tales from Continental romances.

64. Davis gives a detailed account of the plot (*Idea and Act,* pp. 127–30).

65. The hermit Aristo teaches him through autobiography, Lamia by confession, Andruchio by judicial oration, Thomerchus with a sermon, Anthonio by debate, and Porcia with a formal argument drawing on the fundamental places of logic.

66. The clearest and most authoritative study is Robert S. Knapp, "Love

Allegory in John Grange's *The Golden Aphroditis,*" *English Literary Renaissance* 8(1978):256–70, on which I have drawn.

67. The observation is borne out explicitly by Grange's praise of N. O.'s language in courting A. L.: "This praysing of *N. O.* his rolling tongue did encourage him not a little by polished phrase of filed style to feede his Ladies appetites or humors with some one thing or other, whereby he might fancie what fancie most requyred" (sig. F2).

68. A. O.'s miraculous birth is described anagogically (and erotically) in a key passage: while playing with a stray buck (sig. C2v), "I sate me downe likewise to reste my wearied limmes, and played with his hornes in my lappe. But (to be short) he suddenly rising, gan fiercely to pushe at me with his prickyng hornes, and so fiercely pursued his fennishe thrustes, that before I could recouer my feete agayne he gaue me a goring woūd" (sig. C3).

69. Although applicable to the narrative situation, this is also double-edged, for Grange is describing his own aesthetic need for enigmatic prose.

70. "But I beseech you, what Newes al this while at Cambridge? ... *Matchiauell,* a great man: *Castilio* of no small reputation: *Petrarch,* and *Boccace* in euery mans mouth: *Galateo,* and *Guazzo* neuer so happy: ouer many acquainted with *Vncle Aretino:* The French and Italian when so highlye regarded of Schollers?" Gabriel Harvey, *Three Proper and wittie, familiar Letters,* in *Works,* ed. Alexander B. Grosart (London, 1884), 1:68–69.

71. Florence Nightingale Jones, *Boccaccio and His Imitators* (Chicago, 1910), notes that Greene also borrows from the *Decameron* for *Philomela* 2.9 and the ending of *Philomela* (10.8), which mentions 4.2, while *The Spanish Masquerado* of Greene mentions 6.10. Painter uses *Decameron* 1. 3, 5, 8, 10; 2.2, 3, 4, 5, 8; 3.9; 4.1; 8.7; 10.3, 4, 5, 9. Pettie takes sixteen tales from Boccaccio but converts them to long speeches, with the conflicts condensed to quick narrative conclusions. See Jaroslav Hornát, *Philologica Pragensia* 5:214.

72. J.M. Rigg, Introduction to *The Decameron of Giovanni Boccaccio* (London, [1921]), p. xx.

73. Wolff, *Greek Romances,* pp. 370–74. The stories of the second day are exemplary stories of fortune; the stories of the fifth day are about true love rewarded by joy and not suffering.

74. Greene also makes use of Cinthio's *Hecatommithi* for *Philomela* (5.4) and *Planetomachia* (2.2) and Ariosto's *Orlando Furioso* (34.7–43) for *Orpharion.* See Wolff, "Greene and Italian Renaissance," pp. 321–75, esp. p. 346, n. 1.

75. This interest in stability and change is also commented on by Boccaccio in his Author's Epilogue to the *Decameron,* while metamorphosis is the subject of *Decameron* 5.1.

76. John Barsley, *Ovid* (Oxford, 1978), p. 35.

77. The idea of metamorphosis is also the basis of Giovanni Battistia Gelli's *Circe,* a wonderful rhetorical fiction in which Ulysses has great difficulty—and almost no success, except with the elephant—in persuading the animals on Circe's island to undergo another metamorphosis back to men so as to return

home with him. This situational satire—which Swift was to use in *Gulliver's Travels* 4—allows Gelli to make some telling points about the partially tragic condition of man. Henry Iden (Jordan?) translated the *Circe* into English in 1557, but there is no indication that Greene was aware of it. A modern edition is edited by Robert M. Adams (Ithaca, N.Y., 1963).

78. *The .xv. Bookes of P. Ovidius Naso, entytyled Metamorphosis,* trans. Arthur Golding, sig. Cc5; ed. John Frederick Nims (New York, 1965), p. 382.

79. Davis also makes this observation (*Idea and Act,* p. 169). His overall interpretation of *Pandosto,* however, is to see in it an absurd world (pp. 167–70).

CHAPTER 7

1. Lewis, *English Literature,* p. 335.

2. Sidney, *Arcadia:* references are to the text by book and chapter; quotations are from the 1593 composite edition, and the only modern edition (which has occasional errors), ed. Maurice Evans (Harmondsworth, 1977). The 1593 text, the second to be published, bastardizes Sidney's early and late drafts of the *Arcadia,* but it is the one best known to the Tudors and early Stuarts and therefore crucial to understanding the history of humanist poetics. For an account of the early printing history of the *Arcadia* and textual discrepancies between the 1590 and 1593 texts, see William A. Ringler, Jr., *The Poems of Sir Philip Sidney* (Oxford, 1962), pp. 364–80.

3. These persistent interruptions take on the repetitiveness common to jokes. But the invitation to a stag hunt—that is, the temporary surrender of discussion about meaningful action for mere sport—is further complicated by Kalander's subsequent attitude: their gentlemanly host "with a Crossebow sent a death to the poore beast, who with teares shewed the vnkindnes he tooke of mans crueltie" (1.11; sig. C6; 116).

4. Fulke Greville, *The Life of the Renowned Sʳ Philip Sidney* (1652), sigs. L3v, L5v; ed. Nowell Smith (Oxford, 1907), pp. 150, 154.

5. Ornate rhetoric can also deceive in ways we allow or desire, as when Dorus uses a fictional persona to mislead Mopsa while revealing himself autobiographically to Pamela (2.3. et seq.). Sidney's use of humanist rhetoric is, in its many applications, far more sophisticated and complicated than I can treat here and deserves further study.

6. Other examples include the portrait of Philoclea in 1.12 and Zelmane's lament in 2.16.

7. Quoted in John F. Danby, *Poets on Fortune's Hill* (London, 1952), p. 71.

8. Steuart A. Pears, "The Life and Times of Sir Philip Sidney," in *The Correspondence of Sir Philip Sidney and Hubert Languet* (London, 1845), pp. lxv–vi.

9. *Correspondence,* trans. Pears, pp. 183–84.

10. This view is developed in the standard biography by Malcolm William Wallace (Cambridge, 1915). Cf. Samuel A. Tannenbaum: "Modern ethics disapprove of giving costly gifts, even to a queen, when one cannot afford to do so; of marrying for money a child one does not love; of writing impassioned and equivocal sonnets to another man's wife; of living extravagantly with other people's money and dying heavily in debt; and of threatening to stick one's dagger into his father's secretary for reading his letters" (Foreward to *Sir Philip Sidney: A Concise Bibliography,* Elizabethan Bibliographies, no. 23 (New York, 1941), p. viii.

11. William Dinsmore Briggs, "Political Ideas in Sidney's *Arcadia,*" *Studies in Philology* 28:137–61; Richard C. McCoy, *Sir Philip Sidney: Rebellion in Arcadia* (New Brunswick, N.J., 1979), pp. 184 ff. For accounts of the Huguenot theory, see J. W. Allen, *A History of Political Thought in the Sixteenth Century* (London, 1928, 1957, 1960), pp. 302–31, and Michael Walzer, *The Revolution of the Saints* (Cambridge, Mass., 1965), pp. 74–87; primary documents are in Julian H. Franklin, trans. and ed., *Constitutionalism and Resistance in the Sixteenth Century* (New York, 1969).

12. Katherine Duncan-Jones argues convincingly that Sidney was not banished to Wilton from the court, in *Miscellaneous Prose,* ed. Duncan-Jones and Van Dorsten, pp. 34–35; even if, as she claims, political frustration and lack of money were primary causes for his visit, the sprezzatura critics ever since Kenneth Myrick, in *Sir Philip Sidney as a Literary Craftsman* (Cambridge, Mass., 1935), pp. 298–315, have attributed to the *Arcadia* (seen in the parody noted above) assure us that his residence near the Salisbury plains was, for the most part, an enjoyable one.

13. But he goes on to see this as "matchless ... decorum" in "the sweetly constituted mind of Sir Philip Sidney"; he too in the end is one of the idolators. Quoted in Mona Wilson, *Sir Philip Sidney* (London, 1931, 1950), p. 138.

14. Helgerson, *Elizabethan Prodigals,* p. 137.

15. Quintilian, *Institutio Oratoria* 4.4.3–4.

16. Harvey, *Three Letters;* quoted in G. Gregory Smith, *Elizabethan Critical Essays* (Oxford, 1904), 2:263, 264.

17. Greville, *Life,* sig. B6; ed. Smith, p. 11.

18. John Milton, *Commonplace Book,* ed. Ralph C. Haug, in *The Prose Works of John Milton* (New Haven, Conn., 1953), 1:371, 372, 463, 464.

19. Thomas Zouch, *Memoirs of the Life and Writings of Sir Philip Sidney* (York, 1808), p. 155.

20. Julius Lloyd, *The Life of Sir Philip Sidney* (London, 1862), p. 104.

21. Lewis, *English Literature,* p. 339; the point is developed in A. C. Hamilton, *Sir Philip Sidney: A Study of His Life and Works* (Cambridge, 1977), p. 13.

22. Thomas Moffet, *Nobilis; or, A View of the Life and Death of a Sidney,* trans. Virgil B. Heltzel and Hoyt H. Hudson (San Marino, Calif., 1940).

23. Greville, *Life,* p. 6.

24. Wallace, *Sidney,* pp. 19, 17; Lady William Cecil, Lady Nicholas Bacon, and Lady Thomas Hoby, all relations through marriage of William Cecil, Lord Burghley, the queen's principal secretary.

25. Moffet, *Nobilis,* fols. 7–8v, pp. 72–73. This treatise was a private manual of instruction by the tutor Thomas Moffet for his pupil William Herbert, Sidney's nephew, and was composed for him at Wilton after Sidney's death.

26. At Shrewsbury, Sidney had had to attend classes from 6:00 in the morning until 4:30 in the evening from February through November and from 7:00 A.M. until 5:30 P.M. in the remaining months; the sadly incomplete records now at Christ Church do not show us the schedule there or whether, as a member of the ruling class, Sidney was frequently in attendance. "As the favoured nephew of the Chancellor [Leicester], Sidney was probably given many special privileges," Ringler conjectures, "but since he was always a serious student, we may assume that he performed most of the required exercises. The prescribed subjects were grammar, rhetoric, and dialectic." Furthermore, "the most valuable product of his studies and disputations in Oxford was the thorough training he received in logic and formal classical rhetoric" (Introduction to *Poems,* pp. xviii–xix).

27. Ibid., p. xvii. Roger Howell conjectures that Ashton and Philip were acquainted before this time, since Ashton had previously served as a tutor in the family of Sir Andrew Corbett, a member of the Council of the Marches of Wales, like Sir Henry, and his close friend (*Sir Philip Sidney: The Shepherd Knight* [London, 1968], p. 128).

28. Wallace, *Sidney,* pp. 42–43. For a more detailed examination of Sidney's training at Shrewsbury, see F. J. Levy, "Philip Sidney Reconsidered," *English Literary Renaissance* 2:6–7.

29. Howell, *Sidney,* p. 128; Greville, *Life,* sig. B3v. "Though I lived with him, and knew him from a child," Greville adds, "yet I never knew him other than a man: with such staidnesse of mind, lovely, and familiar gravity, as carried grace, and reverence above greater years" (sig. B3v; ed. Smith, p. 6).

30. "Apply your study to such hours as your discreet master doth assign you, earnestly," Sir Henry writes the boy at Shrewsbury, "and the time I know he will so limit as shall be both sufficient for your learning and safe for your health. And mark the sense and the matter of that you do read, as well as the words; so shall you both enrich your tongue with words and your wit with matter, and judgment will grow as years grow in you. . . . Study and endeavour yourself to be virtuously occupied. So shall you make such a habit of well-doing in you as you shall not know how to do evil, though you would." To this letter, his mother adds as postscript, "see that you show yourself as a loving, obedient scholar to your good master, to govern you yet many years, and that my lord and I may hear that you profit so in your learning as thereby you may increase our loving care of you, and deserve at his hands the continuance of his great joy" (quoted in Wallace, *Sidney* pp. 68–70).

31. Further details are in Frederick S. Boas, *Sir Philip Sidney, Representative Elizabethan: His Life and Writings* (London, rep. 1955).

32. Wallace, *Sidney*, pp. 101–2.

33. Richard Carew, *The Survey of Cornwall* (1602), sig. Dd2v.

34. Ovid, *Metamorphoses* 13.169–75; see Dorothy Connell, *Sir Philip Sidney: The Maker's Mind* (Oxford, 1977), p. 103.

35. This passage paraphrases in part Kenneth Muir, *Sir Philip Sidney* (London, rev. 1967), p. 6. But see also Ringler, *Poems*, pp. xx–xxiii; Tresham Lever, *The Herberts of Wilton* (London, 1967), pp. 44–45; and *Correspondence*, ed. and trans. Pears, passim, as well as the biographies of Wallace and Howell and that of Robert Kimbrough, *Sir Philip Sidney* (New York, 1971).

36. "Your purpose is being a Gentleman borne, to furnishe your selfe with the knowledge of such thinges, as maie be serviceable to your Countriee.... This therefore is one noteable use of travaile, which standes in the mixed and correlitiue knowledge of thinges, in which kinde come in the knowledge of all leauges, betwixt Prince, and Prince, the topograficall descripcion of eache Countrie, howe the one lyes by scituacion to hurte or helpe the other, howe they are to the sea well harbowred or not, howe stored with shippes, howe with Revenewe, howe with fortificacions and Garrisons, howe the People warlick lie trayned or kept under, with manie other such condicions which as they confusedlie come into my mynde, soe I for want of leasure sette downe; but these thinges as I said, are those in the first kind which stands in the ballancing of the one thing with the other.

"The other kinde of knowledge is of them which stand in the thinges which are of themselves, either simplie good, or simplie evill, and soe either for a right instruccion, or a shuning example.... the true discerning of mens myndes, both in vertuous passions & vices ... as Germany mee thinkes doth notablie in good lawes, & well administring of Justice, soe yet wee likewise to consider in it, the manie Princes with whome wee have leauge, the places of trade, and the meane to drawe both soldyers and furniture from thence in time of neede" (*Correspondence*, ed. Pears, pp. 195–98; *The Prose Works of Sir Philip Sidney*, ed. Albert Feuillerat (Cambridge, 1912, 1963), 3:124–27.

37. Languet wrote Sidney on 19 November 1573 a letter notable for its eloquence, and on 5 December Sidney replied that he "culled certain flowers, which, as I could do nothing better, I imitated." On 19 December Sidney asks Languet to send him Plutarch in French, and on 1 January 1574 Languet counters by urging him to read instead two volumes of Cicero's letters, "not only for the beauty of the Latin, but also for the very important matter they contain," going on to advise Sidney to practice double translation and approving his plan to study astronomy. Two weeks later Sidney agrees to the suggestion of translating and reading Cicero. Later letters are concerned with the study of geometry (which Languet discourages for men of noble rank) and Greek (which he thinks excessive in Sidney's case, the study of salvation taking precedence). *Correspondence*, ed. Pears, pp. 2, 4, 20, 25–28, 60.

38. In Paris he established ties with the king of France, who created him a baron and a Gentleman of the King's Bedchamber, not only because of his successful personal qualities but also "considerans combien est grande la maison

de Sydenay en Angleterre" (Connell, *Sidney*, p. 60); he also struck acquaintances with Du Plessis Mornay, Francis Hotman, and Ramus. In Italy he met Tintoretto and was painted by Veronese. Other contacts of his tour included Cesare Carafa, Lewis of Nassau, and the humanists Henri Estienne and Johannes Sturm. When at last he returned to England in 1575, no doubt exhausted, nearly two-thirds of his life was over.

39. Historical Manuscripts Commission Reports; Salisbury Manuscripts, 26 October 1569 (London, 1883), p. 439. Geoffrey Shepherd, Introduction to *Sir Philip Sidney: An Apology for Poetry; or, The Defence of Poesy* (London, 1965), p. 9, says Sidney read a number of contemporary and near contemporary authors, perhaps in the original.

40. See *Correspondence*, ed. Pears, pp. 200–2.

41. Cited by Hardin Craig, *The Enchanted Glass* (New York, 1935), p. 163.

42. Danby, *Poets*, p. 50.

43. *Astrophil and Stella* (sonnet 74), sig. D4; *Poems*, ed. Ringler, p. 204.

44. References are to the Ponsonby quarto (1595) and to *Miscellaneous Prose*.

45. B. B., *The moste excellent and pleasaunt Booke, entituled: The treasurie of Amadis of Fraunce: Conteyning eloquente orations, pythie Epistles, learned Letters, and feruent Complayntes, seruing for sundrie purposes. The vvorthinesse vvhereof and profite, dothe appeare in the Preface of table of this Booke* (1567). Helpful analyses of Sidney's debt to the *Amadis* may also be found in John J. O'Connor, *"Amadis de Gaule" and Its Influence on Elizabethan Literature* (New Brunswick, N. J., 1970), pp. 183–201; Robert W. Parker, "Terential Structure and Sidney's Original *Arcadia*," *English Literary Renaissance* 2:72, and Hamilton, *Sidney*, pp. 45–47.

46. Hoskins, *Directions*, ed. Hudson, p. 41. See also Hamilton, *Sidney*, pp. 42–50, 126–31.

47. So Victor Skretkowicz, Jr., "Sidney and Amyot: Heliodorus in the Structure and Ethos of the *New Arcadia*," *Review of English Studies*, 27:171.

48. References are to the Spanish text, Jorge de Montemayor, *Los siete libros de la Diana* (Anvers, 1580); to Yong's edition of 1598, *Diana of George of Montemayor*; and to Yong, ed. Judith M. Kennedy (Oxford, 1968).

49. A. C. Hamilton, "Sidney's *Arcadia* as Prose Fiction: Its Relation to Its Sources," *English Literary Renaissance* (1972) 2:33.

50. Jacopo Sannazaro, *Arcadia*, sig. C6; trans. Ralph Nash (Detroit, 1966), p. 55.

51. Hamilton, "Sidney's *Arcadia*," p. 35.

52. So Jean Robertson, Introduction to *The Countess of Pembroke's Arcadia (The Old Arcadia)* (Oxford, 1973), p. xxv, n. 1.

53. The *Cyropaedia* begins with an exhortation to Cyrus by his father (and a wittier one by his grandfather), continues with the boy's initial address to his troops in imitation of the early lessons (1.5.6–11) and his father Cambyses' final

counsel (1.6.12–16), and concludes with Cyrus's own long oration of blessing and legacy to his sons in turn. Xenophon's two chief concerns in the education of Cyrus are justice—"The boys go to school and spend their time in learning justice; and they say that they go there for this purpose; just as in our country they say that they go to learn to read and write" (1.2.6)—and hunting [as an early analogy to warfare], 1.4.7). Embedded tales are not without humor, as in the schoolroom disputation on well-fitting and ill-fitting tunics (1.3.16–17). Rhetorical precepts are tested by action: Cyrus's military prowess is seen in his capture of the first and second camps of the Assyrians (4), while his more private concerns are tested in the settlement with Croesus and his comforting of Panthea (7) (Xenophon, *Cyropaedia*, trans. Walter Miller, Loeb Classical Library [New York, 1914]).

54. Robertson, *Old Arcadia*, p. xxvii, notes Sidney's eclectic use of tags from Livy, Plutarch, and Tacitus as well.

55. Aristotle, *Politics*, trans. H. Rackham, Loeb Classical Library (Cambridge, Mass., 1932, 1977).

56. Plato also established aristocracy as the ideal form of government (*Republic* 8–9, 544C–579D).

57. Aristotle, *Ethics*, trans. H. Rackham, Loeb Classical Library (Cambridge, Mass., 1926, 1975).

58. Polybius writes of Arcadia, as Sidney may have known, as a cold, gloomy, primitive land, bare and savage, only potentially salvational after the coming of the Messians (*Historia* 4.20.3; 21.5; 33.3; 70.1, 77.8–10), an interpretation reinforced by Ovid, but in an imaginary time (*Fasti* 2.289 ff.); Vergil softens Arcadia into a land significant for its sense of purity and musical sweetness and places it in a Utopian space (*Eclogue* 10). The popular Elizabethan concept of Arcadia was that of a fool's paradise.

59. Henricus Stephanvs, *Platonis opera quae extant omnia* (1578).

60. P. Friëdlander, *Plato: The Dialogues, Second and Third Periods*, trans. Hans Meyerhoff (London, 1969), 3:432.

61. Plato, *Laws*, trans. R. G. Bury, Loeb Classical Library (Cambridge, Mass., 1926, 1967).

62. Plato, *Republic*, trans. Paul Shorey, Loeb Classical Library (Cambridge, Mass., 1930, 1978).

63. Plato, *The Statesman*, trans. Harold N. Fowler, Loeb Classical Library (Cambridge, Mass., 1925, 1975).

64. Cicero, *De Re Publica*, trans. Clinton Walker Keyes, Loeb Classical Library (Cambridge, Mass., 1928, 1977).

65. Cicero, *De Legibus*, trans. Clinton Walker Keyes, Loeb Classical Library (Cambridge, Mass., 1928, 1977).

66. The first person to suggest this was Friedrich Brie, *Sidney's Arcadia: Eine Studie zur englischen Renaissance* (Berlin, 1918), p. 130.

67. Cicero, *De Officiis*, trans. Walter Miller, Loeb Classical Library (Cambridge, Mass., 1913, 1975).

68. The matter is more fully discussed in Alan Sinfield, "Sidney, du Plessis-Mornay and the Pagans," *Philological Quarterly* 58:32–33.

69. Arthur Golding, on the title page of the English translation he accomplished or completed, *A Woorke concerning the trewnesse of the Christian Religion* (1587).

70. Robertson (*Old Arcadia,* pp. xxvii–xxviii) also suggests current historical treatises that Sidney read, such as Guicciardini, *La Historia d'Italia* (1569), Contarini and Donato Giannotti's treatises on the republic of Venice, the *Vindiciae Contra Tyrannos* (1579), and George Buchanan, *De Jure Regni apud Scotos* (Edinburgh, 1579).

71. Peter Heylyn, *Microcosmvs* (1621), sig. Cc4v; quoted in Hamilton, "Sidney's *Arcadia,*" p. 33. Richard Hakluyt dedicated his *Voyages* to Sidney as the secretary of eloquence (1582 ed.), while George Whetstone writes, "His *Archadia,* vnmacht for sweete deuise; / where *skill* doth iudge, is held in Souereigne price" (*Sir Phillip Sidney, his honorable life, his valiant death, and true vertues* [1586], sig. B2v). As late as 1686 a temperament so remote as that of William Winstanley, in *The Lives Of the most Famous English Poets,* gives Sidney exceptional space and devotes his commentary exclusively to "that incomparable Romance, entituled, *The Arcadia*" (sig. F8v).

72. Sidney to Lanquet, Padua, 4 February 1574, in *Correspondence,* ed. Pears, p. 28. He continues, "Inter Aristotelis opera ego praecipue politica ejus legendo puto, quod eo scribo, quoniam me ad moralem philosophiam animum adiungere suades"; "Of the works of Aristotle, I consider the politics to be the most worth reading; and I mention this reference to your advice that I should apply myself to moral philosophy" (trans. Pears).

73. We have been further misled because Banosius dedicated his edition of the works of Ramus to Sidney and because Sidney appointed as his secretary William Temple, also identified with Ramism. Gosson's dedication of *The Schoole of Abuse* and the *Apologie* to Sidney, whose consequent scorn Spenser writes about to Harvey and whose own *Defence of Poesie* refutes, shows us how seriously we are to take Banosius; as for Temple, we have no records of his Ramism being a condition of employment or a qualification for the job. The case for Sidney as anti-Ramist, on the other hand, is patent throughout the *Arcadia,* where figures of speech are always used to convey philosophical and logical ideas, not added as a "stucco decoration" as Mario Praz has claimed among others (in "Sidney's Original *Arcadia,*" *London Mercury* 15:511). This problem is discussed at length by Richard A. Lanham, *Sidney's Arcadia: The Old "Arcadia"* (New Haven, Conn., 1965), pp. 332–44, and Neil L. Rudenstine, *Sidney's Poetic Development* (Cambridge, Mass., 1967), chap. 5.

74. Hoskins, *Directions,* p. 41. Boas adds, "he was specially drawn to Aristotle" (*Sidney,* p. 19).

75. *Correspondence,* ed. Pears, p. 208; quoted in Boas, *Sidney,* p. 196.

76. "Bulephorus, meanwhile, expresses Erasmus's point of view in countering with a very different conception. He insists that a writer must follow the bent of

his own nature and talent, that imitation does not involve a pedantic memorizing and copying of words and phrases, but a personal transmutation of them; it is 'that which culls from all authors, and especially the most famous, what in each excels and accords with your own genius,—not just adding to your speech all the beautful things that you find, but digesting them and making them your own, so that they may seem to have been born from your mind and not borrowed from others, and may breathe forth the vigor and strength of your nature' " (Rudenstine, *Sidney's Poetic Development,* p. 136).

77. Ben Jonson, *Timber; or, Discoveries* (1641), sigs. O1v; P4v; also quoted in Hudson in his Introduction to Hoskins, *Directions,* p. xxii.

78. Jon S. Lawry, *Sidney's Two "Arcadias": Pattern and Proceeding* (Ithaca, N.Y., 1972), p. 26; cf. David Kalstone, *Sidney's Poetry: Contexts and Interpretations* (Cambridge, 1965), p. 85. Duncan-Jones in *Miscellaneous Prose,* p. 17; see also Stephen Orgel, *The Jonsonian Masque* (Cambridge, Mass., 1965), p. 55.

79. Duncan-Jones provides a rhetorical analysis of the Alençon letter in *Miscellaneous Prose,* pp. 44–45; on the Irish letter, Edward Waterhouse, then secretary of state for Ireland, wrote Sir Henry that young Philip "had framed an answer in way of discourse, the most excellently (if I have any judgement) that ever I read in my life" (quoted in *Miscellaneous Prose,* p. 4).

80. Richard A. Lanham, "*Astrophil and Stella*: Pure and Impure Persuasion," *English Literary Renaissance* 2:107. Cf. William Cherubini, "The 'Goldenness' of Sidney's *Astrophel and Stella:* Test of a Quantitative-Stylistic Routine," *Language and Style* 8:47–59. Cherubini uses a computer to isolate and compute various schemes. Sherod M. J. Cooper also finds, for tropes, metaphor, synecdoche, and metonymy, and for schemes the following: diacope, paroemion, asyndeton, homeoptoton, paronomasia, threnos, bdelygmia, orcos, procthesis, ecphonesis, hypophora, epitheton, procatalpsis, and parenthesis (*The Sonnets of "Astrophel and Stella"* [The Hague, 1968], chap. 4). The fullest treatment, however, remains Robert L. Montgomery, Jr., *Symmetry and Sense: The Poetry of Sir Philip Sidney* (Austin, Tex., 1961).

81. See, for instance, Arthur F. Kinney, "Parody and Its Implications in Sidney's *Defence of Poesie,*" *Studies in English Literature* 12:1–19.

82. Myrick, *Sidney as Craftsman,* chap. 2. Howell claims (*Sidney,* p. 176) that even the digression near the end has the form of a classical oration. See also *Miscellaneous Prose,* ed. Duncan-Jones and Van Dorsten, p. 64; and the provocative study by Margaret W. Ferguson, "Sidney's *A Defence of Poetry*: A Retrial," *Boundary 2* 7:61–95.

83. Evans, ed., Introduction to *Arcadia* p. 15.

84. Cicero, *De Oratore,* trans. Sutton and Rackham.

85. These remarks summarize a detailed study by Michael McCanles, which he has been kind enough to share with me in manuscript.

86. Aristotle, *Rhetoric,* trans. John Henry Freese, Loeb Classical Library (Cambridge, Mass., 1926, 1975).

87. Sidney, *Correspondence* 35, in *Prose Works,* ed. Feuillerat, 3:122.

88. Some of the preceding remarks paraphrase Nancy Rothwax Lindheim, "Sidney's *Arcadia,* Book II: Retrospective Narrative," *Studies in Philology* 64:162–63. This is an important study of Sidney's novel.

89. I am indebted in the foregoing remarks to a fine essay by Lorna Challis, which develops each of these points at greater length; see "The Use of Oratory in Sidney's *Arcadia,*" *Studies in Philology* 62:561–76.

90. See Brother Simon Scribner, *Figures of Word-Repetition in the First Book of Sir Philip Sidney's "Arcadia"* (Washington, D.C., 1948).

91. Other models for forensic orations are in Quintilian, *Institutio Oratoria,* Books 4, 5, and 7.

92. Walter W. Greg, *Pastoral Poetry & Pastoral Drama: A Literary Inquiry, with Special Reference to the Pre-Restoration Stage in England* (London, 1906), pp. 319–34; C. R. Baskervill, "Sidney's *Arcadia* and *The Tryall of Chivalry,*" *Modern Philology* 10:197–201.

93. Goldwell writes, "Then proceeded Master Philip Sidney in very sumptuous manner with armour part blue and the rest gilt and engraven, with four spare horses having caparisons and furniture very rich and costly, as some of cloth of gold embroidered with pearl, and some embroidered with gold and silver feathers very richly and cunningly wrought; he had four pages that rode on his four spare horses, who had cassock coats and Venetian hose of all cloth of silver laid with gold lace, and hats of the same with gold bands and white feathers, and each one a pair of white buskins. Then had he a thirty gentlemen and yeomen, and four Trumpeters who were all in cassock coats and Venetian hose of yellow velvet laid with silver lace, yellow velvet caps with silver bands and white feathers, and every one a pair of white buskins; and they had upon their coats a scroll or band of silver which came scarf wise over the shoulder and so down under the arm, with this poesy or sentence written upon it both before and behind, *Sic nos non nobis*"; see Wallace, *Sidney,* p. 265. The £ 42.6s. is the debt Sidney owes Richard Rodway, merchant tailor of London (ibid., p. 158). Wallace also sums the entertainment, from accounts by Laneham and Gascoigne, on pp. 154–55.

94. In Holinshed's *Chronicles* (1587), sig. 7L1v; quoted by Duncan-Jones, *Miscellaneous Prose,* p. 4.

95. John Drinkwater, Biographical Introduction to *The Poems of Sir Philip Sidney* (London, 1910), p. 8. So Moffet: "Vix emenso vitae sexennio, morbilli et variolae, ceu cuniculis quibusdam, formae dignitatem, & schema everterant: nec ita tamen quin deceret illum aeque reliquus ornatus, atque insuper doceret: non esse tanti faciendum formae flosculum, sed illam animi venustatem aestimandam"; "When he had scarce completed six years of life, measles and smallpox laid waste, as with little mines, the excellence and the fashion of his beauty; and yet not in such wise that the residue was unbecoming to him; and by the same token it showed, moreover, that the flower of beauty ought not to be held in price but that grace of soul ought, rather, to be esteemed" (*Nobilis,* fol. 7; p. 71).

96. Wallace, *Sidney,* p. 121. James M. Osborn, *Young Philip Sidney, 1572–1577* (New Haven, Conn., 1972), p. 70.

97. *State Papers, Ireland, Elizabeth,* 1 June 1570 (London, 1860), p. 430; also quoted in Wallace, *Sidney,* p. 86. *Cottonian MSS., Vespesian,* F. 12, f. 179, also quoted in Wallace, *Sidney,* p. 150.

98. Although this was finally granted him after he had requested it for two and a half years.

99. Margaret A. Dana, "The Providential Plot of the *Old Arcadia,*" *Studies in English Literature* 17:57.

CHAPTER 8

1. In "Renaissance Poverty and Lazarillo's Family: The Birth of the Picaresque Genre," *PMLA* 94:877–78, Javier Herrero traces attitudes of More and Vives in the Spanish *Vida.* For a sensible and thorough analysis of the conscious planning and artistry of the *Vida,* showing how it is much more than a rogue's random adventures, see A. D. Deyermond, *Lazarillo de Tormes* (London, 1975).

2. Herrero develops this point, ("Renaissance Poverty," p. 876).

3. Quoted in ibid., pp. 876–77.

4. Quoted in ibid., pp. 877.

5. Miguel Giginta, *Tratado del remedio de pobres,* (Coimbra, 1579), p. 88; Herrero, "Renaissance Poverty," p. 885, n. 11; trans. Herrero, p. 880.

6. The point is made by Dale B. J. Randall, *The Golden Tapestry* (Durham, N.C., 1963), p. 61.

7. Cf. R. O. Jones, Introduction to *La Vida de Lazarillo de Tormes* (Manchester, 1963), p. xxviii.

8. Giginta, *Tratado,* pp. 87–88; quoted in Herrero, "Renaissance Poverty," p. 886, n. 21; trans. Herrero, p. 883.

9. Rowland adds a short, final chapter in which Lazarillo finds drinking companions in Toledo who finally move on. Since he has a daughter and household of his own by then, Lazarillo forsakes their friendship to continue his hypocritical existence (*Pleasaunt Historie,* sigs. H5v–H7v).

CHAPTER 9

1. Cicero, *In Pisonem,* trans. N. H. Watts, Loeb Classical Library (Cambridge, Mass., 1931, 1964); cf. fragment 1 with Erasmus on the dawn of humanism.

2. R. G. M. Nisbet, Introduction to his edition and commentary on the text of Cicero, *In Pisonem* (Oxford, 1961), p. xvi.

3. Thomas Nashe, *Summers last will and Testament* (published 1600), sigs. H1–H1v; 3:283–84. References to all of Nashe's works are to the first editions and to *The Works of Thomas Nashe,* ed. Ronald B. McKerrow, rev. F. P. Wilson (Oxford, 1958). Occasionally McKerrow and Wilson transcribe incorrectly the quartos I have used. I have slightly modernized the titles of Nashe's works.

4. G. R. Hibbard, *Thomas Nashe: A Critical Introduction* (London, 1962), p. 114.

5. A. K. Croston, "The Use of Imagery in Nashe's *The Unfortunate Traveller,*" *Review of English Studies* 24:96, 90.

6. Lewis, *English Literature,* pp. 410–11; Hibbard, *Nashe,* p. 127.

7. Agnes C. Latham, "Satire on Literary Themes and Modes in Nashe's *Unfortunate Traveller,*" *English Studies,* 1948, p. 86.

8. Juvenal, Satire 1, line 30. Nashe's relationship to Juvenal is taken up later in this chapter.

9. Barbara Green, *Norwich: The Growth of a City* (Norwich, 1975), p. 24. I am grateful to the Norfolk County Records Office for allowing me to examine the many documents dealing with plague in Norfolk during this period; none, unfortunately, deals with the villages with which we know Nashe was associated: Lowestoft (in Suffolk), Rollesby, West Harling; and the deaths of the members of Nashe's immediate family are not described in any extant records I have been able to locate. What we do know—the date of their burials—is in Nashe, *Works,* ed. McKerrow, vol. 5, app. E.

10. Judicio, in part 2 of *The Pilgrimage to Parnassus,* called *The Return from Parnassus* (1602?), sig. B3; quoted in *Works,* ed. McKerrow, 5:150. Thomas Dekker, *A Knight's Conjuring* (1607), sig. L1; rep. in *Works,* ed. McKerrow, 5:152. Michael Drayton, *Elegy to Henry Reynolds, of Poets and Poesie,* in *The Battle of Agincourt* (1627), sig. Dd1v; rep. in *Works,* ed. McKerrow, 5:154.

11. Daivd C. McPherson, "Aretino and the Harvey-Nashe Quarrel," *PMLA* 84:1556.

12. See *Works,* ed. McKerrow, 5:6; there has been no evidence to the contrary, and his conjecture still stands.

13. Herbert Marshall McLuhan, "The Place of Thomas Nashe in the Learning of His Time" (Diss., Cambridge University, 1943), p. 362.

14. Quoted in Hibbard, *Nashe,* p. 89.

15. Michael Ayrton, Introduction to *The Unfortunate Traveller or, The Life of Jacke Wilton by Thomas Nashe* (London, 1948), p. 6; he is speaking especially of this novel.

16. McLuhan, "Place of Thomas Nashe." The bulk of McLuhan's work is on the medieval trivium; the four final chapters are on Tudor Cambridge and, exhaustively, on the Second Sophistic in Nashe's work. I am indebted to McLuhan's work for pointing this out to me, and to M. Thomas Hester for leading me to McLuhan.

17. Philostratus, *Lives of the Sophists* 480, trans. Wilmer Cave Wright, Loeb Classical Library (Cambridge, Mass., 1922, 1961).

18. George A. Kennedy, *Classical Rhetoric and Its Christian and Secular Tradition from Ancient to Modern Times* (Chapel Hill, N.C., 1980), p. 38.

19. Joseph Marshall Campbell, *The Influence of the Second Sophistic on the Style of the Sermons of St. Basil the Great* (Washington, D.C., 1922), p. 3. Thomas E. Ameringer, *The Stylistic Influence of the Second Sophistic On the Panegyrical Sermons of St. John Chrysostom: A Study in Greek Rhetoric* (Washington, D.C., 1921), p. 11.

20. Campbell, *Influence,* p. 9.

21. Dionysius of Halicarnassus, *De Compositione Verborum* 24; trans. Stephen Usher, Loeb Classical Library (Cambridge, Mass., 1974).

22. These remarks are drawn from Campbell, *Influence,* pp. 5–6.

23. St. John Chrysostom, trans. W. R. W. Stephens, in Philip Schaff, ed. *A Select Library of the Nicene and Post-Nicene Fathers of the Christian Church,* 1st ser. (Grand Rapids, Mich., 1975), 9:141–42.

24. Ibid., trans. T. P. Brandram, 9:182.

25. Ibid., 11:401–11, 433.

26. Kennedy, *Classical Rhetoric,* pp. 113–14. Cf. W. Fraser Mitchell, *English Pulpit Oratory from Andrews to Tillotson* (London, 1932), p. 60.

27. G. R. Owst, *Preaching in Medieval England: An Introduction to Sermon Manuscripts of the Period, c.* 1350–1450 (Cambridge, 1926), chap. 8.

28. Quoted and translated in ibid., p. 316, 316n.

29. In a sermon before the canons of St. Victor in Paris (quoted in ibid., p. 312).

30. Owst's term for a sermon where "each letter of sacred names like 'Maria' or 'Jesus,' ordinary nouns like 'Cor,' are made to introduce significant words of their own, thereby supplying the speaker with sermon divisions of a most facile sort" (ibid., p. 329). Nashe delights in wordplay but never as his basic means of organization.

31. Hyperius, *Practice of Preaching,* chap. 15; quoted in Mitchell, *Pulpit Oratory,* p. 52.

32. These are discussed in more detail in J. W. Blench, *Preaching in England in the late Fifteenth and Sixteenth Centuries* (New York, 1964), pp. 105, 106, 107.

33. Ibid., p. 205.

34. Florence Higham, *Lancelot Andrewes* (London, 1952), p. 75.

35. There are several examples in Mitchell, *Pulpit Oratory,* p. 155.

36. Lancelot Andrewes, "Sermon 1 on the Passion," delivered on Good Friday 1597, in *XCVI Sermons* (1629), sig. Gg4.

37. *Sermons,* p. 501; quoted in Blench, *Preaching,* p. 186.

38. *Sermons,* p. 548; Blench, *Preaching,* p. 224.

39. *Sermons* (1675), p. 340; quoted in Mitchell, *Pulpit Oratory,* p. 211.

40. "Imagination quickens fact into art": Stanley Wells, Introduction to *Thomas Nashe,* Stratford-upon-Avon Library, no. 1 (London, 1964), p. 19.

41. Quoted in Mitchell, *Pulpit Oratory,* p. 93.

42. J. B. Steane, Introduction to *The Unfortunate Traveller and Other Works* (Harmondsworth, 1972), p. 35.

43. Chrysostom, trans. Stephens, ed. Schaff, 1st ser., 9:91. Cf. Lancelot Andrewes's sermon on repentance and fasting (Jer. 8:4–7.) delivered before the queen at Whitehall on Ash Wednesday 1602.

44. See *Works,* ed. McKerrow, 4:268.

45. Cicero, *De Oratore,* trans. Sutton.

46. Livy, *History of Rome,* trans. B. O. Foster, Loeb Classical Library (Cambridge, Mass., 1929, 1963).

47. Livy, *History of Rome,* trans. Frank Gardner Moore, Loeb Classical Library (Cambridge, Mass., 1940, 1958).

48. John Carey, in a lecture on Nashe at Oxford on 1 February 1977.

49. Davis makes this point in *Idea and Act,* p. 231.

50. Just why Nashe appeals to a known patron of the arts, who was nevertheless a Catholic, an open supporter of the untraditional Essex, and badly in debt himself, is a nice question; apparently no money was forthcoming—as it hardly could have been from the impecunious Southampton—for the dedication was omitted from the second edition later the same year. For Wriothesley's background, see Lawrence Stone, *Family and Fortune* (Oxford, 1973), chap. 7.

51. Nashe says as much, if the work is actually his, in *An Almond for a Parrat* (1590), sig. A2v; 3:341; nor does he contradict Harvey when, in *New Letter of Notable Contents* (1593), he is accused of following Aretino and Rabelais (sig. B3v). Borrowings in Nashe's works are listed in Werner van Koppenfels, "Thomas Nashe und Rabelais," *Archiv für das Studium der Neueren Sprachen und Literaturen* 207:277–91; see also Charles Whibley, "Rabelais en Angleterre," trans. Marcel Schwob, in *Revue des études rabelaisiennes* 1:1–13, for a general introduction.

52. R. G. Howarth, *Two Elizabethan Writers of Fiction* (Cape Town, 1956), p. 15.

53. Greene, *A Notable Discovery of Coosnage:* references are to the new edition and to Arthur F. Kinney, ed., *Rogues, Vagabonds, and Sturdy Beggars* (Barre, Mass., 1973), where the text also appears.

54. This point is made and developed by Alexander Leggatt, "Artistic Coherence in *The Unfortunate Traveller,*" *Studies in English Literature* 14:35.

55. "The *De occulta philosophia* provided for the first time a useful and—so far as the abstractness of the subject permitted—a clear survey of the whole field of Renaissance magic" (Frances A. Yates, *Giordano Bruno and the Hermetic Tradition* [New York, 1969], p. 130).

56. Similar discussions of the significance of Münster may be found in G. R. Elton, *Reformation Europe, 1517–1559* (London, 1963, 1976), pp. 100–2; and Hans J. Hillerbrand, *The World of the Reformation* (London, 1975), pp. 65–66.

57. This understanding has been offered before, but without much substantiation, by George Saintsbury, *A History of English Literature* (London, 1898; 1920), p. 234; Margaret Schlauch, *Antecedents of the English Novel, 1400–1600* (Warsaw, 1963), p. 212; and Ernest A. Baker, *The History of the English Novel* (1936; New York, 1966), 2:168.

58. Aretino, *Letters* 2, sig. L2 (1609); trans. George Bull, *Aretino: Selected Letters* (Harmondsworth, 1976), p. 181.

59. *The Golden Asse,* trans. W. Adlington and S. Gaselee, Loeb Classical Library (Cambridge, Mass., 1915, 1977).

60. Cf. *The Anatomie of Absvrditie,* sig. B4; 1:24; *Pierce Penilesse,* sigs. H1, H4v; 1:227, 235. Harvey calls Nashe "young Apuleius" in *Pierces Supererogation* (1593); see *Works,* ed. McKerrow, 5:91.

61. As P. G. Walsh, *The Roman Novel* (Cambridge, 1970), p. 180, shows, warnings come to Lucius in *The Golden Asse* before his disastrous adventures; it is a further sign of Nashe's disillusionment that the earl appears *after* some of Jack's most horrible experiences.

62. The earl later catalogues the evils of the major European countries from the traditional Elizabethan viewpoint (sigs. I4–K1v; 2:298–302). The charges frequently resemble those Nashe had already leveled in *Pierce Penilesse* (sigs. B4v–C1v; 1:176–78).

63. David Kaula, "The Low Style in Nashe's *The Unfortunate Traveler,*" *Studies in English Literature* 6:44–45.

64. Madelon S. Gohlke, "Wits Wantonness: *The Unfortunate Traveller* as Picaresque," *Studies in Philology* 73:403.

65. Cf. Boccaccio's and Nashe's uses of nosegays, cartmen collecting dead bodies, and men breakfasting at morning but dead at night (sigs. H3v–H4; 2:286), and Boccaccio's collapsing peasant with Nashe's description of the sweating sickness of 1517 (sigs. C2–C2v; 2:228–30); Boccaccio, *Decameron,* introduction.

66. In his *Annales of England,* John Stow records that 17,893 were recorded dead in 1593 in the city and liberties of London (1601 ed., sig. 406v), 10,675 of the plague. Such sickness may have been very personal for Nashe, given the high mortality rate from plague in Norfolk.

67. According to Graham R. Drake, 5,000 of 15,000 persons in Norwich died during 1578–79, while in 1583 there were 425 deaths there; in 1584, 996; 1587, 471; 1588, 544; 1589, 781; 1590, 896—in all, 8,267 deaths, at least half from the plague between 1583 and 1593 ("Bubonic Plague in Norwich in the Late Sixteenth and Early Seventeenth Centuries" [Thesis, Cambridge University, 1968]).

68. The best recent account of Nashe's activities in 1592 and 1593 is in C. G. Harlow, "Nashe's Visit to the Isle of Wight and His Publications of 1592–4," *Review of English Studies,* 14:225–42.

69. In *The Man of the Renaissance* (New York, 1933; Cleveland, 1958, 1968), Ralph Roeder quotes a plaintive letter of Castiglione, written in late 1552, where even in the Vatican "All I can do is to wash in vinegar, perfume my hands, and commend my soul to God" (p. 419).

70. *A boke, or counseill against the disease commonly called the sweate, or sweatyng sicknesse* (152) describes an epidemic in 1485, which lasted nearly all of August and September, bringing a "souddeine sharpenes and vnwont cruelnes passed the pestilence" (sig. A8v). The author recalls that it "immediatly killed some in opening theire windowes, some in plaieng with children in their strete dores, some in one hour, many in two it destroyed, & at the longest, to thē that merily dind, it gaue a sorowful supper. As it founde them so it toke them, some

in sleape some in wake, some in mirthe some in care, some fasting & some ful, some busy and some idle, and in one house sometyme three sometime fiue, sometyme seuen sometyme eyght, sometyme more, sometyme all, of the whyche, if the haulfe in euery Towne escaped, it was thoughte great fauour" (sig. B1).

71. One of the peculiarities Charles Creighton records is that the sweating sickness was especially fatal to peers and gentry, while the plague killed the lower classes; Wolsey contracted the 1517 sweating sickness three times, although he fled London as soon as it broke out (*A History of Epidemics in Britain* [1891], 1:237–71). A manuscript account of the 1485 outbreak, by Dr. Thomas Forrestier, describes the symptoms: high temperature, sweating, headache, and inflammation.

72. *Opvs Epistolarvm, des.* Erasmusi *Roterddami,* ed. P. S. Allen (Oxford, 1913), 3:46–47; trans. Francis Morgan Nichols (London, 1901–18), 3:1–2.

73. Cf. Holinshed: "But alas! although it be written on the gates grauen in stone, *Iammes ton me a perdeu ton pucellage,* that is to saie; Thou hast neuer lost thy maidenhed: yet if this citie had not beene well furnished and euer at the daie appointed sure of rescue, could not haue continued" (1587 ed., sig. 4K2v). All the chronicles treat Thérouanne and Tournai at greater length and more seriously than Nashe—but we are here in the early, jest-book pages of *The Unfortunate Traueller.* Jane Tross was an actual harlot.

74. J. J. Scarisbrick, *Henry VIII* (Berkeley, Calif., 1968), p. 58.

75. Cf. *Pierce Penilesse* (sig. E2v; 1:186); Ascham's *Scholemaster,* sigs. H3–H3v, I2; Turler notes, "There is an autient complaint made by many that our cuntreymen vsually bringe three thinges with them out of *Italye*: a naughty conscience, an empty Purse, and a weake stomacke: and many times it chaunceth so indeed" (sigs. F1–F1v). Gentillet's discourse on Machiavelli, "A Discourse Vpon the Meanes of Wel Gouerning against N. Macchiavell" (1602) was better known in England in Nashe's time than Machiavelli himself, and Gentillet's description seems especially appropriate to Nashe's depiction: "According to the honour of his nation, vengeances, and enmities are perpetuall and irreconcilable; and indeed, there is nothing wherein they take greater delectation, pleasure, and contentment, then to execute a vengence; insomuch as, whensoever they can have their enemie at their pleasure, to be revenged vpon him, they murder him after some strange & barbarous fashion, and in murdering him, they put him in remembrance of the offence done unto them, with many reprochfull words and injuries to torment the soule and body together; and sometimes wash their hands and their mouthes with his blood, and force him with hope of his life to give himselfe to the divell; and so they seeke in slaying the bodie to damne the soule, if they could" (sigs.Q5–Q5v; trans. Simon Patericke).

76. James Cleland "The Institvtion of a Young Noble Man" (Oxford, 1607), has especially harsh words for Spain (sigs. Ll1v–Ll2). Despite the death of Mary Stuart and the decisive defeat of the Armada, Spain remained a religious and military threat to England.

77. Leggatt's reading of this episode is especially acute. "Our bodies really are vulnerable to the most appalling damage," he notes; and "Sex is just another, slower way in which a body can be wasted and destroyed, till it becomes a piece of rubbish to be popped into the privy" ("Artistic Coherence," pp. 34, 35).

78. The second sentence may be an allusion to Socrates in *Golden Asse* 1, or even to the Sacred Heart of Christ.

79. The full measure of Nashe's charges can be determined by comparing this work with other contemporary accounts of Italy, such as William Lithgow's *Discourse* (1632). His first voyage to Italy (1609) results in some jests (1:1), but he does experience some treachery at Pistoja in a second journey (2:1).

80. A different but valuable interpretation is offered by Ruth M. Stevenson in "The Roman Banketting House: Nashe's Forsaken Image of Art," *Studies in Short Fiction* 17:291–306.

81. References are to the Ponsonby quarto and to *Miscellaneous Prose,* ed. Duncan-Jones and Van Dorsten.

82. Thomas Warton, *History of English Poetry* (London, 1781), p. xxxviii. The best brief discussion of Surrey's classical sensibility is Emrys Jones's Introduction to the *Poems* (Oxford, 1964). Jones sees in Surrey "a new poetic system [in] habits of movement, laws of harmony, verbal colouring, and vocal pitch" (p. xiv), "performances in elocution" (p. xx).

83. Richard Tottel, *Songes and Sonettes* (1557), sig. D2v; Jones, Surrey's *Poems* no. 28, p. 27.

84. Harvey, *Marginalia,* ed. Smith, p. 156.

85. A. B. Grosart, Introduction to *The Complete Works of Thomas Nashe* (London, 1883–85), 6:xi.

86. Lewis, *English Literature,* p. 416.

87. Nashe's unrelieved view of Europe has Elizabethan precedent at least as far back as 1571, when Thomas Fortescue writes in his dedication of *The Foreste* to the Master of the Queen's Wardrobe about his recent trip abroad: "Where a fewe moneths after myne arriuall, the worlde grewe to bee suche, so tumultuous, and troublesome, that no manne could assure hymselfe, or promise him self safe beyng: gates eches where were shutte, tounes and holdes were fenced, castles, and fortes furnished, all passeges straightly, and diligently obserued, the fieldes full of armed menne, readie to the battaile, and in fine, throughout one onely face, and countenaunce of hostilitie. By meanes whereof, the lawes were lockte vp, as if thei neuer had been knowen, iustice was then to none, or sure to fewe menne ministred, all artes Mechanicall, and Sciences surceased, euery corner full of cloase, and wispheryng mutterers, no manne from others malice, or safe, or well assured. In schooles now were the chaires voide of their learned doctours, no man deliuered lawes from Iustinian the Emperour, the solace of the sicke Hippocrates was then, and Galene eke vnknowen, the sciences exiled then, the scriptures were no taught, the tonges were all forgotten, Philosophie, the loue of wisedome, there a straunger. Besides these I nothyng speake of the great number of houses, churches, chapelles, and villages, vtterly wanted, and consumed with fire, of the

wilfull profusion of wine, oyle, corne, and the semblable: of the moste lamentable, and marueilous peniurie, and want of necessarie victualles, of the pitifull complaints of the indigente, and neadie, of the frownyng faces betwixt neighbour, and neighbour, of the little truste the maister had in his seruaunte, the father eke in his childe, or one manne in an other. Thus therfore, when all thynges grewe on, to suche disorder, when policie gaue rome, and place to hostilitie, when armes, and armed menne had all thynges in possession when none liued voyde of feare, when no state was assured, then knewe I not what better dooe, or how better to spende the long, and wearie howers, than at tymes to busie my selfe in some light, and pleasant studie" (sigs. a2–a3). Besides such accounts, the other travel book of the period, William Kemp's *Nine daies wonder* (1600), is a trifling jest book.

88. A colorful account is in A. F. Pollard, *Henry VIII* (New York, 1966), p. 114; the definitive study is Jocelyne Gledhill Russell, *The Field of the Cloth of Gold* (New York, 1969). I am grateful to George Geckle for sharing this work with me.

89. Lucian, *The Dead Come to Life,* trans. A. M. Harmon, Loeb Classical Library (New York, 1921).

90. William S. Anderson, "Studies in Book I of Juvenal," *Yale Classical Studies* 15:90.

91. G. G. Ramsay, Introduction to the Loeb text, p. xxxiii.

92. Peter Green, Introduction to the Penguin translation (Harmondsworth, 1967), pp. 30, 25.

93. The Latin text is from the Loeb, ed. Ramsay.

94. Inez Gertrude Scott, *The Grand Style in the Satires of Juvenal,* Smith College Classical Studies, no. 8 (Northampton, Mass., 1927), p. 12.

95. William S. Anderson traces much of this to Quintilian; see "Juvenal and Quintilian," *Yale Classical Studies* 17:69–86.

96. Green, Introduction (Penguin), p. 9.

97. Gilbert Highet, *Juvenal the Satirist: A Study* (Oxford, 1954), p. 178.

98. Nashe turns to Camden and to a manuscript account of the history of Yarmouth (*Works,* ed. McKerrow, 5:126–27, 380 ff.); see also Hibbard, *Nashe,* pp. 242–43.

CHAPTER 10

1. Edward Andrews Tenney, *Thomas Lodge,* Cornell Studies in English (Ithaca, N.Y., 1935), pp. 1–2.

2. Lodge's play in collaboration with Robert Greene, *A Looking Glasse, for London and Englande,* was staged in the early 1590s by Lord Strange's Men, who acted under the protection of Ferdinando Stanley; *A Fig for Momus* (1595) was dedicated to William Stanley; and his *Prosopopeia* (1596), a work of humanist varying that is also an extended meditation on the Mater Dolorosa, sought patronage from the mother countess of Derby.

3. So the college statutes; see Tenney, *Lodge,* pp. 50 ff.

4. In the dedicatory epistole to *Robert, second Duke of Normandy* (1591), sig. A4; 2:3. References to this and other texts by Lodge are to the first edition (unless otherwise stated) and to *The Complete Works of Thomas Lodge,* 4 vols., privately printed for the Hunterian Club (Glasgow, 1883–87).

5. *Robert, second Duke of Normandy,* sig. A4; 2:3.

6. Stephen Gosson, *An Apologie of the Schoole of Abuse* (1579), sig. M3; in ed. Arthur F. Kinney *Markets of Bawdrie: The Dramatic Criticism of Stephen Gosson* (Salzburg, 1974), p. 133.

7. William Ringler, "The Source of Lodge's *Reply to Gosson,*" *Review of English Studies* 15:164–71.

8. The *Short Title Catalogue* records eleven editions between 1590 and 1634.

9. Jusserand, *English Novel in the Time of Shakespeare,* pp. 204, 214.

10. There may also be some recognition of the earlier poetics of Gascoigne in the fictional levels in Arden, as when Rosalynde playing Ganimede pretends to be Rosalynde.

11. Cf. Greene's comment that "vertue is not perfit without action" (*Euphues his censure to Philautus,* sig. C2; 6:171); and Rabelais, *Gargantua,* chap. 40. In thought, Lodge actually reaches back past Lyly to Rabelais, More, and Erasmus.

12. Nancy R. Lindheim, "Lyly's Golden Legacy: *Rosalynde* and *Pandosto,*" *Studies in English Literature* 15:5–13.

13. Lodge found this act of rebellion, along with Sir John's legacy, Saladyne's withholding of inheritance, the wrestling match, and old Adam Spenser, in the mid-fourteenth-century "Tale of Gamelyn," but Lodge gives all these incidents an implied allegorical and religious signification.

14. For an alternative reading, see Helgerson, *Elizabethan Prodigals,* p. 113.

15. For a schematic discussion of the rhetoric of *Rosalynde,* see H. Ruthrof, "The Dialectic of Aggression and Reconciliation in *The Tale of Gamelyn,* Thomas Lodge's *Rosalynde,* and Shakespeare's *As You Like It,*" *University of Cape Town Studies in English* 4:1–15, esp. the diagram on p. 15. Ruthrof's schemes would align Lodge more closely with Lyly than the present discussion does.

16. I have been anticipated in some of these observations by Louis Adrian Montrose's stimulating essay, " 'The Place of a brother' in *As You Like It,*" which he has shared with me.

17. Wesley Trimpi, "The Quality of Fiction: The Rhetorical Transmission of Literary Theory," *Traditio* 30:28–29; rep. *Muses of One Mind: The Literary Analysis of Experience and Its Continuity* (Princeton, 1983), p. 279.

18. Cicero, *Pro Archia Poeta,* trans. N. H. Watts, Loeb Classical Library (Cambridge, Mass., 1923, 1961).

19. Plato, *Protagoras,* trans. W. R. M. Lamb, Loeb Classical Library (Cambridge, Mass., 1924, 1962).

20. Plato, *Meno,* trans. W. R. M. Lamb, Loeb Classical Library (Cambridge, Mass., 1924, 1962).

21. Plato, *Republic,* trans. Paul Shorey (Cambridge, Mass., 1930, 1978).

22. Cicero, *De Officiis,* trans. Walter Miller.

23. Plato, *Epistle* 7, trans. R. G. Bury, Loeb Classical Library (Cambridge, Mass., 1929, 1961).

24. Cicero, *Epistolae ad Brutum,* trans. M. Cary, Loeb Classical Library (Cambridge, Mass., 1940, 1960).

25. N. Burton Paradise, *Thomas Lodge: The History of an Elizabethan* (New Haven, Conn., 1931), p. 98. For a discussion of Lodge's sources, see Alice Walker, "The Reading of an Elizabethan: Some Sources of the Prose Pamphlets of Thomas Lodge," *Review of English Studies* 8:273, 270.

26. Introduction to Lodge, *Wovnds of Ciuill War,* ed. Joseph W. Houppert (Lincoln, Neb., 1969), pp. xii–xiv.

27. Houppert cites all the passages of the play derived from this source, ibid., pp. 100–4.

28. See the discussion by Tetsumaro Hayashi, *A Textual Study of "A Lookinge Glasse, for London and England" by Thomas Lodge and Robert Greene* (Muncie, Ind., 1969), pp. 6, 8–14.

29. So Paradise, *Lodge,* p. 154; in the absence of specific borrowings, Hayashi ("Textual Study," p. 22) denies the possibility.

30. Quintilian, *Institutio Oratoria,* trans. Butler.

31. *Report on the MSS of the Marquess of Downshire,* ed. E. K. Purness and A. B. Hinds (London Historical MSS Commission, 1936–40), 2:189–90; quoted in Joseph W. Houppert, "Thomas Lodge's Letters to William Trumbull," *Renaissance News* 18:121.

32. Polybius, *Historia,* trans. W. R. Paton, Loeb Classical Library (New York, 1922).

33. *Livy, Ab Urbe Condita,* trans. B. O. Foster, Loeb Classical Library (Cambridge, Mass., 1919, 1967).

34. Strabo, *Geography,* trans. Horace L. Jones, Loeb Classical Library (Cambridge, Mass., 1917); Plutarch, *Moralia,* trans. Frank Cole Babbitt (Cambridge, Mass., 1927, 1969).

35. George Wyndham, Introduction to the Tudor Translations edition of North's Plutarch, p. xxiv.

36. Tacitus, *Annales,* trans. John Jackson, Loeb Classical Library (Cambridge, Mass., 1937, 1962).

37. Herbert W. Benario, *An Introduction to Tacitus* (Athens, Ga., 1975), p. 38. Cf. Norma P. Miller, "Style and Content in Tacitus," in *Tacitus,* ed. T. A. Dorey (London, 1969), p. 106.

38. The title transcribes "pearl" (of great price? at great price?) "written in the Americas"; the actual setting is the imaginary lands of Mosco and Cusco.

39. Lewis, *English Literature,* pp. 424–25.

40. William Warner, *Pan His Syrinx:* references are to the quarto of 1584, and

the modern edition of the 1597 text by Wallace A. Bacon (Evanston, Ill., 1950).

41. The single best study of sources is Claudette Pollack, "Romance and Realism in Lodge's *Robin the Devil*," *Studies in Short Fiction* 13:491–97.

42. Walker lists some specific sources for *Divel Coniured* ("Reading of an Elizabethan," pp. 270–71).

43. Trinity College had more than its share of recusants among Oxford colleges; only a short time before Lodge matriculated, Bishop Horne was demanding that "certaine monumentes tendinge to Idolatrie and popishe or devills service, as Crosses, Sensors, and such lyke fylthie Stuffe vsed in the Idolaters temple ... remayneth in [the] College as yet vndefacd" (quoted in Tenney, *Lodge,* p. 58).

44. Helgerson, *Elizabethan Prodigals,* p. 118; cf. Walker, "Reading of an Elizabethan," pp. 279–80; Tenney, *Lodge,* pp. 111–12.

45. Augustine, *Civitas Dei,* trans. Philip Levine, Loeb Classical Library (Cambridge, Mass., 1966).

46. Davis, *Idea and Act,* p. 82.

47. Lodge may also be using as a model Brian Melbancke's *Philotimus. The Warre betwixt Nature and Fortune* (1583), which in its triadic education of Philotimus, at university, court, and country, employs the same three landscapes as *Evphves Shadow*. Philotimus's "pilgrimage" also moves from a life of earthly despair to enlightened contemplation in the final lesson from Periander—"if they see not within seauen dayes after, they are blinde for euer" (sig. Ff4v)—but the holy dimension drawn from scriptural and patristic writings in Lodge is missing in Melbancke.

48. A useful introduction to the works of this neglected historian is H. St. John Thackeray, *Josephus: The Man and the Historian* (New York, 1929).

49. Alice Walker, "The Life of Thomas Lodge," *Review of English Studies* 10:49.

50. Purness and Hinds, *Report on MSS of Marquess of Devonshire,* 4:215; quoted in Houppert, "Lodge's Letters," p. 122.

51. Quoted in Robin Campbell, Introduction to *Seneca: Letters from a Stoic* (Harmondsworth, 1969, 1977), p. 25.

52. Ibid., p. 21.

53. I follow the attributes listed by Campbell (ibid., p. 16).

54. Anna Lydia Motto, *Seneca* (New York, 1973), p. 49.

55. Motto cites 119 references to Vergil, 30 to Cicero, 28 to Ovid, 23 to Homer, and numerous citations of Callisthenes, Livy, Asinius Pollio, Sallust, and Timagenes among the historians (ibid., p. 79).

56. Isabel Rivers, *Classical and Christian Ideas in English Renaissance Poetry* (London, 1979), p. 48.

57. Marcus Aurelius, *Meditations,* trans. C. R. Haines, Loeb Classical Library (Cambridge, Mass., 1916, 1961).

58. Quoted in Trimpi, "Quality of Fiction," p. 111; rep. *Muses,* p. 360.

CONCLUSION

1. The case for the necessity for the reader's involvement in the texts of Tudor fiction is made perceptively for Elizabethan prose romance by A. C. Hamilton, "Elizabethan Romance: The Example of Prose Fiction," *ELH* 49:287–99, although it is carried much further here.

2. As cited by Jonathan Goldberg in "The Politics of Renaissance Literature," *ELH* 49:537. This is an unusually valuable survey of the state of recent criticism, esp. pp. 515–38 on neo-Marxist criticism and the "new historicism."

3. Stephen Orgel, *The Illusion of Power* (Berkeley, Calif., 1975), p. 26.

4. Arthur F. Kinney, ed., *Elizabethan Backgrounds: Historical Documents of the Age of Elizabeth I* (Hamden, Conn., 1975), and *Rogues, Vagabonds, and Sturdy Beggars.*

5. See especially Louis A. Montrose, "Celebration and Insinuation: Sir Philip Sidney and the Motives of Elizabethan Courtship," *Renaissance Drama*, 8 (1977): 3–35, and " 'Eliza, Queene of shepheardes,' and the Pastoral of Power," *English Literary Renaissance* 10:153–82.

6. Stephen Greenblatt, *Renaissance Self-Fashioning: From More to Shakespeare* (Chicago, 1980), p. 9.

7. Richard Helgerson, *Self-Crowned Laureates: Spenser, Jonson, Milton, and the Literary System* (Berkeley, Calif., 1983).

8. Jonathan V. Crewe, *Unredeemed Rhetoric: Thomas Nashe and the Scandal of Authorship* (Baltimore, 1982), p. 23.

9. William B. Worthen, *The Idea of the Actor: Drama and the Ethics of Performance* (Princeton, N.J., 1984), p. 3.

10. Annabel M. Patterson, " 'Under . . . Pretty Tales': Intention in Sidney's *Arcadia*," *Studies in the Literary Imagination* 15, 1:6; rep. *Censorship and Interpretation: The Conditions of Writing and Reading in Early Modern England* (Madison, Wisc., 1984), pp. 27–28.

11. In a forthcoming *Festschrift* for Herschel Baker, ed. Heather Dubrow and Richard Strier.

12. Greenblatt explains these terms in *Renaissance Self-Fashioning*, p. 9.

13. See Stephen Orgel, "Sidney's Experiment in Pastoral: *The Lady of May*," *Journal of the Warburg and Courtauld Institutes* 26:198–203; rep. *The Jonsonian Masque* (Cambridge, Mass., 1965), pp. 44–57.

14. Cicero, *De Natura Deorum*, trans. H. Rackham, Loeb Classical Library (London, 1933, 1979).

15. Cicero, *Academica*, trans. H. Rackham, Loeb Classical Library (London, 1933, 1979).

16. *LB*, 4:462A–C; trans. Chaloner, sigs. L3v–L4.

17. Copernicus refers to *Academica* 2.39.122 and cites specifically 2.39.123.

18. Mary Mills Patrick, *The Greek Skeptics* (New York, 1929), p. 270.

19. Nashe adapts Sextus's praise of dogs in a passage of a hundred lines in *Summers last will* (sigs. D4v–E1); *Works*, ed. McKerrow, 3:254–56, although he is at least acquainted with his position as early as his prefatory remarks to Sidney's

Astrophil and Stella (sig. A4v; 3:332). See also *Pierce Penilesse,* sigs. B3v, C3v, D1v–D2, F1; 1:173, 185, 188–89, 206. Nashe presumably cites a 1591 translation of Sextus no longer extant. See *Works,* ed. McKerrow, 5:120, 122; Richard H. Popkin, *The History of Scepticism from Erasmus to Descartes* (Assen, Netherlands, 1960), p. 18, n. 5.

20. *Sexti Empirici* (Paris, 1569), sig. ee3v; trans. R. G. Bury, *Outlines of Pyrrhonism,* Loeb Classical Library (London, 1933, 1976).

21. He also undermines humanist rhetoric in much the same way (3.30.267–69).

22. Textual references are to the 1603 edition; to *The Essayes of Michael Lord of Montaigne done into English by John Florio with an Introduction by Thomas Secombe,* 3 vols. (London, 1908); and to *The Complete Works of Montaigne,* trans. Donald M. Frame (London, 1957). Florio's translation had been reprinted by The Modern Library (n.d.). Secombe's transcription has been silently corrected in the citations and quotations. The 1588 edition of Montaigne's *Essais,* published in Paris, the first to include all three books, is a text Elizabethans may well have known, and it also departs from the Florio text. This version reads, "le voyager me semble vn exercice profitable. L'ame y a vn continuel embesongnement, à remarquer des choses incogneues & nouuelles. Et ie ne sçache point meilleure escolle, comme i'ay dict souuent, à former la vie, que de luy proposer incessammēt la diuersité de tant d'autres vies, & luy faire gouster vne si perpetuelle variété de formes de nostre nature" (sig. 5s1).

23. "Les sens sont aux vns plus obscurs & plus sombres, aux autres plus ouuerts & plus aigus. Les malades prestent de l'amertume aux choses douces: par où il nous appert, que nous ne receuons pas les choses comme elles sont, mais autres & autres selon que nous sommes, & qu'il nous semble. Or nostre sembler estant si incertain & controuerse, ce n'est plus miracle, si on nous dict, que nous pouuōs auouer que la neige nous apparoit blanche, mais que d'establir si de son essence elles est telle, & à la verité, nous ne nous en sçaurions responde: & ce commencement esbranlé, toute la science du monde s'en va necessairemēt à vau-l'eau. Quoy que nos sens mesmes s'entr'empeschent l'vn l'autre: vne peinture semble esleuée à la venue, au maniement elle semble plate: dirōs nous que le muse soit aggreable où non, qui resiouit nostre sentiment & offence nostre goust? Il y à des herbes & des vnguéns propres à vne partie du corps, qui en offencēt vne autre: le miel est plaisant au goust, mal plaisant à la veue" (sig. 3V3).

24. Barbara C. Bowen, *The Age of Bluff: Paradox and Ambiguity in Rabelais and Montaigne* (Urbana, Ill., 1972), p. 109.

25. "Iugeons par le ce que nous auons à estimer de l'homme, de son sens & de sa raison, puis qu'en ces grands personnages, & qui ont porté si haut, l'humaine suffisāce, il s'y trouue des deffaurs si apparēs & si apparēs & si grossiers. Moy i'ayme mieux croire qu'ils ont traité la sciēce ainsi qu'vn iouuet à toutes mains, & se sont esbatus de la raison. . . . instrument vain & friuole, mettant en auant toutes sortes d'inuentions & de fantasies tantost plus tendues, tantost plus láches. Combiē de fois leur voyons nous dire des choses diuerses & cōtraires? Car ce mesme Platon, qui definit l'homme comme vne poule, il dit ailleurs apres Socrates,

qu'il ne sçait à la verité que c'est que l'homme, & que c'est l'vne des pieces du monde d'autant difficile conoissance. Par cette varieté & instabilité d'opinions, ils nous menēt comme par la main tacitement à cette resolution de leur irresolution" (sigs. 3N3–3N3v).

26. "Il faut accommoder, mon histoire à l'heure. Ie pourray tantost changer, non de fortuner seulemēt, mais aussi d'intention: c'est vn contrerolle de diuers & muables accidens, & d'imaginations irresoluës, & quand il y eschet, contraires: soit que ie sois autre moymesme, soit que ie saisisse les subiects, par autres circonstances, & consideratiõs" (sigs. 4X2v–4X3).

27. Alois Riehl, *Giordano Bruno,* trans. Agnes Fry (London, 1905), p. 14. Bruno tells the story himself, and summaries of it were and are commonplace.

28. Antoinette Mann Paterson, *The Infinite Worlds of Giordano Bruno* (Springfield, Ill., 1970), p. 34.

29. Quoted in Allen G. Debus, *Man and Nature in the Renaissance* (Cambridge, 1978), p. 102.

30. René Descartes, *Meditationes* (Paris, 1641), sigs. B5–B5v; translated by F. E. Sutcliffe in *Descartes: Discourse on Method and the Meditations* (Harmondsworth, 1968, 1976), pp. 108–9.

31. *Nova Atlantis,* quoted in J. C. Davis, *Utopia and the Ideal Society: A Study of English Utopian Writing, 1516–1700* (Cambridge, 1981, 1983), p. 122–23.

32. Bacon, *Nova Atlantis,* 1638 ed., sigs. Kk4–Kk4v; trans. William Rawley (1676 ed.), sig. Z6v. Rawley's trans. in rep. in The Modern Library, ed. Hugh G. Dick (New York, 1955), p. 576.

33. Davis, *Utopia,* p. 120.

34. Moody E. Prior, "Bacon's Man of Science," in B. Vickers, ed., *Essential Articles for the Study of Francis Bacon* (Hamden, Conn., 1968), pp. 147, 155; quoted in Davis, *Utopia,* p. 120.